363.209 Conti, Philip M.
C

The Pennsylvania
State Police

14566

THE
PENNSYLVANIA
STATE POLICE

THE PENNSYLVANIA STATE POLICE:

A History of Service to the Commonwealth, 1905 to the Present

By
Lt. Colonel Philip M. Conti, PSP (Ret.)

STACKPOLE BOOKS

Published by
STACKPOLE BOOKS
Cameron and Kelker Streets
P.O. Box 1831
Harrisburg, Pa. 17105

363.209
C

Printed in the U.S.A.

Library of Congress Cataloging in Publication Data
Conti, Philip M   1916–
    The Pennsylvania State Police Force, 1905–1977.

    Bibliography: p.

    1. Pennsylvania.   State Police—History.
2. Police, State—Pennsylvania—History.   I. Title.
HV8145.P4C66   363.2'09748   77–12223
ISBN 0–8117–1224–9

To the men and women whose praise-worthy services have contributed to the greatness of the Pennsylvania State Police Force—and to the men who died in the performance of duty upholding its honor

Contents

APPENDIXES

Acknowledgments

I gratefully acknowledge the assistance of John E. Geschwindt, Judith M. Foust, and Louis F. Rauco of the state library staff, and Mary B. Philpott and Thomas Arnold of the state archives and state records center staffs, all of whom encouragingly saw me through months of research.

Thanks, too, go to Major Arthur J. Oldham, Major Ralph D. Gardner, Major Leon D. Leiter, Captain William L. Nevin, Captain Joseph I. C. Everly, Sergeant Paul M. Gilfoyle, Corporal Steven J. Condes, Robert J. Zinsky, Wade S. Kehler, Myron W. Thomas and numerous other members of the Pennsylvania State Police, active and retired, who took the time to answer inquiries and to recall past events and circumstances so that this documentation might be comprehensively and interestingly portrayed.

Not to be overlooked are the photography services of Corporal John S. Balshy, Robert E. Wallick and Lorna G. Sheetz, and the generosity of those persons who offered priceless photographs to enhance this publication.

A special word of thanks is reserved for Sergeant John J. Gallagher of the First Troop, Philadelphia City Cavalry, Fred A. Lumb, Donald W. Adams, Mrs. Nicholas (Ruth Adams) Schilling, Mrs. C. M. Wilhelm, Mrs. Jacob C. Mauk, and Mrs. John C. Groome, Jr.

To my dear wife, Evelyn, and family, I am grateful for the encouragement and confidence they gave me when I most needed boosters.

I do, indeed, give thanks to God for the enduring privilege of association with the "Finest Thing in the World"—as Katherine Mayo designated it—The Pennsylvania State Police Force.

Introduction

In June, 1975, active and retired members of the Pennsylvania State Police gathered at Hershey, Pennsylvania, to celebrate the seventieth anniversary of the renowned organization's founding. As time marches on, they will look ahead to the festivities of a diamond jubilee in 1980. This granddaddy of all state police agencies, though they vary in structure and responsibilities, was given the breath of life in 1905, under the most unusual of circumstances. This first attempt anywhere on the national scene to maintain law and order by way of a state constabulary is a story of courageous men who acknowledged the unique role that was theirs in history, and determinedly took up the challenge of converting unbelievers.

Their tremendous achievement in creating respect for law throughout Pennsylvania's countryside, where none existed, in comparatively few years, falls little short of a miracle. Tribute, indeed, must be paid to Governor Samuel W. Pennypacker whose insistence gave rise to this noble experiment, and Captain John C. Groome, the constabulary's first superintendent, whose ingenuity guided his organization through its formative years as the eyes of the nation remained focused on him and his mounted troopers.

Writer Katherine Mayo, a native Pennsylvanian, living much of her time in the lawless environment of New York State, set about writing a history of the Pennsylvania constabulary with expectation that her book and personal lobbying would encourage the passage of legislation creating a New York State Police Force patterned after the Pennsylvania agency. With an influential lift from former President Theodore Roosevelt and others, Miss Mayo saw her dream come true when the New York constabulary was authorized in 1917—the second such organization in the United States.

11

However Miss Mayo intended her books to be used (she wrote three about the Pennsylvania constabulary), honors must be bestowed on that grand lady for recording much of the constabulary's early history. Except for her writings, the cupboard is rather bare.

Neither the executive offices of the Pennsylvania State Police nor other state sources can presently provide organized historical data to satisfy research needs. Throughout the years, and in increasing numbers in more recent times, literally thousands of requests for research material from high school and college students have found their way to State Police headquarters only to have inexpensive, meager brochures and fact sheets sent to them in reply. Time after time, the inability to refer inquirers to an updated history of the department has been a point of embarrassment for State Police officials. In fact, all during the years of the Force's existence, young troopers themselves have not had the benefit of reading about their organization's history in textbook fashion. They have had to quench their thirst for this valued background information from the reading of Miss Mayo's works and sketchy articles, and listening to the traditional tales of training school instructors and old-timers in the field.

This is not to say that thought was never given to overcoming this embarrassing problem by preparing an adequate documentation. To the contrary, discussions regarding the preparation of a suitable State Police history did take place, but unfortunately without real headway being made. As the years passed, with much more history to be written about, the enormity of such a history-writing task increased proportionately; no remedial alternative surfaced. A bibliography, however, found in the final pages of this publication attests to the wide assortment of official documents and a miscellany of articles written by newsmen and other writers who have considered the State Police a worthy subject at key points in the Force's history, or in the lives of its commanders.

Mindful of this unhappy situation, the thought of writing a State Police history was not a johnny-come-lately one for me. The seeds of this project, in fact, were sown a long time ago. Like a string-saver, I accumulated an assortment of notes, publications, and clippings to fill a four-drawer filing cabinet to overflow. Little of historical importance escaped notice.

A lengthy illness in 1974 and my retirement from the Pennsylvania State Police in 1975, after 37½ years of service, hastened the day for getting the project underway. Bicentennial year 1976, to be sure, presented no more appropriate time for history-writing.

This publication will provide a suitable study base for all students, and non-students, who maintain an interest in law enforcement, particularly, the contributions of the Pennsylvania State Police and the magnificent men who built its worldwide reputation.

Miss Mayo's writings mainly capture the constabulary's early history from the operational point of view—where much of the action was. She was thrilled by the exciting deeds of the troopers and their officers, which in themselves could fill volumes unendingly.

I have elected to take an entirely different viewpoint by telling the State Police story from the lesser-known executive level, where certainly there, too, has been and is excitement of another kind.

Superintendents and commissioners have suffered through distressful experiences to keep the organization moving progressively in the face of ever-increasing demands frequently accompanied by diminishing resources—and, at the same time, cope with the intrigue and personality clashes that all too often confronted them. These latter and shameful circumstances cannot be rightfully labelled as inevitable. Good intentions notwithstanding, these less desirable conditions crept insidiously into the Force, and, for the most part, the tribulations were dealt with by top executives, successfully or not, without attracting public notice.

As I am suggesting, everything has not been peaches and cream for top officers. To offer anything for research that resembles a touched-up photograph would be cheating the researcher. By the same token, this publication is not—and was never planned to be—an exposé to spotlight skeletons in the closet, or satisfy sensationalism. Events are depicted as they happened.

Before getting on with the actual history of the Pennsylvania State Police from the moment of its conception, I have first introduced the reader to the unbelievable lawlessness that existed in Pennsylvania before 1905 to create an appreciation for the need of a state constabulary. Although millions of citizens are very much upset today with their chances of becoming victims of crime, it would be appalling for many to imagine themselves in a land without representatives of the law at all. Regrettably, while a sheriff-constable system did exist in all counties of the state, its ineffectiveness easily gave way to contemptuous wrongdoers and did nothing to bolster public morale. Nevertheless, that is how it was in the pre-constabulary era, when everyone did his unlawful thing almost without fear whatsoever of punishment, and Darwin's newly-propounded theory of the survival of the fittest, as a way of life, was not difficult at all to believe.

The chapters follow the successive administrations of top management, although the two closing chapters dwell on subjects of other interest.

One of the closing chapters bears upon the establishment of the

State Police Civic Association in 1918, its growth and demise. The Civic Association was conceived originally as an instrument to financially care for widows and children of deceased troopers. Later, its purpose was enlarged to provide retirement benefits for those officers and men who survived the rigors of constabulary life to qualify.

The final chapter honors the brave men who were killed in the line of duty. The Call of Honor, an essential ingredient of every trooper's training since the early twenties, contains as one of its pledges, "I must serve honestly, faithfully, and if need be, lay down my life as others have done before me, rather than swerve from the path of duty." Some seventy men, mostly young troopers, drew their last breath of life in the fulfillment of this principle. By their sacrifices, they have inspired fellow troopers to a greater strength of purpose that has rendered certain the greatness of the Pennsylvania State Police Force.

Worthy of mention is the fact that early superintendents and commissioners enjoyed long tenure. Services of pioneers Captain John C. Groome, Colonel Lynn G. Adams, and Colonel Cecil M. Wilhelm span almost a half-century. They were legendary giants in the business. Their string of service was broken only by Colonel Percy W. Foote's nineteen-month stay. Not to be forgotten is the service of Captain Wilson C. Price, who headed the State Highway Patrol for thirteen of that unique organization's fourteen years of existence. In contrast, the twenty-two years since 1955 have seen eight top men in command of the State Police: Colonel Earl J. Henry, Colonel Frank G. McCartney, Colonel E. Wilson Purdy, Lt. Colonel Paul A. Rittelmann, Colonel Frank McKetta, Colonel Rocco P. Urella, Colonel James D. Barger, and Colonel Paul J. Chylak.

Changing times and circumstances—particularly the placing of the commissioner's post on an equal footing with cabinet appointments and the very political nature of these appointments—make it a certainty that the days of long tenure are gone. The records of Groome, Adams, and Wilhelm will remain untouched forever—and that's a mighty long time, as the saying goes.

The opportunity of serving under all State Police heads, with the exception of the department's founder, Captain John C. Groome, and Colonel Paul J. Chylak, whose appointment came in 1977, has filled my life with cherished moments beyond expectation. Abounding with challenges and excitement, the years of association with State Police greats have been an unforgettable experience. To Captain Guy E. Reichard, Comptroller Silvus J. Overmiller, Colonel Lynn G. Adams, Colonel C. M. Wilhelm, Colonel Frank G. McCartney, Colonel E. Wilson Purdy, and Colonel Rocco P. Urella, I am forever indebted. The latter two are the only survivors of this illustrious group.

Throughout this history, wherever research bore fruit, credit has been given to officers, troopers, and civilian employees, by name, for their outstanding, unselfish contributions to the welfare of the Force. It is only proper that each be singled out for recognition; it is truly because of the likes of them that the Force rose to prominence.

To every reader, then, is this documentation commended with sincere anticipation that each chapter will create a deeper appreciation for the highly-regarded Pennsylvania State Police Force.

CHAPTER I

Pre-Constabulary Years Industrial Revolution—Immigration

Except for the horrors of the Civil War, perhaps nothing so affected the tranquility of this nation during the latter half of the nineteenth century and the early years of the twentieth as did the Industrial Revolution. The years of the Industrial Revolution saw the countryside, especially here in Pennsylvania, changed from a basic farm economy to an economy heavily shared by new industry and business. And with this change came turmoil, destruction, and death that shook Pennsylvania society in both rural and urban areas for decades with increasing intensity.

Completely ignoring the strife that accompanied the Industrial Revolution, the 1968–69 *Pennsylvania Manual* summarizes that era in sterile terms,

In 1970 the domestic system of home manufacture still prevailed in Pennsylvania. By 1865 the factory system was fully established, and the foundations of the State's industrial greatness were well laid. The change was most noticeable after 1840. The shift to machinery and factory production came first in the textile industry, and Pennsylvania early assumed leadership in this field, along with New England. By 1860 there were more than two hundred textile mills. Pennsylvania's outstanding industrial achievements, however, were in iron and steel. Its production of iron was notable even in

17

colonial times, and the charcoal furnaces of the State spread
into the Juniata and western regions during the middle
decades of the nineteenth century. Foundries, rolling mills,
and machine shops became numerous after 1840, and by the
Civil War the State rolled about half the nation's iron. The
iron industry aided the development of the railroad age by
furnishing rails and locomotives. The Baldwin Works were
established in Philadelphia in 1842. The Bethlehem Company
was organized in 1862. The Cambria Works at Johnstown date
from 1854 and by the end of the Civil War were the largest
mills in the country. William Kelly, a native of Pittsburgh, is
regarded by many as the inventor of the so-called Bessemer
process of making steel. The iron and steel industry of the
State was a basic factor in the industrial strength which enabled the North to preserve the Union under Lincoln.
Leathermaking, lumbering, shipbuilding, and publishing were
other important fields of enterprise. Tobacco and paper
manufacture were also important. In many of these, Pennsylvania enjoyed a leadership which has since been lost, but the
industrial techniques and often the nationally known firms
themselves originated in the Keystone State. The location of
the State, its rich resources, and the enterprise of its citizens
may be considered the basic reasons for this industrial advance.

In his political pamphlet, *The Constabulary of Pennsylvania,* labor
leader Charles A. Maurer in 1911 had these serious reflections:

Pennsylvania unquestionably leads all other states in her industrial development. The higher the development, the more
keen becomes the struggle between the producer and the ex-
ploiter. This state but a century ago, enveloped in her beautiful mantle of green, her thousands of miles of timber, her
sparkling, well-stocked rivers of fish, her boundless mineral
deposits; her free, thrifty, unsuspecting citizens, Pennsylvania was indeed a fertile field for the serpent-like monster of
capitalism to fasten its fangs upon. From its innocent, worm-
like appearance less than a century ago, only noticeable at a
few spots, it has developed faster than any other monster of
exploitation in the history of the world.
    The cannibalistic nature of the pest, and the glutton-like
manner in which it fed upon its own kind, well nigh ex-
terminated the species, hence those best fitted to survive
developed into a different species, known as the octopus, and
this octopus has encircled the entire State; it has done more; it
has devoured not only the surface, but the very vitals of the

Commonwealth. It has denuded the forests, poisoned the streams with its slime of greed, turned thousands of square miles of the green, velvet-like pasture into barren black desert. It has arrogated unto itself the mineral deposits, worth billions. It has debauched the public officials, from the lowest to the highest. It has enslaved its people, sapped the vitality of its children, and crucified thousands of its daughters on the altar of prostitution. Time and again have the suffering citizens tried to protect themselves against the encroachment of this cruel, hideous monster, and as many times were they crushed, beaten and murdered.

A 1963 Pennsylvania State Police publication has these comments to make:

Pennsylvania's coal fields, iron mills and timber forests played a key role in the Industrial Revolution. Changed in the late 1800s from a largely agricultural state into a complex industrial center, Pennsylvania by 1900 found itself torn by bitter disputes between managers and the laborers they employed by the almost constant violence within the new communities which sprung up around the coal fields, iron mills, textile factories and railroad yards.

By the turn of the century, it was evident that the town constables, sheriffs and similar local officials—who had been adequate to keep the peace in more stable times among homogeneous communities—were overwhelmed in their attempts to cope with the huge foreign-born populations, and hard-pressed to keep order amidst the violent labor troubles of the times.

Today, the problems accompanying any disregard for law and order are referred to well-administered police agencies whose members are trained and capable of dealing with most problems. During the years of the Industrial Revolution, however, police departments were for the most part non-existent. "There was a reluctance to organize police in England and the United States because the police looked too much like the king's army," wrote Thomas J. Fleming.

According to Fleming, it was not until 1829 that the police force of London was unified, and then only because a severe crime wave served as a final persuader. The London Police Department, a concept of Sir Robert Peel, was the first metropolitan organization of record. It was not until 1845 that New York City organized its police department, mainly because of major riots. The same impetus gave rise to police agencies in other U.S. cities. Rioting stemmed for the most part from clashes between immigrants and native-born Americans. In other words, the police forces in this country were originally created in response to massive disorder bordering on anarchy.

The organization of such police forces, however, did not in themselves bring rioting to a halt. Deep-rooted, emotion-packed issues were plentiful on the American scene and once they erupted into incidents endangering life and property the police could do no more than their level best to minimize such losses. And when such efforts failed, state officials had no choice but the costly call-up of their organized militia. The widespread effects of this latter action were to be avoided, if at all possible.

The New York City draft riots of 1863, a three-day upheaval, for instance, are still described as "the most serious challenge to law and order in American history." It is conjectured that the number of dead in New York's draft riots exceeded by far the anticipated number of draftees who would have been killed in Civil War service had the New Yorkers responded lawfully to the call to arms. That is a pitiful conclusion, indeed. The New York police, already organized for eighteen years, were completely overwhelmed, and it was necessary for Union officials in Washington to recall military units from combat zones to a strange battlefield in Manhattan.

On the Pennsylvania scene, police were organized professionally only in Philadelphia and Pittsburgh. All other county areas were served by an ineffective sheriff-constable system. This system was adequate when Pennsylvania's rural population, as Katherine Mayo described it, "came of generations of law-revering stock."

Mayo continued:

But with passing years, all this has changed—changed in part through an influx of foreign immigration great and greater in numbers, less and lesser in understanding of our ways of thought. To such an immigration, liberty had no meaning other than gross license and it gave incredulous laughter to the notion of invisibly guarded law. Looking about them these men saw no gendarmerie, no carabinieri, no uniformed patrol upon the road.

During the 1860s, the ugliness of this situation was made more intolerable by the lawful establishment of private police forces by Pennsylvania corporations seeking protection for themselves—protection that was no where else attainable. The Pennsylvania General Assembly, succumbing to corporate pressures, first passed Act 228, P.L. 225, on February 28, 1865, creating the Railroad Police. This enactment was closely followed by the passage of Act 87, P.L. 99, on April 11, 1866, which authorized "all corporations, firms, or individuals owning, leasing, or being in possession of any colliery, furnace, or rolling mill, within this commonwealth" to create what was to be known as the "Coal and Iron Police." Lamenting this development, Mayo wrote, "In time of turmoil, when the laboring masses rocked in mortal deadlock with the vested interests, the State stepped in to prove her impartial justice by selling her authority into the vested interests' hands!"

These enactments allowed the corporations to appoint, pay and maintain their own police forces by simply applying to the State for commissions conferring police powers upon these men for one dollar a commission. On this point, Mayo commented, "Therefore whenever the miners elected to go out on strike pending the adjustment of a dispute with their employers, they invariably found the power of the State bought, paid for, and fighting as a partisan on their employers' side."

Many of those applying for Coal and Iron Police commissions were described as "common gunmen, hoodlums and adventurers," who drifted in from the unemployed ranks of Pennsylvania's population centers. By their misconduct and abuse of police powers bestowed on them, they too often brought on incidents of violence and terror which they were hired to prevent.

Scarcely had a decade gone by since the formation of the infamous Coal and Iron Police when the activities of the equally infamous Molly Maguires hit Pennsylvania's anthracite coal fields. In his account of the Molly Maguires, Negley K. Teeters had this to say about the terroristic secret society that dominated the political life of several counties in the Pennsylvania coal region,

> Looking backward, we can afford to be more charitable of this harassing and harassed group of Irish immigrants although, obviously, we cannot condone their evil methods of gaining their rights in the labor struggle. No honest critic of labor can excuse the coal barons of the Pennsylvania anthracite region of that era for their exploitive methods nor excuse the dominant earlier settlers of the region—the Welsh and English—for excluding the later Irish immigrants from earning a living in the mines. The story of the Molly Maguires is certainly not one-sided. They resented their economic lot which was a hard one and were particularly determined to undermine the power of the coal companies and their bosses.

The Mollies were infiltrated by a Pinkerton undercover agent,

James McParlan, whose excellent work in disclosing the operations
and deeds of the Mollies lead to their downfall. Teeters wrote:

> Carrying this law enforcement to its necessary conclusion,
> which was ultimately done, required great courage on the part
> of police, jurists, and hundreds of common citizens who were
> called upon to testify at their trials, because of the terrific
> pressure and intimidation. Ten Mollies were hanged on June
> 21, 1877—six in Pottsville and four in Mauch Chunk. This was
> known locally as "Black Thursday." Ten more were hanged
> during the next two years, bringing the total to twenty. Law
> and order were finally established in the region, but it took
> vast sums of money, courage and a sustained determination
> on the part of public officials and citizens alike to demonstrate
> that the forces of outlawry and nihilism have no place in this
> free country.

Teeter's reference to police is undoubtedly a tribute to the Pinkerton agency which again and again surfaces in Pennsylvania history
in connection with major incidents of lawlessness.

"Aside from the hanging of the thirty-eight Sioux Indians at
Mankato, Minnesota (December 26, 1862), this mass hanging is the
largest ever held in this country. It exceeds the witch orgy of New England by one lone victim of the gallows," concluded Teeters' story of
the Mollies.

The phenomenal growth of the railroad system in the country set
the stage for another source of labor difficulties. The most destructive
of the railroad disorders occurred in 1877, and reportedly originated at
Martinsburg, West Virginia, when officials of the Baltimore & Ohio
Railroad announced a second round of wage reductions. The strike
quickly spread to other states.

Local authorities were unable to maintain law and order and it was
essential for state governments to move in the militia. "In Pittsburgh,
Baltimore, and other railroad centers, strikers fought the militia and
troops to a standstill and even into retreat; indeed, the massive use of
armed forces to contain or suppress domestic troubles was a new
experience for the nation," so commented Joseph A. Dacus.

In Pittsburgh sixteen persons were instantly killed by militia
gunfire. Later eight soldiers were killed as was the sheriff of Allegheny
County. Railroad depots, utility buildings and freight trains were
burned by mob action with millions of dollars suffered in property
losses. Dacus reported, "The scenes of pillage witnessed during that
memorable Sunday, July 22, 1877, in the city of Pittsburgh, were such
as were never before witnessed in this country; not even during the war
between the sections (Civil War)."

In Reading thirteen persons were killed and forty-three wounded, including five police officers, one of whom died two days later. Riots occurred at Philadelphia, Erie, Sunbury, Meadville, Altoona, Mauch Chunk, Lebanon, Marietta, Harrisburg, Wilkes-Barre, Shenendoah, Scranton, Hazleton, and Johnstown, all of which communities were occupied by soldiers. At Johnstown several soldiers were killed upon their arrival there by mob gunfire.

The bituminous coal fields and steel industries of southwest Pennsylvania took no back seat in recording their share of murderous disorders. Major rioting took place in Homestead, near Pittsburgh, in mid-1892, some eleven years after the founding of the iron and steel works in that community. There, on July 6, 1892, a pitched battle was fought between the 4,000 members of the Amalgamated Association of Iron and Steel Workers and 300 Pinkerton guards employed by the Carnegie Steel Company officials, spearheaded by the headstrong Andrew Clay Frick. Arthur G. Burgoyne, in his detailed account of the Homestead incident, stated, "Four thousand infuriated steelworkers and three hundred caged Pinkertons were to be left to fight out their deadly quarrel without let or hindrance. The dictates of law and humanity were alike suspended upon that July day—the most unfortunate day in the history of organized labor in the United States."

Before hostilities were ended on that single day three Pinkerton guards and seven workers lay dead. Scores were wounded on both sides. The Pinkerton surrendered their arms and were marched from riverside to Homestead's streets. "By actual count, one hundred and forty-three survivors were suffering from painful wounds and contusions, and those who had by extraordinary good luck, escaped with a whole skin, were half dead from fear and exhaustion, " wrote Burgoyne.

Governor Robert E. Pattison ordered out 4,000 national guardsmen on July 11, and it was not until October 13, after ninety-five days of military surveillance, before the militia was gone from that area. Reportedly, the Carnegie Steel Company suffered a loss of $250,000, while the steelworkers lost $850,000 in wages. The state paid out $500,000 to support the militia action. With costs for extra deputy sheriffs, court costs for prosecutions that followed and the drain on relief funds, the total bill for all concerned exceeded $2,000,000. In his remarks, Burgoyne observed that this bill was, "An enormous sum to be paid for the gratification of Mr. Frick's desire to get rid of unions and unionism."

Burgoyne summed up the Homestead situation like this:

Since labor first organized for its own protection it has passed through no period more prolific in soul-stirring events and significant developments than that extending from July to November, 1892, and including the lock-out at the Carnegie mills, the battle with the 300 Pinkerton guards, the military occupation of Homestead, the trial of labor leaders on capital charges and the ultimate collapse of the Amalgamated lodges for lack of funds to continue the struggle against non-unionism. This was a conflict of far more than local interest. It was watched with anxiety by both friends and foes of organized labor on both sides of the Atlantic; it claimed the attention of leaders of thought in all departments of human activity; it stirred up the British House of Parliament and the United States Congress, agitated the newspaper press of both continents, became an issue in the election for President and is said to have contributed more largely to the defeat of Benjamin Harrison by Grover Cleveland than any other influence.

Although mention so far has been made only of the widely-publicized labor disturbances, the Pennsylvania countryside was equally tormented by a lesser-publicized crime wave. All communities, almost without exception, suffered at the hands of those who murdered and gravely assaulted. Drunkenness, disorderly conduct, gambling and disregard for property rights were common everyday occurrences.

The Black Hand Society plotted almost unhampered in extorting from the more prosperous of the Italian immigrants large sums of money. In some cases, the Italian victims lost all of their worldly possessions to the extortionists. There was little or no thought given to resisting their efforts, once a victim was contacted by the Black Hand. The alternative to resistance was death.

As far back as 1869, the state legislature made some attempts at controlling crime in the rural areas. Reportedly at that time the northwest counties of Pennsylvania were beset by horse thieves and cattle rustlers from bordering Ohio. Yielding to petitions for protection against such forays, the general assembly authorized by the passage of Act 991, P.L. 1002, April 15, 1869 the formation of the Spring Valley Police Company of Crawford County. Again in April of the following year, 1870, the legislators passed Act 1359, P.L. 1486, creating the Conneaut Police Company, also situated in Crawford County. Both companies were brought into existence mainly to recover stolen horses and other property. A third police organization was created in 1872 with the passage of Act 1109, P.L. 1061, on April 3, by the general assembly, which was then and is still known as the State Police of Crawford and Erie Counties. The latter agency was founded for the purpose of recovering stolen horses and other property and for the detection of thieves in Crawford and Erie Counties. Although members of these police companies displayed badges as a symbol of authority, they were unsalaried and wore no distinguishing uniform.

According to a statement made by Captain George F. Lumb some decades later, Sheriff Leonard L. Ray, of Venango County, which lies adjacent to Crawford County, is credited with having suggested the formation of a state police organization to members of the general assembly in 1890.

As long as "liberty had no meaning other than gross license," the plight of crimes' victims was to continue.

At the turn of the century, the population of Pennsylvania, according to the 1900 census figures, was 6,302,115. This figure was broken down into unique categories which would be meaningless in reviewing a more recent population make-up; however, in 1900, these categories provided private and public administrators with data that, at least, had meaning to them insofar as population affected their respective problems:

	Native Born		
Male	2,650,543		
Female	2,666,322	5,316,865	
	Foreign Born		
Male	553,998		
Female	431,252	985,250	6,302,115
	Native White-Native Parents		
Male	1,860,185		
Female	1,868,908	3,729,093	
	Native White-Foreign Parents		
Male	710,528		
Female	719,500	1,430,028	
	Foreign White		
Male	551,591		
Female	430,952	982,543	
	Non-White		
Male	82,237		
Female	78,214	160,451*	

*Negro, Chinese, Japanese and Indian

The "Foreign Born" group constitutes sixteen percent of the state's population. When this group is combined with the "Native White—Foreign Parents" group, the total of 2,415,278 represents thirty-eight percent of Pennsylvania's population. It is natural to assume that the first generation offspring of foreign-born parents would come heavily under the influence of their parents and approach their social problems somewhat in the same fashion. In any case, this high percentage figure of thirty-eight was to be weighed importantly by government authorities in assessing the social problems of their times.

At this point it might be well to review some interesting facts about European immigration to the United States as expressed by Richard Gambino in his documentation, *Blood of My Blood*. Gambino wrote:

> Mass immigration to the United States had been an accepted, even welcomed phenomenon before 1840. There was no anti-immigration response—for two reasons. First, the nation was still expanding its frontiers. There was plenty of room and work for all. Second, these early immigrants were from the British Isles and Northeastern Europe. They were of the same ethnic group as most of the founders of the country—White "Anglo-Saxon" Protestants. In fact, as late as 1864, despite the already active Know-Nothing movement, then aimed at the Irish, the official policy of the American government as written in a law passed that year was to encourage immigration. In the next decades, however, pressure to exclude immigration rose rapidly as the ethnic composition of the immigrants changed. They were no longer predominantly WASP. 1899, when the total United States population was fifty million, Protestants were among the minority (18.5 percent) of immigrants. The majority (52 percent) were Roman Catholics, and 10.5 percent were Jews. In the next eleven years 2,300,000 were to arrive from Italy alone, only 400,000 of these from Northern Italy. And by 1925, there were upwards of five million Italian-Americans, a figure the nativists found alarming.
>
> The Italian percentage of the total immigration to the United States jumped from 6.7 percent in 1821–1902 to 26.9 percent in 1903. In the next decade, an annual average of more than two hundred thousand Italians reached the United States.

This "alarming" situation was eventually to lead to the setting of immigration quotas.

According to Gambino,

The marriage of manual labor and life, so much a part of

Italian-American saga, was begun for many immigrants by a "wedding" that took place even before they reached American shores. For the labor contract that accompanied many of them on the voyage was as binding as any marriage certificate. The contract system was a product of collaboration between steamship carriers, American businessmen, Northern Italian bureaucrats, and Southern Italian opportunists. It was enormously profitable for those who ran it and greatly exploitive of those subjected to it.

In the system, American businesses (urban and agricultural) that needed cheap labor contacted a shipping line engaged in immigrant traffic. This traffic was of enormous proportions. By the year 1900 it had already invested $118,000,000 in the business of carrying immigrants from Europe to the United States.

It would be most difficult for modern-day travelers to appreciate the filthy, intolerable conditions of steerage travel to which European immigrants were subjected. On this point, Gambino wrote:

Conditions of immigrant travel were so bad that, as Terry Coleman records in his book on the subject called *Going to America* (1972), New York City at one point charged ships' captains a ten-dollar fee for each dead passenger. The device failed. Captains merely buried the dead at sea and altered passenger lists to avoid the penalty. Although the United States and Italian governments made other, sporadic efforts to control the abuse of steerage, the appalling conditions continued. The trade was simply too profitable.

Despite the dehumanizing experience of steerage, immigrants heartened by the promises of bread and work were determined to leave behind them the equally unbearable social circumstances in their native lands. Mostly "peasant farmers, fisherman, artisans, and unskilled urban poor," they had for centuries endured the hardships of enemy invasions, ruthless occupations, enslavement, overtaxing, and death. Justice could not be easily explained away to those who suffered such cruelties, nor to their descendants into whose hands tradition passed.
Gambino wrote:

At first the labor movement resented the Italians as cheap labor threatening their uphill attempts to organize and empower the American worker. And, indeed, attempts were made by American companies to use the earlier Italian immigrants as "union busters." Thus in 1874, striking miners turned on a group of Italians imported by the Armstrong Coal

Works in Pennsylvania to be unwitting scabs. Several Italians were killed. In 1907, the Dillingham Commission, established by the United States Congress, reported that "strike after strike in the Pennsylvania coalfields in the 1870's and the early 1880's was smashed when employers brought in Slavic, Hungarian, and Italian labor."

Italians soon caught onto the design to use them as pawns, and turned toward pro-union activities themselves.

As each wave of immigrants came to American shores, its masses had to struggle with predecessors for a decent foothold. And their frequent lawless activities became a matter of deep concern to those who longed to see law and order prevail. In reviewing Katherine Mayo's comments, "To such an immigration, liberty had no meaning other than gross license," it is essential in all fairness to understand, if possible, the adjustment that had to be undergone by the exploited newcomers.

In Pennsylvania, a turning point was reached in 1902. Many sheriffs' deputies and labor rioters were killed in riot skirmishes at Lattimer that year, and the "Great Anthracite Coal Strike," as it was to become known later, was more than Pennsylvania and the nation could endure. This latter strike, because of its own characteristics and spilling-over effect upon the nation, was to give rise to serious thought about the need for a state police to fill the void in law enforcement where it was most sorely needed to cool the heels of both management and labor without siding with either.

In this labor controversy the miners were represented by the United Mine Workers of America (UMW). The UMW was formed at Columbus, Ohio, in January, 1890, by the merger of two organizations: Coal Miners' and Laborers' National Progressive Union and the National Trade Assembly 135 of the Knights of Labor. At the time of the merger the UMW numbered some 17,000 members.

The miners themselves did not enjoy unanimity except on the grounds of their common disaffection for the coal barons for whom they labored. The effects of xenophobia were deeply felt throughout the anthracite region as waves of immigrants arrived on the scene. According to Robert J. Cornell, who chronicled the events of the Great Anthracite Strike,

Prior to 1870 the so-called "English-speaking races"—the English, Irish, Scotch, Welsh, and Germans—furnished practically all the labor supply in the anthracite fields. About 1880, however, the United States witnessed the beginning of mass immigration of Poles, Lithuanians, Hungarians and

Italians, and many of these people moved into the anthracite region. By 1890 these "Slavs" constituted about one-forth of the foreign-born population in the anthracite counties.

Cornell held strongly to the belief that the mine operators may have been responsible for the increased immigration to the coal fields. Such movement helped the operators to keep wages suppressed by irregular work practices—not through the reduction of wages but by virtue of surplus labor. The "Slavs" fared much better than the English-speaking elements because they were accustomed to a lower scale of living.

"In the year of confusion, 1902," reported Katherine Mayo,

the State of Pennsylvania fell victim to what was perhaps the most serious and distressful industrial disturbance yet known to our history. The great Anthracite Strike, begun on May 12th of that year, lasted until the 23rd of the following October. It destroyed the equilibrium of the State at large; it wrecked the peace of seven counties; it took its toll of human lives, and sowed its harvest of pregnant bitterness. It cost the striking miners and their associates some $25,000,000 in wages; it impoverished their relief fund by the amount of $1,800,000; it cost the coal companies $46,100,000 in estimated reduced production; it cost the transportation companies about $28,000,000 in freight losses; and it penalized the country at large by a coal famine and an advance in the price of anthracite. Besides all this, it forced the State, in defense of her laws and her dignity, to call out her entire division of National Guard, at an expense of $996,052.55 of the people's money.

President Theodore Roosevelt intervened in October, 1902, and appointed an arbitration panel acceptable to both sides to investigate the strike's causes and recommend action to be taken in settlement. The president of the United Mine Workers of America, John Mitchell, was instrumental in getting the strikers back to work pending the outcome of the arbitration board's deliberations. The miners went back to work on October 23, and the National Guardsmen were released from their prolonged strike duty. The Anthracite Coal Strike Commission began its work in Washington the following day.

Of John Mitchell, Cornell had this to state, "At a time when organized labor was still struggling for proper recognition by the general public the whole labor movement as well as the miners' union was fortunate in that John Mitchell directed the strike effort and served as spokesman for the cause. His conservative leadership commended itself to the American public who had come to associate unionism with radicalism, and who now could contrast the intemperate attacks on Mitchell and his organization and the seemingly indifferent attitude of the operators toward the public interest with the moderate and conciliatory statements and policy of the miners' leader.''

Before the President's Anthracite Coal Strike Commission, the miners were represented by the renowned barrister, Clarence Darrow, who served as UMW chief counsel.

All of this continuing turbulence and lawlessness in Pennsylvania and elsewhere gave painful evidence to Thomas Fleming's claim that ''a wave of anarchism swept the country just before and after 1900.''

CHAPTER II

Creation of the
Department of State Police
1905

It was during the tenure of Governor William A. Stone (1899–1903) that the Great Anthracite Coal Strike occurred. In his final message to the general assembly in Harrisburg on January 6, 1903, Stone dwelled at length on the subject of this major catastrophe. "The strike of the miners and their associate workmen in the Anthracite Coal Region was probably the most important and far-reaching event of its kind that ever occurred in the State," reported Stone.

Stone explained the sequence of riotous and uncontrollable incidents that prompted his decision to call up the National Guard for strike duty: "The National Guard served for a period of 105 days—the longest period during the last fifty years, excepting the industrial disturbances of 1892 (Homestead) when the National Guard was on duty from July 20 to September 20 and then relieved by the First Regiment Volunteers from September 20 to November 15."

The governor referred to his message to the general assembly at its opening session in 1901, at which time he sought a compulsory arbitration law as a means of settling difficulties between employer and employee. Apparently his recommendation for ending such labor disputes received no favorable treatment from the legislators. In the meantime, the Great Anthracite Coal Strike took place and was being studied by President Roosevelt's special commission. Stone took the occasion of his departure to warn the general assembly that some significant action

Governor Samuel W. Pennypacker (Courtesy of Pennsylvania Historical and Museum Commission)

must be taken by that body to ward off the recurrence of such terrifying events.

The outgoing governor lived to see the creation of the state constabulary under his successor's term of office two years later. Although it was not his proposal for controlling lawlessness in the Commonwealth, he witnessed the fine work accomplished by the state constabulary in seeing to it that the mistakes of 1902 would never be repeated.

Pennsylvania's new governor was Samuel W. Pennypacker, a native son, born in Phoenixville on April 9, 1843. Before his election as governor, Pennypacker was a school teacher, lawyer, author, veteran of the Battle of Gettysburg, and judge.

Katherine Mayo wrote:

> Governor Pennypacker was a student and writer of Pennsylvania history; therefore he abounded in knowledge of causes back of present social aspects in the State. Governor Pennypacker came of old Pennsylvania-German stock; therefore he was a lover of established and prosperous peace. Governor Pennypacker, finally, was first and last a farmer, of traditional farming blood; therefore his sympathies lay with the farmers and he realized with a deep and personal conviction how illogical, how unjust, and how dangerous was the flaccid ignoring by the State of the rights of her country people to protection under those laws and under that government of whose stability they themselves were always the firmest supports.

Just as his predecessor had shown deep concern for labor disturbances in his final message to the general assembly just two weeks before, Governor Pennypacker could not conceal his serious thoughts on this same problem as he delivered his inaugural address on January 20, 1903.

Pointing a finger at the disasters of labor disturbances, Pennypacker had this to say:

> In Pennsylvania conflicts between concentrated capital and organized labor are of frequent occurence and often result in cessation of production, loss of both profits and earnings, violations of the law and disturbance and inconvenience to the community. They present some of the most difficult and complicated problems with which modern administration is confronted. They occur more frequently here than elsewhere because of the great number of our industries requiring the employment of masses of men, many of them born in other

lands, and some of them uneducated, unfamiliar with our language and indifferent to our institutions.

His deep respect for law and order are embodied in his admonition, "No capitalist is strong enough and no laborer is insignificant enough to escape obedience to the law." Pennypacker, an attorney and former jurist, made no attempt to disguise his position that "no man should be permitted to interfere upon any pretence whatever with another who may choose to sell his labor, and violence from whatever source it may come should be promptly and rigidly suppressed, using whatever force may be necessary for that purpose."

Midway through his term as governor, Pennypacker was to see that "force" to which he referred honorably exemplified by the Commonwealth's 228-man state constabulary, to his everlasting credit.

On one occasion after his inauguration, Pennypacker was asked by the deputy secretary of the Commonwealth to sign an armful of Coal and Iron Police commissions. Questions led to the fact that the names on the commissions were supplied by the companies themselves. The episode was ended by Pennypacker's declaration, "Take them away! I will never put the police power of the State in the hands of nominees of one of the parties to a controversy. We must have an independent constabulary."

On March 18, 1903, after a winter of study and deliberation, the Anthracite Coal Strike Commission submitted its report to President Roosevelt. The commission's report found the five-month strike "stained with riot and bloodshed." Brushing aside momentarily the injustices of both sides, the commission blamed the Commonwealth for contributing in no small way to the strike and its consequences by not fulfilling her obligation "to enforce her own laws with her own hand and to protect all of her people." "Peace and order," the commission cited, "should be maintained by regularly appointed and responsible officers and at the expense of the public."

At issue in the coal strike was the role of the Coal and Iron Police, in which the State was justly accused of selling out her authority "into the vested interests' hands!" It was estimated that the Coal and Iron Police by this time numbered 5,000. "Therefore President Roosevelt's Anthracite Strike Commission wrote as the very first of its general recommendations a clear call for legislative action creating a proper executive arm to enforce the laws with impartial might—a call in the name of peace, justice, and the honor of the State, and of the equal good of all men, for the creation of a new thing in the land—for the creation of a State Police," reported Mayo.

"Samuel Whitaker Pennypacker, the new Governor of the Commonwealth," continued Mayo, might have taken all summer to think it over—might, in fact, have taken still another twelvemonth, since the Legislature of Pennsylvania meets only on alternate years. But Samuel Whitaker Pennypacker did not need the time. His mind was already made up. He had worked it out before.

"In the year 1903, when I assumed the office of Chief Executive of the State (he later liked to recount) I found myself thereby invested with supreme executive authority. I found that no power existed to interfere with me in my duty to enforce the laws of the State, and that, by the same token, no conditions could release me from my duty to do so. I then looked about to see what instruments I possessed wherewithal to accomplish this bounden obligation—what instruments on whose loyalty and obedience I could truly rely. And I perceived three such instruments—my private secretary, a very small man, my woman stenographer, and the janitor, a negro. So, I made the State Police."

The general assembly, however, adjourned on April 16, 1903, much too early for Pennypacker to pursue his concept of a state constabulary and seek enabling legislation. Since the state legislature met every other year, Pennypacker had time to contemplate a new department and the strategy required for passage of legal measures in the upcoming 1905 session. He was determined that a state constabulary would see light of day before the 1905 session was adjourned.

The 1905 General Assembly on Janauary 3 opened its first session ceremoniously amidst the trappings of a gala affair. Both the Senate and House occupied their chambers in the new captiol which, although not entirely completed, was readied for the legislators' use. Florists from every corner of the Commonwealth sent flowers to decorate the chambers, and the *Harrisburg Telegraph* described the Senate as "a veritable flower garden."

On that same day, Governor Pennypacker submitted his biennial message to the legislature. Among some twenty recommendations for action by the legislature was the creation of a state constabulary. He briefly summed up the creation and powers of the Coal and Iron Police who exercised the authority of the Commonwealth. He pointed out some recent figures on the issuance of commissions:

1901	570 commissions
1902	4,512 commissions
1903	186 commissions
1904	187 commissions

The reduction in the number of commissions issued during his first two years in office (1903–1904) reflected Pennypacker's distaste for the entire system.

Usually these commissions have been issued at the request of
the companies and have been unlimited in duration. A
practice has recently been instituted in the Executive Department, limiting the appointments to a period of three years,
and requiring the application to set forth under affidavit the
circumstances making the appointment necessary, the capability, and reputation for sobriety and peacefulness, of the
person named, and that he is a citizen of Pennsylvania. But it
needs little thought to see that the system is objectionable
upon principle and is likely to be ineffective in practice. The
act upon which it is based is inartificially constructed and,
were the question raised, would probably be held to be unconstitutional by the courts. Where police are selected, paid
and discharged by the corporations, and bear the name "Coal
and Iron Police," it is evident that they are in effect the
servants of their employers rather than the Commonwealth
whose authority they exercise. The arrest and incarceration
of a citizen for breach of law is one of the most fundamental
and delicate of the functions of sovereignty, and the protection of property and the prevention of breach of the peace and
disturbance are among the most important of its duties. The
one ought not to be delegated and the other ought not be
evaded. To attempt to do so is to abdicate sovereignty and to
accomplish it would seem to be a legal impossibility.

The State stands above interests in controversy and its
powers ought not to be used by either of them. In case of
disturbance, no confidence can be placed in the discreet use
of the power of the State by persons dependent upon others
for their positions. On the other hand, it is the duty of the
State to see to it that the exercise of the franchises granted by
her is not impaired or interfered with by violence. It would be
well for you to consider whether the time has not arrived for
the State to resume these functions and to authorize the appointment by the governor of a constabulary of sufficient
force, say ten in each county, to be used wherever needed in
the State in the suppression of disorder. They could be
utilized in the place of the corporation police, the game
wardens, fish wardens, forest wardens, the officers of the different boards and commissions exercising police authority,
and would enable the executive, in case of emergency, to
"take care that the laws be faithfully executed," as the constitution requires, and they would be likely to inspire a confidence not now felt. The objection to such a course is the
expense. To this objection there are several answers. The
State ought to provide for its necessary work before being
generous, no matter how meritorious the recipients of its
bounty may be. It is doubtful whether the expense of a regular

constabulary would upon the whole, be greater than the occasional calling out of the National Guard, which it would at times obviate. Much of what would be the expense is now being incurred in desultory ways, and the expense of the corporation police comes ultimately from the people. Finally, it may be said that this constabulary could be taken from the ranks of the National Guard, thus starting with a disciplined service, and that no doubt the corporations would be satisfied to be assured of protection to their property and to be relieved of the burden of maintaining their present police.

In this manner did Pennypacker sum up his case and pass on to the legislature a challenge to bring into being a force for good—yet untried by any state in the Union.

Senate Bill 278, creating the State Police, was introduced March 20, 1905, and immediately referred to the Committee on Judiciary General, chaired by Sen. Cyrus E. Wood (R-Westmoreland). The bill was amended by the committee and reported to the Senate floor the following day. The three readings of SB-278 were completed by March 28. Further action on this measure was not taken until April 6, at which time the amended version was passed by a 40–0 vote, and sent to the House. The Senate, heavily dominated by Republicans, consisted of 39 Republicans and 10 Democrats. There was one vacant seat. The vote reflected party line action.

Although Senate action was routine for the most part, a different story unfolded in the House, where opponents to the creation of a state constabulary from both parties were more vocal. Here again, the Republicans dominated the House by an overwhelming membership of 179 compared to 15 Democrats. There were 10 vacant seats. The Senate measure and its companion bill, HB-787, were presented on April 7, and referred to the Appropriations Committee, chaired by Rep. J. Lee Plummer (R-Blair). The second reading occurred on April 10, when the bill was amended and approved for a third reading. The following day, at third reading, Rep. Thomas Hays (R-Butler) spoke against the measure, "Mr. Speaker, this bill I think is just a joke. It was passed out of committee (Appropriations), I think, for the purpose of having a little fun in the House. If it became a law it would cost the State over five hundred thousand dollars. Let us kill it now."

The bill, on motion, was recommitted to the Law and Order Committee, headed by Rep. John Francise (R-Allegheny), and reported back to the floor by the committee the very same day. At third reading, the principal spokesman for the measure was Rep. Frank B. McClain (R-Lancaster), a strong supporter of Governor Pennypacker's legislative programs. McClain referred to Pennypacker's opening address to the 1905 General Assembly, and quoted most of the governor's poignant statements against the corporation police and in favor of a state constabulary so that the Commonwealth could properly assume its obligations. McClain concluded his appeal with some choice words of his own, "The badge of the State's authority should not be given to any except those in the employ of the State and responsible to it for their actions."

One of the most vocal of the opposition group was Rep. William T. Creasy (D-Columbia) who side-stepped the Coal and Iron Police issue and denounced the creation of a state constabulary because of the financial burden on the state in support of the new department. Creasy called for the bill's defeat. Creasy was joined by others who evaluated the bill solely on the basis of its cost and not on its benefits to the state insofar as law and order were concerned. Some House members wanted the bill to specifically do away with the Coal and Iron Police, while others, serving the interests of corporations, were successful in blocking such amendments.

Pennypacker had recommended a constabulary "of sufficient force, say ten in each county." This would have meant a complement of 670. Organized labor, however, fearful that the constabulary would be used as a private army against them, was successful in urging a House amendment limiting the complement of 228 men. This was a considerable reduction in size and satisfied, too, the cost-conscious House members.

The last, but certainly not the least, of serious concerns dealt with the matter of political patronage that might accompany the passage of a bill creating a new department. This concern may have been genuine enough if patronage struggles were inherent with newly-established departments—and apparently they were.

When the heat of accusations of "playing politics" cooled, the bill was finally passed April 12, by vote of 156–28, and sent to the Senate for concurrence with House changes. The Senate voted its concurrence the same day 40–0, and none too soon. The House and Senate adjourned the next day, by predetermined arrangement, ending the shortest session of the Legislature since 1877.

On May 2, Governor Pennypacker signed the bill "that of itself alone was to make him a notable figure in American history," stated Mayo in commenting on this momentous occasion. The enactment of SB-278, from its introduction to signing, covered a period of forty-four calendar days.

The signed measure read as follows:

The Creative Act of 1905

SECTION 1. Be it enacted, &c., That there is hereby created and established the Department of State Police; the head of which shall be the Superintendent of State Police, to be appointed by the Governor, by and with the advice and consent of the Senate, to serve for a term of four years from the date of his appointment, and who shall receive a salary of three thousand dollars per annum, to be paid quarterly upon warrant of the Auditor-General drawn on the State Treasurer.

SECTION 2. The Superintendent of State Police shall be provided by the Board of Public Grounds and Buildings with suitable offices at the Capitol, in Harrisburg, and shall give a bond to the Commonwealth, in the sum of twenty thousand dollars, for the faithful performance of his duties. He is authorized to appoint a deputy, at a salary of two thousand dollars per annum; one clerk, who shall be a competent bookkeeper, at a salary of fourteen hundred dollars per annum, and a competent stenographer, at a salary of twelve hundred dollars per annum.

SECTION 3. He is also authorized to appoint the State Police Force, which shall consist of four companies, or platoons, each consisting of a captain, at a salary of fifteen hundred dollars per annum, a lieutenant, at a salary of twelve hundred dollars per annum; five sergeants, at a salary of one thousand dollars per annum, and fifty men, at a salary of seven hundred and twenty dollars per annum. No applicant shall be appointed to the State Police until he has satisfactorily passed a physical and mental examination, based upon the standard provided by the rules and regulations of the police force of the cities of the first class, in addition to which applicant must be a citizen of the United States, of sound constitution, able to ride, of good moral character, and between the ages of twenty-one and forty years.

SECTION 4. It shall be the duty of the Superintendent of State Police to provide for the members of the Police Force suitable uniforms, arms, equipments, and, where it is deemed necessary, horses; and to make such rules and regulations, subject to the approval of the Governor, as are deemed necessary for the control and regulation of the Police Force. It shall also be the duty of the Superintendent to establish local headquarters in various places. For that purpose he is authorized to do so, by lease or otherwise, so as best to distribute the force throughout the various sections of the Commonwealth, where they will be most efficient in carrying out the purposes of this act to preserve the peace and to prevent crime.

SECTION 5. The various members of the Police Force are hereby authorized and empowered to make arrests, without warrant, for all violations of the law which they may witness, and to serve and execute warrants issued by the proper local authorities. They are also authorized and empowered to act as forest, fire, game, and fish wardens; and, in general, to have the powers and prerogatives conferred by law upon members of the police force of cities of the first class, or upon constables of the Commonwealth; and are intended, as far as possible, to take the place of the police now appointed at the request of the various corporations.

The State Police Force shall, wherever possible, cooperate with the local authorities in detecting crime, and apprehending criminals, and preserving the law and order throughout the State.

SECTION 6. That the sum of four hundred and twenty-five thousand dollars, or so much thereof as may be necessary, be and the same is hereby specifically appropriated to pay the salaries and expenses necessary to carry this bill into effect; the same to be paid on warrant drawn by the Auditor-General upon the State Treasurer, out of moneys in the State Treasury not otherwise appropriated.

SECTION 7. All acts or parts of acts inconsistent herewith be and they are hereby rescinded.

APPROVED—The 2nd day of May, A. D. 1905

SAML. W. PENNYPACKER

CHAPTER III

Department of State Police
Captain John C. Groome
1905–1906

Immediately following the enactment creating the Department of State Police there was national interest generated in this new venture for bringing law and order to rural countrysides. Almost without exception, every segment of the nation was faced with a rural law and order problem similar to that found in Pennsylvania, and Pennsylvania's success with a state police organization was bound to influence the direction of other states.

Pennypacker was conscious of the fact that this noble experiment of his doing could very well be the only accomplishment to bring lasting recall to his tenure as governor. His choice of superintendent was at once the key to any possible chance for success.

On previous occasions while the state police measure was under consideration, Pennypacker had assured the legislators that his appointee would be a qualified person with no political interests. For the better part of two months he weighed carefully the names submitted to him and, on July 1, 1905, offered this unique post to Captain John C. Groome, Commanding Officer of the First Troop Philadelphia City Cavalry.

Groome at first turned down the appointment, quickly admitting that he was not experienced in running a police agency. Pennypacker, feeling certain that his choice was the right one, did not accept Groome's rejection as final, and persisted. Succumbing to the

Captain John C. Groome, Commanding, First Troop Philadelphia City Cavalry (Courtesy of Donald W. Adams)

governor's persuasiveness, Groome agreed to taking on the job, provided he could go about his organizational tasks without political interference of any kind whatsoever; and that he would give up his post, if ever he was disallowed this course of action. "If I take the task of organizing the new State Police, there will be no place in the force for political henchmen or ward politicians, no toleration of wire-pulling in any shape. If, or when I cannot run it on this plane, I shall turn the commission back to the Governor, to dispose of as he pleases," he stated.

Early police forces were filled by political appointments which totally exposed its members to political pressures. It was little wonder that Groome was to demand absolute freedom from politics and political pressure before accepting his unique assignment from Pennypacker to establish a state constabulary in Pennsylvania—the first of its kind in the nation. Pennypacker subscribed to this condition, and acquired a superintendent whose selection was praised in government and public circles.

Reflecting on Pennypacker's choice, Mayo wrote

> (he) offered the appointment of Superintendent of State Police not to a friend of "the machine," not to a vote-bringer, not to a man who had ever served him, not, in a word, to a man of any use under the sun from a "practical" point of view, but to a fundamental and complete outsider.
>
> The choice was a blow between the eyes to the governor's enemies. For the moment they found nothing to say—there was nothing to say that could be said in public. And the press dealt with the news as it stood, without partisan color. "Machine Gets Rap," "Machine Hard Hit," "Out of Politics," read some of the headings, while from all over the State, papers both urban and rural expressed sincere satisfaction.

The *Harrisburg Telegraph* said, "It is fortunate that the experiment . . . is to be carried out under the supervision of an officer of the character and caliber of John C. Groome. . . . Into no better or safer hand could the work of organizing the force be committed and his choice removes any misgivings as to the real aim of the new department."

And the *Pittsburgh Gazette* said, "He has knowledge of military organization and practice, understands the work to be done, and will bring intelligence and integrity to the task. He is not a politician."

Lynn G. Adams, Groome's successor, was later to recall in his memoirs

It was this kind of promise (independence from politics) that attracted men of high calibre to the force from the very beginning. It was this promise, fulfilled, that made the Pennsylvania State Police the finest organization of its kind in the world.

At the time, many thought that Captain Groome was merely paying lip service to a high ideal. In an atmosphere so permeated with politics as Pennsylvania's, they incorrectly presupposed, the new force would quickly become a tool of the party in power.

As the years rolled by, however, and the non-political record of performance grew and grew, all doubt faded that a new kind of police force had, in actuality, been created. Only a loud few, too blind to see, clung to the false notion that the force was arrayed on any other than the side of the law.

John Charles Groome, the eighteenth captain of the First Troop Philadelphia City Cavalry, was born in Philadelphia, March 20, 1862. He was the son of Samuel William Groome, (a descendant of Captain Samuel Groome, mariner, of Ratcliff, Middlesex, England, who settled in Maryland about 1650) and Nancy Andrews Connelly, daughter of Harry Connelly (great-grandson of Colonel John Connelly of the Artillery during the Revolutionary War), of Philadelphia, and a great-granddaughter of the Rev. John Andrews, D. D., Vice Provost and Provost of the University of Pennsylvania from 1789 to 1813. Groome, one of six children, was educated under private tutors and graduated from the Protestant Episcopal Academy, Philadelphia, in 1878.

He went into the iron commission business with his father, but found this not to his liking. One of Groome's first ventures was stock-farming on an estate he purchased in Wythe County, Virigina. He returned to Philadelphia and became associated with Hutchinson and Company, wine merchants and importers.

He was elected a member of the First Troop in 1882, and appointed corporal in 1887 and sergeant in 1889. He was elected cornet in 1894 and first lieutenant six months later. In 1896 he was elected captain, and re-elected to that office in 1901. As sergeant he served with the troop during the Homestead riots in 1892, was in command of the troop in riot services at Hazelton in 1897, and again at Hazleton and vicinity during the Great Anthracite Coal Strike of 1902.

Upon declaration of war with Spain in 1898, the First Troop, under Groome's command, participated in the mobilization of Pennsylvania's National Guard at Mt. Gretna, and was mustered into federal service May 7. On June 17 Groome, as senior captain, assumed command of the calavry squadron, and in company with H Troop, Sixth U.S.

Captain John C. Groome (Courtesy of Mrs. John C. Groome, Jr.)

Cavalry, embarked at Newport News for Porto Rico (now Puerto Rico). On landing at Ponce some eleven days later, Groome was given command of the two cavalry troops, which were at once attached to General Brooke's command at Guayamo, serving together until September 3, when the First Troop was withdrawn from the island.

Groome was chairman of the committee formed in 1899 to sell the old Armory in Philadelphia and to secure a larger piece of ground and construct a new Armory. The First Troop occupied the new Armory on South Twenty-third Street on April 21, 1901.

Each year during Groome's administration, the First Troop received the highest rating in the cavalry for efficiency in the annual National Guard Inspection and on several occasions received the highest rating in the entire division. Groome was an excellent marksman, qualifying with carbine or rifle each during his service with the First Troop.

Groome was an enthusiastic field and trap shot and interested in athletics. He was one of the organizers of the Chestnut Hill Cricket Club and later a member of the Merion Cricket Club. He was one of the organizers of the Philadelphia Polo Club, and a member of the team that played the first polo game in Philadelphia. When the Philadelphia Polo Club was merged into the Philadelphia County Club, he played on the country club team for several seasons; he was captain of the First Troop polo team and country club team which defeated the teams of the Sixth U.S. Cavalry in matches played at Washington in 1896. He was the country club delegate to the Polo Association for many years, and a member of the National Polo Association's executive committee since 1901.

In May, 1888, Groome, then a corporal, was one of a team of six First Troop members selected to represent the troop in cavalry contests held in Atlanta. The team took part in all contests during the two-day event and he won the only race, one mile on the flat, from nine other entrants.

Groome, as a sergeant, with Barclay H. Warburton, Charles F. Henry, Edward Browning, Edward C. Knight, Jr., and William E. Bates, attended the wedding of General E. Burd Grubb, U.S. Minister to Spain and former captain of the First Troop, and Miss Violet Sopwith of Lysmore, Scotland, at St. Stephen's Church, S. Kensington, London, on November 3, 1891. Groome served as General Grubb's best man and his companion troopers were ushers.

Groome was a well-known whip and devoted much time to coaching; he won prizes for four-in-hand teams at the horse shows in New York, Chicago, and Philadelphia. In the spring of 1892 he and Barclay H. Warburton drove the public road coach "Meadowbrook" daily from Philadelphia to Willow Grove and return. In the summer of 1893 he drove the road coach "Alert" for two months daily from the Hollywood Hotel, Long Branch, N. J., to the Monmouth County race track and return. He was elected secretary of the Philadelphia Horse Show Association in 1895 and president in 1899. He was one of six Philadelphians who drove the public road coaches, "Vivid" and "Alert," between Philadelphia and New York daily during the spring months of 1894. One coach departed Philadelphia for New York and one left New York for Philadlephia each day at 8 A. M., and arrived at their destinations at 8 P. M. Seventeen four-horse teams were used each day, and the distance, ninety-two miles, was covered in twelve hours, including thirty minutes for lunch at Princeton. During the following spring, Groome drove the road coach "Champion" daily from the Stenton Hotel, Philadelphia, to the Philadelphia Horse Show at Wissahickon Heights and return, and later in the season drove the "Alert" daily from the Stenton Hotel to Meadowbrook Farms and return. Groome frequently judged the horse shows in New York, Baltimore, and Chicago, and twice judged the horse show held at London's Olympia.

In 1902, Groome left Hutchinson and Company to establish his own wine and import business, Groome and Company, at 1216 Walnut Street, Philadelphia, where he remained until 1914, when he turned to banking and helped form the company of Goddard, Groome, Drayton and Company. He was vice president of this firm for six years.

He was a member of the Radnor Hunt Club, Merion Cricket Club, Raquet Club, Philadelphia Country Club, Philadelphia Club, Rabbit Club, Army & Navy Club of New York, Pennsylvania's Historical Society, Military Order of Foreign Wars and Military Order of the Spanish-American War.

Groome, on April 15, 1884, married Agnes Price Roberts, daughter of Edward and Martha Evans Roberts, of Philadelphia. Three children were born of this marriage.

Groome, with his dark hair close cut and parted in the middle, dark eyes, and a full mustache with pointed tips, was considered by all standards a handsome man.

From his record of activities, Pennypacker had chosen no idle man to serve as his State Police superintendent. It is doubtful that many Pennsylvanians could boast of such accomplishments. He was 43 when he took on his State Police assignment that was to become for him another distinguished career spanning some fifteen years.

Act 227, P.L. 361, of May 2, 1905, carried specific terms with regard to personnel and salaries to be paid. To assist Groome with matters of administration, he was allowed a $2,000-a-year deputy, a

Captain John C. Groome (Courtesy of Pennsylvania State Police)

$1,400-a-year clerk-bookkeeper, and a $1,200-a-year stenographer. The superintendent's salary was set at $3,000 annually. The field forces were to consist of four companies, or platoons, each consisting of a captain, a lieutenant, five sergeants and fifty men. Annual salaries for these positions were fixed at: $1,500 for captains, $1,200 for lieutenants, $1,000 for sergeants, and $720 for privates (as they were to be originally labelled by Groome). The act included a total appropriation of $425,000. Except for those amounts set aside for payroll commitments, Groome had a free hand in expending funds for equipping the force and providing headquarters facilities.

The legislation also provided that the superintendent would be given suitable office space in the capitol at Harrisburg by the Board of Public Grounds and Buildings. This was done. The Department of

State Police was located in the east wing of the new capitol's first floor to the rear of the rotunda's main staircase.

Just one month after his appointment, Groome made one of his first official moves by employing John H. Clarke of Langhorne, Bucks County, as the department's chief clerk. On August 9, Clarke was joined by Alan C. Frazier of Philadlephia—a stenographer-typist.

Immediately following the announcement of his appointment, Groome was flooded with appeals from senators and House members who were acting on behalf of constituents interested in serving with the State Police. Even Pennypacker was not overlooked by the more eager who sought endorsement in high places. Some, perhaps lacking political contacts, applied directly to Groome. By the first of August, more than 1,000 applicants had filed for enlistment. Groome made it quite clear in all public information issuances that no appointments to State Police service would be made before the fall of the year to allow for careful processing, and that no applicant would be given favorable consideration except on his own merits. Political influence would have no bearing on Groome's final selections.

Early application forms were simple; they asked for name, age, height, weight, birthplace, citizenship, marital status, occupation, and military service. Applicants had to be U. S. citizens between the ages of 21 and 40. Pennsylvania citizenship was not a requirement. The following statement appeared in the *Scranton Times* on August 29, 1905: "Men who have served in the regular army, who are physically sound and who are more than five feet six inches tall, stand the best chances of getting appointments on the State Constabulary."

The physical examination form was more like a questionnaire, and called for many points of information already supplied by the application form. The enlistment paper, just as the other forms, was patterned from the military. Although the other forms were altered during the upcoming years, the enlistment paper surprisingly survived as is for more than half a century.

The responsibility for processing the applicants was delegated to Clarke. The setting up of processing centers required considerable travel by Clarke. During September and October, Dr. Francis D. Patterson of Philadelphia visited these centers to examine applicants. The 250 applicants approved by Dr. Patterson were scheduled for mental (written) examinations at Harrisburg, Pittsburgh and Philadelphia on Saturday, November 4. Some 200 successfully met this qualifying step, most of whom also survived final screening by Groome.

One of Groome's early concerns was the location of the four companies. He reviewed available information depicting the centers where his men would be most needed to fulfill their mission. Having developed some ideas on this important issue, he visited those areas in search of suitable buildings. This proved to be a most difficult survey, since it was almost impossible to find buildings ideally suited as barracks. He had no choice except to lease what was available to him and commit himself to a program of remodelling and stable-building. Properties leased were in Punxsutawney, Jefferson County; Greensburg, Westmoreland County; Wilkes-Barre, Luzerne County; and Reading, Berks County.

The services of Dr. C. J. Marshal, a Philadelphia veterinarian, were contracted to purchase horses. Dr. Marshal made two trips to Texas to inspect horses and make selections based on U. S. Cavalry specifications. From the Savage & Conover Ranch of Fort Worth, Texas, 230 were purchased at a unit cost of $115, plus freight and charges for feeding enroute. The horses were shipped directly to each of the four company headquarters.

On August 24, Groome sailed for Europe aboard the S. S. *Deutschland* to study European constabularies as an aid to him in choosing proper uniform wear and adopting the best police procedures he could find. Foreign travel was not new to Groome as he had been to London on at least three previous occasions. For almost one month he visited Ireland, England, Switzerland, France, and Germany. He sailed for home on September 20, aboard the R. M. S. *Oceanic,* somewhat convinced that the Irish constabulary had satisfied his visit more than the others. For those who might be interested, the round trip fare was $476.25 plus steward fees of $29.16. Purchased on the trip were select items of uniform gear for final decision-making back home.

Upon his return from Europe, Groome met with the governor and thereafter focused much of his prime time to the selection of those men who would make up his field force. On November 19, Groome issued General Order #1, announcing his four captains: John W. Borland, 31, 5'8¾", an insurance agent from Mercer, Pennsylvania; Frank D. Beary, 36, 5'7", an Allentown, Pennsylvania, jeweler; William P. Taylor, 30, 5'10½", a clerk from Baltimore, Maryland, and Joseph F. Robinson, 30, 5'7½", a Toledo, Ohio, editor. Taylor and Robinson were residents of Doylestown and Bradford (Pennsylvania cities), respectively, at the time of enlistment. All appointments were effective November 1.

General Order #2, dated November 10, officially recognized the appointment of four lieutenants: Henry F. Egle, 32, 5'8½", a native of Switzerland and an Erie, Pennsylvania, manager; Charles F. Fenerstein, 31, 5'8¼", a salesman from Wilkes-Barre, Pennsylvania; Charles P. Smith, 33, 5'10½", a Philadelphia plumber, and William L. Swarm, 28, 5'7½", a soldier from Pleasant Gap, Pennsylvania. November 11 was indicated as their date of rank.

Captain John W. Borland (Courtesy of Pennsylvania State Police)

Captain Joseph F. Robinson (Court-esy of Pennsylvania State Police)

Captain William P. Taylor (Court-esy of Pennsylvania State Police)

General Order #3, dated December 20, provided for assignments of these commissioned officers:

Troop A, Greensburg
Captain John W. Borland
Lieutenant Charles F. Fenerstein

Troop B, Wilkes-Barre
Captain Frank D. Beary
Lieutenant William L. Swarm

Troop C, Reading
Captain William P. Taylor
Lieutenant Charles P. Smith

Troop D, Punxustawney
Captain Joseph F. Robinson
Lieutenant Henry F. Egle

General Order #4, dated December 20, established the non-commissioned ranks effective December 15:

Troop A, Greensburg
First Sergeant Leonard A. Haskett
Sergeant Thomas M. Harris, Jr.
Sergeant Leon S. Pitcher
Sergeant Lynn G. Adams
Sergeant John P. F. Gorman

Troop B, Wilkes-Barre
First Sergeant Harry C. Dimon
Sergeant Jesse S. Garwood
Sergeant William E. Mair
Sergeant John T. Walsh
Sergeant Herbert P. Hunt

Troop C, Reading
First Sergeant Josiah L. Reese
Sergeant Marshall C. Wilhelm
Sergeant Wilson C. Price
Sergeant John S. VanVoorhis

Troop D, Punxsutawney
First Sergeant George F. Lumb
Sergeant Mathew T. E. Ward
Sergeant William Marsh
Sergeant Charles C. Hoddy
Sergeant Joseph P. Logan

The complement of sergeants at Troop C was not to be filled until January 3, 1906, when Private Thomas F. Wiechard was promoted to sergeant, and given the distinction of having been Groome's first to be honored by promotion.

Although the law creating the State Police gave Groome full authority to acquire a deputy superintendent, he did not do so until December 26, 1905. His reasons for delaying this appointment, when he surely could have used a deputy's assistance during the first six months of organizational pursuits, are not understood. In any case, he did appoint J. Cheston Morris to this post, announcing this action on January 3, 1906, by way of that year's first general order.

This historic appointment went practically unnoticed in the press as evidenced by this succinct acccount in the *Philadelphia Inquirer* on January 4, 1906, "J. Cheston Morris, of Penllyn, who has been appointed Deputy Superintendent of the State Police, reported for duty today."

More copy in the same new release was given to the enlistment of a Bradford salesman, Benjamin F. Rothstein. The 30-year-old son of a millionaire father was to receive $60 a month pay as a constabulary private in Troop D, Punxsutawney. Rothstein was then a member of Company C, Sixteenth Regiment, Pennsylvania National Guard, and expressed his fondness for military life.

Morris was born April 1, 1861, at Philadelphia, the son of a nationally-famous physician, Dr. James Cheston Morris. He attended the University of Pennsylvania from 1875 to 1879 where he received the Bachelor of Arts degree. Morris was an executive with the Pottstown Iron Works, and a member of the Philadelphia Club. It was at the Philadelphia Club, most likely, that Groome came to know Morris well enough to weigh his value as an administrator and teammate, despite the fact that Morris did not come from a military background as was his own. Morris was married to the former Helen Campbell of Philadelphia, and resided at Penllyn, Montgomery County, at the time of his appointment.

On December 15, 1905, at a time when Groome's officers were busily engaged in taking aboard the first complement of recurits, a tri-district meeting of the United Mine Workers was held at Shamokin. John Fahy, president of District No. 9, denounced the constabulary and Governor Pennypacker. In a *Harrisburg Patriot* news account of the UMW meeting, reported on December 16, Fahy is quoted:

> The State Constabulary law, as is the Coal and Iron Police law, is an open insult to the working people of the State of Pennsylvania. I speak of the system, not of the men comprising it. I don't know another State which legalizes men to do what these men can do. There was a standing army of 5,000 men in the last strike maintained by the coal operators. I understand that two of the (constabulary) companies are to be stationed in the anthracite region, the other two companies, I understand, are to be located in the bituminous field. I am sorry that there is not another company to station in Harrisburg to keep watch on the Governor.

By the end of 1905, 133 privates had been enlisted. Together with the commissioned and non-commissioned officers, the field forces then numbered 160. The youngest of this original group was John S. Garland, 21, a native of Chester Centre, who enlisted at Middletown and was assigned to Troop B. The oldest was Barney McNulty, 39, a native of Allentown, who was assigned to Troop A. The tallest was Paul B. Stout, 6′1½″, of Milton, who was assigned to Troop A. The shortest was Thomas C. Lott, 5′5½″, of Philadelphia, who was assigned to Troop C.

TROOP ROSTERS
December 15, 1905

Troop A, Greensburg

Captain John W. Borland
Lieutenant Charles F.
    Fenerstein
First Sergeant Leonard A.
    Haskett
Sergeant Thomas M. Harris, Jr.
Sergeant Leon S. Pitcher
Sergeant Lynn G. Adams
Sergeant John P. J. Gorman
Private Frederick G. Ayers
Private Robert F. Balliet
Private George J. Deegan
Private Frederick G. Denn
Private Harvey Denner
Private Joseph J. Didyoung
Private William J. Ferris
Private Harry F. Fry
Private Frederick D. Frasch
Private John Garscia
Private Emmert W. Gillham

Private Robert Graham
Private Frank A. Hershey
Private George B. Hodges
Private Charles Jacobs
Private Allen G. Lithgow
Private Anthony Lohmiller, Jr.
Private John J. McCall
Private Charles J. McGarigle, Jr.
Private Thomas J. McLaughlin
Private Peter McNelis
Private Barney McNulty
Private John D. O'Grady
Private Michael Podgorski
Private Frank L. Prue
Private John A. Purdy
Private Frank Reed
Private Philip Roller
Private James J. Stinson
Private Paul B. Stout
Private Giles L. Tompkins
Private George W. Wilkinson

Troop B, Wilkes-Barre

Captain Frank D. Beary
Lieutenant William L. Swarm
First Sergeant Harry C. Dimon
Sergeant William E. Mair
Sergeant John T. Walsh
Sergeant Herbert P. Hunt
Sergeant Jesse S. Garwood
Private Frederick E. Borman
Private Joseph D. Carroll
Private Frank M. Class
Private William A. Clark
Private Joseph Cooley
Private John W. Coover
Private Francis L. Drake
Private James D. Dunsmore
Private Ernest V. B. Douredoure
Private James G. Ernst

Private Romanus Fellman
Private George W. Freeman
Private Mortimer C. Funston
Private John S. Garland
Private William Haler
Private Jospeh P. Halloran
Private Charles O. Hart
Private Walter S. Hennig
Private Newton Kelly
Private William Lane
Private William R. MacSherry
Private Francis P. McGinnis
Private John B. Mountjoy
Private Frank J. Murray
Private Alexander C. Reamer
Private Anthony W.
    Shelmerdine

Private Harry Smith
Private Robert G. Tait
Private Leonce J. Tierce
Private Robert E. Tipton
Private Charles S. Weaver

Troop C, Reading

Captain William P. Taylor
Lieutenant Charles P. Smith
First Sergeant Josiah L. Reese
Sergeant Cecil M. Wilhelm
Sergeant Wilson C. Price
Sergeant John S. VanVoorhis
Private Walter W. Ambrose
Private Marvin C. Beck
Private Loyd E. Booth
Private Marshall J. Booth
Private William A. Boyd
Private Alonzo B. Cady
Private John Dugan
Private Ross C. Fetterolf
Private Isaac Fleming
Private Reginald H. Gibson
Private Thomas J. Garrity
Private William R. Johnston
Private Timothy Kelleher
Private William H. Keogh

Private Louis F. Koch
Private Thomas C. Lott
Private Howard G. Mercer
Private George C. Miller
Private Thomas B. Naughton
Private James E. Nilon
Private Mark A. Prynn
Private William R. Smith
Private Walter C. Snyder
Private Thomas Stables
Private Daniel G. Steiner
Private James L. Sullivan
Private Herman Thomas
Private Benjamin F. Tinney
Private Richard H. Tremaine
Private Meyer Van Lewen
Private Maurice J. Welsh
Private Thomas F. Wiechard
Private William E. Wilson
Private Adam Wreath, Jr.

Troop D, Punxsutawney

Captain Joseph F. Robinson
Lieutenant Henry F. Egle
First Sergeant George F. Lumb
Sergeant Mathew T. E. Ward
Sergeant William Marsh
Sergeant Charles C. Hoddy
Sergeant Joseph P. Logan
Private Edward J. Baker
Private Wilbert Brooks
Private Eugene V. Calvert
Private Harry E. Carroll
Private Thomas L. Casey
Private Homer A. Chambers
Private Joseph M. Curts
Private John Devlin

Private Walter W. Duffield
Private Emery Edwards
Private Charles S. Everitt
Private George W. Haas
Private Charles H. Hanover
Private Tyson C. Heller
Private William E. Hess
Private John F. Henry
Private John L. Keogh
Private Frank Kettle
Private Nathan Kohut
Private George H. Koons
Private Lewis E. Lardin
Private Robert Lindsay
Private William E. Lyter

Private Claude R. Masters
Private Joseph R. McIlvain
Private Warren J. Meade
Private William J. Mullen
Private Roy Nevins
Private Charles F. Ohliger
Private Clark Read

Private George S.
   Schollenberger
Private Charles F. Smith
Private Francis S. Strawser
Private James Sutton, Jr.
Private George Wagner
Private Francis A. Zehringer

By December 31, 1906, 272 men were enlisted. Although James M. Boland, a Philadelphian, enlisted on April 2, 1906, was shorter than Lott by one-quarter inch, the statistical limits cited for Garland, McNulty, and Stout held fast. Of the 272 enlisted, 68 were born in states other than Pennsylvania, representing twenty-two states and 25 percent of the enlistments. There were 26 enlistees born in foreign countries—eleven countries in all—representing 9.4 percent of the enlistment figure. Those not native to Pennsylvania made up 34.4 percent of the 1905–06 recruits. It is worthy to note that this noble experiment, the Department of State Police, had such a representative source of manpower.

With a full staff at headquarters and commissioned personnel in the field, Groome was prepared to expedite the purchase of uniforms, ordnance, equipment, and supplies for offices, bedrooms, kitchens, recreational rooms, and stables. Although many items were purchased locally by the field officers, general issue items were purchased by headquarters in bulk from a multiplicity of suppliers. Uniforms were secured from Jacob Reed's Sons, Philadelphia; mattresses and pillows from H. D. Dougherty & Co., Philadelphia; blankets from Thomas Kent Manufacturing Co., Clifton Heights; iron bedsteads from A. J. Logan & Co., Pittsburgh; leggings from Stowasser & Winter Puttee Corporation, Ltd., London; .45 calibre Springfield carbines from the Springfield Arsenal; .38 calibre Colt revolvers from the State Adjutant General; cartridges from the State Arsenal; carbine boots from Francis Bannerman, New York; buckskin gloves from Daniel Hays Co., Gloverville, N. Y.; stable suits and hats, John Wanamaker, Philadelphia; belts, caps, spurs, straps, badges, and collar ornaments from William H. Horstman Co., Philadelphia; handcuffs, billies, and whistles from Edward K. Tryon Co., Philadelphia; saddles and saddle cloths from Mehlbach Saddle Co., New York; saddle racks from Robert A. McCullen, Philadelphia; and horses (as previously mentioned) from Savage & Conover Ranch, Fort Worth, Texas. These represent the major items, and by no means exhaust the list of material needed to equip an organization of its kind for the first time. As Groome later recalled, "I proceeded carefully, there was no precedent,

Troop D recruits await uniforms at Punxsutawney. Left to right: Charles T. Smith, Henry Hilton, Homer A. Chambers, George W. Haas. (Courtesy of Pennsylvania State Police)

nothing to pattern by, and the matter was as new to me as to everybody else.''

When the horses were delivered at troop sites, most stable facilities were yet unfinished and quarters had to be rented from local stable owners.

At Wilkes-Barre it was necessary to temporarily lease office space from the Kulp Detective Agency for $10 a month. (Anthracite was going for $3.50 a ton.) At Punxsutawney, men were initially quartered at the National Hotel until the leased barracks building was readied. While waiting for operational equipment to arrive, the field forces busied themselves with study of criminal law and procedures, caring for the horses and barracks, remodelling buildings and building stables. Chores were endless. Above all else a concerted effort was made to develop a kindly relationship with the people of the local communities.

With everything in readiness, the Department of State Police was operational on March 1, 1906. Before this order was given, however, twelve original members (those enlisted before December 31, 1905) were discharged or resigned.

They were:

Name	Troop	Date of Enlistment	Separated
Captain Frank D. Beary	B	11- 1-1905	2-10-1906
Pvt. Frank M. Class	B	12-15-1905	2-15-1906
Pvt. Harvey Denner	A	12-15-1905	2-10-1906
Pvt. Charles H. Hanover	D	12-15-1905	1- 8-1906
Pvt. Charles O. Hart	B	12-15-1905	1- 1-1906
Pvt. Tyson C. Heller	D	12-15-1905	12-24-1905
Pvt. Peter McNelis	A	12-15-1905	2-10-1906
Pvt. Charles L. Ohliger	D	12-15-1905	2-20-1906
Pvt. Alexander C. Reamer	B	12-15-1905	2-15-1906
Pvt. William L. Smith	C	12-15-1905	2-19-1906
Pvt. Walter W. Duffield	D	12-19-1905	12-25-1905
Pvt. Ernest V. B. Douredoure	B	12-27-1905	2- 1-1906

Captain Frank D. Beary, who resigned, was replaced by a newcomer, James Whit Page, 25, 5'9", a Scranton mining engineer. The first to be dismissed by court-martial decision was Private Douredoure, 22, a native of Philadelphia. He enlisted at Wilkes-Barre with Troop B.

Just a week after the sound of active duty, March 8, Troop C was called to the Cornwall Ore Banks, Lebanon County, where a disorderly strike was in progress. A detachment of two officers, four sergeants, and thirty privates entrained at Lebanon to assist the sheriff who had summoned help. All personnel but one officer, two sergeants, and ten men were relieved of duty two days later, and all were released on March 12, order at the ore banks having been fully restored. This incident was one of more than a dozen major disorder scenes requiring State Police response during the year.

Troop B was moved from Wilkes-Barre on March 27 to the smaller community of Wyoming, across the Susquehanna River, where the officers and men occupied the Hancock Mansion. This was the first of three troop headquarters locations to be changed during the department's early years.

The second of Groome's original commanding officers, Captain William P. Taylor, resigned June 15, 1906, and was replaced by Lieutenant Charles P. Smith who became the department's first commissioned officer to be advanced in rank.

In June, 1906, Groome enlisted a 21-year-old native of Landisville, who was then employed in Philadlephia as a bookkeeper—Samuel B. Nissley. Instead of assigning him to field duty, Groome decided to

Mounted patrol in front of Hancock Mansion, Troop B headquarters, Wyoming, 1907 (Courtesy of Pennsylvania State Police)

keep this promising young man at Harrisburg headquarters to bolster the services of Clarke and Frazier. Groome's appraisal of Nissley's worth was confirmed over and over again as this young man proved himself a most capable administrator.

The spirit of this infant agency was to be dampened by the slaying of two privates on September 2, 1906, at the small mining community of Florence, Jefferson County, near Punxsutawney. The first to die in the line of duty were Private John Henry, 31, of Philadelphia, and Private Francis Zehringer, 34, of Conshohocken.

Sergeant Joseph Logan, of Troop D, attempted to arrest two men charged with murder at Florence, when he was fired on. Logan called for assistance, and was soon joined by a detail of five men. When the detail demanded entrance to the house where the fugitives and others were holed up, they were greeted by a volley of gunfire. Private Henry was killed instantly. Private Homer C. Chambers, of Rochester, Pennsylvania, and Private William A. Mullen, of Harrisburg, were wounded. Although hurt, Chambers, in the face of gunfire, went back to secure Henry's body and suffered additional gunshot wounds. He was hospitalized and not expected to live. But, he did; Groome later praised Chambers for his bravery. Additional help was summoned from Troop D headquarters. A second attempt to rush the entrance of the house resulted in the fatal shooting of Private Zehringer after he had made entry. Nightfall came, and the house was carefully watched until daybreak to make sure that none of the occupants escaped. Gunfire was exchanged periodically throughout the night.

At daylight, amidst a thunderstorm, Captain Robinson decided to dynamite the house. First Sergeant Lumb and Sergeant Marsh, protected by steady gunfire from fellow troopers, rushed the house to secure Zehringer's body, while another detail of men planted the dynamite. Both details retreated to cover after completing their missions successfully despite heavy gunfire from the house. The dynamite was detonated—the house collapsed and burned. Its occupants were dead.

A story appearing in the *Pittsburgh Dispatch* stated, "There was a sad little procession of mounted men who escorted a wagon bearing their dead to the quarters at Punxsutawney, where the bodies of Henry and Zehringer lie in state until Tuesday, when they will be sent to their homes, Privates Kohut and Randolph escorting that of Zehringer, while Sergeant Marsh and Private Lardin will escort the body of Henry to his late home. No services will be held here, but the troop, mounted will act as escort when the bodies are taken to the (railroad) station."

Appearing in the *Punxsutawney Weekly Spirit* was this account:

The funeral procession next day will not soon be forgotten by the thousands from Punxsutawney and neighboring towns who witnessed it. Captain Robinson and Lieutenant Egle rode at the head of the processsion with ministers and prominent residents of the city following in carriages. Two hearses carrying the bodies of the slain troopers followed with four troopers on each side of the hearses, one in each group leading the horses that Zehringer and Henry had ridden, the saddles of which were draped in black. The other troopers, 25 in number, followed on horseback. With bowed heads the great throng watched the procession proceed to the East End depot, from where the bodies were sent to their respective homes over the Pennsylvania Railroad.

There are many differences of opinion regarding the manner of conducting the attack on the house which resulted in the slaughter of three men and the wounding of others, but all

Troop D barracks at Puxsutawney, 1906 (Courtesy of Pennsylvania State Police)

*Private John F. Henry (Courtesy
of Pennsylvania State Police)*

*Private Francis A. Zehringer (Court-
esy of Pennsylvania State Police)*

who watched agreed that the courage and loyalty of the State
Policemen was beyond criticism.

It was the first of many funeral processions to follow.

In an interview some years later, Sergeant Marsh (a lieutenant at
the time of the interview) recalled the incident for Katherine Mayo,
"The Force owes a lot to those two. As for the action itself, if we had it
to handle again, we might handle it differently. But we were young
then, all of us, with much to learn. And those two bore our standard
that day—planted it where it belongs. They taught us to hold the honor
of the Force dearer than life. They gave their own lives to do it, readily
and gladly—and that's all any man can give."

Plans were made by state officials to dedicate the new capitol, at
Harrisburg, on October 4. The new $10 million building, covering two
acres of ground, was designed by architect Joseph M. Houston of
Philadelphia, and follows the classic style of the Italian Renaissance.
The fine statuary in front of the building is the work of George Grey
Barnard, a native Pennsylvanian. The bronze doors were designed by
Otto Jahnsen, and the tile pavement in the rotunda and corridors were
made by Dr. Hugh Mercer, of Doylestown. Paintings by Violet Oakley
decorate the Senate chamber and the Governor's Office. Paintings in
the House of Representatives are the work of Edwin Austin Abbey.
Both Oakley and Abbey were noted Pennsylvanians.

Old State Capitol (Courtesy of Pennsylvania Department of General Services)

New State Capitol (Courtesy of Pennsylvania Department of General Services)

The Vermont granite structure, topped by a magnificent dome and elegantly furnished, is perhaps the most impressive of all state capitols.

The new building replaced the original capitol which was completed in 1819, and burned to the ground at mid-day February 2, 1897, on the eve of the Spanish-American War. The columns of the old capitol, preserved from the ruins, are now in place at the east end of Harrisburg's Market Street bridge across the Susquehanna River. The land area for the seat of state government was given to the Commonwealth by John Harris, Jr.

The Harrisburg Police Department requested assistance from the State Police because of the large crowd of spectators expected in the capital city for this event which featured an address by President Theodore Roosevelt. Groome ordered units from all four troops to Harrisburg, where the State Police detail led the dedication military parade. An estimated throng of 60,000, standing in the rain, witnessed the ceremonies. A Harrisburg editor, William W. Colson, writing about the day's exciting events said, "But it remained for the State Constabulary—two troops of the most brawny Pennsylvanians within the borders of the State, mounted on choice horses and headed by Captain John C. Groome—to make the biggest hit with the President. Clad in dark service uniforms and helmeted after the Irish fashion, their tread and bearing certainly showed them in fine fettle."

The following day this exemplary State Police detail was dispatched to Philadelphia where the men participated in a street parade and governor's review.

By year's end, the four troops had accounted for 808 criminal arrests for forty-five different offenses, with 583 convictions. They patrolled 65,000 miles in twenty counties. The anthracite coal region, served by Troop B, was by far the most disorderly area in the state.

The actions of the troopers in behalf of law and order soon disturbed the radical elements of the United Mine Workers, who wanted no interference with their skulduggery. At union gatherings, resolutions were passed aimed at the disbanding of the State Police, and the support of legislative candidates who would pledge themselves to this end. This harassment continued unabated for more than a decade.

Before the beginning of operational duty on March 1, 1906, a total of 190 men had been signed up by department officials. As stated earlier, 12 of the original recruits were separated and never saw official active duty. This figure was increased by another 53 departures before the end of 1906. Departures, for one reason or another, totalled 65, representing 34 percent, or better than one-third of the number enlisted before March 1. This was a high turnover rate which was to continue for many years. The work was strenuous even for the seasoned career soldier, and most of the recruits had seen military service. Of the 272 men enlisted during the 1905–06 period, there were 76 separations due to death, dismissal, and resignation, leaving a complement of 196 men at the close of 1906. This figure was 32 short of the complement authorized by the legislature.

In his year-end report to Pennypacker, Groome wrote, "In every instance, sometimes with the assistance of the local authorities and sometimes without it, the men of this Force, though few in numbers and always largely outnumbered by the lawless element, have by their coolness, bravery, and good discipline, been able to prevent serious trouble and maintain the peace of the Commonwealth."

A story of this era, which has been told many times, relates to an occasion when the sheriff of Northumberland County called the State Police to report a riot in Mount Carmel and asked for assistance. The sheriff was told that the State Police would be sent to the riot scene immediately, and he, in turn, notified the Mount Carmel authorities to expect help. When the mayor of the town met a lone mounted trooper approaching the community, he asked, "Where are the rest of the men?"

"I was given this assignment. There was only one riot reported," was the trooper's confident response.

CHAPTER IV

Captain John C. Groome
1907–1910

Groome, carefully weighing each administrative move, was slowly shaping the operational function of his infant department. In 1906, he made it clear to his men that two-year enlistments were not to be taken lightly. The enlistment period was to be contract-honored. Being a flexible administrator, however, he recognized that resignations for justifiable causes should be accepted, and permitted his men to do so. But this exit route was not made easy. In his order, Groome stated, "Resignations for cause will be accepted by the Superintendent. Those in good standing will receive 'Honorable' discharges but will forfeit two weeks pay."

He had established daily duty schedules for privates and officers-of-the-day; specified arms, uniforms, equipment and identification markings; set up a procedure for troop commanders in submitting monthly reports covering their operations; issued a policy of granting each man an annual vacation of fourteen days, with pay, during each year of service, and warned all men that after an unauthorized absence of ten days, they would be dropped as deserters.

Groome found to his disappointment that the general assembly had not provided funds to cover costs for medical treatment. Faced with no alternative at this point, he recommended to his troop commanders that each troop provide a fund for handling their medical needs. Aptly, this action was contained in General Order #13.

For the first time since the organization of the State Police, a new governor appeared on the scene. The governor-elect was Edwin S.

Stuart, of Philadelphia. A top-level decision was made to have State Police participation in the inaugural ceremonies on January 15, 1907, for security purposes and to assist the Harrisburg Police Department in handing the problems of this quadrennial day-long event. Units from Troops B and C were detailed to Harrisburg and, in this unprecedented situation, performed exceptionally well—so well, in fact, that no inaugural event has taken place since without State Police participation. Inaugural committees, through the years, have called upon the State Police to satisfy roles of increasing importance.

When Governor Thomas Mifflin, the first governor elected under the 1790 Constitution, was inaugurated on December 21, 1790, the ceremony was brief and held indoors. Inauguration dates were later switched to the month of January, and Governor David R. Porter, on January 15, 1839, was the first to be inaugurated following that change. Growth of the inauguration ceremony was gradual from 1790, and on January 16, 1855, Governor James Pollock took his oath of office in the first outdoor ceremony of its kind, which was far more elaborate than for any of his predecessors'. Inaugural ceremonies more akin to those experienced nowadays are patterned much after the day's events scheduled for Governor John Hartranft's oath-taking on January 21, 1873.

Governor Stuart publicly displayed his satisfaction in the accomplishments of Superintendent John C. Groome by keeping him in this important post.

Groome, who had not severed his relationship with the First Troop, Philadelphia City Cavalry, was honored by the First Troop members in acknowledgement of his twenty-five years of useful service on the troop's active roll. At a testimonial affair, Groome was presented a three-handled silver bowl.

The year 1907 witnessed a continuation of Groome's efforts to establish a sound set of policies to guide his field forces. From the very outset, and for more than half a century, State Police enlistment was open only to single men. Groome cautioned his men that any who married after enlistment would be honorably discharged. He was thoroughly convinced that married men, living away from the barracks, were "not immediately available for service at all times," and were valueless to that extent. In his estimation then, the department was to remain a bachelors' fraternity.

Men on travel status for more than twenty-four hours were allowed $.25 for a meal, $.50 for lodging, and $.50 a day for feeding and stabling horses. A man returning to his barracks within twenty-four hours "must carry rations for himself and horse."

At mid-year, Alan Frazier resigned his post at headquarters.

Samuel B. Nissley was discharged as a private and immediately re-classified as a stenographer-typist to fill Frazier's vacancy.

On September 4, 1907, the young department was to see its third member die from wounds inflicted in the line of duty. Private Timothy Kelleher, of Troop C, "while defending a woman's honor," was fatally stabbed by two assailants in Reading.

After two years of service almost to the day, Captain John W. Borland, of Troop A, resigned on October 31, 1907. To fill his vacancy at Greensburg, Groome called upon Lieutenant George F. Lumb. Lumb was then Borland's lieutenant, having recently arrived from Troop B where he was transferred from Punxsutawney in 1906 after a promotion from first sergeant—just one month after the tragedy at Florence. Lumb, it will be recalled, played a key role, by his daring action, in ending the unfortunate incident which claimed the lives of two fellow troopers. Groome lost no time in promoting Lumb to lieutenant once the opportunity was presented. Now, a year later, he was promoting Lumb again to officially display his confidence in an outstanding officer.

Lieutenant Henry F. Egle also resigned in October. To fill his vacancy, Groome decided in favor of a competitive examination among first sergeants. Heretofore, Groome had promoted non-commissioned officers to commissioned rank without benefit of competition. All first sergeants reported to Harrisburg for the written examination on October 26. The top-scorer, First Sergeant John S. VanVoorhis, of Troop C, was promoted to lieutenant two weeks later.

Just about the time Groome was happily announcing VanVoorhis' promotion, he was by contrast disheartened by his responsibility of reducing another in rank—for the first time. Sergeant John T. Walsh, of Troop B, was reduced to the rank of private.

With the year's end, Groome lost Captain James W. Page, of Troop B, by way of resignation. Page left the constabulary to accept a better-paying position in another state. Groome also accepted on December 31, 1907, "with regrets," the resignation of Deputy Superintendent J. Cheston Morris. Morris, 46, and in poor health, moved to Cheyenne, Wyoming, where he tried his hand at cattle raising.

Placing considerable value on seniority, Groome decided that preference for the Christmas or New Year holiday would be based on seniority, and it was so ordered.

This budding organization, plagued by a high turnover rate and yet unable to fill its authorized complement, patrolled 332,194 miles during 1907. There were 4,388 arrests. Drunk and disorderly charges accounted for 1,107 arrests. There were 691 arrests for assault and battery, and 62 arrest for murder. These crimes of violence shed some light on the behavioral problems facing the constabulary.

During this period, the troop commanders were given authorization to set up substations in troublesome areas to cope with circumstances demanding such special on-the-scene attention. Forty 2- and 3-man substations were operational during 1907. Substations were leased facilities with short term agreements, if there were agreements at all. Substations were discontinued as the need for manpower on site diminished. Men saw substation duty on a rotating basis.

Perhaps the most demanding crime problem of this era was the activity of the Black Hand Society. That secret society of extortionists was operational long before the state constabulary came into being, and thrived on the helplessness of the Italian immigrants in this country. Its activities were by no means confined to Pennsylvania.

The Black Hand hoodlums sought out for their victims the Italian merchants, laborers, and others who were known to possess some degree of savings. Money was extorted from them on the threat of bodily harm or death. The fact that the society was able to carry out its threats without detection and punishment was sufficient for those who were approached; those who valued their lives succumbed to the propositions put to them. Those who dared defy the society swiftly suffered the consequences.

The urgency of this situation increased to a point where those in authority could no longer sit by helplessly. The district attorneys, although few in number at first, called on the State Police to gather evidence against the Black Hand society members, and in 1907 the troopers undertook a campaign of no small dimension to wipe out the influence of that society in the Commonwealth. Encouraged by the State Police and security from harm, victimized Italians and witnesses provided needed evidence. Arrests were made. District attorneys, spearheaded by the effort of Luzerne County District Attorney Abram Salsburg, successfully prosecuted in court. Severe punishment was administered by the courts. The work of the State Police in 1907 went a long way toward wiping out the dreaded influence of the Black Hand in Pennsylvania.

The Black Hand, however, was suspected of having developed an effective, organized, inter-state operation, and is believed to have been the forerunner of the "Mafia" in the United States.

Groome permitted Page's vacancy at Wyoming to ride until March, 1908, when he transferred Captain Robinson from Punxsutawney. Robinson's post at Punxsutawney was filled by the promotion of Lieutenant Josiah L. Reese. Reese, 33, 5'8", a native of Swansea, Wales, England, enlisted from Pittsburgh December 15, 1905. He was

Captain George F. Lumb (Courtesy of Fred A. Lumb)

assigned to Troop C, Reading, and appointed that troop's first sergeant. Groome had lost three of his four original captains in comparatively short order, and now only Robinson remained. Robinson was to remain with the constabulary until 1914 before bringing his excellent career to a close.

Although Groome delayed filling the vacancy at Wyoming, his follow-up on the department's empty number two position was something else. Morris resigned the post effective December 31, 1907, and Groome announced his successor the very next day. On January 1, 1908, Captain George F. Lumb was brought in from Greensburg and appointed the department's second deputy superintendent. Again, Groome manifested his satisfaction with Lumb's stellar performance.

Lumb, 33, was born in London, England, November 10, 1874. He was one of five children born to Isaac and Mary Lumb. In 1880, before his fifth birthday, young Lumb and the Lumb family, a very poor family, set sail for Canada aboard a 3000-ton steamer. The voyage across the Atlantic, according to records, was one of the stormiest.

After a year's stay in Montreal without improvement, Isaac Lumb moved his family to Baltimore, Maryland. There, Mary Lumb, only 39, and an infant daughter died.

After only two years of public school education, it was necessary for George Lumb to leave school and find work. He practically earned his own living from the age of eleven. He sold matches, newspapers, flowers, and soap, and ran errands. He was a waiter and trunk hand, and worked in a Baltimore hat factory until a strike put him out on the street. Then the jobless young man, who too frequently warmed the city's park benches pondering his future, responded to an army recruiting poster, and enlisted in 1893.

His first assignment took him to Fort Sam Houston, Texas, with Troop H, Fifth U. S. Cavalry, where he remained until the outbreak of the Spanish-American War. He was transferred to Company B, Eighteenth U. S. Infantry, for service in the Philippine Islands, where, with the Second Expedition, he was engaged in the seige and capture of Manila. After Manila, he was transferred to Company M, Ninth U. S. Infantry, and saw two more years of action in the Philippines, during which time he won his first promotion for personal bravery.

With the Ninth U. S. Infantry, Lumb was dispatched to China, the wartime scene of the Boxer Rebellion, where he saw action at Tietsin, Peitsan, Peking, Yangsun, and the Imperial City, for eleven months. Before returning state-side, he had participated in twenty-seven battles and engagements overseas. Back home Lumb was assigned to the Thirty-ninth Company, U. S. Coast Artillery, based at Fort McHenry, for three years; he finished his military service with one year in the First Artillery Corps, at Fort Flagler.

During his peacetime service back in the states, Lumb, no idler at heart, took advantage of his comparatively inactive garrison life and devoted all his leisure time to being a student. He was an excellent scholar, and received high grades for his application to study. At Fort Flagler, he had advanced in studies so remarkably well that he was appointed post schoolteacher.

In twelve years of wartime and peacetime service, Lumb rose from a buck private to Sergeant Major of Artillery, the highest honor short of a commission. He returned to civilian life in 1905 and joined his family in Philadelphia where his father had relocated.

The 5'10" ex-solider, having just reached 31, lost no time in applying for membership in the state constabulary as soon as Superintendent Groome publicly announced this opportunity. Groome accepted his application and sent him to Punxsutawney where he was enlisted by Captain Robinson on December 15, 1905, and immediately given the non-commissioned rank of first sergeant, Troop D; he was launched on what was eventually to become a brilliant fifteen year career with the Department of State Police.

Lumb married Ellanora Cain of Harford County, Maryland, on December 12, 1906, in a double-wedding ceremony at Philadelphia, at which time his younger sister married a Philadelphian. This marriage preceded Groome's order regarding the marital status of enlisted men, which was not issued until March, 1907.

It is interesting to note the contrast between Groome and Lumb, both of whom were to work as an effective team for fifteen years in moving an unusual agency from its early beginnings to a place of esteem in the nation's history. Groome was brought up in wealth, a member of a business family, and well-educated in private schools. He married a well-to-do woman, and his prestige as an officer of the First Troop, Philadelphia City Cavalry, made him more than welcome in Philadelphia's social circles. He was an organizer of social groups and an active member in many clubs. Groome was widely known for his many achievements, and it was not surprising to see him come to Governor Pennypacker's attention during the governor's search for a superintendent. The less fortunate Lumb stemmed from humble beginnings: a member of a poor immigrant English family seeking better circumstances in the new world—and not finding them. Lumb was unable to pursue a formal education, and found service in the army a necessity for survival. Although possessing the potential for commissioned rank, he nonetheless ended his military career one notch below that level. He married a Maryland farm girl who came to him with no dowry. They were not caught up in the gaiety of social activities and club life. He was a self-educated, determined, young man, and a complement to Groome who selected him as his top aide.

The continuity of service and suitability of this team remains unmatched in Pennsylvania State Police history. It is fitting that a reputation of this degree shared by two men from differing backgrounds, except for their common interest for military service, should be held in the highest esteem for all times.

Lumb's removal to Harrisburg left a command vacancy at Troop A, Greensburg, which was filled in March by the promotion of Lieutenant Leon S. Pitcher. Pitcher, 33, 5'9", a native of Milford, Delaware, enlisted December 15, 1905, at Greensburg, and was appointed a sergeant. Prior to enlistment, Pitcher served as first sergeant with Company B, First Regiment, Delaware Volunteers, for nine months in 1898, and as a second lieutenant with the same Delaware National Guard unit from 1899 to 1905.

Before the year 1908 was more than a couple of days old, the new administrative team at Harrisburg instituted a training program of weekly schools in each troop. Each troop was already responsible for training newly-arrived recruits on a daily basis, and each recruit remained in training at troop headquarters for a period of four months before seeing substation duty. The weekly school program was intended to upgrade men, on a continuing basis, who had advanced beyond the recruit training stage. It was not Groome's intention to allow his field forces to become less effective through creeping obsolescence. This policy of upgrading personnel by way of weekly schools has survived for more than seventy years—succeeding heads of the department have seen the wisdom of keeping abreast of changing times.

The spring of 1908 was to see the state constabulary forces tied up for some six weeks in the Chester area, where a serious strike of streetcar motormen and conductors threatened the community. At Chester the troopers grew accustomed to sleeping in trolley cars and eating meals in hotels. Both Groome and Lumb attended the needs of this situation by on-the-scene supervision. Lumb was placed in full charge on April 19, and closed down all saloons. His statement at the time was made in anger when he learned that hotel bars were operating in disregard of the mayor's order to remain closed until further notice. Lumb's words reflect law enforcement's thinking in critical circumstances, and are worth quoting:

> A grave mistake has been made by the local authorities in allowing liquor to be sold in Chester at this time. Chester people are apparently peaceful enough but it would not do any good to have a lot of intoxicated men on the streets tonight. As late as 1 o'clock this morning I warned Mayor Johnson that the saloons must remain closed. It seems to me that politics is largely responsible for the condition. The Chester police are giving us little, if any, support. They don't want to fight with the people of their own town.

At the time of his appointment by Governor Pennypacker, Groome had strenuously made his point regarding politics and political pressures—that there was no place in the state constabulary for such influences and they would not be tolerated. Lumb fully subscribed to this position, and at times was more demonstrative of his feelings—his statement at Chester was a mere sample. Later in his career as deputy superintendent he typically displayed his dislike for pushy politicians: when a cabinet member called at this office to persuade Lumb to assign a trooper to him for what appeared to be personal services, Lumb, believing this request unreasonable, denied it. When the cabinet officer reacted in anger and threatened political retribution, Lumb grabbed him by the coat lapels and showed him to the door.

This incident exemplifies the jointly-held contempt of early State Police leaders for overbearing politicians. Some succeeding department heads were just as determined to direct State Police operations despite attempts at political interference; others yielded at times to accommodation.

In mid-summer 1908, Groome encountered another unpleasant personnel transaction. Captain Charles P. Smith, of Troop C, was charged with "conduct unbecoming an officer and member of the State Police," and became the first commissioned officer to face court-martial proceedings. Smith pleaded guilty, and was ordered dismissed by the board. Groome, moved by compassion and Smith's fine record, set aside the dismissal and, instead, reduced him to lieutenant and transferred him to Greensburg. Smith, who was also the first to be promoted in the commissioned ranks, was a Philadelphian. Abandoning his plumber's trade, he enlisted with the State Police at Reading November 11, 1905. Groome commissioned him a lieutenant, whereupon he and Captain Taylor set about establishing an operational foothold for Troop C. Smith's excellent work in this assignment eventually won him a promotion when Taylor resigned, and earned him Groome's favorable consideration at the time of his court-martial. Smith remained with the constabulary until September, 1909.

Smith was succeeded at Reading by Captain Lynn G. Adams, who was promoted and transferred from his post as lieutenant at Wyoming. Adams, 28, 5'10¼", a native of Hopbottom, Susquehanna County, enlisted December 15, 1905, from Scranton. He was enrolled at Greensburg, and given one of the sergeant appointments with Troop A. From 1900 to 1903, Adams served as sergeant with the Thirteenth U.S. Infantry. Much will be written of this great man who rose to the constabulary's highest post with a record-establishing tenure.

The new alignment of command personnel showed Captain Leon Pitcher at Greensburg, Captain Joseph Robinson at Wyoming, Captain Lynn G. Adams at Reading, and Captain Josiah L. Reese at Punxsutawney.

During the course of this year, another important change was made at headquarters. John H. Clarke, the department's first chief clerk, resigned. This important post was then turned over to Samuel Nissley in July. Newly employed to succeed Nissley was stenographer-typist Charles O. Lippy.

Two days before Christmas, 1908, state constabulary opertions in the anthracite region were given a setback by the complete destruction of the Wyoming barracks by fire. The men stationed there responded to the alarm and risked their lives to save one another, their horses and as much equipment as they could. All of the men suffered the loss of

Troop B barracks at Wyoming destroyed by fire December 23, 1908 (Courtesy of Pennsylvania State Police)

Troop B barracks at Wyoming, 1910 (Courtesy of Pennsylvania State Police)

personal belongings. The Commonwealth later collected $5,000 through its insurance coverage at Wyoming; the claim settlement figure of $5,000 when received by the Commonwealth was reappropriated to the State Police in 1909 by the general assembly. Blame for the fire, which levelled the Wyoming frame facility, was laid to faulty flues. Temporary quarters in Wheelers Hotel, at Wyoming, were occupied while a new headquarters building was constructed.

During the year, operations were conducted from thirty-four sub-stations. There were 424,415 miles patrolled, and 5,028 arrests were made. Disorderly conduct led the list of arrests with 1,171 closely followed by 928 charges for assault and battery. There were 401 arrests for larceny and 46 for murder.

As mentioned earlier, the organization of the state constabulary was not a popular happening insofar as the labor element was concerned, and this rather widespread feeling closely related to the year-ending comment by Captain Pitcher at Greensburg, "We have succeeded in gaining the good will of all the respectable citizens and to a great extent overcome the opposition which was manifested toward the troop upon its organization." The problems faced at Greensburg undoubtedly were the same at the other three locations as the state constabulary tried to set its roots in these communities with a degree of acceptance.

In his report to the governor, Groome made four recommendations: (1) that it be unlawful for an enlisted man to resign before the end of his enlistment, (2) that two additional troops be formed, (3) that a pension system be considered along with benefits to widows and men injured in the line of duty, and (4) that the pay of enlisted men be significantly increased. The last remedial action was sorely needed to offset the high turnover rate of experienced men who were being lost to higher-paying jobs in civilian life.

On October 1, 1908, Henry Ford introduced his first Model T, priced at $850. While this may have slipped Groome's attention at that moment, Ford's enterprising accomplishments were to become a big problem for police. Groome and his successors would face this problem soon enough.

The year 1909 was another sorrowful one insofar as the loss of life was concerned: before the year's end, four more troopers were killed in the line of duty. The first two tragedies came in February, just four days apart, and both were accidental shootings. On February 9, Sergeant Mark A. Prynn, of Troop C, was accidentally shot by Private Reginald Gibson, at Gilbertson. Both were in the process of making an arrest. While Prynn was searching a prisoner, Gibson was covering for him. Gibson's horse bolted, his gun discharged accidentally, and Prynn was fatally wounded. Four days later, Private John Garscia, of Troop B, was accidentally shot by Private Fred M. Carlton, at Inkerman, where both were serving warrants. Deaths in the line of duty now numbered five.

Until June 1, 1909, Troop C headquarters was located on the old Seitzinger homestead along the Wyomissing Road, in Cumru Township, Berks County, about one mile from Reading. Captain Adams, however, considered this leased facility inadequate for troop use and headquarters was moved to Pottsville. The mere presence of a State Police troop headquarters or substation provided a feeling of security within the community where they were located. When the barracks at Reading was being moved to Pottsville, this public feeling was manifested to the point that a special delegation of prominent Reading citizens visited constabulary headquarters at Harrisburg to prevent the move if at all possible. A Berks County newspaper described the move as "a dire calamity for the (Reading) area." The constabulary top brass, however, was not dissuaded, and the move was completed as scheduled.

The newly-occupied building at Pottsville was a large, three-story, brick facility which at one time had been a productive mill. Although this leased building was far from being ideal, it was an improvement over the former dwelling at Reading. The general problem of seeking suitable buildings for troop operations was a continuing one in the absence of state-constructed, state-owned buildings which Groome repeatedly sought in vain. Apparently legislative forces in the general assembly, still hopeful of doing away with the constabulary, did not

Troop C barracks at Pottsville, 1910 (Courtesy of Pennsylvania State Police)

Troop B mounted detail at Wyoming, 1910 (Courtesy of Pennsylvania State Police)

want troopers quartered in permanent structures—a move in this direction would be considered counter-productive insofar as their aims were concerned.

A contract was negotiated at Wyoming to construct a new headquarters building for Troop B, which was to be ready for occupancy early in 1910.

On June 30, 1909, Captain Josiah L. Reese resigned his post at Punxsutawney, and Groome moved Pitcher from Greensburg to Troop D. Lieutenant William Marsh was transferred from Troop C and promoted to captain at Greensburg.

Captain Marsh was scarcely adjusted to his new post when a serious strike with accompanying riotous conditions broke out at the Pressed Steel Car Works at Shoenville, Allegheny County, near McKees Rocks. A detachment of troopers was dispatched to the scene to aid the sheriff. Before the detachment could restore order, a mob of 4,000 strikers attacked the troopers. Privates Jack C. Smith and John L. Williams were shot and beaten to death. Three other privates were severely beaten, but recovered from their injuries. The plight of the troopers was plainly viewed by deputy sheriffs, police and plant guards, all of whom were fully armed and stood by without lifting a hand to assist. Six strikers were also numbered among those killed in the incident.

The Pressed Steel Car Works strike was by far the most violent of encounters faced by the constabulary since its beginnings. Although the Troop A detachment was successful in restoring order at the Shoenville plant, a heavy price was paid in the name of law and order. With the deaths of Smith and Williams, the honor roll of deceased now numbered seven. Seven were killed in four operational years. This sacrifice of life, nonetheless, was never to deter a trooper from his appointed task.

Marsh, moved by the hardships of constabulary life, recommended that a retirement-pension fund for long-service or disability in the line of duty be established, and a four-officer committee be formed to work out a plan. He also suggested a modification of Groome's policy regarding marriage, which would permit enlisted men to marry during their second enlistment.

The hard-pressed troopers patrolled 408,016 miles during the year and made 3,799 arrests. Drunkeness and disorderly conduct accounted for 888 arrests. There were 699 arrests for assault and battery, 354 for larceny and 21 for murder. Crimes of violence continued to be the target for the small band of troopers.

Groome petitioned Governor Stuart for an increase in complement to bolster the ranks of field forces which were overwhelmed by the task before them. He wanted an increase in pay which was presently pegged at $60 a month, $18 of which was earmarked for board and lodging, to offset a fifteen percent increase in the cost of living since 1905. Both of these changes were needed to stabilize a dwindling complement. As a further aid, Groome still sought legal means for enforcing an enlistment contract. In spite of his pleadings, Groome met with no success: he could not muster sufficient strength in the legislature.

Up to this point, each troop was responsible for training its own raw recruits. Men seeking enlistment were given a troop assignment, where they were enrolled and trained before seeing actual duty. This training was about as uniform in its methods as a decentralized system might be expected to offer. Groome was dissatisfied with the decentralized program and changed it. Effective January 1, 1910, he designated Troop C, at Pottsville, as the training center for all recruits. After that date, all recruits were sent to Pottsville where they underwent four months of rigorous training before troop assignments were made. This newly-adopted training program remained operational for a decade.

The year 1910 saw the State Police heavily committed to strike duty. It would serve a useful purpose to devote some attention to the most serious of these strikes, since the story portrays the image being solidly built by the constabulary. This account appeared in a State Police publication:

Supt. John C. Groome and Deputy Supt. George F. Lumb lead constabulary forces into Philadelphia during 1910 trolley car strike (Courtesy of Pennsylvania State Police)

In February, 1910, six thousand employes of the Philadelphia Rapid Transit Company went on strike. As was typical of the times, the strike occasioned great disorder. Irresponsible gangs of hoodlums swelled the violent mobs and soon were entirely beyond the control of Philadelphia's 3,300 policemen.

A militia organization known as the "State Fencibles" was called into the fray but was so unimpressive as to allow the mob to cut the buttons from their uniforms and hang pretzels on their bayonnets. The newspapers reported that two days after they had been summoned to duty, the Fencibles were "recuperating in their armory, after being rescued by the police from a mob." City police, strained beyond the limits of their resources, began firing into the mobs, enraging the strikers and resulting in deaths on both sides. Finally, the Governor sent the Pennsylvania State Police.

A newspaper heralded their approach—"The State Mounted Police from the coal regions, hated and dreaded, known as the Black Hussars, are to encamp at dawn this morning at City Hall. They fire to kill and carry automatic guns."

A union leader threatened that the minute the Black Hussars made their appearance on the city streets, he would call out his 100,000 men and inaugurate the bitterest strike any city in the country had ever experienced.

The Philadelphia Director of Public Safety had called on the Governor to send the National Guard, but the Governor objected that such a course was costly and unnecessary.

"When they have eaten up the State Police" the Governor said, "then I will give you the Guard."

Much criticism was levelled at the Governor for daring to send a group of less than 200 strangers to handle a situation that had utterly defeated the efforts of 3,300 trained officers, heavily reinforced and on their own terrain.

The Kensington section of the city was in the heart of the manufacturing region and the center of the greatest and most obstinate violence. This is where the State Police began their work. The city police were withdrawn and the Troopers, mounted on horseback, dressed in their black coats, the dark blue helmets, made their entry.

The entrance of the State Police is recorded with awe by the newspapers and magazines of the day, and the sight was for years etched in the memory of those who witnessed it.

The Troopers advanced slowly, evenly, at a walk in column of two . . . the men, erect on their mounts, looking neither left nor right . . . big black holsters hanging from their hips, and at each saddle, a pair of shining handcuffs. They did not bring their carbines.

Without a word being spoken, a command uttered, or an eye turned, the crowd that came to jeer turned back in silence and disappeared into the alleys, houses and buildings.

As the squadron rode deeper into the district, a man in a crowd of strikers, looking down from a factory window, threw a heavy steel bolt, hitting one of the Troopers in the back. The man ducked back out of sight, but not before he was seen by one of the Troopers who vaulted out of the saddle and made straight into the factory, up several flights of stairs, through the sullen crowd, and singled out the assailant. As if unconscious of any other presence, the Trooper took his man and firmly propelled him through the throng of his mates, down the stairs, out of the building and into permanent custody. The day before, the incident would have meant a riot. This day, not a finger, not a voice was raised to protest the arrest. From this day, the trolley cars were run throughout the district regularly and with perfect safety.

The *Philadelphia Ledger* reported: "The first appearance (of the State Police) here on any serious business awakened for them the respect and admiration of the whole town. It was generally felt, with something like the conviction that is born of respectful fear, that to monkey with one of these strong and steady-looking chaps was to be playing with the proverbial buzz-saw. If you doubt their ability to swing things as they want them to be swung, just journey up to the district and look one of them in the eye. You won't make any impolite remarks to him."

Editorially, another Philadelphia newspaper had this comment to make regarding the effectiveness of the State Police, "They represent no class or condition, no prejudice or interest, nothing but the soverign majesty of the law. Hostility to them is hostility to the people."

Three days after they arrived in Philadelphia, their duty completed, the squadron left for another assignment. Not a single shot was fired by the State Police during the entire tour of duty.

Once again, Groome and Lumb showed themselves no armchair generals as they personally led their field forces in the Philadelphia Transit strike situation and remained with them until their mission was ended.

Before the year was up, the field forces were called upon to quell labor disorders at the Bethlehem Steel plants, the coal fields of Westmoreland, Luzerne, and Lackawanna counties, and the D. & H. Railroad yards located in the anthracite region.

Groome still maintained his status with the First Troop, Philadelphia City Cavalry, with almost thirty years of continuous service to that honored military establishment. National Guard authorities ordered the four Philadelphia troops, the First Troop, Philadelphia City Cavalry, Second Troop, Troop A and Troop G combined to form the First Squadron Cavalry, Pennsylvania National Guard. On May 12, Groome was elected major of the squadron and, at the same time,resigned his captain's commission with the First Troop, and was placed on the Honorary Roll. He was presented on this occasion with a silver tea service.

In August, former-President Theodore Roosevelt visited the new barracks at Wyoming and inspected the troop. He highly complimented the personnel at Wyoming. Roosevelt, from 1895 to 1897, served as president of the Police Commission of New York City, and never relinquished his high regard for those who served the colors of that public service uprightly. Roosevelt drew national attention for his police reforms and crackdowns on corruption and vice in New York City. The one-day visit took place on August 10, a memorable date for the Wyoming barracks.

In October, Groome made another move in his command structure by transferring Pitcher back to Greensburg and Marsh to Butler.

Lumb, who had on many occasions in his lifetime displayed an eagerness for higher education, set his sights on practicing law as an attorney. Having undertaken a course of study, he successfully passed the preliminary examinations before the state's Law Examining Board, and registered as a student at law with William H. Earnest, a prominent Harrisburg attorney. Lumb also purchased a plot of ground at 21st and Walnut Streets, Harrisburg, and announced his intention to build a home on that site, where he would root himself permanently as a citizen of that community to which he took a liking.

The constabulary in 1910 expanded its substation operations by opening seventy-six facilities, the largest number by far to date. The men patrolled 389,805 miles and made 2,983 arrests. Both the mileage and number of arrests were down from the previous year due to a shortage of manpower. Murder, assault and battery, disorderly conduct, rioting, and larceny headed the list of crimes for which arrests were made.

One troop commander, Captain Pitcher, recommended an increase in the number of horses so that each man would have his own mount for better care and handling. Switching horses among the men apparently was a problem from his point of view. His recommendation, however, regardless of its worthiness was subject to the availability of funds—and Groome had none to spare. Nonetheless, as discouraging as it was, troop commanders continued to file their recommendations with Groome. Groome, frustrated in not being able to implement their recommendations, nor his own as a matter of fact, continued to gratefully accept them.

The United States census was taken in 1910, and the following figures regarding the situation in Pennsylvania were released:

Population total	7,467,713	
Native born	4,222,727	55.1 percent
Mixed parentage	511,039	23.6 percent
Foreign parentage	1,295,228	
Foreign born	1,438,719	18.8 percent
Blacks		2.5 percent

Foreign-born and born of foreign or mixed parentage represented 42.4 percent of the total population.

NATIONALITY		
	Foreign Born	Foreign Parents
Austrians	251,773	142,786
English	109,061	78,974
German	195,185	307,324
Hungarian	123,498	54,162
Irish	165,091	268,134
Italian	196,122	95,534
Russian	240,980	138,566
Others	157,009	209,748
	1,438,719	1,295,228

Bruce Smith, an early twentieth century student of police systems and an author, made these comments of this unique department:

Its origin was inspired by three apparent needs. The first was that of a general executive arm for the state. The second was closely related to the disturbed industrial conditions in the coal and iron regions, and the demonstrated incapacity of sheriffs, constables, and the organized police forces of small communities generally, to contend with them successfully. The third arose from a realization that the sheriff-constable system had broken down, thereby exposing the rural districts to the danger of inadequate police protection.

Recognition of all three conditions in Pennsylvania was

to have an important bearing upon later police developments elsewhere, but the rural protection aspect challenged attention from the very outset and has exercised a compelling influence upon state police management in many parts of the country from that day to this. The Pennsylvania force was not evolved in any strict sense of the term. In the terse expression of Governor Pennypacker, it was "made," and in the making, whether from accident or from design, there was a sharp break from established tradition. Schemes of organization and control which had become imbedded in accepted police practice were ignored in the formation of this new body. Its establishment in 1905 marked the beginning of a new era in rural police administration.

The distinguishing characteristic of this force consisted in the extensive administrative powers granted to the superintendent of State Police, who was made responsible to the governor of the Commonwealth alone. From the very beginning it operated as a mounted and uniformed body which, using a widely distributed system of troop headquarters and substations as a base of operations, patrolled the rural and semi-rural portions of the entire state, even to the little-frequented byways and lanes. In its highly centralized administrative powers, its decentralized scheme of structural organization, and its policy of continuous patrol throughout the rural areas, the Pennsylvania State Police constituted a distinct departure from earlier state practice.

Former President Theodore Roosevelt visits Troop B barracks at Wyoming, August, 1910. Standing at center, left to right: John Mitchell, Capt. Joseph F. Robinson, Col. Roosevelt, Lt. John E. Walsh, Rev. Father Curran, Lawrence F. Abbott, Rev. Father O'Donnell. (Courtesy of Pennsylvania State Police)

CHAPTER V

Captain John C. Groome
1911–1915

Early in 1911, the barracks at Punxsutawney rented from the Punxsutawney Fair Association Land Company, which had been declared uninhabitable in 1910, was vacated. Troop D headquarters was moved to a cite near Butler on January 15, where a new building and stables were leased.

This move westward may have added to the personal problems already being encountered by Captain Marsh and, at his request, Groome demoted him to lieutenant and transferred him eastward to Troop B. This transaction was aimed at alleviating Marsh's family hardships.

Although this demotion was made at the request of a member, demotions for disciplinary reasons were not uncommon. There were numerous courts-martial sessions convened to handle complaints of willful wrongdoing. Groome was determined that discipline would be observed—this was not a surprising stand for most of the men who understood the military way of life.

Marsh's situation gave rise to another innovation by Groome. He decided to have the lieutenants compete by way of a written examination for the opportunity of advancement to captain. The exam was conducted at headquarters on January 11, and four days later Lieutenant Cecil M. Wilhelm was promoted and sent to Butler.

A week later Groome changed commands in three of his troops by dispatching Wilhelm to Reading, Adams to Greensburg, and Pitcher to Butler. Robinson did not figure in this series of transfers and remained at Wyoming.

Although none of the years in the young life of the state constabulary could hardly be labelled as dull, the year 1911 sparked new prospects for the organization. With the appearance of a new governor, John K. Tener, and a more favorable makeup in the general assembly new hopes were raised for changes long sought by the constabulary administrators.

On hand for the inaugural ceremonies at Harrisburg on January 17 was a force of ninety-three troopers to see Tener take the oath of office as the Commonwealth's new governor, and to fulfill the manifold tasks assigned to its individual members. The troopers had already established themselves as an indispensable element to be relied upon by any committee on inaugural arrangements.

Governor Tener reappointed Groome to head the Department of State Police, and the Senate responded by confirming his appointment on February 21.

In Harrisburg, a landmark trial of widespread interest was being heard in Dauphin County Court during the weeks of February. To better understand the case, it is necessary to go back to the Florence incident of 1906, in which the first two troopers were killed. It will be recalled that the members of Troop D, in a final action to apprehend the barricaded fugitives, dynamited the house.

During the 1907 session of the general assembly, a bill was introduced in the Senate, Senate Bill 175, authorizing several persons from Florence to sue the Commonwealth for damages to the dynamited home and furnishings. The bill passed the Senate 34–0, on March 26, 1907, but the measure died in the House.

During the 1909 session, Senate Bill 69, covering the same authorization, was introduced and passed 35–0. A month later, the House brought the measure to the floor where it lacked a majority vote and was defeated. The next day, the House moved to reconsider the bill and postponed doing so until March 22. The sponsor of the House bill

Troop D barracks at Butler, 1911 (Courtesy of Pennsylvania State Police)

explained, upon questioning, that a private home was entered by a fugitive. The owners departed at this action, the fugitive barricaded himself and shot it out with the constabulary. The owners were in no way involved in a crime. According to the legislator, the property loss was estimated at $5,800. The measure this time passed the House by a 160–7 vote.

Governor Edwin S. Stuart signed Act 52, P.L. 90, on April 1, 1909, authorizing Mariasunto Acro, Guercio Liborio, Guercio Michalena, Manderina Muzza, Felice Muzza, Cologero Corriero, Guiseppe Caraggi, Stefano Pagano, Salvatore Ballavia, Salvatore Stutto, Francesco Cirranni, Cologero Arno, Guiseppe Cirranni, Carlo Plumeri, and Thomas Murphy to sue the Commonwealth. (How Thomas Murphy got into the picture is not clear).

The trial began on February 14 and lasted a week. Judges Kunkel and McCarrell presided. Representing the plaintiffs was attorney Frank B. Wickersham. He was ably assisted by a blind attorney from Punxsutawney, William M. Gillespie, who impressed the court with his well-prepared braille notes and remarkable memory. Assistant Deputy Attorney General William M. Hargest defended the State Police and the Commonwealth.

The trial was, according to the *Harrisburg Telegraph* story, "without parallel in any court in the United States."

The State Police story was impressively given by Deputy Superintendent Lumb, former Captain Joseph Robinson, Lieutenant William Marsh, Sergeant Homer Chambers, and a number of others present at Florence, who witnessed the slaying of their comrades, Henry and Zehringer, and explained the emotion that prevailed under the circumstances.

After testimony was completed, the judges charged the jury, proposing four questions to them for which written answers were to be given.

1. Did the conduct of the plaintiffs in anyway contribute to the injury of their property? Answer—It did not.

2. Did the State Police honestly believe in the light of the information they had received September 3, 1906, that the dynamiting of the plaintiffs' house was necessary to enable them to effect the arrest of the felon or felons who had taken refuge in the house? Answer—Yes. They acted as wise, prudent and courageous men would have acted under existing circumstances.

3. Did the dynamiting of the house cause the fire which destroyed it? Answer—We believe it did.

4. Did the State Policemen or any of them after they had

obtained entrance to the house deliberately set fire to the house? Answer—They did not.

The jury's verdict exonerated the State Police from wrongdoing and recommended that the plaintiffs be awarded damages. The presiding judges, participating attorneys, the plaintiffs, and the State Police were all satisfied and content with the outcome. The court ordered the Commonwealth to pay the plaintiffs the sum of $3,100. Oddly-enough, death had claimed the life of Mariasunto Acro, the principal plaintiff and property owner, before the trial began.

Appearing now on the Harrisburg scene to lead labor elements opposed to the existence of the State Police was Representative James Hudson Maurer, of Berks County. He remained a thorn in the side of the State Police for eight long years, leaving no stone unturned to see the constabulary dead and buried.

Maurer was born in Reading on April 15, 1864. He was a newsboy when six years of age, a factory-worker at ten, and a machinist's apprentice at fourteen. In 1895, this ambitious young radical was editor and owner of a populist paper, and in 1905 was editor of the *Reading Union Sentinel.* Maurer served as national committeeman of the Socialist Party six times and as a member of that party's state executive committee for six years. In 1906, he was the Socialist Party candidate for governor. Maurer was first elected to the House of Representatives in 1910, and was reelected to the House continuously until 1918, when his tenure came to an end. He was soon elected president of the State Federation of Labor by its members, and it was also in this capacity that he accelerated his attacks upon the State Police. He was an ego-centered individual who realized that the publicity he drew by his attacks on the State Police was providing him public exposure that money could not purchase for him.

Immediately after his election in 1910, Maurer said, "At last I shall have an opportunity to strike a blow at the Cossacks, Pennsylvania's murderous, legalized band of strike-breakers," a statement recorded by his brother, Charles A. Maurer, also of Reading, in a 1911 labor publication.

One of Maurer's first actions as a newly-elected House member was to prepare a questionnaire for mailing to union locals of the American Federation of Labor in Pennsylvania in an effort to secure information damaging to the constabulary and useful to him in the upcoming general assembly session of 1911. In his accompanying correspondence, Maurer wrote, "The stock arguments used by the champions of the constabulary are: They are here to protect life and property and are a panacea for the social evils of the farmer's hencoop." He did receive replies to his questionnaire survey, which he developed for his 1911 crusade against the "Cossacks."

Maurer lost no time in the 1911 General Assembly in introducing a bill to repeal the act creating the Department of State Police. His bill was sent to the Committee on Judiciary General where it died. On the other hand, Rep. V. Gilpin Robinson (R-Delaware), introduced House Bill 216, which probably provoked more debate and controversy than any other piece of legislation considered by the 1911 session, and would, if passed, bring about improved conditions for the constabulary.

There was a constant need to compare State Police salaries with other police agencies already in existence in the Commonwealth to show how underpaid the troopers were by comparison. Groome and Lumb devoted considerable time to such statistical arguments. This struggle continued through the first two decades of the department's history. The force never did grow significantly nor was its compensation plan ever one to boast about—thanks to the activists in the labor movement.

Sensing success at this point, Groome wrote to the House in behalf of HB 216:

> There has been a great deal said about the State Police Force being used to the injury and detriment of the working classes. This all has its origin in a few professional organizers whose very livelihood depends upon disagreements between capital and labor. As a matter of fact there are records in the office which show that the majority of the intelligent working men are in favor of the Department of State Police for the following reasons:
>
> Previous to the creation of this Force, whenever labor disturbances occurred, it was the custom of sheriffs of the counties to swear in great numbers of deputies who were recruited from the ranks of the unemployed in the cities without making any investigation into their previous character, morals or general fitness for the responsibilities that are incidental to the duties of a police officer. These men were armed with Winchester rifles or revolvers, they were undisciplined and as a rule drank excessively, and it is impossible to think that a man of average intelligence would prefer to have such characters doing police duty in the vicinity of their homes, where women and children must come and go on the public highways, in preference to trained men who have to produce bona fide proofs of their excellent character, pass a rigid physical and mental examination and who are responsible to the bonded officers of the Common-

wealth for their actions. It has been the unpleasant duty of the members of this Department on several occasions to arrest deputy sheriffs who were guilty of misconduct and reckless shooting to the peril of the very people whose homes and welfare they were supposed to guard.

Maurer's first major speech against the constabulary came on March 16, 1911, as consideration was being given to Robinson's House Bill 216. He reviewed at length the results of his survey and the many letters testifying to the brutality of the constabulary.

> Gentlemen, in this brief address (which was not brief at all) to you I have proven that the sole purpose of the State Police is to serve that class at whose solicitation they were created, no farmer asked that this department be created; had the farmer asked for it, and were they only to be used to patrol the rural districts and protect the farmer, and not to be used for strike duty, you know the farmers would not get any more consideration on this question than what they have in the past on other questions. Gentlemen, I have now submitted the truth to you. The situation is now in your hands, and if any more evils occur on account of the Constabulary, I hold you responsible.

On that same day, the American Federation of Labor convention, meeting at Philadelphia, dispatched a delegation to Harrisburg so that AFL president Greenawald could address the House and protest House Bill 216. The Speaker explained to the delegation that Greenawald was welcome to address the House but, according to House rules, he could not make any comments referring to any bill under consideration. The delegation returned to Philadelphia. The bill was not called up.

The bill did come up for a vote on March 27, after considerable debate in which many representatives engaged. The vote lacked a consitutional majority, and went down to defeat. On April 3, Rep. H. J. Wilson (R-Jefferson) moved to have the Robinson bill reconsidered. A 125–57 vote brought the defeated bill back. In the meantime, public pressure in favor of the measure had come into play. Finally, on April 25, House Bill 216 was passed by a 113–65 vote.

True to his threat, Maurer had published the names of the representatives not acting favorably insofar as he was concerned. To his colleagues, he predicted, "I will create such a public sentiment that two years hence when you meet again you will be compelled to abolish the Pennsylvania Constabulary."

The Senate concurred with the House. This was the first favorable legislation affecting the State Police since its inception six years earlier. In fact, the only legislation affecting the State Police at all up to that point was Act 198, P.L. 259, May 25, 1907, requiring the department to make daily monetary settlements with the state treasurer and auditor general. This piece of legislation was forwarded to Governor Tener who approved it on June 1, 1911. It was to be later identified as P.L. 551.

Sections 2 and 3 of the creating act of 1905 were amended by the 1911 General Assembly as follows:

SECTION 2. The Superintendent of State Police shall be provided by the Board of Grounds and Buildings with suitable offices at the Capitol, in Harrisburg, and shall give a bond to the Commonwealth in the sum of twenty thousand dollars, for the faithful performance of his duties. He is authorized to appoint a deputy *superintendent,* at a salary of *two thousand five hundred dollars per annum;* one bookkeeper, at a salary of *fifteen hundred dollars per annum,* and one stenographer at a salary of twelve hundred dollars per annum.

SECTION 3. He is also authorized to appoint the State Police Force, which shall consist of four *troops,* each consisting of a captain, at a salary of *eighteen hundred dollars per annum;* a lieutenant, at a salary of *fifteen hundred dollars per annum; a first sergeant at a salary of twelve hundred dollars per annum; four sergeants, each at a salary of eleven hundred dollars per annum; four corporals, each at a salary of nine hundred and fifty dollars per annum; one blacksmith with rank of corporal, at a salary of nine hundred and fifty dollars per annum; and forty-five privates, each at a salary of nine hundred dollars per annum.*

The members of the State Police Force shall be enlisted for a period of two years; and each member of said State Police Force shall receive an increase in pay of five dollars per month during a second continuous enlistment, and an additional increase in pay of five dollars a month during a third continuous enlistment.

The first change in Section 2 adds the word "superintendent" which was not mentioned in the original section, and provides a full title, "deputy superintendent." The second change increases his annual salary to $2,500. While the general assembly was kind to Lumb, a salary increase for Groome was ignored. The third change omits the word "clerk" and provides just for a bookkeeper with a salary increase to $1,500 a year. The stenographer, keeping Groome company, received no consideration.

Section 3 was amended with much double-talk. Although it appears on the surface to bring on great change—it does not in reality. The manpower complement was merely shifted around and the original complement of 228 remained fixed. The first change in this scetion specifies that each field unit will be identified as a "troop." The original act calls for the creation of four companies, or platoons. All official documents since 1905 referred to the units as troops, which was actually not in keeping with the act. Thus the change in 1911 was to bring about a real situation. The next change increased the annual salary of captain to $1,800, and lieutenant to $1,500. Groome had already appointed first sergeants in each troop, who were taken from the complement of sergeants. The new law confirmed Groome's actions by legally separating one sergeant and giving him another title and salary differential. Four new corporal positions were added to the supervisory rolls, and each troop was given a blacksmith with a corporal's rank, at equivalent salary of $950 a year. To accommodate the new corporals and blacksmiths, the complement of privates—a new title—was reduced to 45 per troop, and each private was given a pay increase to $900 a year. Finally, Groome's won his point for a two-year enlistment, and the field forces were allowed longevity pay of five dollars a month, which applied to their second and third enlistments, provided the enlistments constituted unbroken service.

Here are two groupings, for easy comparison:

1905		*1911*	
Superintendent	$3,000	Superintendent	$3,000
Deputy	2,000	Deputy Superintendent	2,500
Clerk (Bookkeeper)	1,400	Bookkeeper	1,500
Stenographer	1,200	Stenographer	1,200
Each company, or platoon		*Each troop*	
1 captain	1,500	1 captain	1,800
1 lieutenant	1,200	1 lieutenant	1,500
5 sergeants	1,000	1 first sergeant	1,200
50 men	720	4 sergeants	1,100
$57 \times 4 = 228$		4 corporals	950
		1 blacksmith (corporal)	950
		45 privates	900
		$57 \times 4 = 228$	

Groome was successful in securing a much needed pay increase for his men and some additional supervisory assistance. His opposition, however, in the general assembly was sufficiently strong to stymie his plans for a complement increase. Groome could take satisfaction from the fact that, after six hard years, he had at least broken the ice. Unfortunately, it was to take another six frustrating years before further benefits were to come to the State Police, during which years the labor activists fought their best legislative battles under Maurer's leadership.

One week after the new law was signed by Tener, Groome issued an order whereby competitive examinations would be conducted in each troop on June 15 to establish a priority list for promotions to the newly-created rank of corporal. His order specified the nature of the examination material and the evaluation process to be observed by troop commanders. The blacksmiths, by virtue of their specific duties, were not required to compete.

On June 23, Groome announced the first group of corporals:

Troop A	*Troop B*
Cleve T. Dent	Charles M. Culver
Carl S. Dressler	Jasper Oftedahl
Philip Roller	Bernard L. McGarry
Robert Graham	George W. Freeman
Walter W. Mallory	William Metcalf
(Blacksmith)	(Blacksmith)

Troop C	*Troop D*
Harvey J. Smith	Henry T. Bland
Harry K. Merryfield	Frank Hauber
Samuel W. Gearhart	Gustave Birmele
(Vacant)	William J. Kenney
Thomas Meikrantz	Charles Simmons
(Blacksmith)	(Blacksmith)

Apparently Groome was beset with requests from privates seeking transfers to another troop, most likely to be closer to home territory. The wishful thinking of the privates in this matter is understandable when one reviews their places of assignment and compares them with their places of residence at the time of enlistment. Nonetheless, at the time of enlistment, it was understood that each man would accept his assignment wherever it took him to satisfy departmental needs. To end all hope for such consideration, Groome signed a general order stating succinctly that inter-troop transfer requests will not be approved. Such a deep-rooted problem, however, could never be completely rubbed out, and the subject of inter-troop transfers was bound to surface again and again with Groome and his successors—and it did.

In 1912, Groome ordered a mutual transfer of troop commanders, sending Pitcher to Wyoming and returning Robinson to his original command of Troop D. Both Troops B and D headquarters were housed in new leased buildings. By contrast, Troops A and C headquarters were occupying dilapidated buildings. Adams was successful in negotiating an agreement with his Greensburg leasor to construct a new barracks and stables near Greensburg, which was to be made available for occupancy in the spring of 1913. This left Groome with only one remaining sore spot for a troop headquarters—Pottsville. The Pot-ttsville barracks, occupied since 1909, was not in good condition at the time of occupancy, and the intervening years brought no improvement.

Urged by his troop commanders to attach more importance to pistol marksmanship and competition, Groome approved the organization of a State Police pistol team. The team for the first time entered the Military Revolver Match conducted by the U. S. Revolver Association, and placed seventh in a field of forty-five teams. Private H. G. Moore won the State Military Championship gold and silver medals for rapid fire at fifty yards.

Strike duty during 1912 was limited. The most serious of that year's crop of strikes took place in the anthracite region where large detachments of men were sent to maintain order. The strike was concluded on May 22 when an agreement between the miners and coal operators was reached. Lieutenant Mair, Sergeant Wisman, and Corporal Graham were singled out for their outstanding performances during the strike. Governor Tener was very much impressed by the manner in which the troopers handled the potentially explosive situation and wrote Groome, "Am especially pleased that none of your good men (and they are all good) have lost their lives or been seriously injured and my hope is that they may come through these trying days without such sacrifice. Please give to them my congratulations and know that whatever can be done by this Department, to assist you and the men under you, to put down lawlessness and to preserve the peace, will be done."

In autumn, Groome defined more clearly a system of patrol zones. Basically, the men were to cover their zones in a ten day period, riding an estimated fifteen miles a day to do so.

At the close of the year, Captain Adams submitted his annual report and mentioned for the first time the idea that the State Police become motorized. He recommended that the State Police purchase five motorcycles for each troop "to facilitate criminal investigations where the time element is so important to a successful conclusion." Here Adams was referring to the importance of response time insofar as successful police action is concerned.

This recommendation of his also reflected the changing times—the gasoline buggies were beginning the replace the horses—and held a prophesy of a time when the State Police would be entirely dependent upon motorized conveyances.

Operating from forty-seven substations, the field forces patrolled 491,398 miles and made 1,144 arrests. Murder, assault and battery, drunkenness, and disorderly conduct continued to dominate the list of crimes for which arrests were made. Statistics were now being kept on the conviction rates following arrests, and in 1912 the conviction rate for all criminal arrests was 80 percent, which by any standards is exceptionally good.

To clear up any misunderstanding about what he expected from his commissioned officers, Groome issued a general order on March 23, 1913, making the lieutenants equally responsible with the captains for the enforcement of orders and discipline. Groome was an experienced taskmaster, as was Lumb, and both realized the necessity of enforcement within the family of troopers before the troop could carry out its enforcement responsibilities elsewhere.

After four operational years without a fatality, the good fortune of the State Police was ended with the death of Private Robert V. Myers, of Troop D, on March 28, 1913. Myers, on flood duty at Sharon where looting was reportedly taking place, was accidentally shot by Private Frank White. For his actions, White was dishonorably discharged.

The new barracks at Greensburg was completed by this time and occupied by Troop A on April 1. With this move, Troops A, B, and D were well-situated. Troop headquarters facilities at Pottsville were lamentable, and Groome continued to devote interest to this problem.

Notwithstanding the shortcomings of the facilities at Pottsville, Troop C continued to be the training center for all recruits. There the newly-arrived troopers underwent four months training in criminal law, game law, fish law, forestry law, care of horses, military drill (mounted and dismounted), and firearms.

Since the 1911 legislation failed to increase the trooper comple-

Troop A barracks at Greensburg, 1913 (Courtesy of Pennsylvania State Police)

50th Anniversary of Battle of Gettysburg, 1913. First from left: Capt. John D. Delaney, state Factory Inspector and Union veteran. Second and fourth: Constabulary Corp. William J. Kenney, Troop D; Pvt. John A. Gallagher, Troop B. Fifth and sixth: Confederate veterans; all others are Union veterans. (Courtesy of Pennsylvania State Police)

ment, another attempt was made to do so in the 1913 General Assembly. Invariably the opposition element in the House would make every effort to discredit Groome and thereby strategically bring about the defeat of any beneficial measures. This was the case in May, 1913, when Groome's reputation as a business man was under attack during a House debate on a bill to increase the state constabulary membership. Rep. Daniel J. Shern (R-Philadelphia), upon questioning, came to Groome's defense, "Mr. Groome conducts a wholesale liquor business at the corner of Camac and Walnut Streets, right below thirteenth, but he only sells to his intimate friends and three or four clubs the highest grades of champagne and the highest grades of wines. And I know whereof I speak, that he has not a saloon upon his books. Superintendent Groome is highly respected in the community."

In private life, Groome was a Philadelphia businessman—wholesale wine-importing business—a family situation into which he was born. He was not actively engaged in the business and considered himself more or less a silent partner.

The general assembly in 1913 passed Act 338, P.L. 528, which was approved by Governor Tener on June 19, and permitted capital punishment to be carried out by electrocution. The bill provided the sum of $50,000 for the construction of facilities at the Western Penitentiary, located at Rockview, Centre County. Prior to the passage of this measure, capital punishment was administered by hanging.

The federal government had already made elaborate plans to commemorate the fiftieth anniversary of the Battle of Gettysburg, at Gettysburg, in July, and the Commonwealth committed its resources heavily to this historical event. Governor Tener ordered the constabulary to police Gettysburg and surrounding country during that celebration. The State Police command post was set up on the Gettysburg College athletic field, and an advance detail from Troop B arrived there on June 25. The remainder of the large task force arrived at Gettysburg on June 28, and the entire detail remaind on duty there until July 6.

At the conclusion of this great celebration, Lt. Colonel Lewis E. Beitler, secretary of the Pennsylvania Commission, wrote to Groome on July 6, on behalf of the governor and the commission, regarding State Police services during the Great Reunion Celebration.

> From your own excellent staff down through your Assistant Superintendent, your Captains and Lieutenants and your men, everyone in your command deserves the highest praise and commendation for their strict attention to duty, their unfailing courtesy and their excellent discretion and tact in so successfully handling the many unusual conditions here confronting them.
>
> This Medal of Gold presented you is accompanied by five Medals of Silver, one each for Assistant Superintendent Lumb, and Captains Adams, Pitcher, Wilhelm and Robinson, as our direct expression to them of our appreciation, and to each of the officers and men of their respective Troops we desire you communicate this commendation of His Excellency and this Commission.

Later, when the Pennsylvania Commission filed its official report, Beitler wrote, "To their already excellent record of service in the Commonwealth since this force was created, Major Groome and every officer and private thereof there present, added a splendid chapter of accomplishment by their intelligent conception and execution of the many new and unusual duties presented by the vast number of sightseers and visitors who, from almost every walk of life, some on foot, others in farm wagons, some by train, others in high-powered automobiles, crowded all the avenues into the borough and early would have congested its streets beyond all control but for the great work there accomplished by this force in this and all other branches of police protection, the unstinted praise so widely given it being most justly deserved."

Referring to the more than fourteen thousand automobiles and other vehicles on the scene at Gettysburg, the Commission report further stated, "yet all following in orderly procession, so prefectly was the traffic being directed by the combined squadrons of the U. S. Cavalry under Major Rhodes, and the State Police, under Major Groome, yet it was not until the midnight hours that all had departed,

the splendid record made being not an accident of any kind whatsoever, with the tons of fireworks and the thousands of vehicles of all
kinds, with their tens of thousands of passengers, and still greater numbers of veterans and others on foot.''

From these generously-worded statements, it was quite apparent
that all elements of the State Police at Gettysburg had held up their end
in seeing to it that the 1913 Reunion of the Blue and Gray was a truly
glorious occasion.

After all units had returned to station, Groome formed a mess
committee in each troop, consisting of a mess steward and two troop
members, who were to be elected by the troopers living in the barracks. Committee members, according to Groome, were to be unmarried and elected by a majority vote. Mess facilities were maintained
only at troop headquarters. Although elections were to be conducted
by the men using the dining room, the hand of the troop commanders in
the selection of committee members was many times in evidence.

Because of the comparatively low pay and job difficulties, the constabulary was still suffering from a high turnover rate. The year 1913
provided an excellent example, when 42 men resigned to accept better-
paying positions. Twenty-five others were discharged and 6 deserted.
This total loss of 73 men represented 32 percent of the trooper complement, if the complement had been filled at 228, which is doubtful. This
condition certainly was a sore point with Groome and Lumb.

There was never a shortage of applications on file at the main offices in Harrisburg, since interest in joining the force ran high then and
has never diminished in seventy years. If anything, interest has been
on the increase. In order to compensate for large loss of manpower, the
State Police continually recruited and trained classes of new arrivals at
the indoctrination center at Troop C, Pottsville. In doing so, the State
Police managed to keep its authorized strength as high as possible.
While this was a source of some satisfaction to the troop commanders,
it was disheartening to them to have good, experienced men leave and
accept as their replacements men who would need months of additional
training and experience to match the effectiveness of their predecessors. As long as the conditions of employment were less than
suitable for retention of manpower, troop commanders would have to
endure this turnover problem—and they did for decades before the
situation became more promising.

On November 22, 1913, Deputy Superintendent Lumb was elected
national commander-in-chief of the American Veterans of Foreign
Service during that organization's annual convention at Newark.
Lumb, in addition to fulfilling his State Police responsibilities,
remained interested in veterans' affairs and active in their behalf. Later

the American Veterans of Foreign Service was to join with the Army of the Philippines and the Foreign Service Veterans to form a new organization—Veterans of Foreign Wars of the United States (VFW). Lumb was one of the early leaders of Harrisburg's Captain Howard L. Calder Post No. 31, VFW.

Since operations began in 1906, eight men had been killed in the line of duty and nineteen seriously wounded, seven of whom "are crippled for life," stated Groome in a report to the governor. On the other hand, Groome was happy to report that, during the same period, no one had died from natural causes.

The field forces, operating from fifty-three substations, patrolled 645,198 miles during 1913, visiting 2,839 towns and boroughs in sixty-six counties. There were 1,960 criminal arrests for eighty-nine different charges, with a 90 percent conviction rate. Crimes of violence continued, although there was evidence that the State Police influence was serving as a deterrent.

Since 1905 the State Police had successfully prosecuted 102 murder cases. One might wonder what society would have had to endure during those years without a State Police force. In 1913, a new statistic appeared: arrests listed for the violation of automobile laws. This newcomer was to become a giant among the statistics as years went on.

During the year, the department received 4,369 requests for assistance from judges, sheriffs, district attorneys, chiefs of police, mayors, justices of the peace, and private citizens. Admittedly, all requests could not be responded to because of limited manpower. "The State Police did the best it could under the circumstances," so said Groome.

Early in 1914, Lumb was admitted to practice law in the Dauphin County courts upon motion of attorney William H. Earnest, with whom Lumb has been studying for some years. This approval action was taken by the Dauphin County courts on February 9. This was a singular attainment, since no top command official of the State Police has ever been a member of the legal profession. Before the year was up, Lumb was further honored by being admitted to practice before the state supreme court. This action came seven months later to the day.

In February, Groome, with regrets, announced the resignation of Captain Joseph F. Robinson, the last of his original troop commanders. Robinson served honorably in this capacity for eight years and four months. His resignation was effective February 28. Robinson was replaced by Lieutenant Thomas F. Wiechard. Wiechard, not yet 36, 5'8", a native of Philadelphia, was one of Groome's original enlistees of December 15, 1905, when he was assigned to Troop C, Reading, as a private. In less than one month he was promoted as the fifth sergeant at Reading to fill that troop's complement of non-commissioned officers. Wiechard was the first of the original privates to be promoted to the rank of captain.

In August, the Pennsylvania Manufacturers' Association, in its *Monthly Bulletin*, published at Philadelphia, publicly expressed comments strongly favoring the State Police. "From various quarters complaints have reached us recently regarding the activities of certain persons who presume to speak in the name of labor and in that name are demanding the abolition of the State Police," the report stated. In the 1914 primary election, abolitionists contacted all candidates for commitments to do away with the state constabulary, or seriously restrict its scope and powers. They demanded the removal of Major John C. Groome in favor of a political superintendent, "more amenable to their influence," and an amendment to the act under which the department operates, prohibiting the constabulary from doing riot duty.

The PMA publication referred to the summer of 1913, when the State Police served at the fiftieth anniversary affair at Gettysburg.

> The attention they received and the admiration aroused by their quiet efficiency at the Gettysburg reunion last summer entitled them to rank as one of the features of a national event which attracted thousands of the most prominent men in the country and exemplified the most wholesome American sentiment. The development of the State Police under Major Groome's direction has been a matter for general congratulations. Wherever his men have gone, they have acquitted themselves creditably and have left behind them grateful recollections of intelligent and courageous service.

The article mentioned that Groome was very much sought after by New York State which was then trying to organize a state police department of its own. Groome, however, was not about to leave his post in Pennsylvania.

Getting back to the troopers, the report stated, "They are one of the greatest blessings the secluded farmers and the inadequately protected small towns of the interior have ever received from the government in Harrisburg and that the limitation of their sphere of usefulness would amount to a triumph for lawlessness throughout the Commonwealth."

The PMA monthly recalled how Groome, back in 1905, accepted his appointment as superintendent on the condition that he should have a free hand in the organization of his force along military lines and that the department should be kept free of politics. The report quoted from a paper which Major Groome read before the Colony Club in New York:

'And notwithstanding the fact that some of our leading politicians did try to control the appointments and to dictate the policy of the department during the first few years, I have always managed to keep the force entirely free from politics and now it is at last recognized all through the state as an absolutely non-political body. In fact, I do not know and have never known the personal politics of any man on the force. Neither of Governor Pennypacker's successors, Governor Stuart or Governor Tener, has ever interfered in any way with the management of the force.'

In comparing the constabulary's limited manpower of 228 officers and men to its task of protecting 8 million people spread out over Pennsylvania's 45,215 square miles, the report said, "Philadelphia has a police department of 3,987 men. Surely, the great state of Pennsylvania, the only state in the Union, which is without debt, can afford a police force of at least 1,000!"

Reference was made to the fact that in the nine years of the force, the Pennsylvania National Guard was not called on once, although it would have been necessary for the governor to do so had it not been for the State Police. Incidents cited were: Mt. Carmel, 1906; Chester, 1908; McKees Rocks, 1909; Philadelphia, 1910; South Bethlehem, 1910, and Shenandoah, and the anthracite fields, 1912. The Pennsylvania National Guard was last called for riot duty in 1902 at Hazleton. It cost the taxpayers nearly one million dollars for eight weeks of duty, exclusive of the personal loss in salaries, wages, or time to the 9,000 officers and men who were kept away from their daily occupations for two months. "This amount would be sufficient to support the State Police for three years, enabling them to accomplish the same results in a much less spectacular way and at the same time to give continuous service in the prevention and detection of crime of all kinds and the protection of life and property and womanhood in remote rural localities which otherwise would never see a uniformed officer of the law."

President Maurer, of the American Federation of Labor, and President Burch, of the United Hatters of America, lodged charges which were threshed out at a public hearing by Governor Tener at Hazleton in June, 1914. This was an open attempt by the "labor agitators" to discredit the State Police.

Concluded the PMA statements:

The men and women in this state who own property or
esteem law and order should combine now in demanding that
the dishonest and hypocritical element in labor organizations
keep its hands off the State Police. It is only necessary that
citizens everywhere who know and appreciate its invaluable
services express themselves vigorously against any plan to
abolish, restrict or hamper the force. The sole purpose underlying the perennial schemes of professional ruffians is to
give lawless methods freer play and lawless men greater opportunities for evil. Let our State Senators and Representatives, whoever they may be, go to Harrisburg next winter
fully assured that the great body of public sentiment in
Pennsylvania is behind the State Police, and let them understand that any truckling to labor bullies, which menaces the
virtue of defenseless women and the safety of life and
property will not be excused or tolerated.''

By 1914 the motion picture industry was picking up a real head of
steam, and Mary Pickford was the nation's sweetheart. Interest was
generated by one picture studio in the production of a documentary
dealing with the deeds and accomplishments of the Pennsylvania State
Police which had received widespread notice throughout the country.
The studio officials dispatched a crew to Troop A headquarters, at
Greensburg, to work out the details for filming. Captain Lynn G.
Adams cooperated with the film-makers who decided to have a script
centered about the case of a child kidnapping, which ended with the
return of the child, and a successfully prosecuted case by the troopers
of Troop A. During the filming of the documentary, the studio crew
was introduced to the troop's mascot—a female beagle that answered
to the name "Mary Pickford." The documentary film, when completed, was shown in theatres everywhere as one of the "selected short
subjects" which were customarily shown with a feature film presentation in those days.

In his year-end report to Governor Tener, Groome lamented the
fact that detached service had to be cut by 50 percent with only twenty-
nine substations operated in twenty-five counties compared to the 1913
figures when fifty-three substations were operational in forty-six
counties. Groome explained, "The number of substations had to be
reduced to a minimum this year owing to want of sufficient funds, as a
large part of the appropriations available for expense of substations
was expended in the six months tour of duty in Erie during the industrial disturbances in that city."

Troopers patrolled 592,031 miles, visiting 2,364 towns and
boroughs in sixty-six counties. There were 2,098 criminal arrests for
seventy-five crimes, and a 75 percent conviction rate. At the year's

end, there were 150 arrestees awaiting court trial compared to only 28 at the close of 1913, indicating a backlog in the courts even then. Owing to limited manpower, only 75 percent of the 3,286 requests for assistance coming from public officials and private citizens could be responded to.

Groome was pleased to report that 156 men were serving a second, third, fourth, or fifth enlistment, mainly because of the 1911 pay increase, and that these men largely accounted for the increased efficiency of the force. While there were no deaths in the line of duty, one man was seriously injured and crippled for life.

Far from the Pennsylvania scene, Austria's Archduke Francis Ferdinand and his wife, the Duchess of Hohenberg, were assassinated at Serajevo, the small capital of the former Austro-Hungarian province of Bosnia, on Sunday, June 28, 1914. This event coupled with the manifold diplomatic failures of that time brought all of Europe to a war which was to last for four years with devastating results, and affect the history of the United States in no small way. The state constabulary would not escape the out-stretching tentacles of World War I, although this eventuality was not a worrisome matter in 1914.

Early in 1915, a change was made at State Police headquarters. In February, Charles O. Lippy resigned as stenographer-typist. He was replaced by Carroll B. Price. Price, a native of Everett and a graduate of Pennsylvania Business College, enlisted December 15, 1912, at 21. His appointment as stenographer took him from the enlisted ranks.

Once again the general assembly was in session—a session that was to witness much controversy over administration attempts to increase the complement and salary schedules of the state constabulary. Midway through the session, House Bill 412, an administration measure, was introduced for the purpose of raising salaries and adding 116 men to the law-restricted complement. The measure was strongly supported by Rep. Richard J. Baldwin (R-Delaware) and Rep. John S. Eby (R-Perry). Opposition to this bill was headed by an untiring labor foe—Maurer.

In a letter, dated March 24, 1915, Deputy Superintendent Lumb stated to the Hon. John S. Eby, a freshman House member, "There has never been a session of the Legislature when the Representatives of the labor faction have not made a general attack concerning the morals and personal conduct of the members of the State Police Force, and this will no doubt occur again when our bill is under consideration." This letter was written in anticipation of a floor attack when HB-412 was released from committee. A strategy to counteract such a labor attack was planned with Rep. Eby, and supported by Rep. Baldwin.

Groome and Lumb were active in seeking the introduction of favorable legislation in support of State Police operations, in contacting legislators for support, and in keeping records of votes cast on such measures to assess the positions of Senate and House members. This was a time-consuming responsibility, but an essential one. The stakes were too high for Groome and Lumb to risk delegating the lobbyist role.

After considerable debate, HB-412 went down to defeat by a 61-125 vote. The successful opposition was spearheaded by Maurer, who repeatedly manifested his obsession for the abolition of the State Police. A Senate measure, SB-120, requiring Pennsylvania residence of one year and no discrimination against married men applying for the constabulary, was also defeated on vote.

Later in the year, the Pennsylvania Federation of Labor published a booklet authored by Socialist Maurer and entitled *The American Cossack*. The booklet sold for 25¢ a copy, or 10¢ in bundle lots of ten or more. The booklet attacked capitalism, particularly in Pennsylvania where the Industrial Revolution's impact was most intense, and the state constabulary:

> A new labor-crushing device must be created; therefore the State Police Department was organized. These police knew very little about the trials and sufferings of the workers. The men selected (for the Force), wherever possible, were ex-U. S. soldiers, trained in the art of murder and who came into contact with the workers only when called upon to beat and kill them. And it may be seen that this Force is of little, if any, use to the State or its citizens, and, above all, does it become apparent that it is a body of cruel men, whose conduct stamps them as partial to the interests of plutocracy; brutal in their dealing with the working class, generally of low character and law breakers when occasion requires. Let us get rid of them that Pennsylvania may return to the old-time peaceful condition.

The booklet recounted the story of a questionnaire distributed by Maurer, as the 1910 Socialist Party's legislative candidate, by which method he sought replies damaging to the state constabulary image. The labor elements, to whom the questionnaires were sent, dutifully replied with information condemning State Police actions in labor dispute incidents as "czarist cossacks." On the other hand, the radical labor activists were characterized as well-behaved. There was no doubt on the part of the respondents that the constabulary was working for the companies.

The publication carried an address by Maurer, in the House, on

March 16, 1911. He was armed with the most volatile replies to his questionnaire. As mentioned before, Maurer's main objectives were the defeat of a House bill favoring State Police salaries and manpower, and the passage of his bill abolishing the department. The 1911 bill was first defeated 70–17 and later passed by a 113–65 vote; the booklet carried the names of those House members who voted for and against the bill on both occasions in an obvious move to discredit house members voting "anti-labor."

The American Cossack contained a number of photographs showing troopers at the Bethlehem Steel plant office building, in 1910, claiming that company officials curried favor with the troopers who were acting as company agents. The booklet also turned to the events of the 1913 legislature when other bills favoring the constabulary went down to defeat under Maurer's leadership.

Groome, justifiably moved by the vicious attacks contained in *The American Cossack,* swiftly replied by printing a document in defense of his department. Maurer was unquestionably the worst of the State Police critics during this era—an unscrupulous politician. His publication, in Groome's statements, was a compilation of untruths simply aimed at the destruction of the State Police by any means whatsoever—the ends justifying the means. Groome wrote, "The apparent object of a book entitled *The American Cossack,* recently circulated throughout Pennsylvania, is first, to advertise its author, Mr. J. H. Maurer, and then, if possible, to prevent legislation tending in any way to increase the numerical strength or the efficiency of the Pennsylvania State Police Force, and while the false, unproven statements and the unsubstantiated charges in the book are not worthy of notice, at the same time, for the benefit of the citizens of this Commonwealth, who may have read the book and in justice to the men on the State Police Force, I feel it my duty to correct some of the statements contained in *The American Cossack.*"

Groome took Maurer's points one by one, refuting his charges by way of official documents. He recounted the deaths and crippling injuries of his troopers at the hands of labor activists, while no worker was illegally killed during any riot control situation. Not one shot was fired by a trooper during riot duty at Philadelphia during the 1910 transit strike, where, according to Maurer, troopers beat and killed workers. As for returning to what Maurer called "the old-time peaceful condition," Groome referred to the Molly Maguire reign of terror in the 1870s; the Homestead riots of 1892 where eight Pinkerton detectives were murdered, and the Lattimer riots of 1902, where many of the mob and deputy sheriffs were killed.

Groome's final statement carried this message, "No honest, law-abiding citizen, no matter what his occupation or station in life, has any reason to fear or to oppose the State Police, as Maurer very well knows."

In May, Groome and Lumb were sent to Washington to testify before the Federal Commission on Industrial Relations. Of this incident, the *Harrisburg Telegraph* carried this item, "The impression made by Major John C. Groome and Captain George F. Lumb, his deputy, in their recital of the activities of the Pennsylvania State Police and their refutation of charges made by labor workers against the organization, likely will induce the Federal Commission on Industrial Relations to make a favorable report on the police system of Pennsylvania."

Bruce Smith later wrote that when Groome testified before the Federal Commission on Industrial Relations and commented on the wide difference in the training and primary purpose of the police and militia, Groome said, "It takes a certain amount of experience to show how many bricks to let a man throw before you attempt to defend yourself, just how many shots to fire, and just how much abuse you will stand before you make a move."

Before the summer was over, Lumb, awakened by a disturbance near his home at Harrisburg, responded to the outcries of a woman in distress. With his automatic in hand, and a flashlight, Lumb encountered a man assaulting a woman. When the man refused to surrender and fled, Lumb fired. The fugitive, wounded in the leg, was later picked up by the Harrisburg city police. A day later, the following editorial appeared in the *Harrisburg Telegraph:*

> MAKE THE STREETS SAFE—Captain Lumb, of the State Police, put a bullet into the leg of a man on Saturday night, who attacked a girl and refused to halt when Lumb attempted to put him under arrest. Captain Lumb is to be commended for the use of his weapon. Attacks of the kind that he interrupted are all too frequent. A few examples such as that set by the State Constabulary officer would teach a very wholesome lesson. Men who have no consideration for the persons of others are entitled to no consideration. The officer who shoots down the fleeing assailant of man or woman need have no fear of public censure. The streets and parks of this city must be made safe for all persons at any hour at all costs.

What a contrasting message that editorial writer published in a highly-respected newspaper to what might be written these days about the same circumstances!

Responding to calls for assistance was not unusual for Lumb. In

1913 and again in 1914, Lumb was summoned by the governor's office to personally restrain and take into custody demented and unruly callers demanding to see the governor. Lumb's office on the main floor of the capitol was handy to the governor's on the second floor, south wing.

In November, Groome established a new policy which, from any angle, would fire a spark of curiosity in the hearts of police administrators. He ordered a procedure whereby corporals were tested semi-annually, in January and July, and, if they failed to pass the test, they were demoted and their vacancies immediately filled by privates who competed for promotion by way of another written examination. Privates had to have at least one year of service to enter competition. Corporal blacksmiths were exempted from this order. Although an examination for promotional opportunities is easily accepted, one wonders what a police department would be like, if rated men had to withstand the pressures of testing to hold their ranks in the face of those eager to take over.

During the year, fifty substations were operational, 667,882 miles were patrolled, and 3,027 arrests made. Among the arrests recorded were 43 for murder, 588 for drunkenness and disorderly conduct, 286 for larceny, 277 for assault and battery, and 194 violations of the auto laws, the latter figure increasing noticeably. There were 2,348 convictions—80 percent of all arrests.

It is interesting to note, as a matter of statistics, that at the ten-year point, there were three original enlistees of December 15, 1905, who were not rated: James G. Ernst, Troop B; Frank A. Hershey,

Captain Leon S. Pitcher meets with anthracite coal miners at Wyoming, 1915 (Courtesy of Pennsylvania State Police)

Troop A, and William E. Hess, Troop D. Ernst was to receive his corporal stripes in 1918. Not rated among the 1906 enlistees were: Thomas N. Boettner, Francis H. Grey, John G. Meyer, Thomas Parkinson, and Ira C. Stevenson. Stevenson was to see a promotion to corporal in 1916, Grey in 1918, both Boettner and Parkinson in 1919.

It was mentioned in an earlier chapter that 65 field men, who had enlisted before March 1, 1906, left the service by the end of 1906, representing a loss of 34 percent. Another 40 left before December 31, 1907—a total loss of more than half. A loss of 10 more in 1908, 27 in 1909, 15 in 1910, brought the total to 157. In five years, 81 percent were gone. Another man left in 1911, 4 in 1913, 2 in 1914, and none in 1915. This brought the total loss to 168, an 87 percent cut after ten years. Only 22 men, or 13 percent of the March 1, 1906, complement, remained on the job after ten years, and most of those men were commissioned or non-commissioned officers who had made their mark.

Some years later, Bruce Smith made an observation bearing on the above statistics by reporting that "Out of the 185 men originally enlisted in 1905, only 10 remain after 18 years. In sixteen years, more than 2,300 men were enlisted in order to maintain a force of from three to four hundred."

In 1915, facilities for capital punishment, as authorized by the 1913 legislature, were completed at Rockview; 4 men died in the electric chair during that first year. A total of 345 more were to meet the same fate before the halting of capital punishment in Pennsylvania in the 1960s.

During these first ten years, eight troopers were killed in the line of duty.

The following tabulation reveals complete and final disposition of all arrests from December 15, 1905, to December 31, 1915, with a remarkable conviction rate of about 82 percent, "indicating careful investigation before making arrests."

TEN YEAR SUMMARY

Charges	Arrests	Convictions	Discharges
Abduction	10	7	3
Abortion	5	4	1
Absconding witness	48	12	36
Accessory to the crime	92	46	46
Adultery	82	50	32
Aggravated assault and battery	641	447	194
Arson	89	50	39
Assault and battery	3,991	3,220	771

Charges	Arrests	Convictions	Discharges
Attempt to kill	249	163	86
Bigamy	4	3	1
Blackmail	52	34	18
Breach of the peace	63	60	3
Breaking jail	16	12	4
Bribery	2	2	
Burglary	521	376	145
Carrying concealed deadly weapons	622	534	88
Cockfighting	38	36	2
Concealing death of bastard child	4	1	3
Conspiracy	213	91	122
Contempt of court	11	10	1
Counterfeiting	14	10	4
Cruelty to animals	162	133	29
Cruelty to children	11	9	2
Deserter, U. S. service	3	3	
Desertion and non-support	256	218	38
Discharging firearms	70	66	4
Disorderly conduct	3,927	3,680	247
Disorderly house	105	88	17
Disturbing public assembly	6	5	1
Disturbing religious assembly	3	3	
Drunk and disorderly	2,234	2,112	122
Dynamiting	32	18	14
Embezzlement	35	27	8
Enticing female	5	3	2
Escaped prisoner	6	6	
Extortion	6	3	3
Felonious assault and battery	272	217	55
Felonious poisoning	1	1	
Felonious shooting	89	66	23
Felonious use of dynamite	9	3	6
Felonious wounding	298	189	109
Forcible detainer	5	1	4
Forcible entry	14	7	7
Forgery	47	38	9
Fornication and bastardy	218	189	29
Fortune telling	1	1	
Fraud and false pretense	542	453	89
Fraudulent use of the mails	4	2	2
Frequenting disorderly house	25	20	5
Fugitive from justice	9	9	

Charges	Arrests	Convictions	Discharges
Gambling	561	520	41
Highway robbery	139	79	60
Horse stealing	93	55	38
House breaking	173	136	37
Illegal car riding	133	122	11
Illegal traffic in drugs	3	3	
Impersonating an officer	23	20	3
Incest	6	1	5
Incorrigibility	52	45	7
Indecent exposure	80	71	9
Inmate disorderly house	237	204	33
Insanity	102	100	2
Interfering with an officer	167	130	37
Keeping bawdy house	19	19	
Keeping gambling house	1	1	
Kidnapping	7	3	4
Larceny	2,210	1,656	554
Larceny by bailee	7	7	
Lewdness	13	10	3
Malicious mischief	552	459	93
Mayhem	12	7	5
Miscellaneous	167	139	28
Misdemeanor	47	45	2
Murder	396	203	193
Nuisance	61	51	10
Pandering	9	7	2
Pauper	7	7	
Perjury	45	15	30
Pickpocket	12	7	5
Pointing firearms	51	40	11
Poisoning	3	1	2
Rape	225	139	86
Receiving stolen goods	161	110	51
Reckless driving	25	16	9
Resisting arrest	139	115	24
Rioting	563	336	227
Robbery	292	166	126
Runaway	28	26	2
Seduction	6	6	
Selling goods without license	64	61	3
Sending threatening letters	5	4	1
Slander	28	28	

Charges	Arrests	Convictions	Discharges
Sodomy	8	4	4
Surety of the peace	599	512	87
Suspicious character	241	69	172
Threats	250	181	69
Trespassing	985	874	111
Trover	2	2	
Unlawful assembly	5	5	
Unlawful possession of firearms	244	231	13
Unlicensed gypsies	13	13	
Vagrancy	709	648	61
Violation of auto laws	281	262	19
Violation of bail	21	21	
Violation of borough ordinance	12	11	1
Violation of election laws	27		27
Violation of fish laws	514	461	53
Violation of forestry laws	18	15	3
Violation of game laws	456	422	34
Violation of health laws	14	14	
Violation of immigration laws	9	9	
Violation of liquor laws	647	480	167
Violation of livery laws	40	38	2
Violation of medical laws	4	3	1
Violation of mining laws	20	20	
Violation of parole	10	9	1
Violation of postal laws	2	2	
Violation of quarantine laws	3	3	
Violation of revenue laws	1	1	
Violation of Sabbath laws	295	294	1
Violation of school laws	50	40	10
Violation of shipping laws	2		2
Wife beating	2	1	1
Witness	90	56	34
Totals	27,660	22,608	5,052

CHAPTER VI

Captain John C. Groome and Captain George F. Lumb
1916—1919

In the spring of 1916, the troop command structure underwent another change. Captain Wiechard resigned his post at Butler on May 31, "to accept a more remunerative position." Groome promoted Lieutenant William E. Mair, then assigned to Troop B, and gave him the Troop D command June 1. Mair, 34, 5'7", a native of Philadelphia, enlisted December 15, 1905. From 1899 to 1902, Mair served with Troop L, Second U. S. Cavalry, and held the rank of sergeant. Groome, in recognition of this military record, appointed him a sergeant at Troop B, Wilkes-Barre.

The devastation of World War I was continuing into its second year with no end in sight. To the contrary, additional countries were being sucked into this world-embracing holocaust, and it was just a matter of time before the United States would be committing its manhood to "a war to end all wars."

Deputy Superintendent Lumb, with his military background and keen perception of our country's needs, decided to do something significant in behalf of preparedness. The following account of Lumb's actions and accomplishments was authored by Mark T. Milnor, one of Harrisburg's ablest attorneys and Lumb's colleague:

> The war in Europe had been in progress since August 4, 1914, and all was not going well with France and her then Allies. Trouble was brewing with Mexico and units of the

Pennsylvania National Guard were on the Mexican border. It was quite apparent to many that the United States would be drawn into armed conflict against Germany and her Allies in the not too distant future, and our country was woefully unprepared.

Early that summer (1916), Captain George F. Lumb, a resident of suburban Harrisburg, a practicing attorney and deputy superintendent of the Pennsylvania State Police, conceived the idea of starting a military class for the instruction of young men to be the nucleus of a skeleton regiment in case of need.

Milnor cited Lumb's military record and recalled the fact that Lumb had been serving as Groome's deputy since January 1, 1908.

With this background, he was every inch a soldier, an excellent instructor, strict disciplinarian and with it all, a wonderful personality.

The idea was broached and appealed to a number of men, married and single, and after considerable preliminary sparring, the organization began to take form and evolve into a preparedness class, absolutely self-governing and domestic in its nature, but essentially military.

The class met one night each week on the second floor of the old City Grays' Armory situated at the southwest corner of Second and Forster Streets, an old, rather dilapidated frame building, to transact business, elect such new members as needed to fill vacancies, and for the purpose of infantry drill and to acquire the ability to take command of a body of men in the military sense.

During the first weeks, the instruction was limited to close order drill; then followed the manual of arms with wooden guns,and finally with rifles procured through the Harrisburg Rifle Association, either on a rental or purchase basis.

The organization adopted a set of by-laws, elected officers, and gave itself the name, "The Harrisburg Military Association."

The original members of the Association were William S. Bailey, Esq., M. B. Doughton, R. J. Elrick, Samuel W. Fleming, Jr. (acting Leiutenant), J. Clarence Funk, Esq., Farley H. Gannett, Theo. J. Gould, John A. F. Hall, Esq., F. D. Harry, Dr. M. V. Hazen, John C. Herman, Graham R. Hurd, Esq., Dr. Harry M. Kirkpatrick, Mark T. Milnor, Esq., G. W. Moffatt, Lew R. Palmer, Frank Roth, Jr., Theo. E. Seelye (acting Captain), Edward J. Stackpole, Jr., T. L. Welles, Doughlas D. Storey, Esq., Ehrman B. Mitchell, Ray Clark, J. Montgomery Trace, John McI. Smith, Esq., Archibald G. Knisley, Jr., George Kunkle, Jr., Esq., William Lutz, Dr. George Moffitt, Coyle Kennedy, C. A. Emerson, Paul Hooker, Dr. William L. Keller and Walter Johnston.

This list of prominent men of Harrisburg, who joined Lumb in this farsighted purpose, would most certainly qualify for the area's "Who's Who."

Others joined the Association during its brief existence, but we do not have any list thereof except those above listed, and it would be manifestly unfair to those omitted by including others from memory only.

The members of this Association attended the weekly classes religiously, drilled earnestly and for long hours, and all the purpose of being prepared in some degree for what might happen and did happen the very next year, and it all paid off. Many of its members applied for admission, were accepted, were commissioned as Second Leiutenants and saw service either in this country or in France. Others joined the Navy or other branches of the Armed Services and saw similar service. Some were wounded in action. Some were decorated for valor. Others did not enter the military service for good and sufficient reason. The basic important thing, however, was that here was a group of men who were willing to voluntarily give one night per week to prepare themselves to defend their country in time of need.

And credit for motivating this band of business and professional men, The Harrisburg Military Association, went to the state constabulary's number two man who was yet to further display his competence as a leader of men under the most trying of circumstances.

Making her appearance on the Pennsylvania scene about this time, was a gracious lady—Katherine Mayo. Miss Mayo, a journalist and miscellaneous writer, was born in Ridgway, Pennsylvania, in 1867. In August, 1913, while visiting Miss M. Moyca Newell, a lifelong friend, at Bedford Hills, New York, she was extremely moved by the vicious killing of a young construction foreman who was delivering a payroll to carpenters working on the Bedford Hills estate. The youthful Sam Howell, before death, had identified his three assailants, but the sheriff-constable was "too timorous to apprehend them."

For eleven years the Pennsylvania State Police had proven its value and still remained the only organization of its kind in the nation. Miss Mayo was determined that New York State should follow the footpath of Pennsylvania and bring protection to the rural citizens of

Portrait of Miss Katherine Mayo (Courtesy of New York State Police)

New York. Howell's death was to catapult the author and M. Moyca Newell into an unrelenting crusade.

Miss Mayo studied the origin and achievements of the Pennsylvania State Police, and her findings were published in *Justice To All*, the first of three books about the unique constabulary written by this champion of law and order. Through her efforts, much is known about the early years of the constabulary and the men who contributed to the organization's glorious history.

Miss Mayo took Albany by storm and enlisted the aid of former President Theodore Roosevelt, who, on November 10, 1916, wrote the introduction to *Justice To All*. Roosevelt, who admired the men of the constabulary, had this to say:

> To Americans one of the unpleasant features of governmental advance during the last thirty years has been the fact that most of it has been made outside of United States. We usually have to go to the Old World, or else to the newest world of Australia, or else to our friend and neighbor on the north of us, Canada, to help us out in dealing with the puzzling and important problems, whether social or industrial, that confront us; and the people of the Old World and the newest world do not often come to us in similar fashion. If we desire to learn about cooperative marketing for farmers, or industrial insurance, or old age pensions, or the proper encouragement and control of corporations, we have to go to Germany, or Denmark, or Australia, or some other nation. These nations do not have to come to us.

Arrest of kidnapper at Wyoming, 1916 (Courtesy of Pennsylvania State Police)

There are, however, a few exceptions to this rule. It was this country which led off in the establishment of the great natural reservations for wild life; Yellowstone Park can stand as the type. Moreover, much the greatest State or inter-State park in the neighborhood of a great city is the Palisades Park near New York, which, from every standpoint, if far ahead of anything any other country can show. Finally, the State Police of Pennsylvania, under its Superintendent, Major John C. Groome, has furnished a model which is to be studied everywhere; and we Americans ought to be pleased that it is no longer necessary to study the excellent Canadian Northwestern Police, or the excellent Argentine Police, when we desire to find how the elementary needs of our several States can best be served in the matter of securing law, order and justice.

The Pennsylvania State Police is a model of efficiency, a model of honesty, a model of absolute freedom from political contamination. One of the great difficulties in our large States has been to secure an efficient policing of the rural sections. In communities where there are still frontier conditions, such as Texas and Arizona, the need has been partially met by establishing bodies of rangers; but there is no other body so emphatically efficient for modern needs as the Pennsylvania State Police. I have seen them at work. I know personally numbers of the men in the ranks. I know some of the officers. I feel so strongly about them that the mere fact that a man is honorably discharged from this Force would make me at once, and without hesitation, employ him for any purpose needing courage, prowess, good judgment, loyalty, and entire trustworthiness. This is a good deal to say of any organization, and I say it without qualifications of the Pennsylvania Police.

The Force has been in existence only ten years. It has cooperated efficiently with the local authorities in detecting crime and apprehending criminals. It has efficiently protected the forests and the wild life of the State. It has been the most powerful instrument in enforcing law and order throughout the State.

All appointments are made after the most careful mental and physical examination, and upon a thorough investigation of the moral character, and the past record, of the man. All promotions have been made strictly from the ranks. The drill is both mounted and dismounted. The men are capital riders, good shots, and as sound and strong in body and mind as in character.

This is the Force which Katherine Mayo describes in a volume so interesting, and from the standpoint of sound

American citizenship, so valuable that it should be in every public library and every school library in the land. In the author's foreword the murder of gallant young Newell, and the complete breakdown of justice in reference thereto under our ordinary rural police system, makes one's blood boil with anger at the folly and timidity of our people in tamely submitting to such hideous conditions, and give us the keenest gratitude to the founder of the Pennsylvania State Police. This was a case of ordinary crime, in which the sheriff and county constable were paralyzed by fear of a band of gunmen. Other forms of crime are dealt with in connection with industrial disturbances. The author shows how until the State Police Force was established the State, in times of strikes, permitted the capitalists to furnish their own Coal and Iron Police, thus selling her police power to one of the contending parties, that of the vested interests.

The author also shows after the establishment of the Pennsylvania State Police this intolerable condition was ended; local demagogues and foolish or vicious professional labor leaders in their turn attacked the Pennsylvania State Police with the foulest slander and mendacity, because it did impartial justice. The prime lesson for all true friends of labor to learn is that law and order must be impartially preserved by the State as a basis for securing justice through the State's action. Justice must be done; but the first—not only the first, but a vital first—step towards realizing it must be action by the State, through its own agents, not by authority delegated to others, whereby lawless violence is summarily stopped. The labor leader who attacks the Pennslyvania State Police because it enforces the law would, if successful in the long run, merely succeed in reentrenching in power the lawless capitalists who used the law-defying Coal and Iron Police.

No political influence or other influence avails to get a single undesirable man on the Force, or to keep a man on the Force who has proved himself unfit. I am informed and fully believe, that not a single appointment has ever been made for political reasons. The efficiency with which the Force does its duty is extraordinary. Any man who sees the troopers patrolling the country can tell from the very look of the men what invaluable allies they are to the cause of law and order. In the year 1915 the Force made 3,017 arrests and secured 2,348 convictions—80% of convictions. The men are so trained and schooled in the criminal laws of the State that they know just what evidence is necessary. They deal admirably with riots. Perhaps there is nothing that they do better than the protection of women in sparsely populated neighborhoods. Small wonder that the criminal and disorderly classes dread them and eagerly hope for their disbanding!

Year by year the efficiency of the Force has increased and its usefulness has correspondingly increased. All good citizens in Pennslyvania should heartily support the Pennsylvania State Police. The sooner all our other States adopt similar systems, the better it will be for the cause of law and order, and for the upright administration of the laws in the interest of justice throughout the nation.

Roosevelt personally saw to it that each member of the New York legislative chambers was presented with a copy of Miss Mayo's book. This action, in support of Miss Mayo's crusade, heavily influenced the judgment of the New York legislature as it pondered and approved the establishment of the New York State Police in 1917—the second such organization to be formed in the nation's history.

When Katherine Mayo died in 1940, twenty-three years later, the New York State Police honored her by designating twenty-five troopers as pall-bearers and escort at her funeral. At the age of 72, she was buried at Bedford Hills, New York, the scene of Howell's murder. She was truly a great woman, and law enforcement, in general, owes her a debt of gratitude for the influence she brought to bear in behalf of law and order—not only in New York State but in several states shortly after her first book was published.

Much of the State Police manpower was committed to a lengthy trolley strike in the Wilkes-Barre area, which tied up forces from all four troops from March 31 through much of the summer months. Troop D forces returned to Butler on June 1, Troop C was released on June 5, and Troop A—not until July 14. Troop C was called again to furnish assistance to Troop B until the strike was settled. There were forty-seven arrests made in connection with the strike. Property damage to trolleys from stoning and dynamiting was high.

Actually, the trolley strike in Wilkes-Barre got underway in October, 1915, although the State Police was not committed until the spring of 1916. After months of turbulence and violence, the mayor of Wilkes-Barre, who had been adamant in his stand to go it alone, reluctantly asked for State Police support, which was readily given. And, needless to say, the State Police did a magnificent job in restoring law and order after its extended stay in that city.

Katherine Mayo had this to say about the 1916 Wilkes-Barre trolley strike, because of its unusual effect upon incidents occurring elsewhere in the Commonwealth:

In the spring of 1916, while the disgraceful conditions at Wilkes-Barre were holding in that vicinity all four troops of the State Police, trouble broke out near Pittsburgh, at the extreme opposite end of the State. No part of the Force could be withdrawn from the eastern service to meet this latter need; the result would have been intolerable. Therefore, for the first time in over ten years, it became necessary to call upon the National Guard for police duty.

The following statement, furnished by the Adjutant General's office under date of October 19, 1916, covers this event:

"Unfortunately the four Troops of the State Police were all busily employed in protecting the interest of the public in Wyoming Valley during the street car strike last spring, when the emergency arose in the Allegheny County (Pittsburgh) district. Therefore no State Police were available for service.

"The Governor then decided that it was necessary to call out a portion of the National Guard of the State for the purpose of protecting the citizens of the towns of Wilmerding, Turtle Creek, Braddock, and E. Pittsburgh, who were being intimidated by irresponsible mobs, largely composed of foreigners.

"For this purpose the Governor directed the Adjutant General to call out and place on active duty in the field of disturbance four troops of cavalry and one regiment of infantry. A second regiment of infantry was mobilized, six companies of it at their home station and six companies of it at regimental headquarters, which was on the main line of the Pennslyvania Railroad, at Greensburg, within an hour's run of the affected district. These troops were kept on duty from May 2d until May 19th.

"All the bills for this tour of duty have not as yet been audited, but the approximate cost to the State for transportation, subsistence, and pay will amount to about $57,000 while the cost of material and stores rendered unserviceable by this tour of duty will approximate $20,000 additional."

"Therefore," wrote Miss Mayo, "the cash cost to the State for those seventeen days of Guard Service was about seventy-seven thousand dollars, or over a quarter of the entire sum required to maintain the whole State Police Squadron for a year."

Trolley and coal operations appeared to be the principal industries suffering from the effects of labor disturbances of major proportions during this era.

It is also worthy noting that the movement of troopers, their horses and supporting equipment to distant points in response to need was accomplished by railroad. If regular runs were insufficient to meet the need, special trains were put to use. Time and considerable effort were therefore required to mobilize men and equipment for large-scale operations, and much credit must be extended to those who managed such affairs so effectively.

Groome urgently recommended to Governor Martin G. Brumbaugh that the State Police complement be increased, "so as to give more adequate protection to the citizens of the Commonwealth at a time when war threatens the nation and the National Guard is expected to be called away for Federal Service." Groome said that a bill to meet this recommendation would be sent to the general assembly for consideration in 1917.

"Great difficulties," Groome told Brumbaugh, "are besetting the Force. High wages throughout the State cause a great deal of dissatisfaction and unrest resulting in many resignations, over 37 percent of the entire strength having left during the year (1916) to accept better-paying positions. This results in financial loss on account of transportation to barracks (apparently this was a recruiting cost), uniforms made for recruits and the time of officers and non-commissioned officers devoted to the instruction of the new men. Experienced men leave the Force to accept better-paid positions with private corporations, many, as a result of their training, going in an executive capacity."

In 1916, one of the more radical labor organizations, the Industrial Workers of the World (IWW), made its appearance in Luzerne and Lackawanna counties. IWW workers were subjects of numerous complaints by United Mine Workers who were molested and threatened by clubs and weapons. Troopers of the Wyoming barracks were frequently called to the collieries to quell disturbances created by the IWW. The IWW was intent on making mining operations as difficult as possible for the owners, resorting to violence of any kind to achieve its objective. The organization wanted to create the image of being the miners' friend, and that its tactics would lead to higher wages more swiftly than the strategy of the United Mine Workers.

There were 2,827 arrests for eighty-nine different crimes. Calls for assistance from public officials and private sources numbered 4,352. Once again, there was no chance of fulfilling all these requests.

Groome reported some satisfaction over the conditions of all barracks buildings, which he described as "permanent" and "in excellent repair." After much complaining about the Pottsville barracks and its dilapidated condition, Groome's reported, "The old mill buildings used as a barracks and stables by this Troop since 1909 have been repaired and added to, and are now in good condition, but eventually new quarters will have to be secured for this Troop."

Commenting on the achievements of Governor Samuel W. Pennypacker, the following statement appeared in the *Pennsylvania*

Magazine, published by the Historical Society of Pennsylvania, "In 1916 it was written, 'No finer example of practical wisdom in the maintenance of law and order, without taking sides in a controversy, can be found in any State, and the results as attested by eleven years of experience have justified the Governor's sagacity.'"

In the closing pages of *Justice To All*, Katherine Mayo drew this stirring conclusion about the men she observed so closely, which is worthy of repeating:

> If you hear a calumny, a charge, an imputation against one trooper, and tell it to another, officer or man, you will see in the look on his face, before the grave, reserved speech leaves his lips, that the thing is as deeply personal to himself as his own soul. Whatever touches the honor of the Force touches him, and the very quick; for the honor of the Force is the honor of every man in it.

Her observations surely reflect the comradeship that existed between the men, and their united respect for the Force, itself. Such a fine relationship goes a long way in explaining how so few accomplished so much.

Contained in his autobiography, which was written about this time although not published until 1918, are these statements by Pennypacker, bearing upon Groome's selection and achievements:

> The legislature, also, upon my urgency provided for a state police or constabulary, and here the same kind of question arose. (Pennypacker here referred to the political issue that accompanied the creation of the Department of Health during the same legislative session of 1905). Such a body, if organized upon political lines, would have tremendous power over the state and would be correspondingly dangerous. After talking over a number of persons, some of them connected with the Guard, and consulting with several persons, I tendered the position to John C. Groome, captain of the City Troop, who accepted. He proved to be just the man needed, of the right age, slim, erect, quick to see and to act, possessing rare combination of decision of character and sound judgment. I told him I wanted a police force and absolutely nothing else. Not a man on the force was selected upon the recommendation of anybody. The men were all chosen upon the results of physical and mental examination and what political or religious creed any of them professes is officially unknown. Groome has made the constabulary famous all over the United States. Two hundred and forty in number they

have maintained the peace within the state as was never done before. Not once since has it been necessary to call out the National Guard, and that vast expense has been saved. While organized labor has unwisely assailed them as "Penny-packer's Cossacks," one of the greatest of their merits has been that they have saved labor from the oppression of force and have done away with the kind of police intervention which came from men employed by the corporations (Coal and Iron Police).

New York State in 1917 was in the throes of serious debates as public officials argued the burning issue of a state constabulary for the Empire State. The New York State General Assembly asked for testimony from the Keystone State regarding the effectiveness of its constabulary, and Lumb was given this all-important assignment. The following article, captioned, "Fighting for Law and Order," appeared in the *Philadelphia Inquirer*, February 17, 1917:

It is good to know that the Deputy Superintendent of the Pennsylvania State Police Force who went to Albany to answer questions regarding the Mounted Constabulary of the Keystone State was able to give a good account of himself. The bill to give New York a force of this kind has the support of the best people of the Empire State and it is being pressed with the approval of Governor Whitman, but those who do not favor the measure seem to take delight in misrepresenting its character. This was shown at the committee hearing when Socialists and those who assume to represent certain labor organizations heckled the Deputy Superintendent of the Pennsylvania Constabulary. But Mr. Lumb was able to hold his own and prove that the organization of the mounted force in this State has given the people of the rural districts a protection which they have never had before.

It is strange that the purposes of the mounted police should be so persistently misrepresented and misunderstood. Its sole function is to conserve law and order. It aims to give the rural districts the same kind of protection which city dwellers now receive from the local police forces. The claim that it is intended to be used against labor organizations is perfectly preposterous. It is and it has been used against law-breakers of every description, and if labor organizations contemplate breaking the peace or violating the law, then assuredly they may expect to come in conflict with the State Constabulary in the country just as they may expect to come into a clash with the police in the city if they attempt to violate laws or ordinances here.

The Socialist Mayor of Schenectady was one of the most pronounced opponents to the New York bill. He said that in his opinion it was unnecessary to pass such drastic legislation. He said that the better way of coping with threatening labor disturbances was to keep strikebreakers away from the scenes of strikes. Here again is the common error of supposing that the main purpose of a State Constabulary is to fight strikers. It is nothing of the kind. It is true that if there is a disturbance of the peace and the disturbers happen to be strikers that the State Constabulary—in the country—will be called upon to restore law and order. But it is perfect folly to say that there is any discrimination in the matter of keeping the peace.

To try to make the establishment of such a force appear as a class measure is all wrong. It is an inexcusable perversion of the truth. We predict that a State Constabulary will be eventually established in New York and in all of the progressive States of the Union. It may be delayed by foolish opposition, but it cannot be prevented much longer.

And it was not!

Dedicated, too, to the formation of a state constabulary in New York State was Dr. Lewis Rutherford Morris, chairman of the Committee for a New York State Police. In the April, 1917, issue of *Realty Magazine*, Dr. Morris had this to say about police protection for those moving to rural areas:

Now, to every man who is himself of any value to the community, there is one thing more vital even than fresh air and green fields—more vital by far than the whole list of modern conveniences put together. Without this necessity, life in the outlying and sparsely settled districts is nothing less than a continual condition of fear and peril for the inhabitants.

That one thing is protection to his women and children, and to life and property in his neighborhood. This he usually utterly sacrifices when he leaves town and goes to live in rural parts.

Praising the achievements of the Pennsylvania State Police, Dr. Morris continued:

In Pennsylvania, eleven years since, the State formally recognized the right of all the people, without distinction of location, condition, or calling, to active and adequate protection under her laws. It was felt that the State could no longer stand by and see her peace maintained or broken, see people living in safety or in danger, her laws respected or scorned, according to the fancy or the strength of the evilly inclined. Pennsylvania recognized the truth that a State, by making laws for her people and demanding their obedience thereto, incurs the obligation to make her people due return. She must give them the benefit of those laws enforced. And, in order that she might have means to fulfill this duty, she created a State Police.

The pleadings of Dr. Morris, Katherine Mayo, M. Moyca Newell, and others of sincere purpose were to be rewarded when a New York State Police agency came into existence in 1917.

The Pennsylvania General Assembly was convened in 1917, and once again the proponents of State Police expansion were hopeful of success. Not since 1911 were they given anything to cheer about. In 1917, they struck pay-dirt. Not only was the Force given a much-needed salary increase, but for the first time since 1905 there came an increase in the complement.

After the introduction of the bill to bring about these changes, heated debates followed. Opposition members in the House made their usual charges, again including disparaging remarks about Groome. They laid claim to the fact that Groome spent all his time in Philadelphia away from his office, while Lumb remained at his desk and was the real work-horse in seeing to State Police affairs. There was some basis for these charges, since Groome did not reside in Harrisburg, and Lumb did. Groome did spend most of his time in Philadelphia, and Lumb did remain at his desk to handle the day-to-day operational problems. When Groome came to Harrisburg, he would often remain overnight at the Lumb family residence. The charges, however, were not substantive. Whatever working arrangements were agreed to by Groome and Lumb, they were paying off, indeed. Both men got along most satisfactorily—each recognizing the others position and capabilities. Groome was an excellent administrator and handled his liaison duties with governors and legislators tactfully. He was an appealing personality—waxed moustache and all. Even his cigarettes were of a special blend. Lumb tended store in Harrisburg, and was content with his assignments.

A *Harrisburg Telegraph* columnist once wrote, "As the right hand man of Superintendent John C. Groome, of the State Police, Captain Lumb has conducted the affairs of that organization so as to merit the commendations of all those who have had business with the Department. He is always at his post, and he is one of the most reliable men in what is considered the most reliable organization every created by the State."

In any case, the attack upon the superintendent this time got nowhere, nor did any other arguments stymie eventual passage of favorable legislation. Swinging to the support of the State Police bill were a number of anthracite region legislators, who had previously aligned themselves with the labor bloc. Katherine Mayo commented on this position change, "In 1913 and 1915, when attempts were made to improve conditions in the State Police by increasing its complement and salary structure, the Luzerne County assemblymen voted solidly to block such moves. In the 1917 session of the general assembly, however, there was a different story. Impressed by the conduct of the State Police during the lengthy Wilkes-Barre car strike (which was brought to an end in 1916), five of the eight legislators, representing a strong labor consituency, voted for an increase in the Force and a pay raise for all ranks."

It is also interesting to note that Rep. Richard J. Baldwin who diligently supported favorable State Police legislation in the 1915 General Assembly session, was Speaker of the House for the 1917 session. Undoubtedly, in this influential position, he contributed much to the passage of Act 36.

On April 12, 1917, Governor Martin G. Brumbaugh signed into law Act 36, P.L. 54, which was brief and to the point:

SECTION 1. Be it enacted, That on and after the approval of this act, the superintendent and deputy superintendent of the Department of State Police, and the officers and enlisted men of the State Police Force, and their salaries, shall be as follows:

A Superintendent of State Police, at six thousand ($6,000) per annum.

A Deputy Superintendent of State Police, at three thousand five hundred ($3,500) per annum.

Four captains, each at twenty-four hundred dollars ($2,400) per annum.

Four lieutenants, each at eighteen hundred dollars ($1,800) per annum.

Four first sergeants, each at thirteen hundred and fifty dollars ($1,350) per annum.

Sixteen sergeants, each at twelve hundred dollars ($1,200) per annum.

Thirty-two corporals, each at eleven hundred dollars ($1,100) per annum.

Two hundred and seventy privates, each at ten hundred and twenty dollars ($1,020) per annum.

SECTION 2. That the officers and enlisted men of the State Police Force shall receive an increase of sixty dollars

($60) per annum during continuous service, after two years; and an additional increase of sixty dollars ($60) per annum during continuous service, after four years: Provided, This section shall not apply to the superintendent and deputy superintendent of the Department of State Police.''

This amending legislation changed the salaries and complement of the Force to this extent:

1911		*1917*	
Superintendent	$3,000	Superintendent	$6,000
Deputy Superintendent	2,500	Deputy Superintendent	3,500
Bookkeeper	1,500	Bookkeeper	1,500
Stenographer	1,200	Stenographer	1,200

Each Troop		*Each Troop*	
1 captain	1,800	1 captain	2,400
1 lieutenant	1,500	1 lieutenant	1,800
1 first sergeant	1,200	1 first sergeant	1,350
4 sergeants	1,100	4 sergeants	1,200
4 corporals	950	8 corporals	1,100
1 blacksmith corporal	950	67 privates	1,020
45 privates	900		

57 × 4 = 228 complement

82 × 4 = 328
　　　　2　(2 troops with 1
　　　　　　extra man)
　　　330　complement　(an
　　　　　　increase of 102)

The act also provided a longevity consideration of $5.00 a month after the first two-year enlistment, and an additional $5.00 a month after the second two-year enlistment. To qualify for service pay, a man had to have continuous enlistments. The superintendent and his deputy were denied service pay benefits.

While this momentous action was being taken by the Pennsylvania General Assembly, the Congress of the United States made history on April 6, 1917, by declaring war on Germany.

Six days after the declaration of war, Lumb resigned his post as deputy superintendent. It is believed that he did so to rejoin the military service and fight for his country as he had so gallantly done before. But, for whatever reason, his resignation was not accepted, and he remained with the State Police to serve his Commonwealth and nation in another way.

Two other measures were passed by the legislature before

adjournment, which had a bearing upon State Police operations. Act 201, P.L. 600, dated June 7, contained a number of wartime guidelines, and provided that state employes entering military service would have one-half of their salaries paid to their dependents during the period of service, but not to exceed $2,000. The other measure, Act 314, P.L. 814, dated July 11, required the State Police to assist the State Highway Commissioner who was authorized to use prison labor.

Slowly, but surely, directives would stem from headquarters, putting the department on a wartime footing. In May, Groome ordered a detail consisting of one sergeant, one corporal, and twelve men to guard the state capitol for an indefinite period. Although no threats to the building were indicated, precautions were considered essential. Since the State Police would be needed moreso than ever to meet the emergency to be created by the call-up of the Pennsylvania National Guard into federal service, a procedure was established for claiming exemption from the draft for all troopers, as draft notices were received. Act 201 also provided that state employes enlisting in military service had a right to return to their jobs. Groome stipulated that all men anticipating military enlistment notify headquarters ten days in advance.

To emphasize the impact of the automobile in 1917, Groome received an urgent request from the State Highway Commissioner to strictly enforce laws governing speed limits, reckless driving, and operating without a license. Special reference was made to speeding violations. Groome ordered his forces to strictly enforce the laws, and to cooperate with the State Highway Department in every way possible.

Groome, a military man from his early years, could wait no longer to offer his services to the U. S. Army. He entered military service with the Signal Corps on October 20, 1917, and was given the rank of lieutenant colonel. That very same day, Governor Brumbaugh appointed Lumb acting superintendent of the State Police Department, a position he was to fill like a champion.

In the meantime, Lumb had applied to the War Department for a commission. He was informed by telegram that he would be commissioned a major, and a confirmation would follow. Lumb informed the governor of this development. Without losing time, Brumbaugh contacted the War Department, asking that the issuance of a commission for Lumb be withheld since he had already lost his superintendent to the war effort, and had no one else to administer State Police affairs. The War Department yielded to Brumbaugh's petition. The commission was never granted.

Before the end of November, Captains Adams, Wilhelm, Mair,

Captain George F. Lumb (Courtesy of Pennsylvania State Police)

Captain Leon S. Pitcher (Courtesy of Pennsylvania State Police)

and Leiutenant John J. McCall had been given army commissions and were on their way to France. Lumb not only found himself alone at headquarters, but was now facing a depleted command structure for his field forces without notice from a practical standpoint. He had no commanders at Troops A, C, and D. The situation in Troop D was further complicated by the loss of Lieutenant McCall, which left that troop with no commissioned personnel. Captain Pitcher was the only troop commander remaining at his post. This situation forced Lumb to quickly visit each troop headquarters to make necessary promotions to fill existing command vacancies.

His troubles did not end there. Upon his return to Harrisburg from this emergency trip to each troop headquarters, he learned that chief clerk Samuel B. Nissley, who had seen service at headquarters since mid-1907 and "had rendered most valuable and efficient service during a period of ten years," was about to become president of a local manufacturing establishment and resigned December 31, 1917 for that purpose.

On December 4, Lumb publicly announced the appointment of the following officers who would serve in an acting capacity:

Acting Captain William Marsh — Troop C, Reading
Acting Captain Wilson C. Price — Troop D, Butler
Acting Captain Charles Jacobs — Troop A, Greensburg
Acting Lieutenant William A. Clark — Troop A, Greensburg

Acting Lieutenant Herbert Smith — Troop C, Pottsville
Acting Lieutenant Paul B. Stout — Troop B, Wyoming
Acting Lieutenant Samuel W. Gearhart — Troop D, Butler

All promotions were effective December 1. The acting lieutenants were ordered to headquarters at Harrisburg December 11 for a day-long briefing before proceeding to their new assignments. All troop commanders were ordered to conduct examinations as soon as possible to fill vacancies created by emergency promotions.

Lumb, after his appointment as acting superintendent, went to Washingon and Philadelphia to offer the services of the State Police to the Chief of the Justice Department's Bureau of Investigation, the Military Intelligence Office of the War College, and the Fourth Naval District. "As a result thereof most cordial and confidential relations were established, and hundreds of investigations have been made in a most satisfactory manner," Lumb later reported to the governor. This is the first mention of this type of law enforcement—or investigative assistance—being engaged in with federal agencies. These were wartime measures of considerable significance since the State Police Department was faced with its own Commonwealth responsibilities without taking on the added burden of assisting federal agencies with wartime demands.

Also passed by the 1917 General Assembly were two wartime measures, which had no direct bearing on State Police operations. They were Act 106, P.L. 192, May 15, creating a state Commission of Public Safety to prepare for the Commonwealth's defense, and Act 347, P.L. 1062, July 18, authorizing the establishment of volunteer police groups. Lumb, however, recognizing the value of State Police expertise, urged his field forces to familiarize themselves with these acts, and assist local home defense units wherever possible with organization and training. It was essential that any activities counter-productive to the war effort be quickly dealt with, and it was Lumb's intention that both of these laws be well-implemented.

Wartime activities at home counter-productive to the national war effort did, indeed, keep the state constabulary busy assisting federal agencies. The radical Industrial Workers of the World (IWW) which appeared on the Pennsylvania scene in 1916, was now branching out its activities to protest wartime actions of the United States, spread discontent among the miners and, in general, hinder the government in the prosecution of the war. IWW members distributed literature among ethnic groups, persuading them not to register for the military draft on June 5, 1917, as one of their overt radical actions. By infiltration, State Police undercover agents secured sufficient evidence to arrest a number of IWW leaders, and reduce the effectiveness of that organization.

A letter from A. B. Bielaski, Chief of the Bureau of Investigation, Washington, D. C., dated September 12, 1917, and addressed to the Commanding Officer at Troop B, Wyoming, expressed the bureau's gratitude for State Police assistance in coping with the IWW.

During 1917, Corporal Robert E. Tipton, of Troop B, Wyoming, was temporarily assigned to the separate State Fire Marshal's Office, headed by G. Chal. Port, for nine months to investigate "an important arson and conspiracy case in Stroudsburg." Two arrests followed Tipton's skillful investigation of this case. It is possible that this type of assistance eventually led to the transfer of the State Fire Marshal's Office to the State Police.

Despite the general assembly's actions with regard to State Police salaries in 1917, Lumb still considered this matter important enough to mention in his year-end report to the governor. Referring to the recent raise, he stated,

> This was most timely in view of subsequent events. Wages have increased to such an extent that unskilled and illiterate laborers receive far greater salaries than the trained and disciplined officers of the State, who receive as Privates the meagre sum of eighty-five dollars per month from which they are required to subsist themselves, pay rent for barracks, laundry, and purchase all clothing except uniforms. Numerous men of training and experience have been induced by larger salaries to leave the Force before expiration of their enlistments thus violating their oath and causing expense incidental to medical examination of new men, transportation and unforms, to say nothing of the efficiency of the Force being impaired as the result of constantly training new men.

Lumb recommended to Governor Brumbaugh that the salaries of privates on first enlistment be raised to "not less than one hundred dollars per month to meet the changed industrial conditions and the high cost of living." By this time, it was apparent that the World War I economy was creating serious problems for the State Police administrators who sought relief from them.

To cite the seriousness of this manpower situation, Lumb reviewed the separations occurring in 1917. Men, who left for better-paying jobs, numbered 41. There were 36 men discharged for disciplinary reasons, and another 27 men discharged during their probationary period for failing to measure up to the department's high standards. Competing with the draft for a better grade of recruit was undoubtedly becoming a noticeable and losing battle. There was a single death, and four men were dropped for desertion. Under Act 201, 24 men entered military service. These combined losses accounted for 41 percent of the department's new 330-man complement.

Notwithstanding administrative problems, this was a banner year for accomplishments. The field forces, operating from sixty-seven substations, patrolled 857,384 miles and made 5,255 arrests. Of these arrests, 4,134 convictions followed, and 428 cases were backlogged in courts. Requests for assistance numbered 7,505, including 503 from federal agencies this time.

Facing the problem at headquarters, Lumb advanced Carroll B. Price to fill Nissley's vacancy on January 1, 1918, and Walter J. Fisher was hired as a stenographer.

Discipline under Lumb was no less enforced than it was during the years before Groome's departure for wartime service. In February, 1918, this determination to preserve discipline was manifested by two summary court trials that ended with the dismissal of two troopers. One was charged with "abusing horses" and "failing to pay just debts"—in that order. The other was brought to department trial following his arrest for "fornication and bastardy." As a side comment, it is doubtful that by today's social standards either man would have suffered the penalty of dismissal.

A severe winter jammed the Susquehanna River with ice, and on February 25 a detachment of troopers was sent to Lock Haven to relieve exhausted Home Guards and local police who were on flood duty in this Clinton County community. Some twenty-six city blocks were inundated by water backed up behind the walls of ice on the Susquehanna's west branch.

The ninth death in the line of duty was recorded on April 28, when youthful Private Andrew Czap of Troop D died from gunshot wounds during a highway robbery incident at Tide, Indiana County. Of Czap's death, Lumb announced: "The hero's death, in the face of overwhelming odds, is in keeping with the splendid records by the members of this Force in all time past. Private Czap's death is a striking example of the fact that one need not go overseas, or don the khaki, to prove his loyalty to his country and his devotion to the Commonwealth of Pennsylvania. It is this unfaltering devotion to duty which has made the Pennsylvania State Police Force an example and a model that other states are striving to exemplify."

By this time, Lumb was feeling the pinch of trying to administer the department's needs singlehandedly, and summoned Captain Leon S. Pitcher from Troop B, Wyoming, to headquarters where he was to serve as acting deputy superintendent effective May 1.

Other changes in command personnel were necessitated by Pitcher's transfer and the resignation of Captain Marsh at Pottsville. Lieutenant Herbert Smith was promoted to acting captain to fill Pitcher's vacancy at Wyoming. Smith, 5'8", a native of Riverside, New

Jersey, enlisted on March 19, 1906, at Philadelphia, and was assigned as a private with Troop B. After less than one year's absence from Troop B, he was returning as its commander. Acting Captain Wilson C. Price was transferred from Butler to Pottsville in Marsh's place, and Lieutenant William A. Clark was promoted to acting captain, and dispatched to Butler. Clark and Price were to continue with long service records, and will be remembered for their achievements. Clark, 5'11½", a native of Philadelphia, was an original enlistee of December 15, 1905, when he was assigned to Troop B as a private.

The scene of disaster was to shift to western Pennsylvania on May 19, when the Oakdale plant of the Aetna Explosives Company, near Pittsburgh, was completely demolished by an explosion, killing more than 100 workers, and injuring another 100. Property damages were estimated at more than $2 million. Here again, the field forces of the state constabulary were summoned to aid local authorities who were overcome by the magnitude of this emergency situation.

The wartime draft was taking its toll on the ever-diminishing band of troopers, and it was essential that, if the life of the constabulary was to be preserved at all for the Commonwealth's benefit, the War Department should be petitioned for consideration. This was done, and the provost marshal general's office notified all Pennsylvania draft boards that present State Police personnel would be exempt from the draft. Future enlistees, however, would not be exempt, and present members who resigned or left the Force for any other reason would be subject to the draft law.

With the passing of one short month, Private John F. Dargus, 21, of Troop A, Greensburg, was to follow Czap in death. Dargus was shot and killed at Struthers, Ohio, on May 31, while in hot pursuit of an armed fugitive wanted for murder in Fayette County. Lumb, in his public announcement, praised Dargus' bravery. Dargus was the tenth to die in the line of duty.

In mid-summer, Lumb had the unpleasant task of confirming the dismissal sentence of a court-martial board in the case of acting Captain Charles Jacobs. Jacobs was charged with "disloyal remarks and conduct to the prejudice of good order and police discipline," and found guilty. His services ended with his discharge on July 15.

Promoted in Jacobs' place at Greensburg was Lieutenant Paul B. Stout. Acting Captain Stout, at 6'1½", was the tallest of the men enlisted on December 15, 1905, and held that record for a long time. He was a native of Milton, and as a private he drew Troop A, Greensburg, as his first assignment. He, too, was to remain for a record of long, honorable service before leaving the scene in 1936.

In June, the personnel of the Jersey Shore substation were

detailed to Loganton to maintain security in this second Clinton County community in short order to suffer disaster. Loganton was almost completely destroyed by fire which brought down thirty-one homes, eight stores, two churches, and thirty-six other buildings. It is interesting to note at this point that fire losses, nationally, set a record in 1918, exceeding all previous losses except for 1906, when San Francisco was destroyed by earthquake and fire.

Very much impressed with the accomplishments of the Pennsylvania State Police, four states—New York, Colorado, Michigan, and Oregon—had established state police forces of their own by mid-1918, thereby endorsing the state police principle conceived by Governor Pennypacker and administered by Superintendent Groome.

The autumn months of 1918 were to bring on a catastrophe for Pennsylvania and the world as a whole—a catastrophe never before visited upon the earth—the Spanish flu. Dr. Ralph Chester Williams, in his history of the U.S. Public Health Service, wrote, "There were reported 4,114,810 cases of influenza and pneumonia in the United States in October, November and December, 1918. The total number of deaths in the United States due to influenza during this epidemic was estimated to be more than 500,000." "This was the most devastating, widespread epidemic of modern times," Dr. Williams stated. "The 1918 pandemic occurred at a time when many physicians and nurses were absent on duty with the armed forces."

A. A. Hoehling, another historian of this world disaster, reported, "By December of that year of mingled victory and catastrophe, 1918, five hundred thousand Americans had perished in a great plague, and nearly twenty million had sickened. The world had never in history been ravaged by a killer that slew so many human beings so quickly, during but a few weeks in autumn."

To emphasize the extensiveness of the disaster, Hoehling stated, "From the jungle to the polar regions, it snuffed out upwards of twenty-one million lives." And Eskimo villages were wipped out. It staggers the imagination to contemplate the fact that twenty-one million lives were rubbed out—not in a decade—but in a few autumn months. Reportedly, only one spot on this earth miraculously escaped the horrible fate of others, totally untouched—the tiny island of Tristan Da Cunha—located remotely in the south Atlantic.

"Pennsylvania was the most severely affected state in the union," stated Hoehling. There were some 350,000 cases of the flu in the state and 36,000 died. More than one-third of this figure died in Philadelphia. Philadelphia was the second hardest hit city in the nation: New York City topped the list. Philadelphia, at the height of the epidemic, numbered 289 deaths in one day—October 6—the highest figure ever recorded. Father Joseph Corrigan and a band of seminarians with horse-drawn wagons, shovels, and kerosene lanterns, walked the streets of Philadelphia, gathering bodies for burial, so states one account. The statistics for "Black Thursday," October 17, in Chicago, cite the death record there of 381 for that day.

Not to escape the calamitous situation, the armed forces of the United States numbered their losses. More than 5,000 sailors and some 25,000 soldiers died before the epidemic was over.

The effect upon life insurance companies was considerable—to put it mildly. According to Hoehling, the Metropolitan Life Insurance Company which he credited with keeping good records paid out $18 million on 85,000 policies.

In Pennsylvania, the work of the state constabulary forces took on a new look. Law enforcement, for the most part, was abandoned in favor of acts of mercy and bravery that escapes justifiable description. "The men worked day and night driving ambulances, taking doctors and nurses to scenes of sickness and desolation in the foreign quarters of the mining regions, nursing the sick and caring for the destitute children of deceased parents," reported Lumb. He praised his men for their "courage and loyalty" during the "terrible epidemic of influenza that swept Pennsylvania during the year."

On another occasion, while visiting the Troop B area, Lumb said, "Due to the unusual conditions under which the Troop was forced to operate, this was one of the most arduous and trying periods in the history of the State Police Force, and the troopers were called upon and performed many unusual duties and rendered public services in many ways, which undoubtedly were not anticipated by the founders of this Department, when the formation of the State Police organization was first conceived."

Dedicated to their work and unmindful of the risks they encountered, eight troopers died of the Spanish flu:

Private Chester A. Kuhns, Troop C, October 6
Private Joseph B. Malloy, Troop D, October 9
Sergeant Zoe A. Remaly, Troop B, October 15
Private George E. Higgins, Troop C, October 20
Private Joseph R. Brown, Troop B, October 22
Private Edward C. Jackson, Troop B, October 23
Private John P. McLaughlin, Troop A, October 24
Private James Walsh, Troop C, December 15

It is most unfortunate that their brave lives, lost for suffering humanity, are not shown on department records as having been lost in the line of duty. This recognition somehow has been given only to those who have died from beatings, stabbings, shootings, motor vehicle accidents, and the likes of that—in other words—violent circumstances. More needs to be written on this subject, and further comments will be reserved for another chapter.

Private Elmer Strohm, Troop C, died of the Spanish flu, on October 31, while on leave of absence in the military service, at Columbus Barracks, Ohio.

Private Joseph A. Snyder, Troop C, was killed in action in France, on October 16, while on military leave of absence. Thus ended the most disastrous year in State Police history. Twelve men were lost to the department: eight from Spanish flu in the line of duty, two killed apprehending criminals, one killed in military action, and another died from the flu while in military service.

The only encouraging event near the year's end was the signing of the Armistice on November 11, which raised hopes for a lasting peace and the victorious return of America's doughboys.

Lumb had reason to complain to the governor about a ruling by the attorney general. "Unfortunately the Attorney General ruled that the words 'other necessary expenses' in our contingent appropriations do not apply to the medical expenses or funeral expenses of men in this Force who were killed, died or injured in the line of duty, and the underpaid men of the Force have been compelled even to pay the expenses of shipping the bodies of their own comrades out of private funds," he wrote. "This and the compelling of officers transferred from one troop to another because of necessary promotions, to pay for the shipment of their personal effects to their new stations (which are not of their own selection) are hardships which ought to be relieved at once by including such expenses in the provisions of the contingent appropriations."

In an obvious move to raise funds to defray hardship expenses for the rank and file, the State Police in 1917 prepared a *History of the Department of State Police,* and solicited advertisement. The sketchy history and photographs accounted for 53 pages of the paperbound volume, while some 250 pages contained advertisements from business and industry throughout the Commonwealth. This is the first evidence of any organized effort toward self-help in light of state regulations that brought no financial relief. It was the front-runner for the organization-wide civic association and the field exhibitions that were to follow.

In order to better cope with the financial hardships befalling the survivors, Lumb asked the troop civic associations to consider some action in behalf of the dependents of the deceased members. In mid-October, he ordered the troop commanders to his Harrisburg office, as directors of the State Police Civic Association. This board of directors, according to Lumb's planning, would be guided by the actions taken by the troop associations in dealing with benefits to dependents. Troop commanders were also urged by Lumb to modify duties for ten days following the flu epidemic's end to provide the men with "much needed rest and recreation."

In *The Plague of the Spanish Lady,* Richard Collier's epilogue contains these observations of the 1918 influenza pandemic:

> Perhaps the most puzzling factor about the Spanish Lady was her impermanence. On the face of it, the most appalling epidemic since the Middle Ages, which cost more than 21 million lives and in some way or other affected over one billion people—then half the world's population—should have imprinted itself indelibly on the public consciousness these fifty-six years past. Yet except to those who suffered it the Spanish Lady is now little more than a folk-memory—as remote from the conscious mind as the Black Death itself. Many readers under sixty can scarcely be aware that such a pandemic ever existed.
>
> Even at the height of the slaughter, there was this same ambivalence. The disease took at least half a million American lives—ten times as many as the Germans took during the war—yet only in the hardest-hit cities did it ever win through to the newspapers' front pages. In those months of 1918, when the Allied troops were engaged in their last great push across the ruined countryside of France and Belgium, it was the crumbling of the Central European empires, the inexorable peace terms of Woodrow Wilson, that always took pride of place. To some medical men, at least, the fate of civilisation hung in the balance, for medicine could do little more than in the Middle Ages, when a red cross painted on the door of a stricken house, with the legend "God have pity on us," was the sum total of medical knowledge. Yet no such stark facts were ever voiced by the world's headlines.
>
> The Spanish Lady inspired no songs, no legends, no work of art. Even fundamental facts were meagre. To this day, no one can say with certainty where the disease began, where it ended, or even which virus was at fault. As one leading authority has summed it up: "The resemblance to the disappearance of the Cheshire Cat in ALICE IN WONDERLAND is striking." And to this day, too, flu remains one of the great medical imponderables: a disease which could, as recently as 1969, cost Britain's economy alone 150 million pounds—and still escape the headlines. Yet, despite the sophistication of prophylactic techniques since 1918, few governments have shown themselves willing to take a positive lead in advocating mass vaccination.

To take but one example: in Britain alone, in 1967, the purely medical cost of influenza—drugs, doctors' time and hospital costs—amounted to 15 million pounds. Yet the medical report which publicized this figure also estimated that if four out of five people had been vaccinated in that year, the total cost could have been cut to 9 million pounds, and, more important by far, many hundreds of lives could have been saved.

But, just as in 1918, all too many authorities tend to regard the ravages of flu not as a challenge but as an uncomfortable truth, consistently to be ignored until too late. The late H. L. Mencken's commentary on the Spanish Lady, written as far back as 1956, sadly remains as true today: "The epidemic is seldom mentioned, and most Americans have apparently forgotten it. This is not surprising. The human mind always tries to expunge the intolerable from memory, just as it tries to conceal it while current."

Oddly enough, in 1976, President Gerald R. Ford unexpectedly announced a program bearing on this flu subject. An Associated Press release appearing in *The Patriot* (Harrisburg) on March 25 told Ford's story:

President Gerald R. Ford announced a $135 million plan to vaccinate every American against a deadly flu virus by next November.

He emphasized that at this point no one could determine the exact extent of the potential threat posed by a strain of flu known as swine influenza that could become epidemic next Fall.

Although there was only one outbreak of swine flu last month (at Ft. Dix, N. J.) the statement said, "present evidence and past experience indicate a strong possibility that this country could experience widespread swine influenza in 1976–77."

"There is no proof that a global outbreak of swine flu virus will occur next season but it is safer to gamble with dollars rather than human lives," the President's health advisers said.

President Ford had his way, and the immunization program was carried out during that historic bicentennial year accompanied by a multitude of problems so bewildering that the program was cut far short of its goal.

No sooner was there evidence of the epidemic's end, when Lumb had to initiate orders governing the State Police role in the inauguration ceremonies for the newly-elected governor, William C. Sproul, whose inauguration was set for January 21, 1919. This was just another worrisome detail on top of all else suffered with wartime pressures, pestilence, and manpower shortages.

In the budget for 1918–1919 biennial fiscal period, the purchase of motor vehicles was mentioned for the first time. In referring to the total budget and "taking into account $13,402.25 turned into the State Treasury in fines, $52,293.45 for salaries not drawn and $1,423.42 refunded on lost property, the expense per year per capita has been six and one-fourth cents for the protection of a mobile, efficient police force to 8,000,000 people of Pennsylvania," so summarized Lumb in his 1918 report.

During 1918, there were 10,017 criminal arrests with a 91.4 percent conviction rate, compared to 5,255 arrests in 1917 and a conviction rate of "only" 85 percent. Lumb considered this activity "remarkable" since each of the four troops was in the hands of an acting captain, and the State Police was assisting federal agencies in meeting wartime conditions in addition to its regular duties. "The high percentage of convictions demonstrates beyond a shadow of a doubt that the men are exceedingly careful in making arrests and that their cases are well prepared before appearing in court for trial."

There were 2,392 arrests for violations of the auto laws, which headed the list of charges for which arrests were made. This figure was closely followed by 2,078 disorderly conduct arrests. These were 84 arrests for murder and 100 attempts to kill. Arrests by nationality and sex were:

Albanian	5	Greek	91
American	5,469	Hebrew	97
Austrian	612	Horwat	44
Belgian	5	Hungarian	75
Bohemian	10	Indian	1
Brazilian	3	Irish	57
Bulgarian	17	Italian	1,035
Canadian	3	Lithuanian	153
Croatian	8	Mexican	40
Danish	3	Negro	616
Dutch	4	Norwegian	2
Egyptian	2	Polish	638
English	23	Rumanian	92
Finn	3	Russian	305
French	8	Scotch	6
German	90	Serbian	64

Slavish	385	Syrian	13
Spanish	9	Turk	11
Swede	9	Ukranian	1
Swiss	2	Welsh	6
			10,017

	Females	652
	Males	9,365
		10,017

Statistics of this type, generated by headquarters' thinking, appeared for the first time. It demonstrated Lumb's desire to have management reporting accomplished at a level heretofore by-passed. For the first time, too, the miles patrolled by the field forces exceeded the one million mark—1,043,889 miles. Fines and forfeitures assessed the men as a result of disciplinary actions totalled $2,525.97, and 32 men were discharged by summary court action, clearly indicating no let down in the department's expectations for good conduct. Additional losses of manpower stemmed from 40 resignations to accept better-paying jobs, 4 allowed enlistments to expire, 31 were dismissed during their probationary period, and 16 deserted. There were 110 men recruited during the year. The loss of 135, on the other hand, left the department with a complement of only 255 at the end of the year.

Lumb recommended in his report that "a reasonable compensation for the arduous and often dangerous service rendered to the Commonwealth," citing the salaries of private corporations, ranging from $100 to $150 per month for untrained special officers and guards for duties "far more limited in scope and requiring a lower degree of intelligence."

Lumb proposed the following wage scale:

	Present	Proposed
Superintendent	$6,000	$6,000
Deputy Superintendent	3,500	4,000
Statistician		2,400
Bookkeeper	1,500	1,800
Stenographer	1,200	1,500
Captain	2,400	2,400
Lieutenant	1,800	1,800
First Sergeant	1,350	1,500
Sergeant	1,200	1,380
Corporal	1,100	1,320
Private	1,020	1,200

This was a modest proposal, costing $125,960 over a two-year period, which Lumb observed, "would be offset by savings," in coping with turnover costs, a point heavily emphasized in previous annual reports.

Headquarters personnel consisted then of an acting superintendent, acting deputy, clerk (who doubled as a bookkeeper), and one stenographer. One stenographer was detached from his troop to serve pressing needs at headquarters. A statistician was recommended by Lumb "to gather important statistics that a force of this size is expected to have available at all times, such as percentages of crime caused by alcoholic beverages, drugs, passion, etc., percentages of crimes according to classification, according to age, according to sex, nationality, and many other facts which libraries and students of social problems are constantly seeking."

The importance of a statistician must have been considerable with Lumb, since he proposed a salary of $2,400, annually, for that post, which was the same paid to a captain.

In what was certainly an impact recommendation insofar as the functional duties of several state agencies were concerned, Lumb sought the formation of a new department which would bring together the forest, fish, and game wardens, the traveling auditors of the Auditor General's Department, the Health Department's field inspectors, and the deputy fire marshals. He felt that placing them under one disciplinary head would be done in the interest of efficiency. Lumb was unquestionably disturbed by the conflicts between other state agencies extensively served by State Police personnel by virtue of their ex officio status as forest, fire, game, and fish wardens. He wrote, "As a result of this peculiar relationship with other departments of the executive branch of this state government much unnecessary travel, correspondence, and expense result, besides occasional clashes of authority and the consequent bad effect upon discipline. Game and fish wardens are mistaken for State Police and 'vice versa.' " His final comment in this stirring recommendation was, "A competent executive to be known as Superintendent of Conservation, Inspections and Law Enforcement, and who should himself be a man of legal training or have such an assistant, could work great benefit through the reorganization of the aforementioned agents of the State, or an official of this kind might be added to the State Police Department either as a superior or subordinate of the Superintendent of State Police."

At the risk of understating a situation at home—it was not an easy year for Lumb and his constabulary field forces.

Notwithstanding the difficulties of his time-demanding wartime post, Lumb embarked on a unique career as author of a textbook on police training. In 1918, after some twelve years of experience in law enforcement—most of which time was spent in top level management—Lumb was determined to share his knowledge and experience with those who might benefit by his writings. Under the title of *Police Training and Survey,* Lumb put together seven lessons, numbering 219 pages, which were published on March 8, 1919, and identified as "A course of instructions filling a long-felt want among Police, Detectives, Sheriffs and Guards in Seven Lessons."

It is believed that these documents, covering a wide range of subjects bearing on police work in general, were among the first ever to be published in this country. These seven lessons bound in a single volume were sold in the United States and in foreign countries where they drew the interest of both local police departments and foreign national police agencies. Brazil and India, it is recalled by one source, were among the countries that purchased quantities of Lumb's publication.

In his textbook, Lumb could not divorce himself from his own personal philosophy and observations about police work. Of the police profession, Lumb wrote, "No calling is more honorable than that of the guardian of the Law." Another worthwhile quote which is certainly timeless in its value was found, "An officer who prevents crime is more valuable than one who detects crime. If you can show the wayward youth the error of his way before he steps across the boundary of Law and Order, you have rendered a valuable service to mankind."

This pioneering effort by a Pennsylvania State Police brass-hat once again confirmed Lumb's outstanding qualities as a leader with an insatiable appetite for service. It was a worthy addition to the long list of his accomplishments.

Persuading the general assembly to make favorable changes in the constabulary organizational structure and responsibilities, following its creation in 1905, was almost an unsurmountable task, except for the 1911 and 1917 sessions when the barriers to progress were encouragingly overcome. By contrast, the 1919 legislature devoted consideration time to State Police legislation which brought about some significant changes in the work to be done by the constabulary.

Gone from the legislative scene were Socialist Maurer and perhaps other anti-State Police radicals. But, to put the situation in a more positive light, it is possible that the legislators, generally speaking, were finally awakening to the true value of this band of dedicated men. This eventuality must have been a source of deep satisfaction for Lumb.

The 1919 legislature passed three measures of special importance, all of which were acted upon in the closing month of the session. The first enactment, Act 179, P.L. 366, dated June 3, brought about sweeping changes. It authorized the creation of a fifth troop in the constabulary and increased the complement to 415 officers and men. It provided for an increase in salaries. It created within the State Police the first bureau—the Bureau of Fire Protection—and authorized for the first time the keeping of criminal records. The passage of this measure was not altogether a smooth journey through the House. The measure, HB-1132, was once defeated and passed later on reconsideration.

Heretofore, the responsibility for looking after the public's interest in the field of fire protection rested with an independent agency headed by the state fire marshal who reported directly to the governor. That agency was established in 1912. Therefore, Act 179 did not actually create a new agency: it moved an agency already in being from independent status to a subordinate one with the State Police. Civilian employes assigned to the State Fire Marshal's Office were given the option of reassignment to the State Police, and some elected to make the move.

The new troop was earmarked for location in Harrisburg, which was an easily understood development, and $30,000 was set aside to put the new group into operations. Under the new arrangement of the complement, each troop was to consist of:

  1 Captain
  1 Lieutenant
  1 First Sergeant
  5 Sergeants
10 Corporals
    (1 a saddler - 1 a blacksmith)
65 Privates
—
83 × 5 = 415

Act 283, P.L. 678, dated June 30, authorized the State Police troopers to arrest, on view, any motorist violating the Motor Code. During this period the automobile was increasingly coming into the picture insofar as the state was administratively concerned. A State Highway Department report regarding its Automobile Division states, "There has been a phenomenal increase in the work of the Automobile Division during the period covered by this report. The Legislature of 1919 enacted a new law affecting the annual license fees for passenger vehicles and commercial motor trucks, the chassis of which weighed less than two thousand pounds, under the terms of which fees are computed on the basis of horse power and at the rate of forty cents per horse power. Commercial vehicles were divided into classes, the fees ranging from twenty dollars for Class AA machines to one hundred fifty dollars for Class F vehicles. These rates became effective January 1, 1920.

"The creation of an inspection force under the Act of 1919 has resulted in the checking of various infractions of the law, including the improper use of tags, lights, and violations of weight limits, etc., and failures on the part of garages to keep proper records, and licensing of second-hand dealers."

It was apparent that the Highway Department was policing its own rules and regulations governing the operation and licensing of motor vehicles. Since some of the duties of the Automobile Division were of a law enforcement nature, it was perceivable that such duties would be thrust upon the State Police, or a newly created highway police force. The latter eventuality was to come to pass. In the meantime, the State Police Department was looked upon for immediate relief.

Act 286, P.L. 710, dated July 1, spelled out in detail exactly what the Bureau of Fire protection would be responsible for doing. Its duties were extensive and geared to serve every political jurisdiction in the Commonwealth. This subject will be covered more thoroughly in another chapter.

The 1917 General Assembly had already adjourned when Governor Brumbaugh appointed Lumb acting superintendent. So Lumb's appointment came as an interim move without the need for Senate confirmation. In 1919, however, the situation apparently called for his confirmation. On June 10, 1919, Governor Sproul officially renominated Lumb as acting head of the constabulary, and submitted his name to the Senate for confirmation. Moments after the reading of his nomination, the Senate moved to executive session, and confirmed Lumb by a 46–0 vote in unusually swift action. This was undoubtedly intended to be a vote of confidence in Lumb who had seen the constabulary through the troublesome war years.

Earlier in the 1919 session, the general assembly passed Act 68, in April, requiring all state agencies to report biennially rather than annually as theretofore prescribed. The biennial reports were to be submitted no later than June 1 of each odd-numbered year and cover departmental activities for the two years immediately preceding. This new reporting requirement coincided with the state's biennial fiscal period.

Act 179, creating a new troop, also specified that the Board of Public Grounds and Buildings would be given the responsibility of erecting a troop headquarters building and stables at Harrisburg. Pending this action by the Board of Public Grounds and Buildings, and since no adequate facility was available for leasing in the immediate vicinity of Harrisburg, Lumb approved the troop's temporary location at Lancaster.

The leased facility was a large, dilapidated farm-house, situated on the New Holland Pike, Mannheim Township, just one-half mile northeast of Lancaster. In its better days, however, the dwelling was familiarly known by local residents as the McGrann mansion.

Acting Captain Herbert Smith was given permanent rank and command of the new troop. To aid Smith in setting up operations by July 1, men were transferred from other troops to form Troop E—six men from the other four troops. Lieutenant Thomas McLaughlin and First Sergeant Albert Carlson were Smith's top aides. Corporal Charles E. Weller was moved in from Greensburg as blacksmith. Troop E, with its twenty-eight officers and men, became operational on July 1. Smith was given two automobiles—a Ford and Dodge—"which were helpful to work performance."

Referring later to his quarters at Lancaster, Smith stated, "It was somewhat discouraging to the new arrivals. The officers and men labored cooperatively to renovate so that living conditions were materially bettered."

There were important personnel changes at headquarters made at this time. Lumb had succeeded in acquiring a statistician. He named Carroll B. Price to that new post. Walter J. Fisher was advanced to chief clerk, replacing Price. The newcomer to the headquarters scene was Guy E. Reichard, a stenographer. Reichard was born in Chanceford Township, York County, on August 17, 1897. The 21-year-old student, 5'10", was appointed by Lumb on April 22, 1918, and assigned to Troop D, Butler. He was transferred to headquarters on April 1, 1919, and given Fisher's vacancy on June 1. Reichard was to remain at headquarters for many years, and achieve an excellent record of service.

Lumb called a troop commanders' conference at Harrisburg on August 11, 1919, at which time the state was reapportioned among the troops. New troop boundaries were established and certain substations were designated for preferential consideration. Changes were effective September 1.

Act 179 provided that the State Police "shall collect and classify and keep at all times available complete information useful for the detection of crime and the identification and apprehension of criminals." In August, 1919, Lumb decided to train men in the fundamentals of fingerprint classification to promote the department's interests in the keeping of suitable criminal records. Appointed to undergo this study and training were: Private Edward E. Beisel, Troop A; Private Stanley J. Collins, Troop C; Private Edward C. Bergan, Troop D; and Private Charles Kunz, Troop E. Training was underway at Troop B, Wyoming, in September.

With hostilities concluded in Europe, and the work of the

American Expeditionary Forces basically completed, the return of servicemen accelerated. Captain Wilhelm was the first of the commissioned officers to report back. He was given his former command at Pottsville on April 3, 1919. Captains Adams and Mair returned on September 1, and switched commands. Adams was sent to Butler, and Mair to Greensburg.

Lumb confessed that one of his most unpleasant duties was to order acting Captains Paul B. Stout and William A. Clark reduced to the rank of lieutenant, after serving so capably under the most trying circumstances. Acting Captains Smith and Wilson C. Price had earlier been given permanent rank by virtue of Pitcher's transfer to headquarters as deputy superintendent, and the creation of a new troop. Clark and Stout were rewarded with permanent rank within two years.

Lieutenant John J. McCall, who had seen action in France as a commissioned officer with the U. S. Army Signal Corps, was unable to return to constabulary duty due to a war-related injury.

Groome, the first to leave for military service, was the last to return. He reported back in December after more than two years of illustrious duty that is truly worthwhile mentioning in some detail.

In November, 1917, just after his assignment to the Signal Corps, Groome was appointed chief of Military Intelligence. Within fifteen days, he organized this agency and had recruited the services of prominent officers experienced in detective work from large international agencies. He prevailed upon four of his state constabulary officers, Captains Adams, Wilhelm, and Mair, and Lieutenant McCall to join him. They were commissioned captains. From every indication, their wartime services for the most part related to Groome's.

Groome was sent overseas in February, 1918. He was appointed to the board that reorganized the air service, and later was given the task of organizing the Military Police Corps which he was to command. Still later, he was appointed acting Provost Marshal of the American Expeditionary Forces (AEF) during which tenure he built the famous Central Prisoner of War Enclosure near Tours, France, which at one time accommodated 10,000 prisoners. The prison camp was considered a model by both the French and British authorities, and they commended Secretary of War Baker who inspected the compound shortly after it was put to use. Groome was promoted to colonel in the Signal Corps September 12, 1918.

When peace was declared in November, 1918, Groome was given the responsibility of looking after the welfare of Americans in Paris. The officers' Leave Bureau was formed, and then a hotel was opened for American officers over which he had supervision.

On the eve of the date set for his return to the United States,

Col. John C. Groome, Provost Mar-
shal of Paris, World War I (Courtesy
of Mrs. John C. Groome, Jr.)

Mrs. John C. Groome in uniform
of Emergency Aid of Pennsylvania,
World War I (Courtesy of Mrs. John
C. Groome, Jr.)

Groome was sent, at the request of Herbert Hoover, then director of the American Relief Administration, to Russia as the head of an expedition to relieve famine suffering. Groome distributed $10 million worth of food there and in the Baltic states.

For his humanitarian services, the Russian government awarded him knighthood in the honored Order of St. Vladimir. The Croix de la Libertie was bestowed upon him by the government of Esthonia. The French government shortly afterward awarded him the Étoile Noire, or Order of the Black Star, "for meritorious conduct of the Military Police." The British government was not lacking in recognition as it conferred upon Groome membership in the Distinguished Order of St. Michael and St. George, one of the most exclusive orders in English knighthood. Groome returned home with the decorations of four foreign governments. Here at home, he was awarded by a grateful nation the Distinguished Service Medal with two clasps.

Recalling Groome's deeds, Katherine Mayo wrote, "At the end of the war and the completion of their service, those officers who had put on the Army uniform returned to the Force, the Superintendent with the rank of Colonel in the United States Army, in which he served with marked distinction in a varied field." In her judgment, Mayo stated that Groome's decorations "suggest in part the reach and importance of the tasks in which he was engaged."

During her husband's absence, Mrs. Groome saw useful wartime service with the Emergency Aid of Pennsylvania. That organization was founded in 1776 by Esther Reed, wife of Colonel Joseph Reed who was serving as General George Washington's military secretary. Then known as the Emergency Aid of 1776, the organization united the ladies of Philadelphia for the purpose of collecting, by voluntary subscriptions, supplies of clothing and money for the army. Enrollment in this volunteer service soon included women from neighboring colonies. The organization remained in existence through World War I.

Upon Groome's return, Lumb, anxious to practice law on a full-time basis, submitted his resignation terminating his services December 31, 1919. Governor Sproul granted him terminal leave from December 23.

The Commonwealth, however, was not finished with Lumb. He was called back into state service in other capacities on two occasions. These situations will be detailed later.

Captain Pitcher also resigned his post at the end of the year to accept appointment as Wilkes-Barre's chief of police at a starting salary of $5,000 a year.

Groome's first general order in December announced Lumb's resignation, the appointment of Captain Adams as acting deputy superintendent, and his permanent appointment as deputy effective January 1, 1920.

On December 1, 1919, Private Stanley W. Christ, 22, of Troop E, died in the Lancaster General Hospital of extensive internal injuries suffered when he was kicked in the abdomen by a horse. His name appears on the department's honor roll of those killed in the line of duty. Christ was the eleventh so honored.

In light of Lumb's departure in late December, the responsibility for preparing the annual report for the governor fell back on Groome, although he had been back to his desk for only a few weeks. Groome reported that his men were heavily committed to statewide strikes in the steel industry in September. Although there was less than a 40 percent walk-out, there was considerable violence. "Communists and anarchists distributed radical literature accusing the State Police of being special police for the protection of corporations and sent into communities for the purpose of compelling men to return to work. The professional agitators of the radical type advocate intimidation to gain their ends."

The governor was reassured that high standards of discipline were maintained. "Great care has been exercised in the selection of personnel from the list of applicants. In this respect, there has been no little difficulty in obtaining recruits that measure up to the Pennsylvania State Police standards of morals, intelligence, courage, and physique.'' This is the first time that recruiting difficulties were faced, and Groome offered this opinion: ''This difficulty is due, principally, to the scarcity of labor and higher rates of pay in every line of industry. Feeling that the present condition as to pay is not normal, changes in the salary scale are not recommended at this time, further that there should be an increase in the pay for continuous service.'' In lieu of changing the basic pay structure, Groome recommended an increase of $5.00 a month after the first year of service and a further increase of $5.00 a month for each year thereafter for a period of five years. This was a new concept of his.

In connection with the manpower problem, it is interesting to note that Captain Wilhelm, after his return from military service, recommended in his year-end from Troop C a reenlistment bonus to combat the high turnover rate. Wilhelm argued that it would be less expensive in the long run to pay a reenlistment bonus than to have good men leave for higher-paying jobs in business and industry.

During the year, motorcycle patrols were established, ''to respond to the growing size of the motoring public.'' Groome stated that the motorcycle patrols were ''modestly effective in curtailing accidents, carelessness and speeding.'' This was particularly true on the state's main highways where patrols were maintained. Limited patrol power, however, was no match for the problem at hand.

Due to manpower and financial difficulties, the system of operating from substations was not a stable one. Sustations were opened and frequently closed in short order. A substation at Harrisburg, for example, was set up on July 15 and closed on August 15, one month later.

During 1919, the field forces patrolled 1,036,436 miles. They made 7,797 criminal arrests. Arrested were 7,307 males and 490 females. The estimated value of recovered stolen property was $103,362.

Recruits during the year numbered 247—a figure that was offset by 187 departures. Reasons for separations were:

Better-paying jobs	81
Expiration of enlistment	15
Disciplinary action	44
Probationary dismissals	27
Desertions	17
Killed in the line of duty	1
Death not in line of duty	2
	187

Plaque presented to Pennsylvania State Police by Miss Katherine Mayo in 1917. Depicted are the flags of major U. S. allies during World War I. Plaque was designed by P. M. Tonetti, a New York sculptor. (Courtesy of Pennsylvania State Police)

The year-end complement of 351 men fell considerably short of the 415 figure set by the general assembly.

When Katerine Mayo was readying her fifth edition of *Justice To All,* she asked Governor William C. Sproul to prepare an official statement for her new edition. Sproul obligingly wrote of 1919—his first year in office:

> During the past year the Pennsylvania State Police has again shown, in a time of uneasiness, its real worth to the State and to the communities. Indeed, there was a period of crisis during the early days of the steel strike when, had we

not been prepared, anything might have happened in the industrial centers in Pennsylvania. At this time conditions were rather different from any which had heretofore arisen here. The American element among the steel workers did not want to strike; and, where they were out-numbered, left their work under protests, and to return to it as soon as they were assured of protection. The active elements in the strike were led by avowed Syndicalists and enemies of our form of government, and the rank and file were made up of aliens who had no knowledge of our Democracy and no respect for our institutions. Everything seemed set for a period of violence and intimidation, and plans had been made for marches and raids upon those plants and those communities in which the workers had refused to strike.

With a knowledge of these conditions our plans were laid in advance, our forces distributed where they would be needed in case of trouble. And when the trouble came they were ready for it. In no single instance did the promoters of disorder get the jump upon the authorities. The sheriffs of the counties and the local officials alike were assured that they would be backed up by the power of the State. General publicity, too, was given to the fact that the State authorities were determined to preserve law and order at all hazards and that the rights of every one would be protected. Our courts having sustained the authority of our peace officers to prohibit gatherings or demonstrations in trouble zones, which might lead to disorderly outbreaks, the burgesses and local police officials were given to understand that they would be upheld in exercising their judgment in these matters. The State Police, as representing the strength and dignity of the Commonwealth, were everywhere in evidence, quietly and inoffensively but firmly and determinedly. The result was that there was very little disorder and very few casualties in a situation which combined all of the elements of danger and which, allowed to develop without interference, might have brought about a veritable reign of terror and destruction in some of the counties.

In meeting this situation and the coal strike which followed before the steel strike had been determined, we depended entirely upon our State Police Force and upon the splendid public sentiment of the people of Pennsylvania which endorsed and upheld the action of the administration. It may readily be seen that without this organized State Police body representing the Commonwealth, hundreds of lives and millions of dollars' worth of property might have been destroyed, the State disgraced, and its law-abiding people humiliated and disheartened. The necessity of calling out the

Reserve Militia was obviated and thus a great expense was saved.

In fact, from a practical standpoint, I am sure that the State Police in the year 1919 have saved for the people of Pennsylvania more in actual expense to the taxpayers than the total cost of the force from the time it was organized to the present date. It is a noteworthy item in the history of this splendid organization that at no time since it was inaugurated has any disturbance in the State gotten beyond its control.

We are strengthening the force, trying to improve its already superb morale, bettering and increasing its equipment and providing superior facilities for the education and comfort of its members. We are also organizing a headquarters division that will possess a bureau of criminal records and information, which will be of great service to the counties and communities of the State. Those who flout the authority of the Commonwealth of Pennsylvania will soon understand that the State Government does not forget; and that those who make trouble here in Pennsylvania and violate our laws will be followed, apprehended, and brought back to justice in Pennsylvania, no matter where they may go.

There will be hereafter no amnesty to offenders against the rights and laws of our people when disturbances are over; nor will the mutations of local politics and the changes of local officials longer serve as a cloak to cover old offenses against our authority. We expect to make our State Police Force even more useful in the future than it has been in its splendid past.

Dated February 3, 1920, Sproul's statement was appropriately titled "The State Police In A Period Of Crisis."

CHAPTER VII

Pennsylvania State Police
Major Lynn G. Adams
1920–1923

With a statistician then at hand at headquarters to evaluate field reports, Groome instituted in mid-January, 1920, a new policy whereby all arrests would be classified by cause: (a) Avarice, (b) Alcoholic stimulant, (c) Drugs, (d) Lust, (e) Revenge, (f) Subnormal mentality, and (g) Recklessness. All criminal arrest reports, according to the new policy, would also note whether the person arrested was a first offender or a habitual offender.

This order, a week later, was followed by companion orders dealing with quarters and meals for field personnel. The first order ended the practice of deducting barracks rental from salaries, and allowed men to remain at any barracks rent free. This was a significant development. For instance, in 1919, a total of $5,121.87 was deducted from salaries for this purpose. The second order established a method for payment of meals to the troop mess funds when stationed at a barracks.

In February, Groome, supported by the inventiveness of Adams, instituted two important changes in State Police procedures.

For a decade, early training of recruits was accomplished at Troop C, Pottsville, with very little change in the training program observed there. The first of the two changes concerned the formalizing of the training program by delegating this important responsibility to a special detail of men, and relocating the training site. After considering the lo-

153

cations suggested for a school, Groome decided to locate at Newville, Cumberland County. A three-year lease was executed with owner George D. Frey for the use of the old Big Spring Hotel and its ten-acre site. The aged hotel was altered to provide administrative offices, a gymnasium, recreation room, dining room, kitchen, and sleeping quarters. The area adjacent to the hotel accomodated the stables, corral, and drill field.

Captain William Mair and Lieutenant Thomas J. McLaughlin were given the assignment of getting the new school on an operational footing. In February, 1920, the first class of thirty recruits began training. Groome appointed McLaughlin the first school commandant. McLaughlin was aided by Sergeant Richard H. Fairservice, Troop D; Sergeant Peter T. Link, Troop B; and Sergeant M. S. Q. Row, Troop A, all of whom served as instructors. Frequent changes in this original administrative crew were to follow before the year was up.

The other change worthy of note concerned the reorganization of the field clerical positions at the five troop headquarters. Because of legal restrictions placed on the department's total complement of enlisted and civilian positions, the clerical work at the troop level since the department's early beginnings was accomplished by enlisted men with some degree of talent and training for office work. With the modification of restrictions on civilian positions by the 1919 legislature, the reorganization then was mainly aimed at picking up enlisted positions which were still limited by law by reclassifying the enlisted men performing clerical chores.

Accordingly Private Ralph H. Stephens was discharged and appointed a stenographer at Troop A; Sergeant Silvus J. Overmiller and Private Jonathan Baddorf were discharged and appointed bookkeeper-stenographer and clerk, respectively, at Troop B; Private Clyde C. Grim was discharged and appointed bookkeeper-stenographer at Troop C; Privates John H. Myers and William Carey were discharged and appointed bookkeeper and stenographer, respectively, at Troop D, and Corporal John R. Price and Private Enos L. Mowrer were discharged and appointed bookkeeper and stenographer, respectively, at Troop E. All discharges were effective January 31, 1920, and the civilian appointments were officially recognized the following day, when all appeared on the departmental headquarters payroll instead of the troop payrolls.

Each of the newly-appointed civilians was permitted to retain his uniform wear, and remain a member of the troop mess. Although they took their daily operational assignments from the troop commissioned officers, as a group they were administratively placed in the hands of the department's statistician. This arrangement was to remain in effect for almost two decades.

Overmiller and Price were soon destined to become important figures at the Harrisburg main offices where both served honorably for many years.

These were to be the final significant actions taken by Groome. He submitted his resignation to the governor—a resignation that was to take effect on the last day of February, 1920, thus ending fifteen history-making years at the helm of the nation's first state constabulary. It was Groome's desire to return to his private business in Philadelphia.

He severed his connections with the brokerage firm of Goddard, Groome and Drayton Company, Philadelphia, where he had served as vice president since 1914, and joined with George W. Kendrick and Company, bankers and brokers.

Of this, Katherine Mayo's succinct summary is most appropriate, "On February 28, 1920, after over fifteen years of such service to Pennsylvania and to the Union as make both forever his debtors, Colonel Groome resigned the Superintendency of the organization that he built, inspired, and so long commanded, in favor of his senior Captain, Major Lynn G. Adams."

Adams' rank of major, just as Groome's rank of colonel, was representative of his promotion to that level during World War I military service. Groome, like Lumb, was to return to state service in another agency, and mention of this will be made later.

Governor Sproul, on March 1, 1920, appointed Lynn G. Adams superintendent to succeed Groome. Begun was the lengthiest tenure by any head of the Pennsylvania State Police—a record of service never to be equalled. Adams was truly a great man and a worthy successor to the State Police Department's top post. Surprisingly, Groome's departure and Adams' appointment received little attention by the press.

In more eloquent terms, this is what Katherine Mayo had to say about Adams' appointment, "The retirement of Colonel Groome is an event that must, whenever it should occur, occasion widespread regret. But, Colonel Groome, through long distinguished service rendered, has won the right to lay the burden down. The officer who now assumes it is one in whose hands the honor of the Force is absolutely safe. The wise policies determined, the lofty and inflexible standard set by the first Superintendent will be carried forward by his worthy successor without a shadow of turning.

"Finally, the present opportunity must not be missed to congratulate the State of Pennsylvania upon its Governor, the Honorable William C. Sproul. Happy is the Commonwealth whose affairs rest in the hands of a man whose ambition and whose pride is to administer them nobly—who has looked, in filling a place of power, not for personal friends, not for political strength or for financial resource, but for

Major Lynn G. Adams (Courtesy of Pennsylvania State Police)

the one man in the country best qualified to service the people's interest, and, through that, the Union."

Lynn George Adams was born in Hopbottom, Susquehanna County, Pennsylvania, on July 8, 1880. He was the son of Simeon Adams and Nina Viola Payne Adams. Simeon, a carpenter and builder, was born July 24, 1855. The Adams family is traceable to a Henry Adams, of Devonshire, England, and his son, John, a millright, who came to the Massachusetts colony in 1650 and died in 1706.

Superintendent Adams' grandfather's grandfather, John Adams, was born in 1745 and died in 1849 at a ripe old age of 104—a family record. He served at Lexington and Concord, fighting with the Sergeant Deliverance Company of Colonel Whitcomb's Regiment. He became a first lieutenant on July 6, 1780, with the Francis Lane Company, a unit of the Worchester Regiment. This same John Adams married Lucy Monroe who died in childbirth. He then married her sister, Joanna, who bore him twelve children. Joanna and Lucy were daughters of Ebenezer Monroe, of Lexington, who was wounded at Lexington. On Ebenezer Monroe's gravestone at Ashbunham, Massachusetts, is written an historical note that he fired the first shot of the Revolution. How authentic this note might be is not known.

A later descendant, Thomas Adams, of Cambridge, Massachusetts, commanded a company of militia from Cambridge during the French and Indian War. Lynn G. Adams, indeed, derived from an illustrious family background, and by his own accomplishments added to his heritage.

Adams attended Dunmore public schools. He left Scranton High School in 1898, before graduation, to join the U.S. Army then engaged in the Spanish-American War. Adams, however, eager to fight did not see front line action. He remained in the army and was dispatched to the Philippine Islands where he did see action during the Philippine Insurrection with Company G, Thirteenth Regular Infantry.

It was said then that promotions to company first sergeant went to the man who could fight his way to the top. Adams, a formidable light-heavyweight boxer and scrapper, fought his way to company top-kick in short order. It is claimed that at 22 he was the army's youngest first sergeant.

He served in the Philippines for thirty months before returning stateside. His company, upon returning home, was temporarily stationed at a west coast military encampment near Alcatraz. According to one account by Colonel William Fisher, a life-long family friend, Adams was a ringleader of a rough-and-tough band of soldiers from Company G, known as the "Dirty Dozen." When they drank, they would fight at the least provocation. During their stay at Alcatraz, the "Dirty Dozen" planned a night on the town. But Adams drew sentry duty that night, and could not accompany the group. A serious fight broke out between the soldiers and a group of sailors and, before the drunken brawl was ended, a number of sailors were killed. Many of the combatants were injured.

Some of the soldiers were arrested and sentenced to prison terms and dishonorably discharged from military service. The penalties were stiff enough, and the sadness of the aftermath was shocking to Adams. The violent-tempered Adams, who did his share of drinking, was thankful for having drawn sentry duty that kept him away from that bloody fracas. He realized full well the disgrace of a dishonorable discharge, and the unfavorable consequences often following one. In his case, enlistment in the state constabulary later on would have been an impossibility. He, then and there, swore never again to drink. That pledge he kept faithfully for the rest of his life. His temper, however, never diminished, and was displayed frequently.

After his honorable discharge from the army in 1903, Adams returned to his education. He attended the Scranton Business School. Later he was employed as a clerk in the storekeeper's office of the Erie Railroad at the Dunmore shops. Here he met another employe, Frank Matthews. By way of the friendly relationship that grew between them, Adams was introduced to Matthews' sister Gertrude, whom he was later to marry. Gertrude Matthews was then employed by Scranton's International Correspondence School. Adams remained with the Erie Railroad until his appointment to the state constabulary. Adams, 26, 5'10¼", a resident of Scranton, was an original member of the Department of State Police. He was enlisted on December 15, 1905, and given an appointment as sergeant by Groome at Troop A, Greensburg.

Adams married Gertrude Matthews, a native of Dunmore, in 1906. The ceremony took place in St. Mark's Episcopal Church at Dunmore. Gertrude was the daughter of Sidney and Sophia Vaughn Matthews. Her parents, as a married couple, came to the United States from England, and were naturalized. Sidney Matthews was a native of Monmouthshire, England, where he operated stationary steam power generators at the Monmouthshire mines. For awhile he followed this same trade here in Pennsylvania's anthracite mines before his employment with the Delaware and Hudson Railroad at Scranton as engineman. Sophia Vaughn Matthews was a native of Hereford, England.

Adams was promoted to first sergeant at Greensburg in November, 1907. Four months later—March, 1908—he was advanced to the commissioned ranks as lieutenant, and transferred to Troop B, Wyoming. In mid-August, 1908, he was given command of Troop C. Captain Adams was transferred back to Greensburg in January, 1911, and remained there until his entry into military life again in 1917 to serve with the American Expeditionary Force in France.

During his years as troop commander at Greensburg, he moved his wife and two children, Ruth and Donald, to Greensburg where he purchased land, just across the roadway from the barracks, and built a modest, frame bugalow. It was here that he was visited by Katherine Mayo, who was searching out material about the constabulary preliminary to her writings that led to the creation of the New York State Police, and spotlighted the achievements of the Pennsylvania constabulary.

Katherine Mayo was very much impressed by Adams and took a liking to him. Adams was a frequent "hero" in her short stories about

Captain William E. Mair (Courtesy of Pennsylvania State Police)

the constabulary case histories. Mayo visited the Adams homestead a number of times. She was always warmly received by the Adams family. At Mayo's invitation, the Adams family visited her at Bedford Hills, New York. The luxurious accommodations of the Newell country estate, serviced by an assemblage of domestics, were breathtaking for the Adams children.

Ruth and Donald Adams recall Miss Mayo, then middle-aged, as an attractive lady "with a capital L." Her snow-white hair, well-groomed, was strikingly beautiful, and a match for her lovely complexion. The author, born to wealth, spoke with a distinctive sound of British aristocracy, and her demeanor was no less royal. She neither smoked nor drank alcoholic beverages. Full-length dresses made up the wardrobe of this medium-sized lady. She, like her companion, Moyca Newell, was totally independent of the fads of the "Roaring Twenties." Miss Mayo travelled in style with a luxury station wagon driven by a French, uniformed chauffeur. For stays in New York City, she maintained a Park Avenue apartment. These are pleasant recalls by the Adams children who admired Miss Mayo as an elegant lady and friend.

In November, 1917, the War Department awarded Adams a captain's commission in the U.S. Army Signal Corps. This account is offered by Katherine Mayo:

His overseas war record shows him, first, as Provost Marshal of the District of Paris, with the rank of Captain, D.M.A., U.S.A. And General Harts, commanding the District, in specially recommending Captain Adams for a majority, dwelt with emphasis upon his "rare good judgment in handling the many delicate problems pertaining to his office," and "his splendid record." Major Adams' later service culminated in his creation, organization, and command of the entire Department of Transportation Guards, under General Atterbury.

Major Adams, according to family records, did not enter into combat and was not specially decorated.

Adams was mustered out of the service July 26, 1919, and returned to the constabulary September 1. Lumb assigned him to Troop D command at Butler, where he served until his call to Harrisburg in the waning days of 1919.

Shortly after his appointment as superintendent, Adams sold his Greensburg bungalow and land, and moved his family to Harrisburg. The former Adams homestead was later acquisitioned by the state as part of the Greensburg barracks property.

On the very day that Governor Sproul announced Adams' appointment as superintendent, he also appointed Captain William E. Mair the new deputy. Mair served with Adams in France during World War I, returning with the rank of major. Mair, now 38, was commander at Greensburg at the time of his upgrading. The handsome Philadelphian was a well-accepted attraction at headquarters.

It is noted that Sproul and Adams did not rely upon seniority in naming Mair deputy superintendent. Wilhelm, who was promoted to captain in 1911, was the department's senior captain. Mair was not promoted to captain until 1916. So Wilhelm was actually Mair's senior in grade by more than five years. Among Wilhelm's close associates, it is recalled that Wilhelm was somewhat upset with this development.

Adams was faced with two important moves stemming from legislative action requiring the State Police to keep criminal records and create a Bureau of Fire Protection. To satisfy the first requirement, Adams created the Bureau of Criminal Identification and Information (BCI & I) and named Captain Wilson C. Price to serve as that bureau's first chief. Price's appointment became effective March 1. On May 7, 1920, Adams brought in Captain Cecil M. Wilhelm to head up the new Bureau of Fire Protection (BFP), as that bureau's first chief.

Because of the special nature by which the BFP was created, the department was furnished a specific appropriation for the new bureau's operations, and the chief was earmarked for an annual salary of $4,000. This figure became Wilhelm's new salary bracket, which was a considerable jump from the $2,400 salary he was drawing as troop commander. The salary of $4,000 placed Wilhelm on the same pay level as the deputy superintendent.

The BFP occupied office space on the first floor of the capitol's north wing, remaining where it had been as the independent Fire Marshal's Office. The new bureau remained in the capitol until 1925 when it was moved to the Yoffee Building, and later to the Blackstone Building. Both office buildings were located in downtown Harrisburg.

The BCI & I at the outset was located on the fifth floor of the capitol's south wing, and remained there until 1934.

With the removal of Adams, Mair, Price, and Wilhelm from field command positions, promotions were given to Lieutenants Thomas J. McLaughlin, Elmer Leithiser, Samuel W. Gearhart, and William A. Clark. Smith moved to Troop A; Clark to B; Gearhart to C; Leithiser to D, and McLaughlin to E, to establish a new complement of troop commanders for the newly-arrived administration.

McLaughlin's vacancy at the Newville training school was filled by the transfer to Lieutenant Oke R. Campbell from Troop D.

By 1920, the motor vehicle continued to make its impact upon the Pennsylvania roadways, and this statement taken from a State Highway Department biennial report reflects the times: "In cooperation with the State Police Department, a standard procedure was developed with respect to the erection of gasoline tanks along state highway routes." This particular statement reflects the work being done by the BFP with regard to the storage and use of inflammable liquids.

The same report contained this recommendation: "Adequate provisions should be made for more rigidly enforcing the motor vehicle laws in view of the abnormal increase of traffic and the unusual number of fatal accidents as a result of the careless and reckless operation of these machines. The scope of the enforcement now in charge of the Department of State Police should be extended."

The State Police was not idle in this area of enforcement, and had laid plans for the purchase of a small fleet of motorcycles, and a system of patrol. During April, 1920, seventy motorcycles were purchased, adding considerably to the mobility of the force. Motorcycle operators were secured by asking the field forces for volunteers. The volunteers, when finally selected, were dispatched to the Newville training school, where instructions in the operations and maintenance of the cycles were undertaken. When this training program was completed, fourteen cycles were assigned to each of the five troops.

The system of patrol was a modest one. Patrol zones were established and owners of telephones along the patrol routes were given steel discs, ten inches in diameter, painted red and white. Calls for patrolmen would be made to these telephone locations, where signs would be displayed. Patrolmen were required to call their stations on viewing a displayed sign. Exempted from this order were plain-clothesmen under specific orders.

On June 16, all troop commanders were notified to report to head-quarters "for the regular Monthly Conference." From this directive, it is taken that Adams did call for monthly meetings with his commanding officers, which was another innovation, since there is no indication of such conferences prior to his appointment as superintendent.

In 1920, the State Police began publishing a *Monthly Bulletin* containing information of public interest, regarding departmental activities. The first issue, Volume I, No. 1, was dated August, 1920. The names of Adams, C. M. Wilhelm, chief of the BFP, and W. C. Price, chief of the BCI & I, were prominently displayed.

Adams was quoted, "Pennsylvania first, not only in manufactur-ing and agriculture, but also in Safety, will be the aim of the Depart-ment. Patrolmen well trained in enforcement as well as knowing the spirit of the law cannot but aid in safety to all."

The BFP engaged in a noble effort to inform the public on the tremendous losses suffered needlessly by fire and undertook a widespread program of education to reduce fires and fire losses.

The BCI & I described its services and pledged its support to all law enforcement agencies by promptly replying to all inquiries for in-formation, and serving as a central repository for criminal records.

To better acquaint himself with the technicalities of criminal iden-tification, Price undertook a series of instructions with Faurot, of the New York City Police Department, and Bodkin, of the Philadelphia Police Department, both of whom were recognized experts in this field. Additional know-how was obtained from other sources that came to his attention. From such training, Price gained sufficient knowledge in this specialty to personally give direction to his new bureau's operations.

Wilhelm's transfer to the BFP was less troublesome to him since he inherited a trained staff that was formerly engaged by the former State Fire Marshal Office and optioned to move over to the State Police.

The second issue of the *Monthly Bulletin*, Volume I, No. 2, continued the same format. This time the name of Deputy Super-intendent William E. Mair appeared in print. The bulletin recounted the problem of tramps. Until 1917, the countryside was bothered by tramps. They were dangerous and feared by farmers. During the war years, the tramp all but disappeared. The post war years, however, saw the tramps returning.

The bulletin indicated that State Police troops were maintaining records on stolen cars, and had men specifically assigned to investigate car thefts.

As early as 1920 the State Police were preaching "safety first" to the rapidly-increasing driving public, and cautioning drivers to remove keys from parked cars, and to lock car doors. The speed limit on "open highways" was then set at thirty miles per hour.

The State Police advocated a state-wide, uniform code of signals for drivers: stop—left arm extended horizontally; right turn—left arm extended and raised at about forty-five degree angle; left turn—left arm extended and lowered at about forty-five degree angle. The adoption of this code was recommended to the public and suggestions for improvements to the code were solicited.

Fire Prevention Day, set aside in October, was proclaimed on the federal and state levels to bolster the fight against the loss of precious resources by fire.

September saw further adjustments in the field clerical forces when Private Blair O'Neal was discharged and appointed bookkeeper at Troop A; Private William Ridgley was discharged and appointed stenographer at Troop B; Private John V. O'Neal was discharged and appointed stenographer at Troop C, and Private William N. Doll was discharged and appointed stenographer at Troop D.

During the opening days of the 1921 legislative session, Governor Sproul submitted Adams' name to the Senate for confirmation to serve from March 1, 1920, "until annulled." On a motion by Senator Richard J. Baldwin (R-Delaware), Senate Rule 38, requiring nominations to be referred first to committee, was dispensed with; and the Senate, voted into executive session, immediately acted on the lengthy list of nominees. Senator Baldwin's motion that the Senate do advise and consent to these nominations was passed by a 46–0 vote on January 25.

Within a ten-day period in May, 1921, Governor Sproul signed into law four measures affecting State Police operations. The first, Act 234, P.L. 550, May 11, permitted appeals from State Police orders and decisions relative to fire prevention. The second, Act 279, P.L. 657, May 16, ordered State Police personnel and all law enforcement agencies to report stolen vehicles to the State Highway Department. The third, Act 297, P.L. 847, May 17, authorized State Police personnel to arrest for shooting at targets or random. The fourth, and most important to State Police operations, was Act 386, P.L. 1061, May 21, creating a School

Troop, adjusting service pay, and increasing the complement to 421 officers and men—an increase of 6.

The school troop was to consist of:

1 Captain at $2,400 annual salary
2 Lieutenants at $1,800 annual salary
1 Sergeant at $1,380 annual salary
2 Corporals at $1,320 annual salary

The enactment provided for a service pay of $60 yearly after the first year of service, and an additional $60 yearly for continuous service for each of the following five years. Again, service pay was not to apply to the superintendent or his deputy.

Captain Herbert Smith was trnasferred to the school at Newville on May 21, 1921, to become the school troop's first commandant. Lieutenant Paul B. Stout was promoted to captain, and filled Smith's vacancy at Greensburg. Smith's initial staff included First Sergeant William E. Rucker, and Corporals Joseph O'Boyle, August Ahlquist, and Alfred W. Northacker.

To review the changes at departmental headquarters, the following roster provides a better understanding of the build-up of administrative forces:

Executive Office

Superintendent—Lynn G. Adams
Deputy Superintendent—William E. Mair
Statistician—Carroll B. Price
Chief Clerk—Silvus Overmiller
Supervising Clerk—Guy E. Reichard
Stenographer—Chester E. Shuler
Clerks—Enos L. Mowrer and Carl A. Knorr

Bureau of Fire Protection

Chief—C. M. Wilhelm
Assistant Chief—Charles D. Wolfe
Investigator—William F. Traeger

Bureau of Criminal Identification & Information

Chief—Wilson C. Price
Assistant Chief—William F. Hoffman
Clerk—Raymond C. Smith

Silvus Overmiller, a native of Stewartstown, York County, was born November 23, 1884, and enlisted January 6, 1909. He was promoted to corporal at Troop B in 1917, and to sergeant in 1919. After his discharge and appointment as bookkeeper and stenographer early in 1920, Overmiller was transferred to headquarters to fill the chief clerk position left vacant by Walter J. Fisher's departure.

Chester E. Shuler, a native of Montgomery Ferry, Perry County, was born August 3, 1894, and employed as a stenographer in January, 1920. He was to become Adams' personal and trusted secretary for seventeen years.

William F. Hoffman, a native of Valencia, Butler County, was born in 1889, and enlisted October 9, 1911. Assigned to Troop D, he was promoted to corporal in 1917, and sergeant in 1918. In April, 1921, he was discharged and transferred to headquarters as Price's assistant chief.

Electing to transfer from the abolished State Fire Marshal's Office to the State Police were two key figures, Charles D. Wolfe, of Williamsport, and William F. Traeger, of Altoona.

In April, 1921, the operations of the BCI & I were expanded, and the following field men were transferred to that agency to augment its work force:

Sergeant Charles Kunz, Troop E
Private Frank A. Hershey, Troop A
Private Thomas H. Doty, Troop B
Corporal Robert L. Evans, Troop C
Corporal Edward C. Bergan, Troop D
Private William P. Henchel, Troop E

A month later Bergan was returned to Troop D, and replaced by Private Martin V. Law of the same troop.

In 1921, it was officially noted that Dr. Frank F. D. Reckord was the department's examining surgeon, and Dr. Frank H. McCarthy departmental veterinarian.

Adams, in March, 1921, set up a formal procedure for the conduct of courts-martial, and in mid-year ordered all troop commanders to set aside accommodations for the use of BCI & I personnel at the troop level.

Later that year, Adams issued an order to overcome any misunderstanding about reinstatement by requiring the following statement to be included in all resignations where the full enlistment period was not observed: "I realize that, through this resignation, I am violating my contract to serve the State faithfully for a period of two years. I never expect to be reinstated with the Pennsylvania State Police Force." There were exceptions made in the case of ill-health, or other compelling and acceptable circumstances.

Adams' general orders throughout his early years reflect his deep

concern for the outstanding services of his men, and his desire to acknowledge these deeds by special awards. Numerous citations were
presented for valor and exceptional performances.

In 1921 Adams prepared an information sheet which was available
for men interested in a State Police career. Because of its importance
to a better understanding of Adams and his recruiting program, the
content is quoted in full:

Sir:—The following information is furnished for the
benefit of prospective members of the Pennsylvania State
Police Force:

The Force is composed of five troops each consisting of
one Captain, one Lieutenant, one First Sergeant, five
Sergeants, eight Corporals, one Blacksmith with the rank of
Corporal and one Saddler with the rank of Corporal, and
sixty-five Privates, enlisted for a period of two years. The
First Sergeants receive a salary of $1,500 a year; Sergeant,
$1,380 a year; Corporals, $1,320 a year, and the Privates,
$1,200 a year during their first enlistment, with an increase in
pay of $5.00 per month during second continuous enlistment,
and an additional increase of $5.00 per month during a third
continuous enlistment. The State supplies uniforms, arms,
and equipment, but the men are required to board themselves.

For the sake of discipline and to obtain the highest state
of efficiency in the Force, as well as a matter of economy to
the men, suitable barracks have been rented, equipped with
all modern improvements, electric lights, baths, steam heat,
etc., and the men are provided with bedsteads, mattresses,
blankets, sheets, kit trunks, cooking utensils, mess outfit, etc.
The men run their own mess, the cost of which is prorated,
and averages about $18.00 per month per man. Expenses are
paid by the Commonwealth when men are on detached
service.

Recruits are enlisted on probation for four months on full
pay, when, if their service is satisfactory, the enlistment is
extended to complete the two years.

Promotions are made absolutely on merit. After one
year's faithful service all men are eligible to take the examination for promotion to fill vacancies in the higher grades.

The duties are principally mounted patrol work, day and
night, enforcing the criminal law, fish, game and forestry
laws, and such other duties as may be ordered.

Applicants are required to pass a physical and mental
examination, be able to ride, of good moral character,
between the ages of twenty-one and forty years, over five feet

six inches in stocking feet, and should forward with their application, at least three letters of recommendation as to moral character and discharge certificates, which will be returned by registered mail.

Members of the United States Army Reserve or National Guard are not considered as applicants for positions on the Pennsylvania State Police Force until honorably discharged.

The Pennsylvania State Police Force requires men of the highest type. Measure yourself and determine your fitness by the following standards:

1. Can you give references as to your moral character?

2. Can you disregard partisan criticism or face death in order to perform your duty?

3. Have you a physique that will permit you to undergo a strict course of training and unusual hardship in the performance of duty?

4. Have you sufficient self-control to refrain from personal vengeance when you are personally insulted and assaulted while in the performance of duty?

5. Do you believe that it is the duty of a police man to enforce the law regardless of class, color or creed?

6. If you sign a contract to serve two years in the Pennsylvania State Police Force, will you do it, and give the best service in your power?

The Board of Buildings and Grounds, ever since the passage of Act 179 creating the fifth troop destined for Harrisburg, was busily engaged in securing funds to build a troop headquarters building and stables for Troop E. Land was secured at 20th and Herr Streets, Harrisburg (Susquehanna Township), and funds were appropriated by the general assembly for the stables. Funds for the barracks building were to follow.

A stables building, constructed of brick, was completed in 1921. A dispute, however, developed in the general assembly, and funds for the new barracks were withheld in favor of allowing the State Police to lease a new building instead. Pending the implementation of the latter plan, Troop E headquarters remained in Lancaster. A substation was established at Harrisburg, and the personnel under the supervision of Sergeant Joseph Merrifield were quartered on the second floor of the new stables building, which was intended for feed and supplies storage. Adams lamented the fact that his horses were better accommodated than his men insofar as housing was concerned in the Harrisburg area. The stable building, without heat and essential accommodations, was no place for winter quarters, and the men were moved to the Progress Hotel, owned and operated by Tony Harlacher, to await the movement of troop headquarters from Lancaster to Harrisburg. This latter movement was not to be made until 1924.

A brief review of the building situation indicated that the Greensburg barracks was suitable, but had suffered considerable damage due to mine cavings; the Wyoming barracks was outgrown, and additional space was needed; the old factory building at Pottsville was "almost unserviceable," and money was being spent to make the building "barely habitable." The high sick leave rate at Pottsville was blamed on building conditions. Troop E, Lancaster, was occupying an antiquated, unsuited farm house, pending better facilities at Harrisburg. Troop D, Butler, alone, was considered satisfactory. Regarding the school facilities at Newville, Adams admitted that the main building was "makeshift at best," and "an old hotel much in disrepair." On the brighter side, "It is hoped that at some future date the Department will be able to supply a building especially adapted to needs of this important part of the service."

In his biennial report for 1920–1921 to the governor, Adams made some interesting observations:

> During the past two years, there has been a steady improvement in the personnel, both in regard to the physical and mental training of the men. A higher standard of physical requirements has been established, and a very thorough course of instruction carried out at the school. The turnover of personnel has been necessarily large. Many men enlist in the State Police through the spirit of adventure and leave the service after completing the regular two-year period of enlistment. Others find the discipline too severe, the work too hazardous and the compensation too small. The largest contributory factor is that men trained in State Police work are in great demand as heads of police departments in towns and corporations where they often receive one hundred to two hundred percent more compensation than they could expect to receive from the State.

Adams described the school as an important facility "for the preliminary instruction of recruits and advanced instruction of men of the Force who aspire to promotion to the higher grades, and where the following courses of instruction were covered: criminal procedure; criminal law; motor vehicle, game, fish and forestry laws; investigation and reporting of crimes; police methods; traffic, crowd and mob control; geography, particularly that of Pennsylvania; transportation; highway system; industrial and political sub-divisions of the State; first-aid to injured; horsemanship, including cavalry drill; care of the horse and stable hygiene; self-defense, which includes the use of weapons, jui-jitsu, wrestling and boxing.''

Insofar as the operation of motorized equipment was concerned, Adams wrote, "There have been some accidents in connection with the use of motor vehicles, particularly motorcycles; however, considering the fact that these machines have been used in all conditions of weather and the number of miles traveled, serious accidents have been few.''

During this period, the department established another formal division to handle the mounting paperwork, the Division of Records, Accounting and Statistics. The principle of this division was advanced by Lumb during his acting stewardship. To this division "was entrusted the compilation, classification and preservation of reports of investigations, statistical data and other valuable records. Division members provided auditing, bookkeeping, reporting, stenographic and filing services.'' There were six members at Harrisburg main offices, and others were stationed at the five troops and the Newville school. According to the organizational structure, the field clerks were still functioning under daily supervision of troop officers, but were administratively under the control of the headquarters division chief at Harrisburg.

Of the BCI & I, Adams commented, "This Division of the Department of State Police provides the rural portions of the Commonwealth and the smaller cities, towns and boroughs with facilities for criminal identification and information equal to the best city police departments in the United States.''

Adams reported that the Bureau of Fire Protection "is empowered to investigate all fires of suspicious origin, make inspection of such buildings as may be deemed fire hazards, promulgate and publish such data as may be of educational value in reducing fire losses, cooperate with local communities in fire prevention, appoint fire chiefs as assistants, and keep records of all fires in the Commonwealth.'' His report praised the work accomplished by the new bureau, and its savings to the Commonwealth by reducing the number of special investigators by fifty percent "with the unusual result of work accomplished at less cost to the Commonwealth.'' He cited these comparison figures:

	Old Fire Marshal Dept. (1918)	*BFP (1921)*
Fires investigated	297	910
Orders issued for removal of fire hazards	2,044	5,143
Inspections for fire hazards	6,052	15,050
Arrests	81	138
Cost	$67,416.67	$50,912.81

The following department-wide statistics were submitted:

	1920	*1921*
Requests for assistance	10,753	15,133
Criminal arrests	8,413	12,948
Conviction rate	84.64%	86.55%
Stolen autos recovered	181	201
Patrol mileage	1,257,715	1,808,415
Value of recovered property	$459,542.34	$664,595.57

Violations of auto laws led the arrests with 1,961, followed by 1,123 arrests for disorderly conduct in 1920. In 1921, auto law violations headed the list with 3,558, followed by 1,285 for disorderly conduct. Violations of liquor laws totalled 774 in 1921, a significant jump from 218 in 1920.

Ages of those arrested were highly centered between 18 and 35, with greater concentration on the 22 to 28 age group. The highest rate involved 24-year-olds. The oldest was 80—the youngest 10.

Causes	*1920*	*1921*
Alcoholic stimulant	879	1,270
Avarice	4,011	5,550
Drugs	1	4
Lust	621	627
Recklessness	1,738	4,289
Revenge	991	1,026
Subnormal mentality	172	142
	8,413	12,908
First offenders	7,809	11,798
Second offenders	207	178
Habitual criminals	397	932
	8,413	12,908
White	7,648	12,162
Black	765	746
	8,413	12,908
Male	7,785	12,162
Female	628	746
	8,413	12,908

	1920	*1921*
Married	3,454	5,767
Single	4,959	7,141
	8,413	12,908

Broken down by nationality, the Americans numbered 13,955 for the two-year period. The Polish figure of 1,557 ran second with the 1,517 Italian arrests closely following. Blacks placed fourth on the list with 1,487 arrests. The classification of those arrested by occupation was headed by laborers, miners, merchants, chauffeurs, farmers, and students, in that order.

In reviewing the outstanding work of the Department, Adams had this to say, "One realizes that none of the 370 (average number on the Force during the two-year period) men has been idle. There are numbers of instances where members of the Force have remained constantly on duty for forty-eight hours or more, and twenty-four-hour stretches of duty are very common." It is to be noted that this evidence of dedication to duty continued unabated for many more years until the five-day work week was officially instituted by Commissioner E. Wilson Purdy in 1963. Duty time was further reduced through labor relations negotiations in the late 1960s and early 1970s between the governor's office and the Fraternal Order of Police.

Back in 1918, Lumb had recommended a statistician to "gather statistics that a force of this size is expected to have available at all times, such as percentages of crime caused by alcoholic beverages, drugs, passion, etc., percentages of crimes according to classification, according to age, according to sex, nationality and many other facts which libraries and students of social problems are constantly seeking." Lumb's desire to have the State Police actively engaged in such statistical reporting to satisfy a demand was meeting with success.

Field Complement

Men available Jan. 1, 1920	351	Men availabe Jan. 1, 1921	340
On military leave	1	Enlisted	326
Enlisted	269		—
	269		666
	621	Separations	264
Separations	277	Trans. to Hdqrs.	10
Trans. to Hdqrs.	4		— 274
	— 281		
	—	Available Dec. 31, 1921	392
Available Dec. 31, 1920	340		

Separations

	1920	*1921*
Better-paying jobs	117	35
Expiration of enlistment	11	7
Death	—	3
Disciplinary action	65	77
Probationary dismissals	62	132
Desertions	22	10
	277	264

The comparatively high number of separations for "Disciplinary action" and "Probationary dismissals" clearly indicated the administration's low tolerance for misbehavior and below-standard performance during and after probationary status, despite the urgency of maintaining a full complement.

This format of reporting statistics by way of the biennial reporting procedure was to remain unchanged for more than a decade.

Population of Pennsylvania

1905	6,983,615
1906	7,119,914
1907	7,256,213
1908	7,392,509
1909	7,528,812
1910	7,665,111
1911	7,770,602
1912	7,876,092
1913	7,981,584
1914	8,087,077
1915	8,192,568
1916	8,298,058
1917	8,403,543
1918	8,509,034
1919	8,614,528
1920	8,720,017
1921	8,845,017

Operational Cost With Average Cost Per Capita

1905	$73,479.67	.0105
1906	213,787.51	.0300
1907	245,282.79	.0338
1908	251,689.31	.0340

Operational Cost With Average Cost Per Capita

1909	241,757.38	.0321
1910	269,153.79	.0351
1911	299,253.11	.0385
1912	309.050.32	.0392
1913	324,876.68	.0407
1914	307,678.98	.0380
1915	325,701.74	.0398
1916	335,595.90	.0404
1917	471,844.50	.0561
1918	513,481.02	.0603
1919	703,363.17	.0816
1920	850,836.23	.0984
1921	926,030.09	.1048

Miscellaneous Statistics

Year	Average Number of Men	Number of Arrests	Average Cost Per Arrest	Percentage of Time on Strike Duty
1905	13			
1906	195	808	$264.58	24.59%
1907	216	4,388	55.90	9.51
1908	221	5,028	50.06	8.33
1909	209	3,799	63.64	12.75
1910	217	2,983	90.24	35.25
1911	200	2,425	123.40	34.77
1912	222	1,144	270.15	23.57
1913	221	1,960	165.75	16.46
1914	225	2,098	146.66	12.30
1915	228	3,027	107.60	9.35
1916	224	2,827	118.71	55.66
1917	258	5,255	89.79	0.5
1918	299	10,017	51.25	0.0
1919	342	7,797	90.21	11.4
1920	404	8,413	101.13	1.6
1921	443	12,948	71.59	0.0027

Manpower for Special Services

	1920	1921
Bureau of Fire Protection	19	20
Bureau of Ciminal Identification and Information	3	10
	22	30

Personnel Statistics

Year	Enlistments	Discharges
1905	164	2
1906	112	74
1907	109	99
· 1908	68	70
1909	127	124
1910	149	136
1911	66	63
1912	74	75
1913	74	75
1914	55	49
1915	46	56
1916	130	131
1917	210	111
1918	108	134
1919	247	189
1920	269	277
1921	326	264

Authorized Complement

Year	Headquarters	Field Forces	Total
1905–1916	4	228	232
1917–1918	4	330	334
1919	5	415	420
1920	44	415	459
1921	58	421	479

When Katherine Mayo's *Mounted Justice* appeared in print in 1922, she made this observation:

> When *Justice To All* went to press, the only State Police Forces in the true sense of the term, on this continent, were the royal Northwest Mounted, the Pennsylvania State Police, and the Texas Rangers. Today, in addition to those three, we have the State Police Forces of New York, Massachusetts, Connecticut, New Jersey, Maryland, West Virginia, Colorado and Michigan, with strongly developed movements in other Commonwealths. On October 11th last (1921) the Commanding Officers of these Forces allied themselves for cooperation, in an Association of State Police Commanders. On February 27, 1922, that body held its first regular meeting—an occasion rich in promise for the weal of the Nation.

It was plainly seen at this point that the idea of a sovereign state relying upon a state constabulary to uphold its laws was "catching on." Pennsylvania's noble experiment had passed the test of effectiveness and endurance and, in so doing, had set the stage for every state in the Union. The Association of State Police Commanders was the frontrunner of inter-state and international organizations designed to facilitate cooperation between agencies in pursuit of their common purposes.

The Prohibition Enforecement Act, introduced by Representative A. J. Volstead, and passed by Congress in October, 1919, was having its effect upon the Pennsylvania scene in the early 1920s, as it was everywhere else in the nation. The manpower-hungry state constabulary, already pressed to enforce the laws of Pennsylvania and maintain safety on its highways, was now called upon to aid federal authorities in coping with the sale of illegal liquor. Statistics will be cited later to show the extent of State Police involvement in prohibition enforcement.

Prohibition was not a happy state of affairs from the general public's point of view, and it didn't take long for bootleggers to become well-organized enough to satisfy the nation's thirst. The success of bootlegers was, to a significant degree, made possible by "cooperating" public officials. Adams, hell-bent on having the laws enforced without fear or favor, abhorred the thought of police involvement in protection and the bribes that were offered.

It was once stated by a family member that any account of Adams' interaction with the Pennsylvania State Police Force, if it was to have authenticity, must consider his hot temper and low tolerance for fools, crooks, politicians, and people who didn't agree with him. Adams was extremely cuatious during the prohibition period to protect his reputation. At one time, for instance, he had an inter-office telephone hookup between his office and his secretary's. If a visitor to his office engaged in any discussions which might lead to embarassment or violation of the law, Adams would depress a foot switch to alert Chester A. Shuler, his secretary. At his end, Shuler would pick up the conversation and transcribe it from stenographic notes for Adams' safekeeping. This, Adams felt, was his insurance against false charges. The prohibition days were trying ones for him, and he wanted no part of the dishonesty in government that accompanied those years. Adams headed the state constabulary all through the fourteen years of prohibition, and emerged with a clean slate.

Adams was described as "a very hard-nosed opponent of any politician who sought to influence the activities of the State Police in any way that could be remotely construed as improper by strict standards." This inflexible stand of his was to lead to certain difficulties during his tenure, particularly with regard to Senate confirmations.

Adams was an active outdoor sportsman, and very much interested in pistol marksmanship. Mid-way through 1922, he established a program for revolver-firing training and efficiency and, with it, an inter-troop revolver match geared to generate keen competition among the field forces. As early as 1911, Adams had recommended to Groome that the men engage in quarterly qualifications instead of annually "to improve marksmanship and ease in handling firearms." Groome was called upon by Adams to serve as a judge for one of these early revolver matches. Groome graciously accepted the invitation and the opportunity to renew old acquaintances. The first officially recognized "Champion Revolver Shot of the Pennsylvania State Police Force" was Private Leo Gratcofsky, of Troop B, Wyoming. Lieutenant Albert Carlson, also of Troop B, was the first to win the Superintendent's Match. These awards followed the first matches held at the training school in August, 1922.

On August 25, 1922, Adams issued a confidential special order officially bestowing on Deputy Superintendent Mair the rank of major. This was the initial use of that rank in constabulary history. By virtue of his military rank, Adams was already commonly known as Major Adams. This rank was held exclusively for the two top positons until 1938, when its use was expanded.

During the calendar year of 1922, records indicate that twenty-seven convicted murderers died in the state's electric chair at the Rockview Penitentiary. Executions were held in every month of that year except for August. This was the highest annual figure recorded since the chair was first put to use in 1915.

In January, 1923, the constabualry forces again joined in the cermonies welcoming a new governor. Newly inaugurated was Republican Governor Gifford Pinchot, of Pike County.Pinchot renamed Adams to the post of superintendent. Adams' earlier confirmation by the Senate in 1921 carried the sweeping provisions of service "until annulled," and, in the absence of any Senate annulment action, his service was continued.

Early in 1923, it became necessary to close down the training facility at Newville. The old building was infested, and could no longer be tolerated for living quarters. The lease expired at the end of March.

Adams pulled Price away from his duties with BCI & I at headquarters to make temporary arrangements for the training school elsewhere. Price situated the school at the Pennsylvania National Guard Military Reservation at Mt. Gretna, near Colebrook. Accommodations provided there by the Department of Military Affairs consisted of tents and military field equipment. On May 1, Price was given temporary command of the school. He was supported by Lieutenants Oke R. Campbell and William E. Rucker.

The general assembly, during the 1923 session, passed four measures of interest to the State Police. Act 183, P.L. 283, May 19, cited duties of the State Police relative to the state's anti-lynching law. Act 230, P.L. 425, May 24, authorized the State Highway Commissioner to appoint employes to enforce provisions of the Motor Vehicle Code. Act 274, P.L. 498, June 7, enacted the state's first Administrative Code with its sweeping changes at all levels of government. Act 296, P.L. 718, June 14, authorized "designated officers" of the State Highway Department to enforce the Motor Vehicle Code.

Acts 230 and 296, in effect, created the state Highway Patrol which was often recommended to take over the responsiblity for safety on the state's expanding highway system in the absence of additional manpower needed by the State Police to do the job adequately. The story of the State Highway Patrol will be reserved for separate chapters. It is sufficient here to point out that in 1937 the general assembly was to see fit to merge the State Highway Patrol and the Pennsylvania State Police, and make of it a new department—the Pennsylvania Motor Police.

Act 274 had more impact directly on State Police operations. It abolished the Bureau of Fire Protection as a specific agency within the State Police. The department was to continue with the bureau's established responsibilities, but there would be no separate budget or other special recognition. The title, "Chief of the Bureau of Fire Protection," was also abolished. The superintendent was free to appoint his own administrator, and call him whatever he wished. The same treatment was given the office of deputy superintendent. Formerly, that office was specifically given legal status, and filled by the governor. Act 274 granted the superintendent the authority to appoint his own deputy, with the approval of the governor. The name of the constabulary, under this same act, was officially changed from the Department of State Police to the Pennsylvania State Police. Although the constabulary was increasingly known as the Pennsylvania State Police, it was not until the passage of act 274 that this name was given official life.

Another point of interest was Article IV, Section 401, of the new Administrative Code, which stated, "The Pennsylvania State Police shall consist of a superintendent, the State Police force as now or hereafter authorized by law, and such deputies, chiefs, statisticians, clerks, experts, and other assistants as the superintendent, with the approval of the Governor, shall deem necessary for the work of the force." By this provision, the general assembly was abandoning its control over specifics within the department, and allowing the executive branch to attend to its own housekeeping chores. The salary of the superintendent was also set at $6,000 a year.

Section 504, of Act 274, also changed the procedure for biennial reporting by state departments. Such reports were ordered submitted to the governor by October 1 of each even-numbered year, covering "the condition, management, and financial transactions of the department," and "such reports shall, except where impracticable, be for the two-year period ending May 31 of the year in which they are made." The transition from the 1919 requirement, involving calendar year reporting, to the 1923 change, involving fiscal year standards, created some difficulty in reconciling and presenting statistics, and other data. Reporting procedures were smoothed out in time for the period beginning June 1, 1924.

After scandalous conditions were disclosed at the state's Eastern Penitentiary, Governor Pinchot called Colonel John C. Groome back into state service by appointing him warden of the troubled prison June 10, 1923. Groome succeeded Robert J. McKenty, who had been warden many years. With this appointment came a renewed association with the Pennsylvania State Police. Groome's official staff at the penitentiary was recruited from members of the constabulary, who were known to Groome as excellent performers. One of his early choices was Captain Herbert Smith, who joined Groome as deputy warden July 18, 1923, and was promoted to chief deputy in October. The confidence Groome displayed in Smith's administrative capabilities surfaced early.

The correspondence between Groome and his successor, Lynn G. Adams, indicated that Groome's recruitment program was open and did receive Adams' full cooperation. This relationship was closely indicative of the respect Adams held for his former boss. Were this not a friendly relationship accusations of "pirating" would have followed closely on the heels of any attempt to persuade top-flight constabulary personnel to leave their posts for penitentiary service.

Groome made many changes at the prison to improve general conditions, security, and reduce idleness. He continued as warden until Febraury, 1928, when he resigned to become vice president of the Boca Raton Corporation, a Florida land development firm. Ill-health, however, cut short his association with that organization. Nonetheless, he did accept Governor John S. Fisher's appointment to the Eastern Penitentiary's board of trustees in January, 1929, his final government post.

Smith, Groome's top aide, officially took over the warden's post in January, 1928, prior to Groome's actual departure. Smith went on to serve as warden for seventeen years, bringing his career there to a close on August 31, 1945, at a time when the United States and its allies were still celebrating the end of World War II. He was then 64.

Training school operations at Colebrook were halted during the summer of 1923, and Price was relieved of these special duties. Insufficient funding made it necessary for the State Police to endure a reduced complement. State Highway Department officials, faced with the problem of organizing the State Highway Patrol, called upon Adams for support. Adams then gave Price the challenging task of putting together this new body of highway patrolmen. Price was given temporary leave from the State Police to undertake the new assignment. As it turned out, the leave was not so temporary, because Price remained with the State Highway Patrol as superintendent until the mid-1930s. Meanwhile, the responsibility for keeping the BCI & I operational passed to Assistant Chief William F. Hoffman.

Corporal Ben F. McEvoy, the school troop's quartermaster, and Private William J. Omlor of Troop B, Wyoming, were the department's 12th and 13th to die in the line of duty. McEvoy, a thirteen-year veteran, was killed on September 21, 1923, as he walked along the roadway to render assistance to a stalled motorist, and was struck by an approaching vehicle. He was the department's first motor vehicle fatality. Omlor died of injuries sustained in a motorcycle accident on October 25, 1923. He was the first motorcycle fatality.

State Treasurer Charles A. Snyder, who was continually at odds with Governor Pinchot, raised an issue at year's end that could have been disastrous, if Snyder had his way. Snyder, according to a story appearing in the *Philadelphia Evening Bulletin* December 20, 1923, and in other newspapers, claimed that Pinchot verbally informed the State Police that if a policeman should violate any other law in prosecuting the State prohibition enforcement act, and was convicted of so doing, Mr. Pinchot would extend the benefit of his pardon power. This controversy led to Snyder's inquiry into the status of the Pennsylvania State Police, and his later claim that the Administrative Code of 1923 actually abolished the State Police. Snyder threatened to withhold State Police paychecks after January 1, 1924.

Apparently the state treasurer was informed by his counsels that his allegations about the illegal status of the State Police were not founded. In any case, nothing further was heard of this matter, and the paychecks continued on schedule.

In his biennial report, Adams again allowed his concern for prohibition enforcement to leak through,

Discipline has been up to the usual high standard. A number of men have been dismissed from the Force by sentence of court-martial, but these cases have been relatively few. One wonders that there have been so when the temptation which these men have been called to face are taken into consideration. There are records of men having been offered bribes amounting to from one to five years' salary to suppress evidence in a single case. The moral and physical courage of the personnel of the Pennsylvania State Police is not surpassed, if equalled, by any other organization in the world.

The size of the Force was reduced below the strength provided by the 1919 and 1921 legislatures. This was the direct result of reduced appropriations for State Police operations. In effect, the general assembly could set back the State Police any time it wanted to by this simple method of restricting its funding. The effects of reduced manpower, however, were statistically minimized by the longer hours and higher workloads undertaken by the men on duty. "The police problem of the Commonwealth demands a full quota of men and an adequate expense appropriation, and it is earnestly hoped that the next session of the legislature will remedy the present shortage," Adams reported.

In defense of his argument for more men, Adams stated further:

Closely scheduled railroad trains, inter-urban trolleys, automobiles and good highways have made the rural inhabitant an easy victim of the criminal. The criminal may now prey on rural districts and hide in the cities. In Pennsylvania, there are hundreds of unincorporated villages made up of alien mine and factory workers that are almost entirely without competent police protection. During the period covered by this report, a consistent endeavor has been made to cover this area with a system of substations consisting of from 3 to 5 men and patrols on foot, horses, motorcycle and automobile. The importance of the uniformed patrolman can not be easily over estimated. He is the eye of the law and to the potential criminal is a visible arm of the law.

With the exception of the school troop, each troop maintained from five to ten substations which were located at various points and moved about from time to time as the needs of the service required. It is noted that the troop commanders, with the superintendent's approval, apparently had no difficulty in making these substation changes compared to the modern day difficulties with politicians and community pressures facing top adminstrators at every turn.

Once again Adams hit at prohibition, "The greatest problem that has confronted the State Police during this period has been in the enforcement of the prohibition laws." Here are some of his observations:

1. Bootleggers can afford the best legal talent versus elected county prosecutors.
2. Many county officials, judges and district attorneys are not in favor of prohibition and their attitudes reflect upon their official acts.
3. Where anti-prohibiton feelings run high, no jury will convict.
4. Juries believe the testimony of bootleggers while setting aside the evidence offered by corroborated testimony of two State Policemen whose character and reputation are beyond reproach.
5. Inadequate fines.
6. Bootleggers pay fines and continue in business, charging fines to "overhead."

Adams' report was especially critical of the operators of the Keystone Brewery, at Dunmore, and the Jenners Brewery, at Jenners. Some headway was made in prosecution, the report states, "But probably the most significant indication is the steady increase in the price of illegal liquor."

Silvus J. Overmiller, on June 1, 1923, was appointed departmental statistician, replacing Carroll B. Price, who resigned. Before the year's end, Adams formed a Division of Secretarial, Accounting, Statistical and Supplies Services, and placed Overmiller in charge with the title of Executive Secretary. There were twenty-nine men in that division—eight at headquarters, four in each troop, and one at the training school.

Adams continued to praise the work of the BCI & I, "giving it a value that can not be measured in dollars and cents."

He noted the efforts of the Bureau of Fire Protection (an identification Adams chose to use) to cope with Pennsylvania's fire losses of some $25 million in 1922 and a slightly less figure in 1923. According to Adams, 75 percent of that waste was believed preventable. In 1922, the bureau investigated 730 fires with ninety-three arrests. In 1923, there were 437 fires investigated with fifty-three arrests.

During this period, the bureau undertook a project to standardize fire hose couplings in Pennsylvania, and recommended a national standard. The bureau cautioned the public about the hazards of improperly installed aerials for radio reception. Some aerials were strung across power lines. The short-circuiting of radio equipment to batteries was cited as another cause for fires. The new age of radio had arrived. The bureau was also instrumental in securing the enactment of ordinances prohibiting or regulating the sale and use of fireworks.

Another innovation in police services was credited to the Pennsylvania State Police in 1923 when the department installed the nation's first statewide police radiotelegraph system. The system, linking low-frequency radiotelegraph facilities at Harrisburg, Butler, Greensburg, Wyoming, and Pottsville, remained operational until 1947.

The network's key station at Harrisburg was located at 20th and Herr Streets, to the rear of the new stable building. A small operations building was built to accommodate the telegraphers. Twin antenna towers were erected on the site. These towering landmarks were symbols of State Police progress in communications for almost a quarter of a century before they were dismantled in favor of improved technological equipment and a new system.

	1922	*1923*
Requests for assistance	19,920	22,773
Investigations	26,916	25,902
Arrests	14,290	12,245
Stolen automobiles recovered	167	140
Percentage of time on strike duby	35.98	.0038
Patrol mileage	1,907,545	1,791,914
Value of recovered property	$298,313.61	$243,116.60
Average cost per capita	0.1088	0.0876
Average cost per arrest	$63.83	$64.82
Average arrests, per man	39.31	41.93
Operational costs	$912,148.17	$793.687.86

*   *   *

Violations of auto laws	4,525	2,476
Disorderly conduct	2,290	1,386
Violation of state liquor laws	1,350	3,875
Gambling	740	1,177
Larceny	436	197
Assault and battery	425	237
Cruelty to animals	11	392

*   *   *

Youngest arrest	10	10
Oldest arrested	90	99
Highest age group	28	28
	(713 arrests)	(556 arrests)

Prohibition era raid at Dunmore, 1924 (Courtesy of Pennsylvania State Police)

During 1923, the following property was confiscated in connection with illegal liquor operations:

Automobiles	236
Trucks	176
Whiskey, quarts	91,340
Alcohol, gallons	11,228
Wine, gallons	32,154
Beer, cases	3,926
Beer, quarter-barrels	29,313
Mash, barrels	2,908
Cider, gallons	1,730
Stills	761
Miscellaneous, bottles	185

During the reporting period, 193 men were recruited. This figure was offset by a loss of 363 men, 159 of whom left for better-paying positions. There were only 290 men available for duty at the close of the period, a fact that bothered Adams no end.

The growth of the statistical staff at headquarters was reflected in the abundance of statistical tables offered. The State Police continued with attempts to classify crimes by cause, age, sex, nationality, race, occupation, and marital status. New statistical tables were developed for fines collected, case dispositions, assistance rendered and county breakdowns on some of these statistics, the value of which might be questioned. The remarkable factor is the importance attached to work accountability by Adams at that time.

CHAPTER VIII

Major Lynn G. Adams

1924—1930

Another milestone was reached in the amazing lifestory of former Captain George F. Lumb who remained a practicing attorney in Harrisburg. He was admitted to the bar of the state Superior Court March 13, 1924.

During his earlier years in the legal profession, Lumb, an observant and understanding man that he was, witnessed the difficulties of the large Italian community in Harrisburg with legal matters. Determined to assist the Italians in their plight, resulting mainly from a language barrier, Lumb learned their language well enough to represent them in and out of court. It was said of him that, "He, indeed, did have quite a few Italian clients who greatly liked and respected him."

Lumb prospered as an attorney, and shared offices with Senator George L. Reed in the State Theatre Building. For a time he was special counsel for the Harrisburg Railways Company. Not to overlook his many other activities, Lumb was a past master of Robert Burns Lodge No. 464, F. and A. M., and of the Harrisburg Lodge No. 301, I.O.O.F. He was past president of the Harrisburg Rotary Club and Rotary district governor. Lumb was described as an eloquent speaker by those who recall his appearances on the rostrum.

Pennsylvania State Police Training School, Hershey (Courtesy of Pennsylvania State Police)

As a citizen, Lumb was particularly interested in the welfare of boys, and for many years taught a class of boys at the Grace Methodist Church Sunday school at Harrisburg. As a husband, Lumb devoted much time to the tender care of his ailing wife, who fell gravely ill with tuberculosis in 1922. This situation placed a tremendous burden on Lumb, both financially and physically. Nontheless, as a father, he was a guiding light for his only son, Fred, who recalled that in spite of the demands upon his father's time. "He remained a wonderful father to me, spending ample time with me. He taught me cribbage, seven-up, how to shoot, the fundamentals of boxing, the value of exercise, care in grooming, gardening, and the value and rewards of being intellectually curious."

Back at the capitol, Superintendent Adams, bent on restoring the services of the school troop, was fortunate in acquiring the use of a large, frame building on Cocoa Avenue, Hershey, in the spring of 1924. The building was owned by the Hershey Estates, whose officers allowed the State Police to occupy and use this facility, its auxiliary buildings, and grounds with a rent-free agreement. This arrangement continued for thirty-six years until the State Police in 1960 moved to a newly-constructed, state-owned building, also situated in Hershey. Until the kitchen and dining room facilities could be established in the newly-acquired building, the school troop personnel and recruits shared their meals with the State Highway Patrol whose training school was located in the Hershey Inn, less than a mile away.

Other important moves were made in 1924. Troop E headquarters was moved from Lancaster and temporarily quartered in the new stable building at 20th and Herr Streets, Harrisburg. When efforts by the Bureau of Buildings and Grounds to purchase the Progress Hotel failed, plans were approved to have a new building built by the Allison Hill Real Estate Company, of Harrisburg, and leased to the State Police. The leased building, located at 18th and Herr Streets, Harrisburg, was completed and occupied by Troop E November 1. Five years passed before Troop E, originally intended for Harrisburg in 1919, arrived finally at its destination.

Troop C, located in the old, dilapidated three-story, factory building for so many years, which was at last declared unsanitary and no longer habitable, moved to improved quarters in West Reading. Reading was the original site for Troop C, back in 1905.

Records indicate that Adams instituted a competitive examination program for advancement of lieutenants to captain. Heretofore, exams were held only up to the rank of lieutenant. The first exam for aspiring lieutenants was conducted August 24, 1924.

According to an account by Chester A. Shuler, Adams' secretary, the month of August was eventful for another reason, "Adams and I had a miraculous escape from serious injury or death. We had just been sitting in his office and a few minutes after we left there was a thunderous explosion followed by a great clattering of broken glass and a mighty thud. The end of an air drill tank, just outside the capitol wing where work was progressing, exploded and was hurled through the large window of his (Adams') office, thence through the door and clipped off one of the big chandeliers. It fell to the floor at a spot where all the captains had assembled the day before a conference. Glass was showered over his private office. It was a narrow escape for several." Deputy Superintendent Mair was also close at hand when this accident occured on August 14.

The year 1924 saw the deaths of three more troopers in the line of duty. Private Francis L. Haley, Troop E. was shot and killed as he pursued a bank robber on October 14. Sergeant Edwin F. Haas, Troop B quartermaster, was accidentally shot on Ocotober 17. Private Bernard S. C. McElroy, Troop D, died on December 20, from injuries sustained in a motorcycle accident. They were the 14th, 15th and 16th added to the list of those who gave their precious lives to public service.

In 1925, the State Police needed facilities for maintaining and repairing the ever-growing fleet of motorized equipment which consisted mainly of Harley-Davidson motorcycles. A repair shop was established in one of the Highway Department's metal sheds situated on grounds adjacent to the new Troop E stable building. Assigned to duties there were Privates Frank R. Cooch, Guy E. Heckman, Miles L. Motter and Raymond Boxler. Whenever occasions demanded it, Heckman doubled as an aide to Adams. The increasing reliance upon motorized equipment to meet the demands for service was met with a decreasing importance of the horses. To reflect this changing set of circumstances, the stalls in the west wing of the Troop E stable building were removed, the roof was braced, and the floor cemented. This remodelled area then provided indoor storage for twelve passenger cars.

The 1925 session of the general assembly produced only one measure affecting State Police operations. Passed was Act 177, P.L. 314, April 27, amending the Administrative Code and specifying the appointment procedure and term of the superintendent, and increasing the salaries and service pay for the field forces.

The act specified that, "The Superintendent of the Pennsylvania State Police shall be appointed by the Governor for a term of four years from the third Tuesday of January next following the election of a Governor and until his successor shall have been appointed and qualified." Longevity, or service pay, was increased to $120 after the first, second, and third years of service, and another $60 a year after the fourth, and fifth years.

At mid-year, Private Lewis M. Whitecotton competed successfully for single honors during the annual pistol matches, and was proclaimed the department's new revolver champion.

During the early years of prohibition, Adams authorized the formation of a special detail of troopers to gather evidence and conduct raids. The men assigned to this detail were expert motorcyclists, and capable of moving swiftly to any point in the state. They were familiarly known as the "Flying Squadron." The squadron's record for effective enforcement was widely acclaimed. The squadron, however, was not to remain a separate unit for long. Adams, more cautious than ever to avoid the possibility of bribes and misdirection of the department's enforcement program, decided to disband the Flying Squadron before strong temptations could overtake its members.

On December 10, 1925, Private Bertram Beech, Troop D, Butler, became the seventeenth to die in the line of duty, and the fourth to be killed in a motor vehicle accident. The vehicle in which Beech was a passenger collided with a Baltimore & Lake Erie Railroad freight train at McCoytown Crossing, Pine Township, Mercer County.

Before the year was up, Adams undertook a new program for identifiying the members of the force, who at this point carried their badges as their sole identifiers. This was an acceptable practice for men in uniform, but lacking insofar as plainclothes personnel were concerned. To provide an effective backup identification system, Adams ordered an identification card prepared for each man, bearing his photograph, thumb-print, and signature. The card was authenticated by Adams' signature, and the department's seal. The fold-type document was mounted in a leather pocket case for easy carrying. This same method of identification, with slight modification, was continued in use until 1975 when plastic laminated cards with color photographs were substituted by Commissioner James D. Barger.

The close of the year was to see another change in top management. Deputy Superintendent William E. Mair resigned his post, effective December 31, to accept appointment as chief security officer for Westinghouse at Pittsburgh. The new appointment carried, among other benefits, a better salary. For the next six months, Adams was to serve without the direct support of a deputy.

Early in February, 1926, Adams ordered a reapportionment of his troops and reset their boundaries.

In his biennial report for the period ending May 31, 1926, Adams once again was critical of reduced appropriations which forced the State Police to operate with an average of only 281 filled positions. "This shortage in number has been a severe handicap to the operations of this Force as will be shown from time to time in the body of this report. Every attempt has been made to make up in quality what has been lacking in quantity and as a consequence the character of the personnel has been kept up to a very high standard."

Continuing, Adams stated, "The Training School, at Hershey, has clearly demonstrated its value not only as a means of educating the police officer as to the technicalities of his work, but also as a means of determining the personal character of the recruit. Never in the history of the Force has it had to pass through such a trying period as the last four years." Continuing instruction and drill customarily carried on in the field was seriously impaired by extra work and the shortage of manpower in the face of prohibition, and other heavy demands for services.

Adams, still proud of the loyalty and honesty of his field forces, deplored the temptations thrown into the faces of police officers everywhere by the circumstances of prohibition. He lost no time in citing his men for meritorious services and valor as a public manifestation of his gratitude.

Although Adams commented on the temptation of prohibition bribes that faced his field forces, he made no official mention of those that he himself faced occasionally. On one such occasion, Adams was approached by a well-known public figure who implied that it would be worth $150,000 to an eastern bootlegger to have his illegal operations overlooked. The offer was made cleverly enough to avoid arrest for attempted bribery. Nonetheless, the message was clear to Adams—and just as swiftly put aside. Adams held in the highest esteem those who shared his obsession for honesty in the police family.

One unfortunate troop clerk, who had succumbed to bribery, was found guilty in 1926 of passing on to local bootleggers information regarding raid plans. An example was made of the clerk by having him formally drummed out of the service at a military troop formation. Thus was displayed Adams' intolerance for any dishonest member of the force.

The backlog in the courts, and lost man-hours in court attendance were highly criticized by Adams.

> The effectiveness of the organization is greatly hampered on account of the time that it is necessary for men to spend in court as witnesses. An investigation of one day may and often does result in a policeman's being held up as a witness for five or six days during preliminary hearings and court trials. There have been times during the past two years when nearly the entire Force has been removed from effective police duty in this manner. The organization should be kept strong enough to afford a reserve to meet these conditions.

Adams was complimentary about the services of his two bureaus, the BFP and the BCI & I. The BCI & I was increasing in value "as it acquires age." A total of 230 persons were identified, by way of fingerprints, as having previous arrest records. BCI & I personnel were given the additional assignment of visiting county jails and prisons to fingerprint and photograph inmates. Total individual criminal prints on file numbered about 45,000. "There is a great necessity of a definite law requiring the photographing and fingerprinting of persons arrested. The establishment of a State Bureau of Criminal Identification by a law requiring the compulsory fingerprinting of suspects and convicts and the cooperation of all police departments in the Commonwealth would be of inestimable value in law enforcement," recommended Adams.

The BFP, during the biennial period, investigated 903 fires and arrested 180 persons for arson. The bureau, now armed with authority to supervise the construction and operations of dry-cleaning and dyeing establishments, materially reduced the hazards of this industry. During this period, safety solvents were introduced to dry-cleaning to replace highly volatile and inflammable liquids. The bureau also cooperated with Penn State College researchers in an extensive farm survey, concluding that a high percentage of farm fire losses were due to spontaneous combustion of crops. A program was developed to inform farmers of methods aimed at avoiding these causes for fire.

Statistics

	Year ending May 31, 1925	Year ending May 31, 1926
Requests for assistance	21,473	21,683
Investigations	23,764	24,045
Arrests	12,269	11,342
Stolen automobiles recovered	156	192
Percentage of time on strike duty	.004	5.82
Patrol mileage	1,781,827	2,003,798
Value of stolen property recovered	$233,582.66	$256,380.91

Arrests

Liquor laws	3,513	2,717
Gambling	2,513	1,597
Disorderly conduct	1,558	2,188
Automobile laws	956	947
Cock-fighting	324	1
Larceny	296	379
Assault and battery	247	261

Causes of Crime

Alcoholic stimulants	894	997
Avarice	7,825	6,637
Drugs	2	4
Lust	414	480
Recklessness	2,694	2,716
Revenge	367	413
Subnormal mentality	73	95

Confiscated Property
Liquor Laws

Automobiles	274	177
Trucks	97	53
Stills	581	438
Whiskey, quarts	14,353	20,674
Moonshine, quarts	73,682	66,523
Alcohol, gallons	28,526	29,761
Beer, barrels	25,321	24,306

Beer, cases	4,305	3,772
Wine, gallons	31,624	33,503
Cider, gallons	6,058	7,065
Gin, quarts	1,512	622
Jamaica Ginger, quarts	6,053	745
Brandy, quarts	451	32
Miscellaneous, quarts	1,045	492
Mash, barrels	3,306	3,963
Coloring, quarts	29	38
Slot machines	—	50
Punch boards	—	36

The youngest person arrested in both years was 10. The oldest in the first period was 78—the second period 80. There were 565 30-year-olds in the first period, and 516 28-year-olds in the second period, representing the highest number in a single age group. The ratio of males to females arrested was 10 to 1. During these years, the nationality leading the list of those arrested was American, with the Italians, Polish, and Blacks following in that order. By occupation, laborers and miners continued to head the list.

Personnel Statistics

	1924–25	1925–26
Available June 1	246	274
Enlistments	224	138
	470	412
Separations	196	140
Available May 31	274	272

Separations

Better-paying positions	42	32
Expiration of enlistment	4	11
Deaths	5	1
Disciplinary action	25	27
Probationary period dismissals	118	67
Desertions	2	2

Headquarters Personnel

Available June 1	52	54
New appointments	13	14
	65	68
Separations	11	18
Available May 31	54	50

It will be recalled that Adams lost his deputy at the close of 1925. For the next six months, he managed the department's affairs without the benefit of an official assistant. On July 1, 1926, Captain Cecil M. Wilhelm was named to fill that vacant post. What prompted Adams to delay this important appointment is not clear. Wilhelm remained Adams' deputy until the Pennsylvania State Police was merged with the State Highway Patrol in mid-1937.

Following the transfer of Wilhelm from the BFP, management of that bureau fell to J. William Morgan. A title change, however, was made for Morgan. While Wilhelm was identified as the bureau's chief, Morgan was given the title of fire marshal. Authority for Adams' action was contained in the newly-adopted Administrative Code of 1923. William F. Traeger was upgraded to supervisor of investigations. Morgan and Traeger were civilian employees of the abolished State Fire Marshal's Office, and transferred to the constabulary. Their promotions in the bureau were effective July 1, 1926, as was Wilhelm's change of status.

The 1926 departmental pistol matches brought to the forefront a new champion—Captain Jacob C. Mauk. Mauk, later in his career, was to serve as deputy commissioner, and much more will be written of him.

Adams continued to express hope for a new Troop E headquarters building at Harrisburg, to be constructed by the Commonwealth next to the new stables at 20th and Herr Streets. This project, although it had at one time been given the general assembly's blessing, was never to become a reality. The general assembly was content to have Troop E operations continued in a leased facility at 18th and Herr Streets, which the troop was then occupying, and Adams could not budge the legislators from that position.

In 1927, four more troopers were killed in the line of duty. Private Claude F. Keesey of Troop C, Reading, died of injuries sustained in a motor vehicle accident on January 4. Private Thomas E. Lipka of Troop E, Harrisburg, died on April 3: he was also a victim of a motor vehicle accident. Sergeant John M. Thomas, another motor vehicle accident victim, succumbed to injuries on May 8. He had been assigned to the training school. The last of the four, Private John J. Downey of Troop A, Greensburg, was shot and killed on August 22.

The general assembly, during its 1927 session, passed three pieces of legislation affecting State Police operations. Act 270, P.L. 414, April 27, redefined and broadened the powers and duties of the State Police with regard to the recording of criminal identification data and its obligation to interstate, national and international systems and to local law enforcement agencies. Act 291, P.L. 450, April 27, redefined and broadened the department's powers and duties with respect to fire prevention. The law gave the department control over the appointment of fire chiefs and assistants, and made compulsory the reporting of fires to the State Police. Fire insurance companies and associations were also bound by law to file reports. Act 452, P.L. 886, May 11, constituted a new Vehicle Code which cited the authority of State Highway Patrolmen and at the same time enabled members of the State Police and the Highway Patrol to weigh motor vehicles and trucks.

A major effort was made in 1927 to codify all rules and regulations, and publish them for departmental use in a more orderly manner. After twenty-two years of accumulation, a system was much in need. Included in this package of rules and regulations were a number of formal lectures written by the superintendent on subjects regarding behavior and performance of duty. General Order No. 1, dated May 1, contained a lengthy list of forty-seven articles governing the enlistment, behavior, discipline, and operations of the State Police. Although the order was still burdensome in certain respects, it was an improvement. Just for the sake of pointing up some of its provisions, Article #31 stated, "Any member of the Force who shall be found guilty of having taken an active interest in politics or who has endeavored to influence the vote of any other person shall be discharged from the Force." Article #34 contained a very pointed admonishment, "Any member of this Force known to have used outside influence for the furtherance of his interest will be considered as acknowledging his incompetence, and will be dropped from the service." These articles reflect Adams' personal feelings about politics and politicians, and the need to keep his command free of political influences.

Article #33 prohibited any enlisted member from marrying without the superintendent's approval, clearly indicating the desire to keep operations as uncomplicated as possible.

Article #39 controlled public relations, "Making public of any reports, statistics or other information in connection with the Force, either in writing or conversation, except by approval of the Superintendent is prohibited.''

About this time in State Police history, giant strides were being made to keep abreast of technological developments in communications. The department had already installed a basic telegraph-typewriter system to link the troops with Harrisburg headquarters. Also operated from Harrisburg headquarters was a State Police radio station WBAK for broadcasting information of interest to the general public. Connnecting all State Police installations, too, was a system of radio communications by way of Morse code. In the area of communications, the Pennsylvania State Police again demonstrated its ability, under excellent leadership, to innovate and lay the groundwork for sister agencies to follow.

According to an article appearing in the 1928 spring issue of *The State Police Magazine,* there were in 1928 a total of sixteen states supporting state police organizations. The noble experiment of 1905 in Pennsylvania, after twenty-three years of operations, was unquestionably an example to be followed in all states sooner or later.

Adams submitted a number of recommendations to the governor in 1928, clearly showing his foresight as a police administrator. He recommended, (1) an appropriation large enough to operate at full strength, claiming that the State Police had not been able to do this since 1919, (2) an expansion of the telegraph-typewriter system to connect with substations and local police departments, (3) the regulation of police uniforms, specifying that private security personnel wear brown uniforms, all municipal police wear blue, and that dark grey be reserved for State Police, (4) the unification of the Pennsylvania State Police and the State Highway Patrol as a move to increase efficiency and reduce operational cost, (5) abolition of Coal and Iron Police by increasing the State Police complement to 1,000 men and limiting the authority of private corporation security police to the role of watchmen, and (6) the passage of a law regulating the sale of firearms and automatic weapons.

Adams' third recommendation regarding police uniforms deserves a comment here. As local police departments were established in the state, there was a natural tendency to copy the methods of the State Police even to the point of duplicating uniform wear. Adams wanted to discourage this trend and yet did not want to risk alienating local police agencies. He, like his successors, would have preferred to have the State Police uniform copyrighted and reserved for its own public image; but, this was, and still is, a preference that could never be realized without creating hard feelings. Today, more than ever before, police throughout the state resemble troopers in many respects, and are often misidentified as troopers. As changes were made in State Police uniforms through the years, it was not long before such changes would appear in other departments. Reached now is a point of no return.

In his biennial report ending May 31, 1928, Adams reminded the governor that reduced appropriations had forced him to limit his complement to 308 officers and men although the legally-established complement was set at 421. There were serious incidents of industrial strife in western Pennsylvania to which heavy commitments were made with no decrease in the demand for service in connection with criminal complaints. Adams openly admitted that his department could not meet its total obligations. To meet the industrial disturbance incidents with sufficient manpower, he established fifty-three emergency substations in the western and central areas of the state, leaving the eastern portion inadequately serviced. He reported to the governor that prohibition was still a time-occupying pursuit, nonetheless the liquor laws "have been vigorously and relentlessly enforced."

Here are some of the statistics for the two-year period ending May 31, 1928:

Activities

	1926–27	1927–28
Requests for assistance	22,273	29,694
Investigations	22,619	23,678
Criminal arrests	11,879	10,031
Stolen motor vehicles recovered	227	221
Time committed to strike duty	11.88%	38.77%
Patrol mileage	1,821,256	2,069,869
Value of stolen property recovered	$259,568	$289,363
Average cost per capita	.089	.08

Partial Arrest List

Disorderly conduct	2,406	2,283
Liquor laws	1,841	957
Gambling	1,743	746
Motor vehicle laws	968	776
Larceny	534	678
Breaking and entry	532	516
Murder	77	105
Narcotics laws	44	2

The practice of classifying crime by causes, nationality, sex,

Towers of State Police radio station WBAK, Harrisburg, 1930 (Courtesy of Pennsylvania State Police)

marital status, and age, was continued by the statisticians with basically no change in the pattern already shown in previous biennial reports. The total of 21,910 arrests for this biennial period reflected a conviction rate of 82 percent.

The BCI & I reportedly received 4,124 fingerprint records in the period ending May 31, 1927, compared to an increase of 14,673 records by May 31, 1928, which is accounted for by the mandatory submission of records by police agencies under the 1927 law.

The State Fire Marshal reported that in the calendar year of 1926 fire losses in Pennsylvania reached a record level of $31,116,712.

Adams closed his report to Governor John S. Fisher with these comments which bear repeating:

During the past six years, the Force has been compelled to operate with an appropriation far below the amount sufficent to carry a full complement of men and for payment of adequate equipment necessary to efficiently perform the work it has been called upon to perform. As a result, much police work has been left undone, notwithstanding the fact that officers and men have worked more hours in each day than should be expected of them. In order to efficiently carry out the mission of the State Police, sufficient appropriations should be arranged for in the coming biennium to carry a full complement of personnel and bring the equipment up to a standard which will meet modern conditions.

The police problem of today is as different from that of twenty years ago as the condition of human life is different.

Good highways, motor cars and other means of rapid transit have opened up the rural districts to the sudden attack and quick getaway of criminals of the cities. The only effective defense is an adequate patrol and observation system, coordination of all police agencies, and a higher standard of training for all police personnel. The only power that can do this lies with the State; and, to this end, the following program is proposed:

1.   Establishment of motor observation patrols at strategic road intersections, each consisting of two or more State Policemen equipped with a specially designed motor car, carrying a portable radio communications set, suitable arms and other police equipment.

2.   The coordination of all police agencies by the use of telegraph-typewriter.

3.   The establishment of a school for the proper training of all policemen.

To the end that this program may be accomplished, the budget of the State Police for the next biennium is being made up to cover the necessary additional equipment. Acts are being drafted to cover such parts as can not be accomplished without legislation.

On April 19, 1929, the State Highway Patrol mourned the death of Patrolman Russell T. Swanson—the first to be shot and killed in the line of duty. Swanson, of the Erie Highway Patrol detachment, in the act of arresting a trio of fugitives from Minnesota, was shot in the head. The incident occurred near North East, and the details of this killing will be reserved for a separate chapter devoted to the history of the State Highway Patrol.

The State Police, however, was summoned, and Sergeant William

Jones and Private Harold Munsee, of the Lawrence Park Substation, Troop D, led police in the capture of the trio at the North East railroad yards. Arrested were Joe Invie, Samuel Bard, and Fred Halverson. They confessed to the slaying of Swanson, and were sentenced to long prison terms. Jones and Munsee were awarded citations by Adams for their exemplary performance of duty in this case.

The general assembly met again in 1929, and passed five measures affecting State Police operations. Act 153, P.L. 151, April 4, repealed the salary limits for officers and men contained in previous legislation, and led the way for Act 463, P.L. 1538, May 3, which increased those salaries. Act 175, P.L. 177, April 9, better known as The Administrative Code of 1929, cited the powers and duties of the superintendent, and transferred the State Highway Patrol from the Department of Highways to the Department of Revenue, among its many other provisions. Act 403, P.L. 905, May 1, known as the Vehicle Code of 1929, cited the authority of the State Highway Patrol. The Authorization for installing an electrically-operated telephone-typewriter system of communications and funds were provided by Act 55-A, P.L. 36, May 3.

Act 55-A reads as follows:

Section 1. Be it enacted, That the the sum of three hundred and seventy-five thousand dollars ($375,000), or so much thereof as may be necessary, is hereby specifically appropriated to the Department of State Police for the purpose of installing, operating, and maintaining a telegraphic typewriter system linking the central office of said department and the offices of the various organized police forces of the cities, boroughs and townships of the Commonwealth maintaining night offices.

Said appropriations shall be paid out by requisition of the Department of State Police after approval by the Governor on the Auditor General by warrant of the Auditor General and by warrant of the Auditor General drawn on the State Treasurer in the usual manner.

Approved—The 3d day of May, A. D., 1929, in the sum of $260,000. I withhold my approval from the remainder of said appropriation because of insufficient State revenue.

/s/John S. Fisher

Adams' petitioning efforts for such a police communications network was at last bearing fruit, and developments worthy of note will be described later.

The general assembly also passed Act 243, P.L. 546, April 18, better known as the Industrial Police Act, affecting the regulation and authority of Industrial Police (Coal and Iron Police) which, as a group, still constituted a subject for heated debate. This related item appeared in the *Harrisburg Telegraph,* April 24:

> Captain George F. Lumb, local lawyer and former acting superintendent of State Police, returned to the State payroll yesterday as Governor Fisher's personal administrator of the perplexing coal and iron police problem.
>
> Captain Lumb will assume his post May 1, and at once will begin an examination and investigation which will involve every individual in the State who holds a coal and iron police commission.
>
> Captain Lumb will be assisted by Major Lynn G. Adams, superintendent of State Police, and Attorney General Cyrus E. Woods.

Because of later developments, it is interesting to mention that the new Administrative Code of 1929, as did the code of 1923, simply recognized the Pennsylvania State Police as a branch of government responsible to the governor, and did not classify it with other administrative departments. The new code continued to include the term "deputies," technically allowing for more than one deputy, if the superintendent and governor would agree on the need.

During the year, Adams cited Corporal William R. Hanna, for exceptional bravery. Distinguished Service Medals were awarded to Major Cecil M. Wilhelm, Captain William A. Clark, Captain Samuel W. Gearhart, and Captain Albert Carlson, for honest, faithful, and distinguished service. Distinguished Service Medals for valor were awarded to Captain Paul B. Stout, Captain Jacob C. Mauk, Lieutenant Thomas F. Martin, Sergeant Joseph Merrifield, Sergeant Edward T. Cohee, Sergeant Frank Gleason, Sergeant John E. Mullany, Corporal William R. Hanna, and Private David A. Drenning.

Citations for meritorious service, and other qualifications, were awarded by Adams to numerous enlisted men, clearly indicating his interest in officially recognizing praiseworthy efforts of his field forces. He displayed this personal interest early in his tenure, and continued to do so throughout.

Adams, on October 9, issued his General Order No. 14, requiring all members of the department to memorize the Pennsylvania State Police Call of Honor:

> I am a Pennsylvania State Policeman, a Soldier of the Law. To me is entrusted the Honor of the Force. I must serve honestly, faithfully, and if need be, lay down my life, as

Teletype system equipment at State Police headquarters, 1930. Operators are Chester Robenolt, left, and Henry Stone. (Courtesy of Pennsylvania State Police)

others have done before me, rather than swerve from the path of duty. It is my duty to obey the Law and to enforce it without any consideration of class, color, creed or condition. It is also my duty to be of service to any one who may be in danger or distress, and at all times so conduct myself that the Honor of the Force may be upheld.

Recitation of the Call of Honor was a requirement for graduation from the training school and formal ceremonies. This practice initiated by Adams in 1929 is still much a part of the department's ceremonials to this day.

On December 23, just about seven months after Governor Fisher signed enabling legislation, he officially dedicated the State Police teletype system at formal ceremonies held in Harrisburg. The system connected 102 police stations with each other and with State Police headquarters. Zone headquarters were established at Harrisburg, Troop B, Wyoming, Philadelphia City Police headquarters, and the Allegheny County Detectives headquarters at Pittsburgh. The zone headquarters equipment was geared for sending and receiving. Receive-only units were located at 33 stations in the Harrisburg zone, 22 in Wyoming, 16 in Philadelphia, and 31 in Pittsburgh. The system was to become officially operational on January 1, 1930, and administration of the system was entrusted to the BCI & I. Adams praised this system, saying, "It has brought a measure of coordination and cooperation on the part of local police that could not have been brought about in any other way." Adams, who was active in the affairs of the State Chiefs of Police Association, paid tribute to that body by stating that the teletype system was made possible "through the initiative and energy of the Pennsylvania State Chiefs of Police Association who sponsored it before the Legislature."

Four days later, police circles were shocked by the murder of Corporal Brady C. Paul, a member of the State Highway Patrol detachment at Butler. On December 27, Paul, accompanied by Patrolman Ernest Moore, was implementing a roadblock near New Castle. They stopped a car carrying three passengers, later identified as Irene Schroeder, 21, Glenn Dague, 33, and 5-year-old Donald Dague. Irene Schroeder, without warning, fired at both officers. Paul was fatally wounded. Moore recovered and went on to be a captain and troop commander in later years. Schroeder and Dague escaped, and were later captured in Phoenix, Arizona, after a shoot-out with police there.

Oddly-enough the police were tremendously aided in their investigation of Paul's murder and the capture of the fugitives by the very same teletype network that had just been dedicated. Schroeder and Dague were both found guilty, after extradition and trial, and died in Pennsylvania's electric chair. More will be written of this case in the State Highway Patrol chapters.

Prohibition was still demanding much of the constabulary time and, reportedly, one of the largest raids ever conducted by the State Police took place in 1929 at Steelton's west side, just a few miles from the state capital. A detachment of forty mounted troopers from the training school at nearby Hershey provided protection as other troopers with sledge hammers broke down the doors of buildings where illegal liquor and gambling devices were pinpointed by investigators. A participant in the raid stated that seized contraband consisting of moonshine, beer, and slot machines were hauled away in large horse vans. When the preliminary investigation revealed such a large-scale vice operation in Steelton, Adams personally entered into the raid's planning.

Among Adams' innovations was the formation of a special headquarters detective division. For this work, he brought together Lieutenant Harry McElroy from the BFP, and Privates William A. Miller, George V. Stedman, Lewis M. Whitecotton, Russel K. Knies, and Curwen Jones, of Troop E. They were given operational authority on January 1, 1930. It was not until 1935, however, that Adams' action was legislatively confirmed by the general assembly.

An unpleasant task faced Adams early in 1930, when he was informed of possible improper conduct by Captain Thomas Mc-

Laughlin, of Troop A, Greensburg. An investigation immediately led to McLaughlin's court-martial at Greensburg on April 6. Adams was kept informed of proceedings by radio transmissions from the Greensburg operator. Upon being informed that the board had found McLaughlin guilty of the charges lodged against him, Adams ordered McLaughlin's dismissal that very day. This was the third occasion, unfortunately, in twenty-five years, calling for the dismissal of a captain by the superintendent.

Adams' report to Governor Fisher for the period ending May 31, 1930, was somewhat more optimistic in some respects. He stated that increased appropriations had allowed him to raise the average complement of 351 officers and men—an increase of 43 over the previous biennium. These men were assigned to seventy-nine field installations of 3 to 10 men each. These stations were located "at strategic points throughout the Commonwealth where crime seemed to indicate that their personnel was most urgently needed."

Just as he had done on previous occasions, Adams was critical of the rental program for barracks buildings. He was not at all satisfied with the accommodations leased as troop headquarters in most cases, and raised the point that it was impossible to secure adequate rental facilities in localities where they were needed. Troop A headquarters, although habitable, was damaged by mine cave-ins; Troop B was tolerable, but the stables and garage facilities were dilapidated; Troop C was an old residence intended for a private family and very unsatisfactory; Troop D was suitable but the stables and garage did not measure up to the troop's needs. Of the situation at Troop E, Harrisburg, Adams had this to report,"In 1919 began a building program which due to a lack of funds was never completed. A model stable, to accommodate 80 horses, was built, and it was expected that a model barracks would be built the following biennium. However, the barracks has not materialized up to the present time—with the result that Troop E is provided with a stable that is superior to the building in which the personnel of the troop is housed, this building being a leased building and too small for the purpose."

In 1930, the State Police repair shop at Harrisburg was moved from the Highway Department metal shed No. 5 to the west wing of the stable building, which had been converted first to simple storage of motor equipment, and remodelled for use as a repair shop. The original crew of Heckman, Cooch, Motter, and Boxler had been joined in 1927 by Private William E. Aitken who doubled as a trusted aide to Adams and Wilhelm in the absence of Heckman. Heckman, Cooch, and Aitken went on to be sergeants before their retirement.

According to Adams, the school was satisfactory, "But it can not be claimed that they (the school's buildings) are in keeping with the dignity of the Commonwealth and an organization having the prestige of the Pennsylvania State Police." Adams further pointed out to the governor, "Under the circumstances, it would seem that good business and police efficiency demand that the State should adopt a building program to the end that the State Police may be housed in buildings especially adapted to its needs and owned by the Commonwealth of Pennsylvania."

An intense patrol experiment was conducted in Fayette County for three months (October, November, and December) in 1929 to secure reliable data on the effectiveness of adequate patrolling as a crime-preventive measure. Thirty men were assigned to strategic points, day and night. During this period, crime against persons declined by 50 percent—crime against property decreased nearly 49.5 percent.

It is felt that had the personnel been available to continue this experiment, an even greater decrease in crime would have resulted. Certainty of detection, apprehension and conviction inhibit criminals, as the records of this Force abundantly prove; but, it is far better to prevent crime by adequate patrol than by the detection-apprehension-conviction system. The latter system took up 85 percent of the Force's operational time and only 15 percent of the time was given to preventative patrols, whereas these figures should be reversed.

Adams rationalized, "Under the heading of 'conviction' come the expense of court operations, payment of witnesses, juror fees and expenses, and under 'detection' comes the cost of maintaining idle prisoners in jails and penitentiaries. From the material at hand, it is safe to say that if crime could be decreased 50 percent by adequate police patrols, the building program, insofar as penal establishments are concerned, could be materially reduced and probably this reduction would be sufficient to cover the cost of expansion of police forces."

Training, basically unchanged, was continuing at the training school at Hershey. "Each student must qualify with a grade of 70% or better in each subject at an examination held each month, or be dropped as undesirable."

"When the School and faculty are not required for the training of recruits," Adams explained, "special classes are conducted for the instruction of prospective non-commissioned officers and officers, and for the purpose of keeping the older members of the organization informed as to the latest developments in police work. The operation of this School has been of inestimable value in increasing the efficiency of the organization and at the same time raising the morale and esprit de corps.''

Adams' recommendation in prospective were:

1.   The Force should be increased so that a greater amount of preventative patrolling can be accomplished.

2.   The Commonwealth should own the buildings used to house the State Police Force—both stations and permanent substations.

3.   The scope of the police training school should be increased to permit the training of young men who are ambitious to become State Policemen and in this manner establish a reserve of trained men that may be inducted into the Force as vacancies occur and thus keep a maximum number of trained men on the rolls.

4.   To expand the present telegraph-typewriter system to include a number of boroughs that are not a present connected and also to make connections with important cities and bordering states that have similar systems.

5.   The expansion of the BCI & I to include specialists in chemistry, pathology and physics—such specialists to be available to serve the various district attorneys throughout the Commonwealth in the investigation of crime.

The BCI & I continued to work with local police in the promotion of its statewide program. The bureau's director was actively cooperating with the Pennsylvania Chiefs of Police Association. The contribution of fingerprint records in 1930 showed an increase of 8,233 over 1929—up 60 percent. A total of 35,899 prints were received during the 1929–30 biennial period.

Fire losses for the 1927–28 period totalled $51,413,932, indicating a decrease of $8,056,404 from the 1925–26 figure of $59,470,336.

Activities

	1928–29	1929–30
Request for assistance	27,175	33,334
Investigations	21,689	29,434
Criminal Arrests	9,839	12,420
Percent of strike time	11.14	.002
Stolen cars recovered	177	256
Conviction rate on completed cases	80.8%	81.1%
Patrol mileage	1,902,259	2,414,196
Value of recovered stolen property	$168,071.83	$232,425.30

Partial List of Arrests

Disorderly conduct	1,778	1,753
Liquor laws	1,278	1,717
Gambling	949	1,021
Breaking and entry	858	1,195
Larceny	780	1,179
Auto laws	614	666

For both years, the age group most arrested was 22. There was an increase in the number of habitual offenders. Laborers and miners headed the list of those arrested. Americans, Italians, Polish, and Blacks, in that order, topped the list by nationality.

Enlistments for this reporting period accounted for 269 men. Separations totalled 155, allowing a net gain in complement, which Adams stated the department could at last afford. Of the men separated from service, 47 left for better-paying positions, and 89 were sent away either for disciplinary reasons or poor performance during their probationary periods.

CHAPTER IX

Major Lynn G. Adams
1930—1937

Although State Police enforcement efforts had done much in the first quarter of the twentieth century to wipe out the notorious Black Hand Society, there were still surviving traces of its operations in Pennsylvania. Private Charles L. Stewart, of Troop A, Greensburg, assigned to a case involving Black Hand activity, was shot and killed while apprehending a member of the society on July 18, 1930. Another young life was yielded to the depraved members of a society that, for too long, extorted and killed, and spread uneasiness among the hearts of those who came to America's shores with profound expectations.

With barely six weeks to recover from this incident, the state constabulary was to learn that its founder, Colonel John C. Groome, died at his Bryn Mawr residence on August 31, 1930, at the age of 68, bringing to a close an outstanding career as soldier, the nation's first State Police superintendent, state prison warden and trustee. For a few months prior to his death, Groome had been virtually bedridden—a victim of arthritis. Groome devoted a lifetime to public service. He was, indeed, a great man.

Adams issued a special order the following day, recognizing in simple terms the death of a man of prominence in State Police history:

> Colonel John C. Groome, born 1862, at Philadelphia, Pennsylvania, was the first Superintendent and the organizer

of the Pennsylvania State Police Force. He built the organization on non-political lines and outlined the policy that has made the Pennsylvania State Police Force comparable with the best police forces in the world. The Commonwealth of Pennsylvania and the Pennsylvania State Police Force owe him a great debt of gratitude. He died August 31, 1930.

As a mark of respect to his memory, the flags at the various barracks of the Pennsylvania State Police Force will be displayed at half-staff for the period of thirty (30) days. During the same period, each member of the Pennsylvania State Police Force will wear a black crepe band four inches wide on the left arm of the uniform blouse with the center of the band midway between the shoulder and the elbow.

Although he certainly deserved special honors at death, it was the Groome family's wish that no military honors be accorded at his funeral in old St. Peter's Protestant Episcopal Church, Philadelphia. Church services, however, were attended by members of the First Troop, the seventy-ninth Division, the 305th Cavalry, and the state constabulary. There were no honorary pallbearers, and at Groome's request the active pallbearers were representatives of the four organizations with which he was affiliated for many years. They were Major Lynn G. Adams and Captain C. M. Wilhelm, Pennsylvania State Police; Captains J. Franklin McFadden and Clement B. Wood, First Troop; Majors R. R. D. McCullough and E. P. Rutan, 305th Cavalry, and Captains Herbert H. Smith and Elmer Leithiser, Eastern Penitentiary. Groome was buried in Laurel Hill Cemetery where private internment services were observed.

Following the pacesetting Pennsylvania constabulary, the New Jersey State Police in 1930 inaugurated a statewide teletypewriter system. The New Jersey system was by design linked to the New York City Police Department's system. Pennsylvania and New Jersey linked their systems, allowing each participating agency immediate general broadcast access to all terminals within the three interfaced systems.

Facing up to the need of expanding this three-party network, invitations were extended to other east coast states to join the network as statewide systems were developed. Established in short order was the Eastern States Police Teletypewriter Net linking Pennsylvania, New Jersey, New York, New York City, Connecticut, Massachusetts, Rhode Island, Delaware, Ohio, Virginia, Maryland, New Hampshire, North Carolina, Vermont, and the District of Columbia. This enlarged network was, indeed, a big step forward in police communications.

Before leaving office, Governor Fisher nominated Adams to

another term as superintendent on January 6, 1931, opening day for that year's legislative session. On January 20, however, the newly-inaugurated governor, Gifford Pinchot, who had been elected to another four-year term after sitting out Fisher's tenure, asked that all of Fisher's nominations be recalled from the Senate. Later that day, Pinchot renominated Adams who was immediately confirmed by the Senate.

Adams and Pinchot, during the governor's earlier term, disagreed on many administrative decisions regarding State Police operations. Pinchot, realizing the value of Adams and setting aside any disagreeable circumstances, did not for one moment delay in reappointing him. This speaks well for Pinchot who will be remembered as one of Pennsylvania's more distinguished governors, and for Adams, too, who had the fortitude to stand up for what he believed best for his command.

The general assembly adjourned on May 28 without passing legislation of any kind directly bearing on State Police operations. The legislators did enact one measure affecting the State Highway Patrol, which will be taken into account elsewhere, and another which, for the first time, regulated the registration, sale, and ownership of firearms. Act 158, P.L. 497, June 11, 1931, better known as the Uniform Firearms Act, was given to the Secretary of the Commonwealth for administrative purposes. The administration of the Uniform Firearms Act was to be transferred twelve years later to the Pennsylvania State Police in 1943.

In order to implement the procedures established by the Uniform Firearms Act, Governor Pinchot again brought Captain George F. Lumb back to the state payroll. Lumb had completed the mission given to him by Governor Fisher in 1929 in connection with the processing of commissions for Industrial Policemen, and now answered the call for public service for the last time at Pinchot's beckoning. Lumb fulfilled his commitment by launching the Uniform Firearms Act with effective results in comparatively short order, and finally set aside his truly commendable career with the Commonwealth for a small handful of years as a private citizen before death claimed him.

Commencing with 1931, the general assembly, although officially scheduled to meet only on odd-numbered years, was called into special sessions regularly throughout the remaining nineteen-thirties and midway through the forties. By this time, the magnitude of the Great Depression was deeply felt, and the ingenuity of the state legislators was hard-pressed to deal with the manifold problems besetting the people of Pennsylvania, as elsewhere in the nation. When the problems of the Great Depression were finally alleviated by another disaster,

Sergeant Timothy McCarthy and Omar (Courtesy of Pennsylvania State Police)

Omar (Courtesy of Pennsylvania State Police)

Omar is decorated at Troop E ceremony (Courtesy of Pennsylvania State Police)

World War II, the "annual" sessions were continued to meet the demands of wartime.

The role of the State Police in labor disturbances never did cease to be an issue in state government circles. At times the issue was a more burning one, and the subject came up for discussion again early in Pinchot's second term. On March 4, 1931, Adams issued his General Order No. 17, which contained the following letter from Pinchot:

> In confirmation of our recent talk regarding the attitude of the State Police toward strikes and strikers, I want to describe in writing the attitude the State Police should take:
>
> 1.   The State Police will take no position, either for or against either side, in any strike, unless in the case of violence.
>
> 2.   The duty of the State Police is to prevent and repress violence on either side without fear or favor in any labor dispute.
>
> 3.   State Police will not be employed in any strike in advance of the commission of an overt act, except by the direct orders of the Governor.
>
> 4.   Request for State Police from any sheriff will not be complied with, except in the case of actual violence, until after that request has been submitted to and approved by the Governor.
>
> 5.   I shall be very glad, indeed, to have you keep me advised as soon as the information reaches you as to any possibility of trouble likely to require the intervention of State Police anywhere in the Commonwealth, or as to any other matter in this connection which, in your judgment, I ought to know.

This directive from Pinchot has basically served as the department's "bible" for labor disturbances ever since.

Another tragedy visited the state constabulary in the spring of 1931. Sergeant Timothy G. McCarthy, of Troop E, Harrisburg, was shot and killed as he boldly attempted to take into custody a mountain resident of Brush Creek Township, Fulton County, who had been described by the sheriff as "a menace to a whole community and all parties are fearful to molest him."

McCarthy was a popular, well-liked member of the department, and his death gave rise to widespread public mourning for this veteran trooper. Because of some of the unusual aspects of this killing, more details will be offered here than has been the case with other fallen comrades. McCarthy, 43, was born at Killarney, Ireland, and to this point was the oldest trooper to die in the line of duty. During World War I, he served with the 102nd Infantry, twenty-sixth Division, also known as "YD"—the Yankee Division commanded by General Clarence Edwards. Honorably discharged from military service, he enlisted with the State Police September 1, 1919.

For a moment, it is necessary to go back to 1929, when Adams undertook the organization of a canine corps of police dogs. Learning of Adams' plans, a longtime friend, Lt. Colonel Hobart F. Hopkins, of the National Guard's 28th Division, donated his four-month-old Shepherd. Given the name of "Omar," the animal soon developed into a fine police dog with special handling at the training school. An excellent working relationship grew between Omar and McCarthy to whom the dog was assigned. On his fatal mission to Fulton County, McCarthy was accompanied by Private Philip A. Duane, Private Russell Knies, and Omar.

McCarthy and his companions were taken to the mountain home of Marshal Lodge on May 12 by the Fulton County sheriff and his deputy. McCarthy, shortly after entering the dwelling, was confronted with Lodge whose arrest he came to make. Lodge, with a revolver concealed from McCarthy's view, fired at point blank range, and swiftly scurried to another room in the house. McCarthy died instantly. Omar entered the house and stalked the killer who then fired at the dog, wounding Omar severely. Before his capture, Lodge had also wounded Private Knies.

The gallant Irishman was buried "amid the most impressive honors ever accorded a police officer killed in the line of duty," so stated an eye-witness to the ceremonies. Omar recovered from his injuries slowly. At formal ceremonies, on November 12, 1932, attended by members of Troop E, Omar was presented a medal of valor—the only animal to be so decorated by the state constabulary—thus giving Omar a special place in its history. Presented was the American Kennel Club Medal of Heroism. Private Knies also recovered from his facial wounds. He was advanced through the ranks to major before his retirement in 1963.

Lt. Colonel Hopkins, who was named an honorary pallbearer at McCarthy's funeral, was instrumental in persuading the Chambersburg American Legion Post to purchase from Tiffany, of New York City, a specially-engraved trophy in McCarthy's memory, to be awarded annually to the best pistol and rifle shot in State Police competition. So ended a sad and unusual episode that struck at the hearts of Pennsylvanians everywhere.

In the winter of 1931, Adams' work schedule was temporarily

interrupted by a broken collar bone. Adams, who enjoyed riding horses, joined with the Beaufort Hunt directed by Harrisburg's Ehrmann Mitchell. While riding "to hounds" at full gallop, his horse fell on a frozen swamp, and Adams was thrown. Luckily for the superintendent, the incident was not a more serious one.

Adams was a dedicated outdoorsman, and welcomed every opportunity to find diversion and relaxation in the beautiful mountain reaches of Pennsylvania. Although he was an excellent shot with a rifle and a cagey fisherman by repute, Adams was rated a top man with the bow and arrow. According to his hunting companions, Adams bagged many a deer with archery gear, and was deeply interested in promoting this mode of hunting.

During 1932, Pennsylvania's public officials were concerned for the movement of the Bonus Army marching on Washington to petition the White House and Congress for a bonus for World War I veterans. The veterans, suffering many hardships of the Great Depression, sought a bonus to help them through those troubled times and as a special consideration for wartime service. Adams was given the responsibility for seeing to the orderly progress of the march through Pennsylvania to and from Washington. He traveled the state to facilitate and direct the marchers. At the Enola railroad yards, near Harrisburg, Adams engaged in a serious confrontation with Pennsylvania Railroad's local officials when they refused to move the bonus marchers. He was successful in his objective to see to it that the march was completed with a minimum of disorder.

During the biennial period ending May 31, 1932, the BCI & I increased its files of criminal records by 55,235, bringing its total record count to 98,848. Of new records received, 21.8 percent of the persons arrested were identified as having previous arrest records. Adams authorized the formation of a photography section in the BCI & I to assist all police departments. The photo section also aided in the production of Wanted Persons bulletins. Directing the operations of the photography section was Samuel Garvin.

Adams also organized a crime laboratory division, which at the outset was of very basic nature. The first of the lab services dealt with micro-ballistics. To provide this service, Adams employed John A. Funck, a graduate of Franklin and Marshall College. Funck was teaching school when he was introduced to Adams. His appointment as micro-ballistician followed, and he was assigned operational quarters at the training school where he remained until the lab was expanded and moved to Harrisburg in 1939.

The teletypewriter system dispatched 81,263 messages, and the number of police departments on-line with the system was increased to 109.

Statistics

	1930–31	1931–32
Requests for assistance	46,028	61,014
Investigations	35,398	31,594
Criminal arrests	17,478	14,358
Stolen automobiles recovered	264	230
Percentage of time on strike duty	.0047	10.8
Percentage of convictions	81.6	81.0
Patrol mileage	2,945,220	3,106,097
Value of recovered stolen property	$234,841.67	$214,945.61
Total fines collected by state	$564,323.51	$330,782.69
Salaries paid	$912,649.39	$850,919.01
Average per capita cost	.11	.107

It is noted that Adams' statisticians were attempting to make a comparision between revenues collected by the Commonwealth in fines from State Police arrests and the salaries paid State Policemen. Setting aside any argument on the validity of this comparison, the fines did substantially support fifty percent of the salaries.

In the second half of the biennial period, only eight student recruits were processed: a near-full complement accounted for this record low. A total of fifty-eight were processed during the biennium compared to ninety-nine separations. Again better-paying jobs, disciplinary action and probationary dismissals accounted for most of the departures.

Partial List of Arrests

	1930–31	1931–32
Disorderly conduct	3,126	2,197
Breaking and entry	2,108	2,105
Liquor Laws	2,056	1,576
Larceny	1,906	1,395
Gambling	1,185	989
Auto laws	754	521
Narcotics laws	8	2
Murder	126	95
Illegal possession of milk bottles*	1	

(*) An oddity

During the biennium, a total of ninety-two aliens arrested for criminal offenses were deported to their prior homelands. Americans, Italians, Polish, and Blacks continued to head the list of persons arrested, by nationality. Avarice and recklessness were leading causes for crime. Single persons committed more offenses than married persons. Again, records showed an increase in the number of habitual offenders (classified as those arrested three or more times).

In his period-ending report to Governor Pinchot, Adams was still critical of the leasing program for State Police field installations, and repeated his argument in favor of crime prevention efforts.

A headquarters roster published in 1931 included the following persons:

Executive Office

Superintendent—Lynn G. Adams
Deputy Superintendent—Cecil M. Wilhelm
Executive Secretary—Silvus J. Overmiller
Chief Quartemater—Guy E. Reichard
Accountant—John R. Price
Police Clerks—Lloyd V. Becker, Herman L. Brieghner and Chester E.
          Shuler
Statistician—Carl A. Knorr
Clerk—Gilbert W. Aungst

Bureau of Criminal Identification and Information

Acting Chief—William F. Hoffman
Assistant Chief—Charles Kunz
Micro-Ballistician—John A. Funck
Operators—Harold Nifong, Paul J. Roche, and Elmer H. Doll
Photographer—Samuel Garvin
Clerk—Ralph L. Fiscel
Stenographer—L. M. Sites

Bureau of Fire Protection

Fire Marshal—J. William Morgan
Supervisor of Investigations—William F. Traeger
Clerks—Ethel M. Wright, Pauline Hanlen, Percy C. Moore
Clerk-Typists—Rose H. Katzen, Alberta L. Cence, Ruth E. Foreman,
          Hazle L. A. Wenrich
Stenographers—Sarah M. Blair, Martha I. Kell, Jane A. Quigley,
          Elizabeth M. Hoster

Troop Commanders

Troop A, Greensburg—Captain Albert Carson
Troop B, Wyoming—Captain William A. Clark
Troop C, Reading—Captain Samuel W. Gearhart
Troop D, Butler—Captain Jacob C. Mauk
School Troop, Hershey—Captain Jasper Oftedahl

In 1932, Adams was able to secure additional office space adjacent to the BCI & I in the capitol's south wing for the Fire Marshal. The bureau was moved out of its leased space in the Blackstone building to the capitol. Although the executive offices were separated from the BCI & I and the Fire Bureau, all branches were at least under the same roof to facilitate administration.

Appearing on the scene in police circles was the polygraph instrument which was accepted as a useful device for investigators. Adams, electing to adopt this instrument for constabulary use, chose John Funck as the department's first operator. Chicago-trained in polygraph operations, Funck provided this special service in addition to his work in micro-ballistics.

Adams' General Order No. 17, dated June 17, 1932, revealed another of his innovations. Adams ordered the formation of a criminal intelligence section to gather information regarding major criminals. This move was particularly aimed at the personalities and operations of gangsters and racketeers who had been abundantly spawned by more than a decade of prohibition. The intelligence files were labelled as sensitive and secret. Information from this source was shared with other law enforcement agencies, but only after permission to release was secured from a limited number of authorizing officers. Like many other procedures established by Adams in the administration of his force, the gathering of criminal intelligence data has developed into a major function of larger police departments everywhere.

As was mentioned earlier, Adams was a formidable light-heavyweight boxer during his days in the U. S. Army. He never lost interest in this sport, and followed the careers of the prominent professional boxers as avidly as most boxing fans could. Adams managed to persuade the world's former heavyweight champion, Jack Dempsey, to visit the training school at Hershey early in 1933. Winter still had control of this area, and Dempsey, who had lost his title to Gene Tunney only a few years before, arrived at the training school accompanied by Adams during a blinding snowstorm. Dempsey, still one of the nation's sports heroes, talked informally with the recruits who were then finishing up four months of a six months training program. Dempsey answered questions put to him, sparred with some of the recruits, and remained to watch several matches between recruits who were eager to impress their distinguished visitor. It was a memorable occasion for the men present at that session.

During the 1933 session of the general assembly, Act 282, P.L. 1139, June 1, was passed abolishing certain fire prevention records and reports required by P.L. 450, 1927, which were found to be redundant.

There were no other measures passed affecting State Police operations. Representative Frederick H. Myers, Jr. (R-Philadelphia), however, introduced House Bill 1377 forbidding the Pennsylvania State Police to enter areas effected by strike or industrial disputes except upon the express order of the governor.

Two years earlier Pinchot had provided Adams with a written directive clearly delineating the steps to be followed by the constabulary in response to requests for assistance in strikes and labor disturbance. Pinchot's order allowed State Police intervention "in the case of actual violence." Myers' proposed legislation was obviously intended to close off that leeway for constabulary action. The Myers bill, however, died in the State Government committee.

Members of the general assembly were faced with the serious effects of an ever-deepening depression. The Commonwealth was losing revenues at a record-breaking pace, and receipts were far below the level required to meet its financial obligations. To find possible solutions to this financial crisis, a resolution was passed calling for a joint legislative inquiry which was to be undertaken immediately. The study, according to the resolution, was to be centered on four important points:

    1.   Elimination of certain functions and services of state government.
    2.   Consolidation of certain functions.
    3.   Elimination of overlapping and duplicating functions.
    4.   Increase of license and service fees.

Adams and his staff were called to testify before the joint committee and supply information regarding constabulary operations. Each of the bureau operations and costs were thoroughly reviewed. There were then 56 persons assigned to headquarters. Undergoing review also were the work and related costs of the field forces then numbering 385. Committee members were not backward in their approach to the likelihood of slashing salaries across the board. Adams argued hard and long against such a move. He knew full well the perennial difficulties en-

countered by the constabulary since its inception because of inadequate pay. He was not about to willingly slide back to such circumstances, and predicted disastrous effects on morale if salaries were not
kept on a comparative footing with other large police agencies. Fortunately for his men, and himself, Adams was successful in sustaining his
argument and preserving the payroll.

As soon as the fast-moving hearings were completed, the joint
committee recommended that certain inspections undertaken by the
Fire Bureau be transferred to the Department of Labor and Industry.
The committee pointed out that the cost of the teletypewriter system,
then amounting to $400,000 a biennium, was not supported at all by
local communities serviced by the system; and recommended that local
governments so served be made to pay a reasonable share. The committee was convinced that considerable savings could be found by
transferring the State Highway Patrol from the Department of Revenue
to the Pennsylvania State Police for administrative purposes, but
allowing for each agency to perform its own duties. It recommended
that the State Police and Highway Patrol jointly use field facilities. A
cut in the rolls of the Highway Patrol to no more than 500 men was also
sought; the Patrol, on March 1, 1933, numbered 528 officers and men.
The transfer of both the Dog Law Enforcement from the Department of
Agriculture and the Division of Safety from the Revenue Department
to the State Police wound up this series of findings.

None of the committee's recommendations was ever carried out
except for the merger of the State Police and the Highway Patrol,
which awaited another four years to materialize, and the joint use of
field facilities.

Before the new year of 1934 was more than a couple of days old,
Adams officially recognized the repeal of the National Prohibition Act
of 1919, which had proven itself a miserable failure from many
viewpoints. He reminded his forces that the misuse of alcoholic
beverages would bring swift disciplinary consequences. His directive
left no room for doubt that drink and duty were not considered com-
patible and such a mixture would not be tolerated. And so the constabulary, like the rest of the nation, went about its business of adjusting to a new way of life with booze moving over the counter instead of
under it.

Before the close of the 1932–34 biennial period, Adams expanded
the functions of his detective division with offices in the capitol. He
placed the micro-ballistics section, now located at the training school,
under the detectives' control although this modest special service was
to be supervised on a daily basis by the commandant of the school.

Adams placed the chief intelligence officer in overall charge of the detectives.

With the rapid advances being made, Adams considered Pennsylvania as "one of the outstanding states in handling police communications. With a teletype network second to none and radio communications with various parts of the State and with other States not equipped with teletype, the system of police communications is improving each year and has more than repaid the Commonwealth since its installation."

The Pennsylvania teletype network connected with New York, New Jersey, Massachusetts, and Connecticut. A connection with Delaware was underway. By radio, Pennsylvania was able to communicate with Ohio, West Virginia, and Michigan. A working arrangement with the bordering state of Maryland was under negotiation.

A total of 114 police departments were on-line with the teletype system, and a move to the use of duplicate paper was in the making so that the system's operators could furnish message copies to 73 additional police departments. During the biennium 123,455 messages were dispatched over the system, representing an increase of 52 percent over the previous reporting period.

An important change at headquarters occurred in early 1934. The office of the executive secretary was abolished. It will be recalled that the executive secretary, Silvus J. Overmiller, was responsible for most of the department's paperwork. Overmiller was then given the title of comptroller and made fully responsible for preparing the budget and all budget reporting documents; compilation, classification and preservation of investigative reports; statistical data; property and other valuable records, as well as auditing, accounting, reporting, stenographic and filing services at headquarters and field locations.

The Fire Bureau accounted for 12,123 inspections and issued 5,309 fire hazard correction orders during the biennium. Arrests for arson then exceeded 200.

The BCI & I received 54,178 criminal records. Of these, 14,072, or 25.97 percent, related to persons having previous arrest records. The recidivism rate was then nearing 30 percent. Total BCI & I criminal records reached the 135,900 mark. The bureau also recorded 74,799 inquiries for information in the two-year period. Because of the expanding services of the bureau, Adams found it necessary to seek out additional office space. Having done this successfully, the bureau was moved to improved quarters on the fifth floor of the capitol's north wing.

Adams continued to petition the governor for new barracks build-

ings owned by the Commonwealth, and lamented the fact that his men
could not engage in any crime prevention program since their time was
completely occupied with investigations and arrests. He praised the
mobility of the State Police in providing better statewide coverage.

Statistics

	1932–33	1933–34
Requests for assistance	61,285	59,317
Investigations	36,419	34,417
Criminal arrests	12,195	10,663
Recovered stolen motor vehicles	124	100
Percentage of time on strike duty	1.5%	10.14%
Conviction rate on completed cases	75.59%	77.88%
Patrol mileage	2,993,619	3,022,502
Value of recovered stolen property	$109,658.25	$147,207.77
Fines collected	$251,442.55	$101,314.21
Average cost per capita	.102	.105

Partial List of Arrests

Larceny	1,584	1,833
Breaking and entry	1,923	1,578
Disorderly conduct	1,041	1,218
Gambling	1,081	839
Liquor laws	1,080	298
Narcotics laws	2	3
Murders	114	102
Automobile laws	292	268
Arson	262	136

During the first year of the biennium, thirty-seven alien-arrestees
were deported and ten during the second year. Such was the disposition of their cases. It is noted that at this point a greater percentage of
persons arrested were classified as "Americans," with a correspond-
ing drop in other nationalities. Avarice and recklessness were listed as
the major causes for crime. Single persons outnumbered married
persons arrested, and males outnumbered females better than 10 to 1.

The complement of enlisted personnel was basically a stable one
during the reporting period. There were only fifty-four men recruited
and trained in comparison to a low separation figure of forty-one.
There was no noteworthy change in the complement at headquarters.

On September 10, 1934, death claimed the highest ranking trooper
to date under unusual circumstances. First Sergeant James A. Seerey,

of Troop B, Wyoming, an outstanding horseman and popular figure in the constabulary, died of injuries when his horse fell on him during mounted drill. Seerey, 42, a native Philadelphian, was a fourteen-year veteran with the constabulary.

The State Police later in 1934 engaged in what was destined to be one of its most widely-known murder cases—"The Case of the Babes in the Woods." John Finch, a Harrisburg newsman, retelling forty years later the story of the mid-state crime that shocked the nation, wrote, "In an era of well-known murder cases, the Babes in the Woods murders shared the spotlight with other infamies of the time—including the Lindbergh baby kidnapping/murder—the trial of which would begin only five weeks after the Babes in the Woods case emerged."

The bodies of three children, all girls, were found near Pine Grove Furnace, Franklin County, on November 24, 1934, by local woodsmen.

The State Police entered the case soon after notice of the discovered bodies had been made to the Carlisle police. Although the case was supervised by Major Cecil M. Wilhelm, deputy superintendent of the constabulary, the investigation was primarily the responsibility of the department's chief of detectives, Lieutenant H. E. McElroy.

Within hours of the discovery of the "Babes," the bodies of a man and a woman were reported found in a deserted Pennsylvania Railroad station at Spring Meadows, near Altoona. Both were believed to be victims of a suicide pact. An attempt by investigators at first to link this incident with the death of the three girls was fraught with doubts.

After hundreds of interviews across the country by Pennsylvania State Police investigators, with the cooperation of other police departments, the solution to a mystery that enkindled the interest of a nation began to develope. The deceased found near Altoona were identified as Elmo J. Noakes, 32, of Roseville, California, and his 18-year-old niece Winifred Pierce.

Police learned that Noakes, a widower of two years, fled his home in California with his niece, who had been keeping house for him since mid-summer of 1934, and his three daughters. The daughters were later identified as Norma, 12, Dewilla, 10, and Cordelia, 8. Medical examiners and police attributed the deaths of the three girls to strangulation or suffocation.

Piecing together precious bits of information, the State Police were satisfied that Noakes hurriedly left California with his niece to overcome family objections to their affair. Their cross-country escapade took them to Philadelphia and to southcentral Pennsylvania, where Noakes, convinced of the hopelessness of finding employment and support for his niece and daughters, plotted the beginning of the end for the five runaways. The three girls were murdered and tenderly placed together on the ground under a blanket in a wooded area some twenty feet from the roadside. Noakes abandoned his 1929 Pontiac sedan in a field near McVeytown; it was the identification of this vehicle that led police to the swiftly-developing solution to this headlined mystery. With a secondhand rifle, purchased with their remaining few dollars, Noakes shot his niece and then himself.

The three girls were buried in Westminster Cemetery, at Carlisle, in a grave donated by the cemetery management. The three white caskets were purchased with funds raised by the Carlisle American Legion. Several days later, Noakes, an ex-Marine, was buried in a gravesite near his three "Babes." The State Police officially closed its files on a murder case involving an unusual love affair and reflecting the despairing times of the Great Depression.

Before the year's end, another motor vehicle fatality was to be noted in the constabulary registry. Private Floyd W. Maderia, of Troop B, Wyoming, was killed in an automobile accident on December 11, 1934.

A 1934 roster of command personnel indicated the following line-up:

Department Headquarters
Superintendent—Major Lynn G. Adams
Deputy Superintendent—Major C. M. Wilhelm
Comptroller—Silvus J. Overmiller
Chief Quartermaster—Guy E. Reichard

Bureau of Criminal Identification and Information
Chief—William F. Hoffman
Assistant Chief—Charles Kunz

Bureau of Fire Protection
Chief—William F. Traeger

Troop A, Greensburg	*Troop B. Wyoming*
Captain Jacob C. Mauk	Captain William A. Clark
Lieutenant Charles C. Keller	Lieutenant William D. Plummer
Troop C, West Reading	*Troop D, Butler*
Captain Samuel W. Gearhart	Captain Jasper Oftedahl
Lieutenant Edwin C. Griffith	Lieutenant Thomas J. Boettner

Troop E, Harrisburg   *Training School, Hershey*
Captain Paul B. Stout   Captain Thomas F. Martin
Lieutenant Montgomery B. Bennett   Lieutenant Andrew H. Hudock
                                         *Lieutenant Harry E. McElroy

*(*)*Lieutenant McElroy was actually directing operations of the Detective Division, and carried on the records of the training school because of complement restrictions. A 1935 law later permitted his transfer from the school to the Detective Division which was then officially established.

On January 15, 1935, George H. Earle III, who became the first Democratic governor in this century, was inaugurated. Earle grew up in a family identified with Republicans for many years. He, however, supported Franklin D. Roosevelt in 1932 and was elected as the state's thirty-second governor two years later on the Democratic ticket. The swing to the Democratic party made a remarkable change in the composition of the Pennsylvania Senate and House. In 1933–34, Republicans controlled 43 seats in the Senate and 139 in the House. The Democrats provided token opposition with only 7 senators and 65 House members. When Earle took office, he had the support of 19 Democratic senators and 117 House members. The Republican membership in the general assembly dwindled to 31 senators and 88 House members.

It was evident that the merger of the State Police and the Highway Patrol was being considered by some members of the general assembly. In April, Senator George W. Woodward (R-Philadelphia) asked for Adams' opinion on this proposal. Adams replied on April 18:

> I am in a very peculiar position. I believe that greater police efficiency would be obtained if these two organizations were one. At the same time, I realize that the enforcement of the traffic laws of the Commonwealth are a "headache" and I am personally very happy without these duties.
>
> Obviously, being one Department of the State Government, I cannot recommend taking the duties from another Department, even though so doing would bring about an economic saving in cost of operation—and it undoubtedly would.

Although Adams' reply was not intended as an outright endorsement of the merger, his words could hardly leave much doubt in the mind of the reader—Senator Woodward.

The general assembly, although it took no direct action on the merger in its 1935 session, did pass four measures affecting the State Police to some degree.

With the election of Earle and an overwhelming number of Democratic senators and House members, labor had secured at last a better springboard for legislation more favorable to its interests. Labor groups had made no bones about their dislike for the Coal and Iron Police. The Coal and Iron Police, in spite of the Industrial Police Act of 1929, still constituted a group to be reckoned with; according to an Associated Press release, they "were the uncontested law enforcers in many Pennsylvania towns." And, it was then time to wipe them out.

Act 156, P.L. 348, signed by Earle on June 15, 1935, repealed all enactments: P.L. 225, 1865; P.L. 99, 1866; P.L. 214, 1925; P.L. 546, 1929—and thereby abolished the Coal and Iron Police. Corporation forces were retained for security purposes, but their former powers under law were terminated. This was, indeed, a long-awaited victory for the labor movement.

Act 379, P.L. 1169, July 18, adjusted the State Police complement and officially established a detective division. This action legally gave life to a division already existant under Adams' wise guidance. This act reduced the school troop complement by one lieutenant, and increased the complement of each of the five troops from sixty-five privates to forty first-class privates and forty second-class privates. This change boosted the complement of privates in each troop from sixty-five to eighty. This added a total of seventy-five men to the complement. Act 379 authorized the detective division to have one lieutenant, two sergeants and ten detectives—a total of thirteen men. The act, in effect, increased the State Police complement by eighty-seven men rather than eighty-eight since the lieutenant position was a transfer and not a new creation.

Act 379 set the salaries of first-class privates at $1,400 a year, and second-class privates at $1,080 a year. The detective division salaries were fixed at $2,400 for the lieutenant, $1,700 for each of the two sergeants, and $1,500 for each of the ten detectives.

With official recognition then given the detective division, Adams added to the original 1930 complement five more men, one from each of the five troops. They were: Privates James Griffith, Troop A; Robert Musser, Troop B; Anthony C. Parry, Troop C; William L. Nevin, Troop D; and Frank G. McCartney, Troop E. Adams did not, however, transfer these men to the detective division immediately. Official transfers came later with a number of changes in detective personnel.

Lieutenant McElroy, a native of Marietta, was born September 28, 1892. He joined the constabulary August 1, 1917, and was assigned by Lumb to Troop B, Wyoming. After promotions to corporal, sergeant and first sergeant, he was transferred to the training school in 1927 and promoted to lieutenant. McElroy remained at the school until Adams officially appointed him head of the detective division July 19, 1935.

Earlier in the 1930s, Adams had strongly recommended the use of the training school for the training of all police officers. The general assembly, taking his recommendation to heart, passed Act 411½, P.L. 1314, July 18. The act mandated the conduct of courses of instruction for municipal police at the training school, established standards for applicants, set a fee for municipalities not to exceed $40 a month, and appropriated the sum of $20,000 for the 1935–36 fiscal year to cover costs of salaries for added instructors and other employes to carry out the new program.

Act 355, P.L. 1056, July 16, (section 1218) cited the authority of police officers, including the State Police.

At the urging of Adams, Earle was persuaded to reaffirm the fact that politics was to remain out of the State Police and that this policy of long-standing had the governor's backing. On September 27, 1935, Earle issued the following message which was directed to all officers of the State Police and the State Highway Patrol:

> I urge and encourage every one of you to exercise your rights as citizens by casting your ballot. However, I am determined that politics must not be permitted to interfere with the safety of our citizens.
>
> You are, therefore, notified that political activity of any kind by any member of the State Police or the State Highway Patrol will be cause for summary dismissal. At the same time, I pledge myself personally to uphold any member of the State Police and Highway Patrol who is subjected to political pressure from any source in his efforts to discharge his duty.

The message was understandable enough.

The early days of 1936 were to witness the death of another great man in State Police history—Captain George F. Lumb—whose impressive career with the constabulary and elsewhere in state government is worthy of remembrance. Lumb, 61, died at his Harrisburg residence of January 14, after some years of ill-health which forced him from public life. Private funeral services were held at the Grace Methodist Church, where he had been an active churchman for years. Lumb was buried in Shoop's Church Cemetery, at Harrisburg.

The following first-person comments on his death, which are

quoted in part, appeared in the *Harrisburg Sunday Courier* on January 19:

> A movie man looking for a thrilling plot would find it in the life of Captain Lumb. But above all that, I knew him as the kindest and most considerate of men; gentle, companionable, friendly. I shall feel his presence beside me when next I toss a line overboard from a Chesapeake fishing boat—but I shall no longer hear his good-natured chiding, his illuminating tales of far horizons, his mirth-provoking but always barbless witticisms, and I shall miss them.

Lumb was survived by his wife, Eleanor, and a son, Fred. Mrs. Lumb, who suffered from tuberculosis since 1922 and was tenderly cared for by her devoted husband, went on to outlive him by twenty-nine years. Eleanor Lumb succumbed to her illness on October 24, 1965, and was buried in the family plot in Shoop's Cemetery. In 1919 and 1920 she was president of the Penbrook Community Civic Club and active in community affairs in the Harrisburg area.

In 1936, the move toward use of passenger cars for trooper transportation to replace horses and motorcycles was on the upswing. Funding was provided to make such vehicles available to the field forces on the basis of two cars for five men.

In his biennial report to Governor Earle, for the period ending May 31, 1936, Adams advocated the expansion of radio to patrol vehicles. In order to provide statewide coverage, he cited the need for five additional broadcasting stations. He pointed out that 173,174 messages were dispatched by way of the teletype system, indicating an increase of 40 percent from the previous period.

The training school included courses of instruction in crime laboratory services, which had been "unusually successful" in crime detection. Adams reported that municipal police officers were undergoing training at the school in compliance with the 1935 statute.

By 1936, the BCI & I had organized branch services in all five troops. The bureau was given full responsibility for all crime investigation reports and the index system, and was publishing a monthly bulletin for Pennsylvania's police agencies. A total of 60,546 fingerprint records were received during the biennium, bringing the bureau's total to 176,216. Of the newly-received records, it was noted that 27.5 percent of those arrested had prior arrest records. Adhering to a new policy of accepting fingerprints from non-arrestees on a voluntary basis for emergency identification purposes, 7,185 "personal" prints were processed. Of these, 3,914 prints were submitted by state institutional employes on the Department of Welfare payroll.

Activities

	1934–35	1935–36
Requests for assistance	59,203	56,027
Investigations	33,941	29,683
Criminal arrests	11,726	9,655
Stolen vehicles recovered	110	107
Percentage of time on strike duty	9.92%	2.57%
Conviction rate on completed cases	80.6%	83.7%
Patrol mileage	3,596,842	3,064,798
Value of recovered stolen property	$128,987.25	$111,588.02
Cost per capita	.108	.104

Partial List of Arrests

Larceny	1,769	1,432
Breaking and entry	1,601	1,602
Disorderly conduct	1,475	1,071
Gambling	1,277	1,376
Murder	142	77
Liquor laws	618	224
Auto laws	259	171
Narcotics laws	2	6
Arson	106	171

The creation and effective use of the State Highway Patrol alleviated much of the constabulary's concern for auto law enforcement, although troopers continued to arrest violators on the roadways. State Police concern for liquor law violations was also diminished by the state's Liquor Control Board agents.

New enlistments during the biennium were outnumbered by separations 26 to 46. Only three men successfully completed training in the 1935–36 period. A "tight" budget evidently compelled Adams to operate with a force short of its legal strength.

During the calendar year of 1936, executions at the Rockview Penitentiary dropped to the lowest figure in twenty-one years. Only one person died in the electric chair that year.

The following is a 1935–36 listing of the office personnel assigned to each of the five troops:

Troop A, Greensburg
Principal Police Clerk Blair E. O'Neal
Principal Clerk-Stenographer James K. Seacrist
Special Stenographer-Clerk Frank Hamm
Special Stenographer-Clerk Percy C. Kratzer

Troop B, Wyoming
Principal Police Clerk Frank M. Barry
Principal Clerk-Stenographer George R. Naugle
Special Stenographer-Clerk Leo A. Garvey
Special Stenographer-Clerk Stanley A. Gabrysh

Troop C, West Reading
Principal Police Clerk Raymond S. Herb
Principal Clerk-Stenographer Paul E. Levan
Special Stenographer-Clerk Samuel A. Ely
Special Stenographer-Clerk Denver B. Barne

Troop D, Butler
Principal Police Clerk C. C. Bowman
Principal Clerk-Stenographer Carl A. Kennedy
Special Stenographer-Clerk Ambrose E. Bergan
Special Stenographer-Clerk Homer S. Hammond

Troop E, Harrisburg
Principal Police Clerk William N. Doll
Principal Clerk-Stenographer Fred J. Denn
Special Stenographer-Clerk W. Earl Gulden
Special Stenographer-Clerk Robert P. Maffet

In 1931, Governor Pinchot wrote to Adams, outlining his thoughts about the attitude the State Police display toward strikes and strikers. In his directive Pinchot specified that any request for assistance from a sheriff "will not be complied with, except in the case of actual violence, until after that request has been submitted to and approved by the Governor." Although the directive was stated clearly enough, situations arose where the position of the State Police was questioned. To clear up these misunderstandings, Adams submitted two questions to Attorney General Charles J. Margiotti, asking for Margiotti's opinion. Adams' questions were:

1.   On many occasions and also during labor disturbances, sheriffs of counties have called upon the State Police

for assistance, indicating the situation was beyond control, and with the approval of the Governor, such assistance was furnished. Under such circumstances, shall the State Police act under the instructions of the sheriff or shall the State Police act under instructions of their superior officer carrying out the policy of the Governor, assuming that the known policy of the Governor does not coincide with the known policy of the sheriff?

2.   Should the State Police on arrival at the scene of the disorder learn that the measures taken by the sheriff did not adequately cover the situation as regards the preservation of law and order, or in the opinion of the State Police officer in charge, were too harsh or burdensome, are the State Police authorized to act independent of such sheriff?

Margiotti's reply, better known as Opinion No. 208, was dispatched to Adams on September 11, 1936. Margiotti's preliminary comments dealt with the powers and rights of the governor and the authority and duties of the State Police, which formed the basis for his official opinion:

> Therefore, in response to your first inquiry, you are advised that when the sheriff of a particular county calls upon the State Police for assistance in preserving law and order, such request should be addressed to the Governor, and that the State Police should act under the instructions of their superior officer who is carrying out the policy of the Governor.
>
> In answer to your second question: if the State Police, upon their arrival at the scene of disorder, learn that measures taken by the sheriff to preserve law and order are not adequate, or that such measures are too harsh or burdensome, or that law and order can be better preserved by other means, it is the duty of the State Police to formulate and carry out their own orders as to how the situation must be handled, and in so doing they may act independently of the sheriff. It may be that, upon arrival of State Police at the scene of disorder, they find the sheriff has issued a proclamation defining the activities of persons in and about the scene of disorder, or had issued orders as to the manner in which peace officers and others must conduct themselves. The sheriff by proclamation can in no way limit the superior authority of the Governor; and his agents, the State Police are not bound thereby, but may perform their duty in such manner and make regulations for the conduct and activities of persons in and about the scene of disorder as they, in their discretion, deem proper.

It has not been the policy of the Commonwealth to interfere with local authorities in enforcement of the laws and the handling of local officers, unless assistance is asked in the manner above outlined. However, the Governor as the chief executive officer and the highest civil and military authority within the Commonwealth may at any time that he believes the enforcement of the law and preservation of peace and order is being handled inadequately, or that the interests of the public demand it, supercede the local sheriff and send in the State Police to take charge of the situation. In such cases, the local officers and authorities are likewise subservient to him and his orders and his representatives, and the State Police are not bound by any proclamation or other order that the sheriff may issue.

When requesting assistance, the sheriff, according to Margiotti, must submit his request to the Governor and "clearly specify that the situation is beyond his control and that the sheriff specifically asks the Governor to take charge of the situation by sending the State Police, the National Guard, or both." State Police top officials have scrupulously observed Margiotti's guidelines ever since they were issued.

Adams, in October, 1936, moved Gearhart from Reading and gave him command of Troop E, at Harrisburg. Gearhart replaced Stout who had retired in April. Gearhart had commanded the Reading troop from May, 1920, until his transfer to Harrisburg. The sixteen-year tenure was one of the longest on record.

His command at Harrisburg was cut short when Adams again transferred him. This time he was temporarily placed in charge of the detective division operations. This move was made just prior to the State Police-Highway Patrol merger in 1937.

In late 1936, the general assembly met for its second special session during that year. Governor Earle took advantage of this session to submit Adams' name to the Senate for confirmation as State Police superintendent from November 15, 1936, to the third Tuesday of January, 1939. Adams' nomination was given to the Senate on December 1. He was confirmed five days later.

The events of mid-1937, however, were to change the course of Adams' career and his Senate confirmation to serve as superintendent until the third Tuesday of January, 1939, was not to be fulfilled.

In early spring of 1937, the Ohio Valley was devastated by major flooding of the Ohio River, and in an unprecedented move, Adams dispatched a constabulary force to Louisville, Kentucky, to assist in rescue work and guard against looting. The detachment remained in the flood-ravaged area until waters subsided and local authorities were in a position to maintain order. It was a fine gesture—and more than a gesture—for Pennsylvania to rush to the assistance of another state momentarily facing a hardship beyond its limits to cope with.

In April, 1937, the constabulary witnessed the loss of two more troopers in the line of duty. Private John E. Fessler, of Troop E, Harrisburg, was shot and killed on April 22, while apprehending William Yeager, of Cooper Township, Montour County. Private Joseph A. Hoffer, of Troop A, Greensburg, was shot and killed on April 27, during a shoot-out following a jail break in Fayette County.

During its regular 1937 session, the general assembly passed a number of measures affecting the State Police. There were eight acts in all, numbering from 448 through 455. The last of these, Act 455, had the greatest impact upon the constabulary's future.

On a number of occasions the merger of the State Police and the State Highway Patrol was recommended for both effectiveness in law enforcement and economy. Governor Earle favored a merger of the two agencies and encouraged his supporters in the general assembly to draw up the necessary bills. The first to be introduced was Senate Bill 782 which quickly drew fire from the state's automobile clubs. A news item appearing in the *Harrisburg Telegraph* February 27, 1937, stated:

> Opposition to Governor Earle's proposed merger of the State Police and the State Highway Patrol was voiced by the Legislative Committee of the Pennsylvania Motor Federation meeting last night in the Harrisburger Hotel. Two reasons for this opposition were expressed by R. B. Maxwell, of Harrisburg, general manager, who contended that not only will the merger be financed by money taken from the Motor (license) Fund, but the two units have separate and distinct duties—one to battle crime and the other promote safety.

The Senate conducted public hearings on this bill. Some witnesses opposed to the merger were concerned for the use of motor license fund monies for other than traffic-related matters, which echoed the argument of the automobile club officials; others were simply against any legislative move that would smack of extending the State Police. Former members of the constabulary expressed their interest in maintaining the constabulary as a separate organization which they fondly served and sentimentally wanted preserved. Some witnesses argued that federal funds would no longer flow to the Commonwealth, if a merger were to take place.

Proponents of the merger counter-argued that: (1) federal funds would not be affected; (2) the Motor License Fund would be tapped only to the extent necessary to support highway safety activities, and (3) efficiency and economy in government demanded such action.

There remained in the legislature sufficient oppositon to having the Pennsylvania State Police enlarged by absorbing the Highway Patrol, since this is what would appear to have occurred, if the name of the Pennsylvania State Police was to be passed onto the proposed new agency. The use of the Highway Patrol title was equally shunned by those who favored the Pennsylvania State Police identity. As a compromise to both sides in this issue and to placate the automobile clubs on the use of the motor licence fund for a department which would also be engaged in general police duties, the sponsors of the bill adopted the name—Pennsylvania Motor Police.

On May 18, 1937, the Senate approved SB-782 by a vote of 28–19, and sent the measure to the House. The companion House Bill 2373 was referred to the Committee on State Government and finally released to the floor for consideration on June 4. After brief debate, following closely the points already mentioned, the House voted 143–49 in favor of the merger. The House vote came just one day before general assembly adjournment, and the bill was signed by the House Speaker on adjournment day, June 5.

The legislature-approved measure amended the Administrative Code of 1929 to reflect the consolidation of the Pennsylvania State Police and the State Highway Patrol and to identify the new organization as the Pennsylvania Motor Police; to increase the complement of the new agency to 1,600 officers and men; to set the commissioner's salary at $8,000 a year; and to limit appointments to one deputy.

It is noted that the new department head was to be titled "commissioner." Both the State Police and Highway Patrol were headed by a superintendent. Until this time, according to the Administrative Code of 1929, the former State Police superintendent had the authority, with the approval of the governor, to appoint "deputies." This authority, however, was never exercised. The newly-approved measure specifically restricted the commissioner to one deputy. This restriction remains in effect to this day, although considerations have been given to having this limit removed.

Almost one month went by before Governor Earle signed the merger bill into law. During this period, Earle and his advisors were faced with the decision of naming a commissioner to head the new department, since the new agency would officially come into being the moment Earle affixed his signature to the bill. Adams was top man in the State Police and Captain Earl J. Henry was acting superintendent

of the Highway Patrol. Appointing either of these men to the commissioner's post could have created conflict and apparently this
bothered Earle who turned his attention elsewhere. Among those
under consideration was Captain William A. Clark, of Troop B,
Wyoming. Clark, a popular figure in the anthracite region of northeast
Pennsylvania, had been troop commander since 1920 and had established an excellent reputation.

Earle decided in favor of Clark, and Clark was informed that he
would be the first commissioner of the Pennsylvania Motor Police.
This message reached Clark late in the evening of June 27, allowing the
Troop B commander and his family some brief moments for rejoicing.
By nine o'clock the following morning, however, a public announcement came from the governor's office appointing retired Rear Admiral
Percy W. Foote instead. It is entirely possible that Earle's advisers
convinced him in the final moments to go for someone having no ties
whatsoever with either the constabulary or Highway Patrol. In any
event, Foote was in—Clark was out.

Clark was very much disappointed with this unexpected turn of
events and on the verge of quitting his post. Allowing time for tempers
to cool, he did not quit, and went on to serve his department well until
1945.

Earle signed the merger bill on June 29, 1937, which became Act
455, P.L. 2436. On that same day he also signed into law: Act 448, P.L.
2403, citing certain duties relating to fires and fire protection; Act 449,
P.L. 2410, updating the statutes relating to the training school; Act 450,
P.L. 2412, authorizing the use of Motor License Fund for partial funding of Pennsylvania Motor Police operatons; Act 451, P.L. 2420, regulating hours of rest and vacation time for the new agency personnel;
Act 452, P.L. 2421, modifying enforcement responsibility for the dry
cleaning trade; Act 453, P.L. 2423, establishing a retirement system for
the Pennsylvania Motor Police and making membership in the system
mandatory, and Act 454, P.L. 2433, updating the statutes governing the
keeping of criminal identification records. The enactments amending
statutes already on the books were basically essential to reflect the
name of the new department.

Also passed by the 1937 General Assembly was Act 211, P.L. 774,
signed by Earle on May 21, establishing a Pennsylvania Turnpike Commission and authorizing the commission to build and maintain a toll
roadway between Middlesex, Cumberland County, and Irwin, Westmoreland County. Although this legislation held no particular significance to the State Police at the time of passage, the opening of the toll
roadway in mid-1940, however, was to bring about an important
change in the alignment of field forces.

At the time of the merger, the Pennsylvania State Police numbered about 375 officers and men who were significantly outnumbered by the Highway Patrol's 650 officers and men.

Before proceeding with the history of the Pennsylvania Motor Police, it would be well to have a better understanding of the State Highway Patrol. The next chapters will be dedicated to that purpose.

CHAPTER X

State Highway Patrol
Captain Wilson C. Price
1923–1927

A quote from the *Boston Globe,* which was picked up by the *Harrisburg Patriot* on June 9, 1975, went like this: "After the devil made the automobile, he couldn't think of anything to do for an encore except invent the atom bomb."

The World War I years saw a tremendous increase in the number of motor vehicles on the American scene, and this first product of the "devil," as the *Boston Globe* writer put it, amazingly took the country by storm after the war's end. Pennsylvania was busily engaged in building highways to accommodate travel by motorized equipment, a responsibility resting with the Department of Highways, which was organized in 1903. Pennsylvania was then, and still is, one of the nation's leading road building states.

The Department of Highways was faced with not only providing adequate roadways for the motor age, but also governing the behavior of those who operated motor vehicles, and maintaining essential records of both equipment and operators. In earlier chapters, it was noted that the state constabulary was looked to by the Department of Highways to enforce its rather simple regulations regarding speed and general highway usage, to cooperate with that agency in the recovery of stolen vehicles and to apprehend those guilty of such thefts. But the state constabulary, limited by its law-bound complement and already overburdened responsibility for enforcing the state's criminal laws, was in no position to be of effective assistance with regard to the state's motor code. The constabulary officials did the best they could under the circumstances, and that was it.

This was a matter of serious concern to Superintendent John C. Groome, acting Superintendent George F. Lumb and Superintendent Lynn G. Adams, all of whom were most willing to commit themselves and their constabulary forces to the fight against lawlessness of any kind. Their individual efforts to convince the general assembly to increase the constabulary manpower limits were repeatedly denied. Elements in the general assembly were yet skeptical about the growth of the constabulary, particularly those legislators who were heavily influenced by the labor lobbyists.

There was an alternative to an increase in the constabulary complement to enforce the motor code. State Police officials and the Highway Commissioner, sensing the futility of expanding the constabulary in behalf of highway safety, jointly recommended the formation of a separate organization specifically geared to handle the problems of a motoring public. Governor Pinchot and his Secretary of Highways Paul D. Wright were convinced that this alternative plan did have a chance of surviving legislative debate, and pursued the passage of enabling legislation.

There were men in private life interested, too, in the advancement of highway safety. Dr. William S. Cook, a Beaver Falls dentist and the first president of the Beaver County American Automobile Association (AAA) club, was very much interested in the formation of the state highway patrol. Sharing his thoughts in this matter was Homer H. Swaney, a Beaver Falls attorney. Swaney, often in Harrisburg to represent local utilities in matters before the Public Utility Commission, was well-known to Governor Pinchot and other heavyweights on the political scene. Swaney was influential enough to get the Cook-Swaney ideas of a state highway patrol introduced into the political arena where action would be taken. Although credit for the establishment of the highway patrol can not be given to any one man—or two—tribute should be paid to these two Beaver County professionals who were instrumental in moving state officials toward a keener handling of the highway safety problem. After the patrol was organized, Cook and Swaney were rewarded by the establishment of a patrol substation at Beaver Falls rather than at the county seat or elsewhere in the county.

The general assembly in 1923 reacted favorably to this approach and passed three measures: Act 168, P.L. 259, May 18; Act 230, P.L. 425, May 24, and Act 296, P.L. 718, June 14. Cautious to keep members of this new organization from being identified in any way with the State Police, the enabling legislation was carefully worded to identify the Motor Code enforcers as "designated officers" of the Highway Department. The designated officers were empowered only to arrest for violations of the Motor Code. They were not given the authority to make criminal arrests. Denying them this authority and calling them designated officers, in the opinion of the legislators, were sufficient safeguards against any mistakened association with the constabulary. At last the highway officials were given an opportunity to form an enforcement organization that would put teeth into the rules and regulations they saw fit to promulgate.

Highway officials had no experience in patrol organization. Neither was there such an organization in being elsewhere in the nation to emulate. So, whether or not the members of the general assembly liked it, Secretary of Highways Wright turned to Superintendent Adams for constabulary assistance and guidance.

Adams selected Captain Wilson C. Price for this liaison role. Price at the time was chief of the BCI & I. Adams relieved Price of this primary responsibility and gave him a full-time schedule to build a worthwhile agency. Adams felt it in the best interests of the constabulary to have an effective counterpart in the area of highway safety with which the constabulary could cooperate in areas of mutual concern.

Price had already established for himself an excellent reputation for his constabulary services. He was one of the original group of hearty souls that joined the constabulary on December 15, 1905. He was then a senior officer with eighteen years of experience under his belt.

Price was born in the District of Croagh, Union of Ballycastle, County of Antrim, Ireland, August 13, 1881. He was one of nine children born to Alexander and Ellen Corry Price. Accepting the possibility of a better life in the new world, as did many other Irish families, Alexander Price, his dear wife Ellen and the first four children born to them set sail for American shores in August, 1886. Young Wilson Price was then nearing his fifth birthday, and celebrated it aboard ship.

As the ship carrying the Price family neared the Philadelphia harbor to which it was destined, the ship was caught up in a severe storm, suffered damages and had to be abandoned. Fortunately, another vessel in the shipping lanes spotted the sinking ship and hastened to the rescue. By way of "breeches buoys," all passengers of the doomed vessel were transferred to the rescue ship in a heavy sea that made rescue no simple task. Ellen Price, faced with the loss of all their worldy belongings, managed to cling to two silver candelabra that

Captain Wilson C. Price (Courtesy of Major Walter E. Price)

had been in the Price family for years and held sentimental value, if nothing else. (The candelabra remain in the possession of Price family survivors to this day.) The rescued Price family was set ashore at Philadelphia on August 18, 1886.

Young Wilson had very little formal schooling. Strongly desiring an education, however, he undertook a series of correspondence courses from the International Correspondence School at Scranton.

He became an apprentice machinist and pursued this occupation until he was overcome by the promises of a more venturesome life in the U. S. Army. The United States in 1899 was then faced with dealing with insurgent forces in the Philippine Islands. Price, not yet 18, misrepresented his age and enlisted with the Army on June 6, 1899.

Price, as an infantryman, saw action in the Philippines and later bravely served in the Boxer Rebellion in China where he earned a recommendation for the nation's highest military award—the Congressional Medal of Honor. Because of some misunderstanding in the handling of this recommendation through military channels, Price was instead awarded the United States Certificate of Merit by President Theodore Roosevelt on March 10, 1902.

Authorities, however, who were interested in Price's military deeds, for more than two decades pursued a course of righting what was considered a grave wrong. In 1924, the following letter, summing in detail Price's heroic accomplishment, was written by Philip Dorr, Price's Highway Patrol adjutant, to Congressman C. C. A. Baldi, Jr., of Philadelphia:

Relative to your interest in the case of Wilson C. Price, who served in Company F, 9th Infantry, U. S. Army, from 1899 to 1902, I have gathered the following facts.

Price enlisted at Philadelphia on June 6, 1899, and was assigned to Company F, 9th Infantry, which regiment was then serving in the Philippines. He joined his company at San Fernando, Luzon, in September, 1899, and took part in the advance on and capture of Angeles, the eleven engagements incident to the holding of this place and the advance on and capture of Tarlac, at that time the capital of the Philippine Republic and the headquarters of the Insurgent forces.

In June, 1900, the Boxer uprising having broken out in China, the lives of all foreigners in North China being placed in jeopardy and the American and other legations in Peking being in a state of seige, the 9th Infantry was ordered to China for the purpose of protecting American citizens and relieving the seige on the U. S. Legation. On July 9, 1900, the transport Logan, bearing the 9th Infantry and other troops, arrived at Taku, China; the troops were disembarked and proceeded to Tien Tsen where it was found that a state of war existed between the various powers and the Imperial Chinese Government and that a battle was inevitable.

On the morning of July 13, the allied forces, of which the 9th Infantry was a part, attacked the walled city of Tien Tsen. During the battle which ensued, the 9th was ordered to the right flank of the Japanese in an effort to quell a heavy enfilading fire, this movement was hampered and eventually stopped by a series of water filled ditches, and as ammunition was running low the Regiment found itself in a very dangerous position. At this point Lieutenant Lewis B. Lawton, adjutant of the 1st Battalion, who had been sent to the rear by his Commanding Officer in an effort to secure reinforcements and ammunition, came running across the field toward the front line. He was seen to stagger and fall, then regain his feet and come forward; again he seemed to receive a heavy blow and fell, was unable to rise but began to crawl forward and fell into a ditch near where Price was lying and firing toward the Chinese line. Price immediately went to the assistance of Lt. Lawton and found that he had been severely wounded in the right arm, right breast, the foot and head. While Price was administering first aid to this officer, the Chinese began an encircling movement which gave them direct fire down the ditch in which the Americans had sought shelter; when Price noted this he immediately began, with the tools at hand, namely a mess pan and bayonet, to dig a trench and construct a traverse for the protection of this wounded man. As the work on this trench progressed, Price was able to bring two other wounded men into its protection; one of these men, Private Hammons of Company F, had a gunshot wound of the groin and the other, a Private from Company C, had a gunshot wound of the jaw.

Through the medium of this crudely constructed trench and traverse, Price was able to protect these men from the Chinese fire and undoubtedly saved their lives. When eventually relieved of their position, the wounded men were evacuated to the hospital and Lt. Lawton made the following recommendation.

Lawton recommended the Medal of Honor for Price's heroic efforts on July 13, 1900. Lawton cited as witnesses Major J. M. Lee, 9th U. S. Infantry and Private Packett, Company C, 9th Infantry and himself. For some unaccountable reason the recommendation was changed by Lt. Colonel C. A. Coolidge to read "Certificate of Merit" instead of Medal of Honor and Price received the Certificate of Merit in 1902. Price went on to fight in the battles of Yang-Tsun, Ho-Sie-Wu, Matow, Tung-Chow and Peking. Attempts were made by friends to restore the original recommendation for the Medal of Honor, apparently without success.

More will be reported on Price's military awards as the subject surfaced later in his police career.

When the Ninth Infantry returned to duty stateside, Price was transferred to the Quartermaster Department at Fort McPherson, Georgia. Price's military career came to a close with his honorable discharge from the army on June 5, 1902.

He returned to his machinist occupation at Philadelphia, and on April 5, 1905, married Rebecca Sheppard Ely. The Sheppard and Ely families came to Philadelphia from England. Three children, Walter Earl, Isabel Ellen and Robert Alexander, were born to Wilson and Rebecca Price. Isabel Ellen died at the age of 4.

When recruiting for the new constabulary was underway, Price again succumbed to the challenges of adventure and applied for membership in this unique organization. He was interviewed by Captain William P. Taylor, at Reading, who was very much taken with Price's military background. After consultation with Superintendent John C. Groome, Taylor approved Price's appointment to the constabulary and granted him an outright non-commissioned rank of sergeant effective December 15, 1905. Price was assigned to Taylor's Troop C at Reading.

Price was promoted to first sergeant on September 15, 1909, transferred to Troop A, Greensburg, on January 17, 1910, promoted to lieutenant and transferred to Troop B, Wyoming, on June 15, 1916, promoted to acting captain at Troop D, Butler, on December 1, 1917, transferred to Troop C, Reading, on June 1, 1918, and transferred to Troop A, on April 1, 1919. Later that year, he was given permanent hold of the captain's bars on September 1, at Troop B. This ended his field tour of duty.

On March 1, 1920, Adams saw fit to bring Price to State Police headquarters and give him command of the newly-organized BCI & I. To better equip him for this command role, Price received special training with criminal identification experts with the New York City and Philadelphia police departments.

When the State Police training school was closed at Newville, Price was temporarily taken from the BCI & I to head up a training school for recruits at the Pennsylvania National Guard Reservation at Mt. Gretna.

Price obediently accepted Adams' order to assist the Highway Department with the formation of a new agency specifically trained to patrol Pennsylvania's thoroughfares. The assignment, intended to be a provisional one at the outset, took up the remaining years of Price's police career. The Highway Department furnished Price with offices on the third floor of temporary building No. 1 behind the state capitol. Later he was moved to third floor accommodations in temporary building No. 2. These temporary buildings, numbering six in all, were erected immediately to the rear of the capitol to satisfy a need during World War I; though intended as temporary structures, they were not demolished until after World War II. Highway Patrol headquarters remained in temporary building No. 2 until the agency's merger with the State Police in 1937.

Public announcements made by Governor Pinchot and Highway Secretary Wright in newspapers throughout Pennsylvania heralded the formation of a 100-man highway patrol unit. Interested young men were invited to apply for membership. The summer of 1923 witnessed the response of some 2,500 men. In the absence of special application forms of its own, the Highway Department drew forms from the State Police; all forms concerned with the processing of applicants were borrowed from the State Police.No proof of age was required, which gave rise to the temptation to misstate age for the sake of eligibility at 21. Misstatements of age were disclosed many times in later years when correct ages had a critical bearing upon retirement benefits.

Since Price was given the job of putting together a unique outfit, it was only natural that he would draw upon the experience of another unique agency to which he belonged—the Pennsylvania State Police— and to enlist the support of constabulary management whenever and wherever it was needed. The most impressive of applicants were notified by mail to report to the nearest State Police troop headquarters for screening. There they were interviewed by non-commissioned officers and given a preliminary physical exam which was limited to the measurement of height and weight; eyesight was checked and notice made of any significant infirmities. A written test was not part of this initial recruiting effort everywhere. Recruits in the Harrisburg area, however, do recall undergoing a brief written exam and a physical exam by a doctor. In Harrisburg, Price had contracted the services of Dr. S. J. Roberts who remained the Highway Patrol medical officer for more than a decade.

After screening through processed applicant reports, Price selected 125 and directed them to report to a training site at Colebrook. Colebrook was a geographical point for the National Guard Reservation at Mt. Gretna. Price was acquainted with this military site earlier in 1923, and prevailed upon the state's adjutant general for the use of National Guard facilities until other arrangements could be made. Men heading for Colebrook for the most part had to entrain for Harrisburg and take another train from there to Colebrook. A mile-walk faced each recruit from Colebrook to the Mt. Gretna training site where they were greeted by Price in civilian dress and a five-man staff of State

Police non-commissioned officers. Training began in mid-September, 1923.

The original group of 125 men forming this semi-military patrol outfit was housed in tents, 5 men to a tent. Included in this complex were tents for mess, headquarters, staff, post exchange and a wash tent with outside showers featuring running cold water. Two large tents were later set up to house the newly-purchased motorcycles. Instruction classes were held in the mess tent.

Each recruit was given fatigue clothing and an old State Police uniform without identifying patches, cap or coat ornaments, and assigned a motorcycle.

The first instructors were First Sergeant August Alquist, Troop E, and Corporals George A. Amick, Troop A, Edmund Roos, Troop B, James J. Hughes, Troop C, and Edward J. Price, Troop D. A modest course of instructions included studies in the motor laws, criminal procedure and criminal law, geography of Pennsylvania, spelling, arithmetic, motorcycle operations and maintenance, calisthentics, and military foot drill. Responsibility for motorcycle instructions rested with representatives of the Indian Motorcycle Company. Firearms training and report-making were conspicuously absent at Mt. Gretna.

Kitchen police and fatigue duties occupied a share of training time. Cutting fire wood daily was a major undertaking. One wood pile was described by a trainee as "big as a house." Much of the wood, it was suspected, was destined for fireplaces in Harrisburg. As temperatures dropped during the fall months, wood-burning stoves were placed in the tents and recruits tended these fires through the day and night. Discipline was strict and training was rugged—both of these factors accounted for a high attritional rate. Before the training program was over, almost half of the class was gone. Only sixty-eight stalwarts saw the seven-week period to its conclusion.

During the final week of training, the recruits were measured for new uniforms. The class broke up at Mt. Gretna on Monday, November 5, 1923. The discordantly attired band of cyclists left Colebrook early Monday morning and arrived at their destinations the same day. The patrolmen were accompanied by their State Police instructors who rode back to their respective troops in motorcycle sidecars. Their teaching assignment was finished with the end of this first class.

Unfortunately, no special importance was attached to this history-making class, insofar as ceremony was concerned. The recruits finished their schooling on November 5, they were given their assignments—and dismissed. They left in five groups, each heading for a State Police troop destination. There were no graduation exercises—

no ceremony whatsoever to mark this historic occasion. Class members did not recall any officials present at Mt. Gretna to bid them farewell or wish them well; no certificates were issued.

Once at their State Police locations, the patrolmen awaited the arrival of their uniforms and equipment. Patrol operations were to get underway on December 1. During this waiting period, patrolmen attended makeshift schools. Most of this month-long wait, however, was given to fatigue duty for State Police personnel, including the cleaning of stables, grooming horses and "everything else they could think of for us to do." No one was permitted liberty, except for an emergency. The patrolmen were pleased no end to leave behind that type of work, once their regular patrol duties were begun.

On November 22, Highway Secretary Paul D. Wright informed the public that the State Motor Patrol operations would commence December 1. According to Wright, patrolmen would be quartered in twenty-six cities and towns with patrols covering a radius of thirty miles. "The sole idea of the legislation in providing for this Motor Patrol," said Wright,

> is to safeguard the lives and property of those who use the roads in Pennsylvania. It is the hope of the Highway Department that the Motor Patrol will not be compelled to make wholesale arrests. No person who obeys the laws of the Commonwealth and the rules of the road need fear members of the Motor Patrol. Other persons, rightfully, will be dealt with according to law.

Wright went on to cite those things to which drivers should be particularly attentive to avoid arrest. He noted that:

> when a motorist is stopped by a patrolman, his driver's card will be punched that thereafter it will be a record against him, and this record will also show on the cards filed at Harrisburg.
>
> The Department will be particularly severe on reckless drivers. The law gives the Highway Commissioner power to revoke a license without warning, and cases of glaring recklessness when reported to Harrisburg will be followed immediately by loss of the offender's license.

Uniform equipment was delivered too late to meet the December 1 date. Uniforms were of grey whipcord. The breeches had a black stripe down the sides. The uniform coat had a choker collar. The cap and coat ornaments were keystone-shaped with "SHP" and a number. Other items of equipment included a service revolver and holster, leather storm coat, short rain coat and matching storm pants, puttees and fatigue clothing. Recruits were required to purchase their own shoes and socks. This was thoughtfully done at the Mt. Gretna post exchange prior to their departure.

The *Lebanon Daily News* on December 4 carried this item, "Lebanon motorists will probably encounter officers of the new State Highway Patrol today or tomorrow when they get out on the state highways. Owing to the delayed delivery of the new grey uniforms the patrolmen could not get out for duty on Saturday, the date scheduled for their start on the job."

With reference to the patrolman's limited power to arrest, the *Lebanon Daily News* stated, "In some counties, it was said yesterday, sheriffs may deputize the patrolmen, giving them power of arrest within the county. Department officials, however, would not say that such plans have been under consideration." It is understandable that Highway Patrol and Highway Department officials would not comment on such a development because of an obvious clash with certain members of the general assembly. Nonetheless, the curb on the power of arrest was swiftly overcome by the eventual deputizing of all patrolmen by sheriffs in counties to which they were assigned.

In this same newspaper on December 10 appeared this observation, "While the new organization will not officially serve in any campaign to run down liquor law violators, it is understood it will cooperate with other police agencies in such efforts and will transmit any information gained on law breaking in this respect to enforcement officers. A watch will be kept on trucks suspected of transporting liquor and data on such activities will be turned over to the State Police." It was now clear that the new Highway Patrol was not simply confining itself to the narrower responsibility of making the highways safer, regardless of the legislative objectives which brought the agency into existence.

Some patrolmen operated from State Police substations where they shared facilities and enjoyed an excellent relationship with State Police personnel. Others were sent to leased substations where they were on their own. There were fifteen substations at the outset. Price, by way of his own system of evaluation, appointed certain patrolmen to service as officers-in-charge of their substations. In the absence of any field sub-divisions, Price directed operations from Harrisburg and almost single-handedly supervised such operations as well as one man could be expected to do.

Said one patrolman:

We did not know the highways, had never been in a JP's (Justice of the Peace) office, had never been instructed on how to file a charge or testify. We just had to feel our way around. We had been furnished with some old State Police patrol reports to make up and send to Harrisburg daily. We had no typewriters. As a matter of fact, we had no telephone for some time. No one remained on station on reserve anyway since we all went on patrol afternoons and evenings. It was a good thing the public did not know how dumb we were. We learned through trial and error.

At one substation the men assigned there rented a typewriter. They shared the cost and its use. Since training did not include typing instruction, the men typed the hard way. Some were zealous enough to attend a nearby business school when time off permitted.

The early patrol had no regular working hours nor workdays. The patrolmen worked each day until they were tired. They worked seven days a week and put in long hours. Occasionally some would sneak off a day, trusting that no emergency would point up an absence. Later, however, Price did establish regular working schedules which included a day off each week. A practice was soon adopted statewide whereby each patrolman would stop at a local post office at the terminus of his patrol zone to assure his supervisor that a patrol had indeed been completed.

Although Price was in command of the Highway Patrol operationally, the Patrol was structurally placed under the wing of Benjamin G. Eynon, the Highway Department's Register of Motor Vehicles, for administrative purposes. Eynon was most helpful to Price during the early stages of the Patrol's formation.

Also lending a supporting hand to Price during these early days was Philip J. Dorr, 27, a handsome, zealous Motor Vehicles office employee. Dorr joined forces with Price in November, 1923. Price, early in 1924, cited his need for an adjutant, and with Eynon's approval the post went to Dorr. In May, 1924, Dorr was given the rank of captain.

Price also looked to members of the original class for supervisory assistance elsewhere in his budding agency. In February, 1924, he handed out a number of non-commissioned ranks based upon his own judgment of performances. There was no competitive testing.

In preparation for another class of recruits to up the Patrol's complement, Price arranged with the Hershey Estates to secure the use of one of the Hershey Inn buildings situated in the center of that candy-making community. The training and motorcycle repair facilities were to remain here a short time under the command of Lieutenant John

Marshall, a constabulary officer borrowed by Price. Selected to assist Marshall were young Highway Patrol corporals, David E. Miller, of Munhall, Allegheny County, and Lawrence Brosha, of Antes Fort, Lycoming County. Marshall taught criminal law; Miller handled the motor vehicle law class, and Brosha, a school teacher by earlier profession, held classes in geography, English, spelling, penmanship and arithmetic. Training was not formalized. The instructors planned their programs individually as they saw fit.

The second class was underway in March, 1924. Recruits reported to Hershey training quarters where they were greeted "coolly," given brief instructions and then examined by Dr. Roberts. Supplies and equipment were distributed to each by constabulary Quartermaster Sergeant Edwin Griffith, of Troop E.

Again, the attritional rate was high. Training ended without ceremony. The trainees, after two months, were given their assignments and sent on their way.

The constabulary training school was also moved to Hershey in 1924 and located in a Hershey Estates building on Cocoa Avenue, about a mile from the Highway Patrol school. Before a kitchen and dining room facilities were established at the constabulary school, State Police recruits shared these accommodations with the Highway Patrol. Because of the rugged training at the constabulary school, many of the trainees there welcomed the opportunity to take on kitchen police duties at the Highway Patrol school just to get away from the saddles and give their sore rumps time to be comforted. The two schools engaged in sports competition until the patrol school moved to a new location in Harrisburg.

Classes continued at the patrol school in Hershey during 1924, and command later that year passed to Sergeant James H. Marshall, of Bloomsburg. Marshall was formerly a member of the constabulary, later served a short term with the New Jersey State Police and then joined the patrol. He was known to Price and was swiftly advanced to corporal and sergeant.

Charles F. Schroeder, of Erie, a motorcycle dealer, was enlisted in 1924 to head up the motocycle maintenance program at Hershey. He was appointed corporal.

A 1924 report indicated that during the year 9,460 arrests were made for motor law violations. In addition "an incalculable amount of good was accomplished by the hundreds of warnings issued daily to motorists guilty of minor violations." More than a quarter of a million driver license applicants were examined. Complaints received and investigated by the patrol numbered 2,350. The patrol collected more than $15,000 in protested checks which had been submitted to the

Highways Department for car registration payments. The report continued:

> In addition, forest fires have been prevented, lives saved, and criminals apprehended. In the year and a half that it has been in operation, the record of the Pennsylvania Highway Patrol for law enforcement has been watched with the greatest interest by other progressive states, and at least four commonwealths have already adopted a similar plan, using the Pennsylvania force for their pattern. The patrol is no longer an experiment. It is a success. And every citizen of Pennsylvania may well be proud of its achievements.

In 1925, Price promoted Miller to lieutenant and sent him to Greensburg as inspecting officer for the western half of the state. John R. Standiford, of Glen Rock, York County, was promoted to lieutenant as inspecting officer at Hershey for the eastern half of the state. Others promoted to lieutenant were Lawrence Brosha, who supervised all supply operations, and John W. McCarthy, of Wellsboro, Tioga County, who was given statewide supervision of the driver examination program. Training in motorcycle operations was in the hands of Sergeant William F. Mote.

With four lieutenants, Price then had divided his control. His two inspection officers provided closer field supervision. As yet, Price had established no troops, and he was stressing the need for 250 to 300 men.

During the general assembly session of 1925, freshman Senator Howard I. Painter (R-Butler) introduced Senate Bill 1202 transferring the State Highway Patrol from the Department of Highways to the Pennsylvania State Police. The bill was promptly referred to the Law and Order Committee where it never again saw the light of day. This was the first of other attempts to bring these two police agencies together.

For public enlightenment, Highway Patrol officials published a 118-page document providing interesting information about the Patrol. *Educational Review of the Pennsylvania State Highway Patrol,* as it was titled, carried this foreword:

> If such a thing were possible we wish every one of the two million motorists in Pennsylvania could spend a day on the road with the State Highway Patrol. Only by personal contact with the men themselves and observation of the work they are performing, can one fully understand the need for such a force and the benefits resulting from it.

We believe an experience of that sort would give the average citizen an entirely new conception of the State's work in making the highways safe and a far clearer vision of his own responsibilities as a driver.

Unfortunately it is impossible to give all motorists such an opportunity. But it is the intention of this book to convey, as vividly as words and pictures can do so, an idea of the purpose and method behind the activities of the State Highway Patrol. We hope every man and woman who reads these pages will gain a new appreciation of this fine body of men.

Highlighted, too, was the "Aim of the Patrol": "To familiarize motorists with the State Highway Rules. To emphasize the importance and necessity of Safety First. Safety not only for yourself, but for your fellow-motorist and for the person on foot. To be obliging and accommodating. To render assistance wherever necessary. To be a gentleman on all occasions and under all conditions. To enforce the Motor Laws of Pennsylvania."

The following "Don'ts for Motorists" was featured:

Don't drive with poorly adjusted brakes.

Don't stop your car with all four wheels on the main highway.

Don't drive with only one headlight or with glaring headlights.

Don't attempt to pass another machine anywhere a white line is painted on the highway, at a crest of a hill, at an intersection of two roads, or on a railroad crossing.

Don't attempt to pass another machine unless the highway is clear of machines traveling in the opposite direction for at least two hundred feet; three hundred is safer.

Don't attempt to pass a line of machines and failing in the attempt, cut into the line you are endeavoring to pass. Await your turn to pass a slower moving vehicle.

Don't stop or park your automobile anywhere within a white line, even though you can get your machine entirely off the highway; it is against the law and extremely dangerous.

Don't attempt to pass another machine without signaling your intention, not only to the operator in front, but also to the one that may be following.

Don't forget the speed limit, especially in boroughs and towns you are passing through.

Don't race with another motorist and never try to race with a train to the railroad crossing.

Don't take a chance. Be sure; otherwise you endanger the lives of those in your own car, and also the lives of others.

Don't pass a trolley car loading or discharging passengers.
Don't cut corners on any city street.
Don't forget to keep your lights focused and to carry extra
bulbs.
Don't forget to notify the Automobile Division of the Department of Highways of any change of address. They need it
to send you your application for renewal of license.

The *Educational Review* included some details about the training, which are worthy of mention:

The course includes instruction in the state motor laws, criminal procedure, Pennsylvania geography, simple arithmetic, examination of operators, forms and reports, practical first aid, care and operation of motorcycles and automobiles, and adjustment of headlights. In short, the men are given sound training and experience in handling such situations as will arise when they are graduated to road work. Good food, a daily physical drill, and regular hours, under strict military discipline, put the men in the pink of condition.

Supplementing the classroom work, the "rookies" are sent out on day and night road detail with experienced men, both to observe and to be observed.

A helpful part of the instructions is a series of lectures, demonstrations and written tests given by officials of the Bureau of Motor Vehicles, who came out from Harrisburg, several times a week. These men with their first-hand knowledge of the conditions which must be met in the detailed work of the Department, are able to give the recruits a thorough understanding of the reasons back of forms and regulations.

At the end of the eight weeks' period of training, a final examination is given, which usually weeds out a number of recruits. The young man who comes through as a patrolman must have something more than average ability and brains. During the first week or two (after graduation) he usually goes out on patrol accompanied by a seasoned man. At the end of that time he is sufficiently experienced to meet emergencies cooly and is ready to do his bit in making Pennsylvania highways safe to drive.

The back cover of this paper-bound publication carried a letter, dated May 22, 1924, from Superintendent Wilson C. Price to Mr. J. B. McNaughton, of the Indian Motorcycle Company, Springfield, Massachusetts, in which Prince praises highly the 150 Indian motorcycles in use by the State Highway Patrol. His final sentence, "We are very much pleased with this type of motorcycle and do not hesitate to recommend it to anyone in need of a good, durable, economical and efficient piece of equipment," is a clear-cut endorsement of a product. More recent Pennsylvania State Police practices prohibit the endorsement of any product regardless of its value to law enforcement. Although the worth of an equipment item may be outstanding, any favorable comments by members of the Pennsylvania State Police are made privately to those concerned, if made at all. Members violating this policy do so at the risk of disciplinary action.

In the *Saturday Evening Post* issue for March, 1925, an article captioned, "Driver Tests," contained these important comments in defense of testing operators:

> That the examination and license system for all operators of motor cars affords more protection from street and highway accidents that can be had by any other means is apparently accepted as a fact by all automobile, highway and traffic authorities. Why? Every other element of highway safety is inconsequential compared with the human element. The road-bed, the curves, the warning signs, the signals, the police system and the automobile itself may be one hundred percent perfect according to present standards, and yet the human element, in the form of a reckless, careless or physically or mentally deficient driver, will instantly reduce all these safeguards to complete impotence and make the highway a path of peril to all who happen to share it with him.
>
> The net of all automobiles and highway experience enforces the conclusion that a denial of the rights of the highway to all who are, for any reason, unfitted to drive on it with reasonable safety to themselves and others, is the only effective means of controlling the human element. A perfunc-

State Highway Patrol Training School, Hershey, 1924 (Courtesy of Pennsylvania State Police)

Formal inspection at State Highway Patrol Training School (Courtesy of Mrs. Lawrence Brosha)

tory, for-revenue-only operator's license system is worthless; to be effective it must involve the careful and impartial examination of every applicant, a practical driving test in traffic, and reexamination at reasonable intervals, to guard against driving disabilities which did not exist when the first examination was made.

The *Saturday Evening Post* writer was, indeed, a keen observer of the situation as he beheld it in the mid-twenties, and his words of wisdom have not diminished in value through the decades. The "path of peril," whatever the circumstances, is still the blameful handiwork of the human element for the most part. The worth of the work undertaken by the Pennsylvania State Highway Patrol and continued by the present-day Pennsylvania State Police remains unquestioned.

Late in 1925, Harry A. Edie, of Stewartstown, York County, was moved in as the school's acting first sergeant. Instructors were: Earl J. Henry, of Conestoga, Lancaster County, Arthur J. Oldham, of Confluence, Somerset County, and Fred G. McCartney, of Glasgow, Cambria County—all corporals.

The Hershey Estates required the use of the school building for community purposes, and the patrol school, in 1926, was temporarily moved during the warm months to its former outdoor location at Mt. Gretna. The motorcycle repair unit, however, was reestablished in Highway Department tin shed #4, at 20th and Herr Streets, Harrisburg, adjacent to the constabulary repair shop. In late summer, the school was moved to the leased Harrisburg Childrens Home, at 19th and Swatara Streets, Harrisburg. The new commanding officer was upgraded Lieutenant Edie. Henry, Oldham and McCartney were promoted to sergeant. Henry remained at the school as acting first sergeant. Oldham and McCartney joined Lieutenants Miller and Standiford as aides in the field inspection program.

Lieutenant McCarthy resigned his post in 1926, and the driver examination program fell to Lieutenant George H. Keller, of Pine Grove Mills, Centre County.

Patrolmen committed to the driver exam program in 1926 processed more than 300,000 applicants. They failed 25 percent of the applicants on first examination and 3 percent were permanently rejected. Examinations were conducted at 100 different locations in the state, and the schedule at each point was tailored to acommodate the anticipated workload. These points were served by traveling exam details and, with few exceptions, were not permanent Patrol stations or substations.

By that time, the Patrol force numbered some 230 men, operating from forty-six stations and substations "which are dotted all over the state."

State Highway Patrol Training School, Harrisburg, 1926 (Courtesy of Pennsylvania State Police)

During those early years of the Patrol, Price formed a special group known as "The Flying Squadron." Made up of six exceptionally-trained non-commissioned officers equipped with the best in high-powered motorcycles, this squadron was called into service on short notice to augment regular patrols where troublesome traffic conditions demanded special treatment. The squadron under the direct supervision of Patrol adjutant Captain Dorr won much deserved praise for its effectiveness in promoting highway safety.

Not until 1927 did Price establish his first troops. Through the earlier years, Price was apparently content to supervise statewide Patrol operations from Harrisburg with the aid of his two inspecting lieutenants and two sergeants. With the growth of the Highway Patrol, however, it was inevitable that he would have to draw upon the pattern and experience of the constabulary for guidance. And, he did. The first two troops, A and B, were established at Harrisburg and Greensburg, respectively. These were also sites of constabulary troop headquarters.

With the establishment of the first two troops in April came the first field promotions to the rank of captain. Captain John R. Standiford was given command of the Harrisburg troop and Captain David E. Miller the Greensburg troop. The new table of organization called for two inspecting officers within each troop. Lieutenants James H. Marshall and George N. Pickering, of Germantown, Philadelphia, supported Standiford at Harrisburg; and Lieutenants John M. Bender, of Sharpsburg, Allegheny County, and William B. Smoot, of Girard, Erie County, were Miller's aides.

Upgraded at the same time were Captain Lawrence Brosha, Supply Officer, and George H. Keller, Examining Officer. Keller operated from headquarters situated at Bellefonte, and was assisted by Lieutenant Charles J. McRae, of Port Allegany, McKean County. Mechanical Inspector Charles F. Schroeder was promoted to lieutenant. Lieutenant Harry A. Edie commanded the training school. There were four captains and seven lieutenants in the corps of commissioned officers.

Price and Dorr were the only officers at Patrol headquarters. Assisting them in administrative matters were four civilian employees, all from Dauphin County:

Principal Clerk Harold H. Flack
Stenographer-Clerk Rebecca Klawansky
Account Clerk Mrs. C. A. Books
Clerk-Typist Helen J. Bechley

Appearing on the scene in August, 1927, were the first men to hold the official rank of first sergeant. Promoted were: First Sergeant Arthur J. Oldham at Greensburg; First Sergeant Joseph G. McCann, of Patton, Cambria County, at Harrisburg, and First Sergeant Earl J. Henry at the training school.

The field clerks, mechanics and some custodial employees were given enlisted status, and drew the same pay and allowances received by the patrol members empowered to arrest. This policy continued for some years, after which time these classifications of employees were given civilian titles and their pay structure differed from the enlisted compensation plan.

Mess facilities were maintained at troop headquarters and the training school. Cooks and waiters were not classified as state employees, but were instead paid from the mess fund where employment was held. It was not until the mid-1930s that cooks and waiters were picked up as state employees and allowed the privileges of that status.

The Highway Patrol and the constabulary differed somewhat in the handling of their mess facilities. The Patrol members were furnished quarters and meals in kind where such state accommodations were available. The constabulary troopers, who drew a higher rate of pay, reimbursed the troop mess funds for any meals served them each month.

The Highway Patrol first sergeants were responsible for mess operations and management of kitchen and dining room personnel. Perishable food items were purchased from local vendors after competitive bidding and issuance of short-term contracts. Canned and nonperishable commodities were bulk-purchased in Harrisburg and requisitioned by the field mess stewards.

As it was mentioned earlier, prominent persons interested in Price's military achievements continued to petition Congress and the War Department in his behalf, seeking for him the Congressional Medal of Honor. During World War I, Congress brought into existence the nation's second highest tribute for valor—the Distinguished Service Cross. By authority of Congress, permission was granted to award the Distinguished Service Cross retroactively to those who qualified. It was determined by the War Department that Price had qualified for this award and, on February 14, 1927, Secretary of War Dwight A. Davis awarded to Price the nation's second highest award "for distinguished gallantry in the Battle of Tien Tsin, China, July 13, 1900." This was truly a belated joy and source of pride for Price and the Price family. His friends, however, amid satisfaction did not give up their pursuit of the Medal of Honor.

One of the most unique situations in police circles arose in 1927, since it is rare, indeed, for a top police official to be publicly charged for allegedly "fixing" a traffic arrest. In this case, the son of an Allegheny County court judge was arrested on a charge of driving while under the influence of intoxicants by a State Highway Patrolman from the Butler barracks. Reportedly, a Certificate of Intoxication was submitted by the arresting officer and withdrawn by Captain David E. Miller, troop commander at Greensburg. In a case deeply invaded by political overtones, Miller was cited for malfeasance in office and tried in Butler County court in December, 1927, on that charge. He was found guilty. A sentence of four-months imprisonment and a $200 fine plus court costs was imposed by Judge Vidal. Fellow Highway Patrolmen, sympathizing with Miller's plight, voluntarily contributed to a fund in support of Miller's defense.

Miller appealed the Butler County court action to the state Superior Court (*Commonwealth* v. *Miller*, 94 Pa. Super. 499, 1928). The Superior Court upheld the lower court's disposition, and in an opinion written by Judge Robert S. Gawthrop the court concluded that "the troop captain of the State Highway Patrol, securing withdrawal of information against one charged with 'Driving While Under the Influence,' though there was ample evidence to warrant information, was subject to indictment for malfeasance in office." The case was returned to the lower court.

Subsequently, Miller was placed on probation and paid the fine and costs. Miller continued to serve in his same capacity as troop commander without agency disciplinary action. Perhaps Price and Highway Department officials, because of the political intrigue involved or for other reasons not disclosed, did not feel obliged to punish Miller.

Discipline in the Highway Patrol was much patterned after the constabulary practices. Price was brought up under Groome, Lumb and Adams, all of whom believed in rigid adherence to principles of good conduct. Highway Patrolmen were summarily dismissed for wrongdoing. Patrolmen headed for inevitable dismissal were dispatched to Harrisburg with their motorcycles and equipment, generally accompanied by a non-commissioned officer, where motorcycles and equipment were exchanged for a notice of separation.

Two unusual conditions existed in the Highway Patrol under Price's supervision, which are not easily explained. Price prohibited patrolmen from carrying a gun when off duty, and would not authorize the use of sirens on motorcycles or passenger vehicles. It was no secret that the legislators wanted patrol members to be dedicated only to highway safety. Undoubtedly, Highway Department officials wanted it that way also. The legislators might have foreseen the tendency of patrolmen, who were trained police officers, to emulate the constabulary troopers in criminal matters; and, feeling as they did, worked out an arrangement with Price to prevent such a development. If true, such action could justify Price's policies of no guns off duty and no sirens. These policies remained in effect throughout the life span of the Highway Patrol.

On February 27, 1927, the Highway Patrol recorded its first death in the line of duty. Dead was Patrolman Martin A. Hanahoe of Troop A. Hanahoe, attempting to apprehend a fugitive from justice, was forced off a highway near Towanda, Bradford County, and struck a telephone pole. The motorcycle accident occurred on October 16, 1926. In critical condition, Hanahoe spent the few months following his accident in the Robert Packer Hospital at Sayre, where he died.

Before the year 1927 was up, the Highway Patrol sadly noted another death in the line of duty. Corporal Vincent A. Hassen, also a Troop A member, was thrown from his motorcycle on December 26, in the city of Milton. He was taken to the Geisinger Hospital at Danville; he died the following day. Rightfully labelled a "killer," the motorcycle was to carry many dedicated patrolmen to their deaths before its use was wisely discontinued.

CHAPTER XI

State Highway Patrol
Captain Wilson C. Price
Captain Charles H. Quarles
Captain Earl J. Henry
1928–1937

The reputation of the Highway Patrol continued to grow, and by 1928 there were on file 6,500 applications for appointment to the force which then was supporting a payroll of about 400 patrolmen and employes.

There were yet only two troops, each consisting of a captain, 2 lieutenants, 12 sergeants, 30 corporals and 75 patrolmen. Patrol zones, extended to 100 miles, were manned without concern for weather conditions. The driver examination unit was supervised by a captain and a lieutenant. In 1928, 116 patrolmen were committed to this special program. Traveling details consisted of 2 corporals and 4 patrolmen. Large examination details, numbering more than 10 at times, were permanently operational at Pittsburgh and Philadelphia. Special-duty personnel saw to training, supply and motor equipment maintenance.

In March, with the approval of Governor John S. Fisher, Dorr was reclassified from adjutant to deputy superintendent. This was the first evidence of some reorganization activity.

On June 1, 1928, the driver examination program headed by Captain Keller was given troop status and designated Troop C, Bellefonte. Each of the three troops was divided into two divisions, and this is the formal table of organization for all branches of the Patrol:

Troop A, Harrisburg	*Troop B, Greensburg*
1 Captain	1 Captain
2 Lieutenants	2 Lieutenants
1 First Sergeant	1 First Sergeant
8 Sergeants	8 Sergeants
30 Corporals	30 Corporals
78 Patrolmen	78 Patrolmen
Division #1 - 14 stations	District #1 - 12 stations
Division #2 - 16 stations	District #2 - 16 stations

Troop C, Bellefonte
1 Captain
2 Lieutenants
6 Sergeants
16 Corporals
75 Patrolmen
District #1 - 9 stations, plus travel points
District #2 - 9 stations, plus travel points

Training School	*Supply Unit*	*Repair Unit*
1 Lieutenant	1 Captain	1 Lieutenant
1 First Sergeant	2 Sergeants	1 First Sergeant
2 Sergeants	2 Corporals	4 Sergeants
2 Corporals		4 Corporals
20 Patrolmen		6 Patrolmen

In connection with the reorganization, Price promulgated the "Regulations of the Pennsylvania Highway Patrol," which he also identified as Bulletin No. 34, dated June, 1928. Much of the material paralleled the constabulary regulations, which was understandable.

Price limited the ranks to superintendent, deputy superintendent, captain, lieutenant, first sergeant, sergeant, corporal and patrolman—not at all unlike the constabulary. "The entire Force constitutes one body and any of the officers and men may at any time be placed on duty day or night, temporarily or permanently, in uniform or plain clothes, anywhere within the State without regard to territory or duty to which they are assigned," was a statement plainly put.

According to Price, the force was to be officially known as the State Highway Patrol, and its duties were:

> To patrol the state highways
> To enforce the motor vehicle laws
> To protect life and property

One regulation provided that "Members of the Patrol shall be appointed for a period of years, depending entirely upon the attitude of the individual towards his work." In this respect, the Patrol differed with the constabulary which adhered to a two-year enlistment period. Another regulation stated that "Patrolmen appealing for aid to persons outside the Department when disciplined for misconduct or for assistance toward promotion will be regarded as incompetent and will be immediately dismissed from the service." This was the same philosophy held by Groome and continued with equal vigor by Lumb and Adams.

Price revealed that it cost the Commonwealth of Pennsylvania approximately $400 to train a patrolman. The processing of a patrol applicant included a written exam, a physical and background investigation. Of the latter point, Price stated, "The character investigations constitute one of the most important functions of the Patrol and should be conducted in a conscientious and thorough manner."

More in the form of a lecture rather than a regulation, Price had this to say:

> Show no favoritism, ignore outside interference and above all refuse to withdraw informations (arrest data) that have already been filed. This provision, however, does not mean that an agreement cannot be reached and compromise made with reference to disposition of certain informations filed. Headquarters reserves the right to have certain cases discharged that warrant such action.

He admonished his men with these words, "The practice of threatening motorists with arrest or further prosecution is prohibited. If any action is contemplated, it is not necessary to hold 'curbstone court.' The Justice of the Peace or sitting magistrate will decide on the evidence submitted."

On most major roadways today, signs indicating a minimum speed are much in evidence. Apparently slow drivers in the twenties were considered a hazard to be reckoned with also, according to Price, "The 'hearse driver' operating a motor vehicle at fifteen (15) or twenty (20) miles an hour should be considered as great a menace as that particular motorist, who weaves his way in and out of congested traffic, thus endangering life and limb of other users of the highway."

On the subject of Courtesy:

> A man can be a Patrolman and a gentleman at the same time. In the Pennsylvania State Highway Patrol, honesty,

loyalty and courtesy are the principal virtues, and a man who does not possess all of them will soon find himself on the outside. It is easy to be courteous to everybody without exception. Courtesy is in no way a sign of weakness. On the contrary, it is a sign of strength of character, self-confidence and self-respect.

On the all-important subject of firearms:

The Superintendent will not hold to censure or other punishment, a Patrolman who fires his revolver while in the performance of duty, for any of the following purposes:

To defend another person unlawfully attacked from death or serious injury.

To effect the arrest or prevent the escape, when other means are insufficient, of a convicted felon or of a person who has committed a felony in the Patrolman's presence.

To kill a dangerous animal, or to kill an animal so badly injured that humanity requires its relief from further suffering. When in doubt, DO NOT FIRE.

The pamphlet-size regulation document also cited the arrest authority of the Patrol contained in Section 1215 of the Motor Code (Act 452, P.L. 886, May 11, 1927), and a detailed program of activities and studies for the Patrol training school.

Highway patrolmen point out dangers of improperly adjusted headlights (Courtesy of Pennsylvania State Police)

In 1928, Pennsylvania's motor vehicle registrations topped 1,600,
000. It was during that period the state undertook one of its major steps
in the direction of highway safety when it instituted the official motor
vehicle inspection program. Appointed the first year, as official inspection stations, were 7,000 auto dealers, garages and service stations.

The year 1928 held much sadness for members of the Highway
Patrol as they buried with honors three patrolmen who died in the line
of duty. Killed in motorcycle mishaps were:

Patrolman Sharon C. Wible, Troop B, on February 6
Patrolman Andrew W. Miller, Troop A, on April 1
Patrolman Jay F. Proof, Troop A, on August 29

After previously applying its efforts to examine the fitness of
operators, the Highway Department turned its attention to another side
of the safety program—faulty vehicles. Pennsylvania pioneered in
both of these programs to its everlasting credit. Although the supervision of this inspection program and enforcement of its rules and regulations were not shouldered by the Patrol at the outset, these
responsibilities were soon to pass to the Patrol, after significant irregularities crept into the initial program that called for stern measures.

The general assembly, in its 1929 session, undertook a major revision of the Administrative Code of 1923 and enacted the Administrative Code of 1929 (Act 175, P.L. 177, April 9). Insofar as the Patrol was
concerned, the code's principal provision was the transfer of that
agency and the Motor Vehicle Bureau from the Department of Highways to the Department of Revenue. Ben Eynon, Price and their
respective staffs on June 1 found themselves working for a new boss—
Revenue Secretary Charles A. Johnson. Basically, the move was void
of any significant changes in Patrol activities; the Patrol had established itself under Price's leadership and there was no inclination to
interfere with its progress.

Price welcomed his son, Walter, to the enlisted ranks of the Patrol
in June, 1928, bringing to the Patrol a unique father-and-son combination. Young Price had earlier taken on the job of motorcycle mechanic
with the Patrol, gaining for himself a storehouse of knowledge about
his father's famous agency before attaining minimum age for enlistment.

On September 1, 1929, Price set up his fourth troop at
Williamsport. Command of that newly-formed troop was handed to
Captain John M. Bender. Bender's lieutenants were Charles H.
Killian, of Warren, Warren County, and James H. Marshall. First

State Highway Patrol top officials at entrance of Training School, Harrisburg. Front row, left to right: Capt. Philip J. Dorr; Benjamin G. Eynon, Commissioner of Motor Vehicles; Capt. Wilson C. Price; Walter W. Matthews, Director of Safety; Capt. Lawrence Brosha; Lloyd Persun, Asst. Registrar of Motor Vehicles. Second row: Lt. George N. Pickering; Capt. George H. Keller; Lt. Charles F. Schroeder; Capt. John R. Standiford; Capt. John M. Bender. Third row: Lt. Charles J. McRae; Lt. Walter B. Smoot; Capt. David E. Miller, Lt. Harry A. Edie; Lt. James H. Marshall. (Courtesy of Mrs. George H. Keller)

Sergeant Frank T. Crum, of Derry, Westmoreland County, was fourth in the troop command structure. Troop clerks were Myron W. Thomas and Carlton W. Mendenhall. The Patrol continued to grow under the auspices of the Revenue Department.

The Patrol in 1929 saw two of its members shot and killed in the performance of duty, in separate incidents. On April 19, at North East, Patrolman Russell T. Swanson, in a routine traffic check, had stopped a Lincoln sedan bearing Minnesota plates and occupied by three male passengers. In the absence of any identifying papers, Swanson directed the driver to the nearest magistrate. Enroute Swanson pulled alongside the vehicle to offer additional directions and was shot in the head. When his murder was disclosed to the constabulary stationed at nearby Lawrence Park, effectiveness of the troopers was exemplified by the swift apprehension of the murderers, who were eventually tried and given long-term prison sentences for their brutal crime. State Police Sergeant William Jones and Private Harold Munsee were awarded citations by Superintendent Adams for the apprehension of Swanson's killers. Swanson was the first martyr to the Patrol cause.

On December 27, Corporal Brady C. Paul, accompanied by Patrolman Ernest C. Moore, was participating in a roadblock intended to cut off robbery suspects who had escaped capture in Butler. At New Castle, Paul and Moore stopped a Chevrolet sedan with Ohio registration. A man, woman and young boy were occupants. The operator could produce no evidence of ownership, but before the patrolmen could proceed further, the woman repeatedly fired a revolver, fatally wounding Paul. Moore was felled by a head wound; he recovered and went on to become a troop commander in later years.

An interstate search for the fugitives led to their capture in Arizona, after a shoot-out that cost the life of a deputy sheriff. Captured were Irene Schroeder, 21, and Glen Dague, 33. Both were extradited to Pennsylvania to stand trial for Paul's murder. They were convicted in 1930 and died in Pennsylvania's electric chair on February 23, 1931, less than two years after Paul's slaying. Schroeder and Dague were the 208th and 209th persons to face electrocution in Pennsylvania for a capital crime; Schroeder was the first woman to go that route.

The determination of both Price and Adams to obtain first degree murder convictions against Schroeder and Dague in the Paul case was underscored by their petition to the attorney general for a special prosecutor. They recommended and secured the appointment of the distinguished trial lawyer, Charles J. Margiotti of Punxsutawney. The results of the trial attest to his talents in court. Margiotti, in 1935, became Governor Earle's attorney general.

In police circles, a return of the swift justice meted out to Schroeder and Dague would be welcomed. While capital punishment remains a matter for serious debate, the cold-bloodedness of Brady Paul's slaying, and the slaying of all guardians of the law under somewhat similar circumstances, warrant the severity of capital punishment—a viewpoint that is upheld by the overwhelming majority of peace officers who lay their lives on the line every day of duty, fulfilling their sworn obligation to protect their communities from the scourge of crime.

It is worthwhile mentioning here that State Highway Patrol personnel were often called upon by the constabulary to assist in the conduct of large-scale illegal liquor and gambling raids where constabulary manpower was inadequate for effective carrying-out of raid plans. The Patrol supported other constabulary criminal law enforcement activities when needed. Once again such cooperation reflected the congenial relationship that existed between Price and Adams at the very top of the two state agencies. Most members of the general assembly, who would not cast a vote for extending the complement of the State Police, apparently were not disturbed with this type of joint effort. On the other hand, those same legislators would have blown the lid off the capitol had Adams and Price ever joined forces in labor disturbance incidents. Adams and Price, knowing this, of course, were not the kind of men to push their luck beyond a point of no return. Mutual assistance was definitely selective.

On October 14, 1929, Patrolman Wells C. Hammond of Troop D was killed in a motorcycle accident. He was the third patrolman to meet death in the performance of duty that year. It was also the second consecutive year in which three such deaths were put into the records. Six deaths in two years gave Highway Patrol officials much to worry about; accident prevention dominated their planning.

Nevertheless, multiple deaths continued. Two deaths were recorded in 1930 and another two in 1931—all the result of motorcycle accidents in the performance of duty. The honored dead were:

Corporal Thomas E. Lawry, Troop D, on January 31, 1930
Patrolman Arthur A. Koppenhaver, Troop D, on July 13, 1930
Patrolman Thomas B. Elder, Troop B, on March 22, 1931
Patrolman Orville A. Mohring, Troop A, On December 11, 1931

A single motorcycle mishap was recorded in 1932, when Patrolman Joseph A. Conrad of Troop E met his death on August 30.

In earlier chapters, mention was made of the difficulties Groome, Lumb, and Adams encountered in their attempts to have the general assembly act favorably on a State Police capital budget calling for new state building construction. Ever since 1905, the State Police hierarchy had to content itself with leased facilities, mostly of unsuitable qualities, from which constabulary operations were conducted. Some legislators, hopeful that the constabulary would disappear, had no intention of giving that agency the permanency of state-owned buildings, and such feelings prevailed for a number of decades. Except for a stable building at 20th and Herr Streets, Harrisburg, World War II was to come and go before a permanent structure was legislature-approved and built.

The Highway Patrol was more fortunate—at least to this one extent. The Revenue Department, the parent organization, had access to motor license funds—a procedure that gave that agency leeway to build and to increase the Highway Patrol complement with due consideration, of course, to the availability of motor license money. (It

New State Highway Patrol Training School, Harrisburg, 1931 (Courtesy of Pennsylvania State Police)

will be recalled that the constabulary could not increase its complement except by way of legislative enactment.)

Price, with Revenue Department approval, went about the construction of a three-story building at 21st and Herr Streets, Harrisburg, to house Troop A, the training school, and the supply unit. A smaller building was erected behind the barracks for motorcycle maintenance. An expanse of open grounds east of the barracks was adapted for motorcycle training; another portion was given to a modern pistol range. All in all, the buildings and grounds constituted an up-to-date police facility for administration and training unmatched anywhere. The newly-acquisitioned facility was formally dedicated in 1931 by a party of state officials headed by Governor Pinchot. Within two years, the patrolmen and trainees voluntarily contributed time and effort to the construction of a large, outdoor swimming pool that added immeasurably to the Patrol's recreational program.

At this point in the organization's history, the Patrol took on additional chores, and the Revenue Department changed the label to State Highway Patrol and Safety. Price became the deputy commissioner of Motor Vehicles, a position he held jointly with superintendent of the State Highway Patrol.

In May, 1932, Price brought into being his fifth troop—Troop E, at Philadelphia. Captain William J. Ruch, of Germantown, Philadelphia, was appointed troop commander. Ruch, at 23, had enlisted with the constabulary on August 1, 1920, and resigned after a brief three-month stay to accept a better-paying job. He later joined the Highway Patrol in 1924. Ruch's two lieutenants were George N. Pickering and John L. Rendt, of Emporium, Cameron County. First Sergeant Harold V.

Piersol, of Phoenixville, Chester County, completed the command structure at Philadelphia.

This is the Patrol command roster of May, 1932:

Superintendent - Captain Wilson C. Price
Deputy Superintendent - Captain Philip J. Dorr

Troop A, Harrisburg
    Captain John R. Standiford
    Lieutenant Harry A. Edie
    Lieutenant Joseph G. McCann
Troop B, Greensburg
    Captain David E. Miller
    Lieutenant Earl J. Henry
    Lieutenant Arthur J. Oldham
Troop C, Bellefonte
    Captain George H. Keller
    Lieutenant Charles J. McRae
    Lieutenant Warren C. A. Bear
Troop D, Williamsport
    Captain John M. Bender
    Lieutenant Charles H. Killian
    Lieutenant James H. Marshall
Troop E, Philadelphia
    Captain William J. Ruch
    Lieutenant George N. Pickering
    Lieutenant John L. Rendt
Training School, Harrisburg
    Lieutenant John Grance
Supply Unit, Harrisburg
    Captain Lawrence Brosha
Mechanical Unit, Harrisburg
    Lieutenant Charles F. Schroeder

The Patrol payroll then carried 395 officers and men, a figure that did not include clerks, mechanics and others performing specialized duties.

Late in the summer of 1932, Price was recognized in a special way by the State Police high command. On August 25, the State Police field exhibition was held at Greensburg. As part of the program, forty state troopers and forty highway patrolmen, in full uniform and attuned to the occasion, formed an honor guard as Superintendent Lynn G. Adams awarded to Price, before a capacity public audience, the constabulary's Distinguished Service Medal. This was a befitting tribute, indeed. After eighteen years of service with the constabulary and almost ten years as the Patrol's superintendent, Price was officially still a commissioned officer on the constabulary rolls.

This situation, however, was remedied the following year, when on May 31, 1933, Price resigned as a member of the State Police to terminate his dual role and, at the same time, allow Adams the opportunity to fill his vacancy. Price was then placed on the retirement rolls of the State Police Civic Association.

Interestingly enough, the two police agencies were subjects of legislative action during the 1933 session of the general assembly. Senator John J. McClure (R-Delaware), on April 11, introduced Senate Bill 1030, calling for the transfer of appropriations for the Highway Patrol from the Department of Revenue to the Pennsylvania State Police. This bill, if approved, would have facilitated the transfer of the Patrol to the constabulary. After considerable debate, the bill was referred to the Finance Committee and dropped from the calendar by Senate action two weeks later.

Probably the most far-reaching change ever attempted was contained in Senate Bill 595 introduced by Senator George Woodward (R-Philadelphia) earlier in the session, whereby the State Highway Patrol and various municipal police departments would be abolished and all transferred to an enlarged Pennsylvania State Police with supporting funds contributed by the municipalities concerned. Needless to state, that bill was too, too much and died in the Appropriations Committee.

In the 1933 session, Senate Bills 371 and 372, and House Bill 1426, all aimed to consolidate the State Highway Patrol and the State Police, were defeated on vote or died in committees. Nonetheless, such activity in the legislative halls was indicative of the rising interest in bringing these two agencies under one roof.

In 1933, the Highway Patrol celebrated its tenth birthday. As part of the birthday celebration, special recognition was given ten members of the Patrol, who numbered among the original sixty-eight in 1923. They were:

> Captain John R. Standiford, Troop A
> Captain David E. Miller, Troop B
> Captain George H. Keller, Troop C
> Captain Lawrence Brosha, Supply
> Lieutenant Harry A. Edie, Troop A
> Lieutenant Arthur J. Oldham, Troop B
> Lieutenant Charles J. McRae, Troop C

Ten original Highway Patrol members are honored at 10th anniversary at Longwood Gardens, 1933. Left to right: Capt. John R. Standiford, Lt. Harry A. Edie, Sgt. Charles V. Varner, Corp. John D. Kime, Capt. George H. Keller, Corp. John P. Peck, Capt. David E. Miller, Capt. Lawrence Brosha, Lt. Charles J. McRae, Lt. Arthur J. Oldham. (Courtesy of Mrs. George H. Keller)

Sergeant Charles V. Varner, Troop A
Corporal John D. Kime, Troop A
Corporal John P. Peck, Training School

Formal ceremonies were held at the Longwood Gardens, near Kennett Square, Chester County. Deputy Secretary of Revenue Clyde Shaeffer assisted Price in presenting each man with a star uniform insignia. Representing ten years of service, the stars were to be worn on the blouse sleeves just above the cuffs. Attending the ceremonies were members of Troop A, Harrisburg, and Troop E, Philadelphia. Ceremonies included a review of the two troops by Price and revenue officials. With a few exceptions, the men honored that day continued service until retirement. Oldham, McRae and Kime attained the rank of major with the Pennsylvania State Police before their careers closed.

Two deaths in the performance of duty were sadly noted during 1933. Patrolman Charles E. Householder of Troop A was killed in a motorcycle accident on August 20 and Patrolman Herbert P. Brantlinger of Troop B was shot and killed in a service station holdup on September 3. Brantlinger was the third and last patrolman to be murdered: preceeding him in 1929 were Patrolman Russell T. Swanson and Corporal Brady C. Paul.

On December 15, 1934, the State Highway Patrol and Safety was given division status within the Bureau of Motor Vehicles by revenue officials in what was seen as a major organizational change.

During the changes in the 1930s, there was a shifting and assigning of responsibilities to the State Highway Patrol and Safety, which are worth looking at for a better understanding of the broadened scope of operations. The following material quoted from the 1935–1936 *Pennsylvania Manual* explains:

> The patrol is also responsible for the enforcement of the liquid fuels tax law, the testing of headlights and brakes, the examination of all applicants for operators' licenses, the examination of official motor vehicle inspection stations, the weighing of suspected overloaded trucks and the general enforcement of peace and safety on the highways.
>
> The functions of the Division of Safety are to create and develop methods for insuring the public safety; to revoke and suspend registration and operating privileges for proper cause, and to conduct hearings in connection therewith; to receive reports of accidents and to compile accident statistics; to approve lighting devices and other equipment; and to organize and promote periodic campaigns for the inspection of lighting devices, brakes, and other safety appliances on motor vehicles.
>
> All work, such as the preparation of reports, analyses of accidents, development of exhibits, done for the purpose of carrying out the recommendations of the Governor's Highway Safety Council, is handled by this Division. It devolves upon the Division to establish and maintain relations with other states in connection with operators' examinations, accident reporting and statistics, general enforcement methods and such other special problems as may be necessary.

Earlier it was mentioned that the official motor vehicle inspection program begun in 1928 was not initially given to the patrol for supervision. Supervision was placed in the hands of civilian inspectors who, soon enough, allowed irregularities to sprout to the point where this all-important program's future lay in jeopardy. Revenue officials quickly reacted to this situation by transferring custody of the inspection program to the State Highway Patrol. Under the Patrol's supervision, the rules and regulations were strictly enforced and the program was given new life.

Enforcement of the program, insofar as the operations of inspection stations is concerned, remains to this very day with the Pennsylvania State Police. Although there have been discussions from time to time regarding the transfer of this duty from the State Police, there is doubt that the program can survive without the authority of uniformed and trained troopers.

On January 15, 1935, Pennsylvania welcomed a new governor, George H. Earle. Earle was considerably interested in highway safety and some important achievements in this field can be attributed to his tenure in office. It is possible that he favored consolidating the Patrol with the constabulary upon his taking office as governor, or acquired a strong taste for this movement during the ensuing months. Certainly the unfavorable Patrol activities of 1936 could have been persuaders. In any case, the legislation to bring about this merger in 1937 was a strongly supported administration measure.

Price's friends, who never lost interest in seeing the Medal of Honor bestowed upon Price, came close to fulfilling their mission in 1935. On April 29, Congressman C. Elmer Dietrich introduced House Bill 7787, authorizing the President to present, in the name of Congress, a Medal of Honor to Wilson C. Price:

> Be it enacted by the Senate and House of Representatives of the United States of America in Congress assembled, that the President is authorized to present, in the name of Congress, a Medal of Honor to Wilson C. Price, formerly a private in Company F, Ninth Infantry, U. S. Army, who, in action involving actual conflict with the enemy at Tien Tsin, China, on July 13, 1900, distinguished himself conspicuously by gallantry and intrepidity at the risk of his life above and beyond the call of duty.

Disappointingly, the measure failed to move successfully through both chambers, and no further attempts in pursuit of this objective were undertaken.

On October 7, 1935, Head Police Clerk Harold H. Frack resigned the post he held with the Patrol for ten years. He was replaced by Russell Wrightstone, of Lemoyne, Cumberland County.

One of Price's final important actions was the establishment of a troop at Franklin—Troop F—the sixth and last troop to come into being before the merger. Captain Bender was moved from Williamsport to Franklin to pioneer the troop there. Already stationed in the new troop's jurisdiction were Lieutenants Oldham and Herman J. Roush, of Hummelstown, Dauphin County. Troop F's first sergeant was Alfred G. Wissinger, of Scalp Level, Cambria County. To support this undertaking, Troop Clerk Myron W. Thomas was borrowed from Williamsport and Troop Clerk Clyde Borror from Greensburg. Troop F became operational in February, 1936.

Thomas was shortly thereafter called to Harrisburg for duty at Patrol headquarters, and Borror was returned to Greensburg. Both were replaced at Franklin by Michael Donick, Jr., and William F. Falger.

During the early months of 1936, rumors of wrongdoing by a number of Patrol officers led to a full-scale investigation. Heading the investigation was James C. Taylor, a principal enforcement investigator for the Revenue Department. Price, whose very make-up was action-oriented, was privately criticized for not spending enough time at his desk with administrative chores and disproportionately attending to field activities. Understanding Price's background with the military and constabulary, it is not too difficult to accept the merits of this criticism.

Price, accepting responsibility for having allowed misconduct by a less than firm management policy, resigned his post on February 29, 1936. At 55, Price saw his police career of thirty-one years come to a disappointing end. Brokenhearted, he brooded over this outcome—a condition that surely contributed to his death in 1937. Captain Dorr, Price's deputy, resigned two weeks later, on March 16, 1936.

Following Price's departure, revenue officials called on

Final assembly of State Highway Patrol officers, 1937. Front row, left to right: Capt. John R. Standiford, Capt. Lawrence Brosha, Capt. J. G. McCann, Capt. George H. Keller, Capt. Charles H. Quarles (Supt.), Capt. William J. Ruch, Capt. Earl J. Henry, Capt. Arthur J. Oldham. Back row: Capt. T. N. Boate, Lt. John D. Kime, Lt. G. N. Pickering, Lt. Frank C. Miner, Lt. John Grance, Lt. Melvin H. Snavely, Lt. W. C. A. Bear, Lt. H. J. Roush, Lt. H. A. Edie, Lt. Fred McCartney, Lt. Charles McRae, Lt. A. H. Kratzke, Lt. C. S. Graeff, Lt. J. C. Bricker, Lt. Charles F. Schroeder, Lt. Ray Hoover. (Courtesy of Capt. Fred G. McCartney)

Lieutenant Earl J. Henry, training school commander at Harrisburg, to administer affairs pending the appointment of a new superintendent. Lieutenant Joseph G. McCann was moved into headquarters to assist Henry.

Appointed superintendent on April 13, 1936, was Charles H. Quarles, a former assistant commandant of the Valley Forge Military Academy. Reportedly, Quarles' selection followed a recommendation submitted to Governor Earle by Lt. General Milton Baker, an influential military and political figure in Pennsylvania.

One month later, Quarles promoted Henry and McCann to the rank of captain. Henry returned to the training school. Quarles retained McCann's services at headquarters. Captain John M. Bender terminated his services that same month, and Lieutenant Oldham was named his successor at Troop F. Oldham was promoted to captain later in September.

Changes continued through that fateful year. Troop D was moved from Williamsport to Kingston on July 1, and Captain Keller was given command. Troop C at Bellefonte was then headed by Lieutenant McRae, and it remained in his command until the merger in mid-1937.

In August, Captain David E. Miller closed out his career, and the reins at Greensburg were taken up by Captain William J. Ruch, who was transferred from Troop E, Philadelphia. In coordination, Captain Standiford was transferred from Harrisburg to Philadelphia. Troop A, Harrisburg, remained without a captain until January, 1937, when Captain T. N. Boate, of Harrisburg, assumed command. Lieutenants James H. Marshall and Charles H. Killian resigned on September 30.

One officer, pinning his hopes on more lenient treatment or spitefully striking out at the Price family, recommended to Quarles that young Price be dismissed. In reply to this recommended action, Quarles asked for a reason. The reason given—Walter Price, then a sergeant, was the former superintendent's son. Quarles, in a creditable judgment, labelled the reason as insufficient and small. Sergeant Price remained; the officer did not. Sergeant Price continued to serve honorably until mandatory retirement age of 60 in 1969. He had by then attained the rank of major and commanded Area II—Pennsylvania's northeast counties—with offices at Wyoming, where his illustrious father served many years before as troop commander.

By the year's end, the State Highway Patrol had experienced a complete change of command at the top and at every troop headquarters. It would be difficult to deny the impact of these events of 1936 upon those to take place the following year. The year 1937 had scarcely gotten underway when Quarles resigned his top Patrol post on Feburary 28. Again, revenue officials pointed to Henry and asked him to serve as acting superintendent pending merger with the State Police—a move that then appeared inevitable. Henry lost no time in making three personnel changes favorable to the officers concerned. He moved Captain McCann to Greensburg, Captain Ruch back to Philadelphia and brought Captain Standiford to headquarters as his acting adjutant.

Throughout the turmoil of 1936 and 1937, Captain Brosha and Lieutenant Schroeder were the only officers to retain command of their special duty posts. In fact, both headed their units from the moment they were instituted through the early years of the merger. Troops A, C, D and F saw many months during 1936 and 1937 without a captain as senior officer. Troops B and E, and the training school enjoyed more stability of command.

The Highway patrol management was not generous insofar as the rank of captain was concerned. From 1923 to 1937, a period of fourteen years, only thirteen men were honored with this rank, which was indeed a small figure considering the existence of headquarters, special services and six troops. They were:

> *Captain John M. Bender*
> *Captain Thomas N. Boate*
> *Captain Lawrence Brosha*
> *Captain Philip J. Dorr*
> *Captain Earl J. Henry*
> *Captain George H. Keller*
> *Captain Joseph G. McCann*
> *Captain David E. Miller*
> *Captain Arthur J. Oldham*
> *Captain Wilson C. Price*
> *Captain Charles H. Quarles*
> *Captain William J. Ruch*
> *Captain John R. Standiford*

When Governor George H. Earle signed Act 455 on June 29, 1937, bringing together the Pennsylvania State Police and the State Highway Patrol, they found a new identity with the Pennsylvania Motor Police.

But, before the new organizational name could be familiarized by the general public, and within five days of the disappearance of the Highway Patrol from the state scene, Wilson C. Price died at his Harrisburg residence. His death on July 4 was attributed to a stroke. During the sixteen months since his resignation, Price brooded over his separation from the Patrol and was in ill-health.

Price did, however, cling desperately to one slim hope. Shortly after his resignation, he was approached by former governor Gifford Pinchot who informed him that he had every intention of running again for governor and promised, if elected, to put Price back at the Patrol superintendent's desk. Price did not live to see the next gubernatorial campaign, however, nor did the aging and remarkable Pinchot ever rise again to political prominence. But he did live to see his Highway Patrol, as an entity, close its doors.

Price guided the Patrol from 68 men in 1923 to more than 500 at the time of his resignation. "The State Highway Patrol was known as a model organization and many states patterned their highway patrol systems after the force Price built up," was a comment appearing in the *Harrisburg Telegraph* on the occasion of Price's death.

In private life, Price was a benefactor to the poor, the needy and the "underdog." In his final years, Price devoted time to the underprivileged in Harrisburg's Edgemont area. He was an active member of the Shriners' Irem Temple and the Sojourners. This cribbage-loving Irishman, who made his mark in law enforcement in Pennsylvania and abroad, was buried in Oakland Park Cemetery, at Frankford, Philadelphia. He was survived by his widow Rebecca and two sons, Walter and Robert.

The Patrol command structure at the time of the merger was as follows:

> Captain Earl J. Henry, Acting Superintendent
> Captain John R. Standiford, Assistant Superintendent
> Captain Lawrence Brosha, Supply Officer
> Lieutenant Fred G. McCartney, Training School
> Lieutenant Charles F. Schroeder, Mechanical Unit

Troop A, Harrisburg
Captain T. N. Boate
Lieutenant Charles S. Graeff
Lieutenant John D. Kime

Troop C, Bellefonte
Lieutenant Charles J. McRae
Lieutenant Harry A. Edie
Lieutenant Warren Bear

Troop B, Greensburg
Captain Joseph G. McCann
Lieutenant John Bricker
Lieutenant Ray Hoover
Lieutenant George N. Pickering

Troop D, Kingston
Captain George H. Keller
Lieutenant Atreus H. Kratzke
Lieutenant John Grance

Troop E, Philadelphia
Captain William J. Ruch
Lieutenant Melvin H. Snavely
Lieutenant Frank Miner

Troop F, Franklin
Captain Arthur J. Oldham
Lieutenant Herman J. Roush
Lieutenant Albert L. Flick

The years 1934 and 1935 slipped by without a death in the line of duty. These were indeed rare years in the history of the Highway Patrol. The last three deaths in the Patrol's history came in 1936 and 1937. Killed in a motorcycle accident on June 4, 1936, was Corporal Joseph L. Fulton of Troop C. A motor vehicle accident took the life of Sergeant Joe B. Champion of Troop B on July 15, 1936. The last name to be added to the Highway Patrol honor roll in its waning days was that of Patrolman J. Lee Clarke of Troop E, who was killed in a motorcycle accident on March 1, 1937. During the Highway Patrol's brief existence of fourteen years, a total of nineteen dedicated, young men met violent deaths in the carrying-out of their sworn obligations.

CHAPTER XII

Pennsylvania Motor Police
Colonel Percy W. Foote
1937–1939

During the month of June, 1937, events of far-reaching importance took place, which were deferred from an earlier chapter, and it would be well to review them now for a better understanding of developments to follow.

The spring of 1937 witnessed major strikes in the steel industry that rocked the nation. In June, Pennsylvania was beset by the ugliness of the prolonged strike settlement, and conditions were especially critical at the Bethlehem Steel Company plant at Johnstown. Employees of the steel firm and operating employees of the Conemaugh and Black Lick Railroad, serving the plant, went on strike. Some workers, having suffered through years of the Great Depression, were not strike sympathizers and threatened to disregard picket lines. Faced with the threat of serious disorder at Johnstown, Earle declared martial law on June 19, and ordered out a State Police-Highway Patrol task force of 525 men. The job of maintaining law and order rested with National Guard Colonel Augustine S. Janeway. Adams commanded the State Police forces, while Captain Earl J. Henry saw to the activities of the Highway Patrol.

At Johnstown, Adams, who had for years been unfairly labelled by unions as anti-labor, was confronted with labor's strong man, John L. Lewis, with whom he seriously disagreed regarding State Police activities in maintaining the peace. Lewis responded swiftly by appealing to the governor for prompt intervention. Earle, having no intention of shaking labor's support of his administration, sided with Lewis. Adams was clearly disturbed by Earle's phone orders which Adams considered legally improper.

For years, Adams and his predecessors lived by the policy that neither side in a labor dispute should be favored by constabulary action. Adams, true to this tradition, was privately critical of Earle's judgment in yielding to what he considered labor pressures at Johnstown.

Martial law was lifted on June 24; Adams was recalled to Harrisburg. The State Police force, then reduced to 200 men, was turned over to the custody of Captain William A. Clark who was brought in from Troop B, Wyoming. Apparently the association between Clark and Lewis over previous anthracite coal region issues led to respect for one another, and the Johnstown incident was eventually brought under control without serious harm to persons, although a dynamite explosion on June 28 destroyed the steel plant water mains.

Adams, who often had indicated his approval for the State Police-Highway Patrol merger whenever this issue arose, reasonably held hopes of commanding such an expanded agency. Foote's appointment to that post instead was a disappointment to him. Adams resigned from state service just hours before the official debut of the new force rather than serve in a secondary slot. Persuaded by Governor Earle and Attorney General Charles J. Margiotti, Adams withdrew his resignation, and agreed to become Foote's deputy.

Appearing on the Pennsylvania scene in mid-1937 was the 1,025-man Pennsylvania Motor Police; gone were the Pennsylvania State Police and the State Highway Patrol. The Pennsylvania Motor Police was not the only new item to be pondered by all concerned—for the first time in Pennsylvania's law enforcement history the man at the top was an "outsider." The constabulary and Patrol had known no top officials other than those who rose through the ranks—one of their own. Governor Earle may have been wisely counselled in appointing an impartial administrator to avoid trouble, but he also ran the risk of failing the new Motor Police Department by placing its reins in the hands of someone strange to the law enforcement field.

Although his official appointment dated back to June 29, 1937, 58-year-old, retired Rear Admiral Percy W. Foote, U. S. Navy, was not sworn in until July 6. Administering the oath of office was Commonwealth Secretary David L. Lawrence. Present for this occasion were Governor George H. Earle, Attorney General Charles J. Margiotti,

Lynn G. Adams and Cecil M. Wilhelm. The general assembly had adjourned one month earlier, permitting Earle to give Foote an interim appointment and postpone any Senate confirmation action until the legislators returned to their desks in 1939.

Foote was born at Dellaplane, Wilkes County, North Carolina, August 13, 1879. He was the son of Major James H. Foote, a Confederate soldier and one of the founders of Wake FOrest College, and Susan Hunt Foote. The Foote family emigrated from Cornwall, England, and numbered among its greats Rear Admiral Andrew Hull Foote, U. S. Navy, who commanded the U. S. Naval gunboat flotilla on the Ohio and Mississippi Rivers during the Civil War. Susan Hunt Foote was a great-granddaughter of Nathan Hunt, a Philadelphian and leader in the Society of Friends, who founded Guilford College near Greensboro, North Carolina, under the auspices of the society. Her great-great-grandfather was Captain John Bryan, of Chester County, an officer in General Washington's Revolutionary Army.

Foote was educated in North Carolina public and private schools, and graduated from the U. S. Naval Academy in June, 1901. During his forty years of active service with the navy, Foote commanded vessels from a tug to a battleship, and rose through the ranks from midshipman to rear admiral. Soon after his graduation from the Naval Academy, Foote aided in the transport of army personnel to the Panama Canal Zone in 1901 and to China during the 1905 riots in Shanghai.

During World War I, Foote commanded the U. S. Naval Transport *President Lincoln*, which was then commissioned to carry American troops to France. The ship accommodated 5,000 men. After safely delivering some 25,000 soliders to France, the ship's luck ran out: on May 31, 1918, about 500 miles out of Brest, France, on a return trip to the United States, the *President Lincoln* was struck by three torpedoes fired from the German submarine *U-90*. The damaged ship, afloat for only eighteen minutes, then sank in Atlantic waters. Foote stayed aboard until the last lifeboat had been launched and then pulled a drowning seaman to safety.

Of the 715 men aboard ship, only 26 lives were lost. Credit for the comparatively small loss, if it can be considered as such, was attributed to Foote's excellent emergency preparedness and discipline. The Navy Department later commemorated this event by authorizing an oil painting dramatically portraying the final moments of the *President Lincoln*. For this exceptional performance, Foote was awarded the Distinguished Service Medal by the secretary of the navy.

From 1918 to 1921, Foote was aide to the Navy Secretary Josephus Daniels, and later chief of staff of the Fourth Naval District at

Colonel Percy W. Foote (Courtesy of Pennsylvania State Police)

Philadelphia. In 1932 and 1933, he commanded the battleship *Arkansas* and the training squadron of the U. S. Fleet, which was made up of two battleships, eight destroyers and a total complement of 2,500 officers and men.

On shore, Foote was for five years industrial manager of the U. S. Naval Gun Factory, at Washington, D. C., employing some 8,000 workers. For three years, he was U. S. Naval Inspector of Engineering and Ordnance Materials at the General Electric Company facility, Syracuse, New York. He is credited with developing a number of devices for naval ordnance and ordnance stores, some of which saw longtime usage by the navy. While at General Electric, he made extensive studies of electrical machinery for propelling battleships. His recommendations largely influenced the adoption of such equipment by the Navy Department, and earned him a letter of commendation.

Foote married Genevieve Clary, of Great Falls, Montana, on October 1, 1910. Born to them were a son, Thomas Clary Foote, and a daughter, Diana Harrison Foote. Thomas, choosing not to follow in his father's footsteps, served as an officer with the U. S. Army Field Artillery.

Closing out his naval service in June, 1936, Foote established his retirement residence at Drexel Hill, Delaware County, not too distant from Governor Earle's home at Haverford.

Foote, for several weeks prior to his appointment, was secretary of a special state commission to study whether state government should control the oil industry. He resigned his $5,000-a-year job to become the first Motor Police head. According to Act 455, creating this new entity, Foote was to be identified officially as the "Commissioner." Foote took upon himself the rank of colonel, and commissioned Adams a lieutenant colonel. Foote was salaried at $8,000 annually, and Adams at $7,500.

Wilhelm was kept on as chief of staff with the rank of major. Former Highway Patrol officer personnel were not included in the command hierarchy. Henry was returned temporarily to the training school, at Harrisburg, and Standiford was retained at headquarters as top advisor on traffic matters.

The early Motor Police headquarters staff included the following:

> Colonel Percy W. Foote—Commissioner
> Lt. Colonel Lynn G. Adams—Deputy Commissioner
> Major C. M. Wilhelm—Chief of Staff
> Captain John R. Standiford—Assistant Chief of Staff
> Lieut. Elmer W. Faber—Aide to Commissioner
> Silvus J. Overmiller—Comptroller
> Guy E. Reichard—Chief Quartermaster
> John R. Price—Accountant
> C. A. Knorr—Principal Statistical Clerk
> Chester A. Shuler—Advanced Steno-Secretary
> Dorothy B. Young—Advanced Steno-Secretary
> Gilbert W. Aungst—Head File Clerk
> Russell Wrightstone—Head Police Clerk
> Herman L. Breighner—Senior Police Clerk
> Harold J. Berrean—Clerk Class A
>
> *Bureau of Criminal Identification and Information*
> William F. Hoffman—Director

Charles Kunz—Supervising Fingerprint Operator
John A. Funck—Micro-Ballistician
Paul J. Roche—Fingerprint Identification Clerk
Elmer N. Doll—Fingerprint Identification Clerk
Samuel Garvin—Senior Photographer

Bureau of Fire Protection
William F. Traeger—Fire Marshal
Ralph D. Gardner—Senior Investigator

Detective Division	*Mechanical & Supply Units*
Lieut. Harry E. McElroy	Captain Lawrence Brosha
	Lieut. Charles F. Schroeder

Training School
Captain Thomas F. Martin

On July 21, 1937, Foote issued his first general order dividing his new department into four districts with headquarters at Greensburg, Harrisburg, Wyoming and Philadelphia. Included within the district structures were the eleven troops Foote inherited from the constabulary and the Highway Patrol. Since the constabulary troops were lettered from A to E, and the Patrol from A to F, Foote had to eliminate the duplicate identifications. The constabulary troops held seniority and rightfully deserved priority in retaining their original identity. Foote acted accordingly and re-identified five Patrol troops as G, H, I, K and L. Troop F remained unchanged. Command of the districts and troops was committed to:

District No. 1

Captain Jacob C. Mauk—commander
Lieutenant Martin J. Crowley—Troop A, Greensburg
Lieutenant Andrew J. Hudock—Troop D, Butler
Captain Arthur J. Oldham—Troop F, Franklin
Captain Joseph G. McCann—Troop H, Greensburg

District No. 2

Captain Earl J. Henry—commander
Lieutenant Charles C. Keller—Troop E, Harrisburg
Captain T. N. Boate—Troop G, Harrisburg
Lieutenant Charles J. McRae—Troop I, Bellefonte

District No. 3
        Captain William A. Clark—commander
        Lieutenant Charles S. Cook—Troop B, Wyoming
        Captain George H. Keller—Troop K, Kingston

District No. 4
        Captain William J. Ruch—commander
        Lieutenant Melvin H. Snavely—Troop L, Philadelphia
        Captain William D. Plummer—Troop C, Reading

When Foote relieved Clark of his Troop B command, at Wyoming, to head up the new District 3, headquartered also at Wyoming, he brought to an end Clark's record-setting tenure as a troop commander. Clark, promoted to captain by Superintendent Adams, took command of Troop B on March 1, 1920. He guided Troop B operations through 17½ years—an achievement not equalled by another troop commander.

The following personnel, omitting those previously identified with the headquarters staff, were carried on the clerical and accounting division payroll during the early days of the merger:

        B. E. O'Neal—Principal Police Clerk
        F. Barry—Principal Police Clerk
        R. S. Herb—Principal Police Clerk
        C. C. Bowman—Principal Police Clerk
        William N. Doll—Principal Police Clerk
        Edward P. McBreen—Private
        Benjamin P. Bretz—Corporal
        L. V. Becker—Radio Announcer
        R. B. Young—Senior Steno-Clerk
        F. Hamm—Special Steno-Clerk
        P. C. Kratzer—Special Steno-Clerk
        L. A. Garvey—Special Steno-Clerk
        S. Gabrysh—Special Steno-Clerk
        D. B. Harne—Special Steno-Clerk
        A. E. Bergan—Special Steno-Clerk
        S. A. Ely—Special Steno-Clerk
        H. S. Hammond—Special Steno-Clerk
        R. P. Moffet—Special Steno-Clerk
        W. E. Gulden—Special Steno-Clerk
        J. K. Seacrist—Principal Clerk-Steno
        G. R. Naugle—Principal Clerk-Steno

P. E. Levan—Principal Clerk-Steno
C. A. Kennedy—Principal Clerk-Steno
Fred J. Denn—Principal Clerk-Steno
Michael Donick, Jr.—Clerk C
William E. Boniger—Patrolman
S. J. McKenrick—Troop Clerk A
Donald D. Brink—Patrolman
Sidney C. Deyo—Patrolman
John U. Colligan—Troop Clerk A
Clyde Borror—Troop Clerk B
Oscar E. Scott—Patrolman
Harry L. Price—Troop Clerk A
George R. Gibboney—Troop Clerk B
Joseph F. Hughes—Troop Clerk A
Carlton L. Mendenhall—Troop Clerk B
Charles A. Givler—Patrolman
Delbert A. Johnson—Troop Clerk A
William J. Maher—Troop Clerk C
Thomas P. Cahalan—Patrolman
David J. Falger—Troop Clerk B
William F. Falger—Troop Clerk A
Myron W. Thomas—Troop Clerk A
Joseph J. Lennon—Troop Clerk C
Harry R. McKenna—Patrolman
J. C. Taylor—Chief Enforcement Officer
A. Melnick—Fireman
E. Mae Twigg—Advanced File Clerk
Jeanette Sheridan—Principal Stenographer
Robert J. Franklin—Expenditure Record Clerk
Elizabeth J. Hicks—Junior Payroll Clerk
Jane M. Heefner—Bookkeeping Machine Operator
William C. Burton—Bookkeeping Machine Operator
John H. Klinger—Typist Clerk
Gretchen L. Knox—File Clerk
Elma Hoppes—Senior Stenographer

The use of enlisted men in clerical positions was not uncommon in either State Police or Highway Patrol history. Enlisted men were pulled from field duty to assist the permanent office forces when the pressure of paperwork demanded such action. Other enlisted men who were disabled in the line of duty were given desk jobs rather than being forced into disability retirement.

At the merger, members of the State Police and Highway Patrol did not enjoy equal pay plans. (The difference in each organization's handling of quarters and meal allowances was brought out earlier.) Additionally, it was no secret among Patrol members that the troopers generally had a better pay scale to look to. There was every indication, too, that both organizations were underpaid when compared with major police departments elsewhere in the country.

Recognizing these circumstances, Foote set up a board to study a new compensation plan. Appointed to the board on October 11, 1937, were Major C. M. Wilhelm, Captain Earl J. Henry and Captain Samuel W. Gearhart. The board did confirm the fact that the State Police and Highway Patrol payroll figures by comparison with other agencies were lower and, as a remedial measure, structured a pay scale carrying an increase for all ranks. The board also recommended that certain bureau and division directors at headquarters be given commissioned ranks in keeping with their command responsibilities in a semi-military department.

The board, in another recommendation, advocated the adoption of a subsistence allowance plan that had found favor with the New York and New Jersey State Police agencies. The subsistence allowance was not a payroll item. The allowance was processed monthly by way of individual vouchers. The allowance was not then subject to federal income tax. Neither did the allowance contribute to benefits in the state employes' retirement system. This allowance system, as cumbersome as it was to process, remained in effect until the 1960s when the Internal Revenue Service regulations made a change necessary. This subject will be pursued in due course.

The pay board recommended the use of two enlisted ranks—private first class and private second class. Recruits upon graduation from the training school would be promoted to privates second class and given an increase in pay. Subject to satisfactory performance of duty, all privates second class were to be granted automatic promotion to privates first class after three years of service. This promotion, too, was to be accompanied with a jump in pay.

The longevity features of the new pay scale, however, were not liberal. Basically, longevity was geared to five-year increments, and as time went on this extended period between pay-raises became an item for discontent. Later, too, there was to be dissatisfaction with the ranks of private second class and private first class.

Foote accepted the board's entire package. All employees shared in a more generous pay plan. Some command officers were promoted and key civilian employes were given commissioned ranks. As one might expect, Foote's new payroll and subsistence allowance program, although generally beneficial, was critically reviewed by the malcontents.

Soon after his appointment, it was noted that Foote placed much reliance upon Clark's advice insofar as field operations were concerned. This was a strange and unexpected development, since Clark was at one time destined to be the first Motor Police commissioner, and at the last moment lost out to Foote. Observers noted that Clark spent much time in Harrisburg at Foote's invitations. It was no secret that Adams and Wilhelm were irritated with the thought of being by-passed on serious field issues. Nonetheless, Foote continued to lean on Clark for counselling.

Still bothered by his differing views with Earle on labor issues and now disenchanted with his role in Motor Police affairs, Adams submitted his resignation to Earle on October 21, 1937. Rumors circulated through the capitol that he had resigned as deputy commissioner. Questioned by reporters, Adams refused to either confirm or deny the rumors, allowing the governor the opportunity to make a public announcement. Again, Earle and Margiotti urged him to withdraw his resignation and remain at his post. This time, however, Adams held to his decision, stating that he had given serious thought to entering private business as a gun shop operator, a plan that never materialized. Whatever his reasons for departing, Adams never publicly revealed them.

On October 22, the *Harrisburg Patriot* carried Margiotti's comments, "Pennsylvania has suffered a great loss by the resignation of Major Adams. He has won international recognition as an outstanding police official. Under him Pennsylvania has developed the greatest police organization in America. I sincerely regret his resignation." It was well known at the capitol that Margiotti respected Adams as a topflight police administrator.

Recalling this incident, Donald Adams said of his father, "Although Dad was often accused of being anti-labor, I am sure he was not. He was definitely a man of the 'peepul.' It was just that he was for law and against law-breakers. Riotous mobs, no matter how just their cause, were law-breakers, as he saw it."

The day after Adams' resignation was accepted Foote moved in Wilhelm as deputy commissioner. In his parting comments to Foote, Adams had strongly endorsed Wilhelm as his successor. Although Wilhelm was immediately advanced to the deputy post, Foote did not commission him a lieutenant colonel until the end of the year.

Following his resignation, Adams was appointed Dauphin

County's chief investigator. In 1938, he worked closely with a special grand jury probing charges against high officials of Earle's administration, which did not set well with the Democrats. The investigation, set off by Attorney General Charles J. Margiotti, led to a number of arrests and convictions.

At the same time that Adams was preparing to depart from state service, rumors were circulating that Captain Gearhart was also planning to resign. Gearhart had been brought to headquarters to direct the detective division operations shortly after Foote's tenure was underway, temporarily taking the command from McElroy. Before his transfer to headquarters, Gearhart commanded Troop E at Harrisburg for a brief time following Captain Stout's retirement. Rumors again were well-founded. Gearhart resigned on November 1 to accept the post of superintendent of the Lower Merion Township police department. Following Gearhart's departure, McElroy once again took over the detective division reins, and was promoted to captain on April 1, 1938.

Consideration was given by Foote to changing the uniform for the Motor Police. Adopting the uniform of either the State Police or the Highway Patrol would have indicated, perhaps, the favoring of one agency over the other; Foote already had his work cut out keeping dissention, which was already evident, from blossoming into a greater problem for him. Changing the uniform, then, was almost a must for Foote.

Both the constabulary and the Highway Patrol had stayed with the high collar blouse, breeches and puttees, although a distinction between organizational personnel was easily made. Foote's final decision basically changed the blouse and not much else. He selected an open collar blouse requiring a uniform shirt and tie. Retained were the breeches and puttees. The State Police campaign hat was picked for head wear, which did not seem to disturb the former Patrol members, who apparently had some liking for the traditional constabulary campaign hat. The sam browne belt and holster of black leather followed the State Police type as did the issue shoes. The new uniform was dark grey with specially designed metal buttons and very little trim. The keystone patch, identifying lapel and collar ornaments, revolver and whistle completed the uniform equipment. Unlike the two former organizations, the official badge was not displayed as part of the uniform wear: the badge and identification document were pocket-carried. Delays in tailoring schedules prevented statewide display of the new uniform until mid-1938.

The new police agency was not yet two months old when it

chalked up its first death in the line of duty. Pfc. John J. Broski, an old B-Trooper, was cut down by shotgun fire during a tavern holdup on August 14, 1937. Before the year was up, another motorcycle fatality was recorded. Pfc. John D. Simoson of Troop E-1, a former Highway Patrolman, was killed on December 1.

Facing Foote was the tremendous job of recruiting and uniforming men to fill the newly-ordained complement of 1,600. Just prior to the merger, a number of recruit applicants were in the stages of processing for the constabulary. Mindful of the new manpower complement, Foote had every intention of continuing with the acquisition of these additional men. A class of 57 was called to the training school at Hershey, on September 1, 1937, to undergo training basically attuned to constabulary operations.

Shortly after the merger, a massive campaign was underway to recruit some 500 men, authorized by Earle, to fill the ranks of the Motor Police. By December, 1937, the processing of 280 applicants drew to a close. The training schools at Harrisburg and Hershey were totally inadequate to accomodate a class of that size. To overcome this problem, Motor Police officials negotiated for the use of the abandoned Albright College campus at Myerstown.

On December 13, 1937, an advance group of 77 recruits was called to Myerstown. This group was called early to ready the abandoned facilities at Myerstown, which sorely needed attention. Manpower was also borrowed from the class at Hershey to meet a January 1, 1938, deadline. On January 1, the main body of the first Myerstown class, numbering 193 men, arrived. This class, then totalling 270, undertook the serious business of training for Motor Police duties.

The 57 recruits at Hershey in the meantime had completed their six-months training in February. They were, nonetheless, kept on at the school for another month to see to the fatigue chores and assist Troop E personnel with police duties, pending the graduation of the Myerstown class. It was planned that both classes would graduate in joint ceremonies.

Both classes, numbering 313 men after attrition, graduated at exercises held in the State Forum building, at Harrisburg, on March 31, 1938. The graduates received their diplomas from Governor Earle amid the praise and applause of many state and local government dignitaries. Honor graduates from Myerstown were George A. Panrock, Walter A. Wise and George P. Stock, ranking in that order.

Having passed a competitive examination at Myerstown, 27 of the graduates were dispatched to the training school at Hershey to undergo additional training which included the specialty of criminal investigation. The rest of the Myerstown class was assigned to the field for three months of on-the-job training to qualify for the rank of private second class.

The 57 men, who had completed a seven-months stay at the school and graduated with the Myerstown class, were assigned to field installations as criminal investigators. Honor graduates from that Hershey class were Mauro Forte, Robert L. McCartney and Arthur R. Gore.

On April 1, 1938, before the bunks had a chance to cool off at Myerstown, another 249 men reported to the training campus there. After three-months training, 238 men graduated at formal exercises also held at the Harrisburg Forum building on July 6. Again the diplomas were handed out by Earle with dignitaries everywhere in evidence. Honor graduates were James Burkholder, George W. Pinkerton and Joseph Dussia.

Earle, referring to the Motor Police merger in his graduation comments, said:

> I realize the necessity of morale and of discipline and I realize more that we had the sacred duty of saving lives in Pennsylvania, primarily from highway speeding and also through prevention of crime. I thought that in this great state with the tremendous population of ten million—that our police force was divided into two units which made it brittle in operations, and there were other inefficiencies besides that. I want to say here that I did recognize the magnificent traditions of the Pennsylvania State Police before I came here— the courage and training. But I did feel that two forces under two different commanders could not possibly achieve the efficiency of one force under one commander. Some men were only trained for highway patrol and other men were only trained for criminal work and you suddenly had a tremendous burst of deaths on the highways or criminal activity and you could only throw half your force into the breach, whereas, if we have one great force trained in every department it would be very much more flexible and very much more efficient.
>
> So, after a long struggle in the legislature we put that (the merger) through. It was a very hard thing to do. I don't understand yet the reasons for the opposition, but it was sincere opposition, a lot of people thought, and a lot of the members of the legislature thought that divided, it was a better force. But we finally won out on that. Then the second thing to do was to get the men off those man-killing motorcycles. They are very destructive to the bodily welfare of our policemen and, they

can't be used in very wet weather without grave danger of serious injury to our Motor Policemen who ride them.

In his commencement address, Foote revealed, "It certainly should increase your self-pride and confidence to know that you and the class that preceded you composed about 500 men who were picked out of 4,000."

This second Myerstown class was also committed to three months of on-the-job training before leaving behind their recruit label. Many graduates of both classes found their way back to the training school, at Hershey, to qualify for private second class in lieu of the on-the-job route.

The honor graduates of both classes went on to achieve exceptional careers. Notably were Pinkerton, who attained the rank of major and headed the traffic bureau before retirement, and Dussia, who held down the deputy commissioner post for six years with the rank of lieutenant colonel.

The two Myerstown classes were the largest ever to be graduated in State Police history. To provide an adequate corps of instructors for these classes, Motor Police officials drew on seasoned field supervisors who had proven themselves worthy of the task at hand. Selected were:

Lieutenant C. S. Cook
Lieutenant A. H. Kratzke
Lieutenant F. G. McCartney
Lieutenant C. S. Graeff

Troop A, Greensburg
Sergeant W. R. Hanna
Sergeant F. J. Gleason
Corporal H. C. Johnson
Corporal W. B. Kunkle

Troop B, Wyoming
Sergeant J. Carr
Sergeant S. S. Smith
Corporal J. F. Santilli

Troop C, Reading
Sergeant R. L. Davis
Sergeant R. Simmons
Corporal W. P. Snyder

Troop D, Butler
First Sergeant E. J. Donovan
Sergeant H. W. Pierce
Corporal C. E. Stacey

Troop E, Harrisburg
Corporal A. B. Snyder
Corporal A. Verbecken
Corporal W. Kasparavich

Troop F, Franklin
Corporal P. E. Carlson

Troop G, Harrisburg
First Sergeant J. J. Toohey
First Sergeant W. J. Bynane
Sergeant J. S. Rhine
Sergeant A. H. Shuller
Corporal M. J. Wicker
Corporal W. A. Ent

Troop H, Greensburg
First Sergeant F. T. Garnow

Troop L, Philadelphia
Sergeant C. A. Lipp
Sergeant E. R. Rubincam

Troop K, Kingston
First Sergeant F. T. Crum
Sergeant W. M. Smith

Foote had then completed the major portion of his gigantic recruiting effort. Not having quite attained the 500-man goal, he took on an additional class on October 1, 1938. That class of 37 men graduated on March 31, 1939, after six months of training at the Hershey school.

In his form letter acknowledging Motor Police applications from hopeful young men, Foote had these interesting words of wisdom to impart, "Experience has demonstrated that alert young men who desire to lead an active life succeed as Motor Policemen, while the 'drones' who will not devote their efforts toward self-improvement fail in this as well as in any other vocation."

On January 1, 1938, the districts, then changed to squadrons, became operational with the appointments of Major Jacob C. Mauk (PSP) at Squadron 1, Greensburg; Major Earl J. Henry (SHP) at Squadron 2, Harrisburg; Major William A. Clark (PSP) at Squadron 3, Wyoming, and Major William J. Ruch (SHP) at Squadron 4, Philadelphia. To provide administrative balance, each major was assigned an aide from the opposite service. In other words, a former State Police major had as his aide a former Highway Patrol captain and vice versa. This made a neat compromise package as Foote walked the tight rope. Also promoted to major was Captain Thomas F. Martin of the Hershey training school. All received their commissions from Foote in a simple ceremony in the commissioner's office. Receiving his commission as lieutenant colonel on this same occasion was Deputy Commissioner Wilhelm.

In November, 1937, Foote enlisted Captain Amberse M. Banks, a former U. S. Navy pilot, to study the feasiblity of organizing an aeronautical unit to aid Motor Police ground forces and add to the department's effectiveness. Banks, during his brief Motor Police service, piloted small fixed-wing aircraft, and introduced a new technique to police work that was not to be fully pursued for another thirty years, when the helicopter craft came into its own outside of military services.

A change in headquarters personnel was made necessary by the sudden, unexpected death of Captain John R. Standiford on January 15, 1938. Standiford, 50, had been serving as assistant chief of staff, and was primarily responsible for traffic administration. A veteran of World War I, Standiford served with the Army's Third Division Regulars. Standiford's place was taken by Captain Thomas N. Boate.

Foote, fully convinced of the merits of a physical fitness program, established a medical unit. The unit, founded in January, 1938, was responsible for overseeing a physical fitness program and attending the medical needs of the men. Appointed as first medical officer was Dr. David A. Johnston, a native of Hazleton and assistant surgeon at the Hazleton State Hospital. To better carry out his program in a semi-military outfit, Johnston on January 17 was given the rank of major. Enlisted in May to aid Johnston was William T. McAlpin, a retired U.S. Navy chief pharmacist mate, who was given the non-commissioned rank of sergeant. Johnson and McAlpin prepared a schedule of physical examinations and toured the department statewide.

One of Foote's innovations was the publishing of a departmental news instrument entitled *The Bulletin*. *The Bulletin* was distributed twice a month, and the first issue, Volume 1, No. 1, appeared on January 1, 1938. This house organ, however, barely outlived Foote's administration. The final edition, Volume II, No. 4, was printed February 15, 1939. Lieutenant Elmer Faber, departmental publicist, was the publication's editor.

Commissioner Foote, by way of Personnel Order No. 9, dated January 3, 1938, officially brought into being the communications division which began operations on February 1. To head operations, Detective Donald E. Wagner was promoted to lieutenant and transferred to the new division. Transferred to the communications division at the same time were:

> Private Troy A. Moats—Troop A
> Private Lewis W. McChesney—Troop B
> Private Stanton L. Bast—Troop C
> Private Sherman G. Bassler—Troop D
> Private Charles L. Hoffman—Troop E
> Private Robert L. Bomboy—Troop E
> Private Chester B. Robenolt—Troop E
> Private Henry D. Stone—Troop E
> Private John H. Williams—Troop E
> Private Hugo J. Tacchi—Troop E

Five permanent and two mobile radio stations were then operational:

> Station WBA, at Harrisburg
> Station WJL, at Greensburg

Station WBR, at Butler
Station WDX, at Wyoming
Station WMB, at Reading

Harrisburg station WBA was the key-station. Also located at Harrisburg were two mobile stations, WAMF and WPIB. These rolling command posts were swiftly moved to any emergency site when needed.

Among other things, Earle will be remembered as a strong advocate for highway safety. He set a fifty-mile-an-hour speed limit on all state highways and directed the Motor Police to vigorously enforce that speed limit. Emphasis was placed on investigating accidents and reporting them in detail. The accident report forms were cumbersome, requiring information of all sorts; the form was kept in use for some thirty years until it was finally simplified in the 1960s and a uniform report form was established by law for all Pennsylvania police departments.

To further implement the wishes of a safety-conscious governor, Foote established driver clinics at Philadelphia and Pittsburgh manned by Motor Policemen. The clinics were rehabilitation centers for "accident repeaters," who were identified as drivers involved in two or more accidents in a single calendar year. Special equipment was put to use in determining a driver's limitations and deficiencies and rehabilitation efforts were highly successful. The clinic program was continued for many years, but plans for the expansion of the program never materialized.

Later in his adminstration, Earle was boastful of the fact that highway fatalities in Pennsylvania were reduced 35 percent despite the increased volume of traffic.

To adequately equip the Motor Police for its mission, Foote ordered a large fleet of passenger cars in 1938. The 267 police cars, painted white with PENNSYLVANIA MOTOR POLICE lettered on the doors, were soon called "ghost cars" by the public and press. The patrol vehicles were equipped with under-the-hood mounted sirens, and a red-light, intended to bring another car operator to a halt, mounted on the crown of the right fender. The glare of the sun on the white auto hoods, however, was more than the eyes of the operators could withstand, even with sun-glasses, and an order was issued to have all hoods repainted black. For almost a decade, the ghost cars with black hoods remained a symbol of the State's authority on the highways. Passenger cars continued to be the basis for patrol operations as the Department phased out the "man-killing motorcycles."

Although the detective division at headquarters was doing a commendable job, statewide coverage was a drawback. To provide the division with field reinforcement, Foote, on March 1, 1938, added two detectives to each of the squadron headquarters staffs. The following were selected by Foote for promotion to these new posts:

Squadron 1, Greensburg
Detective Charles J. Hanna—Troop A
Detective George W. Kercher—Troop A

Squadron 2, Harrisburg
Detective Carl E. Hartman—Troop E
Detective Reagle O. Parsons—Troop E

Squadron 3, Wyoming
Detective Richard H. Jones—Troop B
Detective Charles Hartman—Troop B

Squadron 4, Philadelphia
Detective John F. McDevitt—Troop C
Detective Benjamin O. Lichty—Troop C

In June, 1938, Foote brought in additional outside assistance. Employed as special assistant to the commissioner was retired Captain Leo F. S. Horan, U. S. Marine Corps. Horan, 54, a member of the Philadelphia Bar since 1919, was assigned to basically personnel administration, devoting most of his brief services to updating court-martial procedures and improving methods for evaluating performance. Assigned to assist Horan was John R. Price, departmental accountant. It was at this point that personnel matters were divorced from the comptroller's area of operations and placed in the hands of another supervisor. It was not until later, however, that the personnel division was shown on any table of organization as an entity.

Two additional personnel changes on the headquarters roster are worthy of mention. Lieutenant Charles Kunz on June 15, 1938, retired from the BCI & I where he had spent seventeen of his thirty-one years of service with the force. Promoted on July 1, 1938, to lieutenant was Detective Wallace H. Smith, who was then Foote's secretary.

In July, 1938, the Motor Police was directed by Earle to move a large task force to Gettysburg for the seventy-fifth anniversary of the Battle of Gettysburg. The event was labelled as a reunion of the Blue and Grey. Honor guests at the reunion were some 2,000 Civil War veterans. There was an intense interest in that observance and large

State Police Detail, 75th Anniversary of Battle of Gettysburg, 1938. Gov. George H. Earle and Col. Percy W. Foote are shown at center. National Guard Maj. Gen. Edward C. Shannon is at left. (Courtesy of Pennsylvania State Police)

crowds were expected to attend the battlefield ceremonies—and did attend. Featured was the lighting of the Eternal Light Memorial by President Franklin D. Roosevelt on July 4. Mr. Roosevelt also delivered the dedicatory address.

A 495-man task force under Major Henry's command took over full responsibility for the policing of Gettysburg and its surroundings from June 29 to July 6, and did a magnificent job of it. Just as the infant constabulary in 1913 earned the nation's tribute for its handling of the fiftieth anniversary in Gettysburg, so did the newly-organized Motor Police efficiently conduct itself and reap commendation.

Other officers on the task force staff were:

> Captain T. N. Boate—Adjutant
> Lieutenant Donald E. Wagner—Communications Officer
> Lieutenant Elmer W. Faber—Public Relations Officer
> Major David A. Johnston—Medical Officer
> Lieutenant Wallace H. Smith—Secretary
> Captain Guy E. Reichard—Quartermaster
> Captain William F. Traeger—Fire Marshal

Major General Edward C. Shannon commanded the Pennsylvania National Guard support forces.

By way of General Order 24, dated July 19, 1938, Foote established an elaborate competitive examination and promotion system which recognized the problems of the merger and gave equal opportunity to former State Police and Highway Patrol members. The promotion of men was a sensitive issue then, and harsh feelings continued to exist for years. It was the continuing problem of administrators to keep cool heads during the long adjustment period to sustain morale at the best level possible.

In Foote's early plans to divide the department into four districts, or squadrons, each headed by a major, it was also his intention to have each squadron consist of five troops. Since the constabulary brought with it five troops and the Patrol six troops, for a total of eleven, Foote was faced with the ambitious and dubious transaction of instituting nine new troops.

On August 11, 1938, Foote issued Special Order 4, ordering into existence the following troops as soon as possible:

First Squadron
Troop A, Greensburg (formerly A)
Troop B, Washington (formerly H)
Troop C, Punxsutawney
Troop D, Butler (formerly D)
Troop E, Erie (formerly E)

Second Squadron
Troop A, Harrisburg (formerly G)
Troop B, Chambersburg
Troop C, Hollidaysburg
Troop D, Williamsport (formerly I)
Troop E, Harrisburg (temporary)

Third Squadron
Troop A, Hazelton
Troop B, Wyoming (formerly B)
Troop C, Towanda
Troop D, Blakely-Olyphant
    (formerly K)

Fourth Squadron
Troop A, Philadelphia (formerly L)
Troop B, Lancaster
Troop C, Reading (formerly C)
Troop D, Bethlehem
Troop E, Pottsville

Once again the identity of the original constabulary troops was preserved. The above list did not quite reach the twenty-troop mark, and Foote's efforts were never destined to make it.

One of the most lamentable developments associated with Foote's 1938 reorganizational plan was the creation of two troop headquarters in Luzerne County—Troop A, at Hazleton, and Troop B, at Wyoming. The northeastern counties, making up the Third Squadron, hardly constituted an area large enough for four troops and, certainly, in the views of other commissioners to follow, there was no reason whatsoever for two troops in one county. Splitting the county administratively and statistically has been a headache for all commissioners.

Political pressures of the Earle administration's labor factions are

believed responsible for Foote's misdirection. And his successors, almost without exception, have attempted to some degree to have the
Hazleton troop headquarters abolished in favor of an adjustment ending the sharing of Luzerne County's law enforcement problems. Each
attempt, however, has met with strong political opposition despite the
savings to be derived from such a consolidation of resources without
any sacrifice whatsoever in police services. Governors, unfortunately,
respond to the bull-headedness of politicians, and the wishes of police
commissioners have been brushed aside. Ironically, it has been the appointed commissioners who have had the welfare of Luzerne County at
heart moreso than the misguided, elected representatives.

Other counties in the state, according to Foote's organizational
plan, were divided between adjacent troops. Allegheny, Indiana, Westmoreland, Northumberland, Lackawanna and Bucks counties also
saw shared jurisdiction. It was in Luzerene County, only, that two
troop headquarters were situated. Gradually, succeeding commissioners recognized the inefficiency of split-commands and did away
with them. But the only surviving trace of split-commands is found in
Luzerne County.

When the general assembly met in special session, at Earle's calling, the governor submitted Foote's name in nomination to the Senate
on September 27, 1938, for confirmation. The nomination was referred
to the committee on Executive Nominations. Foote was confirmed on
November 21, 1938, by a 40–1 vote to serve from June 29, 1937, until
the third Tuesday of January, 1939.

Flavel M. Williams, a technician and a Foote appointee, worked
closely with Sergeant Joseph G. Burkhart, of the Quartermaster division, to develop a spectroscopic camera. By mid-1938 their experi-
mentation successfully resulted in a much-heralded prototype
reportedly capable of night photography and automatically calculating
speed of violators. But his new enforcement device, for some reason,
was never produced for practical application in the field. Williams,
who had been given by staff personnel the nickname "Infra-red,"
terminated his services with the close of the Foote administration.

Motor Police officers and men were saddened by the accidental
deaths of Privates Joseph F. Williams and Charles H. Craven on
October 8, 1938, in the line of duty. Both died from injuries resulting
from a four-car collision near Gettsyburg, while on patrol. Although
multiple deaths from gunfire in single incidents had occurred before in
State Police history, Williams and Craven were the first multiple
fatalities in a single motor vehicle accident.

By November 1, 1938, Foote had managed to see eighteen of his troops organized, and the following roster reflects the command structure as Foote's term of office was coming to a close:

Squadron 1—Major Jacob C. Mauk
          Captain Joseph G. McCann
Squadron 2—Major Earl J. Henry
          Captain Charles C. Keller
Squadron 3—Major William A. Clark
          Captain George H. Keller
Squadron 4—Major William J. Ruch
          Captain William D. Plummer
Troop A-1, Greensburg—Lieutenant Martin J. Crowley
Troop B-1, Washington—Lieutenant Frank L. Garnow
Troop C-1, Punxsutawney—Captain Arthur J. Oldham
Troop D-1, Butler—Lieutenant Andrew J. Hudock
Troop E-1, Erie—Lieutenant Herman J. Roush
Troop A-2, Harrisburg—Lieutenant John D. Kime
Troop B-2, Chambersburg—Lieutenant Atreus H. Kratzke
Troop C-2, Hollidaysburg—Lieutenant Harry A. Edie
Troop D-2, Williamsport—Lieutenant Charles J. McRae
Troop A-3, Hazleton—Lieutenant John Grance
Troop B-3, Wyoming—Lieutenant Charles S. Cook
Troop C-3, Towanda—Lieutenant Albert L. Flick
Troop D-3, Blakely—Lieutenant John J. Tomek
Troop A-4, Philadelphia—Lieutenant Melvin H. Snavely
Troop B-4, Lancaster—Lieutenant Fred G. McCartney
Troop C-4, Reading—Lieutenant Edwin C. Griffith
Troop D-4, Bethlehem—Lieutenant Frank C. Miner
Troop E-4, Pottsville—Lieutenant John C. Bricker
Hershey Training School—Major Thomas F. Martin
                        Lieutenant James J. Tooey
                        Lieutenant Emmett J. Donovan
                        Lieutenant William R. Hanna

The broad headquarters staff consisted of:

Colonel Percy W. Foote—Commissioner
Lt. Colonel C. M. Wilhelm—Deputy Commissioner
Captain William F. Hoffman—Director, BCI & I
Captain Lawrence Brosha—Quartermaster & Mechanical Unit
Captain William F. Traeger—Fire Marshal
Captain T. N. Boate—Traffic Officer

Six new lieutenants are promoted, December, 1938. Front row, left to right: Col. Foote, Lt. Frank L. Garnow, Lt. Stanley S. Smith, Lt. Norman E. Annich, Lt. Col. C. M. Wilhelm. Back row: Lt. Emmett J. Donovan, Lt. James J. Tooey, Lt. William R. Hanna. (Courtesy of Pennsylvania State Police)

Captain Amberse M. Banks—Aviation Unit

Captain Guy E. Reichard—Chief Quartermaster

Captain Harry E. McElroy—Chief, Detective Division

Lieutenant Charles F. Schroeder—Quartermaster & Mechanical Unit

Lieutenant Warren C. A. Bear—Traffic Office

Lieutenant Ralph D. Gardner—Bureau of Fire Protection

Lieutenant Ray Hoover—Traffic Office

Lieutenant Elmer W. Faber—Public Relations Officer and Commissioner's Aide

Lieutenant Donald E. Wagner—Communications Officer

Lieutenant John A. Funck—Micro-Ballistician (Crime Lab)

Lieutenant Wallace H. Smith—Secretary

Lieutenant Stanley S. Smith—Questioned Documents Examiner (Crime Lab)

By executive order, Foote raised the maximum height for recruit applicants to 6'2'', effective December 5, 1938. The minimum height remained at 5'8''.

At the request of the Secretary of Property and Supplies, Foote placed First Sergeant Donald H. Austin in command of the Capitol Police Force on December 30, 1938. Prior to that assignment, Austin was carrying out staff duties at headquarters.

The November, 1938, general election saw the defeat of the Democratic party as it tried desperately to overcome the effects of scandal and hold to another four years. The Republican party standard-bearer, Arthur H. James, led his party to victory and power in Pennsylvania, a state that was to remain in Republican hands until January, 1955.

On January 17, 1939, Earl's term arrived at its final day, and with it ended the nineteen-month career of Commissioner Percy W. Foote, an "outsider," who did remarkably well in wrestling with the challenging task of the merger. He gave to his new-found organization the strength and stability to see better days ahead.

CHAPTER XIII

Colonel Lynn G. Adams
1939–1943

Victorious by a comfortable margin over his Democratic party opponent, Charles Alvin Jones, in the 1938 election, Arthur H. James, a former "breaker-boy" in the Luzerne County anthracite coal mines, was sworn in as governor on January 17, 1939. On that same day, he resigned his state superior court judgeship. Although he was much criticized for not leaving the superior court to campaign for governor, James stubbornly refused to yield to such criticism.

James and Major Clark shared parallel careers in Luzerne County, and as lawyer and police administrator, they became close friends. According to family sources, James consulted with Clark regarding the appointment of a Motor Police commissioner for his upcoming term of office. James was torn between Adams, who, in James' opinion, was unfairly treated by the Earle administration, and Clark, a personal friend. It is said that Clark, had he pursued the post, could have had the appointment. Clark, however, had the greatest respect for his former superintendent and disliked the role of being Adams' competitor; the nod went to Adams.

On inauguration day, January 17, James submitted to the state Senate for confirmation a list of cabinet nominations. Included in the listing was Adams who would serve as commissioner of the Pennsylvania Motor Police until the third Tuesday of January, 1943. The names were referred to the Committee on Executive Nominations. Senate Rule 38 was set aside and the nominations, favorably reported back by the committee, were subject to floor action that same day. Senator Harry Shapiro (D-Philadelphia), speaking for the minority, stated that he and his Democratic colleagues were prepared to vote on all cabinet appointees except two: Lynn G. Adams and William J. Hamilton, Jr. The Democrats apparently had not forgotten Adams' role in the 1937–38 investigation of high officials of the Earle administration, nor had CIO labor leaders set aside their disagreement with Adams on the handling of labor disorder incidents.

James' cabinet members were confirmed by a 47-0 vote, and the two exceptions were tossed back into committee. This was a disappointing development for the veteran police administrator. Content to abide his time, James appointed Wilhelm as acting commissioner to oversee Motor Police operations.

The Motor Police added another name to the honor roll of those men killed in the line of duty. Corporal George D. Naughton of Troop B-1, Washington, a former constabulary member, was shot and killed on January 20, 1939, as he and his companions attempted to serve an arrest warrant.

On May 5, 1939, in a notable move, Wilhelm issued General Order 25, establishing new responsibilities for the BCI & I. In his order, Wilhelm put under the BCI & I director's wing the:

1. Identification Division
2. Detective Division
3. Criminal Intelligence Division
4. Crime Laboratory

The general assembly adjourned *sine die* on May 29, 1939, and two days later James gave Adams an interim appointment as commissioner. On May 31, Adams returned to the Motor Police as top man this time, to remain there for almost four years as that agency's administrator.

Adams, who had for many years shared an excellent relationship with Wilhelm whom he warmly addressed as "Mark," kept Wilhelm on as his deputy. This move was not unexpected. During constabulary days, Adams and Wilhelm worked very well as a team. Each respected the other and their friendship at the top was a warm, cordial, cooperative one. Interrupted only by Adams' separation during the Earle administration, the Adams-Wilhelm team was to endure through the better part of fifteen years before dissolution.

Both men were later aided by BCI & I director Captain William F. Hoffman who was given the added post of office administrator. With the departure of Captain Horan at the end of the Earle administration,

Adams appointed John R. Price supervisor of personnel, a position he was to hold for almost a decade.

Chester E. Shuler, who had served as Adams' trusted secretary for almost two decades, saw Adams in action from a unique vantage point. Wrote Shuler, who ended his state service in early 1938:

Colonel Lynn G. Adams (Courtesy of Pennsylvania State Police)

My admiration for Colonel Adams and his work with the Pennsyllvania State Police is great. I had the privilege of working with him almost from the day he was made acting deputy superintendent, and shortly afterward superintendent, in 1920, until his retirement in 1937. During all of that time I knew him as a man of honor, fairness, courage and ability. He always stood behind his men as long as they were in the right. He constantly refused to allow politics to dictate the policies of the Force.

Adams was not to change his views toward politicians and blocked any moves aimed at influencing Motor Police operations. His attitude was very simply displayed in this brief incident: Retired Army Lt. Colonel Hobart Hopkins, an Adams' family friend, who was then active in American Legion affairs, visited Adams. Hopkins informed Adams that he had been approached by the widow of a trooper who was shot and killed in the line of duty a few years earlier. She wanted a scholarship for her daughter, a high school senior, and was sure Adams could secure the scholarship for her through Senator Harvey Taylor (R-Dauphin)—a legendary powerhouse in Republican circles. Knowing full well that a phone call to Senator Taylor would bring favorable results for the widow, Adams nonetheless informed Hopkins that he would not make the call and preferred to donate from personal funds to the young girl's education. Adams, according to Hopkins, was convinced that a phone call to Taylor would generate a call from the senator within a week, asking for a favor in return. In Adams' view, few circumstances were to be more abhorred than owing a politician a favor, or more pitiful than a man who placed himself in such circumstances in the first place. At Adams' suggestion, Hopkins called Taylor and secured the scholarship.

During the month of June, James signed into law three measures which had passed through the legislative mill and affected Motor Police operations. Act 306, P.L. 660, June 21, added to the Motor Police list of responsibilities the return of escaped convicts. Act 378, P.L. 1080, June 26, authorized the return of parole violators at penitentiary expense. Act 400, P.L. 1135, June 27, regulated the annual inspection of school buses by the Motor Police.

With Adams' appointment as commissioner, the Motor Police Department had been in existence for two years, and gave every indication of weathering the problems of the merger. To satisfy his curiosity about the department's progress, Governor James asked Adams if he would prefer to see the Pennsylvania State Police and State Highway

Patrol go their separate ways again, or remain consolidated. Adams readily replied that he wanted the merger continued. Adams favored the merger and had, from time to time, recommended it. Therefore, the merger was, in his view, an agreeable event, and his appointment to head the Motor Police did not in any way alter his expectation of improved law enforcement at the state level.

During his tenure as State Police superintendent, Adams had displayed considerable interest in organizing an effective crime laboratory to give the field forces an added dimension in their investigation of crime incidents. Adams had enlisted the aid of John Funck as a micro-ballistician, who carried on his work at the Hershey training school facilities. After the merger, Foote, on March 1, 1938, commissioned Funck a lieutenant. Sergeant Stanley S. Smith, who was the department's expert on questioned documents and handwriting, had been moved earlier by Adams from Troop B to the Detective Division at Harrisburg to further develop his specialty. Smith's promotion to lieutenant was also seen during Foote's tenure.

Dissatisfied with decentralized lab services, Adams was determined to see a modern centralized facility at the Harrisburg barracks. He contracted for the building of a wing onto the barracks for this purpose. Pending the completion of this wing, Adams, on October 21, 1939, announced that the crime lab would be officially located at Squadron 2, headquarters at Harrisburg. Moved to that location were Lieutenants John Funck and Stanley S. Smith. Added to this complement were two chemists, Privates Christopher Bomberger and Elmer Bottiglier, both of whom had graduated with the first Myerstown class and had agreed to serve in the new lab's chemistry section.

The crime lab became operational during the early days of 1940, at which time Adams moved Detective Sergeant Lewis M. Whitecotton to the lab to supervise administration as first sergeant. The new facility was then staffed to provide services on demand in chemistry, questioned documents, polygraph, and micro-ballistics to state and local police. A few months later another chemist was added to this staff, Private Peter Strickler, also a graduate of the first Myerstown class, who was willing to lend his talents to upgrade the lab's capabilities.

To more effectively utilize space, the Mechanical Unit was moved from its building at Squadron 2 headquarters to the west wing of the stable building at 20th and Herr Streets which had been occupied years earlier by constabulary mechanics. This consolidated unit was supervised by Lieutenant Charles F. Schroeder and First Sergeant Oliver D. Thomas. Shortly after this transfer, Adams negotiated a Works Progress Administration (WPA) project to enlarge the repair shop by enclosing the courtyard area between the stable wings and providing the department with up-to-date equipment to move from a motorcycle to an automobile repair facility. Motorcycles were rapidly being replaced by passenger vehicles for patrol duty.

Horses formerly stabled at 20th and Herr Streets were moved to the Hershey training school. None were kept outside of Hershey, except for a few "high school" horses at Wyoming. Eventually, all were stabled at Hershey, which allowed stable facilities in the field to be remodelled for auto repair or storage areas.

With the Motor Police complement suitably resting close to the 1,600 mark, there were no recruit classes called during 1939. The training school facilities during that year were largely turned over to the extended training of men in the two Myerstown classes and training of municipal police officers.

At the top of 1940, Adams revamped his squadron structures as follows:

First Squadron
Troop A, Greensburg
Troop B, Washington
Troop C, Punxsutawney
Troop D, Butler
Troop E, Erie

Third Squadron
Troop A, Hazelton
Troop B, Wyoming
Troop C, Blakely-Olyphant

Second Squadron
Troop A, Harrisburg
Troop B, Chambersburg
Troop C, Hollidaysburg
Troop D, Williamsport

Fourth Squadron
Troop A, Philadelphia
Troop B, Lancaster
Troop C, Reading
Troop D, Bethlehem

Gone from the former structure were troops at Towanda and Pottsville, reducing the number of troops from eighteen to sixteen. was a trend away from Foote's goal of twenty. Still remaining, however, was the sticky problem of having two troops in Luzerne County, and it was obvious at that point that neither Adams nor his successors were going to find the elimination of one troop there an easy hurdle to jump.

Because of the unique situation that existed with Troop E, Pottsville, it is worthy of mention. The Pottsville troop with its two substations had but a single county to patrol—Schuylkill. How Foote justified that troop's existence is not known, although it is likely that local politicians had a strong hand in that planning. Adams, in the opinion of his staff, acted properly in doing away with the Pottsville troop—a troop that should not have seen daylight in the first place.

Early in 1940, Adams set about investigating allegations that Major William J. Ruch, Squadron 4 commander at Philadelphia, was involved in politics and misused his authority. Satisfied that these allegations were well-founded, Adams summarily dismissed Ruch. Amid denials and protests from Democratic party circles, Adams would not rescind his dismissal order. Lieutenant Melvin H. Snavely and First Sergeant Harold V. Piersol, reportedly linked to the Ruch case, were transferred out of Philadelphia. This case was never forgotten by Ruch or others concerned with it: fifteen years later the subject of Ruch's dismissal was again raised in high places with surprising results. Major Henry was shifted from Squadron 2, at Harrisburg, to fill Ruch's vacancy at Philadelphia. Captain Charles C. Keller was promoted to major and filled Henry's spot at Harrisburg.

In the early months of 1940, two more names were added to the honor roll. Killed in the line of duty were Pfc. Frederick J. Sutton and Pfc. George J. Yashur. Sutton, a member of Troop A-2, was shot and killed on January 3, as he attempted to serve a bad check warrant at McConnellsburg. Yashur, a member of Troop B-3, met death as he was directing traffic in flood-stricken Kingston on April 1.

Because of the relatively high turnover in personnel, it was essential that Adams consider another recruit class to bring his depleted ranks to full complement. On August 1, 1940, 150 men underwent training at the Indiantown Gap Military Reservation. Once again the training school at Hershey was inadequate for such a large recruit assembly.

After three months of extensive training, the class was dismissed without formalities and sent to the field to undergo on-the-job training until February 1, 1941. The austerity associated with the final days at Indiantown Gap is not quite understood, when one compares it with the elaborate fanfare attending the graduation of the two Myerstown classes at the Harrisburg Forum with dignitaries galore on hand to witness the handing out of diplomas. Thus the third largest class in State Police history, up to that point, entered upon the stage and left it almost unnoticed.

In mid-1940, the state saw the Pennsylvania Turnpike's 160-mile stretch from Middlesex, Cumberland County, to Irwin, Westmoreland County, opened to the public. It was decided by the Turnpike Commission and Governor James that full responsibility for safety along this modern roadway would rest with the Motor Police. Adams, on October 1, responded to that call by moving Troop B, Squadron 2, from Chambersburg, reestablishing a special patrol troop at Bedford, which would retain its identity as B-2. The troop's former duties were then divided between Troop A-1, at Greensburg, Troop A-2, at Harrisburg, and Troop C-2, at Hollidaysburg. This transaction did not disturb the complement of existing troops.

Following the merger, the Motor Police executives occupied the same suite of offices in the capitol's east wing to the rear of the rotunda. An increase in the number of headquarters personnel to handle the added workload, however, made continued occupation of these offices impractical. After thirty-four years at the same stand, the executive offices were moved in 1940 to the third floor of the capitol's north wing. There the executives and headquarters personnel were given what amounted to luxurious accommodations by comparison. Both the executive offices and the special services were then in the north wing with only two floors separating them. Years were bringing them closer. These quarters were occupied until 1963, when a new move finally brought them together in a leased building nearby.

When the 1941 session of the legislature was underway, James lost no time in re-submitting Adams' name to the Senate for confirmation to serve until the third Tuesday of January, 1943. The Committee on Executive Nominations this time decided to keep Adam's nomination bottled up for the remainder of the session. Thus Adams went on to serve until January, 1943, without benefit of confirmation during his come-back years as head of the state's top law enforcement agency.

Reflecting the seriousness of state business and the threat of war, the general assembly remained in session for 196 calendar days—the longest session in 100 years. During that period, the legislators passed three measures bearing on Motor Police operations. Act 91, P.L. 207, June 25, regulated payments into the retirement fund by members while in military and naval service. Act 117, P.L. 249, July 3, specified retirement system rights and obligations of members in active wartime service. Act 189, P.L. 494, July 24, appointed a representative of the Motor Police to the Pennsylvania Highway Traffic Advisory Committee to assist the U. S. War Department.

The general assembly, which usually met every other year, was then meeting every year in response to special calls. In fact, the general assembly met every year from 1931 to handle the unique problems arising from the Great Depression and was at this point knee-deep in the involvements of another fast approaching world-wide disaster—World War II.

Further reflecting the seriousness of the situation at hand, Adams, on August 12, issued an order creating an emergency troop in each squadron "for the purpose of assembly in the event of an emergency requiring such a force." These were not additional troops but rather a composition of handpicked men from each troop in each squadron specially trained to cope with foreseeable wartime problems at home should the state militia be pressed into federal service.

During the brief special session of 1940 and the lengthy regular session of 1941, Adams advocated changing the name of the Pennsylvania Motor Police to Pennsylvania State Police. His efforts, however well-meaning they were, received little or no notice.

Although the general assembly was busily engaged in what could be considered "heavyweight matters," Adams was a subject of diversion for a few legislators. For example, on June 12, 1941, a resolution was introduced in the House by freshman Representative Thomas J. Heatherington (D-Allegheny) calling for a five-member committee to examine the Motor Police investigation of the Rachel Taylor murder at Penn State College. Rachel Taylor, a Penn State student, was murdered on March 28, 1940, in the State College vicinity, and no arrests had been made. For more than one year, that murder and subsequent attacks upon women in the State College area frustrated Motor Police investigators who were then personally supervised by Adams at the scene.

The House resolution made reference to the Senate's refusal to confirm Adams and questioned Adams' qualifications. There was no doubt that the resolution's author was more interested in cutting down Adams than he was in the unsuccessful investigation of a murder. The resolution was read a second time on June 16, when it was referred to the Committee on Rules. There the resolution died.

Adams continued his deep interest in seeing the Motor Police communications systems improve with the state of the art. Transmission speed of teletypewriter equipment was increased from forty to sixty words per minute, and tape-cutters and automatic transmitters were installed at major linking centers at Harrisburg and Wyoming. New base stations and mobile units were added to the radio system statewide for better coverage.

On June 17, 1941, Pfc. Thomas P. Carey of Troop C-4, Reading, died of poisonous fumes inhaled at the scene of a motor vehicle accident and fire. Three months later, Pfc. Wallace F. Ely of Troop D-2, Montoursville, died on September 14 as the result of injuries suffered in a one-car crash. Both deaths occurred in the line of duty.

During those days of the Motor Police, there was mutual concern among its members for acquiring adequate life insurance coverage. Life insurance premiums for police officers were generally higher than for other occupations or professions, and most companies would not offer double indemnity policies. Members of Squadron 2 voted to form an immediate relief fund to supplement whatever life insurance coverage each member could afford. The constitution and by-laws of the Squadron 2 Pennsylvania Motor Police Immediate Relief Fund were adopted on February 8, 1941, and the organization came into being on March 1. The first officers of the fund were Major Charles C. Keller, president, and Sergeant William A. Ent, secretary-treasurer.

The first death benefit assessment followed the death of Private William F. Schmidtmier on December 27, 1941. The sum of $1,795 was paid to Schmidtmier's beneficiary. Additional assessments were made to create three accounts to accommodate multiple deaths, and payment was pegged at $1,000. This figure was later raised to $1,500 and then to $1,750. The subject of payment in the event of suicide was thoroughly argued, and it was overwhelmingly decided that payment would be made for any cause of death. Immediate relief funds sprung up in all squadrons—each administered separately.

On December 7, 1941, the nation was horrified by the Japanese attack on Pearl Harbor. The following day, at the urging of President Franklin D. Roosevelt, Congress declared war on Japan. On December 11, Congress declared war on Germany and Italy in response to declarations of war by those two nations. The nation was fully committed to winning a two-theatre war and winning a lasting peace for mankind. And the Motor Police had to contribute its share to the nation's all-out mobilization effort.

During World I, the general assembly enacted legislation allowing for half-salary payments to be made to state employees engaged in active military or naval service. Payments were made to family dependents. The state entered into deficit spending to support that measure. That enactment was still on the books with the United States entry into World War II.

Because of their police training, military-like discipline and supervisory capabilities, Motor Policemen were in demand by the military, and offered commissions that were tempting, indeed. With military pay and allowances plus half-pay from the state, men were handsomely compensated for their dual roles—officers in the military service and state employes on military leave.

It did not take the general assembly long to realize the impracticality and unreasonableness of continuing such a generous policy in the face of large-scale mobilization. On April 21, 1942, the legislators passed Act 19, P.L. 50, considerably limiting state aid to dependents and taking into account military pay and allowances. The rush into uniform was curtailed. Those on military leave at the time of the law's res-cission were unquestionably discontent with that development on the home front, but were left with no choice but to fulfill their military obli-gations until relieved of them. Many returned after World War II to their former status with the Motor Police, others remained in military service to which they apparently took a liking.

Still the Motor Police complement was riddled by draft call-ups. The loss of personnel was deeply felt. Adams had no alternative but to cut back on services by withdrawing from boroughs, townships and cities where organized forces could manage somehow to look after their own welfare. He cancelled all revolver target practice sessions to conserve ammunition and maximize patrols.

On February 5, 1942, Adams created the Executive Service Sec-tion to provide security at the capitol and governor's mansion. This group was housed with the BCI & I for administrative purposes.

Most of Adams' final year at the helm was spent bolstering the country's wartime efforts at home. The Motor Police took on the se-curity of critical defense plants and aided federal agents in curtailing subversive activities of suspected enemy sympathizers. Patrol activities were sacrificed for more pressing demands on the home front. Adams faced unusual circumstances confidently and guided the Motor Police successfully in meeting departmental obligations with honor and dignity.

The year 1942 was marred by only one death in the line of duty. Pfc. Dean N. Zeigler of Troop A-2, Harrisburg, died on October 17 of injuries suffered in a two-car collision a week before.

On the political scene, Major General Edward Martin decisively trounced the Democratic party candidate, F. Clair Ross, at the November general election. The 63-year-old governor-elect, who was serving as the state's adjutant general and heading Pennsylvania's military efforts, was hardly to be denied an election victory. It is doubt-ful that any Democrat could have defeated Martin.

As Martin awaited his inaugural day, January 19, 1943, he was in-formed by his advisors that none of his cabinet appointees would be confirmed by the Senate if Adams was found among them. To avoid such an unpleasant situation from arising, Adams prepared to leave of-fice with the end of James' term.

Before leaving office, James took the time to publicly recognize Adams' distinguished service by awarding him the Pennsylvania Meri-torious Medal. Adams was the first State Police officer to receive the medal since it was instituted in 1938.

Adams, at 63, resigned on January 19, closing out his tenure as commissioner at three years and seven and one-half months. He had previously served as constabulary superintendent for seventeen years and four months. His combined years in both posts was one-half month shy of twenty-one years, exceeding by far tenure of any other. And it is a certainty that his record will hold up for all time.

Notwithstanding the long, tiring hours at his work, Adams was indeed generous with his "spare" time in behalf of his church and community. Adams was vestryman and senior warden at St. Paul's Episcopal Church, Harrisburg, "for what seemed like decades," it was said. He gave much of his life to promoting the Boy Scout movement in this country, firmly believing in the proper upbringing of the nation's most valuable resource. Adams travelled to England to learn scouting principles and procedures from the Boy Scout founder, Sir Robert Baden-Powell. Having gained this training, Adams became one of the first scoutmasters in the United States long before the movement was fully established. He was chairman of the first Boy Scout circus held at Harrisburg's Farm Show building in 1930. In 1934, he was elected to the Boy Scouts of America executive board.

Adams was a family man, and a niece, Esther W. Watrous, had this to write of him, "He enriched our lives with story telling; his patience, advice and cautioning; his gentleness; his leading us in song, in target shooting and in wholesome conversation. He established the right, the just in our code of life; obedience to law and dedication to high principles; in faith in God and in service and support of our church and our fellowmen. Always setting the example—his life was a beacon and shines as such in our memories."

Adams remained active throughout his "retired" days.

CHAPTER XIV

Pennsylvania State Police
Colonel Cecil M. Wilhelm
1943–1955

When it became publicly known that Adams was leaving his post with the termination of the James administration, it was generally accepted that his desk would be taken over by Wilhelm. No rumors to the contrary circulated. Governor-elect Edward Martin was only two years Wilhelm's senior—both came from military backgrounds, both held top level state government positions and were well known to each other. Martin was inaugurated on January 19, 1943, and true to expectations announced Wilhelm's appointment to succeed Adams. His name and those of other cabinet appointees were submitted to the Senate for confirmation. The Senate, acting swiftly and favorably, confirmed all appointees on inauguration day.

At 61, Wilhelm took his oath of office on January 20, 1943. He was the oldest ever appointed to the office of superintendent or commissioner; when most men were ending their police careers, Wilhelm was leaning into a new and challenging turn in his, that would see him through twelve years as top administrator.

Wilhelm was born in Reading on October 21, 1881, the son of Washington Irving Wilhelm and Mary A. Marshall Wilhelm. The Wilhelm family history in America dates back to the early 1800s. Washington Irvin Wilhelm, named for the celebrated American author, was a bicycle manufacturer at Reading. He promoted and competed in bicycle races and was widely acclaimed for his achievements. Mary, his wife, was a pioneer woman cyclist at a time when the home constituted a woman's domain. Considering that the bicycle of her time was designed with the very large front wheel and a much smaller rear wheel, her skill at riding was no insignificant accomplishment.

Young Wilhelm attended public schools. He played sandlot baseball, played football for Hamburg High School and was an excellent horseman. His education continued at the Carroll Institute and Pennsylvania Military College. At the military college, he was a member of the varsity football team. A teammate, Cecil B. DeMille, went on to become one of Hollywood's founders and its most famous film producer and director. Oddly enough Wilhelm and DeMille were born the same year and died the same year.

Wilhelm was West Point bound. The outbreak of the Spanish-American War, however, interrupted that course. A member of Company E, Fourth Regiment, Pennsylvania National Guard (Pennsylvania Volunteer Infantry), Wilhelm was called into federal service in 1898 and saw action in the Spanish-American War's Puerto Rican campaign. He remained in military service until early 1905.

In 1904, Wilhelm married Eva Gertrude Neiman, of Reading. Born to Eva and Cecil Wilhelm were four children—William, Marshall, Robert and Evelyn.

After military service, Wilhelm took up clerical chores with the P. & R. Railroad at Reading until the organization of the new state constabulary came to his attention. He applied for enlistment, and was quickly accepted by Groome. Wilhelm was enlisted by Captain William P. Taylor, at Troop C, Reading, on December 15, 1905, and, at Groome's direction, given non-commissioned rank of sergeant. Wilhelm was numbered among the original constabulary enlistees signed up that day.

On October 1, 1906, Wilhelm was promoted to first sergeant and transferred to Troop B, at Wilkes-Barre. He resigned from the constabulary on April 30, 1907, and was reenlisted on August 15, 1907, with the same rank of first sergeant. He was reduced to sergeant on January 2, 1908 and replaced by First Sergeant William E. Mair. A month after his transfer back to Reading on January 11, 1909, he was promoted to first sergeant. Before that year was up, Wilhelm was promoted to lieutenant and moved to Troop D, Butler.

Wilhelm, at Groome's direction, competed with other lieutenants in a written exam on January 11, 1911, at Harrisburg, to fill an upcoming vacancy created by Captain William Marsh's request for voluntary demotion and transfer to cope with family hardships. Wilhelm received

Colonel Cecil M. Wilhelm (Courtesy of Pennsylvania State Police)

the top grade and was promoted to captain on January 15, four days later. A week later he was transferred back to his original troop at Reading—this time as commanding officer.

Wilhelm, at Groome's urging, accepted a captain's commission in the U. S. Army Signal Corps on November 27, 1917, and was sent to France for World War I duty with the American Expeditionary Forces. He later saw service with the Military Intelligence Division, and was promoted to major. He returned from military service on April 3, 1919.

In 1919, the legislature shifted the independent Fire Marshal's Office to the State Police as a bureau. Implementing the law, Adams created the Bureau of Fire Protection in 1920 and, on May 7, appointed Wilhelm first director of the new addition to the constabulary. On July 21, 1923, Adams gave Wilhelm the added responsibility of serving as the department's director of Wireless Communications. When Major William E. Mair resigned his post as Adams' deputy in 1926 to accept a security post with Westinghouse, at Pittsburgh, Adams, after some delay, appointed Wilhelm as his top aide effective July 1,1926.

Eva Gertrude Wilhelm died, at Harrisburg, on July 3, 1932. A year later, Wilhelm married Lola F. Brandt, a Harrisburg nurse. Lola Brandt, the daughter of William and Florence Cochlin Brandt, was formerly from Scotland, Franklin County, where the Brandt family lived for many years. From this second marriage, two children were born— Mary and Richard Lawrence.

Wilhelm served as Adams' deputy until the State Police-State Highway Patrol merger in July, 1937. Following the merger, he was given a new post as Motor Police chief of staff. Adams resigned in a huff as deputy commissioner on October 21, 1937, and Commissioner Foote picked up Wilhelm as his deputy that same day.

When, in 1939, Governor James was unable to secure legislative backing for Adams' appointment as commissioner, James called on Wilhelm to serve as acting commissioner. Wilhelm was acting commissioner until Adams' interim appointment on May 31, 1939, and then was kept on as deputy commissioner.

Wilhelm was a quiet man, and given to little conversation. As commissioner, his favorite reply to inquiring newsmen was, "No comment." He was a man fully dedicated to his work, and found no time for hobbies in his life. Wilhelm was modest and never known to talk about himself. A cousin once wrote that "Martie," as Wilhelm was known to him, "carried his modesty to a fault."

Wilhelm, who smoked cigars unceasingly, once tried his hand at golf, but gave it up quickly. He took up fishing, but that was no lasting activity either. Unlike Adams, Wilhelm was not the outdoors type. At one time, however, it was told that he was persuaded by Adams and others to accompany them to Eagles Mere, Sullivan county, for trout fishing—Wilhelm made the first catch.

Wilhelm's second son, Marshall "Bud" Wilhelm, enlisted in the state constabulary, and with Wilhelm's appointment as commissioner there came into existence an unusual father-son relationship for the first time in State Police history. A similar relationship was to occur again thirty years later. Such a situation did exist, however, in the State Highway Patrol during the tenure of Superintendent Wilson C. Price: his son, Walter, was a member of the Patrol.

Wilhelm, who could in many ways be called a "loner," had few intimate friends. His closest companions were Tom Francis, a Harrisburg automobile dealer, and Homer Moyer, a local newspaper executive.

On May 23, 1930, he was awarded the Pennsylvania State Police Distinguished Service Medal, and later awarded the American Legion Distinguished Service Medal. In his lifetime, Wilhelm was much-honored by government and civic organizations for his outstanding work.

Wilhelm held memberships with the Spanish-American War Veterans, American Legion, Pennsylvania Chiefs of Police Association, and International Association of Chiefs of Police. In Masonic circles, he was a member of the Pulski Lodge 216, F & AM, at Pottsville; Harrisburg Consistory; Rajah Temple, at Reading, and the Zembo Temple Luncheon Club, at Harrisburg. Wilhelm was also a member of Harrisburg's Trinity Methodist Church.

Wilhelm was not successful in quickly acquiring a deputy commissioner: Governor Martin was indecisive on this appointment. The post was sought after by Major Jacob C. Mauk, commander of Squadron 1, at Greensburg. Some prominent state officials felt that the job should go to Major William A. Clark, commander of Squadron 3, at Wyoming. Clark, it will be recalled, had a shot at the commissioner's post under Governors Earle and James; he was again being considered for an important appointment.

State Supreme Court Chief Justice George W. Maxey, who had the highest regard for both Mauk and Clark, phoned Clark about the appointment. Maxey informed Clark that Mauk, seeking the deputy post, had visited his office. Clark steadfastly refused the support of influential friends, believing wholeheartedly, according to his family, that any appointment, if it was to come, must come without solicitation. Others, eager for advancement in the State Police, however, did not play the game by Clark's rules. Clark's position strengthened Mauk's candidacy, and it is believed that Maxey contributed to Mauk's eventual appointment.

Mauk's decision to seek the deputy post is not to be looked upon with disapprobation—for the appointment would surely have gone to some ranking officer from the department's rolls. The post was a better-paying one and any successful effort to gain appointment would be financially rewarding, if nothing else. The two top posts, because of the high salaries and power of office, would henceforth be considered political plums worthy of harvesting by aspirants. As will be seen, some campaigns have been bitterly fought, and the deep wounds of battle never healed.

In this particular case, bitterness was absent. Clark, although qualified, did not want to make a contest of it. He was a highly-principled man and not about to surrender his principles even for a better-paying position. Emphasis has been placed on Adams' stubborn attitude toward politics and politicians, but there is reason to judge Clark even more stubborn on these points than his former mentor. At any rate, the appointment went to Mauk on April 16, 1943, after three months of deliberation by Martin and Wilhelm.

Filling Mauk's vacancy at Greensburg was newly-promoted Major William F. Hoffman. Hoffman for many years had headed the BCI & I operations at headquarters. The BCI & I post went to Captain Harry McElroy, who was supervising detective division affairs at headquarters.

Mauk was born at Sprankle Mills, Jefferson County, on October 9, 1893. He was one of six children born to W. Lyman and Anna Caylor Mauk. His father was a farmer and lumberman. When still a youngster, his parents rented their farm and moved to northern Michigan where they purchased large tracts of land for timbering. In Michigan, game was plentiful, and it was there that Mauk learned the art of hunting, a sport in which he never lost interest.

Mauk's only brother, Harry, joined the constabulary in 1909, and an injury suffered while training horses forced him to resign from the State Police. Soon thereafter Harry was commissioned captain with the Jones and Laughlin Steel Plant and headed the plant security police force. Mauk joined the security police force at J. & L. and worked for his older brother. Seeing no opportunity for advancement, Mauk left J. & L. and enlisted in the constabulary, at 23, on April 2, 1917.

His education was limited to the eighth grade; however, he was eager to continue his studies by attending night school.

He was assigned to Troop A, Greensburg, as a private. Mauk was promoted to corporal on August 1, 1918, to sergeant on July 1, 1919, and to first sergeant at Troop A on September 16, 1920. Adams advanced him to commissioned rank as lieutenant on December 1, 1923, and transferred him to Troop B, Wyoming. During Mauk's tenure at Wyoming, Gifford Pinchot, a resident of Milford, Pike County, was

Lt. Colonel Jacob C. Mauk (Courtesy of Pennsylvania State Police)

elected governor. Mauk was often called upon to provide security for the governor and his family, and a warm friendship developed between the governor and the young constabulary lieutentant.

On October 16, 1924, the Ebensburg Coal Company in Cambria County was robbed and an American Express guard murdered. Mauk, on detached duty from Wyoming, was given this case assignment by

Adams. During the course of the investigation, Mauk had the pleasant occasion of working closely with the mine manager's secretary, Carrie Short, whom he courted.

After successfully closing the Ebensburg case, he returned to Wyoming. On June 1, 1926, Adams promoted him to captain and returned him to western Pennsylvania as commanding officer, Troop D, Butler. On September 27, 1927, he and Carrie Short were married.

At Butler, Mauk actively engaged in the search, apprehension and prosecution of Highway Patrol Corporal Brady Paul's murderers. Paul was shot and killed by Irene Schroeder and Glenn Dague in 1929.

Prior to his inauguration the second time as governor, on January 20, 1931, Pinchot, who had befriended Mauk, offered him the post of superintendent. Willing to serve Adams loyally, Mauk declined the offer with sincere appreciation, and promptly reported this transaction to Adams. Following his inauguration, Pinchot retained Adams in office.

Mauk remained at Butler until his transfer to Greensburg in September, 1932. He served as troop commander at Greensburg through 1937 when, on January 1, 1938, Commissioner Foote picked him as one of the four squardron cammanders with the rank of major. Mauk's squadron post was located at Greensburg.

Mauk was regarded as an expert pistol shot; he won many honors during his career both as an individual and team competitor. As squadron commander, he formed a team of revolver sharpshooters, which for years swept all honors.

During ceremonies at Gettysburg in mid-1938, commemorating the seventy-fifth anniversary of the famous battle, Mauk and his crack pistol team were assigned as bodyguards to President Franklin D. Roosevelt. Serving with Mauk were: Sergeant T. E. Jones, Sergeant Lewis R. Feloni, Corporal Walter B. Kunkle, Corporal Thomas E. Eshleman, Private Clarence C. Snipas, Private Bruce Burtner, Private Robert C. McKee and Private William A. Stile.

In 1939, Mauk was called upon to serve as special bodyguard to King George VI, of England, and his queen, the former Lady Elizabeth Bowes-Lyon, who toured the United States and visited Pennsylvania.

Mauk, a strapping six-footer and much like Adams, was an outdoorsman. He enthusiastically looked to hunting and fishing for recreation. Many a night was spent with companion Fred Gardener hunting coon in the mountain woods surrounding Harrisburg. Hunting and fishing took him to his brother's Sullivan County home where Harry settled after his retirement. Mauk was a sports fan and followed baseball in particular.

Wilhelm, a dedicated work-horse, completely dominated his

adminstration and delegated little of significance to Mauk. Yet Mauk doggedly held to his post and served Wilhelm loyally without complaint. Headquarters observers, however, sincerely felt that Mauk was not wholly content with his role as deputy at the outset.

Mauk was considered a policeman's policeman by the field forces. He was line-oriented and successfully met the challenges of criminal investigations, arrests and prosecutions, for which he was much honored. The drastic change to headquarters staff chores has often been difficult to adjust to for many field officers, and it is likely that Wilhelm's administrative habits contributed to Mauk's discomfiture. During the latter years of his tenure, Wilhelm's age and poor health made the delegation of responsibility necessary. Mauk fulfilled his obligations enthusiastically, and faithfully supported Wilhelm until 1955 when both were forced to retire from state service.

Wilhelm found himself in command of a fast-shrinking complement of Motor Policemen. The last recruit class to clear the training school on March 31, 1942, saw only 49 men added to the department's rolls. Because of wartime conditions, no further recruit classes were in view. Already 196 men had entered military service, and others, qualifying for retirement, were seeking better-paying jobs in defense industries.

Faced with this manpower shortage, Wilhelm issued an order prohibiting resignations "except for a good cause." As a result of this order, men qualified for retirement simply deserted. After an absence of ten days without authorized leave, each man was dropped from the rolls on the grounds of job abandoment. Since the State Police Civic Association and the state retirement system were compelled to legally honor bona fide retirement requests, despite the circumstances of separation, Wilhelm's order was easily circumvented. Wilhelm, nonetheless, was determined to keep the ruling in effect for the duration of the war. It's provision, of course, was helpful in retaining those who valued an honorable discharge record at separation.

On April 22, 1943, the legislators passed Act 42, P.L. 67, providing for pay increases and advancement in rank for members in active wartime service. This enactment preserved trooper benefits which would be recognized upon a return to police service after military discharge.

A more agreeable general assembly in 1943 also acceded to Wilhelm's petition to have the Pennsylvania Motor Police name changed to Pennsylvania State Police. Act 52, P.L. 94, April 28, amending the Adminstrative Code, made this name change possible. Acts 53 through 63, April 28, amended laws to reflect the name change. And Act 216,

P.L. 485, May 21, amending the Penal Code sections relating to the Uniform Firearms Act, transferred enforcement of that act to the State Police. Wilhelm gave this responsiblity to the BCI & I.

Some of the 1943 personnel changes worthy of note saw the retirement of Captain George H. Keller, one of the few remaining original members of the State Highway Patrol, on September 18. Retiring, too, was Comptroller Silvus J. Overmiller who, on October 10, brought to a close a distinguished career going back to 1908—thirty-five years earlier. At the close of the year, Lieutenant John A. Funck, who was in military service, resigned in favor of continuing that status. Having understudied micro-ballistics with Funck, First Sergeant Lewis M. Whitecotten was promoted to lieutenant and filled Funck's vacancy at the crime lab. Funck's polygraph duties were picked up by Detective Sergeant Freeman B. Ramer.

Replacing Overmiller at the comptroller's slot was Overmiller's assistant, Edward P. McBreen, a career employee at headquarters. McBreen was born at Mahanoy City, Schuylkill County, on September 10, 1910. The son of Dr. Philip McBreen and Emily Timm McBreen, he was educated in the Tamaqua public schools, Beckley College, and Temple University. McBreen began his constabulary services in 1924 and was transferred to the comptroller's office in 1926.

State Police operations in May, 1944, were curtailed to supply a trooper task force for the thirty-sixth Annual Governors' Conference held at the Hotel Hershey. The four-day conference was underway on May 28. Troopers were kept busy transporting their VIP passengers to nearby Harrisburg, Indiantown Gap Military Reservation, Philadelphia and the Gettysburg battlefield, where special ceremonies and events crammed the governors' schedules. New York Governor Thomas E. Dewey, a presidential hopeful, was perhaps the most prominent visitor at that conference which dealt mainly with wartime and post-war needs.

On June 1, 1944, the State Police table of organization reflected no change although there were changes in personnel. Headquarters still consisted of six bureaus and divisions: BCI & I, Quartermaster, Communications, Bureau of Fire Protection, Traffic and Comptroller. The BCI & I was still responsible for overseeing operations of the Identification Division, Detective Division, Criminal Intelligence Section, Crime Lab and Executive Service Section.

The field forces were divided into the four squadrons and sixteen troops. Operationally, there were eighty-six substations. Because of wartime demands, the authorized complement of 1,600 officers and men was reduced to 1,129, and further reductions were expected. By that time, 265 enlisted men and 28 civilians were on military leave. The State Police had already suffered three war fatalities.

The department was burdened by the additional responsibility of assisting federal agencies in the war effort. And rearing its ugly head at this stage was the major social problem-to-be—juvenile delinquency.

As an advancement in communications, the State Police had just completed a one-year experiment with two-way radio. The station-to-car and car-to-station system try-out in Lancaster County was declared a success.

The BCI & I criminal files then numbered 359,411. Record checks of fingerprints received annually indicated that more than 40 percent of the arrestees had prior records. This rate of recidivism was on the increase.

The State Police state-wide teletype system boasted of 115 terminals, and during the 1942-44 period 464,821 messages were dispatched.

During the 1942-44 period, State Police traffic patrols covered 25,974,866 miles and arrested 55,797 operators for roadway violations. Patrols investigated 21,163 accidents which accounted for 1,371 fatalities. Patrol mileage and arrests were down considerably in view of wartime rationing of gasoline and tires. Automobiles were difficult to procure and those already in the State Police patrol fleet had to be used as sparingly as possible. Patrol vehicles, normally traded at 60,000 miles, were to see 100,000 miles and more.

During the same period, there were 22,009 criminal arrests. Burglary, disorderly conduct and larceny headed the crimes committed. Most arrests, by far, fell in the 21 to 30 age group.

The State Police then owned two buildings. One, at Harrisburg, was acquired from the State Highway Patrol. The other building was located at Philadelphia. Wilhelm was critical of the state's leasing program and lamented the fact that the State Police recorded ownership of only two buildings; he submitted an ambitious building program to the Post-War Planning Commission. Also recommended to the governor for post-war planning was a statewide two-way radio system for all mobile patrol units and a filled complement of 1,600 positions as soon as possible.

Captain T.N. Boate resigned on October 31, 1944, leaving the directorship of traffic operations vacant. Wilhelm moved Major Earl J. Henry from Squadron 4, at Philadelphia, to headquarters where Henry headed the traffic bureau until 1955.

The command personnel at headquarters and the field as of December 1, 1944, included:

Commissioner—Colonel C. M. Wilhelm
Deputy commissioner—Lt. Colonel Jacob C. Mauk
BCI & I—Captain Harry E. McElroy
          Lieutenant Paul J. Roche
Quartermaster—Captain Guy. E. Reichard
Communication—Lieutenant Donald E. Wagner
Fire bureau—Captain William F. Traeger
          Lieutenant Ralph D. Gardner
Traffic—Major Earl J. Henry
          Captain Lawrence Brosha
Comptroller—Edward P. McBreen
          John R. Price (Personnel Director)
Squadron 1—Major William Hoffman
          Captain Joseph G. McCann
    Troop A, Greensburg—Captain Andrew J. Hudock
    Troop B, Washington—Lieutenant Daniel Augustine
    Troop C, Punxsutawney—Lieutenant Jackson Dodson
    Troop D, Butler—Captain William R. Hanna
    Troop E, Erie—Lieutanant John C. Bricker
Squadron 2—Major Charles C. Keller
          Lieutenant W. C. A. Bear
          Lieutenant Ray Hoover
    Troop A, Harrisburg—Lieutenant John D. Kime
    Troop B, Bedford (Turnpike)—Sergeant Albert Shuller
                    (acting)
    Troop C, Hollidaysburg—Lieutenant Herman Roush
    Troop D, Williamsport—Lieutenant Frank C. Miner
Squadron 3—Major William A. Clark
          Captain Charles J. McRae
    Troop A, Hazleton—Lieutenant John Grance
    Troop B, Wyoming—Lieutenant Charles S. Cook
    Troop C, Blakely—Lieutenant John J. Tomek
Squadron 4—Captain William D. Plummer
    Troop A, Philadelphia—Lieutenant James J. Tooey
    Troop B, Lancaster—Lieutenant Fred G. McCartney
    Troop C, Reading—Captain Edwin Griffith
    Troop D, Bethlehem—Lieutenant Melvin Snavely
Training School—Major Thomas F. Martin
          Lieutenant Emmett J. Donovan
Crime Lab—Lieutenant Lewis M. Whitecotton
          Lieutenant Stanley S. Smith

Captain Plummer was given command of the Fourth Squadron to fill

Henry's vacancy, and promoted to major shortly after this roster was published. A number of key officers shown on earlier rosters were serving in the armed forces.

Early in 1945 the number of volunteer departures and draft calls reached more critical proportions. A record number of 329 officers and troopers were then in the armed forces. Wilhelm petitioned the military authorities in Washington to halt the drain of troopers so that some semblance of security could be maintained in Pennsylvania. Military authorities, recognizing the state agency's effective defense role, responded favorably. No volunteer enlistments would be accepted and draft calls would cease as long as troopers remained employed with the State Police. That action permitted Wilhelm to preserve a battered complement yet large enough to carry out some of the department's wartime obligations creditably.

Wartime conditions created another internal problem which bothered Wilhelm. A shortage of men being quartered at state-owned and leased barracks jeopardized the department's goal of at least

"Ghost" car, mid-1940s (Courtesy of Pennsylvania State Police)

breaking even on expenses. The loss of men to the war effort was further complicated by the number of men marrying and living away from the barracks. To study this particular problem, Wilhelm appointed Lt. Colonel Mauk, Captain Fred McCartney and Lieutenant Kime. Nothing of significance, however, resulted from the study— changes were to come much later.

The 1945 General Assembly session found the legislators very active in dealing with matters affecting State Police affairs. Seven laws were passed falling into this category. Act 211, P.L. 538, May 15, amended P.L. 1019 (1933) relative to payment for removal of fire hazards. Act 239, P.L. 583, May 16, provided additional credit for war veterans taking examinations for State Police enlistment. Act 262, P.L. 620, May 16, amended P.L. 450 (1927) relative to removal or change of building fire hazards by political subdivisions. Act 267, P.L. 627, May 17, amended P.L. 787 (1937) relative to removal of fire hazards. Act 336, P.L. 834, May 22, restored retirement rights and specified time for rejoining retirement system after military service. Act 375, P.L. 945, May 24, amended P.L. 280 (1931) relative to payment of costs for eliminating fire hazards. Act 442, P.L. 1388, June 4, provided for troopers' right of appeal to Court of Common Pleas of Dauphin County when aggrieved by action of the commisioner. The latter action by the legislators was a landmark development in employer-employee relations.

The nation was shocked on April 12, 1945, by the news of President Franklin D. Roosevelt's sudden death at his "Little White House" at Warm Springs, Georgia. Death came to the nation's only fourth-term President at 3:35 p.m. central war time, following a massive cerebral hemorrhage. His death came on the threshold of Germany's defeat, and two weeks before the opening session of the United Nations at San Francisco on April 25.

The slow-moving train carrying the President's body left Warm Springs on its twenty-three-hour run to the nation's capitol—his flag-draped casket watched over by an honor guard of soldiers, sailors and marines. Thousands of mourners along the route of travel bid farewell to the man who saw them through the Great Depression and a yet unended world war. Brief funeral services in the White House east room preceded the trip to Hyde Park, New York, where the body of President Roosevelt was buried on the grounds of his ancestral home, as the nation mourned a great President. For many young Americans, there was no other.

Allied forces, having landed on the beaches of Normandy, advanced eastward across the European continent with tremendous success, albeit with heavy casualities. Nonetheless, the German army was routed and surrendered on May 7, 1945, to bring one theatre of war to a victorious end.

The curtain dropped on the forty-year State Police career of Major William A. Clark, who, on June 30, 1945, elected to retire. Clark, a beloved man in the anthracite region, was an orginal Groome appointee on December 15, 1905. His service of forty years was exceeded by only one other—Wilhelm. Following on the heels of his retirement, no less than half a dozen testimonial dinners were held in Clark's honor—a fitting response from the people he served so well and for so long.

On August 6, 1945, the encore invention of the devil (according to the *Boston Globe*)—the atom bomb—was detonated above Hiroshima, Japan, with devastation never before known to man. Dead were 78,150. Thousands were injured and left homeless. Many victims linger to this day with their afflictions. According to a news story appearing in the *Harrisburg Patriot* on August 6, 1975, "120,000 more have died since from radiation poisoning, leukemia and other complications."

Three days later, August 9, another atom bomb was targeted on Nagasaki, Japan, with equally devastating results. Shocked by the destructive capability of this new type of bomb, Japanese authorities surrendered on August 15. Instruments of surrender were signed aboard the battleship *Missouri,* at Manila, on August 19.

Thus ended World War II which, according to a War Department report in June, 1946, accounted for 396,637 American dead. The number of wounded and missing in action boosted the casualty total to more than 1 million. Ten members of the State Police were killed or died during World War II service.

According to an article appearing in the *Veterans of Foreign Wars Magazine,* December, 1975, Navy Department records credit the USS *Concord* with firing the last salvo of World War II as bombardment of the Kurile Islands ended. Serving aboard that four-stack light cruiser as communications officer was Lieutenant Fred A. Lumb, son of the former constabulary-great, Captain George F. Lumb.

With cessation of war, hopes for an early return of troopers and the lifting of wartime restrictions were enkindled. Wilehlm looked forward anxiously to normal circumstances that would make State Police operations less troublesome. Slowly these hopes were realized.

Following Germany's surrender, General Lucius D. Clay was appointed deputy chief of the United States military government in Germany. Recruited to serve as advisors to Clay in police matters were nationally-known police adminstrators. Among them was retired

40th Anniversary Dinner, Harrisburg, 1945. Left to right: Col. Lynn G. Adams, Col. Cecil M. Wilhelm, Lt. Col. Jacob C. Mauk. (Courtesy of Pennsylvania State Police)

Civil Aeronautics Administration class for State Police investigators, Harrisburg, 1946. Front row, left to right: J. W. MacFarlane, Pa. Aeronautics Commission; Kenneth Aldrich, CAA; W. L. Anderson, Pa. Aeronautics Commission; James V. Benard, CAA; John Rodgers, Sr., CAA. Back row: Joe Wiliams, Pa. Aeronautics Commission; Pfc. W. S. Hall; Det. George V. Stedman; Pfc. E. M. McGroarty; Pfc. T. W. Bell; Pfc. E. A. Fagnani; Tom Womer and Robert E. Zook, Pa. Aeronautics Commission. (Courtesy of Pennsylvania State Police)

Colonel Lynn G. Adams. Adams, holding the rank of brigadier general, served in this consultant post for several months before returning to his home and retirement. That was his final involvment with government service.

By this time, State Police administration found itself bogged down by a hodgepodge of general orders, special orders, bulletins and lectures which had accumulated through the years. Even with a noble attempt at indexing, the directives were searched only with difficulty and served no immediate purpose to anyone. Wilhelm, on April 2, 1946, appointed a board to review general orders, update those that still had value and weed out those possessing none. Appointed to the board were Lt. Colonel Mauk, Major Henry, Captain McElroy and Lieutenant Faber. Some progress was made by this board of officers. It was not until fifteen years later, however, that Commissioner Frank G. McCartney successfully tackled this long sought-after project by directing the reorganization of all directives—culled, master-indexed and readily searchable.

In 1945, the State Police took on another specialized task when it was asked by the Pennsylvania Aeronautics Commission (PAC) to assist with the investigation of plane crashes. Wilhelm assigned Detective George V. Stedman to the job of establishing a working relationship with PAC Executive Director William L. Anderson. Soon therafter Pfc. William S. Hall and Pfc. T. W. Bell were added to this new aeronautics detail, each given one half of the state to cover. In 1946, the detail was expanded with the addition of Pfc. Edward M. McGroarty and Pfc. Edward A. Fagnani, and the state was then divided into four sections for improved coverage. Men chosen for this duty were all licensed pilots with commercial, Civil Air Patrol or military experience, and were later given non-commissioned ranks. Training was provided by the Civil Aeronautics Administration, Civil Aeronautics Board, Flight Safety Foundation and Cornell University's Crash Research Institute.

Hall replaced Stedman as supervisor when the latter retired in 1950. Others who saw duty with this detail, as the complement was necessarily changed from time to time, were Stanley Kramer, Paul Mato, Earle Moore, Richard Skillman, Leonard Chehutski, Bernard Chaback, James Summerson, Joseph Yaskus and Nicholas Pauley. The aeronautics detail remained in existence until 1972 when civilian inspectors were employed by the newly-formed Pennsylvania Department of Transportation. State Police personnel then assigned were returned to regular field duty.

Late in 1945 and in early 1946, the State Police rank and file was solicited by officials of the Fraternal Order of Police (FOP) to join that organization. Theretofore, troopers were little organized other than belonging to squadron immediate relief funds and troop civic associations. The only statewide organization was the State Police Civic Association which mainly provided for a pension.

The FOP was not something new. The organization had been in existence for some years. The FOP had its roots with the Pittsburgh Police Department in 1915, when the Allegheny County Court of Common Pleas granted a charter to Fort Pitt Lodge 1, on November 17, 1915. According to that charter, the FOP "is formed for the purpose of social enjoyment, and benevolent, charitable and educational undertakings among policemen."

The idea of organizing police officers who were overworked and underpaid spread from municipality to municipality in Pennsylvania and then to other states. In 1917, a national Grand Lodge was founded. The Pennsylvania Lodge was not organized until July 24, 1934. By that time, the FOP had organized most of the police family in Pennsylvania except the State Police. And in 1946, this matter was diligently pursued. The first Pennsylvania State Police lodge formed was Pioneer Lodge 37, at Philadelphia. Lodges at Wyoming, Hazleton and Blakely followed. Keystone Lodge 41, at Harrisburg, was organized September 4, 1946.

Wilhelm, following the pattern of most police adminstrators, was not in favor of the FOP and made no secret of it. He informed his officers that they were not to join ranks in the FOP and should discourage members of their commands from joining. Despite Wilhem's proclaimed hostility, some officers did enroll with the FOP as charter lodge members, and the influence of the FOP spread swiftly throughout the State Police.

During the summer of 1946, Wilhelm and Governor Martin contrived a program for bringing troopers to the Indiantown Gap Military Reservation for weekend encampments. The men would undergo rifle range instruction, military drill, inspection and generally enjoy the benefits of such an unusual gathering of field personnel. As planned, one-half of the field forces arrived at Indiantown Gap for a four-day weekend. The other half encamped the following weekend. Wilhelm and his staff officers were satisfied that lasting benefits would derive from these encampments. If annual encampments were thought of at the time, none was ever scheduled again.

While encamped at Indiantown Gap, the rank and file was informed in small groups and without fanfare that Wilhelm was dead-set against infiltration by the FOP. Troopers, however, were not discouraged by his position. If anything, Wilhelm's publicized stand created a breach between him and the field forces that was to endure.

During the summer of 1946, Wilhelm was to see one of his post-war recommendations realized. After successfully testing mobile radio units in Lancaster County for a year, Wilhelm wanted the system adopted statewide. On July 9, 1946, Wilhelm signed a service contract with the Bell Telephone Company of Pennsylvania for a statewide radiotelephone system. The Bell Company agreed to install all the system's equipment and maintain it. Although equipment ownership remained with the phone company, the State Police Department was given operational control of the system. The original radio system contract called for 73 base stations and 250 mobile units. The FM system operated on two frequencies, providing for base-to-base, base-to-mobile, mobile-to-base and mobile-to-mobile communications capabilities. Provisions of the contract allowed for expansion of the system as future conditions dictated.

In 1946, crime lab services were expanded by the addition of a photography section. Trooper George Kurteson was moved from Reading to the crime lab for this purpose. Also added to the lab staff was Trooper Edward Crowthers who understudied micro-ballistics with Whitecotton.

In November, 1946, Attorney General James H. Duff lead the Republican party to a lopsided victory over John S. Rice, the Democratic candidate, by a 1,828,462 to 1,270,947 vote. Duff became the third Republican governor in a row since the Democratic party takeover of capitol hill under Earle.

Duff was inaugurated on January 21, 1947, amid the usual festivities. Again there was no doubt that Wilhelm would be kept on as commissioner. Wilhelm and Duff's other cabinet appointees were nominated and confirmed by the Senate on January 21. These remarks by Senator John H. Dent (D-Westmoreland) were made in the Senate at voting time:

> Mr. President, we come across the name of Cecil Marshall Wilhelm. In various counties throughout the state there are complaints that the State Police force of the state of Pennsylvania is too often used as an arm of the party in power, and that they are used to intimidate the men and women who are in the liquor business, and that at election time they visit these places and by inference threaten the welfare of those tax-paying citizens if they do not do the things that are suggested.
>
> I would suggest to Colonel Wilhelm that he, too, is an

agent of the people of Pennsylvania and that, of all the places
it would be criminal to allow partisan politics to participate,
would be in the police force of this state of Pennsylvania.

Since the Republicans controlled the Senate by a 34–16 count, it is
doubtful that confirmation could have been blocked even if the
Democrats had mounted an opposition attempt. But, Dent's words
forecasted a fateful occasion that Wilhelm would face one day.

The first special order issued in 1947 called for Lieutenant John A.
Carr's suspension, pending his court-martial. Carr was the first officer
to face court-martial action since the early 1930s. Although Major
William J. Ruch was dismissed by Adams in 1940 for what the latter
considered improper conduct, Ruch's case was not disposed of by a
court-martial board. Traditionally, the accused officer would have his
case go to a court-martial board. In Ruch's case, however, Adams decided to do otherwise.

The general assembly in its 1947 session passed four pieces of
legislation affecting State Police operations. The first two saw
increased benefits in the retirement system. Act 267, P.L. 625, June 16,
increased state retirement annuities and further regulated allowances.
Act 315, P.L. 720, June 20, provided for payment of tax on premiums
of foreign casualty insurance companies into state annuity accounts.
That legislative action created a third source of income for individual
retirement accounts, which would utimately increase monthly pensions for those qualifying. The other two enactments concerned
enforcement. Act 390, P.L. 935, June 25, authorized search without
warrant to assist the Department of Revenue in collecting the cigarette
tax. Act 497, P.L. 1199, July 2, authorized enforcement of the Fuel Use
Tax Act to assist the Department of Revenue.

The general assembly, sitting in one of its longer sessions, closed
shop after 162 calendar days. The procedure for recording the length of
a session by calendar days, however, came to an end with the 1947
session. Beginning with the next session 1949, duration of a session
would be tallied by the number of legislative days.

Implementing the provisions of Act 497, the State Police engaged
in unusual activities in support of the Revenue Department's enforcement of the Fuel Use Tax Law. Revenue provided the State Police with
a cruiser-type boat for patrolling the Philadelphia port areas of the
Schuylkill and Delaware Rivers and checking all liquid fuel shipments
received by Pennsylvania distributors. Assigned to this special "navy"
duty were four full-time State Policemen.

In mid-1948, the three FOP lodges at Wyoming, Hazleton and

Pennsylvania State Police harbor cruiser, Philadelphia (Courtesy of Pennsylvania State Police)

Blakely, dissatisfied with the insurance coverage provided by the squadron immediate relief system, decided to join forces for a second source of coverage. This was the initial movement in FOP circles toward the goal of additional survivor benefits. A total of 191 members enrolled in this new fund. The first assessment at $3.00 a member was paid to B. J. Jacoby's beneficiary on September 20, 1948. The check amounted to $573.

The FOP movement spread rapidly, and by 1949 there were fifteen State Police lodges in existence. The subject of adequate insurance coverage was still a matter of considerable importance to troopers in all lodges. Witnessing the action of the three lodges in Squadron 3, FOP leaders advocated the formation of a statewide FOP Immediate Relief Fund that would allow for larger death benefit payments.

In early 1949, the organization of the FOP Immediate Relief Fund was completed. Membership applications, accompanied by an initial fee of $6.00, were processed in March. Death benefits were to be paid on the basis of $3.00 multiplied by the number of members at the time of a reported death. The fund's first secretary-treasurer was Charles A. Givler, of Frank Albert Memorial Lodge 43 at Wyoming. Following

Givler's resignation in mid-1957, that post went to Steven J. Condes, of Keystone Lodge 41 at Harrisburg.

The first assessment for the new group was paid to the beneficiary of Frank S. McGregor, of the Swanson Memorial Lodge 48, at Erie, on April 30, 1949. At McGregor's death, there were 611 members carried on the immediate relief fund rolls, and his beneficiary of record was paid $1,833.

The legislators, sitting in what was a comparatively short 1949 session, were active with regard to State Police matters. Act 43, P.L. 396, April 6, clarified P.L. 450 (1927) regarding appeals to fire prevention orders. Act 192, P.L. 776, April 28, increased the commissioner's salary to $15,000 a year and the deputy commissioner's salary to $8,500. Act 268, P.L. 956, May 9, obligated the State Police to assist the Department of Public Instruction in preparing text books on the subject of fire prevention. Act 402, P.L. 1342, May 14, permitted State Police to inspect dry cleaning and dyeing plants. Act 425, P.L. 1438, May 18, increased the State Police complement to 1,800 officers and men, the first manpower increase in twelve years. (The figure of 1,600 was set by the general assembly in 1937.) Act 568, P.L. 1903, May 27, enacted the Military Code of 1949 exempting members of the State Police from militia duty except by voluntary enlistment.

If anyone was to list Wilhelm's achievements in order of importance the list would most likely be headed by his successful work in constructing new barracks buildings for his field forces. For years the field forces were compelled to occupy leased facilities of questionable accommodation. Wilhelm diligently pursued his building program with the governor's post-war planning board, and his determined efforts put the field forces into new construction.

New troop headquarters buildings were completed and occupied in 1949 in Washington, Butler and Lancaster. New buildings at Reading and Hollidaysburg were soon under construction. Proposed buildings in Punxsutawney, Montoursville, Philadelphia and Bethlehem were nearing approval stages. Wilhelm was to see all of these new buildings dedicated before his tenure was up. This building program alone would earn him a niche in State Police annals. During that period, the General State Authority (GSA) was responsible for constructing all new state buildings. The State Police program was thus committed to GSA officials with whom Wilhelm worked feverishly to move construction as swiftly as possible.

Each of the new buildings proposed by Wilhelm featured a professionally-designed driver examination course. Theretofore, it was customary to exam driver applicants by directing them along on-the-street routes. This procedure was not safe, nor did it reveal the driver's true capabilities under controlled circumstances. The off-the-street courses were a boon to the exam program in Pennsylvania. Later commenting on a First Place Award presented to the Commonwealth of Pennsylvania by the National Safety Council for its contributions to traffic safety, Wilhelm stated, "The modern special driver courses for examination of motor vehicle operators at our various barracks were contributing factors in placing Pennsylvania again foremost in highway safety activities."

Another feature of each of the new barracks buildings, according to Wilhelm's plan, was a cell-block. The cell-blocks were designed to accommodate a few prisoners overnight. This practice of retaining prisoners, however, was short-lived and dropped in favor of immediately committing prisoners to the county prisons, regardless of the hour of the day or night. Abandoned cell-blocks were later converted to storage areas or utility rooms.

Wilhelm continued Adams' interest in an effective detective division. Serving in this capacity in 1949 were:

> Detective Sergeant Russel K. Knies
> Detective Sergeant Freeman B. Ramer
> Detective Sergeant Benjamin O. Lichty
> Detective Sergeant George V. Stedman
> Detective Frank G. McCartney
> Detective William L. Nevin
> Detective Anthony C. Parry
> Detective Arthur W. Shulenberger
> Detective Roy O. Wellendorf
> Detective James F. Murray

Captain Harry E. McElroy headed the BCI & I and directed all detective division operations. This cadre of investigators was many times commended for its accomplishments. With the exception of Stedman, all were to see commissioned rank before final separation: Knies was later promoted to major, Ramer to lieutenant, Lichty to captain, McCartney to commisioner, Nevin to captain, Parry to lieutenant, Shulenberger to major, Wellendorf to deputy commissioner, and Murray to lieutenant.

Wilhelm, in 1949, expanded polygraph operations by adding another trained operator—Detective Nevin. The state was divided between Ramer and Nevin: Ramer covered the eastern half and Nevin the western.

PENNSYLVANIA STATE POLICE
DETECTIVE DIVISION
1949

CAPT. HARRY E. McELROY
CHIEF

DET. SGT. FREEMAN B. RAMER

DET. SGT. RUSSEL K. KNIES

DET. SGT. BENJ. O. LICHTY

DET. SGT. GEO. V. STEDMAN

DET. FRANK G. McCARTNEY

DET. WILLIAM L. NEVIN

DET. ANTHONY C. PARRY

DET. ART. W. SHULENBERGER

DET. ROY O. WELLENDORF

DET. JAMES F. MURRAY

Detective Division, 1949 (Courtesy of Pennsylvania State Police)

Wilhelm, the headquarters staff, and all who knew him were saddened by the untimely death of Captain Guy E. Reichard, on April 6,
1950, at 52. Reichard, serving as Chief Quartermaster, was spearheading Wilhelm's building program with GSA. A heart attack cut short his
distinguished career, and Wilhelm lost a most capable staff officer.
Reichard was highly respected on and off the job. He was active in the

Masonic Order and the *Harrisburg Zembo Pep-er* had this to say about Reichard, "Some more than others have the privilege and the opportunity of serving. None has given more of his time, energy and wise counsel to Zembo Temple than Noble Guy Reichard. As an aide to many Potentates, the knowledge of Shrine procedure he acquired was invaluable to all. He gave unstintingly, always remaining quietly in the background; he shunned the limelight. Zembo Temple will miss his guidance and wisdom." Those comments could have been appropriately transferred to his State Police career at headquarters where for thirty years he quietly and efficiently supported superintendents and commissioners.

In 1950, the list of State Police retirees having grown to a signficant number, there was interest displayed in an organization for retired members. Attempts to organize were fruitful and the Retired State Police Association of Pennsylvania was incorporated on June 24, 1950. The organization's first president was Herbert Smith, a former captain.

The association's charter cites these purposes, "The objects of this Association shall be to foster fellowship amongst its members, to keep alive the memories of service when members of the Pennsylvania State Police, to promote the welfare of its members and to inculcate a spirit of friendly cooperation with members of the Pennsylvania State Police Civic Association." Since retired members of the department, in most cases, were drawing a Civic Association pension in addition to a state retirement annuity, their interest in maintaining ties with the Civic Association was understandable. Retired members were represented on the Civic Association board of directors, a circumstance that permitted them voice and vote regarding pension matters.

In 1950, the United States was deeply involved in settling an explosive situation in a divided Korea. The United Nations officially recognized and supported South Korea in that dispute. Despite UN reconciliation efforts, the North Koreans crossed the 38th parallel on June 25, 1950, to open the Korean War. The period of peace following World War II was, indeed, a short one. The three-year war was not to affect State Police affairs to the extent that World War II did. Troopers were lost to the draft and reservists were called up; nonetheless, Wilhelm was spared the severity of World War II conditions.

On July 24, 1950, the State Police was to suffer its first death in the line of duty in eight years. Pfc. John A Ditkosky of Troop A-2, Harrisburg, was struck by a truck and killed as he was questioning a stopped motorist.

In November, 1950, Superior Court Judge John S. Fine again led the Republican party to victory, defeating Democratic party candidate

Richardson Dilworth by only a narrow margin. Fine was the fourth in a string of Republican governors. The small margin of victory, however, was a point of deep concern for Republican leaders, and their worries were well-founded as the election results of 1954 will disclose.

Again there was little doubt that Wilhelm would be retained by Fine—and he was. Wilhelm and the entire Fine cabinet were nominated on January 16, 1951, inauguration day. The Republican senators with an edge of 30-20 over their Democratic colleagues still lacked sufficient votes to confirm. After considerable Senate delay, Fine's cabinet was confirmed on February 26. Thus three Republican governors in a row had seen fit to honor Wilhelm with successive appointments as head of the state's top police agency.

Fast approaching his 70th birthday, Wilhelm was continuing to set records as the oldest commissioner to hold office and the oldest member of the State Police in terms of service. It was widely known that he wanted very much to observe a fiftieth anniversary as a member of the State Police—a date that would fall on December 15, 1955. Fine's term of office would end in January, 1955, just short of Wilhelm's anniversary date. Thus he would need support from another governor.

Wilhelm, by successive appointments, was then closely allied with influential Republican leaders. He was most cooperative with them in matters affecting State Police operations, a point that did not set well with many. Adams, although retired, had not lost his interest in departmental affairs, and was disturbed by Wilhelm's about-face from the strong Adams policy of no politics. Adams cautioned Wilhelm on this point as one friend to another. Wilhelm, however, had a goal in mind and, to that end, was putting all his eggs in one basket—a strategy that was not to pay off for him.

Through his successive appointments, Wilhelm retained Mauk as his deputy. Mauk had served him loyally and well, and there was no reason for making a change at the deputy post. This relationship, however, was also to affect Mauk's status with the department later.

The legislators in 1951 sat through the longest session of the general assembly on record. The call to order came on January 2 and final adjournment on December 22, after 109 legislative workdays for the Senate and 99 for the House. The session fell just days short of taking up the entire calendar year. That record session was the forerunner of numerous lengthy sessions which have become the rule rather than exception.

Nothwithstanding their lengthy session and the attendant bickering, the legislators narrowed their consideration of State Police business to five items. Act 4, P.L. 28, March 19, created the State Council of Civil Defense for the purpose of assisting in the coordination of the state and local activities related to national and state civil defense. Act 9, P.L. 53, March 22, gave sweeping control of special fire police to the State Police. Act 14, P.L. 57, March 22, imposed duties for regulating fireworks. Also passed before adjournment but not signed by the governor until later were Act 561, P.L. 2016, January 14, 1952, authorizing the transfer of regular police and auxiliary police during disaster and emergencies under State Police direction, and Act 609, P.L. 2150, January 18, 1952, increasing the deputy commissioner's salary to $10, 000 a year. By raising the salary of the deputy commissioner, the legislature opened the door for heated contests of another kind.

In order to assist in the implementation of Act 4, the State Council of Civil Defense called on Wilhelm to assign a liaison officer to serve with SCCD. Favorably responding to that request, Wilhelm gave the new post to Captain Jackson Dodson. Council Director Richard Gerstell, Ph.D., agreed to reimburse the State Police for the liaison officer's salary. This arrangement between the State Police and SCCD was to continue through 1970 with a number of commissioned officers and non-commissioned officers succeeding Dodson.

Act 561 was meant to sharpen the efficiency of law enforcement in the state, generally, in the event of wartime disasters. The United States was involved in a Korean conflict and such legislation reflected government concern for preparedness at home should hostilities develop into nuclear warfare.

The new barracks buildings at Reading and Hollidaysburg were completed and occupied in 1951, as Wilhelm with deserved pride witnessed his construction program continue fruitfully. Construction at Bethlehem, Philadelphia, Montoursville and Punxsutawney was completed in 1952. The Bethlehem barracks was dedicated January 26, and cost $375, 957. Philadelphia, the largest and costliest at $500,251, was dedicated March 31. Montoursville, the least expensive at $312,863, was dedicated September 1. And Punxsutawney, built at a $387,331 figure, was dedicated October 3, closing out a big construction year for the State Police.

Captain McElroy, who had distinguished himself as longtime head of the detective division and the BCI & I, was seriously ill through much of 1952. Illness brought about his retirement on December 1. His retirement was cut short by his untimely death on March 14, 1953.

The general assembly in 1953, in a not-so-long session, approved two measures bearing on State Police operations. The first was in response to Wilhelm's appeal for more men: Act 254, P.L. 1006, July

29, increased the State Police complement from 1,800 to 1,900 officers and men. Act 361, P.L. 1273, August 21, regulated the business of private detectives in what was to be more familiarly known as the Private Detective Act of 1953, which imposed duties on the State Police for screening applicants for appointment by county courts.

The Korean War, which had been prolonged by the entry of Chinese armed forces in support of the North Koreans, was finally brought to a close by the signing of an armistice at Panmunjom on July 27, 1953. A Defense Department report released on July 22, 1954, listed U. S. casualties at 142,067, including 23,345 dead, 12,954, missing in action and 105,768 wounded. Peace again was achieved. But, the period of peace was not to see many years before the nation would be sucked into the quicksands of southeast Asia—into a shameful Vietnam War that would see disastrous conditions arise at home and on the battlefront.

In the opinion of Detective William Nevin, an opinion that was shared by many rank and file members of the State Police, the titles of Private First Class and Private Second Class did not uphold the dignity of the field forces—particulary during court appearances. During his term as president of FOP Keystone Lodge 41, Nevin petitioned Wilhelm to drop those titles in favor of "Trooper." Wilhelm partially accepted Nevin's recommendation by abolishing the "First Class" and "Second Class" classifications and allowing the general title of "Private" to remain in effect.

On November 2, 1953, the State Police was to record the death of another trooper who was slain in the line of duty. Dead was Trooper Floyd B. Clouse, 29, of Troop D, Butler. Clouse, in company with Corporal Harold G. Rice, was serving a disorderly conduct warrant on Edwin C. Stanyard, of White Township, Beaver County. Stanyard unexpectedly fired at the two, killing Crouse instantly and seriously wounding Rice. Rice, however, was able to return fire and killed Stanyard. Dr. H. E. Douds, a Beaver Falls physician, had accompanied the troopers to the Stanyard residence, and waited outdoors. The doctor's on-the-scene treatment of Rice was credited with saving the corporal's life.

Douds, as a youth, had been a motorcycle enthusiast, and enjoyed above all else to be associated with Sergeant Frank Garnow and other State Highway Patrolmen assigned to the Beaver Falls Substation. His affection for the State Police never diminished. As a practicing physician, Douds saw to it that troopers and their families received the best of treatment, and refused payment. The Beaver Falls physician was later commended by State Police authorities for sponsoring a

Clouse Trust Fund for the deceased trooper's family. Dr. Douds, not unlike many other unsung private citizens, was and still is a down-to-earth State Police booster.

Throughout the years of association with troopers in western Pennsylvania, Douds enjoyed warm friendships, but none as warm and enduring as his friendship for Corporal Joseph Dussia. He and Dussia, who was appointed deputy commissioner in 1967, grew to be inseparable companions.

The biennial report for the period ending May 31, 1954, revealed some interesting items. (The format for reporting statistics had not changed from that initiated by Groome during the constabulary's infancy.) State Police patrols in the two-year period traveled 41,453,910 miles. Arrested for traffic violations were 287, 464 operators. Speeding arrests alone accounted for 87,328. A total of 803,796 driver applicants were examined. Of this figure, 269,969 were failed. In operation as of May 31, 1954, were 10,379 official inspection stations, all of which were supervised by State Police uniformed personnel. Troop B, Squadron 2, was then patrolling 327 miles of the Pennsylvania Turnpike which had been extended eastward to King of Prussia and northward to Scranton.

Also opened to vehicular traffic was the Schuylkill Expressway linking Valley Forge with downtown Philadelphia. That new roadway was soon to be a point of much criticism for its inability to accommodate the daily volume of traffic to which it was exposed.

Wilhelm reported with pride that his troopers had suppressed the general prison riots of January, 1953, without loss of life or serious injury.

With the imput of 158,911 criminal records, the BCI & I files had exceeded the half-million mark with 562,963 individual records. There were 29,808 criminal arrests by State Police personnel, and the percentage of convictions remainded at a high 88.7 level. Burglary, larceny and disorderly conduct led the list of crimes committed. Juvenile delinquency and malicious mischief arrests exceeded the 1,000 figure, clearly indicating a sharp rise. The highest count of arrests fell to those in the 14 to 21 age group with age 16 carrying the highest total, reflecting the activities of juveniles. Crimes were still being classified by cause with avarice and recklessness heading the list. There were 9,299 first-offenders and 5,493 arrestees were classified as habitual criminals, or recidivists. Males continued to outnumber females in the commission of crimes; and single persons surpassed married persons in the arrest column 2 to 1. For the first time in annual or biennial reporting, the State Police discontinued identifying arrestees by nationality, and rightfully so, since that table of arrests served no practical purpose whatsoever.

On October 18, 1954, a class of recruits was convened at the Hershey training school, and for the first time in State Police history a black applicant was enrolled. Undergoing training was John R. Dudley, of Wilkes-Barre. Dudley for six years served in the armed forces and was a corporal at separation. He was a waiter in a Luzerne County country club when he came to the attention of Governor Fine. Reportedly, it was Fine who pressed the issue with Wilhelm and "sponsored" Dudley's enlistment. Upon graduation from the training school, Dudley was assigned to Troop A-4, Philadelphia. He resigned two years later—September 4, 1956.

At the polls in November, 1954, George M. Leader, the Democratic candidate for governor, soundly defeated Lloyd H. Wood, his Republican opponent, by a 1,996,266 to 1,717,070 vote count. After sixteen years of Republican control, the seat of power in Pennsylvania was to rest again with Democrats. The Democrats took control of the House, but remained the minority party in the Senate.

Prior to his election as governor, Leader served four years in the Senate from York County, and was well acquainted with the political scene at the state capitol. It was thought certain that Leader would not retain Wilhelm as commissioner, but there were those who sympathized with Wilhelm's aspiration to realize his fifieth anniversary and wanted him to remain in office long enough to see that day. Divided feelings ushered in 1955.

Wilhelm, on January 1, 1955, transferred Captain Albert F. Dahlstrom from Troop C, Hollidaysburg, to headquarters where he would direct BCI & I affairs. During the two-year period following McElroy's retirement, operations of the bureau had been supervised by Mauk, who did so in addition to discharging the responsibilities of deputy commissioner. Ordinarily, Wilhelm would have gone to BCI&I commissioned ranks to fill McElroy's vacancy; however, it was rumored that he did not do so in order to head off possible internal strife. The fact that he finally appointed an "outsider" to the bureau tended to confirm that rumor.

CHAPTER XV

Colonel Earl J. Henry
1955–1959

Governor George M. Leader took his oath of office on January 18, 1955. He was only the second Democratic party standard-bearer to do so since the turn of the century.

The new governor made no overt or immediate move to replace Wilhelm, although it was strongly suspected that he would. Evidence of any decision by Leader was not to be seen until March. A meeting was reportedly held in March at the home of James A. Finnegan, Leader's Commonwealth Secretary, which was attended by the governor and Major Earl J. Henry. Finnegan was a close friend of former Major William J. Ruch, who was summarily dismissed from his post as squadron commander at Philadelphia by Adams in 1940. The firing came on the heels of an investigation which revealed, at least to Adams' satisfaction, that Ruch was politically involved with leading Democrats in the Philadelphia area. Usually such firings followed a court-martial, but in Ruch's case there was none. This unusual firing was further complicated by the fact that Ruch at the time of his dismissal had not served sufficient time to qualify for pension.

That meeting was called to serve two purposes—replace Wilhelm and get Ruch back on the job. Henry and Ruch were fellow officers with the State Highway Patrol, and an excellent relationship was shared by them. Henry was offered the position of commissioner on condition that he reinstate Ruch immediately, thus righting what was considered a wrong. Henry agreed to that condition.

It would be grossly unfair to leave the impression that Henry was selected simply because he agreed to reinstate Ruch. Henry had been a senior officer with the Highway Patrol and twice served as acting superintendent of that agency. His outstanding services with the department since the merger were a credit to him, and Henry, indeed, merited the consideration given him for appointment to the top post.

Wilhelm, his hopes for an extension lost forever, was forced to resign his post on March 31, 1955, bringing an illustrious career to an end just short of fifty years. Then 73, Wilhelm was not in the best of health and the strain of office was evident. It would be unkind to presume that Wilhelm was let go because of his Republican alignment. After all, he was older than most active public office-holders and Leader very likely wanted a younger, more vigorous commissioner to lean on. Wilhelm, throughout his terms as commissioner, and particularly during his latter years, did not leave his office much: he was desk-bound and the field forces saw very little of him. He had grown to be more of a symbol to the field forces than an active leader.

Some headquarters staff members recall Wilhelm's display of relief at his separation. He was described as content to lay aside the robes of responsibility in favor of a more restful way of life to which he was deservingly entitled.

Wilhelm joined Groome, Lumb and Adams in the legendary ranks. His record of service, spanning almost fifty years, will unquestionably stand for all time. Wilhelm served as acting commissioner for four months in 1939 and as commissioner for twelve years and two months. Total time as top administrator added up to twelve and one-half years, ranking him third in terms of longevity: first place is held by Adams with almost twenty-one years, and Groome comes up in second place with fourteen years and eight months. It is doubtful that these standings will ever be disturbed. Wilhelm was the last of the original enlistments of 1905 to terminate services with the State Police. Others had long preceded him into retirement. His retirement, regrettably, was not a lasting one. Death overtook this great man in four years.

A native of Conestoga, Lancaster County, Earl Henry was born on May 1, 1896. He was one of six children born to Mr. and Mrs. Albert L. Henry. Henry attended the Millersville public schools and graduated from the Pennsylvania Business College, at Lancaster.

During World War I, Henry served with the Thirteenth Field Artillery, Fourth Division. With his fellow "Ivy Troopers," he saw combat in the second battle of the Marne, Vesle and Toulon sectors, and the St. Mihiel and Meuse-Argonne drives. At the close of the war, Henry remained with the Occupation Forces in Germany.

Colonel Earl J. Henry (Courtesy of Pennsylvania State Police)

After military service, Henry attended Millersville State Teachers College, where the strapping, six-footer won varsity letters in football, basketball and track. In 1920, he was captain of the Millersville College eleven. Throughout his life, Henry pursued an active interest in target shooting and was known as a skilled marksman.

The Department of Highways in 1923 organized the State Highway Patrol which became a matter of interest to Henry. In October, 1924, he enlisted with the Patrol, beginning a career in law enforcement that was to see him through the next thirty-five years.

Because of his college training in the teaching profession, and after only a brief tour of duty as a highway patrolman, Henry was transferred to the Patrol training school in 1925 to serve as an instructor. He

was soon promoted to corporal. Henry's prowess on the gridiron accounted for the Patrol team's unbeatable record in its inter-agency
competition with the state constabulary school squad.

In 1926, Henry was promoted to sergeant, and picked up the additional duties of acting first sergeant at the school. Henry was one of
three men promoted in August, 1927, to the permanent rank of first
sergeant—a rank that was not previously recognized by the Patrol although it was used unofficially.

In February, 1929, Henry was promoted to lieutenant and moved
to field duty at Greensburg. The Highway Patrol that year underwent
major changes to improve its effectiveness. One administrative change
moved the Patrol from the Highway Department to the Department of
Revenue.

Henry was returned to the training school at Harrisburg in
October, 1935, as commanding officer of that facility. At the invitation
of J. Edgar Hoover, director of the Federal Bureau of Investigation,
Henry underwent twelve weeks of training at the FBI Academy in
1935. At the time, he was the only Highway Patrol or State Police
graduate of the prestigious National Police Academy. Soon after his
return from the FBI Academy, Henry enrolled in special traffic safety
courses at New York University.

When Highway Patrol Superintendent Wilson C. Price resigned
his post in February, 1936, Henry was called in by Revenue Department officials to administer affairs pending the appointment of a new
superintendent. He fulfilled those duties for two months. Soon after
the appointment of Superintendent Charles H. Quarles, Henry was elevated to the rank of captain, and remained commandant of the training
school.

Quarles held the superintendent post for less than one year, and
resigned in February, 1937. At that point, the merger of the Highway
Patrol and the State Police was a certainty. Revenue officials, faced
with that eventuality, withheld naming Quarles' successor and, instead, preferred to once again call on Henry to carry out the duties of
the Patrol's top post in an acting capacity. Henry remained in that
status until the merger in July, 1937.

Governor Earle appointed retired Rear Admiral Percy W. Foote
commissioner of the newly-organized Pennsylvania Motor Police in
mid-1937. Before the year's end, Foote decided to divide the new
agency into four squadrons, each to be headed by a major. Henry was
one of the four men chosen by Foote to fill those new positions—all of
whom were promoted to major on January 1, 1938. Henry was assigned
to Squadron 2 at Harrisburg.

Henry remained in Harrisburg until Major Ruch's dismissal at Philadelphia in 1940 by Commissioner Lynn G. Adams. Adams then moved Henry to Squadron 4 at Philadelphia.

Following the resignation of Captain T. N. Boate, who directed the department's traffic program, Henry was transferred to headquarters to head the traffic bureau in November, 1944. He remained in that position until Governor Leader appointed him to his cabinet as State Police commissioner in 1955.

Henry was married to the former Catherine Burgwald, of Titusville, Crawford County. The couple had no children.

To the field forces, Henry was a popular figure and his appointment was well-received. During his years as a field officer and director of traffic, he frequently visited field installations and mingled with his men socially. Henry was considered "one of the guys." This was in sharp contrast to Wilhelm who remained detached from the main stream and disallowed field personnel the opportunity to warm up to him as they did with Henry. Generally, to the man, Henry's appointment generated a feeling that then holding the seat of power was someone who had an appreciation of their problems and wants, and would do something about them. It was simply a matter of waiting for the new commissioner to produce.

Governor Leader submitted Henry's name to the Senate for confirmation on March 28, 1955. Unanimous confirmation was given by the Senate that same day, and Henry was sworn in by Deputy Commonwealth Secretary Henry E. Harner in a simple ceremony witnessed by Leader and Mrs. Henry.

Very little press notice was given Henry's appointment, and surprisingly less was given to Wilhelm's departure after a record-setting career. An editorial appearing in *The Patriot* (Harrisburg) edition of March 30, 1955, noted Henry's confirmation, stating that he was also given

> virtually unanimous approval of those members of the force who have known and worked with him for a long time and who appreciate the zeal he has displayed in working for the continued improvement of the organization.
>
> Henry joins the brief list of distinguished men who have commanded the world-acclaimed force since John C. Groome organized it shortly after the turn of the century.

On the heels of Henry's cabinet appointment, the traffic bureau operations fell into the hands of Captain Thomas P. Cahalan, Henry's top bureau aide.

Although Henry's career up until the time of his appointment was not allied with politics, Henry was to get his fill of politics soon thereafter. His first ordeal concerned the appointment of a deputy. That post was held by Mauk whom Henry respected. The relationship between both men was amicable and Henry wanted his former boss retained as deputy. But, Mauk's association with Wilhelm through many years of Republican state control was to prove counterproductive for Mauk at that point. Henry's move to keep Mauk on the job met a Democratic party stonewall.

Mauk was to survive Wilhelm by only sixty days. He was forced to leave his post on May 31, 1955, at 61—a departure that was accompanied with embitterment. Mauk's colorful, thirty-eight-year career was a distinguished one. His final twelve years as deputy is a record tenure second only to Wilhelm's deputyship.

Mauk was a lifetime member of the National Rifle Association. He was also a member of the Harrisburg Elks Lodge, Harrisburg Kiwanis, Progress Fire Company, International Association of Chiefs of Police, and the Pennsylvania Chiefs of Police Association. At Greensburg, he had been president of Kiwanis.

After his departure from the state scene, Mauk was offered several important federal government positions, but accepted none. His retirement, given to travel with his beloved wife, was unexpectedly ended by illness in five brief years.

Supposedly with support from Senator Joseph M. Barr (D-Allegheny) and Pittsburgh Mayor David L. Lawrence, Leader gave his approval to the appointment of Frank G. McCartney to the vacant deputy post. McCartney, a former State Police detective sergeant, had earned for himself a valued reputation in the criminal investigation field in which he excelled and in the area of industrial security management. His services with the constabulary and the merged police agency spanned twenty years.

With Leader's blessing, McCartney reported to Henry. The latter, however, steadfastly declined to accept McCartney as his top aide. Although Henry harbored no ill-feeling toward McCartney and recognized his qualifications, Henry was not about to set precedence by giving the number two spot to anyone who had not been a commissioned officer. Traditionally, the deputy post was always filled from the ranks of commissioned officers. Although Henry may have had anxious moments about refusing the governor's nominee, he was more concerned for the negative reaction from his officer complement.

Henry's firm decision brought about a stalemate. If he would not accept McCartney, he would get no one else. Faced with this dilemma,

Henry called upon Captain Dahlstrom to sit in as acting deputy, pending further developments. McCartney, disheartened by the unfavorable turn of events, vowed to be back. Dahlstrom was destined to serve as acting deputy for almost one year before eventually succeeding to the post officially.

True to his word, Henry lost no time in preparing the way for Ruch's reinstatement. On July 1, 1955, Ruch returned to the State Police payroll with the rank of major—the same status he held at the time of his controversial dismissal in 1940. After an absence of some fifteen years, Ruch, then 58, was once again an important figure in the State Police hierarchy.

Ruch's longtime separation from the day-to-day operations of the department, however, left him behind the times. That situation in itself limited the assignments Henry could provide for him. Ruch was appointed Henry's itinerant representative continually visiting field installations. Good-natured and always a pleasing personality, Ruch found little difficulty in settling down to business and securing for himself the cooperation of those about him. Reports of his inspections and personal interviews with officers and enlisted men were considered helpful to Henry.

In August, 1955, State Police field forces, Civil Defense workers and National Guard units saw emergency duty in the Commonwealth's northeast area as heavy rainfall accompanying hurricane Diane swiftly raised streams and rivers to flood stage. Unofficially, there were ninety-three deaths reported in eastern Pennsylvania. Hardest hit was Camp Davis, a private summer camp near Stroudsburg, Monroe County, when flash-flooding of the Brodhead Creek inundated the camp site as campers slept. The bodies of thirty-one Camp Davis victims were recovered. Officials described flood damage the worst in fifty-two years as estimates hit the half-billion dollar mark. Governor Leader lost no time in ordering the immediate evacuation of 10,000 children encamped in the Pocono Mountain resorts.

Henry was yet to confront another controversy with political overtones. In September, 1955, Governor Leader urged the dismissal of Comptroller Edward P. McBreen. McBreen's dismissal was made apologetically and without bitterness. McBreen accepted the reason given him—his post was to go to someone more acceptable to the Democrats.

Richard J. Shaffer, McBreen's top assistant, was considered by most headquarters staffers as the heir apparent in the event of McBreen's retirement. He was eminently qualified by the Civil Service Commission for the accounting position. The appointment of an outsider, however, put an end to that speculation. McBreen's replacement was John Grillo who, supposedly, came with the sponsorship of the influential John R. Torquato, secretary of Labor and Industry.

Serious and continuing difficulties arose between Grillo and Shaffer. This was typical of conflicts between career executives and political appointees frequently occurring in state government offices. But, at State Police headquarters it was an unusual experience. Grillo sought Shaffer's removal to the Wyoming Barracks, indicating the heat that was generated. Henry, wanting to keep Shaffer's valued services nearby and not subject himself to criticism that was bound to stem from those who supported Shaffer in this discordant episode, transferred Shaffer to the Hershey training school instead. The fact that such a move was forced upon the commissioner was significant enough.

Grillo, who was not content to play the passive role traditionally observed by comptrollers before him, was bound by his actions to create discord at headquarters and in the field. And he did. His tenure, however, was to continue through the Henry administration.

Appearing on the scene as legal counsel for State Police was Deputy Attorney General Frank P. Lawley. Lawley was appointed to his Justice Department post in March, 1952. Once given his assignment, Lawley took an active role in State Police affairs.

Governor Leader, young and energetic, held high one of his campaign objectives to reorganize the Commonwealth government into an effective, professionally-managed complex. He brought aboard men like Dr. James C. Charlesworth, of Temple University, and Dr. John H. Ferguson, of Penn State University, and many other notables in the field of public administration, who were expected to provide leadership in achieving that prime objective. The all-powerful Office of Administration (OA), an outgrowth of that effort, adopted controls over the administrative departments, boards, and commissions under the governor's jurisdiction. OA's principal reforms dealt with the budget, financial management, personnel and systems analysis. Other areas of responsibility concerned staff assistance to the governor and the executive board.

The controversial OA appointed methods management personnel in most of the state agencies under the governor—men and women who crossed lines of command in working directly with OA. Some of those so-called "efficiency experts" themselves brought unnecessary problems within agencies mainly because of their lack of diplomacy in selling their missions, or OA's mission. The unfriendly term, "egg-head," was soon to become a favorite title throughout capitol hill for OA personnel.

Departments and agencies, once autonomous in their operations, were then made to knuckle under. None was more autonomous than the Pennsylvania State Police, and the problem of adjustment stared Henry in the face.

The 1955 General Assembly session produced six measures of interest to the State Police. Act 83, P.L. 259, July 7, commonly known as the Heart and Lung Act, authorized payments for certain injuries to State Policemen who were previously excluded from such coverage. Act 128, P.L. 321, August 9, provided for additional credits to applicants who had served in any armed conflict. Act 257, P.L. 866, December 15, eliminated from the authorized State Police complement of 1,900 officers and men all troopers assigned to duty with the Pennsylvania Turnpike Commission. That enactment, for all practical purposes, raised the manpower ceiling by 175 men. Act 446, P.L. 1387, April 4, 1956, changed the state's pay plan from twice a month to biweekly, effective June 1, 1956. Act 592, P.L. 1761, approved May 28, 1956, provided $3 million for a new training school, and new buildings at Blakely, Erie, Greensburg, Carlisle, Chambersburg, Ebensburg, Somerset, Lewistown and Mercer. And Act 657, P.L. 1959, approved June 1, 1956, increased the salaries of the commissioner to $20,000 and the deputy to $13,500.

During the 1955 legislature, House Bill 2083 was introduced, calling for an increase in the number of deputy commissioners. The bill passed the House and was sent to the Senate. In the Senate, however, there was serious objection to the fact that the bill did not limit the number of deputies. Since there was little sentiment in the Senate to deal with the subject anyhow, the bill was referred to the Committee on Rules where it died.

One important comment can be made about the 1955 session's stamina. It was a marathon legislative exercise lasting from January 3, 1955, to May 22, 1956, during which time the House conducted business for 168 legislative days and the Senate 159. The legislators set a new record.

During the calendar year of 1955, seven men died in the electric chair at the Rockview Penitentiary. The last was executed in September. That was the heaviest schedule in eight years and the final year to have more than two executions take place. Only seven more were to take place between 1956 and 1962 when capital punishment in Pennsylvania was halted.

On the lighter side, and before the close of the year, members of the Pennsylvania State Police celebrated the fiftieth anniversary of their department's founding. It was in 1905 that the state constabulary was born and its first members enrolled. Gathered at the Hershey Park Golf Club on December 15, 1955, were 500 guests. Attending were Governor Leader, Henry and former commissioners Lynn G. Adams and Wilhelm. Adams and Wilhelm were among the thirteen original members honored on that occasion. Others were: James Sutton, Jr., Herbert P. Hunt, Frederick E. Borman, William A. Clark, James G. Ernst, James L. Sullivan, Eugene V. Calvert, Thomas L. Casey, Homer A. Chambers, Francis S. Strawser and Anthony Lohmiller, Jr. Sutton, the oldest at 84, was flown from his home in Miami to join the festivities.

Leader was the principal speaker. His address, for the most part, was a litany of the improvements his administration had secured for the State Police. More notable were: legislation exempting the turnpike detail from the authorized State Police complement, a new policy for purchasing new patrol vehicles yearly, and the introduction of a modified uniform for summer wear and a fur cap for winter use.

Although funds were set aside by the legislature for the building of a new training school, the site for the new facility was still undecided. The deteriorating school building was located in Hershey and had been at the Cocoa Avenue location since the move from Newville in the early 1920s. Surveys found land sites in the Hershey area either too costly or undesirable. State Police officials soon looked to outlying areas and found suitable ground near Hummelstown.

The possibility of the State Police moving from Hershey aroused certain directors of the Hershey Estates. It was their contention that the State Police school had been a landmark in Hershey for many years and a major tour attraction, and should not under any circumstances be moved elsewhere. Following a series of debates on that issue, the Hershey Estates board of directors, offered the State Police a prize twenty-eight-acre tract of land for one dollar. The hilltop location east of the Hershey Hotel offered a magnificent view of the Hershey community and its surroundings, and presented an ideal spot for a new school. The State Police gratefully accepted the offer, thus making it possible for the training school to retain its Hershey address. It is believed that responsible Commonwealth officials would have considered too costly the purchase of that prime acreage at its true market value. The Hershey Estates directors were, indeed, generous.

Payroll records of May 31, 1956, indicate that there were 2,131 employees, enlisted and civilian, enrolled with the State Police. Their assignments were broken down like this:

Executive Office—9
Accounting, Secretarial and Clerical Division—132
Bureau of Criminal Identification—26
Bureau of Fire Protection—4
Communications Division—12
Quartermaster, Mechanical and Service Division—103
Field Forces—1,845

In 1956, OA undertook a massive project to reduce the several thousands of job classifications to a basic 1,600. OA also noted that the State Police pay plan allowed very little financial gain for men promoted to higher ranks. A series of flat-amount salary increases had compressed the schedule to a point where there was no substantial incentive for promotion.

By August 1, 1956, the new state compensation plan was put into effect. To give the State Police plan an incentive spread, men in the higher ranks were granted sizeable pay adjustments compared to little

State Police-Highway Patrol uniform display at 50th anniversary, Hershey, 1955 (Courtesy of Pennsylvania State Police)

or nothing for men in the lower grades. That situation brought about widespread dissatisfaction, to put it mildly. Rationalizing efforts by OA personnel did little to salve the hurt feelings. The reclassification plan also removed from the enlisted ranks certain specialists who were assigned civilian job titles. Most notable in that class was Major David A. Johnston, who was reclassified to Physician I. Nonetheless, officers and men alike had the greatest respect for Dr. Johnston, and continued to address him as "major," until his retirement in the 1960s.

Somewhat related to the compensation plan was Lieutenant Nevin's continued interest in having the title of "private" dropped in favor of "trooper." He had approached Wilhelm with partial success, but his recommendation to Henry was ignored. Through mutual acquaintances, Nevin petitioned Bruce Smith, a nationally-known figure in police administration, who had been retained by OA for consultation on State Police matters. Smith, finding favor with Nevin's one man crusade, persuaded OA officials to go along with the recommended change. And, so it was that the "trooper" title was adopted officially, although it had been in common use by the news media and in government circles.

Bruce Smith's survey of State Police operations accounted for some other important changes. He noted that the troop mess accounts were running in the red. Troopers were remaining single for shorter periods after enlistment, and maintaining family residences. No longer was the barracks the center of social life as it had been known for so many years since 1905. As a result of Smith's study, all dining rooms were closed. The men and women employed in food services were reclassified to other positions, mainly in office and quartermaster activities. The vacated kitchens and dining rooms were soon converted to much-needed offices. The closing of dining rooms was reflected in minor adjustments in the payment of quarters and meal allowances monthly to enlisted personnel. These monthly payments continued to be exempted from federal income tax.

Meanwhile, Henry still had to content himself with an acting deputy commissioner. During this period, Dahlstrom took advantage of his acting tenure to seek out influential support for a permanent appointment, which was as natural as night follows day. His efforts, however, were met with serious competition from Major Andrew J. Hudock, squadron commander at Greensburg. There were times when it appeared that Hudock would successfully outstrip Dahlstrom. But, that was not to be so. At long last, supporters for McCartney removed all roadblocks to another's appointment; the job on June 13, 1956, went to Dahlstrom, who by that time had garnered both political backing and

Lt. Colonel Albert F. Dahlstrom (Courtesy of Pennsylvania State Police)

Henry's favor. Dahlstrom was sworn into office by Commonwealth Secretary Henry E. Harner.

A native of McKeesport, Allegheny County, Dahlstrom was born on September 17, 1895. Following a three-year hitch in the U. S. Army, he enlisted in the constabulary on April 1, 1920, and underwent training at the newly-organized training school at Newville. One year later he was promoted to corporal and to sergeant on January 1, 1924. Dahlstrom was assigned to Troop E, Harrisburg, and later promoted to first sergeant and lieutenant. Wilhelm upgraded Dahlstrom to captain on January 1, 1953, and transferred him to Troop C-2, Hollidaysburg, as troop commander. On January 1, 1955, Henry called Dahlstrom to headquarters at Harrisburg to direct operations of the BCI & I.

Dahlstrom was a charter member of Keystone Lodge 41, FOP,

having joined the ranks of the FOP in 1946 when Wilhelm was viewing such action as hostile. Dahlstrom was also a member of the Harrisburg American Legion Post 27.

To fill Dahlstrom's vacancy as director of the BCI & I, Henry promoted Lieutenant Ralph D. Gardner to captain and transferred him from the Fire Bureau. In the Fire Bureau, Sergeant Lawrence Priar was promoted to lieutenant. During that same period, Lieutenant Freeman Ramer retired, and the department's polygraph operations again fell to a single operator—Lieutenant Nevin. Later, two-man operations were restored when Lieutenant James Murray was brought into the polygraph program.

The subject of promotions was a sensitive one for Henry. For one thing, there were many officers eagerly looking to him for advancement for the comparatively few vacancies that cropped up in the higher grades from time to time. The filling of each vacancy was a painful exercise for him. To avoid such pressures and reduce decision-making to a minimal level, Henry introduced a policy never before resorted to by a State Police head—promotions to captain and major would be given to officers solely on the strength of time in grade. Seniority then became the all-important criterion; consideration of abilities, leadership and other command qualifications was out the window. One needed only to be senior in grade to know where he stood in line for advancement. It was a highly predictable situation, and one that drew fire from many quarters in that the policy did nothing to motivate the younger element, especially those men who were bent on making their marks before reaching "old-timer" status. Henry remained hide-bound to this policy, although there were occasions when he saw fit to do otherwise for special reasons of his own.

On May 13, 1956, another death in the line of duty was recorded. Trooper Joseph F. McMillen died of injuries sustained in a head-on collision with another vehicle.

The detective division as it was originally put together by Adams back in the 1930s operated well as it was designed to do during its first dozen or so years of existence. Men assigned to that division performed excellently as skilled crime investigators and upheld the traditions of that field of police work. As time went on, however, abuses slowly crept into the use of the detective title. The basis for such abuse was principally one of finance: detectives drew a sergeant's pay. Troopers and corporals, who managed to find themselves assigned to the governor's office as bodyguards, mansion guards, reception room guards, or accepted comparable assignments with the lieutenant governor and attorney general, lost no time in using these influential positions to secure for themselves a reclassification to detective. Accompanying the reclassification, of course, was a jump from trooper or corporal pay to sergeant pay. That was an ideal shortcut to financial gain—a gain that many of the men concerned might have found difficult to achieve by way of the regular promotional system.

The abuse became widespread and a point of ridicule by the rank and file. Often men with detective rank were jokingly asked if they were "real detectives or steeringwheel detectives." Confronted with this situation and a need to remedy it, Henry simply petitioned OA to abolish the detective series. His petition was granted. All men holding detective titles were reclassified to non-commissioned rank. Some suffered a loss in pay, others did not. The deepest hurt, of course, was suffered by the "real" detectives who took pride in their achievements and, for all of that, found themselves victims of circumstances. Nonetheless, most of them appreciated the fact that Henry had to do something to stifle abuse.

In some political quarters Henry's move was unfortunately misunderstood as a drive to make the State Police an all-traffic force. This point was to become one of the issues underlying a proposed legislative study of the department's operations.

In addition to those improvements covered by Leader at the fiftieth anniversary affair, Henry could boast of others before his first two years drew to a close. The State Civil Service Commission was called on to administer written examinations to recruit applicants and provide the State Police with an elegibility list from which applicants would be taken in numerical order for further screening. A program was developed for the training of civilian fingerprint classifiers to reduce the number of enlisted men committed to BCI & I duty. The alphabetical index system, then numbering close to one million cards, was transferred from old-fashioned box files to modern, rotary files. That timesaving change would lead to other BCI & I improvements in later administrations.

In September, 1956, Henry issued two orders worthy of note. The first abolished the use of the "squadron" label in favor of "district." To carry that change one step further, the title of "squadron commander" was replaced with "district inspector." Henry, who was formerly a squadron commander, apparently had personal reasons underlying the issuance of that order. Henry created a special board by his second order—a board charged with the responsibility of reviewing and updating general orders. Such an update was long overdue. Appointed to the board were Captains William F. Traeger, Elmer W. Faber, Thomas P. Cahalan, and Ralph D. Gardner, and Management

Analyst M. W. Thomas. Thomas, a highly-qualified, career employee, was Henry's trusted aide for many ears dating back to the days of the Highway Patrol.

Although the Retired State Police Association was organized in mid-1950, it was not until October, 1956, that the association members decided to hold their first annual banquet. Edwin J. Stroman was then president. The big event was held at the Penn-Harris Hotel in Harrisburg. Prior to 1956, association meetings were mainly concerned with business matters.

At the close of the year, Lieutenant Donald E. Wagner retired. His vacancy as State Police communications officer was filled by Sergeant Robert L. Bomboy. Bomboy was promoted to lieutenant in January, 1957.

At the top of 1957, Henry was discomforted by a serious confrontation with Major Thomas F. Martin, training school commandant. Henry ordered Martin's transfer to headquarters, appointing him field commander. Having been promoted to major in 1938, Martin was senior in grade. On January 17, Henry transferred Major Charles C. Keller to the training school. Martin, the school commandant for some twenty-four years, refused his new assignment, according to accounts of that incident, thereby creating an awkward situation for all concerned. Heated conferences ended with Martin's decision to retire on February 27, at 65. Gone from the scene was the training school's most notable and colorful figure.

Martin, a native of Shamokin, was born of Austrian immigrant parents on August 5, 1891. He was a graduate of Shamokin High School and Oberlin Academy. He saw military service with the U. S. Cavalry from 1911 to 1914. At 23, Martin enlisted with the state constabulary on July 1, 1915, and was assigned to the Butler troop. His police career was interrupted with World War I service short of one year, after which he remained in the Cavalry Reserves until 1928. Martin rose steadily through the ranks. Adams promoted Martin to captain in 1932 and gave him command of the training school. Foote upgraded him to major in 1938. His long career spanned almost forty-two years, and his tenure at the training school—twenty-four years—established a record for continuous service in one command position. While at the school, Martin was awarded the State Police Distinguished Service Medal and an honorary degree of Doctor of Law from St. Vincent's College. Martin, a devout Catholic, was a member of St. Joan of Arc Church, Hershey. Like many of his constabulary comrades, his retirement was regrettably brief.

Following Martin's departure, Henry and Keller reorganized the

training school staff of administrators and instructors in what was then
labelled as the biggest shake-up ever seen at that institution.

In July, 1957, Personnel Director John R. Price retired. He was replaced by Sergeant John H. Klinger, a move that placed personnel matters for the first time in the hands of a non-commissioned officer. Only
during the brief tenure of Captain Horan was Personnel, as a separate
unit, supervised by a commissioned officer.

Major Thomas F. Martin (Courtesy of Pennsylvania State Police)

Klinger, a native of Hummelstown and a twenty-year veteran with the force, distinguished himself as Personnel Director during his five-year tenure, for which he was deservedly promoted to lieutenant and captain before his retirement.

Through many consecutive sessions of the legislature, the State Police FOP lodges, which had increased their membership and influence since their modest origin back in the Wilhelm years, labored and lobbied for a mandatory retirement law. They sought mandatory retirement at age 60 for all enlisted men. That joint effort was successfully concluded with the approval of Act 360, P.L. 682, by Leader on July 10, 1957. The act, which was to become effective January 1, 1958, excluded the commissioner and deputy commissioner.

The act included a special provision that allowed enlisted men beyond 60 to remain on the job, if they had not yet served out twenty years. It will be recalled that Ruch, at 58, was reinstated in 1955. He would have reached mandatory retirement age before finishing his twenty years, falling short of pension requirements. After having gone to the trouble of seeing to Ruch's reinstatement, it was not the intention of state officials and the legislature to see him numbered among the two-time losers. Thus came the saving provision in Act 360 that served no other purpose.

Although Henry had nothing whatsoever to do with the legislation's passage, the law was passed nonetheless in his administration and he had the obligation of carrying it out. The first group already beyond 60 felt the axe on January 1, 1958. Mandatory retirement, in spite of scattered discontentment, became an accepted procedure. It was, however, to be contested in the courts later.

Other relevant enactments by the 1957 General Assembly were: Act 40, P.L. 98, April 30, amending the Private Detective Act of 1953 to include members of the State Police; Act 122, P.L. 245, June 5, requiring insurance companies to report fire losses to the State Police, and Act 359, P.L. 679, July 10, imposing duties on the State Police relating to the sale and use of air rifles.

Introduced in several previous sessions were measures authorizing State Police use of radar for speed law enforcement. It was not until 1957, however, that any success at all was evidenced, when the House passed a radar bill. The bill was then sent to the Senate and hastily referred to the Committee on Highways chaired by Senator George N. Wade (R-Cumberland), where the bill was never to see the light of day.

Sponsored by Senator Thomas A. Ehrgood (R-Lebanon), a resolution was passed by the Senate, enabling the Joint State Government Commission to study State Police operations. Rumors that a "bad morale problem'' existed in the State Police were common, and it was Ehrgood's contention that improvements could be made by Henry.

The Senate resolution in part read as follows:

> Resolved that the Joint State Government Commission be directed to make a comprehensive study of the problems of the Pennsylvania State Police with a view to increase its morale, efficiency and incentives, giving particular attention to:
>
> (1) The pay scale or a possible family allottment pay for married members of the Force,
>
> (2) A compulsory retirement at age sixty, as recommended,
>
> (3) Modern, new and radical use of technological changes and equipment,
>
> (4) The reorganization of the Pennsylvania State Police and increasing the size thereof along with the study of the State Police functions,
>
> (5) Any other pertinent matter which the Commission deems appropriate to the State.

The resolution provided that the Commission's report be submitted to the general assembly no later than January 31, 1959. The resolution was adopted on May 29, 1957, prior to the passage of the compulsory retirement act.

Needless to report, Henry was not pleased with that turn of events, nor with his inability to deliver the goods expected of him by the rank and file. Frustrated and unhappy about his growing unpopularity, Henry withdrew from public appearances and less was seen of him as his term drew on. He owed much to the staff officers at headquarters, who picked up the mantle of responsibility. Captains John D. Kime and Thomas P. Cahalan were his outside representatives, and Captain Harry B. Kerns looked after many in-house chores. In a not-too-unexpected move, Henry rewarded these men by promotions to major in July, 1957. In a companion move, changes were made in the organizational structure to provide the basis for the newly-created positions. The new posts were: Chief of Field Forces, Chief of Supply Services and Chief of Special Services, to which Kime, Kerns and Cahalan were assigned, respectively.

Kerns and Cahalan managed to fill their new roles without much trouble dogging their trails administratively. Poor health, however, overtook Kerns before Henry's term ended. Kime, who became Henry's troubleshooter, was to encounter more unpleasant duties relating to discipline. But, being an obedient officer, he fulfilled the assignments Henry gave him. Unhappily, that new role thrust upon him by Henry was to importantly affect Kime's career in later years.

Midway through the year, the Fire Bureau which shared accommodations on the capitol's sixth floor with the BCI & I was moved to the South Office building. That move permitted both bureaus to better handle their expanding operations.

Shortly after that move, Fire Marshal Captain William Traeger was suddenly taken ill and died. The loss of Traeger, who spearheaded the State Police fire protection efforts for so many years, was deeply felt. Succeeding Traeger as state Fire Marshal was Captain Lawrence Priar. Advanced, too, was Lieutenant Jack Sacriste.

In 1957, a sudden attack upon the United States and the horrors of nuclear warfare were still very much the concern of federal and state officials, as the Soviet Union and the United States engaged in a critical nuclear arms race. Responsibility for dealing with that possible threat was left to the military and the Office of Civil Defense. Here in Pennsylvania, as in other states, The National Warning System (NAWAS) was installed. The State Council of Civil Defense (SCCD), headed by Dr. Richard Gerstell, arranged with Henry to have the Pennsylvania NAWAS terminals installed in each of the troop headquarters buildings, where desks were manned around the clock. Terminals were also installed in the Selinsgrove and Lehighton Substations as backup points for the State Council's area offices located in those two communities.

NAWAS is a two-way voice system which is instantaneously activated and designed as the nation's early warning system in the event of enemy attack. The State Police, in accepting the system, assumed full responsibility for fanning out the warning to local and state emergency forces. Added benefits, however, derived from the system. Military authorities allowed NAWAS to be used for statewide communications between State Police field installations during emergency incidents in which field forces were deeply involved. Critical strikes and floods in the late 1960s and early 1970s were typical incidents to be covered in later chapters. Later when SCCD's eastern area office was moved to Hamburg and the western area office to Indiana, State Police backup terminals were installed at the Hamburg and Indiana Substations.

On October 16, 1957, members of the State Police and the populace of Pennsylvania's northeast region were saddened by the death of retired Major William A. Clark. Clark was a beloved figure in the coal regions where he continued to be active in community affairs after retirement. Major Arthur J. Oldham, district inspector at Wyoming, notified Henry of Clark's death. Not completely understanding, perhaps, the importance of Clark's death to the coal region people, Henry missed the boat by disallowing a military funeral conducted by State Police personnel. Some resentment was publicly expressed as a result of Henry's decision. Nonetheless, a funeral, the likes of which are not often seen anywhere, was held for Clark, a devout Catholic. Impressive in the funeral procession was the corps of nurses from the Pittston Hospital where Clark served on the board of directors. Civil and military officials were everywhere in evidence as they joined the throngs gathered to reverently honor Clark—a soldier, police officer and humanitarian. Notably numbered among the mourners was 78-year-old Lynn G. Adams.

Death again visited the State Police family with the brutal slaying of Trooper Phillip C. Melley of Troop C-4, Reading, on November 3. Melley was killed by a shotgun blast at the hands of a Boyertown teenager.

The momentum of Wilhelm's building program was to continue through Henry's administration. A new substation building was completed at York; included in that project was a modern off-street driver examination course. Contracts were awarded for a new barracks at Greensburg, and new substation facilities at Ebensburg, Mercer, Lewistown and Somerset.

The pride of the State Police, however, rested with the contract award for the new training school at Hershey. The much-awaited groundbreaking ceremony took place on July 17, 1958. General State Authority's executive director, A. J. Caruso, was program chairman on that occasion. Governor Leader and Senator Harvey M. Taylor (R-Dauphin) turned ground with a steel shovel, as Democrat Leader and "Mr. Republican" exchanged quips. State officials acknowledged the generosity of the Hershey Estates for donating the twenty-eight-acre site for the new school. Mr. John B. Sollenberger, president of the Hershey Estates, was spokesman for the Hershey interests. Others speaking briefly were Major Charles C. Keller, school superintendent, and Commissioner Henry. The new building was scheduled for completion in two years. In his comments, Taylor disclosed the fact that U. S. Senator Edward Martin, a former governor, wanted the new school located at the Indiantown Gap Military Reservation.

Before Henry's term was up, plans were also made to have all troop headquarters and substation buildings equipped with emergency power gear to permit uninterrupted services.

Criminal records processed by the BCI & I during the biennial period ending May 31, 1958, indicated that 63 percent of all those arrested had previous criminal records—an alarming rate of recidivism.

To satisfy some reasoning, the Executive Board on January 18, 1957, changed the name of the BCI & I to Criminal Coordinating Division. The former label had been in continual use since 1920.

During the same reporting period, the number of radio-equipped patrol vehicles jumped to 540. Operational were eighty-one base radio stations.

The teletypewriter center, long located at Troop A, Harrisburg, was moved to the basement of the capitol where a modern "torn-tape" system was installed. A full duplex circuit linked the State Police with the Bureau of Motor Vehicles to speedily handle requests for operator and registration data.

During the biennial period, traffic forces patrolled 53,794,944 miles. Patrols accounted for 282,134 traffic arrests, 110,441 of which were speeding charges. Patrol forces were called upon to investigate 53,988 rural motor vehicle accidents which took 1,999 lives. The training school graduated 192 State Police recruits, and trained 196 municipal police officers and prison guards.

Of serious concern to State Police administrators has been the problem of reducing the number of substations in some counties where

State Sen. M. Harvey Taylor breaks ground for new State Police Training School, Hershey. Left to right: GSA Executive Director A. J. Caruso, Maj. Charles C. Keller, Gov. George M. Leader, Col. Earl J. Henry. (Courtesy of Pennsylvania State Police)

the figure was considered high. In Schuylkill County, for example, there were three substations located at Pine Grove, Schuylkill Haven and Tamaqua. After much political haggling, Henry was successful in getting the number cut to two substations. Henry's successors in office were to find this problem a frustrating political battlefield. Politicians who claimed to be economy-minded yielded swiftly to the unreasonable position of misguided back-home leaders—and still do.

By mid-1958, it was no secret that Henry had decided not to seek reappointment. He was tired of his job and looked forward to its end. His decision left open the door for any and all aspirants, and by election time there were a few. Dahlstrom headed the list, and there was reason to believe that Deputy Attorney General Frank P. Lawley had thrown his hat into the ring, according to the State Police grapevine. Not to be overlooked was Frank G. McCartney whom Henry had thrust aside for deputy.

The year 1958 saw three deaths in the line of duty. The first to die was Trooper Charles S. Stanski of Troop A-2, Harrisburg, who met death in an auto crash on January 23. Four months later, Trooper Edward Mackiw of Troop B-1, Washington, was struck down as he directed traffic at an accident scene on May 3. The last to die was Trooper Stephen R. Gyurke of Troop B-2 (Turnpike), who was crushed by a tractor-trailer as he questioned a stopped motorist on August 21. This was the first time in almost two decades that more than one name was added to the honor roll in a single year. It was also the last time multiple deaths were recorded.

At the November polls, the Democratic party gubernatorial candidate, Mayor David L. Lawrence, of Pittsburgh, defeated his Republican opponent, Arthur T. McGonigle, by a slim margin of 76,083 votes. Lawrence's victory, in unprecedented fashion, brought Democratic administrations back-to-back. The Democratic majority in the House, which was lost to the Republicans in 1957, was regained by a 108 to 102 edge. The Senate, however, remained under Republican control 28 to 22.

As a result of the election, McCartney was reportedly in line for the commissioner post and considered by other contestants as the man to beat. McCartney became the common enemy, and attempts were made to discredit him as a bona fide appointee. As the post-election days wore on, bitterness was a predictable eventuality—a bitterness that was to linger. In early December, all speculation was ended by Lawrence's announcement that McCartney would be his State Police commissioner. McCartney's foes, however, did not give up the contest with that announcement. They knew that McCartney still had to face

Senate confirmation, and no time was lost in plotting his downfall. Such actions only added to the bitterness that already existed.

Even in his final days, Henry was not to find comfort. Senator Ehrgood was still pushing for a legislative study of the State Police: Ehrgood was dissatisfied with an earlier study made by the Joint State Government Commission, and was critical of Henry. Henry publicly responded to Ehrgood with heated comments of his own. Ehrgood stated that before introducing another resolution for a State Police study, he would confer with the incoming commissioner—Frank G. McCartney. The young senator sought McCartney's cooperation.

From that point on, Henry's interest in departmental affairs rapidly dwindled. He vowed to have nothing to do with the upcoming inaugural ceremonies nor the 1959 Farm Show detail, both of which required considerable planning and large manpower commitments. Dahlstrom, with the aid of headquarters and field officers, looked to those major obligations.

Major Harry B. Kerns, one of Henry's trusted aides, retired in December because of ill health, after twenty-five years of service. Lawrence and McCartney had persuaded Leader to halt any promotions or transfers within the State Police until January 20, 1959, when the incoming administration would officially take over. Thus, Kerns' vacancy was not filled and Lieutenant William J. Garrick was appointed acting chief of general services.

Henry's resignation on January 20, 1959, at 62, brought to an end a long and distinguished career that began with the State Highway Patrol in 1924. He and Mrs. Henry remained residents of Harrisburg. Henry, after brief appointments with the federal government and private enterprises, withdrew from all activity—a status he was to enjoy for only twelve years.

CHAPTER XVI

Colonel Frank G. McCartney
1959–1963

Sleet, rain, snow and icy streets greeted inaugural day for Pennsylvania's fortieth governor. These conditions on January 20, 1959, were serious enough to convince the inaugural committee and State Police commanders to alter the day's schedule. The ceremonies were hastily moved to the Farm Show arena, and the inaugural parade—a highlight of such quadrennial affairs—was cancelled. Spectators, content with the warmth of an indoor inauguration, jammed the Farm Show arena to see David Leo Lawrence sworn into office. That was the first time that the governor's office was to be occupied by a Roman Catholic.

The Patriot (Harrisburg) on January 21, reflecting the abandonment of the specially-constructed facilities in town, lamented, "The snow-covered outdoor inaugural site in front of the Capitol was a scene of icy loneness."

The Senate, having received Lawrence's nominations for cabinet appointments, met in an afternoon session shortly after the inaugural ceremonies were completed to consider the new governor's official family-to-be. By four o'clock, all had been confirmed except Frank G. McCartney, Lawrence's choice for State Police commissioner. Late in the afternoon eighteen cabinet colleagues were sworn into office in the House chamber as McCartney stood aside.

According to reports, McCartney's confirmation was held up at the request of Senator Edward J. Kessler (R-Lancaster). The State Police grapevine attributed Kessler's action to State Police officers who were either unhappy with McCartney's appointment or wanted to keep their own chances for appointment alive. Republican spokesmen were clear to state that McCartney's character was not a matter of scrutiny—simply his qualifications for the high post. At the inaugural ball, McCartney greeted friends who shared his disappointment. To them he expressed confidence that the Senate would act favorably.

Lawrence, reacting to this setback, designated Deputy Commissioner Dahlstrom acting commissioner, pending the outcome of the McCartney hassle. Dahlstrom, however, was deprived of any right to promote or transfer. Dahlstrom supporters remained hopeful.

Before inaugural week was out, tragedy struck at the Knox Coal Company mines at Port Griffith, Luzerne County, on January 23. A January "heat wave" melted ice and snow along the Susquehanna River basin bringing the level of the river and its feeder streams to flood stage. Swift river waters washed through the mine ceiling at Port Griffith, flooding operations. State Police troopers at Wyoming joined in rescue efforts and, with the help of special equipment aboard a Civil Defense rescue truck, managed to save the lives of thirty-three miners. Twelve trapped miners died. McCartney was later to award a citation to the officers and men of Troop B, Wyoming, for their decisive action at the disaster scene.

After weeks of delayed Senate action, Senator Harold E. Flack (R-Luzerne) proposed a compromise to Lawrence wherein Dahlstrom would unquestionably be confirmed as commissioner and McCartney given the deputy post. Lawrence refused to consider any compromise, and was obviously prepared to sit out the controversy. Neither Lawrence nor McCartney during the waiting period risked the issuance of any public statements bearing on the Senate's actions.

Just prior to inauguration day, the FOP state lodge meeting in Philadelphia fully endorsed McCartney's appointment. The state lodge, representing a membership of 16,000, "thought McCartney eminently qualified for the job." Spearheading the FOP action was John J. Harrington, state president and a Philadelphia police sergeant, who continued to throw his weight in favor of McCartney.

In mid-February, McCartney was called before the Senate committee for questioning. His advocates were eventually successful in urging Kessler to withdraw his opposition. Through committee action by Senator William Z. Scott (R-Carbon) and Senator John T. VanSant (R-Leigh), McCartney's nomination was moved to the Senate floor on February 23 where it received unanimous approval.

McCartney, on February 25, was sworn into office by Judge James C. McCready, of Carbon County, as Governor Lawrence and Mrs.

Colonel Frank G. McCartney (Courtesy of Pennsylvania State Police)

McCartney looked on. Standing close by were the McCartney children; the five redheads all but stole the show. John Scotzin, a prominent capitol hill newsman, described the event as "one of the biggest seen in the governor's reception room." Well-wishers jammed the room.

Scotzin, in a later column, speculated on the rolling of heads in the wake of McCartney's confirmation, "It was no secret among Republican senators, nor with McCartney who frequently appeared on the Senate sidelines to check his delayed prospects, that 'certain officers' were responsible for his status as the only unconfirmed member of Gov. Lawrence's cabinet." But McCartney was to display the virtue of patience in office—there was no purge to satisfy sensationalism.

Frank Gerald McCartney, 50, a native of Coaldale, Schuylkill County, was born on March 31, 1908. He was one of six children born to George and Margaret McCartney. Mr. McCartney, a devout Irish Catholic, was born in Glasgow, Scotland. As a youth, he was numbered among the Irish immigrants who sought their fortunes in the Pennsylvania coal mines. He settled in Coaldale where, by apprenticeship and perseverance, he became a respected mining engineer. There, too, he married Margaret O'Brien.

McCartney attended St. Mary's Church school, at Coaldale, where he also served as an altar boy. Described as an industrious lad, he peddled newspapers after school hours to earn spending money. Leaving St. Mary's, he enrolled at Coaldale High School, and participated in football, basketball and track competition. Playing an end position for the "Tigers," McCartney excelled in football. A knee injury suffered in football was to bother him throughout his lifetime. (A teammate, John "Kid" Gildea, went on to star for the Pittsburgh Steelers.) McCartney graduated from Coaldale High School in 1927.

Following graduation, he worked at the Lehigh Coal and Navigation Company colliery, performing duties that did not take him into the mines. While thus employed, he enjoyed dancing as a recreational outlet, and was a frequent patron at the nearby Lakewood Ballroom, where big-name bands were regularly booked.

Impressed by the State Police troopers he met in the anthracite region, McCartney decided against following his father's footsteps in the mining industry. He applied for enlistment in the constabulary, and was admitted to the training school by Superintendent Lynn G. Adams on February 1, 1931.

At the training school, McCartney showed exceptional skill in horsemanship; he was picked as a member of the prestigious rodeo stunt-riding team. After graduation, he was assigned to Troop E, at Harrisburg, and annually recalled to the school for several years to participate in the rodeo. His tour of duty in Troop E took him to substations at Lewistown, Muncy, Chambersburg, Gettysburg and Mount Alto. Establishing himself as an outstanding investigator, McCartney was transferred to the detective division at department headquarters in 1935.

After his assignment to the detective division, McCartney married the former Agnes T. Finn, of Wilkes-Barre, a secretary in the Commonwealth's State Department. Miss Finn was one of ten children born to John and Anna Burke Finn. McCartney and his wife took up residence at Harrisburg.

During World War II, he refused to sign a request for deferment from military service—a procedure followed by the State Police to preserve its diminishing ranks. During the war years, McCartney aided the armed forces intelligence services to safeguard defense plants and military installations, and was not called up for military service. Following World War II, he was promoted to detective sergeant and his assignments were centered on anti-lottery prosecutions and special probes. He deservingly won acclaim in 1950 when he spearheaded major raids on lottery and gambling operations in Luzerne County, which resulted in seventy successful prosecutions.

A family death later in 1950 brought him back to Coaldale where he met officials of the Lehigh Coal and Navigation Company, who offered him a position as chief of security. Torn between a continuing State Police career and a tempting offer from the colliery, the detective sergeant faced a difficult decision. The financial burden, however, of supporting four children was a deciding factor. He applied for State Police retirement in 1950 and took up his new post with the large coal firm. Afterward a fifth child, a second son, joined the family circle.

In 1955, following the dismissal of Deputy Commissioner Jacob C. Mauk by Governor Leader, McCartney was notified to report to State Police headquarters as Commissioner Henry's deputy. Henry, as it was reported before, refused to endorse McCartney's appointment. Reluctantly, Leader yielded to Henry's position in this sensitive issue. Angered by this ordeal, McCartney went back to the coal company to reclaim the post from which he had just resigned. He remained there for only three months before joining the state Justice Department as chief investigator. Adding to his prominence as a criminal investigator, McCartney stayed with the Justice Department until Governor Lawrence named him to the top State Police post in 1959. It was Lawrence who had previously supported McCartney's unsuccessful bid for the deputy's job in 1955.

Topped by thinning, short-cut, snow-white hair, the six-foot-one, 205 pound, former football player, in uniform or civilian attire, cut a handsome figure that commanded attention wherever he went. Like his predecessors, except for Henry, McCartney was a cigar-smoking commissioner.

He was a charter member of Keystone Lodge 41, FOP, which was organized in Troop A-2, at Harrisburg. McCartney was active in civic, church, fraternal and police organizations. He held important offices in the Boy Scout and Cub Scout movement, Harrisburg Catholic Forum, United Services Organization board of directors, Knights of Columbus, Carbon-Schuylkill Industrial Development Corporation, Holy Name Society, Police Chiefs Association and Mahoning Valley

Country Club. During his tenure as State Police commissioner, the Mc-
Cartney family retained residence at Lansford, Carbon Couty.

Shortly after his election in November, 1958, Lawrence asked Mc-
Cartney to prepare a list of objectives he would follow were he to be
the next State Police commissioner. McCartney submitted a detailed
formal document to Lawrence, in which he cited an array of changes in
highway safety programs, salaries, equipment, training, personnel, and
crime investigation. Particularly important were his proposed "no-fix"
system for handling traffic violations, use of radar, salary increases,
purchase of more comfortable uniforms, minority recruiting, reactivation of the detective division, revitalization of the crime lab, and
improvements in public relations. Governor Lawrence was impressed
with McCartney's presentation. It is interesting to note how closely

*Colonel Frank G. McCartney, first day at work (Courtesy of Philadelphia In-
quirer)*

McCartney was to follow that outline of objectives through his four years in office. Although time did not allow all his ambitious objectives to be reached, he nonetheless made remarkable progress.

McCartney procrastinated in naming a deputy commissioner of his own choosing. It was never his intention to keep Dahlstrom on any longer than was necessary. Dahlstrom, however, was to serve in that capacity for an entire year before a change was made.

McCartney, if other circumstances could have been put aside, would have given the appointment to Captain John J. Pezzent. Mc-Cartney, a Roman Catholic and the first Catholic to head the State Police, was hesitant about having another at the top with him. Pezzent, a Catholic, was also a coal region native. For many years the State Police hierarchy was predominantly Protestant in makeup and many top officers were members of the Masonic Order; although Masonic membership did not guarantee advancement or special favor, troopers were mindful of circumstances that existed. McCartney did not want to make religion an issue with regard to appointments. Whether he was right in placing that much importance on this point is debatable. At any rate, Pezzent was not named. As it will be seen, four of the next six commissioners to follow McCartney in office embraced the Catholic faith. It seems that the law of averages, given time, will have its way.

A second choice for the deputy post rested with Major John D. Kime, district inspector at Harrisburg. McCartney had Kime's name dropped to FOP state president John J. Harrington to weigh the FOP's reaction. The trail balloon brought back a swift and unfavorable response: the FOP would have nothing to do with Kime. Henry had made somewhat of a "hatchet man" out of Kime, and that reputation was everlastingly detrimental to him: McCartney withdrew further consideration of Kime. Discouraged with his progress in picking a deputy, McCartney put aside the problem and looked to others.

Any visitors to headquarters were greeted by uniformed troopers as they approached a wooden railing and made their inquiries to the ac-companiment of banging teletype machines. The reception area was likened to a precinct police station rather than the antechamber for State Police executive officers. That condition McCartney considered deplorable. Through the capable services of Lieutenant William J. Gar-rick, chief quartermaster, the reception room and executive offices were transformed into dignified settings befitting their purposes. Carpeting, murals, plush furniture and a female receptionist made a world of difference. Favorable comments from all quarters were re-warding enough. Garrick, one of McCartney's key staff officers, was to be a very busy man, indeed, as many of the commissioner's programs

Testimonial dinner for Col. C. M. Wilhelm and Col. Lynn G. Adams, 1959. Front row, left to right: Sgt. Rufus G. Williams, Maj. Frank Garnow, Col. Wilhelm, Col. Frank G. McCartney, Col. Adams, Lt. Col. A. F. Dahlstrom, Sgt. Arthur Shulenberger, Sgt. Charles Harbaugh. Back row: Capt. Wilbur Smith, Tpr. P. M. Conti, Maj. Thomas Cahalan, Capt. Lawrence Priar, Dr. David A. Johnston, Lt. William J. Garrick, Lt. Willian Nevin, Capt. Elmer Faber, Maj. Charles Keller, Lt. Anthony Parry, Sgt. Henry Wellen, Capt. Ralph D. Gardner, Lt. James Murray. (Courtesy of Pennsylvania State Police)

for improving the organization involved inordinate purchasing of material and equipment.

One of McCartney's earliest promotions went to Sergeant John H. Klinger, personnel officer. Klinger was promoted to lieutenant not only in recognition of meritorious services but also to add prestige to the personnel office which was destined to be one of the busier operations at headquarters. Klinger was promoted to captain in less than two years, reflecting McCartney's satisfaction with his outstanding work.

On March 31, 1959, just five weeks after his confirmation, McCartney was honored at a testimonial dinner held at the Stevens House, Lancaster. Hosting the gala affair were officers and members of Conestoga Lodge 66, FOP, representing the Lancaster troop. Among the honor guests was Senator Edward Kessler. That was the first of other testimonials welcoming McCartney to his post.

McCartney had the greatest respect for his former mentors and predecessors, Lynn G. Adams and Cecil M. Wilhelm. In response to his personal feelings for these two giants in State Police history, McCartney, on April 14, arranged for a private testimonial affair to pay tribute to them. Festivities were held in the Colonial Park residence of Lieutenant Anthony Parry. Invited were a few staff officers and former members of the detective division, who, like McCartney, worked closely with Adams and Wilhelm. Needless to state, Adams and Wilhelm were deeply moved by the heartwarming display of affection by those in attendance.

The testimonial affair was held none too soon for the failing Wilhelm. Shortly thereafter Wilhelm was confined to the hospital—a victim of cancer—and on June 14, at 77, he succumbed to his ailment.

McCartney ordered a full military funeral for Wilhelm with family consent. Nothing was overlooked by McCartney to give the former commissioner final honors he so richly deserved. To the sounds of a firing squad and taps, Wilhelm was buried in Camp Hill's Rolling Green Cemetery.

In June, death also claimed Lieutenant Ralph C. Hoover who headed the department's transportation program. Hoover, 55, enlisted with the State Highway Patrol in 1925. He, like Wilhelm, was a cancer victim. Replacing Hoover as transportation officer was Lieutenant Philip F. Chulick.

John A. Bedford, the department's second black recruit, was enlisted on May 13, 1959. Upon graduation from the training school, he was assigned to Troop A-2, Harrisburg. Bedford resigned from the State Police on November 16, 1960.

It griped McCartney no end, even before his appointment, to read newspaper accounts wherein heads of state agencies and district attorneys had "ordered" the State Police to investigate. Within a few months of taking office, a serious school bus accident occurred in the Pittsburgh area, and a newspaper story carried a statement by Traffic Commissioner O. D. Shipley that he had "ordered" the State Police to investigate the accident. McCartney made a daily practice of scanning the state's major newspapers and spotted Shipley's statement. He immediately phoned Revenue Secretary Charles M. Dougherty, Shipley's boss. Out of respect for Dougherty as a friend and fellow cabinet colleague, McCartney politely but firmly made it clear that he resented Shipley's statement, and no one would command the State Police but the State Police commissioner and the governor. Dougherty delivered the message.

Within a week of the Shipley incident, McCartney had another occasion to drive this same point home to a VIP in state government. The Justice Department was evaluating a matter allegedly involving the commission of a serious crime. Attorney General Anne X. Alpern, one of the two females in the Lawrence cabinet and the first woman in the nation's history to be appointed state attorney general, in her news release regarding the incident stated that she was "ordering" the State Police in on the case. McCartney called Alpern, reminding her that she was a cabinet officer of equal, not superior, rank and explained his position concerning the State Police command structure.

For the remainder of McCartney's term, his unbending position was respected by his cabinet colleagues and, in fact, it cannot be recalled thereafter that anyone in state government risked locking horns with McCartney on that score. It must be stated, however, in fairness to those who thoughtlessly resorted to the use of words likely leading to a public misunderstanding, that to command State Police forces was not literally intended at all. Nonetheless, McCartney's sensitivity in protecting his department against a subordinate role can be appreciated, and his stand was probably shared by other commissioners before him, who simply elected to remain silent in facing up to any such statements rather than make an issue of them.

McCartney, surprisingly, revealed a tremendous interest in traffic matters. Having been in the criminal investigation end of law enforcement for a quarter of a century, it was expected that he would give little or no attention to traffic operations. McCartney, however, knew the deep feeling Lawrence had for traffic problems and the need for combatting them. Lawrence had lost two sons in a highway mishap—an event that underscored the governor's determination to see highway slaughter ended. McCartney ordered maximum patrol coverage for holiday traffic and other times when exceptional treatment was advisable. Vacationing was taboo and plainclothesmen were pressed into patrol services. He spent his first July 4th in a National Guard helicopter surveying traffic conditions in central and eastern Pennsylvania, and continued to monitor patrol activities on critical occasions throughout his tenure.

Early in his administration, Lawrence challenged the state with his thirteen-point highway safety program which included among other items, the use of radar, the intoximeter, a no-fix ticket system and a driver re-examination procedure. McCartney spearheaded the drive to get general assembly approval for State Police use of radar. He spent endless hours during legislative sessions lobbying for radar—a battle that was not to end favorably for two years.

The development of the no-fix ticket system was a challenge given to Kime and Garrick. They were successful architects of the system that still remains in effect. The no-fix policy was a morale booster for the field forces and constituted a promise of better days for patrol personnel who for years had been repeatedly wearied by appeals to fix.

McCartney was mindful of the fact that he was soon to inherit the finest training school facility in the country. He wanted the school not only to be housed in the finest building, but also to be matched by quality instruction as well. To assure himself of this goal, he appealed to the Secretary of Education Charles H. Boehm to evaluate the training program and the capabilities of the instructors. That survey was done and remedial measures were taken: instructors underwent special training conducted by the Valley Forge Military Academy Dean of Admissions, Temple University psychologists, faculty members of the Eastern Psychiatric Institute and Millersville State College. Objective testing, teaching techniques, visual aids, comprehension and reading, and behavioral studies to identify problem students were some of the principal subjects taught. Instructors received continuing training at Harvard and the University of Maryland.

The training survey also indicated that streamlining and improved quality of instructions would allow a reduction in time. McCartney followed up on that finding by cutting the training period from six to five months. McCartney's effort to upgrade the school's training output was fruitful, indeed.

To further upgrade the school image, McCartney sought out a change in name. He recommended to the legislature that the name be changed from "Pennsylvania State Police Training School" to "Pennsylvania State Police Academy." The legislators obligingly passed Act 112, P.L. 487, signed by Lawrence on June 29, 1959. Other enactments of the 1959 General Assembly will be listed later.

Prior to McCartney's time, preparation of the budget was a biennial duty of the comptroller's office. The growth of the State Police budget and the problems related to it were considered worthy of separate, full-time attention. With this thought in mind, McCartney found little difficulty in securing top-level authorization to create a Fiscal Office. To fill this new position, he moved Richard J. Shaffer back to headquarters from the Academy where he had been banished earlier by Henry after serious disagreement between Shaffer and Grillo. Thus Shaffer became the department's first fiscal officer with the responsibilities for preparing a meaningful budget reflecting McCartney's objectives and to counsel the commissioner on broad fiscal matters in dealings with the governor's office and the legislature.

Although the new fiscal officer relieved the comptroller of budget responsibilities, the latter was still occupied with accounting, payroll and processing of payable accounts. Although accountable to the department heads, all comptrollers were directly assigned and guided by the secretary of administration who, in this case, was Dr. David H. Kurtzman, a key figure in the Lawrence cabinet. McCartney did not consider Grillo an acceptable comptroller in his view. Taking his case to Dr. Kurtzman, McCartney persuaded him to transfer Grillo to another state agency and assign a replacement comptroller more agreeable to the State Police headquarters staff. This Dr. Kurtzman agreed to do—and did. Incoming comptroller was John Bringman who from early 1960 to 1969 went on to serve the State Police most commendably.

Because of wise counseling and personal diplomacy, McCartney throughout his tenure enjoyed an excellent relationship with the governor's office, the secretary of administration, the budget secretary and leaders of the House and Senate appropriations committees. McCartney's programs to generally modernize the State Police agency as swiftly as possible received wide support at all levels of government. Not once was McCartney hampered by a shortage of operational funding.

Blessed with that good fortune, the delivery of material and equipment to the field quartermasters reached proportions never before witnessed by staff and line personnel. Filing cabinets, electric typewriters, tape recorders, motion picture projectors, surveillance cameras, portable "handitalkie" units, office furniture, bedroom furnishings, handcuffs and office supplies, just to name a few, were part of the shipments to reach the field. Replaced were the worn-out chrome badges. The new gold badge was impressively designed and issued with a leather carrying case. At McCartney's order, Garrick surveyed the age of all service revolvers. About 700 old models were withdrawn from service and replaced with new .38 Colt Specials. Snub-nose revolvers and holsters were purchased for officers and plainclothesmen. Thermofax copy machines were purchased for each troop office. Chief clerks were pleasantly surprised by the receipt of such modern and useful equipment "without our even asking for them. Something funny is going on at headquarters."

Soon after his confirmation, McCartney was interviewed by Scotzin who wrote, "His announced plan to visit every troop and substation in the state will get under way this week, beginning with the Harrisburg and Lancaster areas. His inspecting purpose is to 'meet the men and tell them what I expect of them and what I'll do for them.' "

True to that commitment, McCartney set out on his troop and substation visits. Some locations were revisited, but all were visited at least once during his early tenure. From his personal observations and conversations with the field officers and men, McCartney determined their needs. During those tours, Kime was a frequent companion.

Contract tailors measured line forces for new summer uniforms with trimmings to brighten the appearance. Washable and cooler shirts replaced those that required costly drycleaning. New straw hats were purchased and issued. Officers were decked out in new uniforms fashioned after the military-look. Gone were the old sambrowne belts. Cap visors for all ranks above lieutenant were bedecked with the military brass "scrambled eggs." Gold ornaments and identifying trimming set off the uniforms. Bright black and gold shoulder patches replaced the drab blue and grey patches. The organization from top to bottom had a new look—practical and comfortable.

McCartney did not limit his time away from his office to field visiting. He accepted just about every speaking invitation that came to his attention, simply to tell the State Police story to every possible audience, large or small, and gain public support for his department. He actively participated in the affairs of the International Association of Chiefs of Police, the Pennsylvania Chiefs of Police Association, and worked closely with neighboring state police heads in the free exchange of information. The Pennsylvania State Police, once held to itself, was rubbing elbows with fellow agencies up and down the east coast. McCartney's energy was without bounds.

Almost from the department's inception, promotional examinations were prepared and administered by State Police commissioned personnel. That system was not entirely free of criticism. In order to substitute a procedure holding greater promise for fair play, McCartney turned to the State Civil Service Commission (SCSC). That agency was already preparing and administering entrance examinations for State Police applicants with apparent success. SCSC officials considered McCartney's proposal and took on the job. Reasonable weights were assigned to test results, performance and evaluation, and seniority. Higher grades included points for oral board interviews, which at the outset included non-police board members. That board makeup, however, came under fire and McCartney yielded to a board composed of State Police officers instead.

McCartney's first year in office saw many complaints arrive in the mail regarding the conduct of Justices of the Peace acting on traffic arrests. Investigations in most cases determined that the complaints were generally well-founded. McCartney reported his findings to the governor's office and recommended that the legislature study means for upgrading the minor judiciary in Pennsylvania. Although no action was immediately in evidence, action was taken eventually, as outcries of incompetence swelled. (Several years later, legal steps were taken to abolish the JP system and replace it with a system of district magistrates who are trained and closely supervised by the county president judges. Far from being a perfect setup, the new system is a significant forward step from the days of the Justices of the Peace.)

Busily pursuing his promise to visit all field installations, McCartney stopped at the Punxsutawney barracks, where he was greeted by Captain Charles Hartman. Opening the commissioner's car door was Corporal Bernard V. Johnson who asked if he could shake the commissioner's hand, "I've spent twenty-nine years in the State Police and this is the first time I've ever seen a commissioner." (This story was told by *Philadelphia Inquirer* reporter Saul Kohler in the TODAY supplement, June 25, 1961.)

While at Punxsutawney, Captain Hartman asked McCartney to move him closer to his home area in the east. McCartney agreed to consider that request if and when a vacancy in the east was to come up. A vacancy did occur in June, 1959, and McCartney moved Hartman to Troop A, at Harrisburg.

The State Police was called upon in September to join federal agencies in providing a large security task force for visiting Russian Premier Nikita Khrushchev. Khrushchev's U. S. tour included a two-day stay at Pittsburgh, his only Pennsylvania stop, where the Russian dignitary visited the Mesta Machine Company plant at West Homestead, and was honor guest at a luncheon at the University of Pittsburgh. McCartney personally supervised State Police participation in that event of world interest.

The 1959 General Assembly remained in session for an entire year. The House recorded 120 legislative working days, the Senate 114. In addition to passing an act changing the name of the training school, the legislature enacted the following laws affecting State Police affairs: Act 78, P.L. 392, June 1, revising membership in Class C (Retirement System), effective August 1, 1959, to include only those having police powers; Act 113, P.L. 488, June 29, amending the Administrative Code to reflect the training school's name change; Act 327, P.L. 838, September 8, making unlawful for State Police, or any state agency, to refuse employment to members of the Pennsylvania National Guard not on extended active duty; Act 455, P.L. 1334, October 21, entitling FOP representatives to leave of absence, with pay, to attend state and national lodge conventions or conferences; Act 533, P.L. 1518, November 19, establishing procedure for furnishing abstract of accident investigations for a $3.00 fee, and Act 696, P.L. 1916, December 17, authorizing the carry-over of unused annual and sick leave entitlements and setting limits.

During the session, House Bill 2022 was introduced permitting the commissioner to retain members who have reached compulsory retirement age. The bill was sent to the Committee on State Government. Contacted by committee members, McCartney stated that he was not in favor of having this judgment rest in the hands of the commissioner. The bill died in committee.

Before his first year was up, McCartney was elated with the

Executive Board's approval of his request for an across-the-board pay increase for his troopers. Happily, McCartney notified his forces that salaries would be increased by $300 a year, effective December 1, 1959, and the subsistence allowance jumped by one dollar a day, retroactive to July 1, 1959. That meant an annual increase of $665 a year per trooper. Paychecks reflecting the payraise were distributed before Christmas.

January 5, 1960, was to see an unusual event in Pennsylvania history. The general assembly adjourned its 1959 session and opened its 1960 session on that same day. Under a new state law, the general assembly in 1960 began its first annual session. Since 1879, the legislature had met only during odd-numbered years except for special sessions. According to the legislative change, however, the legislators could consider only fiscal matters during even-numbered years. All other considerations had to await sessions held in odd-numbered years. Because of that limitation, there were no measures passed affecting State Police operations in 1960.

Before adjourning its 1959 session, the legislature approved an ambitious capital expenditures budget for State Police construction, calling for new troop headquarters buildings at Wyoming, Dunmore and Erie, a new facility at Harrisburg to house the Supply and Transportation Units, and ten driver examination points. A previous attempt by Henry to get a sorely needed troop headquarters building at Erie ran short of funds.

In January, 1960, Ruch, who had seen some controversial days during his broken years of service, was required to turn in according to the provisions of the mandatory retirement act which had been specially engineered for his sake. Ruch's retirement presented McCartney with his first opportunity to appoint a major of his own choosing, and there was little doubt in his mind to whom that appointment would go. McCartney's respect for Pezzent had not diminished.

Also retiring in February was Major Charles C. Keller, Academy superintendent. McCartney was anxiously awaiting the completion of the new Academy building, only a month away, and considered Pezzent a good choice to succeed Keller. When he discussed this move with Pezzent, however, he was disappointed with the captain's decision: Pezzent did not want the Academy post. Nonetheless, in January he was given the promotion to major and put in command of District 4 with headquarters at Reading. Meanwhle, McCartney designated Captain Peter Carlson acting superintendent and put aside his search for Keller's successor until another time.

On various occasions during 1959, McCartney had informed

Lt. Colonel Charles Hartman (Courtesy of Pennsylvania State Police)

Dahlstrom that he was not to be his deputy for four years and would appreciate Dahlstrom's resignation, undoubtedly hoping that Dahlstrom's departure would hasten his appointment of a successor. Dahlstrom, instead, refused to resign and appealed to McCartney to keep him on. This indecision could no longer be tolerated by McCartney. On February 2, 1960, McCartney notified Dahlstrom by letter that his services were being immediately terminated. Dahlstrom, 64, had joined the constabulary in 1920 and served for almost forty years.

Then, facing up to a vacancy in the office next door, McCartney decided to give the deputy post to the nearby Harrisburg troop commander, Captain Charles Hartman, after a final look at other possible choices. Hartman was a compromise in McCartney's judgment. He had worked with Hartman in the coal regions and believed him to be an honest, sincere police officer. McCartney knew Hartman to be a non-Catholic and even in later years admitted that he never was aware of Hartman's political leanings. In fact, he cared less, since his primary objective was simply to appoint a good man to back him up—and he honestly believed that Hartman might fill the bill. Hartman was sworn into office on February 4, 1960, just two days following Dahlstrom's firing.

Hartman, 53, was born at Philadelphia, on February 7, 1907. He was brought up in the Port Carbon area of Schuylkill County. At the minimum age of 21, he enlisted in the constabulary on New Year's Day, 1929. Slightly built at 5'9", he was a truck driver by occupation when he turned to law enforcement as a career.

Most of his service time was spent at Troop B, Wyoming. When the detective bureau was expanded to include field investigators, Hartman was appointed one of the two detectives at District 3 headquarters at Wyoming. He was promoted to detective sergeant in 1946, and to lieutenant in 1952. His first field command came with his promotion to captain in 1958 and assignment to Troop C-1, Punxsutawney. As a personal favor, McCartney moved him to the Harrisburg troop in 1959. Hartman and McCartney were fellow rodeo stunt riders, and worked closely in conducting lottery and gambling raids in Luzerne County. Hartman, during World War II, served as a Coast Guard lieutenant.

He is married to the former Marie Nalbaugh of Nanticoke, Luzerne County. They have a son, Charles, Jr.

On the heels of Hartman's appointment, McCartney promoted Captain Russel K. Knies to major and gave him command of the newly-created Sub-District 1 at Erie. At the same time, he moved Major Arthur J. Oldham to District 1, at Greensburg, and Major Harold T. Newman to District 3, at Wyoming, in a mutual transaction.

At long last construction of the new Academy building was completed. The Academy staff moved into the new facility on March 2, 1960, leaving behind the colonnaded, frame quarters where recruits had been trained for more than three decades. For the first time in its fifty-five-year history, the State Police agency was proud possessor of a state-owned Academy. Final building costs approached the $1,500,000 mark.

McCartney was not happy with the title of "student recruit" for trainees, just as he failed to see anything significant about the "Pennsylvania State Police Training School." In a companion move to change the name to "Pennsylvania State Police Academy," which he had already secured from the legislature, he sought Executive Board approval to change "student recruit" to "cadet." Executive Board Amendment 45, dated May 4, 1960, granted McCartney authorization to make the title change. So, "Academy" and "cadet" went hand-in-hand then just as they continue in use to this day.

In a three-way switch of positions in March, McCartney moved Major Thomas P. Cahalan from the Traffic Bureau to District 2—Kime went to the Traffic Bureau—and Major Frank L. Garnow was transferred from District 2 to field commander, Kime's former position.

McCartney, an old trick-rider of rodeo fame, knew of abuses, financial and social, that were part of the rodeo team life-style. Disturbing him, too, was the accountability of rodeo fund solicitations, or rather the lack of it. He was determined to remedy both conditions. He began by first appointing a new Academy superintendent who shared his views on rodeo reforms. This he did by promoting Captain Hilding C. Johnson to major and sending him to the new facility at Hershey. His second move was to have rodeo funds audited, and to set up a system of accountability for rodeo solitications—a system that was designed by Fiscal Officer Shaffer. Unhappily, the audit disclosed one incident of impropriety that lead to the resignation of a troop clerk. Needless to report, those watchdog measures led to some favorable and lasting benefits for the pension fund and improved quality of rodeo presentations.

Shortly after the move into the new Academy, McCartney summoned all district and troop commanders to Hershey for a conference. This was an innovation, and one district commander commented that in his long career, this was the first time that he had ever met jointly with his field command colleagues. This was the first in a series of meetings at the Academy to coordinate field operations by face-to-face discussions with those who shared line responsibility. Also attending the conferences were key staff officers who were available for consultation on program policies. The reaction from field commanders to this new relationship between line and staff was most favorable.

The retirement of Captain Elmer Faber left the department without a public relations officer. Faber had been agency publicist for a quarter of a century. Lacking an officer with credentials for this special field, McCartney turned to the governor's office for approval to employ a professional newsman. Upon approval and with the assistance of Richard Haratine, the governor's press secretary, the new public relations post went to Anthony R. Canniff. Canniff, a native of Philadelphia and a card-carrying reporter, was an ex-Marine and a graduate of Drexel Institute.

McCartney felt that major news items could be better handled through headquarters now that he had Canniff's talents to depend on. Confident of this possibility, he issued a special order setting up guidelines for a new public information program. Unexpectedly, the reaction from the news media was critical. News media leaders charged McCartney with trying to manage the news and delaying the free flow of information. McCartney responded by meeting with news reporters, and with newspaper, television and radio editors, and explaining his position in that sensitive issue. Certain compromises were agreed upon by all concerned and tempers cooled. Canniff, supported by a competent secretary, Betty J. Orlando, of Curwensville, established a public relations program worthy of the nation's leading state police organization.

Earlier in his adminstration, McCartney had made no secret of his intentions to have the detective division reactivated. He petitioned the Executive Board for its approval of his plans for the division. The board, in May, 1960 gave him the green light to proceed. With the approval came a salary scale for the new detective series. Each troop would have a detective sergeant and two detectives and the division would be headed by a detective captain and detective lieutenant.

Selected by McCartney to head the division was Captain George M. Sauer. Assisting him was newly-promoted Lieutenant W. J. Stanton. The selection of field assignments was accomplished through recommendations from district and troop commanders with special consideration for those who previously held the rank of detective deservingly. A screening board of officers was responsible for final selections. With a full complement of fifty-five of the department's top investigators, the detective division began operations on July 28, 1960.

McCartney argued that all non-commissioned ranks vacated as a result of detective reclassifications should be retained in the complement and filled. The governor's office bought his argument thus allowing line personnel additional opportunities for advancement.

Expenditures for the biennial period ending May 30, 1960, totalled $31,284,857.10. Passing through the exam points were 776,667 driver applicants. At the request of the Revenue Department, 10,137 special exams were administered. Traffic patrols arrested 302,883 violators, and criminal arrests numbered 35,550. The State Police patrol fleet covered 68,607,101 miles. A total of 2,109 stolen motor vehicles were recovered, and the value of all recovered stolen property was set at $2,993,475.00.

During the same period, construction of new buildings at Greensburg, Lewistown, Ebensburg, Pittsburgh, Mercer, Trevose,

Somerset and West Chester were completed. The pride of the force, however, was the new Academy. Credit for this remarkable capital expenditures program, of course, goes to Henry's administration.

The number of radio-equipped patrol vehicles was upped to 482, and the teletypewriter system was effectively improved by the installation of new instruments. At the close of the biennial period, there were 12,329 approved official inspection stations in the state closely supervised by State Police inspection station supervisors.

In his biennial report to Lawrence, McCartney referred to the death of two troopers in the line of duty with these comments,

> To this sad note might be mentioned the many Troopers who have been injured, some seriously, in the pursuit of duty during this period as well as in previous periods. It is believed that this risk of life and limb, the long dedicated hours of work, the sacrifice of the pleasures of home and family life, the foregoing of holidays are also worthy of mention, if the true story of the Pennsylvania State Police is to be told. In recognition of this valor and unselfish service, the Commissioner has increased official notice of such deeds which deserve citation and commendation.

Encouraging his field commanders to bring to his attention outstanding deeds of troopers, McCartney launched a program of awards. Critics thought that he was too free with his citations and letters of commendation. It is doubtful, however, that the recipients of the pats on the back from the "boss" shared that view. Mark Twain once said, "I can live for two months on a good compliment." Believing in the wisdom of those words, McCartney was quick to recognize the achievements of his men and to compliment them.

The most newsworthy event opening the new biennial period was the dedication of the new Academy on June 13, 1960. Dedicating the new facility before a capacity audience was Governor Lawrence. In his dedicatory address, Lawrence pledged the use of the new Academy for local police training. That was a commitment McCartney was to seriously follow up in the years ahead. The Academy was designed to accommodate a class of 100 cadets. In attendance at the dedication ceremonies were comissioners of eight state police agencies: New York, New Jersey, Maryland, Vermont, Massachusetts, Ohio, Rhode Island and West Virginia. In addition to Lawrence's principal address, remarks were offered by John B. Sollenberger, Hershey Estates president, GSA Executive Director A. J. Caruso, FOP State President John Harrington and Chief Walter Weir, president of the Pennsylvania

McCartney family at Academy dedication ceremony, 1960. Left to right: Patricia Ann, Col. McCartney, Thomas, Mrs. McCartney, Frank, Eleanore Marie, Mary Margaret. (Courtesy of Pennsylvania State Police)

Col. McCartney and Gov. David L. Lawrence at Academy dedication ceremony, 1960 (Courtesy of Pennsylvania State Polic

Chiefs of Police Association. Music was provided by the State Correctional Institution band from White Hill.

The dedication was, indeed, a prideful moment for McCartney. On that subject, Saul Kohler wrote:

> Col. Frank G. McCartney, the Commissioner of State Police, looks upon the Academy much as a father does upon his child. There is a genuine love for the program and an affection for the men enrolled. But there also is the desire to make the cadets the toughest, fairest and finest police officers anywhere.
>
> Thus, the Academy's goal is more than to turn a man into a cop. Instead, the faculty and officers strive to make a cadet qualified and proud to be a Trooper in the Pennsylvania State Police.

First to graduate from the new Academy was a 62-man cadet class on June 29, 1960. Each new trooper received his diploma from Govenor Lawrence.

On August 5, 1960, after a two-year holiday, death struck again. Trooper Francis M. Tessitore of Troop B-2 (Turnpike) was killed instantly as he was arresting a speeding motorist. He was hit by a teenage truck driver who had fallen asleep.

McCartney demonstrated his desire for a better working relationship with the FOP by instituting a grievance procedure for airing problems arising in the field. Basically, the procedure involved the appointment of one FOP representative in each district through whom grievances would be presented to the commissioner. Although this procedure was an appeasement to the rank and file, there was subdued unhappiness on the part of some commanders who felt that McCartney's move would undermine their authority. Others quietly thought he was yielding too much to the FOP. The procedure was joyfully accepted by the FOP lodges—and it worked, but not without problems.

Although some of McCartney's manifold achievements were publicly noticed, perhaps one of his greatest was quietly introduced and was to become one of inestimable administrative value. Through the long history of the State Police, top administrators had issued innumerable general orders, special orders, memorandums, bulletins, and a hodge-podge of other advisory instruments. Previous department heads had attempted to update those documents and index them. Those attempts, however, bore only modest results which were soon undone by a continuing flow of poorly monitored and classified directives. Line and staff supervisors were extremely handicapped by their inability to swiftly refer to directives having application to given situations.

McCartney felt that the job should be done at any cost once and for all. He directed Lieutenant John I. Grosnick and the Academy staff to review every directive on file, to cull useless ones, and separate those with value into temporary and permanent categories. From this time-consuming effort came volumes of departmental regulations sequentially identifying the directives with permanent or long-lasting value, accompanied by a cross-file master index. Short-life directives were grouped into special orders sequentially numbered by calendar year, and documents conveying solely information of temporary importance were grouped into memorandums which were also sequentially numbered by calendar year. Personnel orders revealing personnel transactions of any kind were similarly identified. A clearing house was established for all headquarters-issued documents to make certain that each was properly identified and the index updated. That achievement was highly acclaimed by field supervisors. Future commissioners were to improve upon McCartney's directive system, but to him goes credit for not permitting the project to go half-done.

To improve the quality of the patrol vehicle and provide maximum safety to operating troopers, McCartney ordered a change in specifications. Included were safety belts, padded dashboards and sun-visors, highway hazard flashers, and high-speed tires. All vehicles, new and old, were equipped with the dome "bubble" beacon light. Also introduced for the first time to add a measure of safety to winter driving were snow tires. The latter innovation eliminated time lost with bothersome skid chains.

Troopers, active and retired, were saddened by the death of former Deputy Commissioner Lt. Colonel Jacob C. Mauk, on November 19, 1960, after a brief illness, at 67. He was highly respected by all who worked with him and knew him during his thirty-eight years of State Police service. McCartney ordered an honor guard at Mauk's viewing and internment. He was buried on November 22, in a St. Mary's Cemetery grave, at Patton, Cambria County. Surviving him was his widow, Carrie Short Mauk.

In the midst of a blinding snowstorm, McCartney abandoned the comforts of his plush office to personally head the State Police delegation to Washington for President John F. Kennedy's inaugural parade in January, 1961. Wrapped in winter garb, the colorful mounted detail took its place in the parade. McCartney, a former rodeo rider, proudly led the Pennsylvania colors past the President's reviewing stand.

Col. McCartney heads Pennsylvania State Police mounted detail for President John F. Kennedy's inaugural parade (Courtesy of Pennsylvania State Police)

In the wake of Major Garnow's compulsory retirement in December, 1960, McCartney decided to abolish the position of field commander, no longer clinging to the value of that position. In its place, he created Sub-District 2, at Montoursville. He gave that command to Captain Paul V. Ryan, promoting him to major in January, 1961. In reality, that move divided the field into six districts.

Major Cahalan, too, left state service in December, 1960, to become executive vice president of the Pennsylvania Bus Association. Replacing Cahalan as District 2 commander was Captain W. M. Smith who was promoted to major.

In January, 1961, the general assembly convened, with the Democrats in control of the House by a 109–101 margin and an even split with the Republicans in the Senate with 25 seats for each party. It was the first time in legislative history that the Democrats ever matched numbers with the GOP in the Senate chamber. With the Harrisburg byways again crowded with legislators, McCartney took up his tireless role of lobbyist for his programs. He wanted radar, more troopers, liability insurance for his men, and a host of other benefits—

many of which the legislators gave him before adjourning in September.

McCartney's one-man battle to secure radar was matched only by Senator George N. Wade (R-Cumberland) who was just as determined to block the legalization of radar. In 1957, the House had passed a bill authorizing the use of radar. Wade saw that the measure got nowhere in the Senate; for that he drew heavy fire from Governor Leader. In a *Harrisburg Evening News* story, Leader accused Wade of "sentencing hundreds of citizens to death." The story also stated "Leader so far has lived up to a promise to send Wade weekly reports of highway fatalities in Pennsylvania."

In July, 1960, McCartney insituted an educational program to acquaint the driving public with radar. In less than a year, more than 25,000 motorists were warned for speeding. Radar demonstrations were conducted for the benefit of legislators and judges. Nothing was left undone to campaign for radar, and McCartney's victory was at last in sight. The general assembly, on April 28, 1961, passed act 48, P.L. 108, amending the Vehicle Code to authorize the use of radar by State Police troopers.

Also passed were: Act 336, P.L. 653, July 14, basing retirement on average compensation of highest five years; Act 356, P.L. 820, July 20, providing public liability insurance coverage while performing duties; Act 430, P.L. 965, August 7, authorizing the Department of Property and Supplies to purchase radio communications system from the Bell Telephone Company; Act 444, P.L. 995, August 18, increasing the State Police complement to 2,100 officers and men (previously set at 1,900), and Act 593, P.L. 1341, September 15, clarifying provisions for disability retirement.

Just as the passage of the radar legislation was a tribute to McCartney's personal lobbying, so was the increase in State Police manpower. McCartney was determined to see both measures passed, and the legislators, happily for him, saw fit to reward his labors.

Early in the year, McCartney had liberalized regulations governing the payment of moving household furnishings for enlisted personnel transferred in the line of duty, and deservingly upgraded all supervisory troop clerks to the Clerk V level. He increased the ratio of non-commissioned ranks to the total complement of troopers to improve field supervision and, in so doing, jump up the chances for promotions.

Of paramount importance to the success of the detective division was the need for an updated crime laboratory. McCartney spared no expenses to equip the lab at Harrisburg with the latest in sophisticated instruments: more than $100,000 went into this renovation effort. Staff members underwent special training by instrument suppliers. Civilian chemists were hired, and the ballistics and questioned document units also enjoyed expanded complements. McCartney officially designated Lieutenant Nevin as the first lab director. This move relieved the detective division of operational control of the lab. Nevin was later promoted to captain. An attractive information bulletin, in color, was prepared and distributed to all police agencies in Pennsylvania, describing the technical lab services available to them, and urging them to freely draw on those services. In a feature article, Saul Kohler wrote, " 'This man (McCartney) has done more for us in two years than his predecessors did in 20,' a veteran State Police officer declared."

The consolidation of substations in some counties, a problem that bothered other commissioners, bothered McCartney. He succeeded in merging the Towanda and Sayre substations at Towanda, improving services for Bradford County. McCartney attempted to consolidate the three substations in Monroe County, but failed for the first time to get needed support from Governor Lawrence. Detailed arguments in behalf of the merger were flawlessly presented, but pressure from politicians and the Pocono Mountains resort owners was sufficient to stay Lawrence's approval, and the project was dropped for the rest of his administration.

During the Leader administration, the UNIVAC computer center was established for the central processing of agency payrolls among other important programs. The State Police continued to prepare its own payroll, and resisted UNIVAC because its managers refused to take on payroll deductions for the State Police Civic Association (the independent pension fund). After continuing conferences, UNIVAC personnel finally agreed to State Police demands.

In May, Major Smith retired to enter private business, leaving a vacancy at District 2. Smith's vacancy was filled by the promotion of Captain Ralph D. Gardner. Gardner's vacated post as BCI director went to Lieutenant Benjamin K. Lee who was promoted to captain. Also leaving state service to accept a position in private business was Captain Lawrence Priar, state fire marshal. Priar's vacated position as head of the Fire Bureau was filled by the promotion of Lieutenant Jackson Sacriste to captain.

At mid-year, the State Police was to learn of the death of another former commissiner, Percy W. Foote, at 81. Retired Admiral Foote died on June 23, 1961, at Charlotte, North Carolina, following a long illness. His commendable State Police services of nineteen months terminated in January, 1939. Foote was recalled to naval duty in 1942, shortly after the United States entered World War II, and remained on active duty until 1946. Surviving Foote were his widow, Genevieve Clary Foote, a son, Thomas, and Diane, a daughter.

In June, 1961, President Kennedy signed legislation setting aside a week in May, annually, as Peace Officers' Memorial Week, beginning in 1962. Kennedy's action ended a three-year campaign by Charles Sussman, a "tenacious" south Philadelphia butcher, to have recognition extended to municipal, state and federal law enforcement officers who were killed or disabled in the line of duty. Sussman had served as a Philadelphia police reservist for three years.

In June, 1961, the U. S. Supreme Court, then popularly referred to as the Warren Court, ruled 5–4 in the *Map* v. *Ohio* case that illegally seized evidence must be excluded from use in state criminal trials. That ruling was the first of many others to be handed down by the liberal Warren Court significantly affecting police procedures. Police were highly critical of these liberal rulings, condemning the court for being overly protective of the accused and less concerned with the question of guilt or innocence. In 1976, the U. S. Supreme Court under Chief Justice Warren Burger, with a more conservative approach to a mounting crime problem, saw the use of seized evidence in a different light than did the Warren Court.

The legislators, during the Lawrence administration, made extraordinary progress in taking over the capitol for themselves. At their urging, Lawrence moved some agencies out of the capitol into other quarters. In a major step to empty the capitol for the general assembly, Lawrence and the legislators approved the construction of another state office building at Commonwealth and Forster Streets, Harrisburg, to house the Highway Department, Revenue Department, Pennsylvania State Police, and some smaller agencies. McCartney's staff personnel worked closely with OA to ensure adequate quarters for State Police headquarters units which were then scattered throughout the capitol north wing basement, third and fifth floors, and the South Office building. State Police top officials were looking forward to the consolidation of these units under more ideal circumstances. The new building, however, was not completed until 1967 (the interim story will be taken up in due time).

Following the reconstitution of the detective division, there surfaced some concern for the disclosure of informers' identities and other confidential data when complete investigation records were supplied to the district attorneys preparatory to trial. To protect this confidential information, only data essential to prosecution was transmitted to the district attorneys. Forms revision met a storm of protest from the District Attorneys Association at an annual state meeting on July 14, 1961, at Wernersville. The association appointed a committee to look into the charges that McCartney's administrative policies were causing a breakdown in the cooperative relationship between the State Police and the district attorneys.

The committee headed by Herbert J. Johnson, Jr., Erie County prosecutor, met with McCartney on October 19. Serving with Johnson were Frederick Brubacker, Berks County, association president; Paul W. Reeder, Lycoming County; Stephen A. Teller, Luzerne County, and Martin Lock, Dauphin County. The meeting accomplished nothing of real importance. McCartney heard the committee's complaint and promised to discuss the matter with Attorney General David Stahl before calling another meeting with the district attorneys. The prosecutors, overwhelmingly Republican, gave McCartney a bad time. Another meeting was held in November, and satisfactory adjustments in the handling of transmittal data were made to bring about "complete accord."

On September 1, 1961, with all state highways legally posted, the State Police equipped with thirty-two radar sets officially launched a

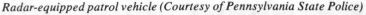

Radar-equipped patrol vehicle (Courtesy of Pennsylvania State Police)

new attack upon speeders. Prior to the start of this program, 330 troopers underwent special training at the Academy: they were instructed in the use of radar, and were provided with strict guidelines to observe. Die-hards in the legislature were forever trying to find fault with radar, and attempts were made unsuccessfully to have the new weapon in the State Police arsenal declared illegal.

McCartney never lost sight of his desire to upgrade the effectiveness of municipal police outside of Philadelphia and Pittsburgh where excellent training programs were on-going. The shortening of the cadet training program to five months allowed for two cadet classes a year at the Academy. During the remaining two months, Academy resources were devoted to a 100-man municipal police class. But that was not enough to suit McCartney, considering the thousands of local police to be reached. He ordered the Academy staff and field commanders to organize municipal police classes in every troop. A forty-hour program was designed to accommodate the local officer in his own backyard where training efforts would not take him away from regular work schedules. The M-40 program, as it came to be known, saw a tremendous acceleration in training. During the first six months of 1962, for example, 1,257 local policemen received training certificates. McCartney was farsighted enough to view universal training of police officers as an essential need—a view that was to be shared by the Pennsylvania Chiefs of Police Association. Mandatory training was still a decade away.

Another death was recorded on October 3, 1961, as motor vehicle accidents continued to take their toll. Killed in the line of duty was Trooper Anthony Bensch of Troop A-3, Hazleton, when a car in which he was a passenger skidded off the highway and struck a tree.

On the lighter side, McCartney sanctioned the formation of the State Police Golf Association, fully convinced that the sport contributed to the morale and physical well-being of his troopers. He had taken up golfing during his tenure as commissioner, and looked forward to an occasional weekend round of golf with friends back home.

Columbus Day, a national holiday, found the State Police capitol offices closed except for Personnel. At work, Director Klinger received a phone call from Deputy Commissioner Hartman asking him to prepare a brief, one-sentence resignation for him, which he would sign as soon as he could arrive at Klinger's office. Klinger reached McCartney at Philadelphia, and gave him the news. Klinger described McCartney as "shocked," and at McCartney's bidding notified Major Kime, the senior officer in the Harrisburg area. Hartman, arriving at the capitol, signed his resignation and left Klinger's office without offering an explanation for his actions. McCartney was hard put to account for Hartman's unprecedented move without explanation or discussing with him the seriousness of his decision to leave beforehand. Repeated attempts by the commissioner to reach Hartman were fruitless.

Rumors of the deputy's resignation reached the press. Hartman refused to talk to reporters or comment publicly on his reasons for leaving his $13,500 a year post. Supposedly, the underlying causes were a serious disagreement with McCartney on policy and McCartney's failure to delegate Hartman authority befitting his status as deputy.

The relationship between McCartney and Hartman was never a warm one. McCartney, anxious to move with many programs, burdened Hartman perhaps moreso than most deputies experienced in the past. Whether he acted out of loyalty to the department or a sense of gratitude to McCartney for his appointment as deputy in the first place, Hartman refused to discredit his former boss or Lawrence. Quiet reconciliation appeals by McCartney and Walter W. Geisey, Lawrence's adminstrative right-arm continued. Hartman was offered his job back and urged to accept—but he declined.

McCartney and Lawrence were well aware of the political developments that could follow this incident—and did. Before the month was out, Republican State Chairman George I. Bloom was screaming for McCartney's ouster in typical out-party fashion, and threatened to have a legislative investigation of the State Police force if Lawrence did not see things his way. Bloom blamed Hartman's departure on disagreements between the deputy and Lieutenant Philip M. Conti, McCartney's administrative officer. Although this barrage of political shouting lasted but a short time, the whole issue was again raised during the following year's gubernatorial campaign.

The problem that confronted McCartney at the outset of his administration—the appointment of his own deputy—was again staring him in the face. Unhappy about that situation, McCartney took no immediate action to name Hartman's replacement. Instead, he called on Kime to sit at the deputy's desk and keep the office going without official label. Six months went by before a deputy commissioner was sworn into office.

Following a three-county pilot program in Bucks, Northampton and Lehigh counties using chemical testing for intoxicated vehicle operators, the State Police, on December 1, 1961, set out on a statewide enforcement effort. Intoxication arrest figures jumped 74 percent in six months, with an overall conviction rate above 90 percent. Receiving instructions in the use of the intoximeter were 2,186 troopers—almost the entire field force. Pending the receipt of their own testing equipment, local police were supported by State Police with both testing facilities and training.

Before the year's end, the State Police had entered into the modern age of electronic data processing (EDP). Card-punching and the processing of arrest reports and statistics became a new way of life at headquarters. Trained earlier at the International Business Machine Corporation's home office at Endicott, New York, were Captain George W. Pinkerton, Lieutenant Philip M. Conti and Sergeant James R. O'Donnell. Charge of EDP operations soon rested with O'Donnell, who underwent continuing instructions as a specialist in this new administrative field.

During Henry's administration, a federal court order made it necessary for the Bell Telephone Company of Pennsylvania to get out of the radio business. The Bell Company for years had maintained a leased radio system for the State Police. The court order permitted a five-year time frame within which Bell was to act. Henry's adminstration came to a close before he could develop a State Police position on this issue.

The State Police was faced with the decision to purchase the system from Bell or look to a qualified leasor. Since the Bell system was antiquated and unworthy of acquisition, in the view of State Police officials, a search for a new leasor was recommended by McCartney. For some reason, OA decided the issue in favor of buying the old Bell system despite the wishes of the State Police communications experts who could foresee nothing but troubles by going that route. Lawrence's administrative aides sought legislative approval of the purchase—and secured it. That action displeased the State Police no end, and feelings were considerably aggravated by the purchase price which was set far above what State Police authorities valued the system. By contrast, it is believed that the scene at Bell headquarters was a happier one.

Having acquired the system, Captain Robert L. Bomboy, State Police communications officer, was given the difficult and disagreeable task of renovating a run-down conglomeration of mobile and stationary equipment, and adding to the state payroll sufficient skilled technicians to do the job. The State Police struggled for years to divest itself of the system's ownership and its inherent problems. Bomboy was then looking at double trouble, since he was also engaged in updating the teletype system to keep abreast of the advancing state of the art; the State Police teletype network needed expansion and automatic switching.

McCartney had already experienced a roadblock by OA staffers when he attempted to secure a small computer to extend data processing programs to include other areas of deep interest to law enforcement; OA was intent on stemming the rush by administrative agencies to enter the computer age. Bomboy's plans for updating the teletype system called for a computer-based operation. To disclose that fact prematurely would only put an end to his plans at the outset. So, he identified the main unit as a "solid state switcher" rather than a "computer." Bomboy's proposal was funded; the new system, a leased General Electric Datanet 30, was on its way. Delivery would not be made until after McCartney's adminstration ended, so the story of Bomboy's solid state switcher will have to await the arrival of McCartney's successor.

For a number of years, the FOP had lobbied for tenure legislation. The organization wanted dismissal, demotion or reduction in pay to come only by way of court-martial proceedings. Although such transactions were never carelessly ordered by any commissioner, job insurance was uppermost on the FOP shopping list. McCartney however, was not convinced that this was the best way for the FOP to handle this matter. He felt that the stigma of court-martial and any court-recommended actions would prove detrimental to dismissed personnel in seeking employment elsewhere. He, nonetheless, was anxious to alleviate FOP concern about summary dismissals and denials of reenlistment, and convince the FOP of his good intentions.

When McCartney entered office, it was the longstanding practice to issue a discharge certificate at the end of each two-year enlistment period. The signing of reenlistment papers accompanied this action, except in rare cases. These procedures not only presented anxious moments for the rank and file, but were also tedious, boring chores for troop clerks. McCartney ordered a halt to such proceedings. A new impressive discharge document, printed on premium bond, was put into use and issued only when a trooper finally separated from the service under honorable circumstances. Gone was the reenlistment document; instead, a trooper's original enlistment papers carried the assurance of continued service so long as his services were not marred by serious wrongdoing. McCartney's changes simplified paperwork considerably, and went a long way toward relieving anxiety. Nevertheless, the FOP persistently pressed for passage of tenure legislation as a more suitable procedure, and the differing views drew fire from the FOP and heated up McCartney's final year in office.

Ever since the merger in 1937, the State Police compensation plan called for the payment of a salary plus an additional daily allowance for subsistence. The salary was paid biweekly, subsistence monthly. The

PENNSYLVANIA STATE POLICE
BUREAU OF DETECTIVES
1962

DET. LT. WILLARD J. STANTON

DET. CAPT. GEORGE M. SAUER

DET. LT. NORMAN P. McFADDEN

DET. SGT. LODWICK D. JENKINS

DET. SGT. ARTHUR SHULENBERGER

DET. SGT. ROBERT McCARTNEY

DET. SGT. ROY O. WELLENDORF   DET. SGT. RUFUS G. WILLIAMS   DET. JOSEPH P. SCHLINGMAN   DET. CHARLES HARBAUGH

DET. GEORGE W. COLLITT

DET. LEWIS R. KISHBAUGH

DET. ARTHUR R. CRONIN

Detective Division, 1962 (Courtesy of Pennsylvania State Police)

payment of subsistence, according to the U. S. Internal Revenue
Service, enjoyed non-taxable status for so long as quarters and meals
were provided to most of the men. In the five years or so preceding
McCartney's years, however, more and more men married and lived

away from the barracks. Dining rooms and kitchens were closed by Leader's administration, bedrooms were turned into offices, and a whole new way of life was being experienced by enlisted men. Analyzing these changes were the watchdogs from IRS. Since the subsistence was nothing more, in their view, than a tax-free income, it was to be taxed as salary. Many conferences were held with IRS officials locally and at Philadelphia to resolve the issue. It was agreed that subsistence would be taxed on a partial basis. The agreement created a bookkeeping headache for State Police adminstrators, and was destined to be further shot down by IRS.

McCartney felt that subsistence, if it was to be taxed, should carry benefits for the trooper insofar as retirement credit was concerned. To this end, he instructed his fiscal officer to draw up plans combining 'salary and subsistence for top level approval. The plans, additionally, were to call for other important adjustments—more frequent increments and longevity considerations. Such plans, however, were long in clearing through bureaucratic red-tape, and did not see light of day until after McCartney left office.

McCartney was also giving serious thought to lifting the entrance requirement that applicants be unmarried. He felt the time had come when discrimination should cease and, at the same time, broaden the recruitment base.

McCartney, during his term of office, encouraged recruiting among blacks. Although few in number, blacks did graduate from the Academy and join the rank of troopers. John A. Bedford, the department's second black trooper, was enlisted May 13, 1959, and resigned November 16, 1960. Benjamin F. Brooks and Richard McDowell, both black, enlisted September 7, 1961, and have become veteran "staties."

Also employed during McCartney's years were female police communications officers (PCOs). Women qualifying were assigned to posts at troop headquarters to relieve enlisted personnel tied down to desk jobs, who were then reassigned to more pressing police duties. As years wore on, State Police commissioners have given much thought to extending this policy to other operational areas to pick up enlisted positions so sorely needed for line duty.

In February, 1962, Captain Klinger retired. His vacancy in the Personnel office was filled by the transfer of Captain R. O. Parsons to headquarters.

McCartney worked closely with the Department of Revenue to produce a fifteen-minute color film entitled, *Pennsylvania State Police*. Costing $7,000, the film was intended to promote traffic safety and enhance an already favorable public image of the State Police. Lieutenant Edward M. McGroarty was technical adviser to the film-makers. Revenue purchased five additional prints at $100 each to facilitate the showing of the film in each district.

The last of three deaths in the line of duty to occur during Mc-Cartney's tenure was recorded on March 18, 1962. Sergeant Edward W. Gundel of Troop C-4, Reading, was cut down by shotgun fire as he was aiding the Pine Grove chief of police in the arrest of a local resident wanted on an assault and battery charge.

To assist the fiscal officer with ever-mounting chores, McCartney brought to headquarters the chief clerk from the Dunmore barracks, Robert J. Zinsky. Zinsky, a graduate of Philadelphia's Girard College and a ten-year office veteran at Dunmore, was one of three talented chief clerks to see their way to headquarters by way of deserving pro-

Lt. Colonel George M. Sauer (Courtesy of Pennsylvania State Police)

motion. A native of Olyphant, Lackawanna County, Zinsky also attended the University of Scranton.

On April 2, 1962, Elmo Smith was the last of 349 persons to die in the electric chair at Rockview Penitentiary. Frank McCoy preceded Smith on January 29. The constitutional question of capital punishment was vigorously pursued, and executions in many states were legislatively abolished.

After six months of managing without a deputy, McCartney put an end to procrastination. He had been more than pleased with the achievements of his chief of detectives, Captain George M. Sauer, and gave the deputy post to him. Sauer was sworn into office on April 13, 1962. Administering the oath in the governor's reception room was Sauer's longtime friend, Judge J. Sydney Hoffman, of the Philadelphia Juvenile Court. His wife Edith and a brother, Sergeant Carl J. Sauer, of the Bethlehem barracks, looked on as Sauer took his oath of office.

Sauer, a native of Philadelphia, was born March 28, 1903. He enlisted with the constabulary on January 1, 1929, at 25, and was assigned to the Reading troop. Oddly enough, he and Hartman were classmates at the training school. At the time of enlistment, Sauer, a former carpenter, was a resident of Conshohocken. He saw duty at Manheim, Shamokin, Doylestown and Coatesville. At Manheim, he met Edith M. Nissley whom he eventually married.

Sauer was appointed a detective at Philadelphia in 1941, and promoted to detective lieutenant in 1954. McCartney advanced him to captain in January, 1960, and gave him command of his home troop at Reading. Searching for a competent officer to head his reactivated detective division, McCartney asked Sauer to give up his post at Reading and take the headquarters assignment. Sauer agreed and helped shape the new division.

Sauer, then 59, faced compulsory retirement in March, 1963. His appointment as deputy, however, exempted him from such retirement for as long as he remained deputy. Sauer opted not to remain, as it will be seen.

In August, 1962, McCartney promoted Lieutenant W. J. Stanton to captain and head of the detective division, replacing Sauer. Stanton had served as Sauer's assistant ever since the division's reactivation.

During the year, the State Police built up its inventory of anti-riot equipment and supplies. Civil disorders were on the upswing, and a bitter lesson was learned at the University of Mississippi where ill-equipped police officers were handicapped in handling rioting on that campus. Authorities in Pennsylvania were determined that the State Police would not be lacking in ability to maintain the peace in the event disorders spread to Pennsylvania cities and campuses. McCartney's successor carried this preparedness to new limits as disorders became more a part of racial strife throughout this nation.

On April 26, 1962, McCartney received news of the death of another State Police great—Major Thomas F. Martin, at 71. Martin retired in 1957 after a brilliant career spanning forty-two years. He was buried in the Hershey Cemetery. Surviving were his widow, Marie Martin, and a daughter, Mrs. Vivian Memmi.

In May, 1962, in observance of the nation's first annual Peace Officers' Week, McCartney ordered a public ceremony to be held at Fisher's Plaza to the rear of the capitol. The ceremony was scheduled for noon to allow capitol hill employees to witness the State Police honor its members who died in the line of duty. A large detachment of troopers from the Harrisburg and Lancaster areas made an impressive sight as they marched with military precision to the plaza and stood at attention as Deputy Commissioner Sauer solemnly announced the names of the sixty-eight fallen troopers. A firing squad and taps added to the brief, emotion-packed ceremony viewed by a throng of spectators. Capitol flags were flown at half-mast.

In his biennial report to Lawrence, McCartney noted that State Police expenditures for the period ending June 30, 1962, amounted to $37,620,098.61. This period covered twenty-five months instead of twenty-four as a result of Act 1, approved June 1, 1961, changing the former biennial fiscal period to an annual period to bring the state into step with the federal government.

Radar and the use of plainclothes patrols were among the tactics used to reduce highway fatalities by 255 deaths from the previous biennial period. Administered were 675,734 driver examinations, and 548,570 visual re-examinations under Lawrence's thirteen-point traffic safety program. Garage inspectors supervised 13,049 official inspection stations—some 700 more than the 1958-1960 period. There were 379,409 traffic arrests with the conviction rate still running high at 97 percent. Speeding accounted for 171,126 arrests. Total patrol mileage jumped to 76,223,058 miles.

Additional technicians were assigned to the crime lab, and the polygraph program was expanded to four field examiners who were home-based at Blakely (Dunmore), Greensburg, Lancaster and Washington. A twenty-year graph compared growth in the number of criminal fingerprints processed by the BCI annually from 42,187 in 1942 to 79,106 in 1962. A total of 2,296 stolen motor vehicles were recovered, and the total value of all recovered stolen property was estimated at $3,084,779. There were 38,352 criminal arrests. Burglary, disorderly conduct and larceny dominated the field. Juvenile offenses, including malicious mischief, were markedly on the rise.

In July, 1962, the activities of the Fifty-fourth Annual Governors' Conference dominated the scenes at Hershey and Harrisburg for five days. A 250-man trooper detail, operating a 150-car pool, was summoned to provide security and give VIP-treatment to visiting state executives. Sixty new Cadillacs were shipped in from the General Motors Detroit plant to give the governors plush accommodations. Tours took the governors to York, Gettysburg and Philadelphia. The State Police also scheduled a rodeo performance in the Hershey stadium for their entertainment. The gathering of so many troopers for this special occasion during the Fourth of July holiday time provoked some critical comments from the press. This was the first Governors' Conference to be held in Pennsylvania in two decades. (Bicentennial year 1976 was to see another in Pennsylvania hosted by Governor Milton J. Shapp.)

By mid-year, the 1962 gubernatorial election campaign was heating up as Congressman William Scranton, the GOP candidate, wrestled with Democrat Richardson Dilworth, ex-mayor of Philadelphia. In unprecedented fashion, the Republican campaigners targeted McCartney and made the State Police an unreasonable issue. The scabs were knocked off old sores with a vengeance. To these was added another incident when Major Pezzent and Captain Lawrence Sapudar locked horns over duty responsibilities. Having been previously rebuked by McCartney for the unreasonable transferring of troop personnel, Sapudar quit in a huff in June, bitterly denouncing McCartney.

The Republicans were swift to play up Sapudar's attack. On that issue, the *Allentown Chronicle* had this to say editorially on June 30, 1962:

> Because he (McCartney) was appointed by Gov. David L. Lawrence he is regarded as fair game for political attack, as demonstrated from time to time by such worthies as George Bloom, state Republican chairman.
>
> Politics was not mentioned in the Sapudar attack on McCartney. But we have wondered ever since it came whether the retired captain might have said and done what he did with the idea it might put him in a favorable light when and if the Republicans have reason to cast about for a new commissioner after the November election.
>
> And then we have asked ourselves whether he might have been induced by someone in the Republican party to let loose his blast with a hint or a promise of consideration for the commissionership if Scranton beats Dilworth.

Later in the campaign, Sapudar's name was linked with others aspiring to succeed McCartney.

Managing the Scranton campaign was attorney Walter E. Alessandroni. McCartney recalled that at one time he and Alessandroni had seriously argued about the prosecution of a well-known racketeer in the Reading area. Alessandroni was then serving in the U. S. Attorney's Office in Philadelphia. McCartney, certain that the Republican campaign strategy of singling him out as an issue was no mere coincidence, earnestly believed that Alessandroni was, indeed, digging at old wounds; it is entirely possible that he was right.

During the campaign, Scranton appeared before a session of the FOP state convention at Erie in July in a purely political address. He tried to rationalize why "this law enforcement agency of the Commonwealth (State Police) has become important in this campaign." He promised, if elected, to sign into law tenure legislation placed on his desk by the general assembly, and made other promises as well to generally remedy the conditions he judged the troopers were suffering at the hands of the Democrats. In unprecedented action, he was dragging into the political arena the FOP which embraced the majority of the rank and file. By way of contrast, the Pennsylvania Chiefs of Police Association in convention at Pittsburgh in August unanimously passed a resolution commending the State Police for "outstanding leadership in the field of law enforcement."

Malcontents within the FOP, encouraged by the pasting McCartney was taking at the hands of the Republicans, jumped on their soap-boxes. Such conduct, however, in one case exceeded bounds and clearly violated departmental regulations governing proper demeanor. McCartney, having already established avenues for FOP grievances, was incensed by the trooper's misconduct. Findings of an investigation supported a court-martial hearing, and McCartney proceeded with such preparations. He notified the governor's office of his planned actions. Geisey, however, notified McCartney that Lawrence wanted the matter dropped. Visibly unhappy with that decision, McCartney nevertheless was obedient. Some years later, McCartney had the occasion to meet the trooper who narrowly missed facing court-martial and possible dismissal. The trooper apologized and admitted that he had been "used."

Traditionally, troopers worked six days a week, and seldom were holidays considered anything but another work day. McCartney felt that improvement could be made here to ease working conditions. He applied to the governor's executive board for authority to grant his men thirteen legal holidays each year. Authority was granted him, and effective with Labor Day, 1962, all troopers had thirteen time-off holidays coming to them. Since it was essential to maintain adequate services on holidays, it was not in the cards for all troopers to be at home. For those required to fill holiday rosters, which included most, compensatory time-off was taken later. That, again, was a first in State Police history.

In September, McCartney closely cooperated with U. S. Secret Service agents to provide adequate security for President John F. Kennedy, who was scheduled to make a four-hour visit to Harrisburg on September 20. President Kennedy was the highlight attraction at a Democratic party $100-a-plate dinner in support of the campaign. The dinner program held at the state Farm Show arena was concluded without incident. Letters, complimenting the State Police troopers and detectives, were swift to come from the White House. It was the last time President Kennedy visited the Harrisburg area: an assassin's bullets were to end his young life fourteen months later at Dallas, Texas.

Scranton soundly trounced Dilworth 2,424,918 to 1,938,627 at the November polls. The margin of victory was the largest since 1946 when Duff defeated Rice. Many Democrats believed Dilworth a poor standard-bearer, and gave him little or no chance whatsoever of keeping the Democrats in control of state government for a third time in a row. Odds-makers overwhelmingly picked Scranton to win, and it is doubtful that the McCartney and State Police campaign issues were at all needed except to satisfy Alessandroni.

Fully realizing that he was then a lame-duck cabinet officer, McCartney nonetheless held to the responsibilities of his office until the end.

On December 6, an explosion at Robena #3 mine near Carmichaels, Greene County, killed thirty-seven miners. McCartney ordered a task force to the scene. It was the worst Pennsylvania mine disaster since 1940. The following day, a freak snowfall all but buried the western half of the Pennsylvania Turnpike, stranding some 2,000 motorists from Carlisle to Irwin. McCartney again saw that State Police resources were not lacking in alleviating hardships. He personally saw to it that plans for the upcoming 1963 Farm Show and Scranton's inauguration measured up to acceptable standards. Kime was given overall command of inauguration day activities.

In November, the FOP had entered suit for the dismissal of Majors Kime and Oldham, claiming both to be 60 and past the mandatory retirement age. The Justice Department, however, stated that both men had misstated their ages at the time of their 1923 enlistments in the

State Highway Patrol, and had in recent years corrected retirement records. Kime, born February 5, 1904, was 58. Oldham, born July 16, 1903, was 59. Both careers continued without interruption. Kime and Oldham were not unique in that regard. The Personnel Office verified that many officers and enlisted men had misstated their ages and corrected them before retirement rather than act fraudulently.

In November, Major Hilding C. Johnson, 60, resigned to meet mandatory retirement requirements. McCartney filled Johnson's vacancy at the Academy by promoting Captain Paul A. Rittelmann to major.

The State Police grapevine was busy carrying stories that Scranton had promised the State Police top post to Lieutenant William B. Cooper, and Alessandroni had Pezzent in mind for the job. In December, after naming most of his cabinet members, Scranton pulled a surprise by appointing a three-man committee to help him come up with a commissioner. Grapevine constituents believed this was a way out for Scranton and Alessandroni to save face with Cooper and Pezzent. Appointed to the "Blue Ribbon Panel," as this committee was commonly referred to, were Dr. Eugene S. Farley, president of Wilkes College; Adolph W. Schmidt, president of H. W. Mellon Educational and Charitable Trust, and a member of the state planning board; and Elias Wolf, chairman of the board of Metal Edge Industries, and co-chairman of the Greater Philadelphia Movement.

State Police officers with the rank of captain and above were invited to apply for the commissioner's job. Applicants were required to submit a 300-word statement citing their qualifications. Carmen Brutto, a well-known political reporter at the capitol, humorously wrote of this procedure in his *Sunday Patriot-News* column on December 23, entitled "In 300 Words or Less, And No Box-tops Needed." Later the field of applicants was widened: applications were also accepted from non-State Police sources. Some 200 applicants found their way to the screening committee.

Appointed to handle the screening chores for the Blue Ribbon Panel were John W. Ingram, executive director of the Pennsylvania Economy League; Larry Young, of the Pennsylvania Economy League; and William Wilcox, excutive director of the Greater Philadelphia Movement. Governor Lawrence designated Conti as liaison.

During the final days of screening, Scranton called in Professor A. F. Brandstatter, of Michigan State University's police administration department, to assist with final evaluations. It was Brandstatter who introduced the name of E. Wilson Purdy, St. Petersburg, Florida, police chief, and a former student of Brandstatter's at Michigan State.

The committee contacted Purdy for biographical and experience data. Purdy, needless to say was taken unawares, and had reason to ponder the possibility of another change in his life.

The screening committee had then reduced the number of quality applicants to fourteen, and on January 11, 1963, all were interviewed. The number was further reduced to five finalists: E. Wilson Purdy, Major John Pezzent, Captain Benjamin O. Lichty, troop commander at Philadelphia; Lieutenant John I. Grosnick, and Philadelphia Police Inspector Albert H. Trimmer. All five were interviewed by Scanton that very same day.

One finalist, a State Police officer, during his interview asked Scranton why he had so forcefully dragged the State Police into the election campaign. Since the department for the first time in its long history had been subjected to such treatment, the question put to Scranton was one that bothered many State Police officers. Scranton, so the story goes, replied succinctly that there was an election to win. In other words, the end justified the means. The fact that Scranton had opened the door to repercussions apparently did not bother him. Little did he know then that the State Police would again be incised by political butchery during his term of office, and that his own appointee would not survive the bloodletting.

The fact that Scranton's final choice, and the committee's, was an outsider apparently was a point of anxiety to him, since he withheld making any immediate announcement. Perhaps insecure with the course he had taken, he did not announce Purdy's appointment until just hours before his inauguration four days later.

The following is a complete listing of officer personnel as of December 1, 1962:

Colonel Frank G. McCartney
Commissioner

Lt. Colonel George M. Sauer
Deputy Commissioner

Major Ralph D. Gardner	Commander, District 2
Major John D. Kime	Traffic Officer
Major Russel K. Knies	Commander, Sub-District 1
Major Arthur J. Oldham	Commander, District 1
Major John J. Pezzent	Commander, District 3
Major Paul A. Rittelmann	Academy Superintendent
Major Paul V. Ryan	Commander, Sub-District 2
Major Singleton Sheaffer	Commander, District 4

Captain Robert L. Bomboy	Communications Officer
Captain John Chrin	Commanding Officer, Troop A-1
Captain Abram W. Corbin	Commanding Officer, Troop D-4
Captain William R. Engle	Commanding Officer, Troop C-1
Captain William J. Garrick	Chief Quartermaster
Captain Richard D. Gray	Commanding Officer, Troop A-2
Captain John C. Grey	Commanding Officer, Troop D-2
Captain Benjamin K. Lee	Director, BCI
Captain Benjamin O. Lichty	Commanding Officer, Troop A-4
Captain Joseph F. McIlvaine	Commanding Officer, Troop A-3
Captain Frank McKetta	Assistant Academy Superintendent
Captain Ernest C. Moore	Commanding Officer, Troop B-1
Captain William L. Nevin	Director, Crime Lab
Captain Reagle O. Parsons	Personnel Officer
Captain Roger E. Pflugfelder	Commanding Officer, Troop E-1
Captain George W. Pinkerton	Assistant Traffic Officer
Captain Walter E. Price	Commanding Officer, Troop B-4
Captain Jackson E. Sacriste	Fire Marshal
Captain Vincent R. Scolere	Commanding Officer, Troop C-3
Captain Albert H. Shuller	Commanding Officer, Troop B-2
Captain George A. Sifter	Commanding Officer, Troop D-1
Captain Willard J. Stanton	Chief of Detectives
Captain Clarence F. Temke	Commanding Officer, Troop C-2
Captain Rocco P. Urella	Commanding Officer, Troop C-4
Captain John F. Yaglenski	Commanding Officer, Troop B-3
Lieutenant John W. Adams	Assistant Personnel Officer
Lieutenant John A. Aumon	Troop C-4
Lieutenant Andrew Baigis	Troop D-4
Lieutenant William I. Banzhaf	Troop A-2
Lieutenant Christian M. Bomberger	Crime Lab
Lieutenant John M. Bosak	Engineer
Lieutenant Charles J. Buchinsky	Academy
Lieutenant Frank J. Cannon	Troop A-4
Lieutenant Philip F. Chulick	Transportation Officer
Lieutenant Philip M. Conti	Administrative Officer
Lieutenant William B. Cooper	Troop A-2
Lieutenant Edward H. Crowthers	Crime Lab
Lieutenant Henry B. Daubenspeck	Troop D-2
Lieutenant Robert L. Dunham	BCI
Lieutenant Joseph Dussia	Troop E-1
Lieutenant Charles S. Graci	Fire Bureau
Lieutenant John I. Grosnick	Academy

Lieutenant Albert L. Henry	Troop A-4
Lieutenant John F. Helfenstein	Troop B-1
Lieutenant Howard M. Jaynes	Troop C-2
Lieutenant Lodwick D. Jenkins	BCI
Lieutenant Alfred H. Krull	Troop A-2
Lieutenant Adrian J. McCarr	Troop A-4
Lieutenant Norman P. McFadden	Troop C-3
Lieutenant Edward M. McGroarty	Troop B-3
Lieutenant James F. Murray	Crime Lab
Lieutenant Robert W. Musser	BCI
Lieutenant Robert A. Rice	Troop B-4
Lieutenant Louis T. Shupnik	Troop B-3
Lieutenant WIlliam J. Smith	Troop D-1
Lieutenant Joseph C. Snyder	Troop C-2
Lieutenant James A. Straub	Troop A-1
Lieutenant Peter Strickler	Crime Lab
Lieutenant John I. Swann	Troop B-2
Lieutenant Edward J. Switaj	Troop A-3
Lieutenant John E. Thompson	Academy
Lieutenant Alphonse A. Verbitski	Troop C-1
Lieutenant Rufus G. Williams	Detective Division
Lieutenant Clifford G. Yahner	Troop A-1
Lieutenant Joseph L. Young	Troop D-1

The total complement of enlisted men and officers on December 1, 1962, was 2,385. Of these, 185 were assigned to Turnpike duty.

During 1960, 1961 and 1962, statistics disclosed that Pennsylvania's death rate for the number of persons killed per 100 million vehicle miles dropped significantly to 4.0, 3.7 and 3.9, respectively. During these same three years, the national death rates were 5.3, 5.2 and 5.3, respectively. The Lawrence-McCartney team for highway safety was unmatched, and their achievements will long stand as a tribute to the two officials and those who wholeheartedly supported them in this area of public interest.

On this score, the *Allentown Morning Call*, on January 2, 1963, had these editorial comments:

> The governor's tough but fair highway safety program has been one of the major accomplishments of his administration. For a year it made Pennsylvania's highways the safest of any major state. Whatever the records may show, there is no question that it saved lives and tragedies and heartaches.
>
> Gov. Lawrence has many good reasons to look back on

his four years in Harrisburg with justifiable pride. Each of them should be a challenge to the new governor and the new Legislature to continue opening the doors through which this state can move forward.

During McCartney's four years, 457 cadets and 250 municipal police officers graduated from the Academy. Thirty-six foreign police officials from Ethiopia, Brazil, Ceylon, Philippines, Chile, Indonesia, Turkey, Tunisia, Vietnam, Taiwan, Thailand and Afghanistan underwent brief training in support of the U. S. State Department's International Cooperative Administration. More than 62,000 visitors toured the Academy. Select members of the Academy staff trained at the U. S. Naval Diving School, Washington, D. C., to provide the field with SCUBA services; bloodhounds were acquired and housed at the Academy to facilitate the work of line forces. Promoted by McCartney were some 500 non-commissioned and commissioned officers.

The main features of McCartney's capital expenditures program—troop headquarters buildings at Dunmore and Wyoming, and a quartermaster building at Harrisburg—were soon to be under construction. A troop headquarters building at Erie was in final planning.

Deputy Commissioner Sauer, who had two months earlier announced his intention to retire at the close of the Lawrence administration, left for home the day before Scranton's inauguration day.

McCartney remained aboard until inauguration day. He prided himself to his dying day that he had no scandals during his tenure. He had led the State Police through portals into a new era of management and operational techniques. Purdy, his successor, was to keep the ball rolling with significant and lasting improvements of his own. McCartney has some scrapes with the press, the district attorneys and the FOP, it is true, all of which took their toll. Yet, he eminently finished four active years in office, and at 54 left as much a man as he began. On his final day, he left his office before noon with an overcoat thrown over his arm, his head held high. Tears were clearly noticeable to those waving him a farewell. McCartney's trusted aide, Corporal Thomas S. Fellin, awaited him at the capitol's main entrance to take him home.

Retired from the State Police, McCartney went on to become a banker, and an active member of his church, Chamber of Commerce, and Mahoning Valley Country Club. He devoted much time to the Boy Scouts of America, and other youth programs. The former commissioner's capacity for public service never diminished until some ten years later when a rare and fatal illness was to lay still the stout heart of one of Pennsylvania's most prominent citizens.

CHAPTER XVII

Colonel E. Wilson Purdy

1963-1966

The 1963 session of the general assembly was called to order on January 1. Wielding the gavel in the Senate was President pro tem M. Harvey Taylor, and in the House, it was Speaker W. Stuart Helm—both Republicans. The Senate was divided 26–22, the House 108–98, giving the GOP a bit of elbow room in both chambers.

The legislators interrupted their session on January 15 to witness the inauguration of William Warren Scranton, 45, a millionaire and former congressman, as governor of the Commonwealth in ceremonies held at the state Farm Show Building. A State Police detail of some 400 troopers, under the command of Major John D. Kime, was on hand to see all the inaugural day activities carried on without incident.

Scranton submitted to the Senate a list of his cabinet nominations, all of whom had been publicly announced before inauguration day, except for E. Wilson Purdy. Purdy's appointment as State Police commissioner was not announced until three hours before Scranton's swearing in. The Senate on January 15 confirmed twelve of Scranton's cabinet members and blocked four. Numbered among the four was Purdy. The Senate claimed that Purdy's last-minute appointment did not allow time to study the Floridian's background and qualifications.

Since McCartney and Sauer had already resigned and departed from Harrisburg, the State Police agency found itself without a commander—an unprecedented situation. The newly-confirmed Attorney General Walter E. Alessandroni was directed by Scranton to immediately notify Kime that the governor was designating him acting commissioner. A governor's aide was swift to publicly make clear this was not indication that Kime would be Purdy's deputy.

Pending the outcome of Senate deliberations, Purdy remained at his post in Florida. Occasional calls were placed with Kime regarding the status of important State Police matters. Purdy asked Kime to assure everyone at headquarters that he was not coming to Harrisburg to sweep the house clean—as the "new broom"saying goes. This was comforting news at headquarters for those who were awaiting the arrival of this unknown figure—the second "outsider" to head the State Police. It will be remembered that retired Rear Admiral Percy W. Foote, an Earle appointee in 1937, was the first.

Purdy's appointment was a surprise to the State Police force—to put it mildly—since it was expected the job would go to someone from the department's ranks. Most of the officers and men, however, favored giving Purdy a chance to prove himself, and cooperating with

Major John D. Kime (Courtesy of Pennsylvania State Police)

him to that end. The FOP threw its support in behalf of Scranton's nominee and refused to block confirmation.

It took the Senate only two weeks to satisfy its curiosity. Purdy was confirmed by the Senate on January 29 with only one dissenting vote. Purdy took his oath of office in an overcrowded governor's reception room on February 7—the last member of Scranton's cabinet to be sworn in. Commonwealth Secretary George Bloom administered the oath. Scranton pinned on the new colonel's gold badge.

Referring to Scranton's unusual procedure, a prominent Harrisburg reporter, Carmen Brutto, wrote, "Pennsylvania had a contest of sorts to see who was the best qualified cop in the U. S. to become State Police commissioner, and the people who did the sifting of applicants came up with Purdy." Thus began a new State Police administration that was to see life for three years and two months, and die as unprecedently as it was born.

E. Wilson Purdy, a native of Orleans, Michigan, was born April 24, 1919. In an interview with Mike Baxter, of the *Miami Herald,* "Bud" Purdy described Orleans as "a crossroads hamlet of two general stores and a gas station." His father, Wilson Purdy, was a potato warehouser in Orleans. Purdy's paternal grandparents settled in Michigan after moving from upper New York State across Canada by covered wagon. His maternal grandparents came to the United States from Ireland.

Purdy admits that he was ten or twelve years old "before I knew my name wasn't Buddy." The initial "E" was apparently something his mother tacked on to keep him from being called Junior—a name she disliked. A country boy, Purdy grew up knowing the hardships of the Great Depression. He worked the area fruit and vegetable farms on shares to help his family get along. "At our country school, I was the school janitor. It was my job to get up at six o'clock in the morning, get the fires built, bank the fires, sweep the floors, clean the blackboards, chop the kindling and haul the coal. That's how I earned my clothes and whatever I had."

He attended high school in nearby Belding, a town with a population of several thousand, and continued to earn his own keep. According to Purdy, nothing of significance occurred at high school, except that he survived. Completing high school in 1937, he enrolled with Michigan State University's police administration school, a pioneer undertaking in the field of law enforcement. While at Michigan State, Purdy was a member of the Reserve Officers Training Corps (ROTC) program.

In 1942, Purdy graduated from Michigan State with a degree in

Colonel E. Wilson Purdy (Courtesy of Pennsylvania State Police)

police administration. On graduation day, he married the former Jane
Winkels, of Grand Rapids, Michigan, and accepted a commission in
the U. S. Army—a memorable day, indeed. Before graduation, he had
also undergone special training in police community relations at
Michigan State, and one year of police administration student training
with the Michigan State Police.

During World War II, he served with the Army Military Police
Corps from 1942 to 1946—a tour of overseas duty in the Philippines.
Upon his discharge from the armed forces with the rank of captain,
Purdy was accepted by the FBI in 1946, training at the bureau's
Academy at Quantico, Virginia, and serving his apprenticeship in
Washington and Albany before taking on an assignment as special

agent in Miami. After one year, he was moved to St. Petersburg, Florida, where he was rapidly promoted to senior agent, winning for himself a reputation as an excellent investigator and administrator. His twelve-year career with the FBI ended with his appointment as St. Petersburg police chief in October, 1958.

A schoolmaster at heart, Purdy for a year and a half was a member of the St. Petersburg Junior College faculty, teaching in the college's school of Police Administration and Public Safety.

Described as "non-smoking, non-drinking, non-swearing, non-gambling, and non-fooling around," Purdy lived a quiet family life, and enjoyed a round of golf. He was a member of the Church of Christ, Scientist, which he regularly attended with his family. He was an active Rotarian and a member of the Nitram Masonic Lodge, at St. Petersburg. After moving to Harrisburg, he became a member of the Harrisburg Consistory. The Purdys have three children—a daughter, Pamella, the oldest, and twins Katherine and David.

At 43, the new commissioner was representative of Scranton's official family members who were comparatively young by earlier cabinet standards. Also by way of comparison, Purdy stood at 5'9"—a height that falls below the average for State Police commissioners.

Purdy's early advisers thought it important that he know something about Pennsylvania's political environment rather than let him learn the hard way. It was only fair that the new commissioner have a briefing on the bitterness of the recent political storm his predecessor had to weather. This was not an academic pursuit, but rather a down-to-earth disclosure of conditions as they really were. Of prime importance was the fact that Pennsylvania was one of the large states still clinging to the patronage system. He was told that he could expect the politicians and officeholders of all sorts to seek favors: some approaches would bear on promotions, transfers for convenience, transfers for hardships, relocation of substations, leases for new substations, and a host of other intentions. These intentions were not necessarily held in contempt—they were a way of life. In most cases, an inquiring politician was satisfied with an explanation of rules and regulations that applied, and why his request could or could not be complied with; this took him off the hook with his constituents. These and other tid-bits were laid before Purdy, and thus he was introduced to the rough environment in which he as an "outsider" would find himself.

Purdy's earlier experiences as an Army provost marshal, a college student, an FBI agent and police chief, if anything, did not build up any particular tolerance for politicians. It was apparent that he had no special taste for political life, and made no secret of this. In fact, when Scranton interviewed him for the commissioner's job, and he was told that he could have it, Purdy offered to take $18,000, less than the $20,000 annual salary for the cabinet post, if Scranton would move the job out of the cabinet. Scranton, however, could not go along with him on this proposition. (As police chief, St. Petersburg paid Purdy $14,000 a year.)

True to his word, Purdy made no sweeping changes at head-quarters. From every indication, he was satisfied to accept the staff he inherited, and retained Constance Sharpe, his predecessor's secretary.

Tony Canniff, State Police public information officer, resigned, leaving that post vacant. On orders from the governor's office, the commissioner was blocked from appointing a replacement. To continue the release of information of public interest, Purdy called on Lieutenant Conti to handle this responsibility in addition to his other administrative chores. This Conti did with assists from Lloyd Rochelle, of United Press International; Harry Ball, of Associated Press; members of the capitol newsroom corps, and Canniff's secretary, Betty J. Orlando. Conti was to continue with this assignment until 1967, before the appointment of a professional publicist was authorized by Governor Raymond P. Shafer.

Seen more often at headquarters was Lieutenant John I. Gros-nick. Grosnick, it will be recalled, was reportedly one of the finalists under consideration by Scranton's Blue Ribbon Panel. Believing that Grosnick could be materially helpful to him, Purdy transferred him from the Academy to headquarters in June as director of staff services, and promoted him to captain.

Before Purdy could call his first staff meeting, he was directed by the governor's office to hold up on any plans for the new troop head-quarters at Erie. According to plans advanced by McCartney, the new building was to be constructed south of Erie, along U. S. Route 19, on grounds shared by the Department of Highways. This meant moving troop headquarters from Lawrence Park. So, with a new administra-tion in the driver's seat, the politicians made their move to have the new building located at Lawrence Park. For one reason or another, delays were encountered, and it was not until two commissioners later that the new building was finally completed—in Lawrence Park—in 1969.

As predicted, the pitches came in from political sources, and Purdy knew for sure that he had a problem to deal with. Heat was generated over some issues, and the situation did not improve with the passage of time.

In March, the U. S. Supreme Court in the *Gideon* v. *Wainwright* case ruled that an indigent defendant must be offered free legal counsel in all criminal prosecutions. This opinion had widespread impact on the criminal justice system and especially those prison inmates whose cases fell within the purview of this ruling.

In April, Major Gardner resigned to accept a post with the state Harness Racing Commission. Major Ryan was moved from Sub-District 2 at Montoursville to District 2 at Harrisburg to replace Gardner. Sub-District 2 was abolished.

Those close to him at headquarters were aware of the new commissioner's dislike for the district commanders in the chain of command structure. Purdy preferred to deal directly with the troop commanders, and it was just a case of watching him carefully do away with each of the district commands as opportunities were presented. Gardner's resignation reduced the complement from six to five.

Time was swiftly slipping by and Kime was still serving as Purdy's acting deputy. During the three months following oath-taking, Purdy had come to know and respect Kime, and considered him a real asset as top aide. Even before his official takeover, Purdy and Kime had become friendly telephone associates. There was reason to believe that he would have retained Kime as number two man had the choice been his to make.

The politicians, however, were intriguingly at work with other thoughts on that subject. Rumors were aplenty that Scranton would not favor Kime's appointment as deputy, and that left the field wide open for any other appointment. In March, Purdy was prompted by the governor's office to interview Lieutenant William B. Cooper as a possible deputy choice. Cooper was interviewed, but no action followed on the heels of that session. At this point, Purdy reportedly was seriously weighing the appointment of Academy Superintendent Major Paul A. Rittelmann.

In mid-May, Purdy returned from a hurried visit to the governor's office noticeably disturbed. He inquired about Captain Frank McKetta's background, especially with reference to his promotion and transfer to the Academy right after the past election. Conti recalled for him that McCartney, in the waning weeks of his tenure, was undecided between Lieutenants McKetta and Clifford Yahner to fill the assistant superintendent post at the Academy. McCartney thought Rittelman and McKetta would make a better team based on the past favorable relationship between these two men, and so it was that McKetta got the nod.

A news release announcing McKetta's appointment as deputy

commissioner effective May 29 was prepared. Although feelings were not openly expressed, it appeared that Purdy was not pleased with this after-five o'clock development. The State Police grapevine, attributed McKetta's appointment to pressures generated by Senate Majority Leader Albert R. Pechan (R-Armstrong) and House Speaker W. Stuart Helm (R-Armstrong). The records show that McKetta moved from lieutenant to captain to lieutenant colonel in six months, and took over the office of deputy commissioner on May 29, 1963.

Personally hurt by this development, Kime informed Purdy that he would immediately retire, and a companion news release was on its way. Kime, one of two original members of the State Highway Patrol still on the payroll, brought to a close a remarkable career spanning more than thirty-nine years. Unhappily, Kime's years of retirement were too few: he died in 1966, at 62.

Captain George W. Pinkerton, who had been acting director of traffic operations during Kime's prolonged absence from his desk, was promoted to major in June.

As soon as arrangements could possibly be made, Purdy shipped McKetta off to Indiana University, at Bloomington, Indiana, to attend an eight-week course in advanced police administration at the university's department of police administration. The training was completed in September.

At mid-year, the Scranton administration announced that henceforth all applicants for state employment would have to be finger-printed. The fingerprint card, according to the established procedure, was to be searched by the BCI prior to any appointment. This signifi-cant workload was thrust upon the State Police with no preparation or additional resources. Considerable time was required for the BCI to train fingerprint classifiers and develop a crew sufficiently large to handle the daily input of fingerprint cards effectively without upsetting criminal print operations.

Confident that the department's records system could stand modernization, Purdy called upon the executive offices of the Interna-tional Association of Chiefs of Police (IACP), at Washington, to un-dertake a complete records survey. A $10,000 contract was drawn up for such services. Conti was appointed department liaison. The comprehensive survey by IACP agent Morton Reed was eventually to lead to a complete reform of the reporting system—a major achieve-ment for the reform-minded commissioner.

From July 1 through July 3, the nation celebrated the 100th an-niversary of the Battle of Gettysburg with special ceremonies at the battlefield. Just as it had done at the fiftieth anniversary in 1913 and the seventy-fifth in 1938, the State Police agency was not found lacking in providing a detachment capable of securing the greater Gettysburg area for the comfort of hundreds of thousands of visitors and participants. A 195-man detail of handpicked troopers accomplished its mission commendably, again enhancing the department's image.

The complement of district commanders was reduced to four in July by the resignation of Major Oldham at District 1, Greensburg. To him goes the honor of being the last of the original members of the State Highway Patrol to survive time. Oldham went on to become chief security officer for the multinational Armstrong Cork Company, of Lancaster.

Before the month was up, the legislature had passed companion bills granting the FOP the tenure legislation that body had fought so long to obtain. Purdy, sharing McCartney's views regarding this type of legislation, urged Scranton to veto the twin measures. The governor, however, recalled his promise to the FOP during the heat of the 1962 election campaign that he would sign tenure legislation passed by the general assembly. True to his word, Scranton signed the bills into law on July 25. Act 147, P.L. 275, regulated the dismissal, suspension, demotion and reenlistment of troopers. Act 148, P.L. 278, specified that no member of the State Police shall be dismissed or reduced in rank except by court-martial action.

Although these enactments were the only ones passed in 1963 affecting State Police operations to any degree, Senator Wade worked diligently from opening day of the session to have radar enforcement banned. There was room, however, to question Wade's sincerity about opposing radar at all: confidential sources held that Wade was very satisfied with the "mileage" he was getting from his much-publicized stand against radar . . . why let go of a good thing?

Purdy was earlier described as a schoolmaster at heart, and this description became more fitting as time went on. During his own years of training and police service, he had fortunately made solid contacts with administrators at Indiana University, Northwestern University, Michigan State, University of Louisville, University of Southern California and other institutions where a rather wide range of police courses was taught. He lost no time in enrolling key officers and enlisted men in these available courses. Although State Police personnel had been sent to the FBI National Academy before, Purdy was to significantly increase the pace. He left no stone unturned to upgrade the persons upon whom he would depend.

He had already sent McKetta to Indiana University for eight weeks. Off to Louisville University went Captain Rocco P. Urella, troop commander at Reading, for twelve weeks, where he scored exceptional grades and was elected class president. His achievements did not escape Purdy's attention.

Successfully competing, three men were enrolled in the nine-month training program at Northwestern University's Traffic Institute (NUTI). Corporal Albert F. Kwiatek, Corporal George W. Crowthers and Trooper Nicholas G. Dellarciprete started their long assignment away from homebase in September. They were the first in a string of men to study at NUTI. Back in 1940, two troopers trained at NUTI at their own expense. One, George W. Pinkerton, oddly enough had just been promoted by Purdy to major and replaced Kime as traffic operations director. Like Pinkerton, other NUTI graduates were to earn advancement in the State Police hierarchy.

Pinkerton's companion at NUTI in 1940 was George Miller. Both men suffered the loss of seniority because of their determination to attend NUTI. In an interview, Pinkerton recalled the "chitchat" he received from his superior commissioned officer just before he entrained for Northwestern. "Why do you want to go to Northwestern? You're only going to come back and do the same thing you're now doing." These were hardly encouraging words.

In September, Conti was sent to Washington to train in records management at the National Archives. His studies were continued specifically in police records at Indiana University and later at UNIVAC's Washington offices to study the application of computers in the records field.

In a companion move to upgrade the rank and file, Purdy encouraged troopers and non-commissioned officers, as well as officers, to enroll in courses at nearby colleges. Upon his arrival in Pennsylvania, Purdy found few college graduates on State Police rolls. To reverse this trend, he initiated a state-supported program whereby tuition for police-related college courses would be reimbursed, provided passing grades were earned. Work schedules were adjusted to facilitate school attendance. Before his departure from the scene in 1966, Purdy was to see a mass participation in his educational program which in the long run has added immeasurably to the quality of State Police performance. The pride of achievement was everywhere in evidence as credits mounted and degrees were bestowed upon those who persevered.

In a statement prepared for the 1963 summer edition of the *Pennsylvania Chiefs of Police Association Bulletin,* Purdy very pointedly summed up his argument in behalf of education and training:

A police department may possess the best in equipment,

the best of jails and have the best specimens of man on its payroll and yet fail miserably because of a lack of proper training and education. Education and proper knowledge of the matters to be dealt with are the backbone of success and should be part of any practical police budget.

In this area of administration, Purdy lived up to those words with an intensity never before witnessed in the State Police.

September was also to see an important move made at State Police headquarters. The legislators, although they had received Lawrence's cooperation in their move to occupy the capitol, were impatient with the progress made to construct a new office building. They were successful in urging Scranton to immediately move the State Police into a leased building. Negotiations were made with H. and J. Gross, Inc., of Harrisburg, to erect a suitable building at 7th and Forster Streets to house all State Police headquarters units, some of which were located in the upper floors of the capitol, the capitol basement, and South Office Building. The leased building was hurriedly built, and in September the State Police moved in, thus centrally locating headquarters resources for the first time in many years. Provided were 42,000 square feet of working space. The governor and other ranking state officials were invited and attended a private open house program on September 16. During the next two days, State Police families and the general public were invited to inspect the new offices.

Although Purdy was openly complimentary of the services provided him by his secretary, Constance Sharpe, whom he privately addressed as "Sam," he was eager to acquire the added services of a former associate who was well-acquainted with his work style. By September, he had successfully persuaded Miss Grace E. Kenner, his former secretary at St. Petersburg, to leave her post there and work for him, this time not as a secretary but as an administrative assistant with a paycheck to match. Miss Kenner took up accommodations in an inner office of the executive suite, and became a key figure during Purdy's tenure.

Before the month of September was spent, *The Communicator* was published and distributed. It was the first departmental organ since 1939 when *The Bulletin* was discontinued for some reason. The new publication's first staff members were: Richard Solomon, editor; Robert Zinsky, associate editor, and Sergeant George M. Pintarch, photographer. First editions were printed by the printing class inmates at the Correctional Institution at White Hill. *The Communicator* has served a useful purpose continuously to this day. Its value has been recognized by every one of Purdy's successors.

Leased State Police headquarters building, Harrisburg, 1963 (Courtesy of Pennsylvania State Police)

Perhaps one of Purdy's more important moves in the last quarter of 1963 was to introduce a five-day work week for the first time in State Police history. New work schedules went into effect on October 1. Prior to his order, it was not unusual for enlisted men to work six and seven-day weeks, adding up to fifty, sixty and seventy hours. Although the work week was shortened, long hours were continued in most cases to get the job done. *The Communicator* carried this statement:

> Minor difficulties are expected here and there, but these can be expected to be ironed out within several months. The success or failure of the five-day week will depend on how well the men accept or reject it. Until the plan gets rolling in high gear, certain inconveniences will develop. This means that everyone will have to give it all they can to make it work. The plan cannot afford to fail.

Needless to state, the field forces were pleased, and wanted no part of going backward.

In an effort to broaden the recruiting base, Purdy set up a well-advertised recruiting program permitting married men to apply for cadet training for the first time in State Police history. McCartney saw the need for this change—Purdy gave life to the idea. The program was also geared to attract college graduates.

Purdy, impressed with McCartney's directive system, made improvements to the system to advance its utility.

In another innovative action, Purdy retained the firm of McCann

Associates to prepare promotional examinations. Questions were to be taken from specified reading material easily within reach of every enlisted man. Lists of suggested reading were published in advance of examinations to allow time for preparation. Accompanying the listings, however, was a warning that questions would not necessarily be limited to suggested material. "Hitting the books" was a slogan for off-duty hours.

Just before the year's general election, Purdy was to come under fire from Democratic party leaders. Purdy had directed a large-scale investigation of vice conditions in Pittsburgh. On the same day in October that Purdy scheduled raids, Scranton campaigned in Pittsburgh, dwelling at length on vice conditions in that city. Mass arrests followed. Democrats could not buy these events as coincidental, and called the raids politically inspired to defeat Allegheny County District Attorney Ed Boyle. Purdy's denials served no purpose. Additional State Police raids were conducted in the Pittsburgh area in December.

Purdy made no secret of his intentions to put civilian administrators in key positions to replace enlisted personnel assigned to those desk jobs. His first move in this direction was to take Captain Parsons out of the Personnel Office and hire Michael R. Aaronson, 30, of Philadelphia. Aaronson had been a Civil Serivce personnel officer for the city of Philadelphia. Later Sergeant Ray Oberheim was transferred to the Academy and eventually replaced by John E. Millett, who became Aaronson's assistant. Similar changes were to follow in other management areas.

Considerably on the increase during this period were juvenile offenses. Lawless juvenile acts were fast becoming one of the big problems for police. To cope adequately with this menace in a special way, Purdy created a Youth Aid Division at headquarters. The new program eventually extended to the field forces and comprised a notable undertaking by the State Police. To head operations, Purdy selected Sergeant Joseph L. Branigan. Branigan, 49, was sent to the Delinquency Control Institute at the University of Southern California for three months to prepare himself for the job ahead. Corporal John R. Dalinsky was chosen by Purdy to serve as Branigan's assistant in Youth Aid Services. After a promotion to sergeant in 1964, Dalinsky attended a ten-week Youth Officers' Institute at the University of Minnesota to undergo training for his new assignment.

On November 22, the news of President John F. Kennedy's assassination brought operations at State Police headquarters to a screeching halt, just as it did everywhere in the nation. Shots from a sniper's high-powered rifle ended the 46-year-old President's life as his triumphant motorcade moved through the streets of Dallas, Texas. At headquarters, tears were openly shed as the details of the President's death filtered in from the news media.

This article appeared in the December, 1963, issue of *The Communicator,*

> Millions of people throughout the world saw the photograph showing a secret service agent spread-eagled over the body of the fallen President. When the shots rang out, Stewart Stoudt threw his body over the President to protect him. But it was too late. Some of the older members of the State Police force may remember Stoudt as a former member of the force during the late 1930s. He served in Pottsville with Troop C. Stoudt, who is a veteran member of the presidential Secret Service bodyguard, joined the Secret Service in 1940.

The next few days were shared between keeping the State Police operational and attending to broadcasts as President Kennedy's body was flown to the White House, then moved to the capitol rotunda to lie in state, and finally reached its resting place in a sloped gravesite at Arlington National Cemetery, as a nation mourned its loss. It was, indeed, a tragic episode.

The complement of district commanders was reduced by two during the last months of the year. At Sub-District 1, Major Knies retired on November 29, and Major Ryan called it quits on Christmas Day. This left Majors Pezzent and Sheaffer at Districts 3 and 4, respectively, and there was considerable speculation on what Purdy would do about them. By this time, the organizational value of district commanders was obviously spent. Also added to the year-ending list of retirees was Dr. David A. Johnston, who had served as medical officer for a quarter of a century. His resignation was effective December 31.

Purdy closed out the year with another innovation. He firmly believed that the deparment's effectiveness would be enhanced by a thorough audit of field activities on a periodic basis. To this end, he devised a staff inspection program. The program basically called for a traveling inspection team which would take a detailed look at each troop's operations and judge the degree to which each troop adhered to departmental rules and regulations. To head this new venture, Purdy called on Captain Urella, who was transferred in December from his command at Reading and moved to new accommodations at headquarters. There he was to implement the new program and put together the team he wanted to help him get the job done.

Purdy's emphasis on education and training—never diminishing in intensity—saw a contract drawn up with NUTI to conduct a series of two-week courses entitled "Supervision of Police Personnel," for all State Police supervisors with particular stress placed on the training of substations commanders and all commissioned officers. Lieutenants William B. Cooper and Joseph Dussia were dispatched to the NUTI campus at Evanston, Illinois, for a five-week course in police management.

Whatever curiosity had developed over Purdy's eventual disposition of remaining District Commanders Pezzent and Sheaffer was satisfied in January, 1964, when the commissioner transferred both men to headquarters. It was then generally believed that both majors would quit—but neither did. Sheaffer was made executive officer to the deputy with supervisory responsibility over the Planning Divison and Inspection Division. Pezzent headed the new Bureau of Technical Services which embraced criminal identification, communications and central records.

To replace the retired Dr. Johnston, Purdy signed-on Dr. Robert P. Dutlinger as medical officer. Dutlinger, a prominent Harrisburg surgeon, graduated from the University of Pittsburgh Medical School and served with the U. S. Army Medical Corps during World War II. At the time of his appointment, he was associate professor of surgery at the Harrisburg Hospital and Philadelphia's Hahnemann Medical College, and past president of the Central Pennsylvania Chapter of American College of Surgeons. He was later to be elected president of the Dauphin County Medical Society.

As was expected, Purdy announced the abolishment of the districts "to further streamline the organizational structure. Troop commanders will now conduct business directly with headquarters, thus effecting a speed-up of departmental communications and police service." Although the concept of districts was dealt a blow by Purdy, it was to rise again within a few years.

Urella had completed his team makeup and selected Troop D, Butler, in February, for his first inspection visit. Picked as his team members were Sergeant Joseph DiPietro, Sergeant William J. Heuer, Corporal Joseph Ruffa, Corporal William Anselmi and Trooper William G. Grohol. He put the troop supervisory personnel at ease by assuring them that he was not conducting a "snooping" exercise. Although basic standardization of operations for all State Police installations was one of the team's objectives, Urella expressed hope that his tour would disclose methods and procedures that could possibly be used beneficially in other troops as well. Troop members were afforded the opportunity to express, in private, their problems, suggestions and needs. Much was learned from these private sources.

Taking McCartney's basic ideas regarding a new pay plan, Purdy had ordered the project pursued for presentation to the governor. The completed plan combined subsistence and salary, adjusted salaries for each rank, and provided for annual increments through six years and longevity raises at the eleventh and sixteenth years. The plan generally classified the department on a par with state police agencies in New York, New Jersey, Maryland and Michigan. Scranton approved of these changes, and Purdy presented them to the legislature for its consideration.

In February, troopers and officers for the first time in State Police history sported identification name plates displaying last names only. Each man was required to furnish, upon request, his full name and rank. Contacts with the public often involved this exchange of information—for better or for worse.

On March 18, Sheaffer retired to accept the job of chief of security for Dickinson College in nearby Carlisle. This left Pezzent the sole surviving former district commander. Surprisingly, as time went on the relationship between Purdy and Pezzent blossomed into friendship that endured to each other's benefit throughout Purdy's tenure.

Purdy's plan for reorganization at headquarters continued in April with the promotion of Grosnick to lieutenant colonel and his appointment as chief of staff. This position was only once before employed at headquarters, when Wilhelm served as chief of staff for Commissioner Foote. In his new position, Grosnick was to guide operations of: criminal identification, crime lab, central records, communications, quartermaster, planning and research, personnel, finance and data processing.

Also promoted in April was Urella. Urella was promoted to major, filling Sheaffer's vacancy. There was no change in his basic responsibility and he continued to direct operations of the Staff Inspection Bureau.

Of deep concern to everyone in the criminal justice system was the ever-increasing impact of the drug problem as a principal social issue. The State Police for many years scheduled speakers for schools, clubs and other public-spirited organizations on safety education subjects. It was only natural for the State Police then to get into the business of lecturing on the drug problem which was becoming just as alarming as juvenile driving. Purdy arranged to purchase a film on drug addiction that was suitable for lecturing, and the new program was underway.

Combatting the drug problem was a three-fold effort. One aspect was to educate youth to the dangers of drug use. Another was to control the distribution, sale and possession of drugs, which was the main thrust for police operations. Remaining was the rehabilitiation of drug addicts who were either apprehended or voluntarily surrendered to authorities. It had been the contention of State Police administrators that the police should be restricted to the control of drug traffic and leave the other two areas to educators and welfare workers. To fill a void, or to do something helpful in the absence of any other state guidelines, the State Police was to remain in the lecturing field for almost ten years before devoting its full resources only to drug traffic.

Although the State Police had emergency troop procedures in force since World War II, the drills were not specifically geared to the circumstances of a new menace to public peace—civil disobedience incidents. At Chester and Folcroft, both Delaware County communities, State Police authorities were somewhat caught with their pants down. At Chester, a community of some 60,000, including a large black population, the local police were summoned following a tavern incident, and State Police were called in to assist in the restoration of order. Folcroft, with a small population of 9,000, saw a flare-up when blacks moved into a white residential section. In both cases, much criticism was heaped upon the State Police for its improper handling of these two affairs.

At St. Petersburg, Purdy had formally trained his small force in riot control tactics and undertook the sizeable task of training here in Pennsylvania. Although there was some resentment, Purdy pushed his training program, and the benefits of it were to be realized as civil disorders increased in numbers and intensity. Purdy had ordered his deputy, McKetta, to devote almost full time to the development of a riot control manual which was to be later identified as Manual 7-1 and become a "bible" for every man on the job. Following months of concentrated efforts, the field forces were adequately equipped with special gear and trained to humanely and skillfully counter riots with sufficient force to overcome force. Purdy's persistence in this area of law enforcement was to be rewarding enough as time went on.

In April, Purdy announced a new training program to supplement those already ongoing. He arranged with IACP to furnish semimonthly "Training Keys" in sufficient numbers for per capita distribution. The "Training Keys" were a series of instructions on many police-related subjects. IACP had sold this program to other police departments, and Purdy wanted to give it a try. The men, however, felt there was one drawback to the "Training Keys"—they were mainly designed for municipal police use, and State Police personnel had to stretch a point here and there to bridge the difference between operations. After about a year's trial, the series of instructions was discontinued.

In May, the State Police in cooperation with the Pennsylvania Chiefs of Police Association and the National Conference of Christians and Jews conducted its first institute on "Police Responsibility in Race Tension and Conflict." This first undertaking of its kind was attended by Scranton, some 100 police chiefs and all State Police line and staff brass. This institute was the forerunner of an array of State Police institutes: "Institute on Local Government Responsibility in Racial and Community Tensions"; "Dialogue Between Law Enforcement and the Clergy"; "Institute on Police Work with Juveniles"; "Institute on Police Handling of Children and Youth."

The format of the institutes was somewhat varied to accommodate the nature of the audiences. Numbered among some of the groups to be invited to the Academy for institute participation were: Pennsylvania Association of Broadcasters; District Attorneys Association of Pennsylvania; Pennsylvania Motor Federation of AAA Clubs; County School Superintendents and Assistant Superintendents; Pennsylvania Newspaper Publishers' Association; Pennsylvania Society of Newspaper Editors; Pennsylvania Motor Truck Association; Optimist International; and American Association of University Women.

Emergency troop undergoing riot control training (Courtesy of Pennsylvania State Police)

Neither the listing of the institute titles nor the invited groups is by any means all-inclusive. There were many others throughout Purdy's tenure, and no better purpose would be served by a lengthier listing.

While holding to the belief that the force's internal success could be achieved by training, Purdy was equally convinced that public support was critical to total success. Purdy wrote for *The Communicator* in October, 1963:

> There is no phase of our operations in which the cooperation of an interested and willing public is not needed. How many more crimes could be solved if a willing citizen would come forth as a witness? How many lives could be saved if even one interested citizen recognizes the need for an effective traffic safety program? How many acts of vandalism and more serious offenses could be prevented if the energies of youngsters throughout the State were guided by us in the proper channels? Each of us, then, must direct our efforts to selling this "product" of law enforcement in the most efficient manner possible, but in the most attractive manner possible, as well.

Unquestionably his series of institutes was intended to do exactly what he was recommending to his men—sell the "product" of law enforcement. The effect of the institutes was widely felt, and the image of the State Police as the state's leading law enforcement body was grossly enchance. Purdy was "riding high."

Another veteran officer, Captain Benjamin K. Lee, 60, retired on May 2. Filling his position as director of criminal identification operations was Conti. Purdy then ordered that both central records and criminal identification records be merged into a new unit, the Records-Identification Division (R. & I.) which took in some 125 enlisted men and civilian employees. Enlisted men were limited to key supervisory positions in R. & I.

Through an excellent relationship with Trooper Edwin Grazer, Safety Education Officer at Troop B-4, Lancaster, planning was undertaken with television Station WGAL to produce in color a videotaped series entitled "Soldiers of the Law." The twelve 15-minute segments were then shown on Station WGAL weekly on Saturdays through August 15. The WGAL managers were kind enough to make the series available to any television station desiring to schedule it for local viewing. Working closely with State Police at Lancaster were WGAL's Arthur C. Webb III, who directed the series, and script writer Nelson Sears.

Another history-making event took place at the Academy on May

25 as seventy-eight cadets graduated. Numbered among them were forty-five married men. It was the first time in the history of the department that married men had undergone training. Academy instructors shared mixed feelings about the success of taking married men aboard: some felt that they made satisfactory trainees, others believed the men worried too much about their home and family problems and were not as deeply involved in their schooling as unmarried men. But whatever their views boiled down to, the acceptance of married men was an unchangeable factor the Academy staff had to live with. There was no turning back. Time, however, has proven that, married or single, men dedicated to a career will vary little in performance and accomplishment.

With the Academy freed of any training commitments for a few days, Purdy planned with a group of retired troopers to schedule a reunion—a two-day affair at the Academy, May 30–31. Labelled as the First Annual Reunion, the affair was attended by scores of retired men and their wives. Former Commissioners Lynn G. Adams, 84, and Earl J. Henry, 67, were among the honored guests. Representing the retired group on the planning committee were Major Hilding C. Johnson, Captain Peter Carlson, Det. Sergeant William A. Miller and Sergeant and Mrs. Russel Ellis. It was rated a successful venture.

McCartney's capital expenditures program was progressing satisfactorily during Purdy's tenure. The new barracks at Dunmore was under construction at mid-year at an expected cost of $554,300. A new headquarters building at Wyoming was being built at a figure of $278,824. Bids on the new Transportation-Supply building at Harrisburg were opened on May 20, and the low bid was $417,779. The new barracks at Erie was still in planning with John Carver, a Philadelphia architect. Plans still called for the building's location south of Erie; however, this idea was to be abandoned as political pressures mounted to keep the installation at Lawrence Park. Construction on nine driver exam points rested at varying stages.

Captain Stanton was the second officer to graduate from the Southern Police Institute (SPI) at the Louisville University, having completed the long twelve-week course in police science and administration. (Urella was the first to do so.) Others attending the SPI short course were Lieutenants Howard Jaynes and Leon F. Wrona. Captain John F. Yaglenski was the next SPI long course enrollee; he began his studies in September.

For the biennial period ending June 30, 1964, State Police criminal arrests numbered 35,607. Leading the list of arrest activities were burglary, larceny, malicious mischief (mostly juvenile acts), disorderly conduct and larceny of auto, in that order. Received were 70,393 criminal complaints. A total of 2,218 stolen vehicles were recovered, and the value of all recovered stolen property amounted to $4,349,312.

In his report to the governor, Purdy stated that the new Youth Aid Division was operational, and during its first four months youth aid officers screened 1,109 juvenile cases.

Members of the Fire Marshal Division investigated 2,309 fires in which 376 lives were lost. They accounted for 412 arrests for arson, with 243 of those arrested falling in the 13 to 21 age group. The motive in most of these cases was reported to be "for thrill and excitement."

Traffic arrests numbered 409,962. Patrol forces investigated 61,058 motor vehicle accidents, conducted 799,170 driver exams and 308,143 re-exams, and supervised 14,409 official inspection stations, among other accomplishments.

There were 235 cadets graduated from the Academy, and 2,141 troopers underwent in-service training. Trained at the Academy were 247 municipal police officers, while 879 local policemen completed the M-40 training program in the field. Guided tours through the Academy accounted for 50,360 visitors.

Funds totalling $38,666,599 were expended during the period with 62.0 percent going for salaries, 15.1 for travel expenses, 7.0 for motor vehicle fleet replacement, 5.2 for fleet operations and 10.7 for other operating expenses, in rounded figures.

A patrol fleet of some 1,200 vehicles posted a total of 72,746,948 miles travelled.

A concerted effort was made by the FBI and R. & I. supervisors to upgrade the quality of the Uniform Crime Reporting system (UCR). This move was essential to the new look in records management desired by Purdy, and eagerly supported by FBI's UCR supervisor, Jerry Daunt. Extensive training programs were conducted with troop chief clerks. This progressive step had a tremendous bearing on later developments in UCR.

In June, the first graduates of NUTI returned to duty. Returning were Sergeants Albert F. Kwiatek and George W. Crowthers and Corporal Nicholas G. Dellarciprete, all of whom were promoted during their nine-month campus stay at NUTI. Kwiatek and Dellarciprete were immediately teamed up with Pezzent and Conti to expedite the development of the new field reporting system. IACP had fulfilled its contractual agreement, and it was now up to the State Police to proceed with the gigantic task of launching a revolutionary system involving every trooper in the field, at the Academy, and at headquarters.

In a brief ceremony held in the commissioner's office on July 2, retired Major John D. Kime was awarded the Pennsylvania Meritorious Medal for outstanding services. Presenting the medal to Kime was the state adjutant, Maj. General Thomas R. White, Jr. Kime was the fiftieth person to receive this award since it was instituted in 1938, and the second in State Police history: Commissioner Lynn G. Adams was the first to receive the award in January, 1943. Kime had retired in May, 1963, closing out thirty-nine years of service.

In August, another important staff position was filled by a civilian appointee. Replacing Lieutenant Philip F. Chulick as transportation officer was William F. Hoffman. Hoffman, 46, a retired U. S. Army lieutenant colonel, devoted most of his twenty-year military career to Army transportation services in the states and overseas.

The one and only death in the line of duty to occur during Purdy's administration was reported on August 8. Trooper Richard G. Barnhart of Troop B-1, Washington, was killed instantly as he pursued drag-racers and was struck by a vehicle entering the highway from a service station.

During the months of August and September, R. & I.'s criminal identification services underwent history-making changes. Begun back in 1920, criminal identification services were first offered to police agencies by the constabulary, and few changes of any significance were made in operational methods. Filing cabinets and alphabetical storage systems were still in use after forty-four years of experience. As volume storage grew, processing became slower and more difficult.

Taking advantage of the new state of the art, the State Police purchased fourteen electrievers and six rotary index units from Remington Rand at a cost of $114,000. Fingerprint cards, exceeding a million, were transferred to these floor-to-ceiling storage units which were pushbutton-operated and designed to complete a revolution in a few seconds. The ease of filing and searching was a welcome relief to the technicians assigned to this work.

In a companion system conversion, more than a million individual criminal record folders were removed from four- and five-drawer filing cabinets and transferred to open-shelf filing. Prior to doing so, however, the folders were removed from their alphabetical sequencing and sorted in terminal digit order with unlimited expansion capability and security. Without the benefit of an index search first, a file in terminal digit sequencing cannot be located.

These two projects brought the State Police into a modern setting. R. & I. was then geared to effectively handle its ever-increasing workload; and for a few years, its operations were an impressive showpiece for visiting police officials, domestic and foreign.

Records and Identification Division Electrievers. Left to right: Fingerprint Classifiers James W. Seiders, Walter L. Leibig, James D. Carrigan. (Courtesy of Pennsylvania State Police)

In September, the true story of the "solid state switcher" which Captain Bomboy was eventually to secure under lease from General Electric was soon to hit OA. It will be recalled that OA staffers were dead set against computer acquisitions by state agencies. This was essentially done because of cost and the need to protect the centralized operations of UNIVAC. Rather than label the main processing unit a "computer," which it was, Bomboy referred to it as a solid state switcher, thus covering up its true identity from OA. To provide himself with the managerial skills required to cope with the General Electric Datanet 30 computer system, it was a must that Bomboy attend a thirty-day course in computer programming and data communictions at GE's Phoenix, Arizona, installation. When Bomboy's request for thirty-day travel status hit OA, the lid was off and the heat was on. Happily for the State Police—and Bomboy—the contractual agreement with GE was too far gone to rest in jeopardy, and OA found itself with little choice but to go along with the department. Bomboy went to Phoenix.

Regardless of OA's evaluation of State Police trickery in this case, Bomboy's actions with McCartney's blessing before the latter's departure brought the force into the computer age where it belonged. The State Police Department was traditionally an innovator in the police field, and there was no call to change that pace.

The next three to leave for NUTI's nine-month long course were Corporals Paul J. Chylak and Nicholas Kordilla, and Trooper Nick Donatsko. Studies began on September 10, and graduation was scheduled for June, 1965.

In September, Captain Albert L. Henry headed a task force providing security for the 52,000 scouts attending the Sixth National Boy Scout Jamboree at Valley Forge. Visiting the encampment and addressing the scouts was President Lyndon B. Johnson. Arrangement for the President's jamboree appearance was no small undertaking.

After months of experience and planning, electronic data processing (EDP) operations at headquarters were expanded to carry a wide range of programs. Pilot studies were ongoing everywhere as dedicated employees and supervisors inched toward computer-based operations, yet a few years away.

In November, still another civilian was appointed to head the newly-created Bureau of Staff Services. Coming aboard was L. E. Simpson, a former director of public safety at St. Petersburg, Florida. In his new position, Simpson held supervisory responsibility for fiscal, quartermater, personnel, and research and planning operations. Unhappily for Simpson, however, his rocky tour of duty with Staff Services was not a lasting one.

In view of the encouraging progress being made with the new field reporting system, a conference attended by all troop chief clerks was held at the Academy in December. Considered the backbone of paperwork activity in the field, it was essential to keep the chief clerks abreast of developments as they occurred—much depended upon their understanding and support.

With crime on the upswing in the Commonwealth, authorities at all levels of the criminal justice system were at a loss to evaluate crime trends in the absence of any sound statewide statistics. The State Police and the Department of Internal Affairs at the state level did their best to develop a reasonable crime picture, and the larger cities kept abreast of their own crime problems. The legislature, equally concerned for the lack of valid statistics, called for a study of crime statistics, and dumped the job in the lap of the legislative research body—the Joint State Government Commission.

The FBI was strongly advocating statewide systems geared to the national UCR program administered by the FBI. The advancement of technological capabilities for automatically transmitting volume data gave impetus to this far-reaching outlook. The neighboring state of New Jersey had already passed legislation making it binding upon all criminal justice agencies to report to the New Jersey State Police, and resting responsibility with that agency to pass its findings on to the FBI and the governor. Purdy set his sights on duplicating this procedure here at home.

The Joint State Government Commission held hearings and interviewed staff personnel at State Police headquarters, the Justice Department, and Department of Internal Affairs, who were basically concerned with gathering criminal statistics. A proposed budget covering operations was prepared, and it looked very much as though this ambitious undertaking was moving satisfactorily with general agreement that the new Bureau of Criminal Statistics, if it came into being, would be housed with the State Police.

When the extensiveness of the new program was realized, it appeared that Grosnick's cooling interest in taking on this added headache turned to total disregard. At any rate, whatever momentum there was for the adoption of this program slowed down. It did not pick up speed again until William C. Sennett, Governor Shafer's attorney general, through the actions of the new State Crime Commission headed by J. Shane Creamer, gave the idea another lease on life in 1968–1969.

The November elections of 1964 brought the Democrats back in control of the House by a 116–93 margin when the general assembly began another marthon session in January, 1965. House Speaker was Robert K. Hamilton (D-Beaver). The Senate remained in Republican hands 27–22. The fact that the House rested in Democratic hands spelled trouble for Scranton and his administration, and in a particular way insofar as State Police history is concerned.

Throughout the session, four measures were passed affecting State Police operations: Act 85, P.L. 123, June 8, provided for closed secret vote by a court-martial board and required the commissioner to furnish a transcript to the accused; Act 112, P.L. 193, July 9, increased the salary of the commissioner from $20,000 to $25,000, and applied the raise only to persons appointed to the office after July 9, 1965; Act 323, P.L. 657, November 9, authorized enforcement of provisions of the Hazardous Substance Transportation Act; and Act 458, P.L. 1164, December 22, provided for pensions to widows of enlisted members who died in the line of duty prior to January 1, 1938. There were other happenings under the capitol dome affecting the State Police during this session, but they will be taken up in a more appropriate time frame.

Purdy, like commissioners before him, was anxious to see the State Police complement increased. In his case, however, there were added circumstances. Purdy had initiated a five-day work week in the face of increased demands for services, and an increase in manpower was crucial. He ordered the Planning and Research staff, under the direction of Lieutenant Arthur W. Shulenberger, to conduct an extensive manpower study so that he could make a well-supported plea to the legislature for more men. The study was underway, and it was anticipated that the study results would show the need for an unprecedented increase.

EDP requirements were now of paramount importance, and to facilitate coding it was necessary to simplify troop identifications. Troops were, for example, identified alpha-numerical, and EDP wanted identification reduced to one letter of the alphabet. Effective January 1, 1965, all troops received new letters:

	From	To
Greensburg	A-1	A
Washington	B-1	B
Punxsutawney	C-1	C
Butler	D-1	D
Erie	E-1	E
Montoursville	D-2	F
Hollidaysburg	C-2	G
Harrisburg	A-2	H
Lancaster	B-4	J
Philadelphia	A-4	K
Reading	C-4	L
Bethlehem	D-4	M
Hazleton	A-3	N
Wyoming	B-3	P
Dunmore	C-3	R
Turnpike	B-2	T

The original constabulary troops at Greensburg and Butler retained their traditional identity, A and D, respectively. Troops at Wyoming (B) and Reading (C) lost out to EDP.

The year 1965 held a special meaning for the State Police since it was just sixty years ago that the unique Pennsylvania State Police organization was founded. Much was to be made of this anniversary year, and every monthly issue of *The Communicator* carried the banner heading. "1905-Sixty Years of Progressive Public Service-1965."

Appropriate to the beginning of the sixtieth anniversary year, the new barracks at Dunmore was occupied and dedicated on February 25. The list of dignitaries attending the affair was headed by Scranton. The

$605,000 building is located on a six-acre tract of land in the Dunmore industrial park off the O'Neill Highway. Local newspapers, giving their accounts of the dedication ceremony, were quick to rightfully give credit to former Governor Lawrence and former Commissioner Frank McCartney for the new building.

In a companion move, the Daleville Substation located a scant ten-minute run from the new Dunmore barracks was closed. Service to the Daleville area was an obligation for the personnel at Dunmore.

Oddly enough, retired Captain Vincent R. Scolere, who commanded the troop during much of the time the new barracks was to become a reality, died February 26, one day following the dedication of the headquarters building at Dunmore.

Sergeant Michael Donahoe was the second man in the Youth Aid Division to attend Southern California's Delinquency Control Institute for twelve weeks of training. Sergeant Salvador Rodriquez was soon to follow that same route to sunny California as a Youth Aid staff member.

During his early days as commissioner, Purdy's position regarding seniority was soon found out. One of his frequent statements went something like this—a twenty-five-year trooper may not have twenty-five years of police experience, but rather just one year's experience twenty-five times over. This message was plain enough, and there was little surprise when he cut seniority points almost in half for promotional competition. In a slow-growth organization, there were many "oldtimers" who were displeased with that arrangement.

Early in his administration, too, he had ordered an eighty-five-man transfer list which for the most part included men with long service records, who had been stationed at some field installations for enduring periods. This was interpreted as another manifestation of Purdy's disregard for seniority as a consideration for promotion. The eighty-five-man transfer incident enraged the rank and file with long service. This furor was to continue seething and later become a morale issue aired in the general assembly.

In the summer of 1964, however, Purdy did establish a favorable troop of preference transfer policy which would allow men to apply for transfers to other locations of their choosing. Since many troopers had, through the years, come from the anthracite coal region, requests for transfer to the three troops in the northeast were overwhelming, and a priority list was set up for these troops and all others as well.

After one year of inspecting, the inspection team evaluated its findings based on circumstances as the team found them in the field. At staff meetings, and privately, Urella informed Purdy that the morale in the field was not as good as it should be. Purdy's feedback came to him by way of troop commanders—Urella was securing his from the rank and file through the inspection team's private interviews and question-naires. Urella believed his sources to be more indicative of the real situation "out there," and felt that Purdy should take the inspection team's observations more seriously.

Whatever respect Purdy held for politicians was slowly but surely eroding as his tenure wore on. He was confident at the outset that he could cope with politics and politicians, but the manifold approaches were more than Purdy apparently had bargained for. Politicians from both sides of the aisle contacted Purdy frequently to influence transfers and promotions, to stop raids on their pet clubs back home, to "fix" traffic arrests, and for other "good" causes. Had the politicians not gone overboard in their zealous efforts to satisfy the unending demands of their constituents, things might have worked out differently.

Some requests unquestionably bordering political favoritism were especially irksome to Purdy. In response to these, he was accused of being unreasonably curt. It is possible that in avoiding political fa-voritism, the commissioner lost sight of political diplomacy to the point of diminshing whatever dialogue he was enjoying with House members. The ensuing breach somehow was limited to his relationship with House members and not with the senators.

By 1965, conditions between Purdy and the more vocal of the House members had reached a point of no return. On February 2, Rep. Charles J. Mills (D-Westmoreland), John F. Laudadio, Sr. (D-West-moreland), Gust L. Stemmler (D-Westmoreland), and Edward W. McNally (D-Cambria) introduced Resolution No. 6 in the House, call-ing for an investigation of the State Police administration and adminis-trative practices. The resolution read as follows:

> The Pennsylvania State Police Force of the Common-wealth of Pennsylvania has traditionally been one of the finest law enforcement agencies in the world. It has consistently been held in the highest esteem by the public because of the courteous and dignified manner in which its activities have been conducted, and its outstanding record of achievement.
>
> Recently, however, there appear to be disturbing in-fluences in the higher echelons of the force which if allowed to continue, could bring irreparable damage to the reputation and operations of the force.
>
> Morale of the members of the Pennsylvania State Police is, reportedly, at an all time low. Promotions, transfers, assignments and other actions taken by the commissioner and

his administrative assistants have been inequitable and of questionable motivation. Such actions are bound to have an adverse effect on the pride and spirit de corps of the troopers, and when that it gone we can bid farewell to the excellence of the force; therefore, be it

Resolved, That the Speaker of the House of Representatives appoint five members of the House, three of whom shall be of the majority party who shall constitute a committee whose duty it shall be to make a thorough study and investigation of the administration and administrative practices of the Pennsylvania State Police; and be it further.

Resolved, That the committee may meet, hold hearings, take testimony and make its investigation whether the General Assembly is in session or in adjournment. It may issue subpoenas under hand and seal of its chairman commanding any person to appear before it and to answer questions touching matters properly being inquired into by the committee and to produce books, papers, records and documents as the committee deems necessary. Any person who wilfully neglects or refuses to testify before this committee or to produce any books, papers, records, or documents shall be subject to the penalties provided by the laws of the Commonwealth in such cases. Each member of the committee shall have power to administer oaths and affirmations to witnesses appearing before the committee; and be it further

Resolved, That the committee make a report of its findings, together with any recommendations it may have for remedial action or for appropriate legislation, to the General Assembly, as soon as it has completed its investigation.

The resolution, having been properly introduced, was set aside without any immediate action taken. It was not until late June before the sponsors were able to move it successfully.

Turning his attention elsewhere, Purdy joined forces with other state criminal justice agencies to form a committee known as "The Committee for Police and Corrections Staff Development," for the lack of a better name. For at least two years, the committee studied the need for and planned the establishment of a department at Penn State University to handle police and corrections programs. Penn State executives by invitation remained on top of developments and welcomed the opportunity to be of service. The committee was eventually successful in securing a $50,000 appropriation for the Department of Public Welfare to establish a Penn State program. Dr. Charles Newman, of Louisville University, was chosen among an array of candidates to become the first program administrator at Penn State University.

Continuing his interest in police education, Purdy was anxious to see the Harrisburg Area Community College (HACC) take on a planned series of police-related subjects leading to an associate degree. His efforts were not to go unrewarded as HACC's president, Dr. Clyde E. Blocker, announced that the college's curriculum would be expanded in September to include a fulltime law enforcement program. Vern L. Folley, 28, police chief at Albion, Washington, was selected to head the new program.

The momentum generated by Purdy in the direction of police training and education was to influence other state and community colleges to establish associate and baccalaureate degree programs in the fields of police administration and corrections.

In April, Conti was promoted to captain and remained in command of the R. & I. Division. New to the headquarters scene was another April-advanced officer, Captain Joseph Dussia, who was appointed director of the crime lab, replacing Captain William Nevin. Nevin, whose retirement was not to be effective until May, closed out thirty-two years of distinguished service.

In 1965, Corporal Steven J. Condes, of the Harrisburg troop, became the first member of the State Police FOP lodges to be elected to a national office. He was named national trustee. This was a clear indication that the fast-growing FOP movement in Pennsylvania was flexing its muscle on the national political scene.

Activated May 1 was the new computer-based teletype communications system which was long awaited, and once again the State Police was placed among the pioneers in the field of telecommunications. The GE Datanet-30 system was programmed to continually poll a statewide network of teletypewriter terminals at State Police substations and municipal police departments for message sending and switching with remarkable split-second swiftness. The system's memory bank was designed to store stolen car data by direct entry from originating police agencies, which could be searched, modified, and cancelled automatically. The system featured many automatic innovations which all in all gave it the right to be considered sophisticated hardware, and a monumental credit to Captain Bomboy's ingenuity. From this pioneering status was to come one of the nation's truly great computer centers where interfacing with all other major intrastate and interstate data banks leaped from the drawing boards into reality after years of determined toiling by dedicated men and women.

The State Police was to chalk up another "first" as it put into ef-

Gov. William Scranton signs proclamation observing 60th anniversary as Col. E. Wilson Purdy looks on. In traditional uniforms are Corporals Francis N. O'Rourke, left, and Joseph F. Petritis. (Courtesy of Pennsylvania State Police)

fect a statewide system for recording juvenile contacts with the police. The Central Juvenile Index (CJI) was established at headquarters with the cooperation of the field forces and municipal police agencies. "The object is to keep a sharper watch on juvenile offenders and demolish their belief they are 'getting away' with something," explained Purdy. He further explained that the index will provide for the recording of all incidents involving juveniles, even minor incidents, so that police may observe patterns and call in agencies in a position to give proper supervision and guidance. The index was also designed to expunge individual juvenile records as each subject reached age 18.

Proclaiming the week of May 2-8 as Pennsylvania State Police Week, Scranton, with reference to the department's beginning in 1905, stated, "The wisdom of this action has been confirmed time and again by the deeds of the dedicated men whose faithful service has earned an enviable reputation among police agencies everywhere and has written an illustrious history for all Pennsylvanians to note."

The highlight of that week, as messages of congratulations poured in, was a sixtieth anniversary dinner-dance in the Starlight Ballroom, at Hershey. Attending were 600 active and retired members. Former Commissioner Frank G. McCartney and Mrs. McCartney were among the celebrants. Honored were former Commissioner Lynn G. Adams, 84, whose ill health did not permit his presence, and Herbert Hunt, 83, both of whom were original constabulary members of 1905.

In late spring, work on the new field reporting system had progressed to a point where the system was ready for testing. Chosen for the pilot study was Troop J, Lancaster. And on June 1, testing was underway. The new system was intended "to bring uniformity to the processing of reports, make reports easier to prepare, increase usefulness of reports, provide supervisors with review and reference techniques, and end once and for all the many objectional features of our current reporting requirements. The system in pilot study allows for an orderly process of complaints and incidents from the moments of call to the proper completion of police action," so stated *The Communicator* announcement.

In a companion move to simplify the investigation of motor vehicle accidents for all police departments, a uniform accident report form was designed for statewide use. The new report forms were printed and distributed to all police agencies in the Commonwealth in time for the July 1 target date. The revision of this one form was an achievement in itself, and lightened the work of all police officers heretofore burdened with unreasonable paperwork requirements.

Returning from NUTI at this time were Corporals Nicholas Kordilla, Paul Chylak and Nick Danatsko. Kordilla was immediately assigned to the new field reporting system project. Kwiatek was promoted to lieutenant and transferred to Planning and Research. He replaced Shulenberger who had been promoted to captain and moved to the Academy.

Scheduled next to attend the NUTI long course were Corporals Leonard T. Koper, Russell C. Rickert and Vincent Fiorani.

On August 25, the new troop headquarters building at Wyoming was dedicated. It was the second new headquarters building to be dedicated in the anthracite coal region since the beginning of the sixtieth anniversary year. The original headquarters building at Wyoming was burned to the ground on December 22, 1908, and a new colonial-type structure was erected on the same grounds. The colonnaded building familiarly known for more than a half century was torn down to make room for the modern $232,000 structure. The original horse barn had been dismantled in 1955 and replaced by a new quartermaster and transportation building.

Again Scranton headed the list of honored guests attending the dedication ceremonies. And again the local press rightfully gave credit for the new building to former Governor Lawrence and former Commissioner McCartney. Scranton, reportedly, wasn't too pleased with the press coverage at Dunmore, and a repeat performance by the press at Wyoming was understandably more irritating.

The story of new construction, however, did not end there. During the summer months, the new building at 20th and Herr Streets, Harrisburg, also planned by Lawrence and McCarney, was occupied by the Transportation and the Maintenance and Supply Divisions. Division directors, proudly occupying their new quarters, were curious to know when their building would be dedicated. Reportedly, they were told that the building would not be dedicated since the governor's office was displeased with the publicity following the Dunmore and Wyoming dedication ceremonies. In any case, it was most unusual for a new state building costing some $425,000 not to be formally dedicated; it is equally unusual to note that *The Communicator* has never acknowledged the existence of the new facility.

Since the introduction of House Resolution No. 6, the relationship between Purdy and certain House members worsened. The most vocal of the House members was Charles J. Mills, one of the resolution sponsors. Further heat was generated when Mills was arrested on the Turnpike for speeding. Putting aside whatever argument Mills advanced for his actions, Purdy allowed the arrest to stand. Mills retaliated with claims of State Police persecution.

On June 29, Resolution No. 6 was successfully moved to the floor. The resolution passed by a 155-45 vote. Nine House members did not vote. Since there were only 116 Democrats in the House, the outcome of the voting clearly showed that an interest in a State Police investigation had invaded the GOP ranks.

In August, the resolution was amended to increase the five-man committee to ten members. The scope of the inquiry was also enlarged to include the subject of manpower needs. Committee chairmanship went to Rep. Ronald G. Lench (D-Beaver). Other members of the committee were: William B. Curwood (D-Luzerne), Samuel W. Frank (D-Lehigh), Edward W. McNally (D-Cambria), Charles G. Mills (D-Westmoreland), Thomas F. Sullivan (D-Allegheny), William G. Buchanan (R-Indiana), Edwin D. Eshelman (R-Lancaster), Guy A. Kistler (R-Cumberland) and Joseph P. Rigby (R-Allegheny). Sebastian D. Natale, a Harrisburg attorney, was named committee counsel.

The resolution struck a blow at Purdy, and there was speculation on what the investigation would really accomplish other than to publicly harrass Purdy by way of open hearings. Nonetheless, a bipartisan House committee was appointed to hold hearings, and something historically important was underway—the State Police was to be formally investigated by the legislative branch of government for the very first time.

Early in November, Representatives Mills and Curwood stopped by the Academy to pay an informal visit. A hassle developed during that visit wherein the Academy staff headed by Major Rittelmann accused the legislators of using abusive language and disturbing classes, and asked them to leave the Academy. Purdy, who was attending a conference at nearby Hotel Hershey, was informed of the fracas by phone and gave his approval to Rittelmann's ouster order. Enraged by their experience at the Academy, Mills and Curwood carried their story to the press and, needless to say, they were highly critical of the treatment they received.

Resentment against Purdy increased in the House and posters could be seen in many House offices, bearing the slogan, "Purdy Must Go."

Before its investigation could be launched, the committee was faced with a major roadblock when subpoenas were served on Purdy and others, demanding their presence to give testimony. Scranton ordered Purdy to ignore the subpoenas, questioning the legal authority of the legislative branch to make this move. Until this issue could be satisfactorily resolved, the committee was powerless to get on with its task.

Spearheaded by Attorney General Alessandroni, the administration was adamant in its stand that the executive branch did not have to knuckle under the committee's demands. Purdy, on the other hand, held to the argument that the hearings would be helpful in producing legislation authorizing an increase in manpower for the department. He was confident that his manpower study would be convincing evidence, if he was allowed to appear before the committee. Purdy was also secure in the fact that the many advancements made by the State Police under his direction would speak well of his stewardship.

Somehow he managed to convince Scranton that there was nothing to be feared from the hearings. He optimistically held to the belief that some good might come from them—the State Police would come out of these hearings "smelling like roses."

Finally accepting Purdy's position, the governor removed the roadblock, and the House committee was then at liberty to make its moves.

When, in December, the House probe finally underway, Alessandroni was given permission to state before the committee that Purdy's appearance at hearings was strictly a voluntary action and not in response to the committee's subpoena. Appointed to protect the interests of the State Police and the Scranton administration, as a matter of fact, was Deputy Attorney General Perrin C. Hamilton, a Philadelphia attorney.

At Purdy's direction, bureau directors and many troop commanders attended the committee sessions. On December 2, Urella's "hostile" testimony claimed that morale in the department was not good mainly because of differing views with regard to Purdy's transfer and promotion policies. Shortly thereafter, Purdy stripped Urella of his on-the-scene field inspections and restricted him to desk duty at headquarters. Field inspections were turned over to Lieutenants William N. Grooms and Michael Donahoe, who completed the tour at the Reading troop begun by Urella.

Committee time was devoted to claims and counter-claims regarding trooper morale. State Police managers volunteered to appear before the committee to testify to their accomplishments. Purdy presented his appeal in behalf of more men, and backed up his contention with a detailed study prepared by Planning and Research personnel. Hearings were rather routine and soon developed into a humdrum undertaking with little or nothing found newsworthy by the press. Surprisingly, all issues of *The Communicator* went to press without mention of the hearings at all. It appeared that Purdy was very much in control of the situation despite the hostile nature of the whole proceedings at the outset. Meanwhile, the work of the State Police continued as usual.

Perhaps the term "usual" is too loosely employed here. Exceeding the notoriety of goings-on under Pennsylvania's capitol dome, insofar as national interest was concerned, were the 1965 racial riots at Selma, Alabama, and the Watts area of Los Angeles, California, where the confrontation between blacks and police elements left deep scars and foretold of a continuing conflict. The State Police, ever mindful of the large black populations in Philadelphia, Pittsburgh, Chester, Harrisburg and other centers, feverishly sharpened planning and training to meet the real threat of riotous civil disobedience.

In his continuing effort to employ civilian administrators wherever possible to release enlisted personnel, Purdy announced the appointment of John P. Klosterman as director of the Harrisburg crime lab. Captain Dussia was transferred to the Greensburg troop as commander, replacing retired Captain John Chrin. Klosterman's appointment followed a lengthy nationwide search for a qualified lab director. Klosterman, 34, a native of Wisconsin, received his bachelor and master degrees in police science from Michigan State University. He had formerly served with the Michigan State crime lab, and for five years held a post with the St. Louis Police Department crime lab.

At a time when the State Police was observing the sixtieth anniversary of its founding and, at the same time subjected to a much-publicized investigation by a House committee, troopers, active and retired, were saddened by the death of former Commissioner Lynn G. Adams. Adams, 85, died on December 2, at Muncy Valley Hospital.

Adams guided State Police operations for twenty-one years and, as it has been stated before, it is doubtful that this tenure record will ever be approached by another commissioner. He was widely acclaimed as a "tough cop"—"a professional soldier whose distrust of politics with respect to his beloved 'Troopers' was as deep and abiding as his hatred and endless pursuit of those who violated the law," which is the way newsman Walter W. Ruch put it.

Purdy said following the news of Adams' death:

> In my travels and contacts with professional police administrators throughout our nation, I have received numerous inquiries concerning Colonel Adams. It has always given me a special feeling of pride to receive expressions concerning his outstanding contributions to the field of law enforcement in the early professional development of career police service.
>
> Col. Adams has been credited throughout our country for many fine accomplishments. And even though many years have passed since his retirement, he is still held in very high regard by the top men of our profession.
>
> We, of the Pennsylvania State Police, are especially indebted to him for his contribution in establishing the reputation and traditions of our Force, which have proved of great value to us in our present efforts. It is our sincere hope that our accomplishments will measure up to the ideals and standards of this fine man, who had the type of vision and courage that can well serve to inspire all of us today.

The State Police honored Adams in death with a military funeral. Uniformed pallbearers carried him to his final resting place, as a firing squad let go its volleys into a winter sky, and a bugler's lament stirringly sounded throughout the countryside. Adams was buried in the Dunmore Cemetery near the grave of his beloved wife who preceded him in death on February 17, 1965, after a long illness. Surviving Adams were his son, Donald W., and daughter, Mrs. Ruth Schilling, and two grandchildren.

By the year's end, Purdy had completed much of his program for reshaping the department. New bureaus and divisions were busy at headquarters clearly guiding line and staff functions. In the field, line and staff functions were also clearly defined. Each troop commander was administratively assisted by two lieutenants and a first sergeant: one lieutenant directed traffic operations, the other crime operations and all staff responsibilities fell to the first sergeant.

In an interview with Bill Campbell, *Sunday Patriot-News* (Harrisburg) reporter, Purdy noted the Force's anniversary and said he considered the reorganization plan the most important step in his administration. "Underlying the entire program is an effort to establish sound business principles within the organization because, with our present budget, we are big business. We must implement these principles because we, the police service—the same as any other agency—must be accountabe to the people. They are entitled to a dollar's worth of police service for each dollar spent."

Despite the fact that his agency was under investigation, Purdy was highly regarded throughout the nation as a top administrator and educator. He was active with IACP and university committee assignments, and served on numerous police conference panels. As a public speaker, he was in demand, and fulfilled as many engagements as his heavy schedule would allow. Plainly put, he was a popular figure on the national police scene—his name was a household word.

After successful testing at Troop J, Lancaster, Purdy ordered statewide application of the new field reporting system to begin January 1, 1966. Of the many changes wrought by the commissioner, the new reporting system undoubtedly had the widest impact since it touched the daily activities of every man on the job. Extensive training programs had been undertaken to ensure the successful move from the old to the new way of doing business. Manuals were given per capita distribution for easy reference, and new forms were printed in adequate supply. All forms were designed and pre-coded for data processing—and were easily executed by a trooper on the scene with ballpoint pen. The new system was a remarkable departure from the former hardships of accounting for police action, and soon received state and national recognition as a major accomplishment. Many state police and municipal police agencies were later to adopt its features.

On January 6, 1966, a class of eighty-one cadets graduated from the Academy. It was the fifth class to number married men among its ranks. This time there were forty-five married cadets completing the tough training course.

Another uniform change to add to the comfort of the patrol

personnel came in the form of a new lightweight overcoat. For the first time in twenty-nine years, the heavy outer garment was discarded in favor of new material available for uniform wear. The black fingertip double-breasted coat featured a fur collar, epaulet and sleeve tabs, nameplate holder and side vents. Slash pockets cut to the inside were designed for easy draw of service weapons.

The new year saw a continuing enrollment of officer and non-commissioned officer personnel in educational and training programs wherever they were available. Lieutenant Leon F. Wrona was the seventh officer to undergo training at the FBI National Academy. Preceding him at that institution were Commissioner Earl J. Henry, Lt. Colonel John I. Grosnick, Captain Rufus G. Williams, Captain Arthur W. Shulenberger, Detective Roy L. Titler and Lieutenant James D. Barger.

On the national scene, Congressional concern for an upswing in the crime rate resulted in unprecedented appropriations of federal funds to aid state and local police agencies. Established to handle such funding was the Law Enforcement Assistance Agency (LEAA). Although the funds at first were modest enough, appropriations in the immediate years to follow were considerably increased. Federal funds were basically intended to support training and the purchase of equipment, and encourage innovative programs to combat crime.

Early in the LEAA program, funds were set aside for the FBI to develop an ambitious computerized data bank to be known as the National Crime Information Center (NCIC). NCIC was soon to become a household word among police agencies across the nation. The FBI's top NCIC managers were Jerry Daunt and Donald Roderick.

To assist in the development of NCIC, the FBI invited the more progressive state police and metropolitan police agencies to appoint representatives to an advisory group. Forming this first advisory group were twenty-three records officers from the invited police departments. Representing the Pennsylvania State Police was Captain Conti. He was later to be joined by Captain Bomboy as NCIC plans were expanded.

NCIC secured the blessing of IACP officials, and was given technical support by the Institute of Telecommunications Sciences and Aeronomy. Initial data storage was limited to wanted persons, stolen motor vehicles, stolen motor vehicle registration plates, and stolen property. This records base was later enlarged.

For three months the House committee continued with its schedule of hearings dealing mainly with the administration of the State Police and the manpower needs of the force. The hearings had slipped from importance insofar as public notice was concerned, and the investigation itself appeared aimless. The Senate in the meanwhile had passed a bill authorizing an additional 600 troopers.

What had started out as an unspectacular probe, however, took on a new complexion in February, 1966, when Rep. Herbert Fineman (D-Philadelphia) joined the committee as a replacement for Rep. Thomas F. Sullivan. On hand for the committee proceedings on February 22 was an unusual gathering of newsmen and television cameras, creating an atmosphere of expectancy in the hearing room. It was rather obvious that an event of some sort was being staged. One committee member later recalled that Fineman was "going for the jugular vein"—Purdy's jugular vein—that is.

Observers were to find out soon enough when Fineman took up his questioning of Detective Angelo Carcaci. In response to Fineman's inquiries, Carcaci gave testimony implying that the State Police had used illegal wiretapping in some of its investigations on orders from Major Stanton. This news fell on capitol hill like a bombshell. Carcaci was admitted to the hospital with heart attack symptoms, and the committee had to continue its probe without his follow-up testimony. Major Stanton, accompanied by an attorney, answered few committee questions and elected to stand on Fifth Amendment protection in response to most questions put to him.

Scranton, in March, disallowed further testimony by Purdy, or his officers, on wiretap charges. He would permit testimony only with regard to manpower needs. The committee, however, not wanting to let go of a good thing, again beat the drums, demanding that members of the executive branch must honor the committee's subpoenas. As the dispute became more heated, Scranton banned any state employee from testifying before the House committee, claiming the Democratic-controlled probe was designed to embarrass his administration in an election year.

It was obvious that Stanton could no longer remain in command of detective operations, and so it was that on March 12 he was transferred to the Academy to await further developments. Detective operations were turned over to Stanton's assistant, Captain John E. Thompson.

In March, the House committee cited Purdy, McKetta and two detectives for contempt when they ignored subpoenas to appear at a hearing on alleged wiretapping. A hassle between the committee and the Scranton ban was inevitable.

For the first time, *The Communicator* carried an article by Purdy reflecting the seriousness of the House committee hearings. Purdy stated:

> During this difficult period, when the structure of our Organization is being subjected to exploratory surgery and the

progress of our many fine programs, in fact, our entire
mission has been hindered to a dangerous extent, it is impera-
tive that we maintain our faith in the integrity of our Force
and in the urgent and ever-present need for professional law
enforcement in our Commonwealth.

Our high standards of law enforcement have been
designed for the common good of all the people of Pennsylvania. The programs introduced have been designed for the
good of the entire Organization.

It is hoped that your faith and professional manner will
carry us through these trying times.

A suggestion program initiated by Purdy sometime earlier in his
administration was catching-on, and many improvements in departmental operations resulted from the interest generated among the rank
and file. Suggestions finding their way to headquarters through channels also dealt with changes in the motor vehicle and penal codes.
Many of these suggestions were passed on to the legislature where they
were favorably processed.

.Dipping for the last time into his bag of innovative programs,
Purdy ordered the enrollment of civilians to conduct driver examinations. Heretofore, examinations were conducted by enlisted personnel
exclusively. Purdy felt that this was another area where civilians could
release enlisted men for patrol duties. Purdy turned to the State Civil
Service Commission to conduct statewide examinations in May. The
first group of fifty, men and women, was to be hired on July 1, and undergo four weeks of training at the Academy prior to field assignment.
Supervision of their work, however, was to be kept in the hands of
enlisted personnel.

With time running out for Purdy, the controversial issue of where
the new Troop E barracks would be constructed was resolved. The
political forces at Lawrence Park were influential enough to have land
on Route 955, in Lawrence Park Township, where Troop E headquarters had been located for some twenty-eight years, chosen as the
new building site. Thus ended a lengthy dispute that had held up for
years the construction of this new field installation in Pennsylvania's
northwest.

Faced with a gubernatorial election year, the Republican party
leaders could not help but be bothered about the wiretap charges and
the disastrous effects they could have on the upcoming campaign. Lt.
Governor Raymond P. Shafer and Alessandroni were to be the Republican standardbearers for governor and lieutenant governor,
respectively. Republicans strategy in 1962 drew the State Police into
the campaign in unprecedented fashion, and in 1966 the tables could

easily be reversed, unless something was quickly done to terminate this whole matter and save face.

Late in the afternoon of Holy Thursday, April 6, Purdy was summoned to Alessandroni's office. There Alessandroni asked for Purdy's resignation, ostensibly with Scranton's approval. Purdy bargained for a formal statement in his behalf by the governor, which was agreed upon in exchange for his resignation effective Good Friday. Purdy was not permitted to return to his own office to prepare a resignation, but was instead given the run of Alessandroni's office to do so. Purdy's dislike for Alessandroni was no less intense than that of former Commissioner McCartney's.

In a *Miami Herald* interview in 1971, Purdy recalled that Scranton did not fire him personally. " 'Hell, no,' Purdy said, 'Cold as clam. Took my resignation—I submitted my resignation about 5, 5:30 in the afternoon, but he cut my pay off at noon! I didn't get any leave! I didn't get any severance pay, nothing! Cold! And on Good Friday!' "

In a "pro forma" statement released on April 7, Scranton, accepting Purdy's resignation "with deep regret," blamed Purdy's "enemies" for setting out to destroy him, "First, because they wished to get rid of him personally; and, second because they hoped to reinstate outside influences in the operation of the State Police." He further stated, "Make no mistake, this is a sad day for law enforcement in Pennsylvania. The worst kind of politics has won a battle for the lawless element in our society."

A Harrisburg *Patriot* editorial on April 11 had this to say, "For one thing, this makes the second straight Administration in which the State Police and the man who happens to be commissioner have become embroiled in the politics of a gubernatorial election year." The editorial concluded with this observation, "The Commissioner's resignation does not eliminate the need for manpower boosts, the need for answers to the wiretapping controversy and the need to isolate the State Police from the quadrennial buffeting by the political winds."

The string had run out on the "outsider," but not before he had made his presence on the Pennsylvania scene an exciting experience for those who shared in his labors. Purdy's leadership, like McCartney's before him, thrust the State Police into modern times—there to profit from the advantages of every notion coming down the pike geared to the advancement of law enforcement. Put in simplest terms, Purdy, in the hearts of many who served under him, was a good commissioner. The profound effect of his numerous accomplishments dedicated to the department's well-being is acknowledged by the officers and men who have paused to evaluate Purdy's stewardship objectively.

CHAPTER XVIII

Lt. Colonel Paul A. Rittelmann
Acting Commissioner
1966–1967

Purdy's firing left Scranton and Alessandroni facing a critical situation—they had to come up with a replacement commissioner in a hurry. On Holy Saturday, April 8, Majors George W. Pinkerton and Paul A. Rittelmann were summoned to Alessandroni's office for interviews. Apparently McKetta and Grosnick, Purdy's top officers, were immediately eliminated from consideration because of their possible involvement in the wiretap scandal. Scranton, for his own sake and the sake of the GOP gubernatorial slate, had to come up with an officer who was not vulnerable to attack by Democratic party strategists.

Pinkerton was the first to be interviewed. Rittelmann appeared at the capitol as Pinkerton was leaving. The latter went to his headquarters office to await word from Alessandroni. There he met Purdy who had stopped by headquarters to remove his personal belongings. Purdy informed Pinkerton that he had recommended him to Scranton for the commissioner's post because of his many years of experience at headquarters and familiarity with executive operations. Purdy felt certain that Pinkerton would get the job. This, however, was not to be the case. Both men learned of Rittelmann's appointment as acting commissioner by way of a radio news broadcast.

To expediently see him through this crisis, Scranton opted to simply designate Rittelmann an acting commissioner to fill the post for the remaining nine months of his term in office as governor. This course eliminated the need of seeking Senate confirmation, and would facilitate the naming of a commissioner by the next governor—a Republican, hopefully.

Rittelmann was the second officer in State Police history to be officially appointed acting department head and remain in that capacity for an enduring period. First to hold this distinction was Captain George F. Lumb who served as acting superintendent of the constabulary during Groome's two years of military service in World War I. Rittelmann was to serve as acting commissioner for the better part of a year. Others have been temporarily placed in an acting capacity to satisfy short-term needs, but with limited authority and no importance.

Certain title changes were made to accommodate Rittelmann's acting status. McKetta's rank of lieutenant colonel was given to Rittelmann and the latter's major rank became McKetta's in exchange. Rittelmann was acting commissioner—McKetta acting deputy.

Rittelmann was to reap an unexpected bonus from his appointment. For the first thirty days of his tenure, he drew a prorated share of the deputy's legally fixed salary of $13,500 a year. After the thirty days, it was ruled by the attorney general that Rittelman would be entitled to the newly-raised salary for cabinet officers pegged at $25,000. The new salary set by the legislature in 1965 was not applicable to incumbents. This odd development put Rittelmann financially a step ahead of his fellow cabinet members.

There was no denying the honor that came to Rittelman on this occasion. But, a realistic view of his new-found position left little room for celebration as he started his brief tenure with a hot potato on his hands. The problem of disposing of the wiretap charges was now his baby. The announcement of Rittelmann's appointment was accompanied by another by Scranton, stating that Stanton and Carcaci would face State Police court-martial on wiretap charges. This was rather an unprecedented action by a governor.

On Easter Monday morning, there were mixed feelings at headquarters in the wake of Purdy's firing. Some staff members were noticeably shocked and downhearted at Purdy's loss, while others appeared to harbor different thoughts. Typical of the latter was Grosnick who, in scholarly Shakespearean form, was heard to announce, "The king is dead." Coming from a top officer who had benefitted to a great extent by Purdy's three-year stay in Pennsylvania, the words fell on disbelieving ears.

Purdy returned to Michigan and took up a post as security consultant at the Fort Custer Job Corps Center near Kalamazoo. While at the Job Corps Center, he also commuted to teach an introductory course in police administration for underclassmen at Michigan State University, his alma mater.

He remained in Michigan until he was appointed sheriff of Dade County, Florida, on November 23, 1966. He took up his new assignment on December 19, where he has since distinguished himself and advanced law enforcement in Dade County. The *Miami Herald* in 1971 quoted crime writer Ralph Salerno, "If you went around the country and asked for a list of the top 10 (police chiefs), his name (Purdy) would show up on every single one—more frequently close to 1 than to 10."

After ten years in Dade County, Purdy has been elevated to the post of Public Safety Director at $50,000 a year, and proudly states that he has the best police department in the country. He has since earned his master's degree from the Florida International University and, in 1975, was elected president of the Greater Miami Rotary Club. Pennsylvania's loss has been Florida's gain.

Rittelmann, 57, a thirty-six-year veteran, was born November 14, 1908, at Baden, Beaver County, He was one of seven children born to Louis J. Rittelmann and Clara E. Schmitt Rittelmann. Rittelmann's father, a die-maker employed by the National Metal Molding Company, of Ambridge, Beaver County, was born at Pittsburgh. His mother, also born at Pittsburgh, was at one time an employe of H. J. Heinz before her marriage.

Rittelmann attended the Baden public schools and, as a high school student, was required to commute fifteen miles daily to Rochester, Beaver County. Because of the commuting difficulty, he was unable to participate in high school sports, although he longed to do so. He later attended the Pittsburgh Academy, a college prep school, where he hoped to prepare himself for a career in the U. S. Army Air Corps. He was an aviation enthusiast as a young boy, and proudly made his first parachute jump at 17.

His father, however, preferred that young Rittelmann follow in his footsteps in the die-making trade. Yielding to his father's wishes, Rittelmann went to work at National Metal Molding as an apprentice for more than two years. Dissatisfied with the opportunities offered there, he went to Pittsburgh and enrolled in a theatre management training program at the Stanley Theatre. During the course of this training, Rittelmann met several times with constabulary Private Robert McKee, a Baden neighbor and high school chum, who convinced him that an exciting constabulary career was worth thinking about.

Rittelmann did give this idea some consideration and applied. After a delay of several weeks, he was summoned to the training

Lt. Colonel Paul A. Rittelmann (Courtesy of Pennsylvania State Police)

school at Hershey on October 1, 1930, and joined a class of thirteen for six months of training. The class was held over for an extra month to prepare a special exhibition for Governor Gifford Pinchot and his cabinet. Following a delayed graduation on April 22, 1931, Rittelmann was assigned to Troop A, Greensburg, and sent to the Washington Substation. At the time of the State Police-Highway Patrol merger in 1937, the Washington Substation became a part of a newly-created troop, B-1, Washington.

Rittelmann was a member of the constabulary detail in 1937 at the Fayette County jailbreak, when Private Joseph A. Hoffer was shot and killed. Rittelmann was also witness to the slaying of another fellow officer at Clarksville in 1939, where Corporal George D. Naughton was shot by a fugitive. Naughton met his death in the very same dwelling where Joseph Yablonski, his wife and daughter were later slain in 1970. (Yablonski was a defeated candidate for president of the United Mine Workers.)

Rittelmann was promoted to corporal in 1940 and transferred to the Butler troop where he was placed in charge of the Beaver Substation until 1945. In 1945, he was promoted to sergeant and moved to troop headquarters at Butler. It was during this tour of duty that he recalls the unusual, authorized use of scopolamine (truth serum) to successfully prosecute the accused in a rape-murder case.

He was advanced to first sergeant in 1952. Four years later, he was commissioned a lieutenant and transferred to Troop E-1, at Erie. Commissioner McCartney promoted him to captain on January 28, 1960, and transferred him back to his home troop at Greensburg as commanding officer. Impressed with his work, McCartney sent Rittelmann to the Academy, at Hershey, as assistant superintendent to succeed Major H. C. Johnson who was soon to retire at 60. Upon Johnson's departure, Rittelmann was promoted to major on November 29, 1962, and took over the Academy superintendent post.

When governor-elect Scranton, after the 1962 general election, invited officers with the rank of captain and above to apply for the commissioner's post, Rittelmann was one of the officers who did not take up the Scranton invitation. He was content to remain at the Academy.

Rittelmann is married to the former Louise Joan Christe, R.N., a native of Cresson, Cambria County, and a graduate of Pittsburgh's Mercy Hospital School of Nursing. The Rittelmanns reside in Hershey. An avid reader, Rittelmann, oddly enough, enjoys cooking and canning, and is an excellent wood-finisher. He is a member of St. Joan of Arc Roman Catholic Church, Knights of Columbus, Areba Club and the Rotary International.

Surprising many, Rittelmann retained Grace Kenner as his administrative assistant—a post to which she was appointed by Purdy. It became apparent that Purdy's firing satisfied the House Democrats and further changes at headquarters were not sought.

Stanton was officially suspended on April 15, pending the outcome of his case. When summoned for questioning by Rittelmann, Stanton was accompanied by his attorney, Huette F. Dowling, a former FBI agent and former Dauphin County district attorney. Stanton's refusal to answer questions put to him was upsetting to Rittelmann who was inclined to help Stanton if he was only following orders of superior officers with regard to wiretap activities. This unsatisfactory session, from Rittelmann's point of view, left him no recourse but to go ahead with the court-martial proceedings.

Major John J. Pezzent, director of the Bureau of Technical Services, was then the department's senior major. He was contemplating his retirement at 60, a point that would be reached in September, 1966, just a few months away. When court-martial proceedings reached beyond the rumor stage, Pezzent sensed that he might be called upon to head the trial board, and made up his mind that under no circumstances would he spend his last few months on the job attending to something as serious and unprecedented as Stanton's court-martial. He didn't have to wait long for the call from topside. Rittelmann informed Pezzent that he was expecting him to preside over the trial. Being well-prepared for this eventuality, Pezzent declined and terminated his services in May. His State Police career spanned thirty-eight years.

The board was finally made up of Captain John F. Yaglenski, who had primary responsibility as president. Serving with him were Captains Edward Switaj and George Sifter. The judge advocate's job fell to Captain Charles J. Buchinsky, aided by Deputy Attorney General Judson Ruch. Stanton's defense effort was in the hands of Dowling, his civilian counsel, and Lieutenant Charles Graci. For the first time since 1937, a State Police commissioned officer had to lay his reputation on the line before a court-martial board. There was special importance in Stanton's case, since he was the highest ranking officer in State Police history to come before a board.

While the pot was yet boiling, Alessandroni and his wife were killed in a plane crash on May 8, during a primary election campaign in which he was a candidate for lieutenant governor on the Shafer ticket. Three days later Scranton named Edward Friedman acting attorney general. Alessandroni's death came nine days before primary election day. Replacing him on the slate was Philadelphia attorney Raymond J. Broderick.

Stanton's trial, privately conducted at the Academy, began May 10. After a number of tension-filled sessions and the offering of much testimony, proceedings were concluded on June 21, ending the longest court-martial session in State Police history. The trial board acquitted Stanton, and two days later Rittelmann returned him to duty status with all back-pay forthcoming.

The outcome, however, was not that cut and dried, for it was not in the cards for Stanton to have his old job back as head of the detective bureau. Allegedly on orders from the capitol, Rittelmann switched Stanton to the Bureau of Staff Inspection, and Urella was transferred to Pezzent's vacancy. Although Urella was doing remarkably well with the field inspection program, he was considered a hostile witness during the House hearings insofar as Purdy was concerned, and his days as head of that program were numbered. The "shake-up" was not completed until Captain Arthur W. Shulenberger was brought up from the Academy, promoted to major, and given the detective bureau slot. The Academy superintendent vacancy created by Rittelmann's advancement had in the meantime been filled by Captain John E. Thompson's promotion to major. At the Academy, Lieutenant Leon F. Wrona was promoted to captain and designated assistant superintendent. This, in the main, took care of Rittelmann's principal promotional activity during his term of office.

Sergeant Angelo Carcaci, who during these trying months was awaiting court-martial, was spared the ordeal when Rittelmann dropped the charges against him. This was a logical development from the outcome of Stanton's trial. Carcaci did, however, suffer a change in duty assignment and a transfer, duplicating the circumstances in Stanton's case.

Although Rittelmann believed that Stanton would be found guilty as charged, he was relieved at his acquittal. He did not want Stanton to be a political football for following Purdy's orders, if that was so. The trial board apparently felt that Stanton was only following orders, and acquitted him.

Before and during the court-martial proceedings, the attorney general's office directed special Deputy Attorney General Judson Ruch, of York, to research State Police crime investigation reports to determine if there was any evidence of wiretapping during the McCartney administration. This was, undoubtedly, considered a countermeasure to whatever political hay the Democrats were harvesting. The search, however, was negative, and Ruch's work was not to provide the Republicans with the ammunition they were seeking.

Before the House investigation and Stanton's court-martial were actually put behind, the State Police had instituted a number of procedural changes regarding the preparation of investigation reports and the use of discretionary funds. These changes were advocated by officers who served as observers and analysts of all that had transpired. By the end of Rittelmann's time in office, the dust had settled—but injured feelings were longer in the mending.

As though Rittelmann's boat was not rocking enough with the Stanton affair, the voyage was made even more difficult by an incident at Shade Gap. The State Police barracks at Hollidaysburg had been investigating for weeks a case of sniping by an unknown gunman in the mountains of south central Pennsylvania near Shade Gap, Bedford County. The investigation blossomed into a news story of national interest when on May 11 the gunman, then identified as William (Mountain Man) D. Hollenbaugh, 44, kidnapped Peggy Ann Bradnick,

17, of Shade Gap, as she walked home from school, and set off one of Pennsylvania's most involved manhunts. Local, state and federal law enforcement officers joined in the hunt as the allusive ridge-runner, herding his hostage with him, managed to stay one step ahead of the posse. Expert trackers and tracking dogs were enlisted in the search.

A tremendous effort by a 400-man State Police task force finally brought the incident to an end eight days later, but not before the "Mountain Man" had slain FBI agent Terry R. Anderson and a police dog, and wounded another tracking dog. Anderson, highly respected in police circles, was agent-in-charge at Harrisburg. The wounded dog, King, owned by Tom McGinn, died later from his injuries.

Cornered in a mountain farm house at Fort Littleton on May 18 by State Police forces and others, Hollenbaugh was slain in an exchange of gunfire. Peggy Ann Bradnick was found unharmed by her abductor.

In looking over the results of the Shade Gap operations, the State Police hierarchy acknowledged that more time should be spent on planning and training for large-scale demands such as this.

Rittelmann drew considerable flak from the members of the news corps that assembled at Shade Gap to cover the nation's number one story. The acting commissioner, because of the danger involved, prohibited newsmen access to certain zones. Protesting newsmen saw it in a different light. One television newsman, heatedly contesting Rittelmann's limitations, was arrested, making Rittelmann a most unpopular figure with the broadcasters. An Associated Press writer labelled Rittelmann "a militaristic career man who is the antithesis of all the easy-going qualities of his predecessor (Purdy). With Col. Paul A. Rittelmann, you need an appointment to get the time of day."

This controversy led again to discussions dealing with the need for a professional public relations officer on the State Police payroll. Scranton had banned the hiring of a public relations officer to fill the vacancy created by Canniff's resignation at the close of former Commissioner McCartney's tenure. In the meantime, Rittelmann was mindful of the need to maintain a public relations program and, for one thing, continued to hold one-day institutes at the Academy with business and professional groups.

The State Police in May demonstrated its determination to keep abreast of the latest developments in the police communications field by joining the Law Enforcement Teletypewriter System (LETS). LETS, a computer-based network, connects all state capitals in the contiguous United States, allowing for a rapid exchange of data between state police agencies. In the field of communications, the State Police also continued to work closely with the FBI and the other large state and metropolitan police forces in developing the National Crime Information Center (NCIC) which was soon destined to become one of the principal data storage systems for police use.

Rittelmann, a firm believer in Purdy's innovative program of civilian driver examiners, completed arrangements with the State Civil Service Commission to assist with the recruiting and screening of applicants. An initial group of fifty was sought. Training for fifty, all males, was begun in August, 1966, but after four weeks of training at the Academy only thirty-three finished. Graduating on September 15, were:

Chalmers G. Barber	Edward C. Leber
Rudolph Barfafski, Jr.	John J. Lowry
Ora M. Brown	William B. Lutz
Nicholas R. Carlance, Jr.	James R. Lynam
Ernest L. Deem	Richard I. McCane
Benjamin W. Deicas	Peter J. McDonaugh
James W. Drenning	Robert L. McKinley
Robert O. Evans	Royd E. Mortimer
Michael P. Gierlak	Jerome F. Parme
James F. Gingher	Robert L. Riddle
Page J. Glasgow	Richard A. Roberts
Charles H. Graham	Loughrey F. Tyson
Elam L. Grumblein	Richard B. Warren
Arnold P. Henley	William E. Wells
Michael T. Kocha	William J. Williams
John J. Korns	Robert G. Wood

William E. Large

Members of this first driver license examiner (DLE) class in State Police history were immediately assigned to the field, releasing enlisted men for patrol duty, except for the few who were retained as supervisors.

Graduating on June 11 from NUTI were Sergeant Vincent Fiorani, and Corporals Russel Rickert and Leonard T. Koper. Selected to begin the NUTI course in September were Sergeants Bernard G. Stanalonis and Earl P. Wright, and Corporal John Duignan.

In June, the U. S. Supreme Court once again rendered a controversial 5–4 decision, this time in the *Miranda* v. *State of Arizona* case. Continuing its liberal leanings toward the protection of criminals, as police viewed it, the court held that police may not interrogate an individual until he has been informed of his constitutional rights, including the right to remain silent and the right to an attorney.

Louis E. Simpson, a Purdy appointment and director of the Bureau of Staff Services, resigned his post in August to accept a position with the U. S. State Department's Agency for International Development in Liberia, Africa. He was replaced by Fiscal Officer Richard J. Shaffer. Replacing Shaffer in the fiscal office was Robert J. Zinsky.

The general assembly, finally acting on Scranton's request for 600 additional troopers, agreed to give the State Police only 250. Act 6, P.L. 54, signed on August 31, increased the authorized complement from 2,100 to 2,350 officers and men. "Sure I'm disappointed and I won't deny it that we didn't get more State Police. We need 600 more to do the job. I am sure the Legislature in due time will wake up to this," commented Scranton as he signed the measure into law, according to a Harrisburg *Patriot* account. Editorially, the House was highly criticized for playing politics in the face of an obvious acute shortage of troopers, and to the public's detriment.

The 1966 session of the legislature which endured from January 4 to November 15, and included two special sessions called by Scranton, passed only one measure concerning State Police operations.

Grace Kenner, in September, married Major Arthur W. Shulenberger, and resigned her position as Rittelmann's administrative assistant in favor of becoming a housewife. Kenner, a popular figure at headquarters, was the last important link with Purdy's three-year term.

The State Police had already trained men to provide SCUBA diving services to state and local police units, and in October ordered four more men to the U. S. Navy Deep Sea Diving School, at Washington, to undergo four weeks of training. They were Troopers Howard G. Berringer, James I. Illingworth, Francis T. Lynch and Marshall C. McDade.

Facing compulsory retirement at 60, Captain William J. Garrick, chief quartermaster, in November ended 31½ years of state service. Replacing Garrick was Sergeant Frank Forker.

At the polls in November, GOP candidate Raymond P. Shafer defeated Milton J. Shapp, his Democratic opponent, by a comfortable margin 2,110,349 to 1,868,719. With Shafer's victory came Republican control of the House 103–99. The Republicans retained their majority in the Senate 27–22.

Shapp, who had come through a bitterly-fought primary battle with Senator Robert Casey, was a newcomer to the state political scene. The multimillionaire business man was again to try his wings four years later—with surprising success. Among those close to Shapp, it was known that had Shapp won the 1966 gubernatorial election he planned to name Major Rocco P. Urella as his State Police commissioner. The truth of this matter was to become evident four years later.

With the election of Shafer came the quadrennial in-fighting for the commissioner's seat in the governor's cabinet. Mentioned most as top contenders were Lt. Colonel John I. Grosnick, Major Frank McKetta and Captain Joseph Dussia. Shafer, like Scranton, named his cabinet members-to-be well in advance of inauguration day, except his State Police commissioner. Appointed Secretary of Property and Supplies was Perrin C. Hamilton who served as counsel to former Commissioner Purdy during the notorious House committee hearings.

On January 13, a news story confirmed the fact that former Army Lt. Colonel John Eisenhower turned down Shafer's offer to be his State Police commissioner. The son of the late President Dwight D. Eisenhower rejected the offer, stating that he was not interested in a political appointment. John Eisenhower was then vice president of Freedoms Foundation at Valley Forge, and had served as chairman of the state Republican party's primary campaign when Shafer received the party's nomination. Shafer's decision to turn to Eisenhower might well have been his strategy to avoid the pressures put upon him in behalf of aspiring State Police officers.

McKetta and Grosnick were believed to be leading contenders for the appointment. Dussia, with strong support from influential Brig. General Richard K. Mellon, decided to throw his hat in the ring. The contest became a foot race between Dussia and McKetta, who, reportedly, had Senate Majority Leader Albert Pechan's backing. Allegedly, it was Pechan who had successfully prevailed upon Scranton to appoint McKetta as Purdy's deputy. McKetta asked Dussia to back off, but to no avail. Once having decided to make his bid, Dussia was not about to back off for McKetta—or anyone else. As the story goes, Pechan informed Shafer that Dussia could not under any circumstances win Senate confirmation, and that McKetta stood a better chance of confirmation. In a compromise with Mellon, Shafer agreed to appoint Dussia as McKetta's deputy. Dussia went along with the compromise.

Preliminary to the compromise, both McKetta and Dussia were interviewed by Shafer, William C. Sennett and Arthur F. Sampson. The latter two men were destined to be heavyweights in the Shafer administration: Sennett was appointed attorney general, Sampson was to fill the dual role of secretary of administration and budget secretary.

Four days before inauguration day, Shafer named McKetta as his choice for State Police commissioner, claiming that he made a thorough survey of all officers with the rank of captain and above, and came up with McKetta as the best man. Upon learning of this news, Democratic House Minority Leader Herbert Fineman recalled that McKetta had been deputy during the wiretap probe, and predicted that McKetta's confirmation in the Senate might run into trouble. McKetta forces approached Urella, a known friend of Fineman, to smooth the way for confirmation. With the promise of special consideration later on, Urella agreed to aid McKetta's cause.

In gentlemanly fashion, Shafer, before announcing McKetta's appointment, took Rittelmann into his confidence. Rittelmann's history-making term as acting commissioner was entering into its final moments. Much credit must be given Rittelmann for seeing the department through some rough times. Strong-mindedly and firmly he guided its course, not yielding to political favors despite the approaches made to him by elements of both parties. He fully measured up to the responsibilities handed him during a period of crisis.

As one of his final official acts before leaving office, Scranton, on January 16, 1967, joined Shafer in dedicating the new Highway and Safety Building, at the corner of Forster Street and Commonwealth Avenue, in the capital city. The $16.5 million dollar structure took 2½ years to construct. Scheduled to occupy the new addition to the capitol complex were the Highway Department, Pennsylvania State Police, Department of Revenue, Department of Internal Affairs, the bureaus of Traffic Safety, Motor Vehicles, and Weights and Measures, and the State Council of Civil Defense.

CHAPTER XIX

Colonel Frank McKetta

1967–1971

Raymond Philip Shafer took his oath of office as Pennsylvania's thirty-ninth governor on January 17, 1967, in ceremonies held at the state Farm Show Building. His election to this highest state office marked the first time in Pennsylvania political history that a lieutenant governor successfully campaigned for the top job. He was also the first to take the new oath approved by ballot in 1966.

Lieutenant Governor Raymond J. Broderick, the last-minute subsitute for the late Walter E. Alessandroni on the GOP ticket in 1966, took his oath of office before a throng of well-wishers who jammed the Senate chamber for that occasion.

In the afternoon of inauguration day, McKetta and fourteen other cabinet choices submitted to the Senate by Shafer were confirmed by a 48–0 vote. Obviously, the groundwork for McKetta's prompt confirmation was well-accomplished. Confirmation, however, was held up on Major General Thomas R. White, Shafer's nomination for state adjutant general, and David O. Maxwell who was earmarked to be state insurance commissioner. Senator Ernest P. Kline (D-Beaver), minority chairman of the Senate Executive Nominations Committee, said the Democrats did not question the qualifications of White and Maxwell, but wanted further information before lending support to their confirmation.

The fifteen confirmed cabinet members took their oaths of office in the House chamber that same afternoon with relatives and friends in attendance. Among the new officeholders was William C. Sennett, 36, the youngest attorney general in Pennsylvania history.

McKetta was the first commissioner since Wilhelm to be confirmed on inauguration day with cabinet colleagues and occupy his office: Henry was appointed a few months after the Leader administration was underway; McCartney's confirmation was held up by the Senate for a month; Purdy's confirmation also ran into Senate trouble for a few weeks; and Rittelmann finished Purdy's unexpired term.

Enjoying the benefit of the newly created salary scale for cabinet officers already experienced by Rittelmann, McKetta drew $25,000 a year during his four years in office.

McKetta, 49, was born February 19, 1917, in the small Pennsylvania mining community of Wyano, Westmoreland County. He was one of four children born to Frank McKetta and Nancy Gelet McKetta. Both of his parents were born in Galitza, Austria, and at differing times emigrated with their families from Austria to Pennsylvania. According to a story attributed to one of McKetta's uncles, the family name was orginally spelled "Meketta." After the family arrived in the United States, the name somehow was phonetically documented as "McKetta," and remained so.

The elder McKetta, before his marriage to Nancy Gelet, was a circus strongman. He later returned to Pennsylvania, and entered the coal fields as a mining laborer, where he earned and saved enough money to try his hand as an independent mine operator.

Young Frank McKetta attended South Huntingdon public schools and graduated from South Huntingdon High School in 1935. Interested in sports, McKetta participated in football, basketball and boxing programs. While a high school student, McKetta suffered the loss of his father who was fatally injured in a mining accident. Unable to earn an athletic or scholastic college scholarship, McKetta could see no bright future during the days of the Great Depression, and reluctantly went into the mines to financially aid his family. A mine cave-in which almost brought his young life to an abrupt finish was enough to end his career as a miner.

He turned to amateur and professional boxing for a living. McKetta toured the country with a group of boxers, and was ballyhooed by his road manager as "Sunnyboy" McKetta. To spice the fight card, promoters often tagged him with aliases during his two-year boxing career that was dominated by low pay, skimpy food, lousy hotels and prolonged absences from home.

Returning to a boxing club back home, McKetta drew the attention of constabulary Captain Jacob C. Mauk, who was then command-

Colonel Frank McKetta (Courtesy of Pennsylvania State Police)

ing the Greensburg troop. Mauk, determined to interest McKetta in joining the constabulary, continually visited with him at the boxing club and enthusiastically described the excitement of constabulary service. McKetta succumbed to Mauk's recruiting efforts and filed an application. Noting that McKetta was only 20 years old, Mauk slyly changed the date of birth to indicate 21.

After a brief delay, McKetta was cleared at Greensburg by an oral interview board comprised of Superintendent Lynn G. Adams, Captain Thomas F. Martin and Mauk. He was sent to the Hershey training school on September 1, 1937, and became a member of the first Pennsylvania Motor Police class to undergo training after the merger of the constabulary and Highway Patrol. His class was held over and later joined forces with the larger Myerstown class. After seven months of training, he was graduated from Myerstown on March 31, 1938, and assigned to Troop B, Wyoming. He volunteered service with the Turnpike troop and was designated officer-in-charge of the Somerset Substation from 1941 to 1943.

McKetta entered World War II service in December, 1943. His wartime services included assignments in North Africa, China, Burma, India and the United States. Honorably discharged at Fort Custer, Michigan, in April, 1946, he returned to his post with the Turnpike troop. He continued to subscribe to the army correspondence studies as a member of the Reserve Corps. In that capacity, he was advanced to major. After twenty-two years of combined active and reserve duty, he retired from the reserve program with the rank of lieutenant colonel in 1965.

At his request he was transferred to Troop B-1, Washington, in 1947, and again transferred to his home troop at Greensburg in 1951. Having established a reputation for his crime investigations, and with the backing of Squadron Commander Major Andrew Hudock, McKetta was promoted to detective in October, 1952. He was later advanced to detective sergeant in 1954. When Commissioner Henry abolished the detective division, McKetta, as were others, was reclassified to sergeant in August, 1956. He was given commissioned rank as lieutenant in February, 1960, and transferred to Troop E-1, at Erie. In November, 1962, near the close of Commissioner McCartney's tenure, McKetta was promoted to captain and shifted to the Academy as assistant superintendent of that facility. In May, 1963, McKetta was appointed Purdy's deputy, and in 1966 exchanged posts with Rittelmann who succeeded Purdy. The towering six-footer was the tallest of men appointed head of the State Police.

McKetta is married to the former Ann Harsanyi, of Brookline (Pittsburgh), Allegheny County. Ann was one of four children born to John Harsanyi and Ann Birkner Harsanyi. Commissioner and Mrs. McKetta, residents of Camp Hill, Cumberland County, have a son, Frank Stephen.

McKetta is a member of the International Association of Chiefs of Police, Pennsylvania Chiefs of Police Association, Northeast Chiefs of Police Association, National Sheriffs Association, Fraternal Order of Police, American Federation of Police, and Good Shepherd Roman Catholic Church, at Camp Hill.

The day after his oath-taking, McKetta announced the appointment of Dussia as his deputy, stating that he had consulted Governor Shafer with respect to the appointment. Dussia was sworn in as deputy on January 19. It was rumored in the field that McKetta's choice for deputy, had it been his to make, would have been Lieutenant Joseph L. Young of Butler. Young, according to the same rumors, was helpful in securing Senator Pechan's effective support for McKetta's appointments as deputy and commissioner. Dussia's successful appearance in the picture, however, scuttled whatever chances Young might have had for the Harrisburg post. Pechan, in earlier years, had tried to convince both Purdy and Rittelmann that Young should be promoted to captain; both men put aside the senator's petitions. McKetta, within two months of his own advancement as commissioner, promoted Young to captain and gave him command of the Greensburg troop. And, again in less than fifteen months, Young was promoted to major.

The breach between McKetta and Dussia, typically resulting from a heated campaign, was never really bridged during the next four years. Dussia was tolerated, but not taken into McKetta's confidence on important official matters except when necessity removed alternatives. For four years, the relationship between McKetta, Grosnick and Dussia was a strange one, indeed.

McKetta, Dussia, Young and others in State Police history are not to be frowned upon for their aggressiveness in seeking high office. They were victims of a system that transformed the commissioner's cabinet post into a political appointment of importance—a political plum to be snatched by some aspirant.

The commissioner and deputy are both removed by law from the authorized State Police complement; they are not officially numbered among its officers and men. Travel for each of these two men is made over political highways—a condition that has been more frequently in evidence during the last two decades. In McKetta's time, the top post paid $25,000 a year; since then, the salary has been increased considerably, making the job even more appetizing from an income standpoint. Accompanying the salary are the power to dispense favors and generous retirement benefits like frosting on a cake. Unfortunately, heated contests for the top post have damaging drawbacks. They create hard feelings that endure for years, such as was seen in the McKetta-Dussia affair. They divide the department into camps. The winner is a loser in many respects.

McKetta's tenure was to be very much influenced by his former associates in the western Pennsylvania troops. Young and Captain Howard M. Jaynes headed the list of field counselors. Both were to find promotions to major fairly soon. At headquarters, Lieutenant Albert F. Kwiatek was viewed as a center of influence, and in the minds of headquarters staff personnel, he was one of McKetta's chief architects. Kwiatek was promoted to captain at the top of 1968 and to major a year later.

Dussia, 50, a native of West Brownsville, Washington County, was born June 7, 1916. His mother, Bridget Colby Dussia, born at Dublin, Ireland, immigrated to the United States with her family prior to World War I. The Colby family settled near East Lansing, Michigan, and took to farming. Soon thereafter, Louis P. Dussia emigrated from his birthplace at Budapest, Hungary, to the United States, and became a hired-hand on the Colby farm. Louis and Bridget, convinced that their teenage love affair and marriage would not be sanctioned by her parents, eloped to West Brownsville, Pennsylvania. Louis found employment with the Vesta Coal Company, a subsidiary of Jones and Laughlin Steel, where he continued as a miner until he was 70. Joseph Dussia was one of five children born to Louis and Bridget at West Brownsville. An only sister, Mary, and his oldest brother, Louis, died in their teens. His brother, John, also became a trooper and was advanced to captain before his retirement in 1975.

Dussia attended the West Brownsville public schools. As a high school student, however, he went to live with his maternal grandparents at East Lansing, and attended Okemos High School there. At Okemos, he was an honor student, an outstanding football player, and valedictorian of his graduating class in 1933. Because of his achievements in football, Dussia was given an athletic scholarship to Michigan State University where he continued in the sport and graduated with a Bachelor of Science degree in business administration. Dussia admits that his continuing education at Michigan State could not have been possible without a scholarship since his parents, like many others during the Great Depression days, were in no position to underwrite university tuition fees.

During his residence with the Colby family, Dussia was fascinated by the work of his uncle, Steve Colby, who operated a locksmith shop at East Lansing. After high school hours, Dussia would spend much of his time with Uncle Steve, and help run the shop at night. This early interest in locks was in later years to become a major undertaking in Dussia's life.

In 1937, Dussia returned to West Brownsville and enrolled at the Douglas Business College, at nearby Charleroi. By 1938, he had by self-training acquired an exceptional knowledge of locks and a skill for lock manipulation. It was then that he became associated with Harry Miller, a well-known figure in the lock business, who, with his father, had controlling interest in Sergeant and Greenleaf, Inc., Rochester, New York, a leading manufacturer of safe locks.

Responding to recruiting notices by the recently enlarged Pennsylvania Motor Police, Dussia applied and was called to the special training school at Myerstown (the former Albright College campus) on April 1, 1938. In July, his 238-man class graduated at formal ceremonies conducted in the forum of the state Education Building at Harrisburg. The three honor classmen, James L. Burkholder, George W. Pinkerton and Joseph Dussia (in that order) were congratulated by Governor Earle. This class was the second largest ever to be graduated by the state's top police agency.

Upon graduation, Dussia was assigned to Troop C-1, Punxsutawney. He was later assigned to the DuBois Substation where he was promoted to corporal in 1950 and to sergeant in 1954. His promotion to first sergeant in 1959 brought him back to troop headquarters. Dussia was advanced to lieutenant in 1962 and transferred to Troop E-1, at Erie, where he supervised both criminal and traffic activities. On April 1, 1965, he was promoted to captain and given command of the crime

Lt. Colonel Joseph Dussia (Courtesy of Pennsylvania State Police)

lab at Harrisburg. In September of that same year, he was transferred to Greensburg as commanding officer of Troop A-1, replacing Captain John Chrin who retired.

During his tour of duty at Greensburg, it was Dussia and Senator Jack E. McGregor (R-Allegheny) who located the crashed plane in which Attorney General Walter E. Alessandroni and his wife lost their lives. McGregor, Alessandroni's western Pennsylvania campaign manager, notified Dussia that the candidate for lieutenant governor was overdue at Johnstown. Securing a search plane at the Somerset airport, Dussia and McGregor spotted the downed plane and led a ground force to the remote mountain crash area from where the bodies of the deceased were removed with considerable difficulty.

With Commissioner Purdy's permission, Dussia lectured extensively on the subject of safe locks and burglaries, and wrote numerous articles for technical and police publications. Dussia, having secured a financial interest in the Sergeant and Greenleaf firm, was also permitted by Purdy and subsequent commissioners to serve as a board member and paid consultant. (The firm, now located at Nicholsville, Kentucky, is the nation's leading supplier of safe locks.) Dussia has contributed significantly to a number of innovations in lock systems; he is listed by the National Safe Manufacturers Association as one the top five safe and lock specialists in the country.

Dussia is married to the former Esther Colkitt, of Big Run, Jefferson County. They have no children. Mrs. Dussia is the daughter of George H. Colkitt and Zula M. Bonner Colkitt, both of whom were born near Johnsonburg, Indiana County. George Colkitt was a pioneer Ford dealer at Big Run, and later opened a Buick agency at Punxsutawney. At 87, he recalls a time when, as a dealer, he offered free driving lessons with each and every car sold to his rural clients, some of whom had never known what it was like behind the wheel until they purchased a car.

Dussia's only hobby of collecting antique guns (flintlocks, and ball and cap) accounts for the finest privately-owned collection of its kind in the eastern section of the United States, valued at more than a quarter of a million dollars.

He is a member of Saints Cosmas and Damian Church, at Punxsutawney, and holds memberships in the American Association of Criminology, National Locksmith Association, Locksmiths of America, Fraternal Order of Police, International Association of Chiefs of Police, Western Pennsylvania Chiefs of Police Association, Knights of Columbus, Fraternal Order of Eagles, Benevolent Patriotic Order of Elks, Loyal Order of Moose, and the DuBois Chamber of Commerce.

In February, Rittelmann was assigned to the newly-created post of field commander with the rank of lieutenant colonel. In this capacity, Rittelmann worked closely with field officers in meeting their line responsibilities. Much of what Rittelmann was expected to do was transferred from the deputy's office, thus diminishing Dussia's role considerably in the now four-man State Police hierarchy. In the eyes of most observers, Rittelmann's promotion was a just reward for his past services in light of his upcoming mandatory retirement twenty-one months away. Rittelmann could not recall any promise by Shafer, indicating his future role in State Police affairs, when the governor informed him of McKetta's appointment. Nonetheless, he was elated by this unique development, and creditably performed the duties of his office.

February was to see another merited promotion go to Gerald S. Patterson, Butler troop chief clerk. Patterson was transferred to headquarters as director of Maintenance and Supply, replacing Sergeant Frank Forker who retired. Patterson, 46, a native of Columbia Cross Roads, Bradford County, entered State Police service in 1938, a service that was broken by a two-year hitch in the U. S. Navy from 1944 to 1946. He is married to the former Dorna Merritt, of Grandville Summit, Bradford County. They have one son, Gerald.

Early in his administration, McKetta called a daily staff conference which was to be attended by top administrators at headquarters, the Academy and Harrisburg troop. The roll call included some thirty-eight commissioned officers, non-commissioned officers and civilian executives, who were expected to be present at all sessions except for excused absences. Conferences were held whether or not there was business to discuss or information to pass on.

The commissioner, in his judgment, felt that the sessions allowed for a worthwhile exchange of information. The conference attendees differed. To them it was generally a waste of time taken from heavy workloads. Analysts agreed that the costs of the sessions were enormous and out of proportion to any recognizable benefits. Attendants, among themselves, believed that weekly sessions and extra sessions in critical times would be more palatable and practical. Nonetheless, this difference of opinion was never openly discussed with McKetta who presented a rather uncompromising attitude about the whole business, while unhappy attendants filed into the headquarters conference room every workday with a grin-and-bear-it outlook. Notwithstanding the costs or their debatable value, daily conferences were held throughout McKetta's four-year tenure. Succeeding commissioners, however, dumped the daily conference in favor of a more reasonable schedule of staff meetings.

State Police headquarters offices occupy 5th and 6th floors of state Transportation Building (Courtesy of Pennsylvania State Police)

With the completion of the new fourteen-story Highway and Safety Building, the State Police moved from leased quarters to occupy the 5th and 6th floors of the state-owned facility. The large Bureau of Technical Services took up all fifth floor accommodations, while the executive offices and all other bureaus and divisions were allocated space on the sixth floor. This gigantic move was made in May, and a public "open house" program was held in July with Governor Shafer headlining the list of distinguished visitors.

The issue of a State Police public relations officer was finally put to rest with the appointment of E. William Lindeberg as director of public information. Lindeberg, 45, a native of Carbondale, Lackawanna County, and a graduate of Missouri University, took up his new post in May.

At the same time, Personnel Director Michael Aaronson, another Purdy appointment, resigned his job to accept a personnel post with the Philadelphia Board of Education. Succeeding Aaronson was John Millett, Aaronson's assistant. Millett, a graduate of the University of Georgia and the University of Pennsylvania, was transferred from another state agency to the State Police in August, 1964.

Not to overlook an important event, the officers and men of the

Pennsylvania State Police sent congratulations to the New York State Police Department which was celebrating its fiftieth anniversary. The New York force was established in 1917, and patterned after the Pennsylvania constabulary. Colonel George Chandler, one of "Teddy" Roosevelt's Rough Riders, was its first commander.

As the racial riot incidents increased in number on a national scale, the summer months of 1967 became worrisome to the State Police. Of particular concern were Philadelphia and Pittsburgh—Pennsylvania's black population centers. For these two locations, special task forces were organized and operational plans developed. Major Urella was directed to head the Eastern Task Force. Urella's choice was a logical one since most of his outstanding field career was spent in the Philadelphia area. He and Philadelphia Police Commissioner Frank L. Rizzo were close law enforcement associates. Urella and Rizzo with their combined resources and leadership constituted a formidable team that kept eastern Pennsylvania free of major violence. During Urella's absence from Harrisburg, Major Stanton filled his shoes as director of the Bureau of Technical Services. The Western Task Force was directed by Captain Howard M. Jaynes.

Although Pennsylvania was not bothered in 1967 by racial violence, the State Police did have to maintain a sizeable task force drawn from all quarters of the department to patrol roadways in western Pennsylvania and the Turnpike due to a steel haulers strike. In a prolonged strike, steel haulers resorted to threats and violence that disrupted the free flow of traffic along most important roadways. A determined patrol force was instrumental in keeping a very difficult situation from getting out of hand.

In 1967, the State Police joined a number of other large departments as the testing of NCIC operations got underway. Conti and Bomboy continued as departmental representatives as NCIC operations developed favorably into one of the most advanced information systems offered to law enforcement. At first, McKetta balked at the assignment of manpower to NCIC needs, but later recognized the wisdom of remaining effectively associated with NCIC and conceded.

Graduating from NUTI were Sergeants Stanalonis and Wright, and Corporal Duignan. Selected to attend the NUTI course in September were Troopers Ronald Sharpe and Thomas Madden.

At mid-year, the State Police saw a change in comptroller. Comptroller John W. Bringman, after more than seven years of commendable service, was transferred to the Department of Property and Supplies. Replacing Bringman was Henry T. Clayton who formerly held down the comptroller post with the state Department of Justice.

Clayton, 73, more popularly known as "Scotty," already had thirty-eight years of state service under his belt before coming to the State Police. For twenty years he had been director of State Aided Institutions with the auditor general's office. Once retired, he was recalled to serve as comptroller for the Justice Department and the Board of Probation and Parole.

The Bureau of Staff Inspection was further kicked downstairs by McKetta as it descended in importance ever since Purdy's departure. Sergeant William Anselmi, the only original inspection team member, and whatever else remained of the defunct bureau were transferred to the Planning and Research Division headed by Kwiatek. There the team inspectors devoted most of their time to monitoring the new field reporting system.

The 1967 session of the general assembly was another marathon course for the legislators who were called to order on January 2 and remained open for business until final adjournment on December 21. Passed during this session were seven measures affecting the State Police:

> Act 12, P.L. 22, May 3, removing salary of deputy commissioner from legal restrictions,
> Act 48, P.L. 172, July 12, increasing complement to 3,550 officers and men during the 1967-1971 period (1,200-man increase at a rate of 350 per year),
> Act 112, P.L. 175, August 24, authorizing State Police to assist Department of Revenue with inspection of truck hold-down and tie-down devices,
> Act 140, P.L. 321, October 5, eliminating the two-year enlistment,
> Act 239, P.L. 492, October 26, raising fee for copy of accident investigation record to $5.00,
> Act 312, P.L. 671, December 5, amending Tenure Act to exclude cadets and troopers with less than eighteen months service, and
> Act 313, P.L. 673, December 5, establishing an eighteen-month probationary period for cadets and troopers.

All in all, it was a favorable legislative year insofar as State Police affairs were concerned.

McKetta lost no time in setting up recruiting schedules, and reducing the training period at the Academy to three months. This schedule change permitted the Academy staff to process 350 men annually. Each of the new troopers, however, had to undergo an additional month of training upon his assignment to a field station.

Finally facing up to the critical manpower needs of the State Police, which had become a burning issue back in 1965, the legislators, particularly the House members, came through with a significant increase. Signing the bill into law on July 12, Shafer said, "Today marks a giant step forward in this Administration's determination to mount an all-out attack on the twin evils of crime and highway traffic accidents and death. For too long a time, Pennsylvania's State Police have been forced to meet increasing demands for all sorts of services with entirely too few officers and men."

Before the additional 1,200 trooper positions could be filled, McKetta was to see considerable pressure put upon him to enlist blacks. Special recruiting teams were established to travel to black population centers to seek out black applicants. Despite this effort, there was insufficient response, and many blacks who did apply could not measure up to State Police entrance requirements.

Pressure groups suggested that McKetta provide special training for a class of fifty blacks so that they could pass requirements. Some minority spokesmen even went so far as to suggest that the State Police waive requirements in order to satisfy a black quota. McKetta refused to go along with these suggestions. In the first instance, he firmly believed that such training, if it was to be done at all by state government, should be undertaken by the Department of Education and not the State Police. In the second instance, the commissioner was conscious of the demoralizing effects upon the field forces should he yield to the establishment of dual enlistment standards.

It must be understood that McKetta and all State Police executives, as a matter of fact, were not prejudicially opposed to minority acquisitioning as charged on occasions. To the contrary, they were eager to take on blacks by any number provided minimum entrance standards did not have to be watered down or waived. Conflicting with this position was the argument that blacks should constitute a significant portion of every cadet class undergoing training regardless of the means employed.

The minority issue was to linger unresolved and, although it was eventually to be thrown into federal court some years later, circumstances were to keep the pot continuously boiling. Developments will be discussed in later chapters for it was no longer possible for any succeeding administration to escape the minority question in one form or another.

In another move to combat crime in Pennsylvania, Shafer authorized the formation of a Pennsylvania Crime Commission (PCC) within the Justice Department. Shafer named J. Shane Creamer the commission's first executive director. An ambitious young attorney, Creamer was to lock horns with State Police administrators on a number of occasions—eventually with tragic results. In 1968, the legislature was to enact a measure legally constituting the PCC as part of the Justice Department.

Shafer, in a surprise move, designated Major Arthur W. Shulenberger PCC's deputy director. This appointment placed Shulenberger in a ticklish spot of reporting to two bosses—Creamer and McKetta. Creamer's tactics were to lead to a rocky relationship between the two agencies before PCC was many months old. His early demand for a detail of troopers to serve PCC purposes under his direction was strongly opposed by McKetta—and rightfully so. Creamer's persistent demands for State Police personnel through the Shafer administration and into Shapp's were to set off arguments with increasing intensity.

Replacing Shulenberger as head of the State Police detectives was Captain John F. Yaglenski, former commander at Troop H, Harrisburg. Yaglenski was promoted to major.

The year's end was to see ground broken for the much-needed troop headquarters at Erie. The new building was scheduled for completion in November, 1968. And a ninety-six-man cadet class graduated from the Academy in December, marking the first boost in trooper personnel under the new complement.

Having successfully petitioned the governor for authorization to make sweeping changes, McKetta, in January, 1968, announced an array of promotions and transfers. Undoubtedly the most important of his changes was the creation of six area commands—a throwback to the old districts which Purdy abolished. Facing the threat of civil unrest and riots, McKetta believed that area commanders were needed to coordinate field operations in the event of major incidents. Assigned to Area I, at Philadelphia, was Major Urella. The remaining five commanders were drawn from the rank of captain and promoted to major:

> Major William B. Cooper, Area II, at Wyoming
> Major George A. Sifter, Area III, at Harrisburg
> Major John C. Grey, Area IV, at Montoursville
> Major Howard M. Jaynes, Area V, at Washington
> Major Clarence F. Temke, Area VI, at Butler

At headquarters, Kwiatek was promoted to captain and his division, Planning and Research, was placed under the commissioner's wing. Conti was moved from the R. & I. Division to Civil Defense, and replaced by Captain James A. Straub. Captain Robert L. Dunham became Pinkerton's assistant bureau director in Traffic.

Other changes at headquarters found the Detective Bureau renamed Bureau of Criminal Investigation. Established were the new Bureau of Training and Personnel, and the Community Relations Division which included the Youth Aid Services. Major Thompson was shifted from the Academy to headquarters to command the new Bureau of Training and Personnel. Captain Charles J. Buchinsky was named director of training at the Academy, replacing Captain Wrona. Community Relations operations were placed in the hands of Lieutenant Michael Donahoe.

Punctuating a change made at the outset of McKetta's term of office a year earlier, the deputy commissioner was relieved of the "burden" of coordinating field operations and left with workaday duties of lesser consequences. Stripped from Dussia was the authority that once rested in the hands of his predecessors; the field commander acquired Dussia's "burden," under the new table of organization.

On March 17, a 111-man cadet class was graduated from the Academy. Although larger classes had been sent through training facilities set up at Myerstown and Indiantown Gap at the time of the merger in the late 1930s, this was the largest class in history to graduate from the Academy at Hershey.

A week later, April 4, the Rev. Martin Luther King, Jr., 39, was fatally shot at Memphis, Tennessee, where he had gone to assist a strike by black sanitation workers. King, in 1964, was awarded the Nobel Peace Prize. (At 35, he was the youngest Nobel laureate ever honored.) As a result of King's assassination, rioting broke out in more than 100 of the nation's cities. Rioting was especially serious in Pittsburgh where the governor dispatched State Police and National Guard units to assist local police.

Many of the 111 troopers fresh from their Academy training found themselves putting their training to good use in a live situation. Major Howard M. Jaynes was the western Pennsylvania task force commander. State Police forces remained in the Pittsburgh riot areas for a week, during which time they conducted themselves in the finest traditions of the department. Compliments from high sources everywhere, including black VIPs, were heaped upon the State Police task force members for their restraint and professional handling of a highly sensitive situation.

Two months after King's slaying, James Earl Ray was arrested in London and charged with the crime.

Scarcely had the headlines given up the King story when another senseless assassination was to shock the nation—the murder of Senator Robert F. Kennedy, a leading contender for the Democratic Presidential nomination and brother of a martyred President. The alleged slayer, Sirhan Sirhan, was arrested at the Los Angeles shooting scene. Kennedy died on June 6, a day after the shooting.

The recently-organized Community Relations Division, with its members spread throughout sixteen troops, was called upon to devote much of its attention to tension situations involving minority unrest and immediately act to cool off disputants. This division's work was done rather effectively.

To cope with the significant increase in the State Police complement and the need to improve training facilities, authorization was granted to build a large addition to the Academy. The new air-conditioned wing with a projected cost of $1,655,419 was to accommodate an additional 100 men, and include five dayrooms, four classrooms, an auditorium, and an indoor swimming pool. Groundbreaking ceremonies were held on April 30, and completion was expected in October, 1969.

Major John C. Grey, in May, faced mandatory retirement at 60. As expected, his vacancy went to Captain Joseph L. Young. Temke was moved from Butler to Area IV at Punxsutawney, allowing Young to remain with Area VI at Butler.

John Klosterman resigned his post as crime lab director in May, and was succeeded by Lieutenant Lodwick D. Jenkins, who was promoted to captain.

In 1968, the Personnel Office saw a number of changes at the top. John Millett transferred to the State Civil Service Commission in January to become that agency's assistant executive director. Lieutenant Leonard T. Koper took over as personnel director. After only a brief tenure, Koper was moved out and replaced by Lieutenant Bernard G. Stanalonis. In 1976, Millett went on to become executive director of the State Civil Service Commission upon the retirement of Richard A. Rosenberry.

Two important projects were moving ahead in 1968. The first concerned the development of a sophisticated statewide State Police information network as a step beyond what was already in use with the GE Datanet-30 system. Chosen to head this project was James W. Barnes, 45, of Cleveland, Ohio. The other project concerned the upgrading of the radio communications system which was sorely in need of attention in view of the department's growth and the antiquity of the system then in use. Under contract to aid in the design of a new radio system was the Page Communications Engineers firm, home-based at Washington, D. C. Both projects were to have tremendous impact on the department's expenditures pattern; the implementing of such costly systems was surely to shake the department's decision-makers.

During this same period, "seed" money had been secured from federal sources to study the use of helicopters for State Police operations. There was every reason to believe that soon the department would be acquiring a limited number of helicopters to enhance its enforcement capabilities. There was no denying the usefulness of airborne patrols.

The team of Urella and Rizzo continued to successfully sweat out the situation in Pennsylvania's touchy southeast corner through mid-1968 despite the uprisings following King's assassination and the other sensitive issues on hand at Philadelphia. No little credit for the keeping of the peace in Philadelphia and the greater Philadelphia area was due these two police principals—Urella and Rizzo.

Not only had Urella done a creditable job in his area, but it will be recalled that he was called upon by McKetta to smooth the way for his Senate confirmation as commissioner. Rittelmann's upcoming mandatory retirement in November provided McKetta with an ideal opportunity to reward Urella justifiably. Reportedly, the field commander's job was promised to Urella. Meanwhile, Urella was being pressured by VIPs in Delaware County to head up the county's crime investigation team at a salary that was meant to motivate him. When, according to Urella, a firm commitment was sought from McKetta on the field commander appointment, there was hedging; Urella could get no straight answer. McKetta supposedly claimed that it was up to Governor Shafer, and contacts with Shafer came back with the story that it was McKetta's baby. Hurt by the apparent renege and convinced that he was not to be the new field commander in November, Urella resigned in June to become the district attorney's right arm in Delaware County. Replacing Urella at Area I was newly-promoted Major Leroy H. Lilly.

A few weeks later at Springfield, Delaware County, an assembly of law enforcement officers, judges, legislators and top public administrators at the local, state and federal levels jam-packed the Alpine Inn to pay tribute to Urella. It was one of those affairs the likes of which will not often be repeated for a retiring State Police officer. McKetta was not in attendance. Breaking bread with Urella that night, however, was a fellow by the name of Shapp—Milton J. Shapp.

During the summer, short-sleeved, wash-and-wear, "perma-press" shirts were issued to troopers. Adding to the comfort of the patrol forces, authorization was secured to purchase air-conditioned police cars.

Act 235, P.L. 754 was signed into law on July 31, creating the Pennsylvania Crime Commission in the Justice Department, consisting of the attorney general as chairman, and four other commissioners appointed by the governor. This legislative action sanctioned a move by Shafer who, in 1967, had brought PCC into being by executive order.

In lieu of any other procedure for dispensing federal money to state and local police, the PCC was designated as the principal state planning group to qualify the Commonwealth for funding under the Omnibus Crime Control and Safe Streets Act. Thus the PCC, rather than the State Police, served as the clearing house for federal funds. State Police administrators were compelled to submit their proposals through the PCC for funding, and in this way became entirely dependent upon PCC for approval of vital programs. Friction developed between PCC and State Police officials when approvals were unduly delayed or proposals unreasonably questioned. The relationship between the two agencies was never to be a cordial one.

Other measures affecting State Police operations passed by the 1968 General Assembly were: Act 111, P.L. 237, June 24, authorizing collective bargaining between policemen and public employers, and providing for binding arbitration; and Act 376, P.L. 1202, December 12, forbidding the interception of police broadcast messages "for the purpose of aiding himself or others in the perpetration of any unlawful act."

By far the most important of these enactments insofar as the department's future is concerned was Act 111. Binding arbitration brought a new dimension to the relationship between the FOP, representing enlisted officers and men, and the governor's office. Manifold benefits were to flow to the troopers by way of this procedure, which remarkably altered the workday routine and compensation plan.

Because of the many legal problems arising from civil disobedience incidents and the controversial U. S. Supreme Court rulings, the need for counsel was increasingly urgent. To satisfy this need, Richard M. Goldberg, a Wilkes-Barre attorney and executive assistant to the attorney general, was furnished an office at State Police headquarters where he spent a portion of his work schedule. Goldberg, a popular figure at headquarters, began a series of articles in October for *The Communicator* primarily intended to provide troopers with a better understanding of important court opinions and the application of these principles in workaday situations.

In October, the governor's office approved the formation of a State Police Aviation Division, and the purchase of two helicopters was assured for delivery in early 1969. Appointed to head the new division was Lieutenant Nicholas J. Pauley. The first troopers certified as helicopter pilots after undergoing training were: Sergeant William S. Hall, and Troopers James L. Boyle, John W. Neil, Dominick F. Spigarelli and Francis R. Suppok. Supporting the pilots as observer mechanics were: Troopers Freddie W. Bendl, John C. Connolly, Robert L. Eakin and George A. Sommerer. Aviation Division operations were to be supervised by the field commander. Rittlemann, who ever since his youth was an aviation enthusiast, was greatly pleased to have this role in the helicopter program even though he had already begun his career's count-down.

Urella's resignation gave way to speculation on the man who would become Rittelmann's successor in November. Some placed their bets on Major Cooper, others were plugging for Major Pinkerton, and some went so far as to say that Major Young was in the running.

Of the three men, Pinkerton was the only one assigned to headquarters. During the absences of the deputy or field commander, Pinkerton was a regular substitute for both top officers. His appointment as field commander would not come as a surprise. Such appointments, unfortunately, do not come as routinely as all that.

From the standpoint of political clout, the heavy odds were on Cooper. And so it was that McKetta designated Cooper as Rittelmann's replacement. Cooper made it very clear to close associates that he owed no thanks to McKetta for the appointment—he had secured it by his own personal effort. Here are implications that McKetta may have had someone else in mind. At any rate, Cooper became the department's second field commander.

Cooper, 53, a native of Summit Hill, Carbon County, was born June 20, 1915. He attended Summit Hill public schools and graduated from high school in 1933. After graduation, Cooper served a hitch with the Civilian Conservation Corps, one of former President Franklin D. Roosevelt's Great Depression programs. He enlisted in the State Highway Patrol in January, 1937, and was assigned to duty in the northeast coal region. He was promoted to corporal in 1948, to sergeant in 1953, and became the Dunmore troop first sergeant in 1958. Cooper was promoted to lieutenant in 1961, and transferred to Greensburg. Later in 1961, he was transferred to Harrisburg. He returned to the Dunmore troop in 1963, and was appointed troop commander the following year.

During his long service in the anthracite region, Cooper was often called upon to provide services for former Governor William Scranton, who resided in the Dunmore troop area. This association with Scranton began long before Scranton was elected to the U. S. House of Representatives.

In 1964, at Detroit, Cooper was conferred the highest Masonic honor—the thirty-third Degree of the Scottish Rite. He was the first member of the State Police to be so honored.

When McKetta early in 1968 reactivated the area commands, Cooper was one of the six commanders with the rank of major. Cooper was one of three brothers to see service with the State Police.

He is married to the former Kathryn Cordes Rehrig, R. N. Lt. Colonel and Mrs. Cooper are residents of Newton Lake, Lackawanna County, and they have one son, Bennett, an attorney.

Unexpectedly, Pinkerton submitted his retirement papers within the month. His tall, handsome figure was missed by many at headquarters as the new year slipped into view. Promoted to major to fill Pinkerton's vacancy in the Traffic Bureau was Captain Charles J. Buchinsky. Replacing Buchinsky as Academy commandant was Captain Robert L. Brubaker.

Cooper's vacancy in Area II, at Wyoming, was filled by the promotion of Turnpike Troop Commander Captain Walter E. Price to major. Price, the son of former State Highway Patrol Superintendent Wilson C. Price, was soon to face compulsory retirement at 60.

Rittelmann's retirement days were short when Shafer appointed him deputy secretary of health and placed him in charge of the drug control program. Rittelmann served at this post until July, 1971, at which time he closed out 40½ years of state service.

By early 1969, the volume of records entered into the NCIC provided a data base sufficiently large to repeatedly score "hits." Impressed by the successful use of the system, member law enforcement agencies throughout the country relied more than ever upon NCIC to effectively carry out their missions. And so it was with every State Police substation in Pennsylvania.

A change at headquarters in March saw Public Information Officer E. William Lindeberg transferred to the Department of Labor and Industry. Replacing Lindeberg was James D. Cox. Cox, a native of Centre County, was formerly news director for Station WGAL-TV, at Lancaster, for fifteen years of his twenty-three-year broadcasting career. Earlier in his career, Cox was a radio announcer at Altoona, Lewistown and York before joining WGAL-TV in 1952. A veteran of World War II, Cox saw service in Europe as an infantry second lieutenant, and advanced to captain before the time of his discharge from the Army Reserve Corps.

Major Price, 60, retired in March and was replaced at Area II by Captain Edward M. McGroarty. McGroarty, former troop commander at Wyoming, was promoted to major. There was a steady turnover in the complement of area commanders.

On March 24, the Aviation Division officially accepted its first two helicopters from the Bell Helicopter Company, Ft. Worth, Texas, at a cost of $123,243.74. The two Bell Model 47G4A units were delivered to the Harrisburg-York State Airport, at New Cumberland. Division Commander Lieutenant Nicholas J. Pauley based one unit at Washington and the other at Middletown. According to plans, the division was eventually to operate six helicopters purchased at the rate of two a year. At long last, the State Police had become airborne.

The general assembly in 1967 had raised the complement to 3,550 officers and men—a goal that was to be met by June 30, 1971. Overconfident with the success of this manpower move, McKetta began pushing for another increase of 1,800 men by June 30, 1974, bringing the total number of officers and men to 5,350. Seemingly assured that his wishes would be fulfilled by the governor and the legislators, McKetta went ahead with plans to increase the number of field supervisors. In this premature move, he secured permission from OA and topside officials to have a lieutenant in charge of each substation with a

First helicopter lands on Academy grounds, 1970 (Courtesy of Pennsylvania State Police)

complement of at least twenty-five men. Sergeants were to replace corporals by the score and the number of corporals was incredulously upped.

As it turned out, however, the legislators did not see eye-to-eye with McKetta, and his folly in loading the supervisory overhead led to a situation where there were too many chiefs and not enough Indians. It is difficult to understand how OA, and others at the top, gave approval to an unrealistic overhead in advance of the manpower increase which, at best, was highly speculative.

Circumstances later confirmed that the State Police was lucky to see meagre manpower increases through Commissioner Urella's brief tenure and none during Barger's years. It is most difficult to foresee when, if ever, the department's complement will go beyond the 4,200 figure. McKetta, in this light, was to leave behind a serious personnel problem.

In another move, McKetta abolished the rank of first sergeant; the few remaining men in that status were promoted to lieutenant. By this action, each commander had three lieutenants with him at troop headquarters. One headed traffic operations, another crime operations. All other responsibilities were lumped into staff services and turned over to the third lieutenant. The majority of the men falling into the latter category were former first sergeants.

Retirements were stepped up in April and May with the departure of Majors Stanton and Temke, and Captain Jackson E. Sacriste, state fire marshal. Three troop commanders also decided to leave. Promoted at headquarters were Captain Albert F. Kwiatek, 44, who replaced Stanton as head of the Bureau of Technical Services, and Lieutenant Bernard G. Stanalonis, 40, who replaced Kwiatek as director of Planning and Research. Replacing Stanalonis as Personnel Director was Lieutenant Jay C. Hileman. McKetta designated Lieutenant Russell Anderson as the new state fire marshal; however, he was not upgraded in this move. The new commander of Area IV, replacing Temke, was Captain Clifford G. Yahner, 57, former commander of the Hollidaysburg troop.

The new troop headquarters building at Erie was completed in April and dedicated in June. Erie was the last of the troops to acquire a headquarters building worthy of the name. Political interference and bureaucratic red tape dragged this $764,492 capital expenditures project through a decade of discouragement for the officers and men of the Erie troop, who had to put up with unbelievable conditions.

Even with the expanded staff of civilian technicians at the Harrisburg crime lab, a backlog in evidence examinations became a matter

Mobile Command Post (Courtesy of Pennsylvania State Police)

of concern for both State Police and municipal police investigators. The distance of transporting evidence from outlying counties to Harrisburg was also a disturbing factor for many requisitioning lab services.

To improve services, and at the same time shorten the evidence chain, the State Police studied the possibility of establishing satellite laboratories away from Harrisburg. Subsequent plans called for satellite labs at Greensburg and Erie in western Pennsylvania, and Bethlehem and Wyoming in the eastern sector. The first of the field labs was opened for business on July 1, at Greensburg. The other three were to take root within two years. Although limited to certain services, the expansion program nonetheless was welcomed by municipal police. Services not yet available at the satellite labs were obtainable at Harrisburg with earlier exam results in prospect.

In another action to facilitate field operations for state and municipal police, the State Police purchased three mobile command posts. Federal funding for the units was provided through the Omnibus Crime and Safe Streets Act. Completely self-contained, the two-room, thirty-five-foot trailers supplied essential support for command personnel and elaborate communications gear. The three command posts were stationed at Reading, Harrisburg and Washington. Later on, three more units were purchased through the same funding procedure. They were assigned to Butler, Montoursville and Wyoming, thus providing each area command with this type of emergency equipment.

The 1969 graduates of NUTI were Sergeant Francis X. Carroll, Corporal Howard G. Berringer and Trooper Robert E. McElroy. Picked to attend NUTI in September were Corporals Lawrence F. Clark and Warren L. Shaffer, and Trooper Daniel A. Spang.

In October, Major Arthur W. Shulenberger resigned his post as PCC's deputy director and retired from the State Police after thirty-two years of service. Reportedly, his tour of duty with the Crime Commission was not a comforting one.

Also taking leave of the Justice Department was Lieutenant Roy Titler who had been assigned to that agency earlier and took on duty assignments for the Crime Commission from time to time. Working with Titler were three troopers. The troopers remained with Justice throughout 1970 without on-the-spot supervision by a State Police commissioned officer.

Shortly after Shulenberger's departure, J. Shane Creamer, PCC's executive director, left the commission to join a federal task force on organized crime at Philadelphia. Replacing Creamer was Charles E. Rinkevich, a former International Association of Chiefs of Police staffer.

The latest capital expenditures budget included a request for a new State Police headquarters building away from the capitol hill at Harrisburg. The department, now employing hundreds of men and women at headquarters, was sorely in need of elbow room not only to accommodate hired hands but to effectively situate computers, peripheral hardware and other specialized equipment operated by a first-class police agency.

From 1905 to 1963, department headquarters occupied various quarters in the main capitol. In 1963, the commissioner and his staff were swiftly moved into leased quarters at 7th and Forster streets, Harrisburg, so that the capitol office space could be turned over to demanding legislators. Moving from the leased building in 1967, the department was squeezed into two floors of the brand new Highway and Safety Building. The thought of moving again into a building all to themselves was comforting, indeed, to State Police officials. But from the proposal's inception in 1969, there was to follow a series of disappointing delays. Groundbreaking was not to take place until 1976—seven years later.

It was originally decided to locate the new building at Hershey nearby the Academy; however, new thinking on this subject after McKetta's departure altered plans considerably in favor of keeping a Harrisburg address.

Also included in the capital expenditures budget was a new building to house Troop H headquarters at Harrisburg. The present Troop H buiding was constructed by the former State Highway Patrol in the early 1930s and was now judged totally inadequate for expanding operations.

To close out 1969, another change in area commands was made. Major Sifter, 60, retired December 31. Replacing Sifter as commander of Area III was newly-promoted Major Robert A. Rice, former troop commander at Harrisburg.

Before the new year was hardly underway, the director of the Staff Services Bureau, Richard J. Shaffer, retired January 14, 1970, closing out twenty-eight years of State Police service. Maintenance and Supply Division director, Gerald S. Patterson, was appointed to fill Shaffer's bureau vacancy. Replacing Patterson was Edward Boyle, former chief clerk at Wyoming. Boyle was the third chief clerk to merit promotion to a headquarters post. The three civilian executives, Patterson, Zinsky and Boyle, oddly enough assigned within the same bureau at headquarters, form one of the most capable management teams ever found at headquarters.

Earlier in 1970, the nation's newspaper headlines were occupied with the murder of Joseph Yablonski, his wife and daughter at their home in Clarksville, Washington County, on January 5. Yablonski had recently run unsuccessfully for president of the United Mine Workers (UMW). At the time of his slaying, Yablonski was scheduled to testify before a federal grand jury looking into alleged mishandling of union elections. A State Police task force, later joined by FBI agents, linked the deaths to UMW officials, in what can be described as excellent police work. The talents of Special Prosecutor Richard Sprague saw the accused tried and convicted for their participation in the triple slaying.

Another command change at headquarters found Captain Straub leaving his post as R. & I. director to accept an appointment as Harrisburg's new public safety director. Promoted to captain as Straub's replacement was Lieutenant Leonard T. Koper. Koper formerly served with Planning and Research.

The employment of civilians to conduct driver license examinations, a program begun by Purdy, was nursed along by Rittelmann and McKetta in order to release more troopers for patrol duty. A group of 44 driver license examiners (DLEs) completed training at the Academy on March 13. Increased by 44, the complement of DLEs was upped to 107. Whatever else can be recalled of this particular class, it will be remembered as the first to include women examiners. Among the 44 were eight women: Rose M. Bauman, Edna L. Blandin, April D.

Bundy, Theresa M. Dunham, Beverly L. Fry, Florence J. Hoffman, Phyllis C. Kosloski and Clare L. Vail. A small class of three, all women, completed training for the DLE program before the close of June. They were Virginia N. Hartle, Virginia R. Miles and Mable E. Watrous.

The new $1.6 million wing to the Academy was dedicated April 15. This much-needed addition doubled the Academy's capacity for training. Accommodations were available for boarding and training 200 men at what was proclaimed the best police academy in the country. Numbered among the many innovations were an indoor swimming pool and a 250-seat auditorium.

For some months, McKetta had been ballyhooing the department's upcoming sixty-fifth anniversary. At his request, the governor issued a proclamation setting aside May 2 as Pennsylvania State Police Day. Signing the proclamation, Shafer said, "I do this with a great deal of pleasure and pride, for not only is the Pennsylvania State Police the oldest such organization in the country, it is also the finest."

Satisfied that he was doing a good job as commissioner, McKetta not so secretly launched a campaign to succeed himself. The Commonwealth would see a new governor elected in November, and the rumor factory carried claims by McKetta that he expected reappointment regardless of a Democratic or Republican Party victory. He was then serving as a Republican cabinet member. The program for the sixty-fifth anniversary dinner-dance, in the opinion of many attendants, appeared to be aimed more at promoting McKetta's reappointment than observing the anniversary.

In May, the governor launched an intensive drive to cut government spending, and strongly urged all department heads to observe his austerity directive. Searching for areas to reduce spending, it was decided that the pistol matches annually held at the Academy would be dropped for 1970. The intertroop competition, involving traveling time and expense in addition to the cost of ammunition, was a likely candidate for cost reduction. Matches were already on the schedule for May 22, and on short notice the field forces were informed that the schedule was scratched. Succeeding administrations have seen no pressing need for renewing the annual event. The records thus indicate that the inter-troop contest traditionally held each year for more than half a century was last held on June 20, 1969—a victim of changing times.

Throughout McKetta's tenure thus far, despite the recommendations for courts-martial submitted by troop commanders in instances where they judged severe disciplinary action in order, the commissioner would not move in that direction. Open to speculation was

Pennsylvania State Police Academy, Hershey (Courtesy of Pennsylvania State Police)

his desire to be a popular "old man" at the expense of his troop commanders who felt their authority was weakened by the commissioner's unwritten policy. Lesser avenues for punishment were resorted to, none of which involved dismissal.

Later, in an interview, McKetta defended his position by stating that he believed the court-martial system, established by law, was not constitutional. Nonetheless, there is no evidence that he made any effort as commissioner to rectify by legislative action any portion of the court-martial process he held to be unconstitutional.

Earlier in April, a detachment of troopers from Troop G, Hollidaysburg, was summoned to Penn State University to enforce a court order enjoining students from occupying university buildings. Twenty-nine students were arrested in this action, and twelve troopers injured by a rock-throwing mob. Despite the casualties, the troopers exercised restraint and did not resort to gunfire.

Student protests against the Vietnam War continued on many of the nation's college campuses. A protest at Kent State University on May 4 ended when Ohio National Guardsmen opened fire on students, killing four and wounding others. This incident at Kent State, which brought swift condemnation of the Ohio guardsmen, aroused much discussion among law enforcement agencies about over-reacting in tension-filled situations. Needless to report, moves were quickly made to intensively emphasize restraint and review the use of fire power, as riot training continued to be a principal concern for police executives. Excellent training was paying off in Pennsylvania as the State Police moved from incident to incident with cool resolve.

In 1970, McKetta was to launch a controversial program that was destined to draw flak from every direction. A former criminal investigator himself, McKetta, abandoning the time-honored title of "detective," decided to form a new series by another name. He called it his CIS program—CIS standing for Criminal Investigation Specialist. By way of this CIS setup, McKetta advanced men to a higher pay scale, without the benefit of competitive promotional examinations, by simply reclassifying them to CIS I, II, III, or IV, depending upon how they fit into the specifications he had drawn up. OA staff members, convinced of the program's inherent defects, were opposed to this evasive effort to form a massive detective corps. Despite this opposition, McKetta was successful in persuading the governor to go along with him.

In May, 269 men were reclassified to get the new program off the ground. Plans called for the eventual reclassification of some 500 men. McKetta's term, however, was to end before the CIS program was full-blown. Undoing the ill-fated program fell to McKetta's successor, Urella, who was to have no easy time of it. There was no way of eliminating completely the discontent experienced by those who hoped to gain further from the program. Although the controversial CIS program was much criticized, more kindly thoughts should be given to the men who were bounced in and out of the program and were, for the most part, capable investigators. They were, if anything, victims of a well-intended but poorly contrived management plan.

In another ill-conceived action, McKetta inaugurated a Security Agent series involving the men assigned as bodyguards to the governor and lieutenant governor, and as guards at the governor's office and the official residences of these two top state executives. Again, as in the CIS program, the men were recalssified without benefit of competitive procedures to SA-1, SA-2, SA-3 and SA-4 titles, depending upon how they fit into the scheme of things. Considerably smaller in scope than the CIS program, the SA series affected only some twenty-five.

Before the end of May, another round of promotions hit headquarters. Lieutenants promoted to captain were Michael Donahoe, Jay

C. Hileman and Roy L. Titler. Donahoe headed the Community Relations Division; Hileman was personnel director, and Titler supervised the Criminal Investigation Bureau's vice operations. Also promoted was former Sergeant Paul F. Dell who, as lieutenant, continued to be Donahoe's assistant.

The 1970 legislature passed only one measure of any significance for State Police. Act 117, P.L. 351, May 6, transferred 43.19 acres of land in Susquehanna Township, Dauphin County, from the Department of Public Welfare to State Police for the construction of a new Troop H headquarters building.

Created in 1970 was the Bureau of Statistics in the state Justice Department. Enabling legislation, Act 188, P.L. 460, was passed by the 1969 General Assembly during its final workdays, and not signed by the governor until January 13, 1970. This enactment provided for the mandatory submission of Uniform Crime Reporting (UCR) statistics to the Department of Justice. Purdy's original concept back in 1965 of having such a statistics agency operate under State Police auspices did not come to pass: Purdy's enthusiasm for the project was not shared by his successors.

The first director of the Bureau of Crime Statistics was the very capable John Yeager, a nationally-known figure in correctional statistics, who was already on the Justice Department's payroll by virtue of his administrative postion with the Bureau of Corrections.

Whether the Bureau of Crime Statistics should have been housed with the State Police was an issue to come up again in a few years. The main thrust as far as the FBI was then concerned was the formation of statewide systems interfaced with the national system—a long-range objective that deserved law enforcement backing.

McKetta, in June, by way of a formal news release, announced that he was forming a new troop dedicated to the patrolling of Interstate Routes I-79, I-80 and I-81. This was the first new troop to be created in thirty years. Known as "Troop S," the new patrol group was to be manned by 273 troopers and eight civilian employees. The troopers would be volunteers from the other sixteen troops. Scheduled to be operational September 1, to coincide with the opening of I-80, the idea of a new troop was not altogether popular with affected troop commanders, nor with many staff members at Headquarters, who believed that the interstate routes could be well-enough handled by each troop through which the interstate routes coursed, without incurring administrative costs for a new troop. McKetta's plans called for federal funding to support operations; however, his defective funding program never did jell, and the heavy burden of costs from the outset remained with the State Police operational budget.

The last original member of the state constabulary died at Harrisburg on May 31. Sergeant Herbert P. Hunt, 87, enlisted December 15, 1905, and remained with the constabulary for one 2-year enlistment before accepting a job with private industry.

June saw the Aviation Division helicopter fleet doubled with the delivery of two Model 206A Bell Jet Rangers. Trained as pilots for this expanded program were Troopers Harold S. Hartman, Thomas S. Heil, David L. Frey, John J. Donnini, Morris W. Demski, Gerald V. Smathers, Norman M. Sorenson and Clement Laniewski.

Graduating in June from NUTI were Corporals Warren L. Shaffer and Lawrence F. Clark and Trooper Daniel A. Spang. Selected to follow in their footsteps at NUTI in September were Troopers Joseph G. Pandos and Stephen R. Warsavage.

Another June happening was the graduation of a 185-man cadet class at the Academy, marking the largest class to complete training at Hershey.

Except for the heated departures immediately following the passage of Act 360 in 1957, compelling officers and men to retire at age 60, the filing of retirement papers had since become a rather accepted and routine procedure. In July, 1970, however, mandatory retirement was to have a challenger. Testing the law was Captain Joseph McIlvaine, commander at Bethlehem, who refused to submit his resignation. Faced with no other alternative, McKetta prepared an ouster order dismissing McIlvaine. At Bethlehem, the ouster order was delivered by Major Leroy Lilly, Area I commander. Accompanying Lilly was Captain Koper, R. & I. director, who had been ordered by McKetta to assume temporary command of the Bethlehem troop upon McIlvaine's departure. Members of the local news corps covered the unique incident in the department's history, and the affair, according to witnesses, was a cordial one.

Although McIlvaine's determination to appeal his ouster to the Commonwealth Court at Harrisburg was easy enough to understand, observers at headquarters were puzzled by McKetta's action in sending Koper to Bethlehem as temporary commander. Koper, a rookie captain, and director of the largest division at headquarters, was also serving as acting director of the Technical Services Bureau in the absence of Major Kwiatek, who was on an Alaskan vacation. Until Koper's return from Bethlehem in November—four months later—the R. & I. Division was without its director. The results of McIlvaine's legal contest will be reported in later chapters as the drawn-out litigation passed through the courts before final disposition.

In July, the small community of Newville, Cumberland County, was not to overlook the fiftieth anniversary of the founding of the first constabulary training school. This formal training program was instituted by former Superintendent Lynn G. Adams in March, 1920. An historical marker was placed on the site where the old, leased school building once stood. It was a big day in Newville as troopers and citizens recalled the history of State Police training which had come a long way from its humble beginnings at Newville to the nation's most modern facility at Hershey.

At the staff conference on the morning of August 7, McKetta was noticeably disturbed as he hurriedly went through the motions of conducting business. It did not take him long to reveal his source of agitation by criticizing, without mentioning names, those men suspected of playing politics to advance their own interests rather than working for the "team." In a threatening statement, McKetta said that if political maneuvering was not stopped, he would give the matter his "personal attention." He did not elaborate. Staff members speculated that McKetta's targets were members of his own hierarchy—Dussia, Cooper and Grosnick—all of whom were reportedly doing their level best to succeed McKetta. Away from the department, Urella was also considered a contender. Dussia had already announced that he would never serve another four years as McKetta's deputy. In this regard, Young, according to western observers, proclaimed that he would be McKetta's next deputy. The effects of the intradepartmental competition were to be felt throughout the State Police command structure long after the November general election, and weigh heavily until the appointment of former Major Urella was securely his.

Milton J. Shapp had again beaten Auditor General Robert Casey in the spring primary to win the Democratic party nomination for governor. The Shapp-Kline ticket was involved in a hot campaign to wrest the governor's office from the Republicans. GOP standardbearers on the campaign trail with contrasting plans were Broderick and Scalera. Electioneering was bitterly conducted.

McKetta, during this critical period, was highly sensitive of any notoriety that might detract from his chances for reappointment. He was distressed by the unfavorable participation of State Police forces from the Greensburg barracks during the UMW fracas at the Cooney Brothers Mine near Johnstown. McKetta was equally disturbed by the Erie FOP action wherein three troopers retained counsel to challenge disciplinary transfers sanctioned by the commissioner. At a troop commanders conference at the Academy on August 20, the commissioner scolded the officers who were responsible, in his judgment, for letting these situations get out of hand.

As scheduled, Troop S became operational on September 1 with temporary headquarters set up at the Rockview Driver Examination point, Centre County. Plans called for the leasing of a new headquarters building at Milesburg, Centre County. Designated commander of the new troop was Captain Charles S. Graci.

During September, satellite crime labs were opened at Wyoming and Bethlehem. The fourth field lab at Erie was expected to offer its services in early 1971.

Another change at headquarters was the retirement of Major John E. Thompson as director of the Bureau of Personnel and Training. Thompson was replaced by the newly-promoted Major Bernard G. Stanalonis. Replacing Stanalonis as head of the Planning and Research Division was Lieutenant Sidney C. Deyo, Jr., who was promoted to captain.

The general election results on November 3 gave Shapp an impressive victory over his Republican foe, incumbent Lieutenant Governor Raymond Broderick, by 500,175 votes—the largest margin since Republican James H. Duff trounced Democrat John S. Rice by a 557,515 margin in 1946. The Democratic Party was once again to take possession of the state's executive offices after eight years of rule by GOP governors Scranton and Shafer. Shapp was equally blessed with control of the House and Senate, giving the Democrats their first working majority in both chambers since 1936.

It will be recalled that Urella was supposedly headed for the commissioner's office four years earlier had Shapp won the gubernatorial election. Shapp's victory this time rekindled the prospects of Urella's return for headquarters. But regardless of how good Urella's chances for appointment were, a smear campaign was underway to discredit him before Shapp made an official move to announce his appointment. Without foundation, such underhandedness was bound to fail—and it did.

Governor-elect Shapp, on a working holiday with his staff at Southern Pines, North Carolina, announced on December 2 his first two cabinet appointments. Appointed were Rocco P. Urella, State Police commissioner, and J. Shane Creamer, attorney general. Oddly enough, the relationship between Creamer and Urella was a cool one and time brought no improvement. In fact, their relationship eventually strained to the breaking point was to have diastrous consequences for both men.

Not typical of governors-elect before him, Shapp's cabinet appointment of a State Police commissioner was one of his first—not his last. Anti-Urella forces, however, were not easily giving up the ghost. Having failed at preventing his appointment by Shapp, they turned their attention to the senators, hoping thereby to block Urella's confirmation. This action, too, was doomed to fall short of its mark. Urella, a popular figure, was well thought of by senators from both political parties.

McKetta, now facing a lame-duck situation as commissioner, lost much taste for the job. Seldom did he conduct the daily conferences, notwithstanding the fact that he ordered them continued.

The FOP had finally organized its forces to take advantage of the provisions of Act 111 authorizing collective bargaining. Although Act 111 was passed by the legislators in 1968, setting the machinery in motion was a slow two-year process. Nonetheless, collective bargaining sessions on subjects of compensation and working conditions were underway in November. Representing the FOP on its first bargaining team were chairman John R. Schneider, Leo E. Pierce, Paul G. Cotter, Leo O. DePolo, Michael Rebar and Steven J. Condes. Retained as counsel was Howard Richard, a Philadelphia attorney. Spearheading the state's position were Dr. Arthur C. Eckerman, Christ J. Zervanos and Deputy Attorney General Thomas Lane.

When negotiations reached an impasse, the entire matter was placed in the hands of an arbitration panel. Representing the Commonwealth was John M. Felice. The FOP named John Harrington, and S. Harry Galfand, of the American Arbitration Association, was the third panel member and its chairman. Following arguments by both parties, the board submitted its findings on December 21, 1970, which were to historically constitute the first State Police contract under Act 111.

The contract's estimated worth was set at $7,025,000. In addition to an across-the-board salary increase, overtime pay allowances and paid Blue Cross and Blue Shield coverage, the contract raised the ceiling for accumulated sick leave from 90 days to 200 days. This latter provision proved to be of exceptional value to the FOP in later contract negotiations. The contract awarded substantial increases in the compensation plan and work benefits that would have scarcely been acquired other than by binding arbitration. The contract was scheduled to be implemented July 1, 1971.

The governor's office was displeased with the proceedings, especially in light of the FOP representing all State Police enlisted personnel—both officers and men. State arbitrators felt that officers should be considered part of management and separated from the rank and file. This proposal, however, fell flat then and no change in the lineup has been made since.

By contrast, contract negotiations for a new State Police radio system ran into a serious snag. A modern system had been designed by Motorola at a cost of some $40,000,000 for a ten-year period. The only criticism that might be levelled at the new costly system was its extraordinary vaulting from a basic, straight-forward system to one calling for extravagant "bells and whistles"—an elaborate affair with overloading specifications which could have been more economically proffered. The $40,000,000 figure was an inordinate one for officials involved in the approval process to ponder. A more reasonable approach at a lower cost figure might have succeeded in gaining immediate contract ratification.

At any rate, the contract had been approved in form by the Justice Department and was made ready for signature. Scheduled to sign for the Commonwealth were the governor, the secretary of Property and Supplies and the commissioner. McKetta, for unpublished reasons, declined to sign despite the pleadings of Kwiatek who could distressingly envision months and months of arduous work by his bureau's technical staff going down the drain without McKetta's signature.

Faced with a dilemma in its last days, Shafer's administration ultimately decided to let the entire matter lapse into the hands of the incoming governor. This delay, unfortunately was to create an unbelievable situation under the Democrats; the Democrats were to dillydally with this project for four long years.

Contract arrangements for a computer-based teletypewriter system, on the other hand, met with a kinder fate. A contract was awarded to Remington-Rand for two back-to-back UNIVAC 418-III real time computers, and peripheral hardware to handle batch-processing of routine statistical and housekeeping programs. To house all of this sophisticated equipment and provide the critical environment for suitable operations, a special prefabricated building was purchased and erected on property adjacent to the Academy at Hershey.

The new system was identified as the Commonwealth Law Enforcement Network (CLEAN), more popularly known as the CLEAN system. This revolutionary, modern system was to provide rapid teletypewriter communications for all full-time police departments in Pennsylvania, and eventually be interfaced with NCIC, LETS and Bureau of Motor Vehicles. It was truly a boon to law enforcement. Much credit is due those who designed and implemented the system, thus firmly establishing the Pennsylvania State Police as a leader among the country's major departments. Kwiatek was the spearhead for this undertaking.

Subject to mandatory retirement, Captain Robert L. Brubaker, 60, resigned as Academy superintendent November 24. Picked to replace

Computer center for CLEAN system at Hershey (Courtesy of Pennsylvania State Police)

him, and promoted to captain was Lieutenant Leon D. Leiter, a member of the Academy staff.

Members of the State Police were shocked by the slaying of Trooper Gary R. Rosenberger on December 12. Rosenberger, 26, of Troop F, had been engaged in a plainclothes narcotics investigation for several weeks. He was shot nine times and left dead in a shallow stream near Williamsport. Charged with Rosenberger's murder was Barney L. Russell, 19, a Williamsport youth.

An outpouring of some 100 troopers and representatives of twenty-four other police agencies from twelve states paid their respects at Harrisburg where Rosenberger was buried with full honors on December 16. During his final week in office, McKetta presented the State Police Cross to Rosenberger's widow. Instituted by McKetta, the State Police Cross is intended for the next of kin of a trooper killed in the line of duty. Mrs. Rosenberger was the first recipient of this medal at an award ceremony on January 31.

An atmosphere of mixed emotions prevailed at headquarters to greet the new year. McKetta was packing to leave and preparations were being made to turn over reins to a new commissioner. It was a melancholy time for McKetta and those who had worked closely with him. On the other hand. there were men and women at headquarters who welcomed a change and looked forward to Urella's coming.

Rumors were flying that McKetta planned some questionable last-minute promotions. Dussia tried to convince him that such a move, if true, was in poor taste; however, McKetta confirmed the promotions and stated that he would proceed with them. McKetta secured Executive Board approval to form a new area command, Area VII, at Harrisburg, which took in the Turnpike troop and new Troop S. On January 14, less than a week before his departure, McKetta promoted Captain Edward Wojick to major and gave him command of the new area. Also promoted were Lieutenant Michael Honkus who succeeded Wojick as commander of the Greensburg troop, and Lieutenant Charles E. Harbaugh, legislative lobbyist, who continued in his post. Although other promotions were made, these three were the most talked about.

Arousing more emotional reaction from State Police officialdom than McKetta's last-minute promotions were Attorney General Fred Speaker's opinion declaring the death penalty unconstitutional in this state and his order dismantling the electric chair at the Rockview Penitentiary. (Speaker replaced Attorney General William Sennett in July, 1970, when the latter resigned his post.) Speaker's shocking actions with regard to the death penalty came in January, 1971, just days prior to his moving out of office to let his Democratic successor in.

Speaker's opinion and its timing were to set off a fury of activity among police, jurists, prosecutors and legislators who sought to have the death penalty restored. The next five years would be taken up with extensive legislative hearings and court proceedings all the way to the U. S. Supreme court before the issue was to be clarified albeit inconclusively.

In his farewell comments appearing in the January, 1971, issue of *The Communicator,* McKetta stated, "As I go into retirement my thoughts and loyalty shall remain with you always. I would like to take this opportunity to thank each and every member of the Department for the excellent cooperation you gave me during my tenure as Commissioner, and of the warm personal friendship I was privileged to enjoy. I sincerely hope that you continue in this same manner with the new Commissioner so that our ultimate goal of true professionalism may be reached."

McKetta, during his four years, had further developed a number of excellent ideas advanced by his predecessors, McCartney and Purdy. Additionally, he established satellite crime labs, the helicopter program, Community Relations program, and expanded facilities at the Academy. McKetta acted responsibly in fostering the automation of telecommunications and methods for handling police and housekeeping records, and inched the department closer to a modern radio system. These achievements, and others of lesser impact upon State Police affairs, underscore his tenure as commissioner. They will undoubtedly influence operations favorably for a long time to come.

Upon his retirement from the State Police, McKetta reported to Washington, D. C., as chief of the Federal Protective Service of the U. S. General Services Administration, at a salary of $29,100 a year. The GSA agency is charged with protecting all federal buildings in the United States, except post offices, and at that time employed 2,800 guards to do the job.

CHAPTER XX

Colonel Rocco P. Urella

1971–1972

The 1971 General Assembly opened for business on January 5, beginning a session that would not be adjourned until December 28. The Democrats had a shaky margin in the Senate 25–24, but a more comfortable margin in the House 112–90; it was one of the few times that the Democrats mustered more than 135 politicians in both legislative chambers. Chosen Senate president pro tempore was Martin L. Murray (D-Luzerne). Herbert Fineman was retained as House Speaker.

Business was halted on capitol hill January 19 as the Commonwealth inaugurated a new governor, Milton J. Shapp, the first Jewish chief executive in the state's long history. Another first was scored by the Senate that day when it refused to confirm Shapp's cabinet despite earlier rumors that the cabinet appointments would be approved unanimously, and the fact that Shapp was the first Democratic governor to take office with Democratic party control of the Senate. Reportedly, the Philadelphia Senate delegation was unhappy with Shapp's selection of Mrs. C. Delores Tucker and Mrs. Helene Wohlgemuth.

In order to get his administration moving, Shapp designated his cabinet members special assistants to the governor, a status they were to endure for almost a week. The Senate confirmed all appointments January 25. Shapp's cabinet was sworn in at one time as well-wishers jammed the governor's reception room to view the ceremony.

Urella, 52, a native of Mt. Carmel, Northumberland County, was

Colonel Rocco P. Urella (Courtesy of Pennsylvania State Police)

born February 10, 1918. His parents, Pompei Urella and Josephine Clinese Urella, were both born at Montecalvo, Italy, near Naples, and immigrated separately to the United States in 1908. It was not until after both their families had settled at Mt. Carmel that Pompei and Josephine married. Mr. Urella found work in the neighboring coal fields and became a boilerhouse operator. Now 86, he is a victim of black lung. Rocco Urella was the third-born of four children.

Urella attended public schools at Mt. Carmel and, as a young boy, displayed leadership qualities whether he was building a shanty with neighborhood chums or heading a hike through the Mt. Carmel countryside. He was described as rough and tough. At the age of 12, he accidentally fell into a dam near Mt. Carmel's Indian Rocks, breaking through a thin ice covering. Quick thinking on the part of Jack Horner and other companions saved Urella's young life.

He graduated from Mt. Carmel High School in 1936. During his high school days, Urella was exceptionally given to sports, participating in football, wrestling and track. Wrestling by far was his preference, and he was good at it: in 1934, he won the Pennsylvania Interscholastic Athletic Association District 4 wrestling championship and took second place in the state championship finals. Sports-oriented, he gave no more attention to studies than was necessary. In later years, however, he turned bookworm and studied incessantly to gain lost ground.

Having graduated from high school when the ill-effects of the Great Depression were still rampant, Urella, like other graduates, was unable to find a job at home. He went to live with relatives in the Bethlehem-Allentown area where he managed to find employment with a construction contractor.

Brother Anthony, the first to think of joining the new Pennsylvania Motor Police, was called to the training school. There, he decided that he was not cut out for police work, and dropped out of training. Urella picked up where his brother left off, and was enlisted with the Pennsylvania Motor Police January 1, 1938, at Myerstown. Not unlike McKetta before him, Urella, 20, stated that he was 21 to meet the minimum age requirement.

Upon graduation from Myerstown, Urella was assigned to the Philadelphia troop for duty. On an early day off, he visited Mt. Carmel to learn that his sister, Mary, had been bitten by the family dog and received no medical care—apparently his parents had dismissed the incident as too minor. Urella, well-schooled in such matters, insisted that the dog be examined for rabies. Testing revealed that the animal was rabid and Mary underwent the distressing treatment series to successfully ward off rabies. One of the few in that area to undergo such medical care, Urella's sister enjoyed being a local celebrity. His insistence undoubtedly spared her life.

In 1940, Urella was transferred to Media where he remained stationed for sixteen years, rising to the rank of corporal in 1948 and sergeant in 1952.

In 1943, Urella, as the result of an alert wartime identity check at a diner adjacent to a defense plant, flushed out an escaped murderer, Victor Andreoli. Andreoli was serving a life sentence for the holdup slaying of Trooper John Broski. In a shoot-out, Andreoli was killed, Urella was wounded. For his bravery in action, Urella was cited by Governor Edward Martin.

Promoted to first sergeant in 1956, Urella was transferred to troop headquarters at Philadelphia. Two years later, he was commissioned a lieutenant. McCartney promoted Urella to captain in 1962, and gave him command of the Reading troop, where he swiftly earned the reputation of being hard on organized crime in Berks and Schuylkill counties, chalking up more than 300 vice arrests.

Listed among his academic achievements, Urella was a graduate of the Pennsylvania Institute of Criminology, American Institute of Criminology, Philadelphia School-Seminar of Sudden Death, Philadelphia School of Medical-Legal Deaths, and the IBM School of Computer Management. For two years, he studied state and local government at the University of Pennsylvania, and law for two years at LaSalle Extension University. He completed the Northwestern University Police Supervision Course conducted at the Academy.

Following competitive exams in 1963, Purdy picked Urella to attend a twelve-week police administration course at Louisville University's Southern Police Institute (SPI), in Kentucky. There Urella was elected class president and graduated with highest honors. Upon his return from SPI, Urella was promoted to major. Purdy shifted him to headquarters to head up the new Bureau of Staff Inspection. The first of its kind in State Police history, the bureau was designed to perfect operations and cut costs.

Urella figured heavily in the 1965–66 House committee probe of State Police affairs under Purdy's administration. Purdy removed Urella from direct command of staff inspections while the House committee hearings were in progress.

After Purdy's firing, acting Commissioner Rittelmann transferred Urella to the Bureau of Technical Services. In the 1967 contest for the commissioner's job, Urella added to McKetta's chances for appointment by smoothing the way for his Senate confirmation. Had Milton J. Shapp won the 1966 gubernatorial election instead of Raymond P. Shafer, Urella would have been a good bet for commissioner.

During McKetta's first year, Urella wore two hats by also serving as commander of the eastern task force in civil disturbance incidents. In January, 1968, McKetta moved Urella to Philadelphia as commander of newly-formed Area I. He toured the nation's riot torn cities as a consultant for the International Association of Chiefs of Police and the President's Commission on Riot Control. He also attended the New Jersey State School on Riot Control.

Sensing a renege on a promised appointment as field commander upon Rittelmann's retirement later in 1968, Urella separated from the State Police in July, and became director of the Criminal Investigation Bureau in Delaware County.

During the heat of the 1970 gubernatorial campaign, Shapp and Urella renewed discussions concerning his appointment as State Police commissioner. At Shapp's request, Urella submitted a fourteen-page document containing his proposals for upgrading the Pennsylvania State Police. Shapp, apparently impressed with the document was convinced that Urella would be his man in the event of an election win.

Urella is a member of the Pennsylvania Institute of Criminology, Delaware County Chiefs of Police, Pennsylvania Chiefs of Police Association, International Association of Chiefs of Police, Fraternal Order of Police, Southern Police Institute, American Management Association, and the Advisory Council of Delaware County's Community College. He served as police science instructor at the Delaware County Community College and was police consultant for the New Jersey State Civil Service Board. He attends St. Denis Roman Catholic Church at Havertown.

Urella is married to the former Mary Sita of Mt. Carmel, Pennsylvania. Commissioner and Mrs. Urella reside at Ardmore, Delaware County. They had two sons. At the time of Urella's appointment, Rocco, Jr., a LaSalle College graduate, was a medical student at the University of Bologna, Italy; Philip was recuperating from brain surgery at the Reading Rehabilitation Center.

In an interview with *Philadelphia Inquirer* reporter Vincent P. Carocci the day before his confirmation, Urella rejected the term "shakeup" with regard to his reorganization plans. Urella had already moved in Captain Philip M. Conti as his administrative assistant and gave Captain Charles S. Graci relief from his Troop S command, at Milesburg, to take on a special assignment at headquarters. Urella stated that Graci would be temporarily helping out with a new table of organization. The presence of both officers at headquarters gave life to the rumor that major changes were upcoming.

In response to inquiries about Dussia's status, the commissioner-designate stated that if he did retain Dussia, he would be a "working deputy." This comment had an obvious reference to McKetta's designed under-employment of Dussia for four years. Two days after his confirmation, Urella announced Dussia's appointment as his deputy. Dussia was sworn in by Urella on January 27 at a ceremony conducted in the headquarters conference room.

Serving as Urella's secretary was Mrs. Eleanor O. Kelly of Springfield, Delaware County. Mrs. Kelly, a qualified legal secretary, had been a member of the Delaware County Criminal Investigation Bureau staff.

Not at all unexpected, Urella designated Trooper James McCann his aide. McCann, a Harrisburg troop member, was formerly assigned to the Reading troop where he first gained Urella's attention. One of Urella's first promotional orders moved McCann to acting sergeant status, an action that arched eyebrows and would one day lead to a controversy contesting the powers of the commissioner. McCann's general behavior during his special assignment with Urella did not ingratiate him with staff personnel and field commanders. Unfortunately, such conduct was not only a disservice to Urella, but it lay the foundation for repercussions that would surely come.

Urella lost no time in summoning troop and area commanders to the Academy for a conference on February 1. The new commissioner briefly outlined his principle objectives, beseeching the cooperation of every commander and bureau director. Basically, it was a welcoming affair rather than an open forum for police problems. Major Wojick was privately informed by Dussia that he was to establish his area command at Milesburg—not Harrisburg.

Three weeks later, Urella met at the Academy with the fifteen FOP lodge presidents. The commissioner was anxious to win over the confidence of the rank and file as well as the top brass in order to lay suitable groundwork for his own performance. As promised, Urella and his staff met later with representatives of OA to iron out any misunderstandings regarding the implementation of the FOP contract beginning July 1. This history-making contract was of paramount importance to the FOP.

Urella continued to work closely with the FOP, a relationship that was not entirely acceptable to all field commanders. Some thought that Urella was bending over backwards too much to appease the FOP at the expense of field supervisors on occasions. This became a tender spot with them. It was Urella's intention to work with the FOP without relinquishing control at any level of command, in keeping with modern concepts of management. It is regrettable that the commissioned officers who did not grasp his aims failed to make their opinions known to Urella so that he could have set them straight. Time and time again, he stated that he welcomed constructive criticism.

Grosnick, who as Urella's former superior officer had treated him rather shabbily before his 1968 departure, was rightfully uncertain about his role. Without losing time, Urella assured Grosnick that under no circumstances could he expect to be a member of his management team. Not surprised with this appraisal, Grosnick resigned and retired. After his departure, Grosnick was appointed McKetta's assistant with GSA's Federal Protective Service, at Washington, D. C. In March, Conti was promoted to lieutenant colonel and appointed chief of staff— the third person to hold that position in the department's history. Preceding him were Grosnick and Wilhelm.

Lt. Colonel William B. Cooper, whose relationship with Urella was less strained, decided to hang in as field commander and await developments. Although many of Cooper's job responsibilities were restored to the deputy, he was still left with much to do.

Cooper disclosed to Urella an incredible pile of disciplinary cases which McKetta had refused to decide. McKetta allowed these to pile up on Cooper's desk to the latter's embarrassment. Urella named a three-man board of officers to review the cases and recommend dispositions. The cases were belatedly disposed of in short order.

As weeks passed by, Cooper's joviality and good will earned for him Urella's favor. Giving Cooper a clean bill of health, Urella informed him that he would be henceforth considered a member of his management team with full responsibility for his post as field commander. To say that Cooper was a happy man with his new status would be an understatement. As time went on, Cooper was heard to say, "I never had it so good."

Promoted in March also was Lieutenant Stanley S. Cimokowski. Captain Cimokowski was transferred to headquarters to reactivate the staff inspection program—a program which Urella had initiated at Purdy's direction. Even though staff inspections were continued by Rittelman and McKetta, the program's role was a diminishing one during McKetta's tenure. Cimokowski, although not an original member of Urella's inspection team, did serve as an inspector later on; he was well acquainted with operations. The fact that Urella would turn his attention to staff inspections once again came as no surprise. The program's return to bureau status was inevitable.

Urella reassigned Captain Harbaugh to the Bureau of Criminal Investigation. Replacing him as legislative liaison officer was Sergeant Arthur E. Berardi, who was brought in from the Erie troop. Berardi had served as State Police aide for a number of state attorneys general; he was well qualified to handle his new assignment.

The evening of February 8, Urella's son Philip suffered a cerebral hemorrhage. His 24-year-old son died early the following morning. Urella was shaken by this loss which was to overshadow his days as commissioner. Never again was he the happy fellow who just two short weeks before had been confirmed as State Police helmsman. Urella's birthday, February 10, was simply lost to family sorrow.

Undoubtedly the best remedy at hand for Urella during these saddest of days was to concentrate on the administrative problems untidily resting on his threshhold and set into motion new programs of his own authorship. This is exactly what he opted to do.

OA staff members were most anxious to discuss the fate of the ill-conceived CIS and SA programs before anything more was done to implement them. They were not in favor of the two programs in the first place, and were content to know that Urella would move in the direction of abolishing them. It was agreed that an opinion regarding the legality of the programs would first be solicited from the attorney general. Nothing further would be done pending the delivery of that opinion.

At headquarters there was considerable objection to the construction of the new headquarters building at Hershey. With the acquisition of sufficient land from the Harrisburg State Hospital, preference was expressed for the erection of both department headquarters and the Troop H headquarters buildings at the north Harrisburg site. Urella and his staff members went one step further and decided that both facilities should be housed in one large building with significant savings accruing to the Commonwealth. Disposing of the problem of two appointed architectural firms was left to General State Authority (GSA) officials. From this point on, plans called for one multistory building to house department headquarters, Troop H operations, Troop S Harrisburg Substation operations, the crime laboratory and computer center. Ironing out the difficulties and intrigue accompanying these major changes in plans was to take up five more years before groundbreaking in 1976.

Urella had definite ideas regarding the composition of the promotional examinations scheduled for October. Contract arrangements were discussed with Yarger Associates, of Richmond, Virginia. This firm had suitably prepared examinations in previous years, and there was no reason for changing to another. Although he agreed to testing police skills for the most part in the lower ranks, Urella pressed for management qualifications in the higher ranks. He wanted only the best qualified supervisors to rise into command positions. Taking into account Urella's specifications, Yarger Associates proceeded with the examinations which, according to established procedure, were reviewed by a board of officers appointed by Urella. By October, Yarger Associates and the board of officers were satisfied that an excellent set of examinations was readied for competition. All concerned with the examinations had been provided an early listing of recommended reading material to study for successful participation.

One of the most frustrating problems to confront Urella was the massive $40,000,000 radio contract that the Republicans had dumped into Shapp's lap. To work with State Police representatives headed by Captain Robert L. Bomboy, Shapp appointed his counsel and personal friend, Israel Packel. Packel and the State Police locked horns right at the outset of discussions. The State Police pursued the leasing of a system free of the horrors of ownership, while Packel preferred ownership. The contract, already prepared to the point of ratification, called for a lease system; and it was recommended by Urella and company that all of the more costly provisions which could await implementation at a later date be deleted from the contract to make a reduced cost figure more palatable. Following up on this proposal, the State Police and Motorola officials reduced the contract figure to $19,000,000—more than fifty percent off from the original figure. Packel, clinging stubbornly to his ownership proposal, declined to rule the State Police action a legal one. Motorola's staff of legal talent defended the action as legal—Motorola, however, was hesitant to take Packel to task on the question.

Informed of this deadlock, Shapp referred the entire matter to a former associate in the electronics business, for whose expertise in this particular field he had the highest praise. Flown to Philadelphia from Florida, Donald Kirk was closeted with Urella, Bomboy and Conti for two days, reviewing the Motorola contract and the State Police position, generally. Upon his return to Florida, Kirk filed his report with Shapp, lauding the State Police approach to a modern radio communications system and recommending the governor give his approval to leasing. Still Packel would not yield to the modified Motorola contract.

It was finally agreed that the preferred lease system would be allowed the State Police, however, it was stipulated that Bomboy would have to prepare a new set of specifications with legal assistance from the Justice Department and invite new bids. This course, however discouraging it was to the State Police, was followed obediently, and consumed months of laborious revisioning on Bomboy's part before a final proposal was ready for advertising. In the meantime, Urella and his forces kept their fingers crossed that neither a major emergency requiring special radio support would arise nor increasing radio system outages endanger operations.

Strongly subscribing to Purdy's concept that a police officer, in order to proceed with his work with professional bearing, requires more than skill training. Urella went a few steps further. Purdy, and McKetta for that matter, encouraged troopers to enroll in college courses during their off-duty time—Urella also wanted college courses incorporated in the cadet training curriculum at the Academy with accreditation for both skill and academic courses.

To gain support for this move, Urella met with top officials of the state Department of Education, who promised to look into his accreditation proposal and were favorably impressed with the commissioner's education interests. Urella, on March 19, also met with the thirteen state college presidents. Campus disorder, police on campus, drugs, investigation of fires, inspection of buildings, police education and accreditation covered the range of subjects discussed with the amenable educators.

Urella's discussions of his plans with the Academy staff resulted in an agreed need to extend cadet training from twelve weeks to twenty-four. Added to the curriculum were sociology, psychology, English composition and public speaking. Penn State University officials were anxious to furnish a teaching staff for these academic courses and eventually authorized accreditation for all Academy training programs. In due time, Urella was to witness his program blossom into a thirty-credit certification for all cadet graduates. This award would provide each graduate with a sound, encouraging basis for continuing his education after field assignment toward the earning of associate and baccalaureate degrees.

The expanded twenty-four-week training program was planned for a new cadet class scheduled to begin July 29. Announcing this change, Urella said, "The complexities of our society and the demands placed upon today's policemen makes more training and education mandatory. It is for this reason that we have doubled the length of the training period for our cadets and greatly expanded the work in the social and behavioral sciences."

Although Urella's thoughts for reorganizing the department's superstructure were not revealed for some months, the introduction of House Bill 663 by Speaker Herbert Fineman and Representative Harry Comer (D-Philadelphia) on March 30 gave public notice of what Urella might have in mind. The Administrative Code of 1929, as amended, provides that the Pennsylvania State Police shall have only *a* deputy. Bill 663 was intended to remove legal restrictions and allow Urella to appoint more than one deputy. Other attempts had been made in the past to remove this limitation and failed, it was now Urella's turn at bat. But, as it will be seen later, the bill ran into a peck of trouble.

On April 21, a ninety-six-man cadet class completed Academy training. Having accepted Urella's invitation, Shapp addressed the graduating class. After the ceremony, Shapp remarked to Urella that he saw no black faces among those receiving diplomas. He urged Urella to do something about that condition. Since the class make-up had already been decided before Urella's tenure began, he was at a loss to explain the circumstances of this all-white class; however, there was no mistaking the governor's message.

Urella met with representatives of the State Civil Service Commission (SCSC) to review the written entrance examination for cadet applicants to determine what, if anything, could be done to remove obstacles to minority competition. SCSC staffers consented to remove any uncommon words and substitute those more likely to be understood by minority applicants, and generally revise questions for easier comprehension. This was one of many moves made by Urella to comply with the state's affirmative action program—particularly to increase the number of black troopers. The State Police in recent years was a prime target of criticism for its basically all-white complement.

Meanwhile, the much-awaited opinion from the Justice Department regarding the CIS and SA programs was handed to Urella. Attorney General J. Shane Creamer, in his opinion, dated March 10, 1971, referred to Section 711 of the Administrative Code, which provides in part that the State Police commissioner shall:

> . . . make rules and regulations, subject to the approval of the Governor, prescribing qualifications prerequisite to, or retention of, membership in the force; for the enlistment, training, discipline and conduct of the members of the force; *for the selection and promotion of such members on the basis of merit.* . . .

Emphasis was added by the attorney general who went on to cite the fact that rules and regulations governing promotions did exist on the basis of merit, except for the CIS and SA programs. Creamer concluded:

> In view of the above quoted provision of the Administrative Code, it is my opinion, and you are accordingly advised that no legal basis exists by which the two specialist classifications here involved can be justified.
>
> If you desire to continue such classifications, it will be necessary to adopt rules and regulations governing the same, as well as placing such specialist classifications within the competitive examination program. If you do not desire to retain the classifications, the same must be abolished immediately, with the persons so classified reverting to the ranks held at the time of their reclassification, but with no reduction in pay.

Urella harbored no intentions of jockeying rules and regulations to give life to either of these controversial programs. Consequently, he ordered his staff to meet with OA representatives to follow the attorney general's guidelines and abolish the programs. This was accomplished by reverting all reclassified personnel to the ranks previously held at the time of their reclassifications without loss of pay. The mechanics of these personnel transactions were reviewed with the FOP, and it took time to accomplish them. Although Urella pursued legal direction in doing away with these programs, there were lingering hard feelings expressed by some of the CIS and SA personnel who believed that they were somehow cheated, and blamed Urella for all that.

Creamer's appointment as attorney general was a disappointment for Urella and other ranking officials in the state and local police family, who believed that Shapp could have picked someone better qualified for the job. Many wagered that Creamer would fail at his new job and, in their estimation, he eventually did. Even legislators were soon to become disenchanted with the new attorney general.

As time went on, ill-feelings between Creamer and Urella surfaced again and again. In March, Creamer sought Shapp's intervention to secure the services of Captain Roy Titler for duty with the Crime Commission. It will be recalled that Titler had formerly served with the Justice Department when Creamer was PCC's executive director. Owen Morris was now director, having replaced Rinkevich. Urella released Titler under protest.

In April, Creamer, apparently with Shapp's blessing, called a series of meetings with State Police and National Guard commanders to consider the attorney general's drafted document entitled, "State Civil Disturbance Procedures." It is not difficult to imagine the discontent shared by the experienced, career State Police and National Guard officials as they read how Creamer would become the center of authority in civil disturbances. The draft was prepared in secret and its delivery to the officers involved came as a bombshell. They were disturbed no end that Creamer would undertake such a proposal without consulting with State Police and National Guard authorities who represent two of the state's top peace-keeping forces that have borne the burden of maintaining law and order for decades honorably and effectively. In a letter to Shapp, Urella was highly critical of Creamer and his schemes. It is understood that the National Guard hierarchy had nothing kind to say about Creamer either.

Creamer's "State Civil Disturbance Procedures" did not come into being; however, a procedure for dealing with tension situations detected by various state agencies and reporting them to the Justice Department was adopted. This substitute procedure provided for calling together all parties to a tension situation with a view to bringing about some rational settlement before riotous conditions could develop.

By mid-1971, Troop S had not yet completed one year of operations, and Urella was under pressure from staff personnel to do away with this troop. A survey of troop commanders indicated clearly that they did not favor the existence of Troop S and would welcome patrol responsibility for interstate routes running through their command areas. In fact, some were so bold as to claim that they could do a better job of patrolling. In weighing all arguments for and against Troop S operations, Urella took into account most the men assigned to the troop and the effects it would have upon them should the troop be abolished. He felt the troopers would be unfairly treated by a reversal, and that the circumstances were quite different from the case of the CIS and SA programs. Although Urella was inclined toward scrapping the troop, he ruled in favor of the men, stating that he could live with Troop S by keeping operational costs down through the continued use of shared facilities. He dismissed any further attempts to abolish the new troop. It remains in existence today—still a problem child in many respects—but undoubtedly a permanent member of the family.

Urella and troopers everywhere were deeply moved by the accidental shooting death of Trooper Robert J. Lomas, Jr., on June 12, at the Avondale Substation. Trooper John J. Finnegan, whose revolver accidentally discharged, and Lomas were changing shifts at the time of the unfortunate incident.

The cigar-smoking commissioner, a connoisseur of fine tobacco, took on speaking engagements right and left. Gifted with an excellent memory and ability to speak extemporaneously, he won favor with his audiences. He pressed for a close relationship with municipal police forces and urged his men to work cooperatively with members of the news media. "It is incumbent upon the troop and substation commander to know the media representatives in his area and to see that all information concerning State Police activities is made available to them. These contacts should be cultivated, not with the idea of just getting 'publicity' but fulfilling our obligation to inform the public," Urella wrote for *The Communicator*.

More than ever, he wanted the public to be served as never before. During the annual field exhibitions, Urella rode at the head of his mounted troopers as they thrilled audiences everywhere with precision drills and stunt-riding. Few police incidents of importance occurred without Urella's presence at the scene to manifest his interest in the problems facing his men. Urella's popularity mounted swiftly.

Early in Urella's administration, James Cox was earmarked for replacement as State Police public information officer. But, with second thoughts on the subject, the new commissioner decided to keep Cox aboard.

The new FOP contract was put into effect July 1, as scheduled. Contract salary increases and the removal of the deputy commissioner's salary from legal restrictions saw Dussia's salary exceed Urella's which was pegged by law at $25,000. This unusual situation was often a point of private jesting between Urella and his deputy. Dussia offered to split the extra dollars with Urella—an offer readily turned down.

Faced with mandatory retirement, Major Joseph L. Young resigned his post as commander of Area VI in August. Urella promptly filled this vacancy by promoting Graci to major. Graci, however, remained at headquarters on special assignment.

Graduating from NUTI were Corporal Joseph G. Pandos and Trooper Stephen R. Warsavage who, like most of their predecessors, were assigned to Planning and Research. Selected to follow them at NUTI in September was a larger group this time. Urella gave the nod to five men: Corporal Joseph L. Monville, and Troopers John C. Caporaletti, Richard A. Ross, Ronald A. Rostalski and Charles D. Sincavage.

In cooperation with Indiana University's School of Law, at Bloomington, Indiana, Urella established a new program whereby three troopers would study law for three years and, upon graduation, become policeman-attorneys. Their services, according to Urella, would be useful in the areas of training, planning and research, preparing legislation and other advisory situations. First to be selected by Urella for schooling was Corporal Lawrence F. Clark, of the Academy staff. Two others were to be chosen in time to enter Indiana University's Law School in September, 1972.

In September, 1971, dedication ceremonies were conducted for the new Troop S headquarters building at Milesburg, and the new regional crime lab at Erie. The building at Milesburg headed the list as the most expensive rental facility in the field. The Erie lab was located at troop headquarters where adequate space was provided.

Perhaps one of Urella's most important policy changes to date was his decision to take on female troopers. Minority recruiting was an issue facing him almost from the time he took his hand off the bible at oath-taking ceremonies on January 25. While discussions since then mainly dealt with the recruiting of blacks, Urella was mindful that females and Spanish surname applicants were not to be brushed aside. Massachusetts, Connecticut and California had already set precedent by taking on females. Pennsylvania was to join these states.

Announcing this policy change, Urella stated, "Women have long since proven that they are capable of doing nearly every job that a man can do. In police work there are several areas in which women can perform even better than men. Therefore, we have decided to utilize this talent within the organization."

A campaign specifically tailored to recruiting minority representatives was begun, and women for the first time were encouraged to apply. Entrance requirements for women were the same as for men, except for height. Arrangements were completed with the Civil Service Commission to provide the State Police with separate listings identifying men and women, white and black. The first female applicant at Troop H, Harrisburg, on October 1, was Miss Romaine L. Engle, of Hummelstown, a registered nurse.

Urella's long-awaited reorganization plan received Executive Board approval in November, 1971. Two new executive positions were created: Chief of Auxiliary Services and Chief of Field Operations. The chief of staff position was retitled Chief of Administrative Services. The field commander's post also retitled was to be known as Chief of Field Services. Appearing on the scene again, with slight tailoring, was the Bureau of Inspection and Special Investigations. Upgraded to bureau status were the Planning and Research Division and the Community Services Division. The Bureau of Inspection and the Bureau of Research and Development (another name change) were both placed under the commissioner's wing.

Promoted to the newly-created executive posts with the rank of lieutenant colonel were Majors Charles S. Graci and Edward M. McGroarty. Graci was designated Chief of Field Operations, McGroarty was named Chief of Auxiliary Services. Captain Cimokowski was appointed head of the inspection operations. Captains Deyo and Donahoe remained with Research and Development and Community Services, respectively. All three were to be promoted in 1972.

Announcing his plan, Urella explained:

> This new structure will permit more direct supervision and coordination of all activities. It will also allow more concentration and attention to each of the management functions by reducing the span of control exercised by any one individual.
>
> Under the former command structure the Field Commander and Chief of Staff had entirely too many complex responsibilities. They could not possibly devote the necessary time to each individual reporting to them. The Commissioner and Deputy Commissioner were, likewise, too much involved in day-to-day operational details to function fully as overall managers.
>
> You will note that the new structure has a maximum of

State Police top commanders, 1972. Seated, left to right: Lt. Col. Joseph Dussia, Col. Rocco P. Urella, Lt. Col. Philip M. Conti. Standing: Lt. Col. William B. Cooper, Lt. Col. Edward M. McGroarty, Lt. Col. Charles S. Graci. (Courtesy of Pennsylvania State Police)

seven individuals reporting to their superior. This, I am sure, will increase our efficiency and improve our service to the public.

This new table of organization, as is the case with any change from the existing system, will take some time to function smoothly. This transitional period can be shortened considerably if each of us offers his complete cooperation.

This announcement of the new hierarchy made clearer Urella's push to remove legal restrictions to the number of deputies he could appoint. There would be a chief deputy, and each of the four executive chiefs would be subordinate deputies.

This revelation at the outset created no particular stir until two challenges surfaced. Graci, with or without Urella's sanction, reportedly, began to buttonhole legislators for the passage of House Bill 663. In doing so, Graci's lobbying efforts left the impression that he would become the chief deputy. This possibility did not set well with Dussia's many legislative friends—friends who would have no part in any action resulting in Dussia's downgrading.

In another move by black House members, Shapp was told that, if he wanted their support for the multi-deputy bill, one of the five deputies had to be black. Because there were no black State Police commissioned officers to consider, Urella would have had to seek out someone for lateral entry—a prospect that shook the department to its very roots—or, elevate a black non-commissioned officer, which would have been a bitter pill for Urella to swallow. Suggested for appointment was a black captain from the Fairmount Park Police Department.

The hassle created by these two developments, and the absence of a suitable alternative were sufficient to kill House Bill 663 without a decent burial. Urella, a victim of circumstances, who looked like a winner some months before, lost out. A Monday morning quarterback could be heard muttering that Urella's jump from one to five deputies was more than traffic could bear.

In November, retired and active members of the State Police took out time to mourn the death of former Commissioner Earl J. Henry. Henry, 75, died at the Harrisburg Hospital on November 6, after a lingering illness. He was survived by his wife, Mrs. Catherine Henry, two sisters and two brothers. Henry was buried near Pleasantville, Crawford County.

Earlier it was stated that State Police commissioners had often tried to reduce the number of substations in the name of efficiency and economy. Henry and McCartney had met with modest success after struggling with political interference. Others failed completely. Urella, looking for hard-to-come-by-dollars, turned his attention to the list of substations that could be consolidated with others at a savings to the taxpayers and with better service to boot. The substation located at Warrendale, Butler County, was a target. Increased patrols operated from troop headquarters some seventeen miles away were promised. Senator Donald O. Oesterling (D-Butler) decided to give Urella a rough time of it, and put on quite a show for his constituency. But, Urella was not to be denied: the substation was closed on November 18 with toll-free phone service to Butler installed—that area of Butler County has never been served better.

In December, a bitter relationship between Shapp and Philadelphia Mayor Frank Rizzo was reaching a boiling point. Shapp sought Urella's aid in bringing about some settlement of differences. Urella, who had served most of his police career in Philadelphia area, enjoyed the best of relationships with the former Philadelphia police commissioner. Seeking Urella's intercession was a smart move on Shapp's part, and a truce was arranged. This interlude, however, was to last but a short time and then erupt into a situation far worse as Shapp and Creamer moved to investigate alleged corruption in the Philadelphia Police Department.

December 9, 1971, was another dark day for the State Police as its members recorded the slaying of another fellow officer in the line of duty. Corporal John S. Valent, attempting to take a trio of young men into custody for questioning, was shot and killed. One fugitive, Charles Koons, Jr., was killed in a pre-dawn gun battle with state and local police. The other two men escaped and were later captured by Florida State Trooper James Rudd at Quincy, Florida. Mark R. Geddes, 22, and Charles H. Knisely, 20, were extradited and charged with Corporal Valent's murder.

Urella, who lost no time in arriving at the scene of the slaying, stated, "While we are always deeply grieved over the wanton killing of police officers, it is particularly tragic and shocking when death strikes during the Christmas season. I know that I speak for the Department and for the entire police fraternity when I say that our hearts, prayers and thoughts are with Corporal Valent's family during these dark hours." Oddly enough, Trooper Gary Rosenberger was also killed at Christmas—one year before.

Valent, 49, was buried on December 13 with full military honors. Attending his funeral were 300 fellow police officers, who included approximately 100 visiting officers from neighboring state and municipal departments. Among the mourners were Governor Shapp and Commissioner Urella.

The area command vacancies created by the Graci and McGroarty promotions were filled by Captains Joseph C. Snyder and Donald S. Cutting, both 59. Major Snyder moved to Area VI, at Butler, Major Edward Wojick was transferred from Area VII to Area III, at Wyoming, and Major Cutting took over Wojick's slot with his Area VII office reestablished in the Turnpike administration building at Highspire.

All promoted commissioned officers, by virtue of a new policy instituted by Urella, received their commissions from Urella in a befitting ceremony at the Academy. Wives were invited guests for the ceremony and luncheon. Needless to state, this policy was a real morale booster.

Before the general assembly closed shop in December, the legislators passed a measure calling for an increase in the number of troopers. Act 163, P.L. 608, December 15, upped the complement to 3,790 officers and men—a jump of 240 from the previously set figure of 3,550. Since the 233 troopers assigned to the Turnpike troop are not counted in the legislated complement, the total number of officers and men now topped the 4,000 mark for the first time—4,023 to be exact.

At the close of the year, FOP and state negotiations for a new contract reached an impasse just as they did the year before. The matter was then referred to an arbitration board as provided for in Act 111. On the three-man panel, the state was represented by attorney Thomas H. Lane, Dr. Edward B. Shils represented the FOP, and Dr. Walter J. Gershenfeld was selected neutral chairman of the panel. Deputy Attorney General Miles J. Gibbons argued for the Commonwealth; attorney Howard Richard stated the FOP case. By the December 31 deadline, another contract increasing salary and benefits was ready for implementation July 1, 1972. The new agreement was valued at $3,839,000—a figure considerably lower than the 1971 contract cost estimate.

A 187-man cadet class graduated from the Academy on January 12, 1972, setting a new record as the largest class to complete training at the Hershey institution. Another class was called in on January 27 to undergo six months of intensive training. This particular class will be remembered as the first ever to number women among its membership—there were 15 of them.

February was to bear witness to some changes in headquarters personnel. Captain Lodwick D. Jenkins retired as head of the crime lab at Harrisburg. Replacing Jenkins was Lieutenant James Sagans. Three officers heading the Bureaus of Inspection, Research and Development (R. & D.) and Community Services were promoted to major. They were Majors Stanley S. Cimokowski, Sidney C. Deyo, Jr., and Michael Donahoe. Lieutenant Russell Anderson, state fire marshal, was promoted to captain. Captain Frank Micolucci was transferred to headquarters to assist Cimokowski, and Captain Joseph I. C. Everly joined Donahoe.

Ever since his appointment as commissioner, Urella had stressed the importance of working closely with municipal police departments. Capping his efforts to assist municipal police with their training programs, Urella opened regional training centers at Collegeville, Montgomery County, and Greensburg, Westmoreland County. Sergeant Tony Ursi was named supervisor of the Collegeville center, and Lieutenant Earl P. Wright was picked to head the Greensburg center. With three centers at Hershey, Collegeville and Greensburg, the training of municipal police was accelerated.

Urella continued to work with Francis Schafer, executive director of the Pennsylvania Chiefs of Police Association (PCPA), and the chiefs' education committee, to push for legislation making police training a mandatory requirement for appointment. This type of legislation had been a long sought objective by police administrators and, with Urella's backing, it appeared that the chiefs were inching closer to legislative approval.

In April, State Police patrol cars sported a new color combination—blue and gold. These colors replaced the green and white color combination instituted by Purdy back in 1963. Urella believed that the state colors—blue and gold—were worth the trial. The colors later proved to be too dark, and lighter shades of blue and gold were selected. The loud look gave way to the moniker, "Tijuana taxi cab." It was inevitable that more suitable colors would have to follow the discontinuance of blue and gold.

Majors Donald S. Cutting and Clifford G. Yahner, having reached mandatory retirement age in March, resigned their posts at Area VII and IV, respectively. Cutting was replaced by Major Roy O. Wellendorf, Yahner was replaced by Major Edward Fagnani. Other changes included the transfer of Captain Oliver A. Smith to headquarters as state fire marshal, replacing Captain Russell Anderson. Lieutenant William Anselmi was promoted to captain and retained command of the Information Systems Division which houses the complex computer and data processing center. Lieutenant Francis Anzelmi was moved into Personnel as assistant director. Transferred into the Bureau of Inspection was newly-promoted Lieutenant Stephen M. Luchansky who would figure in a major controversy before the year's end.

Still rising in popularity, Urella was honored at a testimonial dinner given by FOP Pioneer Lodge 37. Urella was a charter member of the host lodge. The dinner held on May 8 in Media, was attended by 720 cheering guests headed by the entire Shapp family and House Speaker Herbert Fineman. Such an outpouring of admiration for a man in public office is seldom manifested.

Troopers from the Philadelphia area, in June, were called to a scene of devastation at King of Prussia where the J. Leon Altemose Construction Company was erecting a multimillion dollar plaza. In forty minutes of rioting, hard hat unionists, who were locked in a labor dispute with Altemose, destroyed construction equipment valued to the tune of more than $300,000. Severe restrictions on picketting were placed on the striking workers by the Montgomery County court. To protest these restrictions, a massive demonstration was ordered by labor leaders. Some 30,000 workers were scheduled to march into Norristown, the county seat.

Fearing another King of Prussia incident, Urella summoned his forces to see to it that the Norristown march was a peaceful one. A task force exceeding 1,800 troopers, the largest ever assembled, lined the rain-soaked thoroughfares of Norristown on June 22. Impressed by the State Police show of force, the hard hats, to their everlasting credit, demonstrated peacefully—Norristown was spared a possible disaster.

Another disaster, however, was in the making as Hurricane Agnes, whipping up the eastern seaboard since June 19, continued to drench the countryside with record-breaking rainfall. State Police forces at Norristown were quickly redeployed to flooded areas in Pennsylvania's northeastern and western counties.

As Hurricane Agnes moved off the coast, the eastern states were reckoning with the worst flood in recent history. More than 100,000 homes were destroyed; the death count reached 134. In Pennsylvania, the devastation was unimaginable. Wilkes-Barre and many other communities were practically wiped out. For months, State Police forces were retained in disaster areas to facilitate the movement of rescue and reconstruction efforts. Praises were heaped upon the State Police for the remarkable display of law and order at Norristown and tireless services to flood victims, unselfishly rendered, as troopers themselves suffered household losses. State Police helicopter pilots were heroes over and over again as rescue operations were carried out.

Urella later received the Pennsylvania Distinguished Service Medal from Major General Harry J. Meir, Jr., state adjutant general, during a surprise ceremony at the Indiantown Gap Military Reservation. Meir praised Urella for his outstanding leadership and excellent cooperation with the state's National Guard. Shapp had every reason to be proud of his State Police commissioner.

Honored for their flood services were Lt. Colonel Edward M. McGroarty and Lt. Colonel William B. Cooper who received from Brig. General William J. Gallagher, Meir's deputy adjutant general, the state's Meritorious Service Medal. Working with McGroarty and Cooper in the Wilkes-Barre disaster area were Major Edward Wojick, Captain Mauro Forte and Lieutenant James Klass. McGroarty and Cooper, both of whom had served long careers in the coal region, were considered by Urella as ideally suited for the flood relief program

"Hard-hats" demonstrate peacefully at Norristown, June, 1972, as State Police troopers look on. (Courtesy of Pennsylvania State Police)

Middletown and Harrisburg International Airport are flooded after Hurricane Agnes struck Pennsylvania in 1972. (Courtesy of Pennsylvania State Police)

there. Excused from their headquarters responsibilities, both confirmed Urella's judgment by turning in outstanding records.

A critique of the Norristown and flood operations underscored,
among other things, the need for a modern radio communications
system. Yet, the efforts to secure one were moving ever so slowly because of circumstances already mentioned.

On the national scene, an incident of importance took place at the
Watergate building complex at Washington, D.C., on June 17 that was
to rock the nation. James W. McCord, security officer for the Committee to Re-elect the President (Nixon), and four others were arrested
while breaking into the Democratic National Committee offices. Although Mr. Nixon soundly defeated his Democratic opponent in the
1972 general election, the scandal was to bring about his unprecedented resignation as President and damage Republican election
chances at all political levels for a long time. Effects were noticeably
felt in the 1973 Pennsylvania elections.

The five men attending NUTI graduated in June, bringing the total
number of NUTI graduates to 27. Chosen to follow them at NUTI in
September were Sergeant Thomas J. Hanus, and Troopers Donald C.
Bradbury and Thomas P. Brennan.

A history-making cadet class of 146 graduated on July 7, as 14
women joined the trooper ranks. Honored on this occasion were:
Regina Adams, Jill Bairhalter, Romaine Engle, Judith Galloway, Lucinda Hammond, Kathryn Hosmer, Nancy Lightner, Judith McCarr,
Ann Metcalf, Patricia Moe, Kathryn Neville, Mary Rosetti, Doris Sott
and Barbara Wharrey. Missing was Nancy Wilson who dropped out
midway through training to return to college. Trooper Judith McCarr
was the daughter of former State Police Captain Adrian J. McCarr—it
was the first father-daughter team ever to hit the department. (Father-
son combinations were not unusual at all.) Addressing the cadet graduates on that memorable July day was the governor's wife, Muriel
Shapp. Urella, a diplomat, could have made no better choice.

Also honored in July was Trooper Paul G. Cotter, of the Wyoming
troop. Cotter, a long-time activist in the FOP movement, was elected
state president of the fraternal group numbering some 30,000 members.
He was the first trooper ever to be elected to that high post.

State Police patrol expertise was put to the test on July 8, when a
rock festival at the Pocono International Raceway drew an estimated
crowd of 200,000 fans. Raceway parking attendants were unable to
cope with the flow of incoming motor vehicles, and the rock fans
simply abandoned their vehicles, blocking local routes, interstate highways and ramps in what was described as the worst traffic jam troopers

First class of female troopers, July, 1972. Front row, left to right: Judith McCarr, Mary Rosetti, Doris Sott, State Treasurer Grace Sloan, Patricia Moe, Mrs. Milton J. Shapp, Kathryn Hosmer, Regina Adams, Romaine Engle, Col. Rocco P. Urella. Back row: Lucinda Hammond, Nancy Lightner, Kathryn Neville, Jill Bairhalter, Barbara Wharrey, Judith Galloway, Ann Metalf. (Courtesy of Pennsylvania State Police)

have ever had to face. Their success in restoring order earned them much praise from local authorities and raceway officials.

During earlier months, Shapp had recruited from private industry a task force of topflight managers to study state operations. The purpose of the task force was to cut corners and save the Commonwealth money. A three-man team headed by Bruce Lindsay of Sun Oil took on the State Police survey. One of Lindsay's recommendations was the abolishment of the area commander posts. When rumors of this recommendation hit the field, top officers took to worrying that an avenue for advancement would be gone. Among the worriers was Captain James D. Barger.

Dussia and Barger, longtime associates in western Pennsylvania, were known to be the best of friends as well. It was not unusual to find both men on the phone several times throughout a working day to exchange views on official matters. Neither was it unusual when Barger sought out Dussia's aid for promotion to major at the time of Yahner's retirement. He wanted very much to be promoted before the area commands drifted into a state of limbo. Urella did not want to bypass Captain Edward Fagnani, a senior captain; therefore, the commissioner appointed Fagnani as Yahner's successor. Trusting that he would get a crack at the next opening just months away, Barger continued his appeals to Dussia. Dussia assured Barger that he would be strongly recommended when Major Snyder retired from Area VI at Butler.

Meanwhile, Urella, having been an area commander himself, provided Shapp with sufficient justification to override Lindsay's recommendation and spare the area commands. It is entirely possible that Shapp did not override Lindsay so much as he yielded to one of his stellar cabinet performers.

In August, Snyder, 60, retired. Urella, despite urgings from Dussia and Conti, was uncertain about promoting Barger. Nonetheless, he eventually surrendered to his top officers with the prophetic statement that both would live to regret being Barger fans. Jaynes was transferred to Butler and Major Barger, on August 10, filled the Area V vacancy at Greensburg.

Also promoted in August was Captain Nicholas J. Pauley. The new captain was then commanding operations of six helicopters and their crews of twenty-seven pilots and back-up pilot-mechanics.

During September, Urella elevated his aide, James L. McCann, to the rank of lieutenant and placed him in command of the Executive Service Section which has responsibility for the protection of the governor, lieutenant governor, and their families. Urella's successor was to challenge this promotion in a dramatic series of events.

Successfully competing for the Indiana University law program were Sergeant Howard G. Berringer and Corporal John H. Armstrong. They were scheduled to join Clark at Indiana University in September. The appointment of these two men filled the three-man quota set by Urella for his legal adviser program.

In August, Public Information Officer James Cox acquired an assistant. Named to this post was Thomas C. Lyon, 25, a native of Potter County. Lyon attended Clarion State College and Lebanon Valley College, and came to the State Police by way of Station WLYH-TV, Lancaster-Lebanon.

All during Urella's tenure, he, like his predecessors, was approached continuously by legislators and other political figures for favors. Some requests were easily granted without bending State Police policies. Many politicos who sought cadet appointments to the Academy for friends back home, however, banged up against a stone wall. On this score, Urella was unyielding, as he strictly adhered to the Civil Service call-up listing. Whether he granted favors or diplomatically explained why he could not, Urella maintained a wholesome relationship with the politicians on capitol hill. He was successful in securing desired legislation from the general assembly; State Police appropriations during his tenure were satisfactory enough to live with.

Passed by the general assembly during its 1972 session were two measures worth mention: Act 24, February 17, amending P.L. 450 (1927) relative to fire prevention laws and State Police duties, and Act 349, December 28, increasing the complement to 3,940 officers and men. With some 230 men assigned to the Turnpike troop, the total number of enlisted men reached a record high of 4,177. From circumstances that will be described later, it is not likely that this 4,177 figure will ever be exceeded. That is not an optimistic appraisal, but a realistic one, nonetheless. Urella, during his tenure, was successful in raising the State Police complement by 390 men without fuss nor muss.

In September, a more pleasant set of circumstances welcomed FOP and state negotiations. Encouraged by Urella to accept a reasonable contract offer from the state, negotiations this time ended in an agreement between both parties without resorting to an arbitration panel. Signing for the Commonwealth on September 27, in a unique ceremony, were Governor Shapp, Deputy Attorney General Miles J. Gibbons and Charles R. Bistline. For the FOP, signatures were affixed by attorney Howard Richard, James L. Cannon, Edward J. Goddard, John R. Schneider, Steven J. Condes, James M. Morgan and Leo E. Pierce. The agreement valued at $3,637,000 was to go into effect July 1, 1973.

Promotional examinations were once again prepared under contract with Yarger Associates. Examinations were scheduled for the month of October. Urella's successor made quite an ado over the 1972 examinations.

In October, Urella made his last promotion to the rank of major. Jaynes, 60, retired October 3, and was replaced at Area VI, Butler, by Captain William N. Grooms, formerly troop commander at Harrisburg.

The reduced band of State Police officers assigned to investigate plane crashes and complaints of illegal aircraft operations was reassigned to regular field duties. The program, originally begun right after World War II, was turned over lock, stock and barrel to the Department of Transportation in which the Aeronautics Commission was housed.

For the third consecutive year, a trooper was to give his life upholding the honor of the Pennsylvania State Police. On October 16, Trooper Robert D. Lapp, enjoying a day off, volunteered to accompany a detail of troopers and Lancaster city policemen who were preparing to arrest a fugitive murderer who had escaped from New Jersey authorities. Lapp was killed instantly as he and his companions rushed the door of the fugitive's apartment hide-away. Trooper Joseph J. Wescott was wounded in the exchange of gunfire which ended with the shooting death of the fugitive.

Lapp, 30, a native of Reading, had been a trooper for eight years. He was buried with full honors as some 1,000 police officers, representing 100 departments from nine states, paid their respects. Urella appointed a State Police honor guard of 100 troopers. Lapp was survived by his widow, Margaret Ann, and three children. To aid them financially, a Robert D. Lapp Fund was established by several Lancaster organizations.

The results of Urella's all-out minority recruiting drive were a disappointment to him. Although blacks had applied in larger numbers, they did not fare well with the Civil Service written entrance examination which had been revised considerably by commission technicians specifically to aid minority applicants. Earlier, Urella had promised that, if sufficient qualified blacks passed applicant screening, he would set a goal of fifty for the next cadet class scheduled for mid-January, 1973. Urella met often with Lt. Governor Kline and members of the Task Force on Equal Rights to keep them informed of discouraging developments.

As class time approached, Urella lowered the passing grade for blacks, and yet there were not enough blacks to come close to the goal of 50. Hesitant to risk going too far with dual standards and facing condemnation from the FOP, Urella finally called a class of 150, which was to include 10 white females, 1 black female and 14 black males. This cadet group of 25 minority members was the largest ever assembled at the Academy. Dissatisfied black minority representatives on the state payroll threatened to go to court in an effort to halt the class. The class was convened by State Police, nonetheless, and legal action fell through. Sufficient heat, however, was generated to carry over into the following years when court action was successfully undertaken.

Overriding the events of 1972, was a serious situation taking place in Philadelphia where police corruption charges were being hurled. Governor Shapp, either eager for reelection and desirous of knocking popular Mayor Rizzo out of the box as a competitor, or simply interested in a "clean" police department, decided to launch a state investigation of these charges. He gave this chore to his attorney general. Creamer demanded a staff of troopers to do the job—this aggravated Urella no end. Meanwhile, Republican District Attorney Arlen Specter, at Philadelphia, insisted that his office would conduct an investigation of its own and he, too, demanded a staff of troopers.

Troopers were pitched at Philadelphia from two camps— Creamer's and Specter's. The governor was hungry for reelection, Creamer and Specter were both zealously pursuing young, ambitious careers, and the object of disaffection was Rizzo—Urella's avowed friend.

Throughout the two years of Shapp's tenure, the feuding between Creamer and Urella continued unabated. Shapp knew of this explosive siutation and yet apparently did nothing to arrest it. (It is believed that he could have done so very effectively as the state's chief executive.) The situation in Philadelphia, bristling with intrigue and more demands for troopers, was destined to bring Creamer and Urella to the brink of disaster such as is seldom witnessed between two cabinet officers. Former Attorney General William Sennett, a member of the Crime Commission, commenting later on this situation, stated that Urella and Creamer were "on an absolute collision course" from the moment they were appointed to Governor Shapp's cabinet. (These and other comments by Sennett were made at an Erie Kiwanis Club meeting and were carried in an *Erie Times* story on February 10, 1973.) Most observers agreed that Shapp could have stopped both men in their tracks.

On November 28, 1972, Urella's star fell from the firmament when alleged wiretap evidence was claimed by Creamer's hand-picked troopers at the George Washington Motor Lodge, near King of Prussia, Montgomery County. Creamer lost no time pointing a finger at Urella, and it is not at all certain that he talked to Shapp before notifying the press of his charges.

In any case, three men identified as Lieutenant Stephen Luchansky, Corporal Curtis Guyette and Corporal Metro Kardash, and supposedly working at Urella's direction, were seen fleeing from the motel and subsequently accused of wiretapping Creamer's trooper force. Urella supended all three men without pay pending an investigation of the charge placed against them. Creamer, with Shapp's consent, proceeded with an investigation of the George Washington Motor Lodge incident.

The press was having a field day with this story, and Shapp faced a scandal that could perhaps give his campaign for reelection a serious setback. Some sources publicly called for Urella's dismissal. There was evidence, too, that Creamer would not come through this incident unscathed, as Shapp searched for an escape from his dilemma.

Meanwhile, Creamer completed his investigation, and his findings were turned over to the Montgomery County district attorney for prosecution. Facing multiple charges in the motor lodge incident were Urella, Luchansky, Guyette and Kardash, and John R. Law, Jr., a civilian salesman. McCann, and another trooper, Gerald DeWalt were charged with conspiracy.

Urella reported to his office at 11 o'clock Friday morning, December 29, for what turned out to be his last day at headquarters as State Police commissioner. He was accompanied by his attorney,

Richard G. Phillips, and his son, Rocco, Jr. An appointment had been scheduled with Shapp for 11:30, but a call from the governor's office postponed the meeting until 5. The waiting party passed the time with brief conferences with staff members, during which time some pretense was made to move official matters. It was not a productive effort, however, since Urella was ostensibly preoccupied with a far more important question.

At 6 o'clock, Urella was instructed to meet the governor at the West Shore "mansion" for dinner. Urella then remarked that he was attending his last supper. Phillips accompanied Urella. Both men returned to headquarters about three hours later with a promise from Shapp that a decision on Urella's status would be forthcoming by 9:30. Rumors were circulating that Creamer was resigning and that Urella would be asked to resign. Up to this time, Urella had gone on record publicly stating that he would not under any circumstances resign his post.

The press corps was banging on the doors for news both at headquarters and the capitol. While phone calls had been received by Urella from reporters all day long, the number of calls increased after 9 o'clock. There was constant phone contact between young Urella and Richard Shapp, the governor's son. Richard Shapp was broken up as he reported that his father was about to make the biggest mistake of his life by firing Urella, and he was doing what he could to have Urella kept on—the governor's son was manifesting his sincere friendship for the Urella family. It was apparent on many occasions that a friendly relationship between the Shapp and Urella families did exist. In the course of the evening, young Shapp's running commentaries added up to the fact that Urella would be dismissed and it was just a matter of how the governor was going to phrase his dismissal message. Shapp had promised at dinner that he would read his press release to Urella before handing it out. Richard Shapp stated that his father was "obsessed" with the thought of running for reelection and was giving his decision tremendous attention.

About 11 o'clock, Phillips, impatient from a long wait, called the governor. He was put off with the promise of a call back. Finally, the promised call came through, and then a marathon conversation was underway between Shapp and Phillips. It was apparent that Shapp was intent on firing Urella, but Phillips pleaded Urella's case. Phillips kept talking and, if nothing else was accomplished, it was clear that he had the governor confused. The prolonged conversation ended with an agreement that no release would be made that night, and Phillips and Shapp would be on the phone again early in the morning. Phillips was heading for Chicago in the morning and Shapp was leaving for New Orleans to attend the Sugar Bowl game between Penn State and Oklahoma.

At one o'clock Saturday morning, Jim Cox summoned the press for a conference with Urella. The conference, lasting only fifteen minutes, ended with Urella's statement, "I assured the governor, and let me assure you, that at no time during my tenure as State Police commissioner have I been involved in, or had knowledge of, wiretapping by the State Police."

Everyone associated with these closing moments of Urella's career cleared State Police headquarters at 2:00 A.M. It was a disheartened group to say the least. Conti, reflecting momentarily on the past sixteen emotion-packed hours and a sad farewell, was the last to leave the sixth floor executive suite.

The expected phone call between Phillips and Shapp did not materialize. Instead, Shapp announced over the weekend that he had received Creamer's resignation and dismissed Urella effective January 2, 1973. The *Philadelphia Inquirer,* on December 31, carried this story, "Creamer's resignation as a result of the feud was somewhat a surprise to his staff. But Shapp is known to have been dissatisfied with the attorney general for several months for what he considered Creamer's failure to consider the political implications of his actions." What irony, indeed!

In the wake of Creamer's forced departure, three members of the Crime Commission resigned in protest. Resigning were former Attorney General William C. Sennett, an Erie attorney, Philadelphia Judge Charles Wright, and Harold Rosenn, a Wilkes-Barre attorney.

In the November general election, Republicans gained sufficient seats to again take over the House as the majority party by a margin of 107–94. Although the wiretap charges had been placed in the hands of Montgomery County authorities, Speaker-designate Kenneth B. Lee (R-Sullivan) announced that he would push for a House investigation when the general assembly reconvened in January. If political hay was to be made, the Republicans intended to make it.

In two fast moving years, Urella did much to enhance the State Police image. His principal achievements, excellent and numerous, have been cited one by one. It is doubtful that anyone, setting aside the yet unproven wiretap charges, can reasonably deny him the right of being labelled an outstanding commissioner. The wiretap charges stemming from what one newspaper described as "internecine warfare in Shapp Administration," might very well be tagged as two Shapp mistakes. First, if he ever did demand impeccable behavior of his two cabinet members at the time of appointment, he apparently did not monitor their subsequent actions. Second, he engineered, or allowed to be engineered, a situation in Philadelphia where the State Police was turned into a house divided against itself, and placed Urella and Creamer "on an absolute collision course," as one observer put it.

Soon after his dismissal Urella returned to his former Delaware County post as head of the Bureau of Criminal Investigation, where he was warmly welcomed back.

CHAPTER XXI

Colonel James D. Barger

1973–1977

Faced with a major scandal that led to the departure of two prominent cabinet officials during the final weekend of 1972, Governor Shapp still had to deal with the weighty problem of naming replacements.

Rumors that Lt. Colonel Charles S. Graci was seeking political support for his candidacy were circulating. Former Sergeant Arthur E. Berardi and former Sergeant Julius Trombetta, supported by Sam H. Begler, the governor's personnel secretary, were rumored to be under serious consideration. It was later learned that Berardi could not be immediately reached during that historical weekend. In an interview some months later, Trombetta stated that he was handed the appointment. Trombetta, director of the Bureau of Traffic Safety, convinced that he had nothing to gain by moving from tranquil surroundings to a "hot-seat," declined the appointment. He was already drawing a salary just short of the State Police commissioner's.

Kline, who was on top of developments, made his move by recommending Major James D. Barger, a personal friend. Barger's police services in western Pennsylvania were in large measure spent in Beaver County, Kline's home county. A *Philadelphia Inquirer* article stated that Kline had known Barger for twenty years "since the time I was a news broadcaster in Beaver Falls and he was a State Police corporal." Kline added, "He was—and is—a tough, stern and fair guy who knows his job extremely well. And he is completely honest."

Keeping after-midnight hours, Shapp interviewed Barger and announced his appointment as Urella's successor effective January 2,
1973.

After weighing names suggested to him for the attorney general
slot, Shapp named Israel Packel, who was then holding down a
$37,500-a-year Superior Court seat. Before his appointment to the Su-
perior Court a year earlier, Packel, 65, a Philadelphia attorney, served
Shapp as personal counsel. The attorney general-designate was
scheduled to take his oath of office with Barger at a joint ceremony.

The swearing-in ceremony for Barger was set for ten o'clock Tuesday morning, January 2, just moments before the gavels would pound
the Senate and House to order for their 1973 sessions. Shapp, obviously anxious to get on with a State Police commissioner by avoiding
possible delayed Senate confirmation, opted to take the interim appointment route. Some senators were openly critical of Shapp's last-
minute action to sidetrack the Senate confirmation process. (The subject of interim appointments eventually blossomed into a front page
controversy between Shapp and the Senate.)

Nonetheless, the strapping, grey-haired major was sworn in by
Shapp after some delay, but well ahead of the noonday deadline.

Losing no time, Shapp huddled with his new State Police commissioner and attorney general to lay plans for pursuing the wiretap
case investigation and any prosecutions.

Barger, 52, a native of Boston, Allegheny County, Pennsylvania,
was born May 16, 1920. He was the third of six sons born to Walter L.
and Mary E. Barger.

He attended Fallowfield Township grade schools, and graduated
from Charleroi High School in June, 1938. Upon graduation, he took
on employment with the Peoples Natural Gas Company, where he
remained until his enlistment in the State Police.

He signed up with the State Police, then known as the Pennsylvania Motor Police, on October 1, 1941, less than five months after his
twenty-first birthday. Barger completed police training at Hershey
after six months; he was assigned to Troop D, Butler. The Butler troop
jurisdiction takes in Armstrong, Beaver, Butler, Lawrence and Mercer
counties.

His police career was interrupted by World War II military service
in February, 1944. He served with the U. S. Army Air Corps. During
his assignment with the 100th Bombardment Group, Eighth Air Force,
based in England, Barger flew twenty-seven combat missions as a B-17
bomber tail-gunner. He was honorably discharged in November, 1945,
and returned to Butler.

Colonel James D. Barger (Courtesy of Pennsylvania State Police)

Barger received his first promotion to the rank of corporal in 1952. Two years later, he was promoted to sergeant. Barger's reputation as an investigator was firmly established. When Commissioner Mc-Cartney reactivated the detective division in 1960, Barger was promoted to detective sergeant at Butler. In 1965, he was commissioned a lieutenant and transferred to Troop A, Greensburg, where he headed criminal investigation operations. He was placed in charge of the large Pittsburgh Substation in 1967, just before his transfer back to Butler in early 1968 as staff services officer for Troop D. One year later, Commissioner McKetta promoted him to captain, and gave him command of that troop. In mid-1972, Commissioner Urella advanced him to a top field post as commander of Area V with headquarters at

Greensburg (Area V includes Troop A, Greensburg, and Troop B, Washington).

During the 1960s, Barger enrolled in a number of special training programs. Most noteworthy was his twelve-week attendance at the FBI National Academy from which he graduated in June, 1965. Other programs took him to Western Reserve University, Michigan State University, and Indiana University of Pennsylvania.

Barger's memberships include the FBI National Academy Associates; International Association of Chiefs of Police; Pennsylvania Chiefs of Police Association; Veterans of Foreign Wars; American Legion; and the Loyal Order of Moose. He is a charter member of the State Police FOP lodge at Butler.

Barger is married to the former Dorothy Matheny of Butler; they have two sons, William and Charles. The Barger family resides in Butler.

A few hours before being sworn in as interim commissioner, Barger ordered the transfers of Lieutenant James L. McCann to Troop S, Milesburg; Lieutenant Angelo J. Carcaci from Troop K, Philadelphia, to Troop C, Punxsutawney; Lieutenant Herman J. Faiola to Troop H, Harrisburg; Lieutenant Richard M. Weimer from Troop J, Lancaster, to Troop F, Montoursville; and Corporal Robert M. Flanagan from the Executive Service Section to Troop B, Washington. All were in some way or another associated with Urella during his two-year tenure. Although Barger disclaimed a "purge," the press continued to call his actions just that—as the new commissioner ordered more changes at headquarters.

As early as January 2, there was evidence of Barger's team taking form at headquarters. The *Philadelphia Inquirer* stated: "They say he is expected to install his own men in top positions. One who is expected to stay on is Lt. Col. Joseph Dussia—currently deputy commissioner—who has been a friend of Barger's for more than thirty years."

Within a week, Barger withdrew seventeen troopers from duty with the Republican Philadelphia district attorney, Arlen Specter, who was probing alleged police corruption in Philadelphia. Rep. George W. Gekas (R-Dauphin) forcefully criticized Barger's actions. At a press conference, Barger asked, "Who's Gekas?" This did not set well with Gekas who admitted that he didn't know Barger either.

Gekas soon again complained of Barger's handling of several transfers from the Executive Service Section, and accused Kline of influencing Barger's judgment with regard to changes in the original transfer order. According to Gekas, Kline intervened after one of the troopers, peeved at his transfer, threatened to make "unspecified disclosures," if the order was not changed. Kline denied charges brought by Gekas, claiming that a mistake had simply been made in the transfer order. Kline speculated that "someone" in the State Police hierarchy, whom he did not identify, was leaking information to the legislator.

During his first months in office, Barger drew flak from Henry Young, city editor of *The Patriot* (Harrisburg), who could not endorse Barger's purge activities and highhandedness. Barger overlooked no opportunities to publicly denounce Gekas and Young for taking him on.

Meanwhile, Barger and Packel decided to keep the wiretap investigation in the hands of the Crime Commission with manpower supplied by State Police. Some fifty troopers were assigned to this work force. The state Justice Department was committed to assisting the Montgomery County officials with the prosecution of Urella and others charged with criminal wrongdoing at the George Washington Motor Lodge.

For a change of pace, the spotlight turned to the Academy at Hershey, where on January 10 a seventy-two-man cadet class completed training. Addressing the cadet graduates at commencement exercises was Major General Harry Meir, state adjutant general, who had been invited as speaker by Urella before his dismissal.

From the very first day of Barger's appointment, tension at headquarters was pervasive and intense. The new commissioner, previously identified as a close and trusted friend of Dussia, had yet to inform the deputy that he would keep him in that post. Especially disturbing to Dussia was Barger's unexpected cool treatment that surely pointed to unfavorable developments.

Soon enough the ax fell. Dussia, with support from influential legislators, was not dismissed but reassigned on January 15 as Chief of Field Operations, replacing Graci. Barger appointed Graci head of the Bureau of Staff Inspections—a post left vacant by the retirement of Major Stanley Cimokowski at 60.

Foreshadowing Dussia's ouster were the interviews conducted by Shapp at the capitol. Seen entering the governor's office were Majors Charles J. Buchinsky, John Yaglenski, and Roy O. Wellendorf, Captain George Evan, and Lieutenant John Angell. Shapp's announcement of Dussia's reassignment was accompanied by the news of Wellendorf's appointment as Barger's deputy.

To this day, it is difficult to rationalize Barger's about-face with respect to his avowed friend, Dussia. Dussia was convinced at the time that Kline somehow played a hand in his ouster. Reportedly, Kline had tried to persuade Urella to replace Dussia; however, Urella was not beholden to Kline for anything, and kept Dussia on. The Kline-Barger relationship was "something else."

Wellendorf, 58, a native of South Williamsport, Lycoming County, was born September 12, 1914. He was one of six children born to Nicholas Wellendorf, a baker, and his wife, Rosa Hagmann Wellendorf. Both parents were native Pennsylvanians.

Wellendorf attended the South Williamsport public schools and graduated from South Williamsport High School in 1932. In high school, he engaged in football, basketball and track activities. During the six years before his enlistment with the State Police, he held positions in private industry, the last being with the former Williamsport Wire Rope Company.

He joined the State Police on October 1, 1938. Upon graduation

Lt. Colonel Roy O. Wellendorf (Courtesy of Pennsylvania State Police)

from the Academy, Wellendorf was sent to Troop A-2, Harrisburg, for duty. From September, 1942, to February, 1946, he served in the Army Counter Intelligence Corps, returning to the State Police after his discharge.

In 1947, he was assigned to the Detective Division at headquarters. A promotion to detective sergeant followed in 1954. When Commissioner Henry abolished the Detective Division, Wellendorf lost his detective rating, just as others in that division did. He was reappointed detective sergeant in 1960, when Commissioner McCartney reactivated the Detective Division. He was promoted to lieutenant in 1965, and transferred to Troop J, Lancaster, where he headed criminal investigation operations. Three years later, he was promoted to captain and given command of the Philadelphia troop. In 1969, he returned to headquarters as executive officer of the Bureau of Criminal Investigation. He continued in this post until March, 1972, when Commissioner Urella promoted him to major, and designated him commander of Area III with headquarters at Highspire.

Wellendorf is married to the former Marie Rechel of Williamsport. They are parents of a son, James, and a daughter, K. Ann. The deputy and his wife reside at Harrisburg.

Wellendorf's appointment as deputy automatically carried the rank of lieutenant colonel. His starting salary was set at $25,664.

Although not one of his major problems by any means, Barger did experience some difficulty appointing a secretary. None of the top secretaries in the executive offices would accept his offer. Apparently the turmoil surrounding the commissioner's office was sufficient to raise doubts about the value of such an appointment despite the jump in salary. Barger finally persuaded Mrs. Mary Louise Wise, his former secretary at Butler troop headquarters, to join him at Harrisburg to end that episode.

Earlier in January, Barger had declined an invitation to attend the FOP conference at Reading. Former commissioners customarily spent some time at these conferences, which were more familiarly known as "Round Robins." Reconsidering his position with the FOP, he called a meeting of the lodge presidents at the Academy ten days later, and met with them. Although he indicated a willingness to work with them, he stated that FOP affairs would be conducted through regular official channels, and forbid FOP members the freedom of calling top management. This practice had been permitted by Urella.

Barger, in another surprise move, ordered twenty-five enlisted men to the Academy on Friday, January 26, for special assignment, where they were "forced" to take a modified promotional exam that had been originally administered by the Civil Service Commission last October. The re-exam was handled by a special detail selected by Barger. Even Academy Superintendent Major Bernard G. Stanalonis was not privy to these special arrangements. According to *The Patriot* release, James D. Cox, State Police public information officer, simply stated that an investigation was underway regarding alleged promotional exam "irregularities." Cox was quoted as saying, "That's all I know. I don't know who's handling it or how it's being handled."

Polygraph operators, in early February, were in evidence at headquarters where for two days some of the men participating in the re-exam underwent lie detector testing. It was later learned that Barger had directed Major Charles J. Buchinsky to head this inquiry.

Barger, in the February issue of *The Communicator,* said:

> The results of the last promotion examinations have been voided. Arrangements have been made for another examination to be given the last week in March. Material for this new examination has been given to an out-of-state firm which will make up the test. No member of the State Police, including the Commissioner, or any other state agency will review or have access to the questions and answers prior to the examination.

Barger, on February 5, ordered the court-martial of Lieutenant Stephen J. Luchansky, and Corporals Metro Kardash and Curtis W. Guyette "for major violations of the Code of Conduct as set forth in Departmental Regulations." Allegedly, the three men tapped the phones of other troopers assigned to the Crime Commission. The trio had already been suspended without pay by Urella, pending disposition of charges against them. The court-martial was scheduled for February 26 at the Academy.

On Wednesday, February 7, at 9 o'clock, Barger summoned lieutenant colonels, majors, and captains at headquarters to the commissioner's sixth floor conference room. In the presence of these subordinate officers, Barger tersely announced the formation of three regional commands—western, central, and eastern—and the immediate transfers of Lt. Colonels Joseph Dussia, Philip M. Conti, and William B. Cooper to these new commands. Dussia was moved to Punxsutawney, Conti to Montoursville, and Cooper to Bethlehem. Because of this hasty secret action, no guidelines were at hand; the three officers were to report to their new posts, there to await more definite instructions. The three high-ranking officers were denied the courtesy of private notice. Barger preferred a larger audience to witness their discomfiture, if any.

A year before, the Governor's Management Task Force recommended the abolishment of the area commands as unnecessary. Tongue in cheek, Urella spared these posts. Despite the doubtful value of the area commands, Barger had successfully persuaded Shapp, Kline, and the Executive Board to approve yet another link in the chain of command. Most headquarters observers, however, accepted the fact that the expediency of getting the Urella holdovers out of headquarters and sight was more at issue than the defects of the regional command structure. In a companion move, Lt. Colonel Edward M. McGroarty was shifted to quarters at the Academy. The new table of organization also realigned some of the area boundaries. The Punxsutawney troop was switched to Area VI, Hollidaysburg to Area IV, and Lancaster to Area III. Major Fagnani, the only area commander required to relocate headquarters, was moved from Punxsutawney to Hollidaysburg.

Sharing headlines with news from State Police headquarters, was the action taken by the House of Representatives. On February 6, the House approved a resolution authorizing a five-man committee to study "the efficiency and effectiveness of law enforcement within the Commonwealth." Appointed to the committee were Representatives Eugene R. Geesey (R. Cumberland), H. Joseph Hepford (R-Dauphin), David M. Turner (R-Bradford), Russell J. LaMarca (D-Berks), and Joseph Rhodes, Jr. (D-Allegheny). Hepford was elected chairman, and the panel became popularly identified as the Hepford Committee. With the State Police undoubtedly a major target for the panel's inquiry, there was reason for the entire Shapp administration to be concerned about events to come.

Refusing to resign, Graci was suspended by Barger, without pay, on March 8. He was accused of promotional exam cheating; allegedly, he passed exam answers to his brother Sergeant Vincent Graci. Following one postponement, Graci's court-martial was eventually set for June 11 at the Academy.

Sergeant Arthur E. Berardi, State Police liaison officer with the legislature, who refused to undergo polygraph testing in February, was given a ten-day disciplinary suspension without pay. Berardi, accompanied by his attorney, Edward Friedman, a former attorney general, appealed the disciplinary action to Barger. Barger, on March 16, overruled the subordinate officers who recommended the suspension— Berardi was not implicated in the cheating charges.

Four days later, March 20, Wellendorf informed Berardi that he was immediately relieved of his legislative duties and transferred to Troop E, Erie, effective the next day. Berardi soon thereafter retired, and was later appointed police commissioner for the city of Pottsville, Schuylkill County. Replacing Berardi as legislative lobbyist was Lieutenant Harold Selecky.

With all the transferring of men and the oiling of court-martial machinery, the importance of the Tenure Act of 1963, so bitterly fought for by the FOP, was realized more than ever before. Without the umbrella of protection afforded by the Tenure Act, one might speculate on the wholesale firings that could have been ordered throughout these months of turmoil. Already the State Police had experienced a "shake up" like nothing ever seen before, and more was yet to come. Most of the men involved in the Barger-ordered transactions could well be thankful for the FOP.

On weekends, Barger spent a good bit of his time visiting and inspecting troop headquarters and substations. Dissatisfied with many conditions he saw, Barger lost no time in scolding troop and substation commanders for their faults. There was, indeed, some carelessness in the field, and Barger's chastisements were well-founded. Field supervisors resented Barger's criticisms—not because of the shortcomings he saw and wanted remedied—but because of the rudeness of his reprimands.

Earlier it was mentioned that the State Police, if allowed to do so, intended to consolidate certain substations in counties where one substation could provide adequate services and still save precious funds. Barger proceeded to consolidate in Westmoreland, Chester, and Schuykill counties, and ran head on into another squabble with House members who felt that their bailiwicks were being trampled on. Their interest in votes far overshadowed the need for reducing the cost of government without sacrificing services to the public.

At Chester County, a House resolution called for an open hearing at the Avon Grove High School on March 30. The heated arguments resulted in the offering of a compromise wherein the State Police would forego consolidation if the legislature would appropriate $180,000 to cover the cost of new civilian positions to handle non-police chores at those substations earmarked for consolidation and thereby release troopers from those chores. Legislators promised to consider Barger's compromise offer. House Bill 554, specifically calling for legislative approval before the State Police could close down any field facilities, was never enacted.

On March 8, Barger moved Major William N. Grooms from Area VI to Area VII, replacing Wellendorf at Highspire. Captain George Evan was promoted to major and took over Barger's vacancy at Area V, Greensburg. The command post at Area VI, Butler, was left vacant until April 19, when it was filled by the promotion and transfer of Major Roy L. Titler from the Bureau of Criminal Investigation. Replacing Titler at headquarters was newly-promoted Captain Robert G. Shuck.

As weeks rolled on, Gekas did not let up on his critical observations of State Police management under Barger. Kline frequently jumped into the fracas to vigorously defend Barger. Taking issue with Kline's pot shots, Gekas commented to Carmen Brutto of *The Patriot:* "The politics and other maneuvering within the administration of the State Police are what I have been pointing out to the people of this Commonwealth. It is their State Police, not Kline's."

At a testimonial dinner for Barger held at Butler on March 23, the commissioner lashed out at Gekas and Young. He obviously relished the opportunity to entertain his hometown audience with his needling remarks. Kline was the principal speaker on that occasion, and praised Barger's efforts as commissioner. Sponsoring this social affair was the Butler FOP lodge.

The court-martial of Luchansky, Kardash, and Guyette, begun on March 19, was brought to a close on March 30. A marathon of witnesses appeared at what was the first court-martial in the department's history to be open to the public. After five hours of deliberation, the trial board composed of Majors Grooms and Evan, and Captain John Kistler, handed its verdict to Barger. The prosecutor had been Major Rice. On April 24, the commissioner notified the defendants that they had been found guilty, and dismissed them from the force. All three men, by way of their attorneys, announced that they would appeal the commissioner's actions to the commonwealth court. Luchansky was represented by attorney Wallace C. Worth of Allentown; Guyette by attorney Andrew M. Pipa of Shamokin; and Kardash by attorney Paul Vangrossi of Norristown.

While administrative problems consumed the time of top brass at Harrisburg, the field forces took time to pay tribute to Trooper Bruce C. Rankin of Troop A, Greensburg, who was killed in a motor vehicle accident on April 25, when a truck jumped a medial barrier and struck Rankin's patrol car. Rankin, 26, joined the State Police in 1971. Several hundred state and local police officers attended a military funeral in Brownsville on April 28. Representing the commissioner were Lt. Colonel Joseph Dussia and Major George Evan.

It is interesting to note that the "Commissioner's Corner," a feature article regularly appearing in *The Communicator* since its first publication in September, 1963, was disregarded by Barger after the April, 1973, issue. Apparently, Barger had no interest in continuing that tradition.

On May 4, Lieutenant James L. McCann was reduced in rank to trooper. The demotion, according to an official statement, was based on violations of departmental procedures when McCann was promoted to acting sergeant and lieutenant in 1971 and 1972. McCann had been suspended earlier (March 8 to April 19) by Barger for allegedly interfering with a Crime Commission witness in the wiretap scandal. Continuing to serve as a trooper, McCann appealed Barger's arbitrary demotion order to the commonwealth court.

In the McCann appeal, the commonwealth court on December 5, 1973, held that Barger's arbitrary demotion of the lieutenant was improper and ordered McCann reinstated. Since a demotion, according to the court's decision, can only follow a court-martial, Barger ordered McCann to face court-martial on March 4, 1974.

During the month of May, 1973, the State Police undertook the monumental task of introducing the new state Penal Code to troopers and municipal police officers. The new code, replacing the Penal Code of 1939, was the first general updating of Pennsylvania's criminal laws since 1939. It was scheduled to go into effect on June 6. The designated State Police instructors were deserving of praise for having completed their work so well and on time.

Graci, who had been suspended since March 8, faced court-martial on June 11 on charges of improperly noting answers to test questions, as a member of the State Police promotional board, and passing them to his brother Sergeant Vincent Graci. Major Leroy H. Lilly, and Captains Russell A. Anderson and Robert A. Hauth composed the court-martial board. Serving as trial judge advocate was Lt. Colonel William B. Cooper. Graci, the highest ranking officer in State Police history ever to go this route, was represented by attorney Richard C. Snelbaker, a Mechanicsburg lawyer and former Cumberland County district attorney. The lengthy court-martial proceedings, open to the public, were ended on June 23. On July 17, Barger announced that the trial board had found Graci guilty as charged, and dismissed him from the force. Graci appealed this action to the commonwealth court.

Barger, on June 22, summoned regional, area and troop commanders to the Academy for a conference; headquarters bureau directors also attended. After disposing of what was considered routine business, the commissioner condemned his corps of commanders for poor performances by his standards. He stated that he expected his officers to measure up to their jobs because they were well paid, and discouraged them from looking for any bouquets from him since it was not his nature to give them. Barger said he didn't praise people then—didn't plan to do so in the future.

After the conference, a comparison of feelings left no doubt that a resentful band of commanders went back home. Most felt that Barger underestimated the value of a pat on the back, and failed to recognize that there are other motivating factors more important perhaps than a fat paycheck. This conference incident is recalled because it pointedly disclosed Barger's philosophy of management.

On that same day at Norristown, District Justice George Ziegler dismissed all criminal charges against Urella and others who had been accused by the Commonwealth of wiretapping. Ziegler concluded there was insufficient evidence to refer the case to a grand jury. Two months earlier, Montgomery County District Attorney Milton O. Moss refused to prosecute on the grounds of insufficient evidence. Attorney General Packel petitioned the Montgomery County court to overrule Ziegler's decision. President Judge David Goshens, on September 4, turned down the attorney general's bid to bring the accused men to trial.

A week later, Packel said the state would drop any further attempts to prosecute Urella and six others for alleged wiretapping. According to an Associated Press release, Packel admitted the probability of winning a conviction "is so slight that we should devote our energies to other priorities." And thus the curtain fell on a most unfortunate drama that opened with a few tangling wires at the George Washington Motor Lodge in November, 1972. Yet to be disposed of, however, was the court-martial action taken against Luchansky, Guyette and Kardash. Their appeals were still pending before the commonwealth court.

As State Police authorities were trying to get their house in order, the Hepford Committee was holding public hearings, and had been holding them since March 16. Before the committee completed its work in November, 1974, it conducted twenty-three public hearings, and questioned ninety-eight witnesses. Though committee investigators were principally occupied with State Police affairs, they did look into the activities of other criminal justice agencies. Of particular interest to the State Police were hearings on wiretapping, the solicitation of funds, and the committee's views on revamping the State Police.

With regard to the wiretap episode at the George Washington Motor Lodge, the Hepford Committee reached this conclusion: "It will be recalled that the Committee in its Progress Report severely criticized and assessed much of the blame for the King of Prussia fiasco upon the ill-advised practice of utilizing Pennsylvania State Police as investigators for the Pennsylvania Crime Commission. The resulting position in which the employees found themselves of being compelled to report to two masters, undoubtedly, was a major contributing factor in the debacle."

The Hepford Committee ran into a stonewall with the State Police, however, when it made its recommendations for revamping the sixty-eight-year-old organization. The committee thought it best to reduce the State Police to a highway patrol force and transfer all criminal investigations to a separate state agency.

The committee also condemned the court-martial system: "Impractical and archaic procedural relics of the era of the horse must be eliminated or drastically revised and updated to conform with the jet age concepts of civil rights and administrative and judicial disciplinary procedures."

The committee's work led to the introduction of legislation revamping the State Police along the lines of its recommendations, remodelling the court-martial procedures, and requiring the head of the State Police to be a civilian, prohibiting from holding that office anyone who served on the force less than ten years prior to the appointment. Reflecting unanimous thinking among State Police ranks, Barger voiced opposition to the restructuring of the organization. He stated, too, that the department, realizing the need to do so, had already submitted suggested legislation for changing the court-martial procedures.

The Hepford Committee turned its attention to the solicitation of funds by State Police troopers for the benefit of a private pension fund. As a result of the publicity attending this subject, Barger, on July 5, issued an order prohibiting solicitations for any purpose without the consent of the commissioner. Although Barger's order did terminate the practice, the committee recommended that solicitations be prohibited by law.

Because the FOP State Lodge engaged in soliciting funds for its annual program book, Barger sought the resignations of three troopers holding office with the State Lodge. They were Trooper Paul Cotter, state FOP president; Corporal Paul Bezilla, trustee; and Corporal Steven Condes, guard. Barger's alternative to their resigning was a suggestion that the three request a leave of absence for the duration of their terms as state officeholders.

This head-on dispute with the FOP brought a violent reaction. The FOP lodges recommended to the legislature that Barger's confirmation be held up, and went so far as to demand his ouster as a member of the FOP. A hearing on his ouster was eventually held, but nothing was to come of it. The three men quietly finished their terms of office without further difficulties.

Noteworthy, too, was the effect of the solicitation controversy upon the stability of the State Police Civic Association—the private pension plan—which was still dependent upon income from annual solicitations. This subject will be taken up later on.

The Personnel Division, in June, was raised to bureau status. Accompanying this action was a promotion to major for Captain Jay C. Hileman. On June 22, Henry Young, *The Patriot* city editor, wrote: "The action is believed to be in the nature of a 'reward' for Hileman . . . who allied himself with Col. James D. Barger's purge of the force immediately after the commissioner was sworn into office last Jan. 2. The pending promotion has been handled as 'top secret' within the department on Barger's orders . . . and was not to be announced until the conclusion of the current court-martial proceeding against Lt. Col. Charles S. Graci." Hileman was a key witness in the Graci case.

When calling headquarters for confirmation on the promotion, Young encountered this situation: "James Cox, department public information officer, responded with laughter. He said he didn't think it was true because he had heard nothing about it to that point. However, a short time later, apparently after checking with Barger, Cox admitted *The Patriot's* information was accurate." Young also reported that Barger, enraged by the "leak," ordered an investigation to determine the source.

Hileman filed a libel action in Dauphin County court against Young and the newspaper. On December 20, 1973, Judge Warren G. Morgan, in his opinion, concluded: "Without more, statements that may have been annoying or even embarrassing to the plaintiff are not libelous." Morgan dismissed the suit.

Dissatisfied with the Dauphin County court decision, Hileman appealed to the state superior court. The superior court, on May 16, 1974, upheld the lower court ruling.

The latest NUTI graduates, Sergeant Thomas Hanus, and Troopers Donald C. Bradbury and Thomas Brennan were assigned to headquarters for duty. With their return, the department's list of NUTI graduates numbered thirty. Appointed to the September class at NUTI was Trooper Robert Einsel of the academy staff.

In June, Lycoming County District Attorney Allen Ertel conferred with Lt. Colonel Conti and Captain William Banzhaf, Montoursville troop commander, regarding alleged wiretapping at Williamsport's city hall. He asked for State Police assistance to investigate the matter. Both State Police officers agreed, provided there were no objections from headquarters. A call placed by them to Wellendorf ended with a rejection of Ertel's request; when notified of this decision, Ertel appealed to the governor. Shapp was instrumental in having troopers assigned to the case.

Charged with wiretapping and other offenses relating to this particular incident were Williamsport Mayor John Coder; Public Safety Director John Samony; Police Chief Maynard J. Patterson, and Bell Telephone repairman Charles E. Reeder, Jr. All were eventually indicted and found guilty in what was labelled by the *Philadelphia Inquirer* as Pennsylvania's "upstate Watergate."

Effective July 1, the State Police took over full responsibility from the Justice department for the management of the state's Uniform Crime Reporting System. The legislature had originally given this program to the Justice Department for implementation on January 1, 1971. Difficulties arose, however, when too many municipalities overlooked compliance, and the Justice Department found itself without adequate means for dealing with that problem. The State Police did have this capability with its statewide network of stations and men; headquarters staffers believed the program should have been housed with the State Police in the first place. The passage of Reorganization Plan No. 7 of 1973, P.L. 464, by the legislature on October 10 legally confirmed the transfer of the UCR program to the State Police. Since taking over the program, the State Police has done extremely well with gathering statistics and processing them meaningfully in keeping with the intent of the law.

A class numbering 149 cadets graduated from the Academy on July 11. Included in the class was the largest number of minority members ever to complete State Police training. There were 14 black males, 10 white females, and 1 black female. Verna M. Dorsey of Pittsburgh was the first black female in State Police history to join the trooper ranks. Other female cadet-graduates were: Winnifred J. Booze, Paulette J. Cowell, Dorothy B. Cramer, Antoinette M. D'Agostino, Stephanie K. Griffiths, Barbara A. Heddings, Darlene B. Kalb, Margaret J. Keller, Jacquelyn K. Mertz, and Marilyn D. Reber. Antoinette M. D'Agostino of Harrisburg was chosen class speaker—the first female trooper to be so honored.

In another State Police "first," Commissioner Barger presented a diploma to his son Charles, a cadet class member. Previously, Sergeant

Marshal Wilhelm served during the tenure of his father, Colonel C. M. Wilhelm; however, young Wilhelm graduated from the training school prior to his father's appointment as commissioner in 1943. Also receiving diplomas from their trooper fathers were Michael H. Honkus, son of Captain Michael Honkus, and Thomas D. Rupert, son of Corporal Harry F. Rupert.

One day after Barger fired Lt. Colonel Graci, he suspended Lt. Colonel Dussia for an indefinite period pending the outcome of his court-martial on charges of passing test answers to certain members of the force. Barger did not elaborate on the charges, nor did he set a date for the court-martial. Barger's announcement came on July 17. Dussia declared that during the few days preceeding the announcement he turned down three requests from headquarters for his resignation.

It was difficult to perceive Dussia's guilt, since he had not been a member of the promotion exam board, and had been informed by Conti that the test answers were scrambled out of sequence one month before the tests were held. The scrambling action was explained at Graci's court-martial as part of Conti's testimony.

A week later, Dussia's trial was set for August 6; the Academy was selected as the trial site. Appointed to the court-martial board were Major Sidney C. Deyo, and Captains Earl O. Bergstrom and Stanley B. Kramer. Major Robert A. Rice was named prosecutor. Dussia, represented by Harrisburg attorney Bruce Cooper, asked for a postponement of the court-martial. A drawn-out series of court actions was to stay any attempt by Barger to bring Dussia before a court-martial tribunal. A period of 2½ years was to lapse before the Dussia case was finally disposed of by the courts.

The day Barger suspended Dussia, Wellendorf phoned Conti at Montoursville to order him to Butler as temporary commander of Area VI—Major Titler's assignment to special duty and Dussia's suspension had left the northwestern area without a senior commander. Security preparations were already underway for the 1973 National Boy Scout Jamboree at Moraine State Park, Butler County, and importance was attached to having a high-ranking officer there to give evidence of Barger's interest in the affair.

Barger attended the FOP Round Robin in July. There, he reportedly remarked that he would do away with the regional commanders, if he could. According to FOP sources, Barger also speculated that there would be no lieutenant colonels left on the job by the end of the year—except the deputy commissioner. These rumored statements, to put it mildly, were disturbing to the lieutenant colonels still on active duty. It was known, too, that Barger on occasions publicly complained that his lieutenant colonels were drawing more pay than he was; it was apparently a point that bothered him.

Within a week after Dussia's suspension, a number of legislators, Republican and Democratic, attacked Barger's administration. Senator William B. Lentz (R-Dauphin) called for Barger's resignation. Rep. William F. Renwick (D-Elk) introduced House Bill 1301 limiting the commissioner's authority to suspend troopers under certain circumstances.

From August 2 to 9, a large task force of troopers provided traffic control and security at Moraine State Park, where 44,000 scouts from fifty states and twenty foreign countries attended the national jamboree. Some 20,000 tents, presenting colorful patterns, covered the 4½-square mile park area surrounding beautiful Lake Arthur. Credit for the commendable work accomplished by the task force must be given to Captain Calvin A. Richwine and Lieutenant Newton C. Robbins of the Butler troop. Robbins was nominated for the Pennsylvania State Policeman of the Year Award for his work at the jamboree (the award is annually sponsored by the Pennsylvania District of Exchange Clubs).

On September 8, former Commissioner Frank G. McCartney, 65, died at his home at Lehighton, Carbon County, after a lengthy illness. Members of the State Police and high-ranking state officials took time to pay their respects. An estimated crowd of 2,000, including Governor Shapp, Commissioner Barger, Secretary of Labor and Industry Paul Smith, Secretary of Community Affairs William Wilcox, and former Commissioner Frank McKetta attended the late commissioner's viewing.

Hundreds attended the funeral mass at St. Ann's Catholic Church at Lansford, where Rev. Woodrow W. Jones of Shamokin eulogized his friend of some forty years. He praised McCartney's deeds as a father, police commissioner and civic leader. Then turning to the casket, he bid his personal farewell: "As an old Marine, I pay the highest U.S. Naval Department tribute to you old buddy—Well done, Frank McCartney!" With full military honors, the former commissioner was buried on the slope of Mount Pisgah, in St. Joseph's Cemetery, near Bloomingdale.

Effective September 20, two new captains were added to the roster of top-level executives at Harrisburg and Hershey. They were Captain James J. Regan, Bureau of Criminal Investigation, and Captain Paul J. Chylak, director of Regional Training. In October, Conti was moved back to Montoursville. McGroarty was transferred from the Academy to Punxsutawney to replace Dussia as western region commander.

The new radio system contract, so long awaited, was finally signed by Shapp on October 10. The $33,275,339 ten-year contract was awarded to the Motorola firm. The contract called for Motorola to design, install and maintain the system on a lease basis with option to purchase. Fifteen months were allowed for fulfillment of the contract. Thus ended a laborious effort on the part of Communications Officer Captain Robert L. Bomboy and company that was begun during Commissioner McKetta's tenure.

To provide more rapid SCUBA diving services to state and municipal police, twenty-four troopers—four from each of the six area commands—were trained and qualified at the U. S. Navy School of Diving and Salvaging at Washington, D. C.

In a unique ceremony in State Police history, two troopers were wed on November 24. As odd as this might appear, the event was for real as Trooper Jacquelyn Mertz, 24, assigned to the Milesburg barracks, married Trooper John Evock, 26, stationed at Harrisburg. Trooper Mertz, before joining State Police ranks, was director of women's athletics at Widener College. Although separated by ninety miles, the two continued to serve as fellow troopers, and husband and wife—a combination not without problems.

In November, the State Police was hit with a class action suit instituted by William Bolden III in U. S. District Court at Philadelphia. Bolden, a former Philadelphia policeman, was appointed to the State Police Academy January 27, 1972, and assigned to the Doylestown station upon graduation. Bolden, a black trooper, was discharged by Barger in July, 1973, for violation of State Police Field Regulations having to do with personal indebtedness. Bolden charged, among other things, that he was a "permanent"member of the force on July 27, the date of his discharge, and should have been allowed a court-martial rather than being summarily discharged as a probationary trooper. Barger held that his dismissal order preceded the July 27 date, at which time Bolden was in probationary status. Nonetheless, Barger's judgment in firing a black trooper amidst the turmoil regarding minority hirings by State Police, just days before termination of his probation, was repercussive—at least. Predictably, the State Police was involved in a class action suit that was to shake the force unprecedentedly and keep it shaking for years as the minority issue burned.

U. S. District Judge Clifford S. Green, on March 8, 1974, ordered Bolden reinstated with full back pay. Meanwhile, the class action suit, asking that the State Police observe quotas with regard to hiring and promoting, was continued.

To add to State Police woes, truckers armed with citizen band (CB) radio equipment, unlawfully sped across state highways in violation of the 55-mile-per-hour speed limit set in November to cope with the nation's energy crisis. Barger ordered a crack-down on all speeders, and complained fruitlessly to the Federal Communications Commission (FCC) regarding the truckers' use of CBs in violation of FCC rules. Truck drivers, protesting fuel prices and the speeding crack-down, blockaded sections of Interstate Route 80. Governor Shapp intervened; he secured a promise from truckers to cease blockading public roadways in Pennsylvania.

On January 31, 1974, trucker Ronald Hengst, 33, of Spring Grove, was killed when a rock thrown through his windshield from an overhead bridge near Allentwon caused his rig to go out of control and over an embankment off U. S. Route 22. Fearing more serious incidents, Shapp ordered hundreds of armed Pennsylvania National Guardsmen to patrol highways. Negotiations at the nation's capital eventually brought about an improvement in conditions, although threatened trucker reprisals continued for some weeks. Shapp was instrumental in keeping useful negotiations alive.

Although the FOP and the Commonwealth had reached contract agreement by way of negotiations a year before, discussions for the 1974-1975 contract met a different fate. Failure by both parties to come to an agreement sent the entire issue before an arbitration panel composed of John J. Harrington, police arbitrator; attorney Thomas H. Lane, Commonwealth arbitrator; and Dr. Walter J. Gershenfeld, chairman and neutral panel member. Arguments before the panel were handled by attorney William Myers for the Commonwealth, and FOP legal counsel, Howard Richard. A contract, signed in late December, met the deadline set by Act 111; it carried an estimated value of $4,900,000.

Meanwhile, the Hepford Committee, continuing its hearings, listened to testimony regarding alleged wrongdoing by Lieutenant Angelo J. Carcaci and possible wiretap charges against Barger. Carcaci refused to answer questions put to him by the committee. A House resolution, citing Carcaci in contempt, was voted in December, and when he failed again to answer on January 29, 1974, a warrant of commitment was issued—it was the first time such a warrant had been issued in accordance with an 1842 statute.

Represented by attorneys Morris Gerber and Marc Jonas of Norristown, Carcaci appealed the House action to Dauphin County court where he lost. An appeal to the state superior court ended with that court's refusal to rule on the case. The state supreme court took the matter under advisement, and on October 28, 1974, sustained the House contempt charge. Faced with either testifying or going to jail until November 30, 1974, Carcaci appeared before the committee with nothing of consequence occurring. The case ended with the demise of the Hepford Committee. Referring to Carcaci's legal challenges to the House contempt action, the committee reported, "(they) have had the practical effect of frustrating the legislative process."

On the State Police popularity scale, one might well guess where the name of "Joe" Hepford stood—right at the bottom. In 1976, Hepford ran against Lycoming County District Attorney Allen Ertel for the Seventeenth Congressional District seat; Hepford lost by a narrow margin. It can be safely stated that Hepford attracted few, if any, trooper votes in that district.

On December 26, 1973, Major Robert A. Rice retired to accept a security appointment with a large utility corporation. In a three-way transaction, Major Grooms replaced Rice at Area III headquarters, Harrisburg; Major Wojick replaced Grooms with headquarters at Area VII, Milesburg; and Wojick's vacancy at Area II, Wyoming, was filled by Major Yaglenski. A replacement for Yaglenski in the Bureau of Criminal Investigation was not named.

Also retired on December 26 was Comptroller Henry T. Clayton. Clayton, 77, ended more than forty-two years of commonwealth service begun in 1931—the happiest of which, by his own admission, were the years spent with the State Police. He was one of three state employes who organized the State Employes Credit Union in 1932; his outstanding achievements were manifold. Clayton was justifiably proud of his distinguished service that merited him an entry in the 1974 edition of "Who's Who in Pennsylvania."

Replacing Clayton in January, 1974, was Comptroller Joseph McGlinchey, 53, a native of Pittsburgh. McGlinchey, a certified public accountant, held executive positions with HARSCO, the parent organization of the Harrisburg Steel Company, before coming to the State Police. He is a graduate of Duquesne University.

When the state Senate adjourned *sine die* on December 30, 1973, Shapp continued with Barger's services, and the services of numerous other officials, by way of another interim appointment. The Republican-controlled House, however, remained in continuous session until the 1974 legislature met. This odd situation was to become the center of a year-long dispute contesting the validity of Shapp's interim appointments.

On January 2, 1974, the Republicans lost no time in contesting the interim appointments. Republican Senators Richard Frame (Venango); T. Newell Wood (Luzerne); and Richard Tighlman (Montgomery) filed suit in commonwealth court, and then requested the state supreme court to take jurisdiction to save time. Nevertheless, a decision from the supreme court was not to be forthcoming until October; Barger continued in office.

A Crawford County special investigative grand jury in January recommended that Major Roy Titler, Area VI commander, and former Attorney General J. Shane Creamer be indicted for "obstructing and perverting public justice on or about September, 1971, by suppressing evidence in the investigation of the murder of Philip Earl Cownden." If Barger entertained any thought of transferring Titler to the Bureau of Criminal Investigation at headquarters to fill Yaglenski's vacancy, Titler's involvement in the Crawford County case stayed his hand.

On April 1, 1974, a Crawford County grand jury did hand down an indictment against the two men. A United Press International story stated: "The indictment . . . accused the two of failing to investigate a statement made by Wardrop in a 1972 telephone call and in an unsigned statement which Wardrop was alleged to have made in connection with the Philip Cownden killing." James Wardrop, 34, of Youngstown, Ohio, was indicted for the murder of Cownden. A year later, Crawford County Judge P. Richard Thomas dismissed the indictment against Wardrop, ruling that he had been granted immunity from prosecution in return for his testimony before the Pennsylvania Crime Commission.

In a two-year litigation that took the Creamer-Titler case to the state supreme court, the high court in April, 1976, dismissed the indictments against the two. Its ruling upheld an earlier decision by the state superior court that a two-year statute of limitations had expired—that Crawford County had no jurisdiction in the case. It is noteworthy that during this entire case, involving criminal indictment, Barger did not suspend Titler. His action led to charges of dual standards, because he had suspended Dussia without pay for allegedly violating a departmental regulation—a noncriminal charge.

On January 17, 1974, the State Police mourned the loss of its first helicopter pilot. Trooper Ross E. Snowden, 33, was killed when his helicopter crashed at the Reading Municipal Airport. Killed also in the crash was the airport superintendent, Donald Glass, 47. Snowden, a native of Uniontown, served in the U. S. Air Force from 1959 to 1965 before joining the State Police in 1970. In 1972, he was transferred from the Franklin station to the Aviation Division at Reading. Snowden was buried with full honors at Uniontown. Forming an honor guard were 100 troopers. More than 500 officers, representing forty-five police agencies from five states, attended the funeral. Snowden was survived by his wife, Shirley Ann, and two children.

As a result of binding arbitration at the close of 1972, a new contract effective July 1, 1973, was to carry retirement calculations based on the average salary of the highest three years. The legislature, however, had not passed enabling legislation to put this contract provision into effect. Senate Bill 472 was finally passed by the 1974 General Assembly, and the three-year base became law when Shapp signed Act 31, P.L. 125, on March 1. Passage of the law also removed from the bargaining table any discussions effecting retirement benefits. Henceforth, any attempts to alter the three-year base, for instance, must be done through the general assembly—and the general assembly only.

The long-awaited court-martial of Lieutenant James McCann was conducted at the Academy on March 4. Major George Evan, and Captains Patrick Hankinson and Paul Chylak made up the court-martial panel. Prosecuting the case was Major Edward Fagnani, trial judge advocate. McCann's defense was handled by attorney Wallace Worth, Jr., of Allentown. The proceeding took up but one day.

Barger, on March 15, announced that the court-martial board ruled McCann not entitled to his commissioned rank; he immediately reduced him to trooper. Attorney Worth and McCann filed an appeal in commonwealth court.

In March, the legislature and Shapp locked horns on the issue of capital punishment. The House and Senate passed a measure restoring the death penalty to Pennsylvania. Late March 22, just minutes short of the deadline for final action, Shapp vetoed the bill, fully expecting the general assembly would override his veto. He was right. The House and Senate, in less than a week, voted to override by margins far in excess of those required by law. Pennsylvania became the twenty-third state in the nation to restore the death penalty since the 1972 Supreme Court decision on that issue.

On March 7, Barger filled the vacancy in the Bureau of Criminal Identification by bringing in Major Grooms from Area III. Major Stanalonis was transferred from the Academy to Area III, Harrisburg. Captain Leon D. Leiter was promoted to major, replacing Stanalonis at the Academy. Newly-promoted Captain Earl P. Wright was assigned to the Academy to assist Leiter.

Captain Joseph McIlvaine's case, contesting mandatory retirement at age 60, again surfaced in March with a final determination by the U. S. Supreme Court. McIlvaine lost his case in commonwealth court; he appealed to the state supreme court. Dissatisfied with the supreme court's upholding of the commonwealth court ruling last October, McIlvaine took his cause to the U. S. Supreme Court. In March, 1974, the nation's highest court dismissed the retired captain's appeal. Thus ended McIlvaine's challenge; the mandatory retirement age of 60 remains in effect.

The State Police, always striving for innovation, introduced two new processes. The first concerned the capability for all state police agencies in the United States to make computer-to-computer searches of the Pennsylvania registration and operators data files by way of the National Law Enforcement Teletypewriter System (NLETS). This was a "first" for the State Police. The second, developed after lengthy research with Penn State University scientists, permits the use of neutron activation analysis to determine the use of gunfire in the commission of a crime. It is expected that the use of neutron activation analysis will be expanded in due time to allow the examination of an indefinite number of evidence items found at the scenes of crimes.

Finally settling on a decision that blue and gold did not constitute a satisfactory color combination for patrol vechicles, Barger ordered a change to blue and white. The latter color combination was patterned somewhat after the abandoned green and white configuration that had been in use for several years. The delivery of 800 blue and white patrol cars began in May. It was estimated that two years would be required to phase out the blue and gold vehicles.

Based upon the actions of a Commonwealth Compensation Commission and the expired federal wage freeze, Barger, effective May 1, was one of six cabinet members granted salary increases. Barger's salary was upped to $37,500 a year.

Corporal Lawrence F. Clark, on May 19, completed his schooling at the Indiana University Law School; he became the department's first trooper-lawyer under a program begun by Urella in 1971. Clark passed the Pennsylvania Bar Association exam in July; he was later admitted to the state supreme court bar in October. Two others in the program, Sergeant Howard Berringer and Corporal John Armstrong, returned to Indiana University in September to complete their final year of law studies.

Having heard the appeals of Lieutenant Stephen Luchansky, and Corporals Curtis Guyette and Metro Kardash last February, the commonwealth court on June 18, in a lengthy unanimous opinion, ordered the three men reinstated with full back pay. The opinion, written by Judge Theodore O. Rogers stated: "We conclude that the findings of guilt by the court-martial board were not supported by substantial evidence and that the commissioner abused his discretion by dismissing the appellants on this record.''

Unwilling to immediately take the three men back, the Justice Department asked the commonwealth court to stay its ruling, pending an appeal to the state supreme court. Attorney General Packel, however, reversed that stand and ruled there was no basis for appeal. Barger called Luchansky, Guyette and Kardash back to work July 1. The three men received their back pay less income earned elsewhere during the period of suspension.

For several years, the Pennsylvania Chiefs of Police Association (PCPA), the Pennsylvania State Police, and the FBI planned and lobbied for legislation creating a system for the mandatory training of all police officers. Police had long been criticized for placing poorly trained men in uniform and for the unfavorable consequences deriving from their actions at times. Unable to financially support training facilities of their own, the small police agencies looked to the state for relief.

In June, the general assembly finally passed a mandatory training measure. Act 120, P.L. 359, signed by Shapp on June 18, established a seventeen-member Municipal Police Officers Education and Training Commission, and appropriated funds. Under the law, an officer would be required to complete training within one year of his appointment to a police department or lose his job. Barger was appointed head of the commission. Because of the complicated implementation problems, the new training program was still some time away from being a smooth operation. Steps taken by Urella, with mandatory training almost in view, were a boon to State Police efforts to get a statewide program underway with the least delay.

Trooper Robert E. Einsel completed his NUTI training in June: he was assigned to the Personnel Bureau. Chosen to follow Einsel at Northwestern in September was Corporal James B. Hazen of the Troop S York station.

Honored in June for his direction of State Police operations in western Pennsylvania during the twelve-day truck strike earlier in the year was Major George Evan, Area V commander. Evan received the Pennsylvania Meritorious Service Medal from Brig. General Carl F. Mauger, deputy director of the National Guard's Field Command. The citation noted: ''In conjunction with the National Guard commanders, Major Even welded the state police and National Guard into a cooperative and responsive strike force, capable of assembly and deployment with minimum delay. He displayed exceptional ability through his calm and professional approach to difficult situations and thus gained the immediate confidence of others.''

During the early months of 1974, the Bolden class action suit stirred up a controversy, the likes of which the State Police has never known. Already, federal Judge Clifford Green had ordered Bolden's reinstatement with full pay. He also halted the appointment of cadets and the promotional exams for the ranks of corporal and sergeant scheduled for March, pending disposition of other complaints contained in the class action suit. There were indications that Green would definitely impose a quota system on the State Police with regard to cadet appointments and the promotion of black troopers. Attorneys for the plaintiffs and the FOP pounded out what was considered a reasonable consent decree as a substitute to a lengthy, costly court battle.

On April 15, Barger called to the Academy in a late evening session all field commanders, and one lieutenant, one sergeant, one corporal, and one trooper from each troop. Also summoned were the presidents of all State Police FOP lodges. Some 160 persons were in attendance at this unprecedented conference to consider the consent decree. Briefings were conducted by FOP attorney Howard Richard and Deputy Attorney General Benjamin Lerner.

The consent decree provided that one-third of the qualified cadet candidates will be minorities, and one-quarter of the promotions to corporal, sergeant, and lieutenant will be minorities. This percentage formula was to be followed until minority representation on the force reached 9.2 percent—a figure similar to the general makeup of the state's entire work force. The decree also provided for new examinations, and guidelines for the makeup of oral interview boards and the processing of background investigations. It called, too, for the reconsideration of all minority applicants rejected since June 1, 1970. The decree banned retaliation by the State Police against anyone who opposed police practices challenged in the class action suit.

Concerned about stricter court-ordered guidelines, if the case was allowed to progress through the court and to a court opinion, the assembled trooper personnel voted in favor of the consent decree. Undoubtedly persuasive, too, was Barger's pledge that qualifications for cadet appointments would not be lowered. The consent decree was signed June 20 at Philadelphia. It was, indeed, a momentous occasion in State Police history.

In the wake of the consent decree, new units were formed by the State Police to validate entrance and promotional exams and job descriptions for all ranks—an undertaking that was to consume years of work. Complaints and countersuits were to keep the pot boiling without let-up. The effects of the Bolden class action suit have been widespread, and the end is not yet in sight.

Since the mid-1960s when the drug problem blossomed into alarming proportions, the State Police engaged in a drug education program to acquaint the public, particularly school children, with the horrors of drug addiction. This new undertaking was similar to the traffic safety education program the State Police had conducted for years—and is still conducting effectively. The drug education program, however, upon evaluation, proved to be less effective compared with the effort put into it. And so, in July 1974, the program was abandoned. This move took the State Police out of the preventive phase of the drug problem; its resources were then dedicated solely to the enforcement of the drug laws.

The 1974–1975 fiscal year, beginning July 1, 1974, saw the State Police budget figure top the $100 million mark for the first time in its history.

At the sixty-first annual conference of the Pennsylvania Chiefs of Police Association held at Philadelphia in July, Barger, provoked by comments previously made by Republican gubernatorial candidate Drew Lewis, sharply reprehended the general assembly. According to an Associated Press story, Barger said: "I don't think the general assembly should have their noses in the operation of the State Police. I am in no way trying to run the general assembly, and I would appreciate it if no one tried to run the Pennsylvania State Police as long as I'm here."

His remarks brought immediate reaction from the general assembly. Senate Minority Leader Richard C. Frame called Barger "unbelievably arrogant." In an *Evening News* (Harrisburg) story, Frame reminded Barger that he and the Force were responsible to the people of Pennsylvania, "through the General Assembly which established the department and created the post of police commissioner to enforce the laws passed by the General Assembly."

House Bill 1301, limiting the commissioner's powers to suspend troopers, was defeated in the Senate by a 11–35 vote earlier in July; however, Barger's Philadelphia comments generated new interest in the measure. On July 23, the Senate, in what was considered a direct rebuke to Barger, passed the bill by a 26–20 vote, and sent it to the governor. In predictable fashion, Shapp vetoed the measure.

In August, Barger suffered another setback from the commonwealth court. The court, having heard Lt. Colonel Graci's appeal in February, ruled that there was insufficient evidence to fire Graci. The 6–1 majority opinion stated that the prosecution's evidence "wholly failed to support" the charges against Graci and his subsequent firing by Barger. The court ordered Graci reinstated with full back pay. Graci had been suspended in March, 1973, and faced court-martial in June.

In an August 22 editorial, *The Patriot* stated: "Now that State Police Lt. Col. Charles Graci has been reinstated, it is appropriate to comment on one of the most bizarre house-cleanings we have observed in the Capital City in recent years. Governor Shapp's new broom, Commissioner James Barger, instead of sweeping clean, has raised more than a little dust."

Graci was reinstated three weeks before reaching mandatory retirement age of 60. He retired September 4, after thirty-seven years of service.

Occupying national attention in August was Richard M. Nixon's unprecedented resignation as President of the United States. He resigned on August 9, and was followed in office by Vice President Gerald R. Ford, who became the nation's thirty-eighth President. Because of the workings of the Twenty-fifth Consitutional Amendment, Mr. Ford, oddly enough, ascended to the nation's top offices without election. Faced with the difficult, compelling task of restoring public confidence in the Presidency, Ford is credited with having accomplished this before his days in the White House came to an end in January, 1977.

Although the State Police had been strenuously recruiting minority applicants before, efforts were stepped up even moreso after the consent decree. By September, a total of 6,555 applicants passed preliminary screening. Of this number, 671 were black males, 116 black females, 42 Spanish-surnamed males, and 4 Spanish-surnamed females—representing 13 percent of the applicants certified for the Civil Service entrance examination. There were 5,426 white males, and 266 white females. The written exam was administered by the Civil Service Commission on September 14; 2,314 of the 6,555 applicants failed to show up for this first exam in two years.

In October, Captain Leonard T. Koper was promoted to major and transferred to Area I command at Reading, replacing Major Leroy Lilly who retired in July. Replacing Koper in the R. & I. Division was newly-promoted Captain Benjamin R. Jones. Also promoted to captain was Lieutenant Salvadore L. Rodriquez. Rodriquez, assistant director of the Community Services Bureau, was one of the plaintiffs in the class action suit. Also retired in July was Captain Robert L. Bomboy, director of communications. He was replaced by Robert I. Kimmel, civilian supervisor of radio communications.

In a mutual transfer, effective October 17, Lt. Colonels Conti and McGroarty exchanged regional commands, placing Conti at Punxsutawney and McGroarty at Montoursville.

Governor Shapp, on October 10, signed into law Act 235, P.L. 705, requiring mandatory training for privately employed agents who, as an incidence to their employment, are armed. The measure was to become more familiarly known as "The Lethal Weapons Training Act," inasmuch as the definition of "lethal weapons" was enlarged to include any weapon "calculated to produce death or serious bodily harm." Responsibility for training the estimated 11,000 persons falling within the purview of the law was handed to the State Police.

In an effort to do away with inconsistencies found in the disciplinary system, the State Police introduced a new code for dealing with alleged wrongdoing below the court-martial level. The court-martial system, rooted in law, must be adhered to when proposed punishment involves a reduction in rank, reduction in pay, or dismissal. The new disciplinary code was aimed at less severe punishment. It provided for a uniform statewide system of hearings and appeals, and the assurance of similar punishment for similar violations. In an interview with *Patriot* reporter Carmen Brutto, Barger said that the new system was not the result of several State Police cases highly publicized in recent months, but was an idea he brought with him to headquarters at the time of his appointment as commissioner.

Because of a change in the Pennsylvania Constitution, allowing a governor to succeed himself in office, Shapp ran for reelection in 1974. He handily disposed of his opponent, Rep. Martin Mullen (D-Philadelphia), in the spring primary. His Republican opponent was Drew Lewis, a not-too-well-known candidate. At the polls in November, Shapp, as expected, won the election; his win margin of 299,335 votes, however, was a far cry from his stunning victory in 1970 when his margin topped 500,000 votes. Reportedly, Shapp's popularity in the state was waning, but the shattering effects of the Watergate scandal that cost Mr. Nixon his Presidency undoubtedly favored Shapp's second term try.

The Democrats also scored in the general assembly by increasing their margin in the Senate by a 29–20 count, and wresting the House from the GOP by a count of 114 to 89. Thus Shapp was to commence his second term with an unprecedented total of 144 Democrats in the legislature—about as healthy circumstances as he could hope for.

On October 26, just days before the general election, the state supreme court voided some 600 of Shapp's interim appointments, including the State Police commissioner. The ruling followed a suit filed by three GOP senators in January. Action on the ruling, however, was held up pending a petition for a new hearing requested by the Shapp administration. The court on November 21 denied Shapp's petition for a new hearing. Shapp then designated Barger, and other cabinet members, special assistants to the governor, and directed that their formal duties be carried out by their chief deputies. These duties in the case of the State Police fell to Wellendorf.

On November 30, the Senate adjourned without confirming any of the questioned appointments; the supreme court on December 3 ruled that the appointees were officially out of office. On December 5, Barger's tenure was extended by another interim appointment.

On December 18, the new radio system was formally dedicated by the dispatching of a message from the Academy to Troop J headquarters at Lancaster via a helicopter which was used as a repeater station. Sending the message was Lt. Governor Kline. Barger and Arthur P. Sundry, Motorola's vice president and general manager, participated in this ceremony.

Amidst much speculation regarding the makeup of Shapp's second term cabinet, Shapp announced on December 20 that he had asked Barger to remain as head of the State Police.

Again the FOP and the Commonwealth failed to reach a contract agreement by way of collective bargaining sessions; the matter was referred to an arbitration panel. The panel was composed of attorney Thomas H. Lane, representing the Commonwealth; Edward B. Shils, representing the FOP; and S. Herbert Unterberger, impartial arbitrator and panel chairman. A new contract for the fiscal year beginning July 1, 1975, was signed in December. The FOP won an across-the-board salary increase plus additional fringe benefits. The new agreement was valued at $7,610,000—the largest figure ever scored by the FOP under the provisions of Act 111. In an unprecedented procedure, the contract was later bilaterally amended; the amendments were to take effect January 1, 1976.

At the close of 1974, Eastern Region Commander Lt. Colonel William B. Cooper, 59, retired. He had completed almost thirty-eight years of service.

At the start of his third year as unconfirmed State Police commissioner, Barger was rebuffed by the commonwealth court—another in a series of setbacks. Having heard an appeal by Trooper James L. McCann, a former lieutenant, last December, the commonwealth court on January 16 ruled that McCann was entitled to retain the rank of lieutenant. The court noted that the court-martial charges and specifications did not allege any impropriety or misconduct on the part of McCann, and that former Commissioner Urella's promotion of McCann in 1972 was "lawful and proper." McCann was reinstated as a lieutenant.

Ever since the postponement of Lt. Colonel Dussia's court-martial in August, 1973, his case was brought before the commonwealth court a number of times wherein the suspended officer contended that he could not expect fairness. Hearings in September and November led to a final decision by the commonwealth court in May, 1974, refusing to stop Dussia's trial. Barger then scheduled the court-martial for June 24. Dussia's attorney, Bruce Cooper, readily secured a postponement from the state supreme court which agreed to hear arguments challenging the constitutionality of the State Police court-martial system. Joined by the state and national FOP lodges—the latter through the efforts of national president John J. Harrington—Dussia took his case to the state supreme court on January 13, 1975.

During the period that his case was moving through the courts, Dussia stated that Barger on two separate occasions offered to drop charges against him and award him full back pay, if he would then resign. The first offer was indirectly made to Dussia's attorney by the attorney general. The second was directly made to a state senator from western Pennsylvania—a Dussia sympathizer. In both instances, Dussia, preferring to defend his cause in the courts, flatly refused Barger's proposal.

Shapp, 61, began his historic second term at noon on January 21, 1975. He was the first governor to succeed himself in 100 years of Pennsylvania history. He took his oath of office in a glass-enclosed booth in front of the capitol, as a small crowd of some 1,000 brave souls put up with sub-freezing temperatures and snow to view the inaugural ceremony. Shapp's address took up no more than ten minutes. Before noon in the Senate chamber, Kline, 44, also set a record by becoming the first lieutenant governor ever to succeed himself. Except for changes in the departments of Commerce and Welfare, Shapp's second administration was underway with the same cabinet, although it was marred by bitter Senate confirmation battles.

In February, seven troopers, specially trained at the central lab at Harrisburg in ballistics, and toolmark and document analysis, were assigned to the regional crime labs to beef up the services offered to state and municipal police agencies.

History was in the making on March 6, as 151 cadets began their six months of training at the Academy. It was the first class mustered under the terms of the consent decree, and the first State Police class in two years. Composing the cadet class were 99 white males, 43 black males, 2 Spanish-surnamed males, 5 black females, and 2 white females. The class was scheduled to graduate on August 20.

Efforts by the Conference of State FOP Lodges and six individuals to gain a preliminary injunction in federal court to block the class failed. The reverse discrimination suit challenged the makeup of the cadet class under the consent decree. The FOP lodges asked the U. S. Third Circuit Court of Appeals to overturn the district court's refusal to grant a preliminary injunction. The appellate court, however, upheld the district court's action, but did not preclude the plaintiffs from further developing their case. A suit filed in U. S. Eastern District Court asked the court to set aside the consent decree, charging "fraud, conflicts of interest, misrepresentation and unauthorized stipulations by counsel for the commonwealth." Representing the FOP was Lycoming County District Attorney Allen E. Ertel. On February 19, 1976, U. S. District Judge Clifford S. Green dismissed the reverse discrimination suit, ruling that it was "an improper collatoral attack on the Bolden consent decree."

Finally determining the extent of the State Police budget for the 1975–1976 fiscal period, the governor's office excluded funds to support 200 trooper positions. The number of existing vacant positions at this point exceeded the 200 figure, as a result of attritional losses and the inability to convene regularly scheduled cadet classes to maintain a full complement. What the governor's office was saying, in effect, was that the State Police, even if it could conceivably fill all vacancies during the upcoming fiscal year, would lack funds to fill 200 trooper positions. This was a safe administrative judgement, as it was not likely that all vacancies could be filled in view of the minority hassle.

Although Barger was called before the Senate Appropriations Committee in April to defend his $113.9 million budget for the fiscal year beginning July 1, it appeared that the senators were more anxious to discuss Barger's policy on ticketing legislators for speeding. Barger had eliminated any procedures disallowing a trooper to arrest speeders—no matter who they were. Consequently, a number of "heavy-footed" legislators were arrested for speeding—a matter that provided the press with copy each time an arrest was disclosed, and irritated the legislators no end. Barger denied that he had ordered a special campaign against speeding lawmakers. According to an Associated Press story, Barger said: "All citizens—all I ask them to do is abide by the law. We're the easiest people to get along with." Barger also pleaded his case for more manpower and equipment.

In April, Captain Robert L. Dunham, 60, retired from the Bureau of Patrol. His vacancy at headquarters was filled by the promotion of Captain Albert Marchinetti. Also retired in April, after a lengthy illness, was Lt. Colonel Philip M. Conti, 59, western region commander.

An executive order issued by Shapp in April, aimed at "ending discrimination against persons solely because of their affectional or sexual preferences," touched off an unhappy reaction from members of the State Police, the Bureau of Corrections, and the legislature. In a memo sent to Terry Delmuth, Shapp's aide for human services, Barger denounced the hiring of homosexuals as troopers. The commissioner undoubtedly well represented the feelings of his men. Joining him in protesting such a hiring practice was the state FOP. Legislators threatened to introduce measures in the general assembly prohibiting the employment of homosexuals as troopers or prison guards. Later, the legislators did pass a measure, preventing homosexuals from holding State Police and prison jobs; Shapp vetoed the bill.

Early in 1975, the crime lab at Harrisburg acquired an atomic absorption spectrophotometer—an instrument for swiftly and reliably determining whether a person had fired a gun. Examinations by way of this instrument are far less expensive and complicated than the neutron activation method. Samples for analysis are removed from the hands of suspects by a film lift technique familiar to State Police and municipal police crime investigators, whose efforts are remarkably upheld by this crime lab innovation. Responsibility for this special testing program was placed in the hands of Criminalist II Harry A. Fox.

At the primary polls on May 20, a Constitutional amendment, ending the issue of interim appointments by a governor, was approved by the voters. The amendment called for a governor to fill vacancies within ninety days, and the Senate to act within twenty-five legislative days, or allow confirmation by default. It also provided that some of the appointments may be confirmed by a majority vote rather than by a two-thirds vote. Legislation to determine what appointments would require confirmation and by what vote was left to the general assembly. This voter action ended once and for all the hassle between governors and the Senate over interim appointments—an issue that was particularly intensified during Shapp's tenure.

In May, Major John Yaglenski, 60, commander of Area II, Wyoming, and Captain William J. Anselmi, 50, director of the Information Systems Division, retired. Replacing Yaglenski at Area II was newly-promoted Major Patrick J. Hankinson. Promoted and transferred to the Information Systems Division was Captain Blair E. Swistock.

Graduating in May from Indiana University's Indianapolis School of Law were Sergeant Howard G. Berringer and Corporal John H. Armstrong. The two joined Corporal Lawrence F. Clark on the department's legal staff. Berringer and Armstrong later passed the Pennsylvania Bar exam and were admitted to the bar of the state supreme court.

Although the seventieth anniversary of the founding of the State Police organization fell on May 2, 1975, an official event commemorating this historical milestone was not held until June 7. About 650 persons attended a dinner-dance at the Hershey Convention Center. Governor Shapp proclaimed June 7 "Pennsylvania State Police Day" in honor of the anniversary. All original constabulary members of the 1905 muster were deceased. Present on this occasion was former Major William D. Plummer, 89, the dean of retired troopers. Also attending, were the widows of Colonel C. M. Wilhelm and Lt. Colonel Jacob C. Mauk. Visiting dignitaries included Colonel Eugene Olaff, superintendent of the New Jersey State Police; Colonel Frank R. Blackstone, superintendent of the Ohio State Highway Patrol; Colonel Thomas S. Smith, superintendent of the Maryland State Police; and Lt. Colonel Joseph F. Rowan, deputy superintendent of the Delaware State Police. (Neither Governor Shapp nor Lt. Governor Kline was there.)

In June, the name of Corporal James Hazen was added to the list of NUTI graduates. Hazen was assigned to the Academy. Selected to attend NUTI's September session was Corporal Barry P. Buck of the Community Services Bureau.

On June 25, Deputy Commissioner Wellendorf set up a telephone conference call with all field commanders. Although the conference call was made to discuss foreseeable problems with an upcoming strike of state workers, Wellendorf drifted to the subject of investigating motor vehicle accidents involving troopers who had been drinking. He did not reveal the underlying reason for bringing up this subject: he did, however, issue instructions about the filing of supplemental accident reports.

The following day, Major Charles J. Buchinsky, director of the Patrol Bureau, was suspended with pay, pending an investigation of allegations that certain accident reports were improperly prepared. It was later revealed that Buchinsky, at a conference of command personnel at the Academy on March 28, 1974, supposedly directed that dual standards in the filing of accident reports be observed.

In August, Dauphin County District Attorney LeRoy S. Zimmerman entered the case, leading to the possibility of criminal prosecutions, if such wrongdoing was determined. Zimmerman, in September, petitioned the Dauphin County Court to set up a special grand jury to investigate possible "corruption." The court agreed with Zimmerman; it authorized the probe—the first citizen-controlled investigation of the State Police in its seventy-year history. Attorney General Robert P. Kane, who had earlier in Shapp's second term replaced Israel Packel in that top cabinet post, was very critical of Zimmerman's "unilateral" action in asking for a grand jury probe.

Judge Warren G. Morgan swore in a panel of twenty-three on November 6. The panel, composed of twelve women and eleven men, was headed by Andrew J. Hricak. First Assistant District Attorney Mary H. Leedom was put in charge of operations, assisting was Edwin W. Frese, Jr., Zimmerman's chief deputy. The investigatory grand jury began the questioning of witnesses November 12: more than seventy State Police witnesses appeared before the grand jury through the balance of the year and into early January, 1976.

In another unprecedented action, 50,000 state workers belonging to the American Federation of State, County, and Municipal Employes (AFSCME) began a four-day strike July 1. Contract negotiations with the state had fallen through; the workers voted to strike under the provisions of Act 195, "The Public Employes Relations Act." Some disorder incidents were reported throughout the state, and the State Police arrested seventeen strikers. The Justice Department, in a number of court actions, secured strike injunctions which narrowed the number of workers on strike. This action undoubtedly hastened a two-year contract agreement reached by the state and AFSCME in a marathon bargaining session. Gerald McEntee, AFSCME's state director, said: "The members felt it was the best package that could be negotiated under difficult circumstances."

Editorially, *The Patriot* reported:

> Clearly, what brought the State's first public employe strike to a quick end was the action of the courts in finding that the absence from the job of at least 25,000 of the 50,000 workers constituted "a clear and present danger or threat to the health, safety or welfare of the public," and, in accordance with Act 195, ordering them back to work. How the State would have fared if the courts had been less agreeable or had the union ignored the "return to work" orders is uncertain. Act 195 came through this test but it has yet to demonstrate that its strike provisions would be adequate in the face of a more obstreperous challenge.

In July, a provision of the recently approved constitutional amendment governing interim appointments was unexpectedly exercised by five Republican senators: their move was to force a confirmation vote on Barger and several other of Shapp's important appointments within five legislative days. Reportedly, the upcoming vote on Barger busied Kline who had to salvage at least thirty-four Senate votes in what was judged by newsmen and political observers as a tough uphill battle. Nonetheless, Kline undertook the challenge in what has been described as the most effective bit of "arm-twisting" seen at the capitol in years: one Democratic senator stated that he turned down an invitation to visit Kline's office, since he had no intention of voting for Barger's confirmation. In any event, Barger was confirmed on July 15 by a 39-10 vote, which was five more than the two-thirds majority of thirty-four needed. Another senator, commenting afterward on the Senate action, stated that the vote count was a confirmation moreso of Kline than it was of Barger.

It was rumored that Lieutenant Harold G. Rice of Troop D, Butler, in an unusual move, planned to take court action to gain a promotion to captain. Rice, 57, and a thirty-five-year veteran officer, had been promoted to lieutenant in October, 1964. As senior lieutenant, he had been bypassed for promotion by Barger and his predecessors on a number of occasions. Informed of this possibility, Barger, Rice's former commanding officer, reportedly offered Rice a promotion and transfer to the Academy; Rice accepted.

Rice was promoted to captain in July, replacing Captain Wright at the Academy. Wright was moved to the Turnpike troop. Also promoted to captain in July were Lieutenant Nicholas G. Dellarciprete, Personnel Bureau; Lieutenant Russell C. Rickert, Bureau of Research and Development; and Lieutenant John F. Duignan, Bureau of Community Services.

Graduating in August, was a cadet class of 144. It was the first class convened under the Bolden consent decree, and the first class to complete training since July, 1973. Numbered among the graduates were 39 black males, 2 Spanish-surnamed males, 3 black females, and 2 white females: minority representation followed the consent decree percentage guidelines. Married cadets outnumbered single 90 to 54. Attorney General Kane delivered the graduation address. Barger presented the awards and diplomas except to four of the new troopers who received their diplomas from family members. They were Albert Kwiatek, Jr., son of Major Albert F. Kwiatek; Francis Brennan II, son of Sergeant Francis Brennan; Thomas R. Bell, son of retired Lieutenant Thomas Bell; and Rodney J. Patterson, brother of Trooper Gregory N. Patterson.

In September, a few more changes in the State Police high command were made. Major Edward Wojick, 52, retired as commander of Area VII, and was replaced by the transfer of Major Sidney C. Deyo from the Bureau of Research and Development. Deyo's vacancy at headquarters was filled by the transfer of Major Leonard T. Koper, area commander at Reading. Promoted and transferred to Koper's Area I post was Major Stanley B. Kramer.

On September 4, the regional crime lab at Wyoming was dedicated. The lab, which formerly occupied quarters in the troop headquarters building, was moved into a new one-story building nearby.

As an offshoot of the Bolden class action suit, U. S. District Court Judge Green, in September, ordered the State Police to promote Trooper Richard McDowell, a black, to sergeant and give him back pay of $10,000. McDowell, in 1971, was an aide to former Attorney General J. Shane Creamer. Creamer was unable to secure a promotion to temporary sergeant for McDowell, but Creamer's successor, Israel Packel, persuaded Barger to do so. When Attorney General Robert P. Kane, in 1975, took over the Justice post, he declined the services of McDowell who was then demoted to trooper and sent back to the Lancaster troop. Judge Green ruled that McDowell had been discriminated against by the State Police and failure to promote him "was based on race and race alone."

In a diplomatically handled "no-contest" consolidation of stations in Bucks County, the leased facilities at Doylestown and Quakertown were replaced by a new state-owned building at Dublin. The $648,580 structure was dedicated on October 1. The facility at Dublin includes a driver examination point. Another large station remained operational in lower Bucks County at Trevose.

By far the most important news development in October, affecting State Police affairs, was the state supreme court's unanimous 7–0 opinion, written by Justice Robert N. C. Nix, stating that the court-martial procedure was unconstitutional. The decision followed an appeal by Lt. Colonel Joseph Dussia to the supreme court last January. The court ruled that the court-martial procedure in effect at the time Dussia was charged was unconstitutional in that it permitted Barger to bring charges, and then to decide the final verdict based on the court-martial board recommendations. The State Police, however, felt that the court's decision contained "inconsistencies,"and a petition for reargument was filed with the supreme court within a week—an action that blocked Dussia from returning to work after a suspension period of about twenty-six months.

Meanwhile, Senate Bill 402, which would abolish the court-martial system in favor of an Internal Board of Inquiry, was introduced. Immediate action on the measure, however, was nowhere in sight. The bill called for a three-man board, one appointed by the State Police commissioner, one by the accused, and the third by mutual consent of the first two named. The appointment of the third was not restricted in any way. Any deadlock on the third appointment would be settled by the chief justice of the state supreme court. The board, according to the bill, would determine innocence or guilt of a trooper after a hearing, and prescribe a penalty which the commissioner would be required to observe. The right of appeal was also stipulated.

At year's end, the collective bargaining sessions between the FOP and the governor's office reached an impasse. The issues were once again tossed in the lap of a three-man arbitration panel. The panel was composed of attorney Thomas H. Lane, Commonwealth arbitrator; Edward B. Shils, FOP arbitrator; and S. Herbert Unterberger, the neutral member and chairman. A contract, carrying an estimated value of $4,219,000, was signed for the fiscal period beginning July 1, 1976. In addition to salary increases and the extension of benefits won in earlier contracts, the new agreement included the unprecedented payment for unused sick leave at the time of separation. A two-year provision allowed payment for a maximum of fifty days in the first year and sixty days in the second year of the contract.

The new year, 1976, was hardly underway when a change was ordered in the comptroller's office at headquarters. Comptroller Joseph McGlinchey, by way of a promotion, went to OA's Bureau of Financial Management as chief of Research and Evaluation, ending a two-year assignment with the State Police. Replacing McGlinchey, was William F. Braucher, former assistant comptroller for the Department of Health and the Department of Public Welfare. Braucher, 43, a native of Chambersburg, graduated from Shippensburg State College where he received a Bachelor of Science degree in business education. Fifteen of his sixteen years of state service were spent with the Health and Public Welfare Departments.

The Dauphin County grand jury probe broke into the news again when, on January 13, the grand jury recommended to the court that criminal charges be filed against Barger, Wellendorf, and Buchinsky. In an unprecedented undertaking, the grand jury asked that the district attorney file informations against Barger for perjury before the grand jury and conspiracy to tamper with public records, against Wellendorf for perjury before the grand jury, and against Buchinsky for conspiracy and criminal solicitation to tamper with public records.

Two days later the court ordered District Attorney Zimmerman to proceed with the grand jury's recommendations for prosecution. Governor Shapp followed up by ordering lie detector tests for Barger and Wellendorf—an order that drew fire from Zimmerman and some legislative leaders. Zimmerman went to the state supreme court to contest the Shapp order and lost. Nonetheless, a week later Shapp did withdraw his order. Shapp decided not to take any action against his top State Police officials until a disposition was made of the charges against them. Barger ruled out a resignation.

On February 3, the three officers were arraigned in Dauphin County Court where pleas of innocent were recorded for them. A trial date in March was set.

Attorney John Rogers Carroll of Philadelphia, representing Barger, Harrisburg attorney Smith B. Gephart, representing Wellendorf, and Buchinsky's Harrisburg attorney Arthur L. Goldberg filed pre-trial motions questioning, for a number of reasons, the validity of the charges against their clients. These motions not only put off the scheduled trial of the trio, but eventually led to the case going to the state superior court for the resolution of a "controlling question of law." The defense counsels wanted the higher court to determine whether the allegations against their clients actually constituted "crimes." The case went to the appellate court in May, and arguments were not scheduled for hearing until December 6.

Meanwhile, Barger and Wellendorf remained at their posts; Buchinsky continued on suspension with pay. In June, however, public denunciation of Buchinsky's full-pay status after one year without working, and rumored court action to suspend Barger and Wellendorf, apparently brought about Buchinsky's reinstatement. He, nonetheless, was not allowed to return to his job as patrol director. Buchinsky, a Hershey resident, was instead sent to Butler as commander of Area VI—a decision that did not at all set well with Buchinsky or his attorney. In an exchange, Major Titler was moved from Butler to headquarters.

On February 25, the state supreme court in a written opinion denied the Shapp administration's petition for a reargument in the Dussia case. The court in a 7–0 decision last October had declared the State Police court-martial procedure unconstitutional. Armed with the supreme court's final determination and accompanied by his attorney, Bruce E. Cooper, Lt. Colonel Joesph Dussia appeared at Barger's office on March 4; he stated that he was returning to duty. Barger and Deputy Attorney General J. Andrew Smyser, who represented the administration in this case, were not aware of the supreme court's recent action, although a copy of the court's order had been mailed to the Justice Department. Barger and Smyser agreed on Dussia's reinstatement with full back pay. Barger suspended Dussia on July 16, 1973; he reinstated Dussia on March 4, 1976, sending him to the Academy on special assignment and ending a lengthy, involved court action unmatched in State Police annals.

The supreme court's decision in the Dussia case also left Barger without a dismissal procedure in serious disciplinary incidents. The general assembly's delay in passing on a substitute procedure that would meet constitutional requirements added to Barger's woes. In an interview with reporter John Scotzin, Barger said:

> I hope you see the dilemma this puts me in. I can't sus-
> pend or fire anybody because I can't court-martial under the
> court's order. But the law says the only way to demote or dis-
> miss is through a court-martial. Now, that the Supreme Court
> says that the court-martial is unconstitutional, where the hell
> is justice? I have long been for taking away the discretionary
> power to summon a court-martial. I want the stigma of
> "court-martial" to be removed.

Commenting in the FOP's *National Journal*, past president John J. Harrington stated: "He (Dussia) asked for my help and I gave it to him. I hired Arlen Spector the former District Attorney of Philadelphia as my attorney (at no cost to the FOP) and went as a 'Friend of the Court' into this case." He also said: "When this case started, I told Gov. Milton Shapp that Lt. Col. Dussia would win and I would be with him all the way."

Early in the year, Barger was called on to defend the administration's $124.1 million State Police budget before the House and Senate Appropriations Committees. "Although the Legislature has set the maximum strength of the State Police at 4,173 (including the Pennsylvania Turnpike detail), our authorized complement is 200 fewer, or 3,973. The Office of Administration last year ordered this reduction to meet the spiraling cost of Government. Ironically, just when our most recent studies show that we need 780 additional trooper positions to provide 24 hours patrol coverage for 507 patrol zones," he said in a prepared statement. Barger also projected the loss of another 100 to 120 troopers in 1976 through normal attrition. According to Barger's report, the State Police in 1975 responded to 455,530 incidents, made 31,423 criminal arrests, and accounted for 488,919 traffic arrests.

The State Police, in April, planned the first group of promotions under the Bolden consent decree. Fifteen sergeants were to be promoted to the rank of lieutenant. The state FOP lodges, however, asked U. S. District Court Judge Green to intervene; they declared that the new promotional system was improperly implemented. The FOP questioned particularly the evaluation procedure. The court, however, saw no reason for holding up the promotions. These were the first promotions taken from the eligibility listing furnished by the Civil Service Commission in March, and prepared according to the consent decree guidelines. Later in May, the State Police announced the promotions of seventeen sergeants and eighty-nine corporals.

At long last, contracts were awarded for the new State Police headquarters building. The Harrisburg firm of Lambert & Intrieri was named general contractor for the $8,366,000 project. A ground-breaking ceremony was held on May 20. Officiating were Secretary of General Services Ronald G. Lench; Susquehanna Township Commissioner David A. Smith; Colonel Barger; Lt. Colonel Wellendorf; Major Stanalonis; and Captain Everly, all of whom spaded the earth where heavy construction equipment would take over. Completion of the new facility was scheduled for February, 1978.

Lt. Colonel Dussia, 60, retired June 7, bringing to an end a career that spanned some thirty-eight years of public service. Commenting editorially on this event, the *Punxsutawney Spirit* stated:

> Joe Dussia, who spent many of his thirty-eight years with the Pennsylvania State Police in DuBois and Punxsutawney, was signally honored upon retirement with citations of service from the House of Representatives and the Senate of the Commonwealth of Pennsylvania.
>
> The citations were the first ever issued by the House and Senate to a retiring State Police officer.
>
> In addition to his recognition by the state legislature, the *DuBois Courier-Express* honored Lt. Col. Dussia with the following: "Lt. Col. Joe Dussia is home again."

A controversy centering on the subject of employing homosexuals again flared when Governor Shapp proclaimed June 12 to June 19 as "Gay Pride Week." Particularly disturbed by such recognition of the Gay Liberation Movement were the rank and file members of the State Police.

In January, the commonwealth court had upheld Shapp's executive order ending job discrimination against homosexuals. The ruling followed a suit by a Pittsburgh businessman, asking for an injunction against the Shapp order. The court stated that "the governor is not the chief moral officer of this commonwealth," but did agree to uphold the executive order.

In June, Lieutenant Harold G. Selecky, State Police lobbyist, was promoted to captain; he remained at his assignment. Corporal Barry P. Buck completed training at NUTI, and returned to his post at the Academy. Selected to follow Buck at NUTI in September was Corporal Paul H. Woodring of the Academy staff.

Shapp, on June 24, signed into law Act 101, providing for the payment of $25,000 to survivors of police officers (and firemen) killed in the line of duty. This death benefit was eagerly sought after by the FOP.

A flurry of activity was in evidence at the Academy and the Hershey area as the nation's governors gathered for the Sixty-eighth National Governors' Conference at Hershey's famous resort hotel through the long Independence Day holiday weekend. Interests in the election year and the bicentennial year observances underscored much of the governors' business during the three-day conference. Governor Shapp, conference host, had already tried his wings as a Presidential candidate prior to the conference, and withdrew after evaluating his chances at the upcoming National Democratic Party convention. The governors were treated to trips to nearby Gettysburg and Indiantown Gap Military Reservation, and a special flight to Philadelphia for a breakfast with England's visiting Queen Elizabeth II.

The conference—the first held in Pennsylvania since 1962—was free of any unusual incidents that might have otherwise marred a well-conducted session. None was anticipated—none occurred. A 180-man trooper detail was given security responsibility for the governors during their Hershey stay. Conference officials, impressed by the troopers' services, were generous in praising them.

Wellendorf, on July 21, stepped down as deputy—a post he had held since January, 1973. Major William N. Grooms, director of the Criminal Investigation Bureau, was designated acting deputy. Grooms had filled in for Wellendorf a number of times during the latter's absences; his appointment to the vacancy would not come as a surprise.

Assembled at Philadelphia for the Fifty-eighth Annual Department Convention of the Pennsylvania American Legion, the legionnaires on July 23 awarded their Distinguished Service Medal to Commissioner Barger. The ceremony was held at the Bellevue Stratford Hotel which soon afterward had to close its doors—a victim of the mysterious "Legionnaires' disease" that accounted for some thirty deaths. The sharp drop in revenue because of the negetive reputation the hotel sustained from the "disease" was more than the owners of the renowned hotel could withstand.

The State Police complement of lieutenant colonels was reduced to none with the retirement of Lt. Colonel Edward M. McGroarty on August 3. McGroarty, 60, closed out a career spanning 38½ years of service. Upon his retirement, McGroarty took on a top security post with one of northeastern Pennsylvania's largest banks.

In August, the State Police received fifteen evidence vans—another innovation in crime fighting. The vans, partially funded by a $196,000 grant from the Governor's Justice Commission, were distributed to each of the troops, except Troops S and T. Equipped with all necessary equipment for the gathering, tagging, preserving, and transporting of crime scene evidence, the vans will be made available to municipal police departments as well as State Police field forces. Troopers, specially trained in this type of work, will provide key services to all police agencies seeking assistance.

In August, Shapp filled the deputy commissioner vacancy. Major Grooms, who had been acting deputy, did not get the appointment although it was expected that he might. Reportedly, Grooms was Barger's choice as Wellendorf's successor. Named instead was Major George Evan, commander of Area V at Greensburg. Evan was sworn in by Shapp in a brief ceremony in the governor's reception room. Commenting on Evan's appointment, the governor stated: "Major Evan is eminently qualified to fill this demanding position. He has the training, experience and dedication to help the Pennsylvania State Police maintain its reputation as the finest organization of its kind in the nation." Evan's promotion to lieutenant colonel placed him in the position of being the only man in the department holding that rank. The State Police from 1937 to 1964 was headed by a commissioner and deputy with the ranks of colonel and lieutenant colonel, respectively. The State Police with double the complement of officers and men in 1976 found itself with a similar top command structure.

At the same time, Shapp announced the creation of a new post in the State Police agency—an executive officer—to assist the commissioner with administrative affairs. Supposedly, this new position was the governor's idea, not Barger's. It might have been at this precise point that Barger's days in office were to be numbered. Promoted and transferred to this new post at headquarters was Major Paul J. Chylak, 45, a native of Olyphant, Lackawanna County. Chylak was formerly assigned to the Academy as director of regional training, an important post, where he established himself impressively. His work at the Academy did not go unnoticed by the governor's aides who were directly concerned with the municipal police programs supervised by Chylak.

Lt. Colonel George Evan (Courtesy of Pennsylvania State Police)

Evan, 51, a native of Monessen, Westmoreland County, Pennsylvania, was born on July 16, 1925. He is the son of George and Susan Perverchik Evan, both of whom were born in Czechoslavakia. Evan attended the Monessen public schools and graduated from Monessen High School. After graduation, he attended the Spartan School of Aeronautics at Tulsa, Oklahoma.

In October, 1943, he enlisted in the U. S. Navy; he remained in naval service until his honorable discharge in May, 1946, when he was assigned to the Pacific fleet. After completing military service, he was employed as a steelworker, a trade in which his father was also engaged.

Evan entered State Police service on April 1, 1947. Upon his graduation from the training school, he was assigned to the Harrisburg troop for a short time before his transfer to Troop D-1, Butler. He was later transferred to Troop C-1, Punxsutawney, until April, 1949, when he was moved to Troop A-1, Greensburg. Evan was promoted to corporal in May, 1961. A promotion to sergeant in May, 1964, sent him to Troop B-1, Washington; an advancement to first sergeant in March, 1967, moved him back to Butler. A year later, he was promoted to lieutenant. Former Commissioner Urella advanced him to captain in February, 1972, and gave him command of the Washington troop. Named to replace Barger at Area V, Greensburg, in March, 1973, Evan was promoted to major. As associates in the western troops for many years, Barger and Evan were well known to one another. Evan's field career in the western troops was broken only by a brief tour of duty at headquarters, Harrisburg, in 1962.

An expert pistol shot, Evan was departmental champion for three years and a member of the State Police pistol team from 1957 to 1967.

On June 3, 1974, Evans was awarded the Pennsylvania Meritorious Service Medal by Pennsylvania National Guard Field Commander Brig. General Carl F. Mauger for his outstanding services during the serious truck strikes earlier that year. State Police troopers and National Guardsmen, on orders from Governor Shapp, worked together to cope with threatening situations stemming from the truck strikes.

Evan is a graduate of the FBI National Academy and the FBI Field Management School. He also attended the State Police Command School at Maryland University. At present, he is pursuing a bachelor degree in law enforcement and corrections at Penn State University.

He is married to the former Irene P. Kuzniar, of DuBois, Clearfield County, Pennsylvania. They have one son.

Evan's vacancy at Area V, Greensburg, was filled with the promotion and transfer of Major Homer L. Redd. Replacing Chylak at the Academy was newly-promoted Captain John R. Dalinsky.

President Ford, on September 29, signed into law the Public Safety Officers Benefits Act of 1976, allowing the payment of $50,000 to survivors of a police officer who dies as the "direct and proximate result of a personal injury sustained in the line of duty." This action updated a measure signed by the late President Lyndon B. Johnson, which provided for the payment of $50,000 to survivors only if the police officer was killed while enforcing a federal law. A good deal of credit for the federal enactments is due John J. Harrington, past president of the FOP national lodge.

An historic event took place at the Academy on October 9 as the State Police auctioned off twenty of its forty-five horses. No longer a mainstay in patrolling after the 1920s, the horses were reserved mainly for strike duty, in which they rendered incomparable service, and for exhibitions.

The State Police in the 1920s engaged in intertroop competition in horsemanship and marksmanship as a morale building exercise. These annual contests, drawing considerable public interest, blossomed into an annual field exhibition that toured the state. The first "rodeo," as the exhibition was later popularly known, was held at Harrisburg in 1921. This State Police field presentation was continued for more than half a century until 1974. The last in this long series of rodeos was held at Latrobe on August 20, 1974. It was little realized then by State Police officials that the finale at Latrobe would bring down the curtain for all times. In 1975, Barger notified his field forces that because of budgetary limitations the rodeo would not be held. A similar message followed in 1976. The rodeo—a tradition—fell victim to a serious shortage of both funds and manpower, and passed from the scene.

At the auction sale, James D. Cox, State Police public information officer, announced that the sale did not mean the end of horses in the State Police: he stated that twenty-five horses would be retained to meet commitments for searches, parades, ceremonies, and emergencies. Nonetheless, bidders at the auction could not help but feel saddened as stable after stable was emptied.

The State Police, in late October, announced twenty-five promotions. The order, covering the advancement of nineteen troopers to corporal, included only one black. Community Legal Services counsels Jermaine Ingram and Harold Goodman, however, secured a temporary restraining order from Judge Clifford Green, in federal court, and asked for a modification of the Bolden consent decree. The State Police was accused of effecting "a freeze" during the two years since the decree was signed. On November 29, Green modified the consent decree by ordering promotions of blacks from the top half of the eligibility list instead of the top one-third called for by the 1974 decree. He also upped the ratio of minority cadets to nonminority cadets from 1:2 to 1:1. Barger sought approval from Attorney General Kane to appeal Green's ruling. In late December, however, Kane refused to go along with Barger's request. Kane's action was unhappily noted by Barger at a news conference. It was expected that the FOP would file an appeal, and, if necessary, go to the U. S. Supreme Court to contest what is alleged to be reverse discrimination.

Before the year's end, Lieutenant James Sagans, crime lab director at Harrisburg, was promoted to captain. He was the only man to be promoted from the October list. It was felt that Barger would reconsider the other promotions in keeping with the modified consent decree. Needless to report, the entire issue had shot State Police morale to pieces. Observers maintained it had never been worse.

A supervisory change in the Bureau of Patrol in October saw the retirement of Captain Albert Marchinetti, 60, after thirty-six years of service. Replacing Marchinetti as assistant director of the bureau was Captain Frank Micolucci.

Of principal interest to political observers on the Pennsylvania scene were the general elections, as the Democrats gained a stronger hold on their position at the capitol. The Democrats won at least 118 seats in the House; the Republicans managed to hang on to 84. One seat remained contested. In the Senate, the Democrats scored an edge of 29–19, with 2 seats to be filled by special elections. This was only the second time since the turn of the century that the Republican count in the Senate dropped below 20 seats. And for the first time in memory, Allegheny County was without a GOP senator. The complement of Democratic politicos in the 1977 legislature rose to an unprecedented high of 147. Among the few new Republican senators to be seated was former House member George W. Gekas. It will be remembered that Gekas was an outspoken critic of Barger's policies during the commissioner's first years in office.

As an aside, Michael Cassidy, 21, became the youngest member of the House in that chamber's history. Cassidy, a Penn State University political science major, defeated veteran incumbent W. William Wilt (R-Blair) for the Eightieth Legislative District seat.

When the general assembly convened for its 161st regular session on January 4, 1977, Herbert Fineman was elected to an unprecedented fourth term as House Speaker; Martin L. Murray was reelected as president pro tempore of the Senate. The results of both elections were predictable.

On the national scoreboard, Mr. Gerald R. Ford, who became Vice President and President without having been elected to either office, was denied a four-year term on his own. Defeating President Ford in a close race was Democrat Jimmy Carter, a peanut farmer and former governor of Georgia.

On November 26, Shapp signed an appropriation bill supporting the payment of benefits to disabled troopers and survivors of those who die from nonservice-connected circumstances. Although these benefits were awarded under an earlier FOP contract, payments could not be made until Shapp approved the money bill which the legislators delayed passing.

The state superior court on December 6 heard arguments in which attorneys for Barger, Wellendorf, and Buchinsky asked that the Dauphin County indictments against the three be dismissed. Supporting the indictments was Dauphin County Chief Deputy District Attorney Edwin W. Frese, Jr. Until the superior court published its findings, the case against the three remained uncertain.

During the weeks of September and October, contract negotiations between the FOP and governor's office bogged down; it was necessary to turn matters over to an arbitration panel once again. Serving on the three-member panel this time, were John J. Harrington, FOP representative; attorney Thomas H. Lane, Commonwealth representative; and Temple University professor Joseph Loewenberg, neutral arbitrator and chairman. The panel, in December, after hearing arguments, signed a contract awarding troopers with a "near-record" increase in salary and benefits valued at approximately $6.6 million. The new contract became effective July 1, 1977.

In December, two top posts were vacated by the retirements of Major Fagnani, 58, and Major Kwiatek, 51. Filling Kwiatek's vacancy as director of Technical Services was Captain Nicholas G. Dellarciprete, who was transferred from Personnel and promoted to major. Captain Earl P. Wright, who was transferred from his troop command at Butler and promoted to major, replaced Fagnani as commander of Area IV at Hollidaysburg. Lieutenant James O'Donnell was promoted to captain and designated assistant personnel director; he replaced Dellarciprete.

Other important legislative actions during 1976 included the passage of Act 30 (HB-749) April 7, amending the Crimes Code to permit police departments to record certain incoming telephone calls; Act 81 (HB-1817) June 17, enacting a new Motor Vehicle Code with sweeping changes in the laws for the motoring public in Pennsylvania; Act 254 (HB-1945) November 23, amending the Lethal Weapons Training Act of 1974; and Act 227 (SB-21) November 8, amending the Administrative Code and requiring a simple majority of twenty-six votes in the Senate to confirm the State Police commissioner (and others) instead of a two-thirds vote.

Barger, in January, 1977, approved a list of twenty-six promotions, his first under the modified consent decree. Included in this group were six minority members—five black and one Hispanic. The FOP secured from the U. S. Third Circuit Court of Appeals an injunction blocking the promotions just short of their effective date.

At Bedford, Pennsylvania, on January 16, delegates of the State Police FOP lodges met and voted to pursue their case against reverse discrimination by raising sufficient funds and retaining a prestigious law firm to take the issue to the U. S. Supreme Court. The Washington law firm of William P. Rodgers, a former U. S. attorney general and secretary of state, was engaged. From every indication, the plan of the FOP to fight preferential promotions of minority members to satisfy a racial balance in State Police positions had the backing of Barger. Barger's attendance at the Bedford conference drew flak from Rep. Joel Johnson (D-Philadelphia) who demanded that Governor Shapp dismiss the commissioner for his "racist position." One week later, the U. S. Third Circuit Court of Appeals, refusing to act on the modified consent decree, lifted its ban on the promotions.

As Barger continued his tenure into 1977, he became the first commissioner since Wilhelm to serve more than four years: all others saw their appointments end with four years or fewer. His tenure, however, was to enter a fifth year for a short life. The unsettled indictment, hanging over his head like the sword of Damocles, and his obvious discordancy with Shapp and Kane on the minority issue gave rise to rumors once again that Barger might not be kept on much longer.

On January 18, just two days following the FOP conference at Bedford, which Barger attended, the commissioner submitted his resignation to Shapp, citing "personal considerations" for quitting. The resignation, however, was not publicly disclosed. Shortly after January 18, Major Paul J. Chylak, the department's new executive officer, was reportedly summoned to the governor's office. His appearance there started the State Police grapevine drums to beating news afresh that Barger's end was near and that Chylak would be his successor. This time, however, the rumors were substantive: Shapp confirmed them on February 10 with his announcement of Barger's resignation and the appointment of Chylak to replace him.

The following teletype message was dispatched on February 10 to all State Police installations by Deputy Commissioner Evan:

> The following is the text of the news release issued today by the governor's press office: Quote: Governor Milton J. Shapp today accepted with deep regret the resignation of Colonel James Barger as Commissioner of the Pennsylvania State Police effective midnight, February 14, 1977. The Governor also announced the appointment of Major Paul J. Chylak as acting Commissioner of the State Police. Shapp will submit Chylak's name to the state Senate for confirmation as Commissioner. Unqoute. In his letter of resignation dated January 18, 1977, Colonel Barger cited personal considerations as the reason for his departure. Governor Shapp accepted the resignation with regret and extended best wishes to Colonel Barger.

No matter how carefully the message was worded to indicate a voluntary departure, members of the State Police have not been convinced that Barger willingly left behind his powerful $40,000-a-year post. An unusual arrangement approved by the governor made his

voluntary resignation less convincing: although the commissioner relinquished his post as of midnight, February 14, his resignation from
State Police service was delayed until midnight, February 16, the end
of a pay period. During those remaining two days, Barger was permitted to hang on with the rank of major in order to retire with benefits
allowed enlisted men, which, reportedly, would not have accrued to
him as an ex-cabinet member. According to a story carried by *The
Guide*, a Harrisburg area news weekly, Barger's "two-step" retirement arrangement was slated to net him $6,365 in pay for unused vaca-
tion and sick days.

There are some observations that can be offered as a wrapping for
the Barger years in office. Unlike his predecessors, Barger had more
often seen his disciplinary decisions contested in the courts and
reversed in favor of the appellants. Decision reversals, with or without
court involvement, marked his administration. Also, it was judged by
many members of the department that Barger had outdone former
Commissioner McKetta with respect to favoring men from the western
Pennsylvania troops for promotions. Criticism stemmed, as it might be
expected, from personnel in the central and eastern troops. One
eastern troop lieutenant was heard to ask, "How come all the State
Police brains are out west?" Because of strong feelings on this subject,
the western troops were jocularly referred to as "Barger's Western
ROTC." Spoken in jest or not, the monicker was indicative of lowering
morale at least among those who felt left out.

Barger's tenure by comparison with many of his predecessors'
lacked an array of innovative programs that he could label as his own.
It is difficult to evaluate how much in appropriations, if any, was lost to
him and the State Police because of his many conflicts with the
members of the general assembly; in any case, tighter budgets and rising operational costs unquestionably had some restraining effect upon
the number of innovations that could be afforded.

Barger took with him into retirement an indictment that could
heavily influence his future if a trial and conviction follow.

A review of the problem situations in which commissioners have
found themselves might easily lead one to the conclusion that Barger's,
by far, were the most controversial. Whatever he did, whatever he was
involved in, Barger, indeed gave politicians and correspondents much
to speak of and write about. With little risk of dissent, it can be stated
that Barger, regardless of how situations came about, did not have the
pleasure of many problemless moments. His survival through those
troublous years at the helm was a political wonderment. Barger has
taken a security post with the Oxford Development Company of
Monroeville, Allegheny County. The firm operates shopping malls in a
number of states.

CHAPTER XXII

Colonel Paul J. Chylak

1977–

On February 10, 1977, Governor Milton J. Shapp appointed Major Paul J. Chylak as State Police commissioner to fill the vacancy brought about by Barger's resignation. Chylak was Shapp's third appointment to that cabinet post: in 1971, he named Rocco P. Urella, whose vacancy was filled on January 2, 1973, by Barger's appointment.

Chylak is also the second State Police commissioner to come from Lackawanna County. Adams, in 1905, enlisted from Scranton; he later became constabulary superintendent and State Police commissioner. Former Commissioner Frank G. McCartney, a native of Coaldale, Schuylkill County, was also a representative of the Pennsylvania anthracite coal region. It is fitting in many ways that three commissioners should come from this region which has given the State Police more of its manpower than any one other section of the commonwealth. The coal region has truly been the birthplace of troopers.

Chylak was sworn in by Shapp as acting commissioner in a brief ceremony held in the governor's reception room on February 15. Chylak's wife and two children witnessed the ceremony. Also present was Major Barger. Shapp immediately submitted Chylak's name to the Senate for confirmation. It was expected that the senators would act favorably on his confirmation before the month was up.

Chylak, at 45, is not the youngest State Police commissioner. John C. Groome, in 1905, was 43; George F. Lumb, acting superintendent from 1917 to 1919, was 43; E. Wilson Purdy, in 1963, was 43; and Lynn

G. Adams, in 1920, was 41 and the youngest of all department heads. The oldest to be sworn into office was Cecil M. Wilhelm. In 1943, he was appointed commissioner at the ripe age of 62.

As he assumed top command of the renowned police department, Chylak admitted to the many problems that faced him. In this regard, he unquestionably has the good wishes of his officers and men who are anxious to see the turbulence of recent years terminated.

Chylak, a native of Olyphant, Lackawanna County, was born on May 14, 1931. He was one of two children born to Paul Joseph Chylak and Julia Diachun Chylak. His father was also a native of Olyphant; his mother was born at Winnepeg, Manitoba, Canada.

Chylak attended the Olyphant public schools and graduated from Olyphant High School in 1949, where he was an honor student, president of his senior class, and a varsity basketball star. Chylak was also considered an excellent pop vocalist. In his spare time, he sang with local dance bands that toured Pennsylvania's northeast counties. After graduation, he studied voice at the Scranton Conservatory of Music, and became an apprentice barber in his home community.

In August, 1949, he joined the U. S. Army, and remained in military uniform until December, 1952. He served with the Corps of Engineers in the Pacific theatre of operations.

Upon his return home from military service, Chylak decided on a college career. Although he was determined to get a college education under his belt, he was not sure of the studies he would subscribe to in preparation for after-college employment. It was during this period of decision that Chylak met Trooper Edward "Red" Walker of the local Dunmore barracks. Walker, a seasoned trooper, considered Chylak a promising recruit and never overlooked a chance to convince his young friend that a fulfilling career could be found with the State Police. Walker's persuasiveness was not to be denied.

Chylak enlisted with the Pennsylvania State Police on July 1, 1953. Upon graduation from the Academy, he was assigned to the Turnpike troop. He was promoted to corporal in 1960. Chylak was one of three men picked by Commissioner Purdy to attend the Northwestern University Traffic Institute (NUTI) in September, 1964, where he earned top grades. Upon graduation from NUTI in June, 1965, Chylak was transferred to the Academy as an instructor and promoted to sergeant. He remained there until 1967, when he was moved to the Planning and Research Division at headquarters.

In 1969, Chylak was returned to the Academy to supervise the program development unit. A promotion to lieutenant in 1970 placed him in command of the Academy's training section. In September,

Colonel Paul J. Chylak (Courtesy of Pennsylvania State Police)

1973, he was promoted to captain and named director of the Academy's training division, and later given charge of the department's regional training program—a mandatory training system for municipal police officers. In July, 1976, Chylak underwent a twelve-week course of training at the FBI National Academy, where he also scored top grades. He has accumulated college credits at Penn State

University, Millersville State College, Northwestern University, and University of Virginia.

Chylak attends St. Joan of Arc Catholic Church at Hershey. He is a member of the church choir, Pennsylvania Chiefs of Police Association, American Legion, Fraternal Order of Police, Northwestern University Traffic Institute Alumni Association, and FBI National Academy Associates.

He is married to the former Florence Balchunas of Shamokin, Pennsylvania. Mrs. Chylak, a registered nurse, is a graduate of the Polyclinic Hospital School of Nursing at Harrisburg. It was during her training days at Polyclinic Hospital that she met Chylak, then a young trooper. Commissioner and Mrs. Chylak reside at Hershey; they have a daughter, Lorie Ann, and a son, Gary Paul.

Testifying before the House Appropriations Committee on March 2, Chylak defended the department's record budget request for $137.8 million for the 1977–78 fiscal year. The request was $17 million more than the spending figure for the 1976–77 fiscal period. He lamented the fact that the authorized State Police complement was already short 300 men at a time when departmental studies showed a need for 700 more men to meet demands for service. Chylak admitted that State Police morale "has been affected by federal court rulings requiring promotional preference for minority members."

In March, Chylak promoted Sergeant Joseph A. Robyak, Bureau of Research and Development at headquarters, to lieutenant, and transferred five majors: Major Roy L. Titler was moved from the Bureau of Patrol to Area II, Wyoming; Major Bernard G. Stanalonis, Area III, filled Titler's vacancy; Major Earl P. Wright, Area IV, was sent to Area VI, Butler; Major Patrick J. Hankinson, Area II, went to Area IV, Hollidaysburg; and Major Charles J. Buchinsky, Area VI, moved to Area III, at Harrisburg. In view of the circumstances underlying each of the transfers, the moves were not typical of the changes that soon followed Barger's appointment in 1973.

After a month's delay, the Senate unanimously confirmed Chylak's appointment on March 14. Chylak's salary as commissioner was set at $41,250.

Taking to heart the seriousness of lowering morale among the field forces, Chylak embarked on a five-week tour of all troops in a move to turn the tide. Admittedly lacking a bag of tricks from which to draw swift solutions to nagging problems, he could promise his officers and men nothing more than a sincere approach to possible solutions. Chylak's gentleness and personal diplomacy may well calm the rough waters he inherited until disturbing issues are settled.

On March 31, Shapp appointed Captain Benjamin R. Jones acting director of the state's Drug Law Enforcement agency to fill a vacancy brought on by the departure of Joseph H. Reiter, the agency's former director. It was the second time in the past decade that a governor had assigned a State Police brass hat to another state agency. Governor Shafer had previously assigned Major Arthur W. Shulenberger to the State Crime Commission as assistant director.

Chylak did not appoint a replacement for Jones to direct the Records-Identification Division operations; thus that division, the largest in the department, finds itself without an on-the-spot director. This situation may well indicate Chylak's intention to return Jones to his departmental post as soon as rumored organizational changes in the state's drug enforcement program are completed.

William F. Hoffman, in April, retired as director of the Transportation Division. Chylak named Francis E. Wolfe, a Transportation Division career employee, to succeed Hoffman. Wolfe had been the division's assistant director.

Because of the often repeated controversy stemming from the appointment of commissioners, it was not surprising to see measures concerning the appointment procedure introduced in the legislature. In April, Republican House and Senate leaders sponsored bills calling for a fixed four-year term for the commissioner—a term that would not run concurrent with the governor's. Intended to remove the commissioner from political control, the bills provide that the commissioner cannot be dismissed except for misfeasance in office or neglect of duty. According to the bills, a governor would make his appointment from three names submitted to him by an eight-member independent committee. Both bills, however, are given little or no chance of passage.

The department, in May, paused to honor an old-timer. Death claimed Henry B. Hilton, 92, on May 10 at Punxsutawney. Hilton enlisted with the state constabulary on February 1, 1906, and served until December, 1913. After eight years as a state game protector, Hilton was appointed Punxsutawney police chief—a position he held for twenty-nine years. At the time of his death, he was not only the oldest former member of the constabulary but also Pennsylvania's oldest retired police chief.

Chylak made a major change in the department's command structure in May when he reinstituted the chief of staff post. During his previous service years at headquarters, the commissioner had the opportunity to make his own evaluations of that post and undoubtedly accepted it as essential to efficient State Police management as did Commissioners Purdy, Rittelmann, McKetta and Urella. Barger was at odds with his predecessors on this subject and did away with that position during his administration.

Appointed the department's fourth chief of staff was Major Leonard T. Koper. He was promoted to lieutenant colonel—a rank held by his predecessors. Koper was formerly director of the Research and Development Bureau. His vacancy was filled by the transfer of Major Nicholas G. Dellarciprete from the Bureau of Technical Services. Replacing Dellarciprete was newly-promoted Major John H. Angell, former commander at Troop B, Washington. Angell's vacancy at Washington was filled with the transfer of Captain Keith F. McCully from the Information Systems Division. Captain Russell C. Rickert was moved from Research and Development to the Information Systems Division. Lieutenant Warren L. Shaffer was promoted to captain and replaced Rickert.

It is believed that Koper and Dellarciprete, both NUTI graduates and capable administrators, will be Chylak's principal advisers.

Topping the political events to occur during Chylak's young administration were two involving the governor and the House speaker. In May, the Federal Election Commission (FEC), probing the distribution of federal campaign funds to Shapp in 1976, uncovered irregularities and ordered the repayment of almost $300,000. Shapp, who in 1976 ran for President "only to be woefully humiliated in the primaries," as the *Sunday Patriot-News* (Harrisburg) put it editorially, was not personally accused by FEC officials of wrongdoing. Shapp agreed to comply with the FEC repayment order. During the same eventful month of May, House Speaker Herbert Fineman, serving an unprecedented fourth term as speaker, was found guilty in federal court on two charges of obstructing justice in a federal investigation of medical school admissions. Fineman resigned his powerful post on May 23.

Elected unanimously by House members to fill Fineman's vacancy was Majority Leader K. Leroy Irvis, 57, a Pittsburgh Democrat. Irvis became the first black in Pennsylvania history to preside over the House chamber. Rep. James J. Manderino (D-Westmoreland), 45, was chosen to succeed Irvis as majority leader.

On June 29, the state superior court ruled in a longstanding Dauphin County case involving Colonel James D. Barger, Lt. Colonel Roy O. Wellendorf and Major Charles J. Buchinsky. The trio, in an appeal to the superior court last December, claimed that Dauphin County authorities had improperly convened an investigating grand jury which recommended charges. The court's decision struck down the petition for the dismissal of those charges, and cleared the way for the trial of the three officers—a trial that will set a precedent in State Police history. Both Barger and Wellendorf have retired from the State Police; Buchinsky presently commands Area III at Harrisburg.)

At mid-1977, Chylak's administration is supported by the following list of top figures at headquarters and in the field:

> Deputy Commissioner—Lt. Colonel George Evan
> Chief of Staff—Lt. Colonel Leonard T. Koper

BUREAU OF PATROL—Major Bernard G. Stanalonis
> Captain Frank Micolucci, Patrol Services Division
> Captain Nicholas J. Pauley, Aviation Division
> Lieutenant David G. Miller, Safety Services Division

BUREAU OF CRIMINAL INVESTIGATION—Major William N. Grooms
> Captain James J. Regan, General Criminal Investigation Division
> Captain Robert G. Shuck, Organized Crime Division
> Captain Russell E. Anderson, Drug Law Enforcement Division
>> Lieutenant Kenneth W. Bender
> Captain Oliver A. Smith, Fire Marshal Division

BUREAU OF RESEARCH AND DEVELOPMENT—Major Nicholas G. Dellarciprete
> Captain Warren L. Shaffer, Planning Division
> Lieutenant Joseph A. Robyak, Programming Division
> Lieutenant Edward J. Sabol, Statistical Division

BUREAU OF TECHNICAL SERVICES—Major John H. Angell
> Captain Benjamin R. Jones, Records and Identification Division
>> Lieutenant Harry A. Krytzer
> Captain Russell C. Rickert, Information Systems Division
> Captain James Sagans, Laboratory Division
> Mr. Robert I. Kimmel, Communications Division

BUREAU OF STAFF SERVICES—Mr. Gerald S. Patterson
> Lieutenant Raymond M. Rish, Engineering Section
> Mr. Robert J. Zinsky, Fiscal Division
> Mr. Edward J. Boyle, Maintenance and Supply Division
> Mr. Francis E. Wolfe, Transportation Division

BUREAU OF PERSONNEL—Major Jay C. Hileman
> Captain James R. O'Donnell, Personnel Management Division
> Captain John F. Duignan, Evaluation and Standards Division
>> Lieutenant Robert E. McElroy
> Lieutenant Thomas M. Madden, Recruitment and Development Division

BUREAU OF COMMUNITY SERVICES—Major Michael Donahoe
> Captain Salvador L. Rodriguez, Community Relations Division

PUBLIC INFORMATION OFFICE—Mr. James D. Cox
    Mr. Thomas C. Lyon
COMPTROLLER'S OFFICE—Mr. William F. Braucher
    Mr. Robert A. Miller
LEGISLATIVE LIAISON—Captain Harold G. Selecky
AREA V—Major Homer L. Redd (Greensburg)
    Troop A, Greensburg—Captain Blair E. Swistock
        Mary L. Kurth, Troop Office Manager
        Lieutenant Robert D. Baughman
        Lieutenant James W. Crouse, Jr.
        Lieutenant Dominic C. Fanelli
        Lieutenant Andrew J. Petyak
        Lieutenant Glenn A. Walp
    Troop B, Washington—Captain Keith F. McCully
        Marjory J. Angus, Troop Office Manager
        Lieutenant Joseph W. Barr
        Lieutenant Francis X. Carroll
        Lieutenant Stanley J. Oleski
        Lieutenant William J. Regan
        Lieutenant James A. Rendar
        Lieutenant Marino T. Zarroli
AREA VI—Major Earl P. Wright (Butler)
    Troop C, Punxsutawney—Captain Michael Honkus
        Thomas P. Parise, Troop Office Manager
        Lieutenant Elmer A. Barkay
        Lieutenant Thomas L. Cuff
        Lieutenant Harry S. Ellenberger
        Lieutenant Matthew E. Hunt
        Lieutenant Leslie E. Stilwell
    Troop D, Butler—Captain Robert E. Palladino
        Gary G. Zimmer, Troop Office Manager
        Lieutenant George Babics
        Lieutenant Paul E. Faidley
        Lieutenant Arnold Fonseca
        Lieutenant Joseph A. Sasala
        Lieutenant Francis W. Walton
    Troop E, Erie—Captain Lewis K. Johnson
        Salvatore R. Conti, Troop Office Manager
        Lieutenant Robert B. Gorman
        Lieutenant Charles T. Klodell
        Lieutenant George J. Martin
        Lieutenant Lewis P. Penman
        Lieutenant Herbert L. Stouffer

AREA IV—Major Patrick J. Hankinson (Hollidaysburg)
    Troop F, Montoursville—Captain David C. Martin
        Salvadore Bones, Troop Office Manager
        Lieutenant Charles J. Draus
        Lieutenant Stephen M. Luchansky
        Lieutenant William A. McGlynn
    Troop G, Hollidaysburg—Captain Earl O. Bergstrom
        Joseph F. Heininger, Troop Office Manager
        Lieutenant Vincent Fiorani
        Lieutenant Robert F. Gicking
        Lieutenant Willard E. Heberling
        Lieutenant Andrew S. Mazak
        Lieutenant Raymond J. Mitarnowski
        Lieutenant Charlie M. Wheeler
AREA III—Major Charles J. Buchinsky (Harrisburg)
    Troop H, Harrisburg—Captain Joseph I. C. Everly
        Sarah H. Miller, Troop Office Manager
        Lieutenant Herman J. Faiola
        Lieutenant Frank H. Lewski
        Lieutenant Francis McGann
        Lieutenant Anthony W. Rossi
        Lieutenant Edwin V. Secott
    Troop J, Lancaster—Captain Wayne E. Kerr
        Janet M. Groff, Troop Office Manager
        Lieutenant Frank W. Lesch
        Lieutenant Michael R. Gavitt
        Lieutenant James L. McCann
        Lieutenant Joseph P. Skapik
        Lieutenant Richard M. Weimer
AREA I—Major Stanley B. Kramer (Reading)
    Troop K, Philadelphia—Captain Alexander Balnis
        Bernadette H. Gerhard, Troop Office Manager
        Lieutenant Paul Fedock
        Lieutenant John J. Flannery
        Lieutenant Douglas L. Greenfield
        Lieutenant John J. McKenna
        Lieutenant Joseph P. Zuber
    Troop L, Reading—Captain Joseph M. Kane
        Raymond A. Folk, Troop Office Manager
        Lieutenant Donald W. Holloway
        Lieutenant Stanley J. Pijar
        Lieutenant Harley N. Smith
        Lieutenant Jay R. Zeigler

Troop M, Bethlehem—Captain William J. Walker
Paul F. Hammel, Troop Office Manager
Lieutenant Angelo J. Carcaci
Lieutenant Gerardo N. Catina
Lieutenant Paul S. Fehr
Lieutenant Edward Munchberg
AREA II—Major Roy L. Titler (Wyoming)
Troop N, Hazleton—Captain John J. Turissini
John H.Culp, Troop Office Manager
Lieutenant Joseph S. Kunowski
Lieutenant Roman J. Pawloski
Lieutenant Leon F. Salada
Troop P, Wyoming—Captain Lawrence J. O'Donnell
Martin A. Connors, Troop Office Manager
Lieutenant Edward J. Bloomer
Lieutenant Donald D. Dorris
Lieutenant Stephen M. Haschak
Lieutenant Edward J. Pucylowski
Troop R, Dunmore—Captain Nicholas Kordilla
Sylvia A. Estock, Troop Office Manager
Lieutenant Francis J. Anzelmi
Lieutenant Donald F. McGlynn
Lieutenant Charles Zinich
AREA VII—Major Sidney C. Deyo, Jr. (Highspire)
Troop S, Milesburg—Captain William E. Kimmel
Lee S. Thomas, Troop Office Manager
Lieutenant Thomas R. Berryhill
Lieutenant Ronald J. Dixon
Lieutenant Peter Matweecha
Lieutenant Thomas P. Ziemba
Troop T, Highspire—Captain Newton C. Robbins
John R. Felix, Troop Office Manager
Lieutenant Otto J. Binker
Lieutenant James J. Polichicchio
Lieutenant Edward H. Shevenock
Lieutenant LeRoy R. Strickler
ACADEMY—Major Leon D. Leiter
Wade S. Kehler, Troop Office Manager
Captain Harold G. Rice, Academy Training Division
Captain John R. Dalinsky, Regional Training Division
Lieutenant Donald W. Mahoney, Southwestern Training Center
Lieutenant Michael A. Sabol, Northwestern Training Center

Lieutenant Anthony J. Shubzda, Southeastern Training Center
Lieutenant Tony Ursi, Northeastern Training Center
Lieutenant Emil Suchy, Staff Services Division
Robert P. Dutlinger, M. D., Medical Officer

COMPLEMENT OF FILLED POSITIONS BY RANK
July, 1977

Colonel	1
Lt. Colonel	2
Major	14
Captain	33
Lieutenant	89
Sergeant	273
Corporal	553
Trooper	2,879
Total Filled Positions	3,844

The department's legal complement with the addition of the commissioner and deputy commissioner is set at 4,175 officers and men. With only 3,844 of these positions filled, there are 331 vacancies to which appointments could be made—all things being favorable to such action. This, however, is not the case; conceivably, the situation will get much worse before it gets better.

Meanwhile, construction of the new headquarters building at Harrisburg continues slightly ahead of schedule. The pleasure of occupying the impressive structure as commissioner will go to Chylak. The

Architect's drawing of new Pennsylvania State Police headquarters building (Courtesy of Pennsylvania State Police)

new facility, the first of its kind in State Police history is expected to be completed and occupied in early 1978. That event will be a memorable one for Chylak and all members of the Pennsylvania State Police Force.

Accompanying the occupants of the new building will be the current crop of problems and issues that plague the State Police. The department, however, has come through hard times before with flying colors; there is reason to believe that it will do so again. The "noble experiment of 1905" shall not relinquish its status as law enforcement's standard-bearer in the United States.

CHAPTER XXIII

State Police Civic Association

Before the state constabulary was one year old, two troopers were killed in the line of duty. Death and serious injuries sustained in the performance of rigorous duties were to become a way of life for the members of this young, determined organization. Surviving family members of deceased troopers were woefully unprepared to learn that the State Police was in no position financially to assume payments for funeral and burial expenses for its dead; families and State Police comrades did the best they could under the circumstances. In the absence of funds specifically provided by the legislature for medical care or burial, Superintendent John C. Groome and his four troop commanders improvised troop committees supported by personal funds—a kind of pass-the hat situation. Although no troopers were killed in the line of duty from 1910 through 1917, serious injuries were experienced, and this small band of troopers was moved to see that the best medical care possible was given to its sick and injured members. Medical and burial expenses were met through troop associations.

The State Workmen's Compensation system came into being January 1, 1916, and with its arrival on the scene the plight of the injured and the survivors of deceased troopers was mitigated—not eliminated.

In 1917, acting superintendent George F. Lumb turned to the attorney general for a favorable ruling regarding the use of contingent appropriations for medical and burial expenses. Attorney General Francis S. Brown disappointingly ruled that "other necessary expenses" stipulated in appropriations did not apply to medical and funeral expenses. Lumb complained to Governor Martin G. Brumbaugh, which was nothing more than a futile exercise.

Later in 1917, constabulary officials prepared a *History of the Department of State Police,* and solicited advertisement. The 250-page publication raised money in support of the troop associations. Not completely satisfied with decentralized administration, Lumb ordered his troop commanders to Harrisburg to form a State Police Civic Association (SPCA) to look after the special needs of his officers and men. Appointed to the first board of directors were Captains Leon S. Pitcher, Wilson C. Price, Charles Jacobs and William Marsh. According to Lumb's planning, the directors would be guided by the troop associations.

These were the first bylaws drawn up:

1. This organization shall be known as the State Police Civic Association.

2. All officers, enlisted men and others employed under the act creating the Department of State Police or amendments thereto shall be members of this Association.

3. The officers of this Association shall be a President and Vice President who shall also be Trustees, four Directors and a Secretary who shall also be Treasurer.

4. The Superintendent of State Police, or Acting Superintendent in the absence of the Superintendent from the Commonwealth, and the Deputy Superintendent of State Police shall be ex officio President and Vice President respectively. The Chief Clerk of the Department of State Police shall be ex officio Secretary-Treasurer and shall keep the books and accounts of the Association.

5. The four Captains commanding troops of State Police shall be ex officio Directors of this Association.

6. Three Directors and one Trustee shall constitute a quorum to do business providing that the Directors meeting shall be only at the call of the President or Vice President, or by at least three Directors.

7. Dividends to Troop Civic Associations and benefits to be paid to disabled members are the proper uses to which the funds of the Association may be applied by the Directors but other disbursements may be made at their discretion.

8. All disbursements and distributions of funds must be submitted to the Directors for approval.

9. The purpose of this Association being to render financial assistance or benefits to members of the State Police Force or their dependents, no funds shall be used for any other purpose except proper investments made in the name of

the State Police Civic Association as the Directors may order and the payment of bills.

10. All bills shall be submitted to the Directors for approval and paid when so approved by check signed by the Treasurer and one Trustee.

11. All funds of the Association shall be kept on deposit, in such bank or trust company as the Directors may order, in the city of Harrisburg.

12. An annual statement of receipts and expenditures shall be furnished each Trustee, Director and each Troop Civic Association on the first day of each year commencing January 1, 1919.

13. The Trustees and Secretary-Treasurer shall give a bond in the sum of two thousand dollars each for the proper and faithful performance of their duties. The premium for such bond to be paid for out of the funds of the Association.

14. These By Laws may be amended by a majority vote of the Directors after submitting the proposed amendment to the Troop Civic Associations at least thirty days before the meeting at which the amendment is to be considered.

15. The rejection of the amendement by more than two Troops shall be final.

16. The President and Secretary-Treasurer shall be present at meetings whenever possible but not vote at meetings of the Directors.

17. A copy of these By Laws be furnished each Troop Civic Association.

From Superintendent Groome, then on military leave, the association received shares in Diamond Match Company, West Texas Sulphur Company, Union Bag and Paper Company, Republic Iron and Steel Company, in addition to property deeds and Second Liberty Bonds—all valued at about $63,000. By February, 1918, bank deposits amounted to $5,614.24.

In June, the directors awarded $100 to each of the survivors of Privates Andrew Czap and John F. Dargus who were killed in the line of duty. The sum of $500 was given to each troop association for barracks furnishings, athletic equipment, books and magazines. At a meeting in August, another $500 was distributed to each troop, and a $200 reward was posted for the capture of Walter Richardson, the fugitive-slayer of Dargus. The latter months of 1918 were taken up with the approval of burial expenses for the men who died during the Spanish flu epidemic.

It was not until Lumb issued his General Order 38, dated October 16, 1918, that the State Police Civic Association was officially referred to in a headquarters directive. The order dealt with the trooper deaths during the Spanish flu epidemic. It stated that troop commanders, serving as directors of the association, would be summoned to consider action in behalf of dependents of the deceased.

When the fifth troop, Troop E, was formed at Harrisburg (Lancaster) in 1919, it received from the civic association the sum of $1,000. In 1919, the SPCA directors also set a limit of $125 for burial expenses.

In January, 1920, a committee was appointed to study a pension plan. Committee members were C. M. Wilhelm, Herbert Smith and Walter Fisher. Fisher, a civilian, was SPCA secretary-treasurer. On March 11, the committee proposed bylaws calling for monthly dues of $1.00 for privates; $1.10 for corporals; $1.20 for sergeants; $1.30 for lieutenants; $1.50 for captains; and $2.00 for anyone drawing more than $3,000-a-year salary. Proposed were pensions for disability after ten years of service and for retirement after fifteen years. The retirement pension was to be based on the average pay for the five years preceding retirement (.025 x average pay x years and quarters of service). A limit was placed on average earnings at $3,000 and service at twenty years. Civilian employees were to be eligible for membership in the pension system. The proposed plan was submitted to the attorney general for legal review.

In 1920, committees were also formed to review bylaws amendments, to invest available funds in Liberty Bonds, and to establish a Field Day program. The latter was to become more familiarly known as the State Police rodeo.

Major changes in 1921 saw the board of directors increased to seven by the addition of representatives of the Bureaus of Criminal Identification and Fire Protection, and the clerical division. The board decided to retain legal counsel, and revise the bylaws to permit the purchase of artificial limbs for men injured in the line of duty. A permanent disability pension plan for men injured in the line of duty was approved, allowing monthly payments of $10 for two years of service, $12 for three years, $15 for four years, $18 for five years, $22 for five to ten years, and $25 for ten years to fifteen years. Bylaws were also amended to fix fifteen-year pensions at one-half of five-year average earnings preceding retirement. Silvus J. Overmiller replaced Fisher as secretary-treasurer. Chosen to handle legal matters was Spencer G. Nauman, a Harrisburg attorney.

Based upon legal advice, the SPCA was incorporated and chartered on March 6, 1922. New bylaws were approved. Elected to the board under the new bylaws were:

President Lynn G. Adams
Vice President William Mair
Secretary-Treasurer S. J. Over-
  miller
C. M. Wilhelm - Fire Bureau
Wilson C. Price - B.C.I. & I.
John R. Price - Clerical Division

Paul Stout - Troop A
William Clark - Troop B
Samuel Gearhart - Troop C
Elmer Leithiser - Troop D
Thomas McLaughlin - Troop E
Herbert Smith - School

The first field meet was held at Harrisburg on October 12, 1921. The annual meets were intended to raise money for the pension fund. The first meet, however, ran into a deficit that was carried over until 1922.

In 1922, the Dauphin Deposit Bank was selected by the board as custodian of the association's securities at a fee of forty cents a thousand.

The association in 1923 moved to sell Katherine Mayo's books, written about the State Police, in troop canteens. The books were to be autographed by Miss Mayo, Superintendent Adams, and the troop commanders. The board also decided to sell State Police rings through the canteens. Guy E. Reichard succeeded Overmiller as secretary-treasurer.

A Pennsylvania State Police Contingent Pension Fund was formed in 1924 to handle book and ring sales for the SPCA.

Effective January 1, 1926, the bylaws were amended to raise dues from a previous rate of 1 percent to 2 percent, and, at the same time, increase pensions at the rate of 1 percent per year of service after fifteen, for example—51 percent for sixteen years, 52 percent for seventeen years, and so on to a maximum of 60 percent for twenty-five years of service. Dues assessments were not applicable to amounts earned in excess of $3,000. The 2 percent rate was destined to remain in effect until 1937.

The bylaws were again amended in 1926 to allow payment to survivors of association members who died after they were eligible for pension. The amount was to equal pension payments had they retired when eligible, but not to exceed $1,000. The SPCA board agreed to accept contributions from business firms and individuals, wanting to aid the pension fund financially.

The 1926 field meet, sponsored by Troop C, raised the sum of $10,009. Troop A, in 1927, came up with a profit of $25,000. In 1928, Troop E did not do as well: it turned over $16,314 to the association.

By 1928, after ten years of existence, the net worth of the association was $170,000. There were twenty-seven pensioners on the rolls, drawing $1,930.84, monthly. Since dues received amounted to only $870 a month, less than half of the amount required to meet pension outlay, it was easily seen that extraordinary income was critical to the pension fund's well-being.

In September, 1930, the bylaws were amended to raise the death benefit payment from a maximum of $1,000 to $2,500. A monthly pension of $147.50 was also approved for Thomas J. McLaughlin who was court-martialled and dismissed by Adams. This case is only mentioned to confirm the association's intention to pay pensions to its eligible members regardless of separation circumstances.

By mid-1933, the pension rolls listed thirty-one with a monthly outlay of $2,437.99. This figure was offset by $1,300 in dues—just a little more than 50 percent of the pension obligation. The pension fund was still far from being self-sustaining; thoughts were shifting to a possible twenty-year requirement for pension instead of fifteen. On February 12, 1934, a bylaws amendment, requiring new SPCA members to serve twenty years for pension rights, was approved. The amendment also included an increase in disability benefits.

The board approved the preparation of a *Criminal Digest*. The book, a compilation of criminal laws and comments, was to be copyrighted and sold through the association's contingent fund. Under the revised title, *Pennsylvania Criminal Law and Criminal Procedure,* the first publication was offered for sale in June, 1934, at $2.00 a copy. The foreword was prepared by former U. S. District Attorney and Deputy Attorney General Louis E. Graham: "To the policeman, constable, and sheriff engaged in active duty it supplies a long felt want in furnishing a quick and instant reference to those criminal laws and rules of criminal practice which he daily encounters in the performance of his duties as a law enforcement official. In preparing and publishing this book, the author has done a real service to every police official in Pennsylvania." Credit for directing the book's preparation is apparently to be given to William Hoffman, director of the BCI & I.

On March 2, 1937, SPCA dues were raised to 3 percent, and the amount allowed for funeral expenses was upped from $125 to $350.

Special board meetings were called in June and September, 1937, to deal with the problems arising from the merger of the State Police and the State Highway Patrol. The Highway Patrol had no comparable organization with which to merge. Board members were determined to preserve the association.

By 1938, it was agreed that applications would be accepted from all members of the Pennsylvania Motor Police. A new board of directors was structured:

> First Squadron—Jacob Mauk
> Second Squadron—Charles C. Keller
> Third Squadron—William A. Clark
> Fourth Squadron—William D. Plummer
> Training School—Thomas F. Martin
> Accounting & Statistical Division—S. J. Overmiller
> BCI & I—William F. Hoffman
> Detective Division—Harry E. McElroy
> Pensioners—Lynn G. Adams

The new board officers were: C. M. Wilhelm, president; Silvus J. Overmiller, 1st vice president; William A. Clark, 2nd vice president, and Guy E. Reichard, secretary-treasurer. Commissioner Percy W. Foote was appointed advisor to the board.

Later in 1938, Guy E. Reichard was elected a board representative for the Quartermaster & Mechanical Division; Ralph D. Gardner was elected to represent the Fire Bureau on the board.

At the close of 1938, twenty years after the association was organized, total investments amounted to $494,550; there was a bank balance of $34,218. Membership totalled 1,344. Monthly receipts from dues and investments amounted to $6,768 compared to a monthly pension outlay of $4,502. For the first time, operations were in the black. The payment of dues by way of payroll deductions was begun April 16, 1938, and the future looked promising. The year 1939 held even greater promise, according to the finance committee's report, "The calendar year of 1939 has passed into history as the most prosperous year in your State Police Civic Association."

By 1942, membership in the SPCA included 94.2 percent of the Motor Police complement. During that year, it was decided that the beneficiary of any SPCA member killed in the armed forces would be paid $500. Dues payments by members in the armed forces were waived. Some doubt was expressed concerning the holding of the annual rodeo during the war years. Although it was expected rodeo income would suffer, the board believed the exhibition was "good for the morale of the men." Later, however, it was decided to cancel the annual affair for the duration of the war.

The board's wartime decisions began to backfire as the number of members in military service by 1945 soared to 329 and the pension rolls swelled to 133. In 1945, a worried board raised the rate of payroll deductions from 3 to 4 percent, effective February 1, and the bylaws were also amended to require men in military service to pay SPCA dues. Plans were made to renew the scheduling of the rodeo in 1946.

By 1946, the pension rolls increased to 164; pensioners drew a monthly figure of $16,625. This amount exceeded income from dues and interest earnings despite the increase of dues payments to 4 percent. Operations were once again in the red. The augmentation of $271,772 derived from the 1946 rodeo was a welcome relief.

When Stanley S. Smith joined the board in the mid-1940s, the outspoken director questioned the soundness of the SPCA management. He predicted the pension rolls would soon exceed 600, and that without proper planning the association would be "wiped out." His warnings, tactless though they were, did not fall on deaf ears. In 1960, a wiser investment policy was adopted; the investment fund was increased. To do this, the dues were raised from 4 percent to 8 percent of $3,000. The extra 4 percent income was committed to investments, and men resigning prior to qualifying for pension had their contributions to the investment fund returned to them. As an extra benefit, the insurance coverage was increased to $5,000. In 1969, the 8 percent program was dropped in favor of 4.5 percent of a trooper's base pay instead of the traditionally fixed base of $3,000. Insurance coverage was also increased to $10,000 shortly thereafter. Earnings from stocks and bonds significantly contributed to the association's well-being.

The management of finances rested largely with the Dauphin Deposit Bank of Harrisburg. Accountability and the certified auditing of finances was placed in the hands of Fishel, Baskin & Dunn, a Harrisburg accounting firm.

Legal matter were handled in turn by Harrisburg attorneys Spencer G. Nauman (original counsel), John McI. Smith, James S. Bowman (now commonwealth court president judge), and John C. Sullivan.

The successors to Walter Fisher, Silvus J. Overmiller and Guy E. Reichard as secretary-treasurer have been John R. Price, John H. Klinger, Richard J. Shaffer, and Robert J. Zinsky, the present officeholder.

In mid-1960, when the district commands were abolished, the board makeup was changed. One director was elected from each troop, one from headquarters, one from the Academy, and three from the pension rolls. This change, in effect, gave the field forces greater voting power—a position they felt entitled to for a long time. This new board makeup remained basically unchanged thereafter.

Pension figures were set by the board of directors annually; their decisions followed a fixed formula contained in the bylaws. Because of changing financial factors, pensions varied from a high of $110 a month to a low of $56 a month. The average was approximately $90.

During the 1960s and early 1970s, the legislature, responding to the arguments of State Police management for increased manpower, doubled the department's complement. With added income from dues payments and favorable returns from a growing investment program, the thought that the pension system might one day be entirely independent of the rodeo income was most promising. The annual rodeo income was then averaging some $250,000. Because of the undesirable elements associated with the raising of rodeo funds, it was felt that the sooner the association could stop leaning on this source of income, the better off it would be.

The new course taken by the association enjoyed smooth sailing; success was almost within reach. Unforeseen circumstances in the early 1970s, however, began to rock the boat, and the association's future became a matter of grave concern. No one factor can be singled out as the responsible culprit for what was to take place. At the Academy, cadet classmen were increasingly resisting enrollment in the association. They believed they could invest their money elsewhere with greater return. Ill-founded rumors in the field struck hard at the association's managers. The Hepford Committee's public denunciation of solicitations by police officers, for whatever purpose, was followed by Barger's order banning solicitations by troopers. In 1974, the rodeo was held for the last time. In mid-1974, some 400 young troopers withdrew from the association. There seemed to be no end to the list of unfavorable developments that sent the association into a tail spin.

In one move to put the association back on course, the board of directors asked the pensioners, then numbering 982, to agree to a reduced pension program. The pensioners turned down the board's proposal. The board then circulated an informal questionnaire to all members offering alternative actions that could be taken. Among them was the choice of dissolving the association; it was this choice which received the majority of votes cast.

In September, 1974, the payroll deduction of dues was halted. In May, 1975, by formal ballot action, members voted 2,241 to 614 in favor of dissolution, and the payment of all pensions was put to an end. Reportedly, the SPCA assets then added up to $7,600,000; and "unfunded indebtedness" was estimated at $16,000,000. Most of this indebtedness stems from demands for pension payments and for refunds to active troopers.

The opinions of active members and pensioners, regarding the dissolution process, were worlds apart: agreement was impossible. So the multi-million dollar issue landed in the Dauphin County Court where all parties will have the opportunity to be heard. So far, litigation has been complicated by procedural arguments and by suits and countersuits that will undoubtedly prolong final adjudication of a difficult case by that court.

One thing, however, is certain—an organization begun almost sixty years ago by a band of stouthearted constabulary troopers will be no more. Like some other State Police traditions, the civic association falls victim to changing times with one significant difference—the bitter results of dissolution will not soon be forgotten.

CHAPTER XXIV

Killed in the Line of Duty

CALL OF HONOR

I am a Pennsylvania State Policeman, a soldier of the law. To me is entrusted the honor of the Force. I must serve honestly, faithfully, and if need be, lay down my life as others have done before me, rather than swerve from the path of duty. It is my duty to obey the law and to enforce it without any consideration of class, color, creed or condition. It is also my duty to be of service to anyone who may be in danger or distress. And at all times so conduct myself that the honor of the Force may be upheld.

A history of the Pennsylvania State Police would not be at all properly completed without paying tribute to its courageous men who died in the performance of duty—the men who fulfilled their sworn obligation with their very lives. Their deeds have added immeasurably to the greatness of the Pennsylvania State Police.

A tribute is paid, too, to the survivors of these fallen dead, who suffered not only the loss of loved ones, but have had to endure financial hardship because of inadequate compensation. It is only in recent years that federal and state enactments have given worthwhile consideration to the plight of those left behind. This is a fitting response from a grateful nation. Rev. R. Joseph Dooley, chaplain of the Catholic Police and Firemen's Society, at the funeral of Gail Cobb, the nation's first policewoman slain on duty, said in 1974, "Every time a police officer makes the supreme sacrifice, a part of America dies."

If value is to be placed on the protection of life and property, then the loss of a guardian of the law, wherever it occurs, should be a personal loss to every American; for, indeed, a part of America has died.

The following is a list of those taken from the Honor Roll of the Pennsylvania State Police. Brief biographical data and the circumstances of their deaths have been added to better identify them:

1. Private John F. Henry was born at New York City on August 10, 1875. He served with the U. S. Marine Corps aboard the U.S.S. *Marblehead,* and saw action during the Philippine Insurrection and the Boxer Rebellion in China prior to his enlistment in the State Police on December 15, 1905. He was assigned to Troop D, Punxsutawney. Henry was the first constabulary member to be killed in the performance of duty. He was shot and killed at Florence, Jefferson County, as he and other Troop D members attempted to arrest suspected Black Hand Society gangsters on the afternoon of September 2, 1906. Henry, 31, had completed nine months of constabulary service.

2. Private Francis A. Zehringer was born at Conshohocken, Pennsylvania, on February 18, 1872. He served with Troop D, Fourth U. S. Cavalry and later with the Sixtieth Company, U. S. Coast Artillery prior to his enlistment in the State Police on December 15, 1905. He was assigned to Troop D, Punxsutawney. Zehringer was shot and killed at Florence, Jefferson County, as he and other Troop D members, including Private John F. Henry, attempted to arrest suspected Black Hand Society gangsters on the afternoon of September 2, 1906. Zehringer, 34, had completed nine months of constabulary service.

3. Private Timothy Kelleher was born at County Cork, Ireland, on March 15, 1878. He fought with the Boers during their war with England. In the United States, he served with Troop M, Second Cavalry, and saw action in the Philippines prior to his enlistment in the State Police on December 15, 1905. He was assigned to Troop C, Reading. On September 14, 1907, Kelleher witnessed a woman being attacked by two men; he went to her aid. One of the men plunged a knife into his side. He died instantly. His body was found the next morning on a scrap heap along a railroad enbankment. Kelleher, 29, had completed one year and nine months of constabulary service.

4. Sergeant Mark A. Prynn was born at Tywardreath, England, on November 19, 1879. He enlisted with the State Police on December 15, 1905, and was assigned to Troop C, Reading. Accompanied by Private Reginald Gibson, Prynn, at Gilberton, Schuylkill County, was taking into custody a man wanted on a stabbing charge; Gibson was

covering. When his horse bolted, Gibson's gun was discharged wounding Prynn. He was taken to the Ashland Hospital where he died a week later—February 9, 1909. Prynn, 28, had completed one year and seven months of constabulary service.

5. Private John Garscia was born at Brody, Galicia County, Austria, on January 11, 1874. In the United States, he served with Company C, Ninth U. S. Infantry prior to his enlistment with the State Police on December 15, 1905. He was assigned to Troop B, Wilkes-Barre. Accompanied by Private Frederick Carlton, he was serving warrant at Inkerman, Luzerne County, on February 13, 1909. When Carlton drew his revolver, it accidentally fired, wounding Garscia. He was taken to the Pittston Hospital where he died a week later—February 21. Garscia, 35, had completed three years and three months of constabulary service.

6. Private John L. Williams was born at Bentonville, Arkansas, on December 19, 1879. He served with Fifth Battery, U. S. Field Artillery; Company G, Fifteenth U. S. Infantry, and Company H, Thirty-sixth U. S. Infantry prior to enlistment in the State Police on August 14, 1907. Williams and four other Troop A members were sent to the Pressed Steel Car Company plant at Schoenville, near McKees Rocks, Allegheny County, where a riotous strike was in progress. Enroute they were attacked by a mob at O'Donovan's Bridge, Schoenville. Williams was shot and killed. The incident occurred on August 22, 1909. Williams 29, had completed two years of service.

7. Private Jack C. Smith was born at Beavertown, Snyder County, Pennsylvania, on October 20, 1884. He enlisted with the State Police on January 14, 1909, and was assigned to Troop A, Greensburg. On August 22, 1909, in company with Private Williams and three others, he was dispatched to the Pressed Steel Car Company plant at Schoenville, near McKees Rocks, Allegheny County, where a riotous strike was in progress. Enroute they were attacked by a mob at O'Donovan's Bridge, Schoenville. Smith was shot and killed. The three privates accompanying Williams and Smith were severely beaten, but survived their ordeal. Smith, 24, had completed seven months of service.

8. Private Robert V. Myers was born at Berwick, Pennsylvania, on September 21, 1890. He served with Troop H, U. S. First Cavalry, prior to his enlistment in the State Police on February 15, 1912. He was assigned to Troop D, Butler. On March 28, 1913, at Sharon, Myers was patrolling a flooded district against possible looting, when he was acci-

dentlly shot and killed by Private Frank White. Myers, 22, had completed one year and one month of service.

9. Private Andrew Czap was born at Swoyersville, Pennsylvania, on December 10, 1893. He enlisted with the State Police on August 1, 1917, and was assigned to Troop D, Butler. On April 28, 1918, Czap and two other Troop D members were sent to Tide, Indiana County, to arrest four men wanted for highway robbery. He was shot from ambush. He died at the Indiana Hospital five hours later. Czap, 24, had completed nine months of service.

10. Private John F. Dargus was born at Pittston, Pennsylvania, on July 2, 1896. He enlisted with the State Police on October 1, 1917, and was assigned to Troop A, Greensburg. Dargus, Sergeant Homer A. Chambers and Fayette County Detective Smith were detailed to Struthers, Ohio, on May 31, 1918, to apprehend Walter Richardson, a fugitive murderer wanted in Pennsylvania. In company with local Ohio police, Dargus was shot from ambush and killed, as the detail approached the Richardson hide-out. He was 21, and had completed eights months of service.

11. Private Stanley W. Christ was born at Pine Grove, Pennsylvania, on June 20, 1897. He served with Company A, 108th U. S. Machine Gun Battalion, and saw World War I action in France prior to his enlistment in the State Police on November 1, 1919. He was assigned to Troop E at Lancaster. As he was grooming a new horse on November 21, 1919, he was kicked in the abdomen. After undergoing surgery at the Lancaster General Hospital for his serious injuries, Christ died from complications on December 1, 1919. Christ, 22, had completed only one month of service.

12. Corporal Ben F. McEvoy was born at Harrisburg, Pennsylvania, on August 9, 1883. He served with Company K, Fourth Regiment, Pennsylvania National Guard, prior to his enlistment in the State Police on June 6, 1910. He was assigned to the school troop at Newville. As he walked along the roadway to give assistance to a stalled motorist, near Petersburg, Lancaster County, on September 18, 1923, he was struck by an approaching vehicle. He was removed to the Lancaster General Hospital where he died on September 21. McEvoy, 41, was the department's first motor vehicle accident fatality; he had completed thirteen years of service.

13. Private William J. Omlor was born at Locust Gap, Pennsylvania, on July 1, 1894. He served with the Thirteenth U. S. Railway Engineers prior to his enlistment in the State Police on June 2, 1919. He was assigned to Troop B, Wyoming. On October 25, 1923, while on

patrol near Pottsville on the Schuylkill Haven Road, he collided with a truck, and was thrown from his motorcycle. He died enroute to the Pottsville Hospital. Omlor, 29, was the department's first motorcycle accident victim; he had completed four years and four months of service.

14. Private Francis L. Haley was born at Pottsville, Pennsylvania, on July 23, 1899. He enlisted in the State Police on May 1, 1924, and was assigned to Troop E, Harrisburg. On October 14, 1924, near the Graffenburg Inn, Adams County, Haley attempted to arrest Philip A. Hartman, a suspect in the Abbottstown State Bank holdup, and was shot and killed. He died at the scene. Haley, 25, had completed five months of service.

15. Sergeant Edwin F. Haas was born at Reading, Pennsylvania, on May 12, 1889. He served with the U. S. Navy aboard the U.S.S. *Wisconsin* prior to his enlistment in the State Police on August 5, 1910. He was quartermaster sergeant at Troop B, Wyoming. He was accidentally shot and killed, as he attempted to dislodge a jammed cartridge in his revolver at troop headquarters. Haas, 35, had completed fourteen years of service.

16. Private Bernard S. C. McElroy was born at New Kensington, Pennsylvania, on August 18, 1899. He served with Company B, 604th U. S. Engineers prior to his enlistment in the State Police on January 1, 1923. He was assigned to Troop D, Butler. On December 20, 1924, while on motorcycle patrol, he collided with a passenger vehicle in the city of New Castle, and was seriously injured. He was taken to the New Castle Hospital where he died the following day—December 21. McElroy, 25, had completed two years of service.

17. Private Bertram Beech was born at Ridderminster, Worstershire County, England, on April 21, 1897. He served with the Sixth U. S. Cavalry and the Third U. S. Field Artillery medical detachment prior to his enlistment in the State Police on May 1, 1924. He was assigned to Troop D, Butler. On December 10, 1925, he was a passenger in a patrol vehicle operated by Private John T. Edelman, when the vehicle struck a train at McCoytown Crossing, Mercer County. Beech was killed instantly. At 28, he had completed one year and eight months of service.

18. Private Claude F. Keesey was born at York, Pennsylvania, on May 21, 1903. He enlisted with the State Police on August 1, 1925, and was assigned to Troop C, Reading. While patrolling the Baltimore Pike, one mile west of Media, Delaware County, Keesey's vehicle skidded on the icy roadway, and struck a telephone pole. He was instantly killed. The accident occurred on January 4, 1927.Keesey, 23, had completed one year and five months of service.

19. Patrolman Martin A. Hanahoe was born at Pittston, Pennsylvania, on August 8, 1902. He enlisted in the State Highway Patrol on January 7, 1926, and was assigned to Troop A, Harrisburg. On October 16, 1926, while on motorcycle patrol just north of Towanda, Bradford County, Hanahoe attempted to halt a fugitive suspect in a speeding motor vehicle. During the chase, he was forced off the roadway, and struck a telephone pole. He was removed to the Robert Packer Hospital at Sayre, where he died of his injuires on February 27, 1927. Hanahoe, 24, was the Highway Patrol's first fatality in the line of duty. He had completed one year of service.

20. Private Thomas E. Lipka was born at Exeter, Pennsylvania, on December 29, 1901. He served with the U. S. Marine Corps prior to his enlistment in the State Police on August 1, 1925. He was assigned to Troop E, Harrisburg. While driving his police vehicle on Route 33, near Lykens, on April 3, 1927, the car skidded on the wet road surface, rolled over an embankment, and struck a telephone pole. Likpa, 25, died at the accident scene. He had completed one year and eight months of service.

21. Sergeant John M. Thomas was born at York, Nebraska, on March 31, 1884. He served with the U. S. Cavalry and the U. S. Marine Corps for thirty years prior to his employment with the State Police. He was appointed inspector and instructor of small arms at the training school; he was later given the rank of sergeant. On Ridge Pike, west of Jeffersonville, Montgomery County, on May 8, 1927, the vehicle in which he was a passenger was involved in a three-car collision. The police vehicle was operated by Captain Albert Carlson. Thomas was seriously injured and died before reaching the Norristown Hospital. He was 43, and had completed less than two months of service.

22. Private John T. Downey was born at Bridgeport, Pennsylvania, on March 14, 1896. He served in the U. S. Navy prior to his enlistment with the State Police on June 1, 1924. He was assigned to Troop A, Greensburg. On August 22, 1927, Downey was ordered to assist Sheriff Braun of Allegheny County at Acmetonia, near Cheswick, where an unruly mob had gathered to protest the execution of Sacco and Vanzetti. In an attempt to disperse the mob, he was shot and killed. He died at the scence of the shooting incident. Downey, 31, had completed three years and three months of service.

23. Corporal Vincent A. Hassen was born at LaPorte, Pennsylvania, on June 18, 1903. He enlisted in the State Highway Patrol on December 1, 1926, and was assigned to Troop A, Harrisburg. While on motorcycle patrol on Front Street, Milton, on December 26, 1927, he stuck a parked car and was thrown from his motorcycle. He died of his injuries on December 27, the following day. Hassen, 24, had completed one year of service.

24. Patrolman Sharon C. Wible was born at E. Mckeesport, Pennsylvania, on September 14, 1905. He served with the State Police for one month prior to his enlistment with the State Highway Patrol on July 18, 1927. While patrolling Route 9, three miles east of Girard, Erie County, on February 6, 1928, Wible collided with a motor vehicle, and was thrown from his motorcycle. He died at the accident scene. Wible, 23, had completed six months of service.

25. Patrolman Andrew W. Miller was born at Clearfield, Pennsylvania, on August 13, 1906. He enlisted in the State Highway Patrol on August 8, 1927, and was assigned to Troop A, Harrisburg. While on patrol, his motorcycle skidded on street car tracks in the city of Pottstown, on April 1, 1928; he was thrown to the ground. He was taken to A. C. Shute Homeopathic Hospital at Pottstown, where he died of his injuries a few hours later. Miller, 21, had completed eight months of service.

26. Patrolman Jay F. Proof was born at Terrytown, Bradford County, Pennsylvania, on February 10, 1898. He enlisted in the State Highway Patrol on February 14, 1927, and was assigned to Troop A, Harrisburg. Attempting to halt a speeding motorist on Route 826, in Jackson Township, Tioga County, on August 28, 1928, Proof lost control of his motorcycle, and struck a bridge abutment. He was taken to Arnot-Ogden Memorial Hospital at Elmira, New York, where he died of his injuries the following day—August 29. Proof, 30, had completed one and a half years of service.

27. Patrolman Russell T. Swanson was born at Mt. Jewett, Pennsylvania, on September 12, 1905. He enlisted with the State Highway Patrol on October 3, 1927, and was assigned to Troop B, Greensburg. When operator of a motor vehicle, bearing Minnesota plates, could not properly identify himself, Swanson ordered the driver and passengers to a magistrate's office at North East, Erie County, for questioning. Enroute he was shot and killed. Swanson was the Highway Patrol's first murder victim. At 23, he had completed one and a half years of service.

28. Patrolman Wells C. Hammond was born at Galeton, Pennsylvania, on October 13, 1905. He served with the Twenty-eighth U. S. Infantry prior to his enlistment in the State Highway Patrol on January 4, 1928. He was assigned to Troop D, Williamsport. Hammond resigned on June 15, 1928, and was reenlisted on May 16, 1929, at Williamsport. While on patrol on October 14, 1929, just a mile east of Schickshinny, Luzerne County, Hammond was thrown from his skidding motorcycle into the path of an approaching car, and run over. He died an hour later at the Nanticoke Hospital. Hammond, 24, had completed one year and ten months of service.

29. Corporal Brady C. Paul was born at Hickory, Washington County, Pennsylvania, on November 7, 1900. He enlisted in the State Highway Patrol on January 7, 1926, and was assigned to Troop B, Greensburg.Setting up a roadblock on the Butler Highway, three miles east of New Castle, Lawrence County, Brady, in company with Patrolman Ernest Moore, stopped a vehicle bearing Ohio plates. A woman, one of three passengers, fired a pistol at the two patrolmen. Paul was fatally wounded; he was pronounced dead on arrival at the Jameson Memorial Hospital at New Castle. Moore sustained minor wounds. Paul, 29, had completed four years of service.

30. Corporal Thomas E. Lawry was born at Scranton, Lackawanna County, Pennsylvania, on May 30, 1905. He served with the Pennsylvania National Guard for three years prior to his enlistment in the State Highway Patrol on September 17, 1926. While on motorcycle patrol near Whites Ferry, Sullivan County, on January 31, 1930, Lawry was struck by a motor vehicle driven on the wrong side of the highway. He was pronounced dead at the accident scene. Lawry, 24, had completed three years and four months of service.

31. Patrolman Arthur A. Koppenhaver was born at Tower City, Schuylkill County, Pennsylvania, on March 2, 1908. He enlisted in the State Highway Patrol on June 24, 1929, and was assigned to Troop D, Williamsport. While on patrol, on April 21, 1930, Koppenhaver was struck by a motor vehicle in Nanticoke, Luzerne County, and thrown from his motorcycle. He was removed to the Nanticoke Hospital, where he succumbed to his injuries on July 13, 1930. Koppenhaver, 22, had completed one year of service.

32. Private Charles L. Stewart was born at Reynoldsville, Pennsylvania, on December 18, 1907. He enlisted with the State Police on June 1, 1929, and was assigned to Troop A, Greensburg. While on surveillance duty on July 18, 1930, at the Grandview cemetery, near Monongehela, where a sum of $10,000 was placed in response to a Black Hand Society blackmail threat, Stewart was shot. While undergoing emergency surgery at the Memorial Hospital at Monongehela, he died. Stewart, 22, had completed one year and one month of service.

33. Patrolman Thomas B. Elder was born at Elders Ridge, Indiana County, Pennsylvania, on July 27, 1902. He enlisted in the State Highway Patrol on February 25, 1929, and was assigned to Troop B, Greensburg. While on motorcycle patrol in the vicinity of Connellsville, Fayette County, on January 4, 1930, elder was struck by a drunk driver. In serious condition, he was taken to the Connellsville Hospital. He was later transferred to the Indiana Hospital where he died of complications on March 22, 1931, more than a year after the accident. Elder, 28, had completed two years of service.

34. Sergeant Timothy G. McCarthy was born at Killarney, Ireland, on July 25, 1888. He served for four years with the British Army before coming to the United States. He then served with Battery B, 102nd U. S. Field Artillery, and saw World War I action in France prior to his enlistment in the State Police on September 1, 1919. He was assigned to Troop E, Harrisburg. On May 12, 1931, McCarthy and others from Troop E were ordered to assist the Fulton County sheriff with the service of a warrant on Marshal Lodge, a belligerent mountaineer, at his home in Brush Creek Township. As McCarthy entered the house, Lodge fired a pistol he had concealed, fatally wounding the sergeant. McCarthy, 42, had completed eleven years and nine months of service.

35. Patrolman Orville A. Mohring was born at Wichita, Kansas, on June 18, 1907. He enlisted in the State Highway Patrol on May 16, 1929, and was assigned to Troop A, Harrisburg. While on patrol, on December 8, 1931, he was struck by a motor vehicle at the intersections of 57th and Whitby Streets, in Philadelphia, and thrown from his motorcycle. He died three days later, December 11, at the Misericordia Hospital at Philadelphia. Mohring, 24, had completed two years and seven months of service.

36. Patrolman Joseph A. Conrad was born at Mahanoy City, Pennsylvania, on February 25, 1906. He enlisted in the State Highway Patrol on October 2, 1930, and was assigned to Troop E, Philadelphia. While on patrol, on August 30, 1932, Conrad was struck by a motor vehicle at the intersections of Routes 821 and 222, in Berks County, and thrown from his motorcycle. He was removed to the Homeopathic Medical and Surgical Hospital at Reading, where he died on September 6. Conrad, 26, had completed almost two years of service.

37 Patrolman Charles E. Householder was born at Highspire, Dauphin County, Pennsylvania, on January 1, 1906. He enlisted in the State Highway Patrol on May 15, 1928, and was assigned to Troop A, Harrisburg. While patrolling U. S. Route 120, east of Sunbury, Upper Augusta Township, Northumberland County, on August 18, 1933, Householder was struck by a motor vehicle, and thrown from his motorcycle. He died at the Mary M. Packer Hospital, Sunbury, on August 20. Householder, 27, had completed five years and three months of service.

38. Patrolman Herbert P. Brantlinger was born at Conemaugh, Cambria County, Pennsylvania, on July 4, 1906. He enlisted in the State Highway Patrol on December 7, 1931, and was assigned to Troop B, Greensburg. Patrolling Route 19, in South Fayette Township, Allegheny County, near Bridgeville, on September 3, 1933, Brantlinger

stopped at the Melrose service station to investigate what appeared to be the theft of gasoline and oil. As he approached the station, he was hit by rifle fire. He died at Mercy Hospital, Pittsburgh, an hour later. Brantlinger, 27, had completed one year and ten months of service.

39. First Sergeant James A. Seerey was born at Philadelphia, Pennsylvania, on June 30, 1892. He served six years with the Tenth U. S. Cavalry and one year with the U. S. Infantry, as a second lieutanant, prior to his enlistment in the State Police on February 2, 1920. He was assigned to Troop B, Wyoming. In the afternoon of September 5, 1934, Seerey participated in mounted drill exercises at Troop B headquarters. As he executed a jump maneuver, his horse struck the hurdle; both horse and rider were thrown to the ground. Seerey, 42, succumbed to his critical injuries five days later—September 10. He had completed fourteen years and eight months of service.

40. Private Floyd W. Maderia was born at Reading, Pennsylvania, on March 14, 1900. He served five years in the U. S. Navy prior to his enlistment in the State Police on May 1, 1930. He was assigned to Troop B, Wyoming. While operating a police vehicle on December 10, 1934, the vehicle skidded on an icy street in Minooka, Lackawanna County, and struck a telephone pole. He died at the Scranton Hospital the following day, December 11. Maderia, 34, had completed four years and eight months of service.

41. Corporal Joseph L. Fulton was born at Osceola Mills, Clearfield County, Pennsylvania, on September 23, 1903. He enlisted in the State Highway Patrol on October 1, 1928, and was assigned to Troop C, Bellefonte. While returning a new motorcycle from Harrisburg to Erie, on June 4, 1936, Fulton was struck by a motor vehicle on Route 19, two miles south of Erie, and crushed underneath the vehicle. He was instantly killed. Fulton, 32, had completed seven years and eight months of service.

42. Sergeant Joe B. Champion was born at Doner, Stuart County, Tennessee, on May 15, 1900. He served with the U. S. Marine Corps for three years prior to his enlistment in the State Highway Patrol on October 13, 1024. He was assigned to Troop B, Greensburg. While operating a Chevrolet roadster on Route 8, ten miles south of Butler, Butler County, on July 13, 1936, accompanied by Patrolman H. C. Ross, Champion was struck by another vehicle. Champion was taken to the Butler County Memorial Hospital, where he died on July 15. At 36, he had completed eleven years and nine months of service.

43. Patrolman J. Lee Clarke was born at New Castle, Pennsylvania, on November 7, 1904. He enlisted in the State Highway Patrol on January 11, 1934, and was assigned to Troop E, Philadelphia. While

on patrol, on March 1, 1937, his motorcycle skidded on street car tracks in Reading, Berks County, and struck a coal truck. Clarke was pronounced dead at St. Joseph Hospital, Reading. Clarke, 32, had completed three years of service.

44. Private John E. Fessler was born at Cresson, Cambria County, Pennsylvania, on September 11, 1904. He enlisted in the State Police on March 1, 1933, and was assigned to Troop E, Harrisburg. Fessler and Private Thomas A. Hooper were assigned to assist Montour County Sheriff E. Riley Lindner and his deputy, Joseph Wray, in the service of a warrant on William Yeager, in Cooper Township, on April 22, 1937. Yeager shot Fessler in the abdomen with rifle fire. Fessler was taken to the Geisinger Memorial Hospital at Danville, where he died the following day—April 23. At 32, he had served for four years and two months.

45. Private Joseph A. Hoffer was born at Mount Carmel, Pennsylvania, on November 7, 1907. He enlisted in the State Police on September 1, 1929, and was assigned to Troop A, Greensburg. On April 22, 1927, Hoffer and others from Troop A, accompanied by three Highway Patrolman, were dispatched to Uniontown to apprehend Hamilton Leftwich, a fugitive murderer. As they approached the Leftwich hide-out, Hoffer was cut down by shotgun fire. He died at the Uniontown Hospital on April 27. Hoffer, 29, had served for seven years and eight months.

46. Private John J. Broski was born at Silver Brook, Schuylkill County, Pennsylvania, on October 1, 1896. He enlisted in the State Police on January 10, 1918, and was assigned to Troop B, Wyoming. While conducting an arson case investigation, Broski visited the Boulevard Inn, in Bear Creek Township, Luzerne County, on August 14, 1937. During his stay, two armed men staged a robbery. Attempting to place both under arrest, Broski was critically wounded in the back by a shotgun blast. He died at the Wilkes-Barre Hospital ten hours later. Broski, 40, had completed nineteen years and seven months of service.

47. Patrolman John D. Simoson was born at Luzerne, Pennsylvania, on July 4, 1914. He enlisted in the State Highway Patrol on April 21, 1936, and was assigned to Troop F, Franklin. While traveling through Smethport Borough, McKean County, on December 1, 1937, on patrol, Simoson's motorcycle skidded on a curve; he lost control, and was thrown from the motorcycle. He was pronounced dead at the accident scene. Simoson, 23, had completed one year and eight months of service.

48. Private Joseph M. Williams was born at Republic, Fayette County, Pennsylvania, on May 3, 1912. He was enrolled in the ROTC

program at West Virginia University prior to his enlistment in the Pennsylvania Motor Police on April 1, 1938. He was assigned to Troop A-2, Harrisburg. On October 8, 1938, Williams, accompanied by Private Charles H. Craven, had stopped two vehicles on Route 30, four miles east of Gettysburg, for an identification check, when both were struck by a passing vehicle. Williams was pronounced dead on arrival at the Annie M. Warner Hospital, Gettysburg. Craven was admitted; he succumbed to his injuries three days later—October 11. This was the department's first double tragedy as the result of a motor vehicle accident. Williams, 26, had completed seven months of service.

49. Private Charles H. Craven was born at Emporium, Pennsylvania, on July 19, 1906. He served one year with the Civilian Military Training Corps prior to his enlistment in the State Highway Patrol on October 2, 1930. He was assigned to Troop A, Harrisburg, and then became a member of Troop A-2, Harrisburg, as a result of the merger. On October 8, 1938, Craven, accompanied by Private Joseph M. Williams, had stopped two vehicles on Route 30, four miles east of Gettysburg, for an identification check, when both were struck by a passing vehicle. Craven was taken to the Annie M. Warner Hospital at Gettysburg, where he died three days later—October 11. Williams was pronounced dead on arrival at the hospital. This was the department's first double tragedy as the result of a motor vehicle accident. Craven, 32, had completed eights years of service.

50. Corporal George D. Naughton was born at Sharpsburg, Pennsylvania, on January 12, 1899. He served with the U. S. Army Medical Corps, and saw World War I action in France prior to his enlistment in the State Police on November 1, 1926. He was assigned to Troop A, Greensburg, and then became a member of Troop B-1, as a result of the merger. On January 30, 1939, Naughton and others from Troop B-1 were sent to East Bethlehem Township, Washington County, near Clarksville, to assist local authorities with the arrest of Frank Palanzo, who had threatened his family with a loaded weapon. As Naughton entered the house, he was cut down by a shotgun blast; he was instantly killed. Naughton, 40, had completed twelve years and three months of service.

51. Private Frederick J. Sutton was born at Punxutawney, Pennsylvania, on July 17, 1913. He enlisted in the Pennsylvania Motor Police on September 1, 1937, and was assigned to Troop A-2, Harrisburg. On January 3, 1940, Sutton was detailed to assist Constable R. B. Regi of McConnellsburg with the service of a warrant on Brice Hann. Sutton moved to arrest Hann, when he refused to accompany the police officers; Hann fired on Sutton with a pistol concealed in his

overcoat pocket. Sutton was taken to the Chambersburg Hospital, where he died three hours later. At 25, he had completed one year and four months of service.

52. Private George J. Yashur was born at Junedale, Carbon County, Pennsylvania, on December 31, 1915. He enlisted in the State Highway Patrol on January 13, 1937, and assigned to Troop D, Williamsport, and then became a member of Troop B-3, Wyoming, as a result of the merger. While directing traffic on Market Street, in Kingston, during flood relief work in that city, on March 31, 1940, Yashar was struck by a speeding truck. He was admitted to the Nesbit Memorial Hospital at Kingston, where he died a day later—April 1. Yashur, 24, had completed three years and three months of service.

53. Private Thomas P. Carey was born at East Plymouth, Pennsylvania, on November 9, 1909. He enlisted in the State Highway Patrol on May 2, 1935, and assigned to Troop E, Philadelphia, and then became a member of Troop C-4, Reading, as a result of the merger. On June 17, 1941, Carey and Private J. J. Comerford were dispatched to the scene of an accident near Boltz's Corner, Berks County. Two occupants were trapped in a burning vehicle. Assisting to extinguish the fire, Carey was overcome by poisonous fumes; he was taken to a nearby doctor's office, where he collapsed and died. Carey, 31, had completed six years and one month of service.

54. Private Wallace F. Ely was born at Brooklyn, Susquehanna County, Pennsylvania, on January 24, 1913. He enlisted in the State Police on October 1, 1936, and was assigned to Troop E, Harrisburg. As a result of the merger, he was later assigned to Troop D-2, Montoursville. On September 9, 1941, as he attempted to pass another vehicle on Route 220, near Montoursville, Ely's car spun out of control and rolled over. He was taken to the Williamsport Hospital, where he died of his injuries on September 14. Ely, 28, had completed five years of service.

55. Private Dean N. Zeigler was born at Spring Mills, Centre County, Pennsylvania, on March 25, 1918. He enlisted in the Motor Police on October 1, 1941, and was assigned to Troop A-2, Harrisburg. On October 11, 1942, his patrol vehicle collided with another vehicle on U. S. Route 15, three miles north of Dillsburg, York County. He was removed to the Harrisburg Hospital, where he succumbed to his injuries on October 17. Zeigler, 24, had completed one year of service.

56. Private John A. Ditkosky was born at McAdoo, Schuylkill County, Pennsylvania, on August 29, 1922. He served four years with the U. S. Navy, and saw action during World War II, before his enlistment in the State Police on May 1, 1947. He was assigned to Troop A-

2, Harrisburg. On July 24, 1950, Ditkosky stopped a vehicle on U. S. Route 22, four miles east of Harrisburg. As he checked the operator's identification, he was struck by a passing truck, and instantly killed. The truck driver had fallen asleep. Ditkosky, 27, had completed three years and two months of service.

57. Private Floyd B. Clouse was born at Everett, Bedford County, Pennsylvania, on December 20, 1923. He served three years in the U. S. Navy, and saw World War II action, before his enlistment in the State Police on August 1, 1946. He was assigned to Troop D-1, Butler. On November 2, 1953, Clouse and Corporal Harold G. Rice were detailed to serve a warrant on Edwin C. Stanyard of White Township, Beaver County. As they entered the Stanyard home, Stanyard shot and killed Clouse, and wounded Rice. Returning fire, Rice shot and killed Stanyard. Clouse, 29, had completed seven years and three months of service.

58. Private Joseph F. McMillen was born at Conneautville, Crawford County, Pennsylvania, on January 29, 1930. He served five years in the U. S. Navy prior to his enlistment in the State Police on May 16, 1952. He was assigned to Troop E-1, Erie. On May 12, 1956, as he patrolled Route 955, in Harborcreek Township, five miles east of Erie, McMillen's vehicle was struck by another vehicle approaching in the opposite direction on the wrong side of the roadway. He was taken to St. Vincent Hospital at Erie, where he died a few hours later on May 13. McMillen, 26, had completed four years of service.

59. Trooper Philip C. Melley was born at Summit Hill, Carbon County, Pennsylvania, on December 20, 1915. He enlisted in the Motor Police on December 13, 1937, and was assigned to Troop C-4, Reading. On November 3, 1957, two troopers and a Douglass Township officer sought after an armed Boyertown teenager, who had threatened to kill his father. Melley was sent to the area to assist them. He approached the four in a wooded section of Douglass Township, Berks County, to find the teenager holding the three officers at bay with a shotgun. In an attempt to disarm the young man unharmed, Melley was shot and instantly killed. Melley, 41, had completed twenty years of service.

60. Trooper Charles S. Stanski was born at Plymouth, Luzerne County, Pennsylvania, on September 15, 1928. He served three years with the 814th U. S. Army Engineers prior to his enlistment in the State Police on January 4, 1954. He was assigned to Troop A-2, Harrisburg. In pursuit of a speeding trucker on January 17, 1958, Stanski slammed on his car brakes as he saw a train approaching a railroad crossing in Silver Spring Township, Cumberland County; the patrol vehicle overturned. He was removed to the Harrisburg Hospital, where he

died on January 23. Stanski, 29, had completed four years of service.

61. Trooper Edward Mackiw was born at Scranton, Pennsylvania, on June 10, 1925. He served a year in the U. S. Navy prior to his enlistment in the State Police on October 1, 1949. He was assigned to Troop B-1, Washington. As he was directing traffic at the scene of an accident on the Penn-Lincoln Highway, near Pittsburgh, on May 30, 1958, Mackiw was struck by a passing vehicle. He was removed to the St. Clair Memorial Hospital at Mt. Lebanon, where he died the following day—May 31. Mackiw, 32, had completed eight years and seven months of service.

62. Trooper Stephen R. Gyurke was born at Nettleton, Cambria County, Pennsylvania, on July 3, 1929. He served four years with the U. S. Army prior to his enlistment in the State Police on October 4, 1954. He was assigned to Troop B-2 (Turnpike Patrol). On August 21, 1958, Gyurke was checking the credentials of a stopped trucker, when a tractor-trailer left the main portion of the turnpike roadway, and struck him. He was removed to the Frick Memorial Hospital at Mt. Pleasant, where he died on August 24. Gyurke, 29, had completed three years and ten months of service.

63. Trooper Francis M. Tessitore was born at Nesquehoning, Carbon County, Pennsylvania, on February 3, 1932. He served four years with the U. S. Navy prior to his enlistment in the State Police on October 2, 1953. He was assigned to Troop B-2 (Turnpike Patrol). On August 5, 1960, Tessitore stopped a speeding motorist in Chester County. As he was preparing his arrest report, a truck ran off the roadway and struck Tessitore and the arrested motorist. Both were instantly killed. The teenage truck driver had fallen asleep. Tessitore, 28, had completed six years and ten months of service.

64. Trooper Anthony Bensch was born at Coaldale, Schuylkill County, Pennsylvania, on July 23, 1918. He served for two years with the U. S. Marine Corps prior to his enlistment in the State Police on October 1, 1941. He was assigned to Troop A-3, Hazleton. On October 3, 1961, Bensch was a passenger in a patrol vehicle driven by Trooper Robert Latzo. They were returning to station after a small arms qualifying session at troop headquarters. In an attempt to avoid hitting a deer on Route 940, a mile east of Blakeslee Corners, Monroe County, Latzo lost control of the vehicle on the wet highway and struck a tree; Bensch was thrown from the car. He died at the accident scene. Bensch, 43, had completed twenty years of service.

65. Sergeant Edward W. Gundel was born at Highspire, Dauphin County, Pennsylvania, on July 4, 1916. He served three years with

Troop K, 104th Cavalry, Pennsylvania National Guard, prior to his enlistment in the Motor Police on September 1, 1937. He was assigned to Troop C-4, Reading. On March 18, 1962, Gundel was called to assist Pine Grove Chief of Police Clayton with the arrest of Theodore Kemmerling, a young Pine Grove resident, on an assault and battery charge. Kemmerling was seen entering a building through a window. As Gundel approached the building, Kemmerling cut down the sergeant with two shotgun blasts. Gundel was instantly killed. At 45, he had completed 24$^1/_2$ years of service.

66. Trooper Richard G. Barnhart was born at New Florence, Westmoreland County, Pennsylvania, on May 17, 1927. He served one year with Battery B, Sixth U. S. Army Field Artillery Battalion, prior to his enlistment in the State Police on November 15, 1951. He was assigned to Troop B-1, Washington. On August 8, 1964, Barnhart was investigating a drag race incident on Route 112, near Republic, Fayette County. As he pursued one of the racers, a vehicle entered the highway from a service station and struck the Barnhart vehicle; he died at the accident scene. Barnhart, 37, had completed twelve years and nine months of service.

67. Trooper Gary R. Rosenberger was born at Harrisburg, Dauphin County, Pennsylvania, on August 29, 1944. He enlisted in the State Police on May 22, 1969, and was assigned to Troop F, Montoursville. Rosenberger was engaged as undercover agent in a narcotics investigation. On December 12, 1970, his body was found in a small stream in Old Lycoming Township, Lycoming County, near Williamsport. He had been shot nine times. Barry L. Russell, a 19-year-old Williamsport youth, was charged with Rosenberger's murder. Rosenberger, 26, had completed one year and seven months of service.

68. Corporal John S. Valent was born at Blandburg, Cambria County, Pennsylvania, on July 27, 1922. He served three years with the U. S. Navy, and saw World War II action prior to his enlistment in the State Police on February 1, 1946. He was assigned to Troop G, Hollidaysburg. While on patrol on December 9, 1971, Valent stopped a vehicle with three occupants who stated they were from New York City, but could show no identification. As he attempted to take the trio to the Lewistown Substation for further questioning, Valent was shot twice. He was pronounced dead on arrival at the Lewistown Hospital. Valent, 49, had completed twenty-five years of service. He was the oldest member of the department killed in the line of duty, and had chalked up the longest service record.

69. Trooper Robert D. Lapp, Jr., was born at Washington, District of Columbia, on September 27, 1942. He served three years with

the U. S. Navy prior to his enlistment in the State Police on September 3, 1964. He was assigned to Troop J, Lancaster. On October 16, 1972, while off duty, Lapp stopped at the Lancaster barracks and volunteered to assist fellow troopers and local police with the arrest of Alfred C. Ravenell, an escapee from the New Jersey State Prison, where he was serving a life sentence for murder. As Lapp broke into the unlighted apartment hide-out, Ravenell fired from the the bathroom. Lapp was shot and instantly killed. His slayer was shot down by gunfire at the hands of fellow troopers. Lapp, 30, had completed eight years of service.

70. Trooper Bruce C. Rankin was born at Brownsville, Fayette County, Pennsylvania, on August 20, 1947. He enlisted in the State Police on January 28, 1971, and was assigned to Troop A, Greensburg. On April 25, 1973, Rankin was assigned to patrol Route 119. At a point just south of Greensburg, a tractor-trailer jumped the medial barrier, and collided with Rankin's patrol car. He was instantly killed. Rankin, 25, had completed two years and three months of service.

71. Trooper Ross E. Snowden was born at Uniontown, Fayette County, Pennsylvania, on July 19, 1940. He served six years with the U. S. Air Force prior to his enlistment in the State Police on April 9, 1970. He was assigned to Troop E, Erie, and transferred to the Aviation Division in 1972. Snowden was killed in a helicopter crash at the Reading Municipal Airport on January 17, 1974. The airport superintendent, Donald Glass, 47, an occupant in the helicopter, was killed also. Snowden was the first and only pilot killed in a helicopter mishap. At 33, he had completed three years and nine months of service.

Of the total dead, 55 percent died as the result of motor vehicle accidents, 40 percent died from gun wounds, and five percent died from miscellaneous causes. The youngest to die was State Highway Patrolman Andrew W. Miller; he was 21½ years old. Private Stanley W. Christ, 22, had the shortest service record; he served but one month. Corporal John S. Valent, at 49, was the oldest to die. Having completed twenty-five of service, Valent also had the longest service record. The average age was 30; the average length of service was five years. The highest ranked to die was First Sergeant James A. Seery of Troop B, Wyoming.

When Trooper Ross E. Snowden died in 1974, the department's sixty-ninth year, the Pennsylvania State Police averaged one death a year. The State Highway Patrol, during its fourteen years of existence, saw nineteen men killed. Sixteen died as the result of motor vehicle accidents; three were shot to death. The worst year in the department's long history was 1927, when six men were killed. No deaths were recorded in the eight-year period from 1910 through 1917; it was the longest stretch in which death took a holiday.

The department's most disastrous year, taking into account deaths from all causes, was 1918. In that year, the constabulary recorded twelve deaths. Two were shot and killed, eight died from Spanish influenza, one was killed in World War I action in France, and another died in military service from Spanish influenza.

According to Captain George F. Lumb, acting superintendent during the 1917-1919 period, the eight men who died of Spanish influenza labored through endless hours to aid doctors and nurses caring for epidemic patients, and to aid in the removal of the dead from contaminated quarters. From his account, it would appear that these men gave their lives to suffering humanity in a special way, and should have been listed among the honored dead. This, however, was not done, and some doubt can be raised about the criteria for classifying a death in the line of duty. It is true that these eight men did not die under violent circumstances as did those on the Honor Roll, but their willingness to be exposed to death in another form in public service is also true. How does one measure a hero's death?

In a few Honor Roll cases, death resulted from accidental shootings. Yet, in 1971, for example, Trooper Robert J. Lomas, Jr., was accidentally shot by a fellow trooper at the Avondale substation, as patrol shifts were changing. Because of certain circumstances, his death was not considered duty-related—it was a borderline situation that merits departmental review.

In another accidental shooting case, Private John J. Julo of Troop A-2, Harrisburg, according to departmental records, had failed to qualify with his periodic revolver marksmanship score in 1939, and was put on leave of absence so that he could practice for a passing score. During a target shooting session on August 29, near Lykens, Dauphin County, Julo's gun jammed. As he tried to dislodge the cartridge, the gun accidentlly discharged; Julo was seriously wounded. A companion witnessed the shooting incident. Julo was removed to the Coaldale State Hospital, where he died on September 3.

Although neither Lomas nor Julo is listed on the Honor Roll, records indicate that the state's Workmen's Compensation agency awarded benefits to petitioning survivors. Apparently, the compensation executives found sufficient evidence to classify both incidents as job-related. This would indicate somehow that the department could in the name of fairness take more time to review the circumstances of each incident that arises, and make no final determination until the results of state agency hearings and court actions, if there are any, are fully taken into account.

There are other deaths, too, which did not follow soon on the heels of injury incidents in the line of duty. Because the dates of injury and the dates of death were widely separated, Honor Roll listings were withheld. Again, these could be considered borderline cases. Unfortunately, the job of researching records to single out the men falling into this category would be an impossible undertaking.

Departmental records reveal that literally hundreds of men have been injured and disabled, temporarily or permanently, due to line of duty accidents. Motor vehicle accidents, at times, have averaged one a day, unquestionably contributing to the largest number of disabled troopers. So, the Honor Roll is likened to the tip of the iceberg, which does not reveal the total sacrifice made by troopers throughout the department's long history.

Also to be remembered with respect are the troopers who gave their lives in military service. In this connection, it is regrettable that State Police records have not been dependably kept. In listing those killed in action, therefore, there is a risk of omission for which an apology is made. World War I claimed the life of only one trooper— Joseph A. Snyder of Troop C, Reading. World War II fatalities included seven troopers and a civilian: Frank L. Albert, Joseph J. Haggerty, John E. Hancock, Frank J. Kelly, James A. Rose, Anthony J. Tornetta, and Richard E. Whitman, a police clerk.

Setting aside momentarily injuries and deaths, it would be an oversight not to mention areas of community services in which Pennsylvania State Police troopers engage. They sponsor sports events to raise funds for charitable causes; donate blood for the critically ill; conduct Christmas and other holiday parties for the underprivileged; conduct summertime cadet camps for young boys; coach youth athletic teams; serve as scoutmasters; support church-sponsored activities; give their time to the beneficial work of service clubs and fraternal organizations—to name some of the many ways in which troopers prove their worth as community-minded citizens. They are truly men and women to be honored—even among the living.

Appendixes

DEPARTMENT OF STATE POLICE ENLISTMENTS
1905–1906

Name	Date of Birth and Birthplace	Enlistment Date and Assignment
John C. Groome	Mar. 20, 1862 Philadelphia, Pa.	July 1, 1905 Headquarters
John H. Clarke	Langhorne, Pa.	Aug. 1, 1905 Headquarters
Alan C. Frazier	Philadelphia, Pa.	Aug. 9, 1905 Headquarters
John W. Borland	Sept. 30, 1874 Mercer, Pa.	Nov. 1, 1905 Troop A
Frank D. Beary	Feb. 18, 1869 Allentown, Pa.	Nov. 1, 1905 Troop B
William P. Taylor	Sept. 11, 1875 Baltimore, Md.	Nov. 1, 1905 Troop C
Joseph F. Robinson	Dec. 11, 1875 Toledo, Ohio	Nov. 1, 1905 Troop D
Henry F. Egle	June 9, 1873 Switzerland	Nov. 11, 1905 Troop D
Charles F. Fenerstein	June 10, 1874 Wilkes-Barre, Pa.	Nov. 11, 1905 Troop A

Name	Date of Birth and Birthplace	Enlistment Date and Assignment
Charles P. Smith	Mar. 6, 1872 Philadelphia, Pa.	Nov. 11, 1905 Troop C
William L. Swarm	Aug. 11, 1877 Pleasant Gap, Pa.	Nov. 11, 1905 Troop B
William J. Mullen	Aug. 11, 1877 Catasauqua, Pa.	Dec. 11, 1905 Troop D
Robert F. Balliet	June 13, 1878 Ironton, Pa.	Dec. 12, 1905 Troop A
Leonard A. Haskett	Oct. 23, 1870 Hamilton, N.C.	Dec. 15, 1905 Troop A
Harry C. Dimon	July 15, 1881 Fort Scott, Kan.	Dec. 15, 1905 Troop B
Josiah L. Reese	Mar. 17, 1875 Swansea, Wales	Dec. 15, 1905 Troop C
George F. Lumb	Nov. 10, 1874 London, England	Dec. 15, 1905 Troop D
Thomas M. Harris	Oct. 4, 1871 Marblehead, Mass.	Dec. 15, 1905 Troop A
Jesse S. Garwood	Nov. 18, 1873 Lynnville, Iowa	Dec. 15, 1905 Troop B
Cecil M. Wilhelm	Oct. 21, 1881 Reading, Pa.	Dec. 15, 1905 Troop C
Mathew T. E. Ward	June 21, 1876 Baltimore, Md.	Dec. 15, 1905 Troop D
Leon S. Pitcher	Nov. 3, 1874 Milford, Del.	Dec. 15, 1905 Troop A
William E. Mair	July 12, 1881 Philadelphia, Pa.	Dec. 15, 1905 Troop B
Wilson C. Price	Aug. 13, 1879 Philadelphia, Pa.	Dec. 15, 1905 Troop C
William Marsh	July 12, 1880 Philadelphia, Pa.	Dec. 15, 1905 Troop D
Lynn G. Adams	June 8, 1879 Hopbottom, Pa.	Dec. 15, 1905 Troop A
John T. Walsh	Apr. 29, 1877 Philadelphia, Pa.	Dec. 15, 1905 Troop B
John S. VanVoorhis	Apr. 24, 1880 Pittsburgh, Pa.	Dec. 15, 1905 Troop C
Charles C. Hoddy	Feb. 6, 1873 LaFayette, Ind.	Dec. 15, 1905 Troop D
John P. J. Gorman	Feb. 28, 1870 Philadelphia, Pa.	Dec. 15, 1905 Troop A
Herbert P. Hunt	June 21, 1880 Philadelphia, Pa.	Dec. 15,1905 Troop B

Name	Date of Birth and Birthplace	Enlistment Date and Assignment
Joseph P. Logan	June 12, 1876 Reynoldsville, Pa.	Dec. 15, 1905 Troop D
Frederick G. Ayres	June 27, 1878 Pavonia, N.J.	Dec. 15, 1905 Troop A
George J. Deegan	Apr. 30, 1876 Pottsville, Pa.	Dec. 15, 1905 Troop A
Frederick G. Denn	Oct. 20, 1879 Wilkes-Barre, Pa.	Dec. 15, 1905 Troop A
Harvey Denner	Sept.29, 1880 Philadelphia, Pa.	Dec. 15, 1905 Troop A
Joseph J. Didyoung	Sept. 3, 1870 St. Clair, Pa.	Dec. 15, 1905 Troop A
William J. Ferris	Jan. 20, 1878 Philadelphia, Pa.	Dec. 15, 1905 Troop A
Harry F. Fry	Feb. 27, 1882 Harrisburg, Pa.	Dec. 15, 1905 Troop A
John Garscia	Jan. 11, 1874 Austria	Dec. 15, 1905 Troop A
Emmert W. Gillham	May 12, 1884 Collinsville, Ind.	Dec. 15, 1905 Troop A
Robert Graham	Mar. 11, 1880 Carpenter, Pa.	Dec. 15, 1905 Troop A
Frank A. Hershey	Nov. 3, 1879 Mechanicsburg, Pa.	Dec. 15, 1905 Troop A
George B. Hodges	Jan. 8, 1878 Ryde, Isle of Wight	Dec. 15, 1905 Troop A
Charles Jacobs	Aug. 9, 1876 Mannheim, Germany	Dec. 15, 1905 Troop A
Allen G. Lithgow	Sept. 19, 1881 Baltimore, Md.	Dec. 15, 1905 Troop A
Anthony Lohmiller, Jr.	Sept. 29, 1877 Danville, Pa.	Dec. 15, 1905 Troop A
John J. McCall	Aug. 22, 1870 Philadelphia, Pa.	Dec. 15, 1905 Troop A
Charles J. McGarigle	Nov. 8, 1876 Philadelphia, Pa.	Dec. 15, 1905 Troop A
Thomas J. McLaughlin	Dec. 2, 1881 Philadelphia, Pa.	Dec. 15, 1905 Troop A
Peter McNelis	Sept. 28, 1876 Upper Lehigh, Pa.	Dec. 15, 1905 Troop A.
Barney McNulty	Nov. 20, 1866 Allentown, Pa.	Dec. 15, 1905 Troop A
John D. O'Grady	July 24, 1878 Philadelphia, Pa.	Dec. 15, 1905 Troop A

Name	Date of Birth and Birthplace	Enlistment Date and Assignment
Michael Podgorski	Sept. 8, 1878 Austria	Dec. 15, 1905 Troop A
Frank L. Prue	May 4, 1879 Bradford, Pa.	Dec. 15, 1905 Troop A
John A. Purdy	Feb. 10, 1882 Pine Station, Pa.	Dec. 15, 1905 Troop A
Frank Reed	Feb. 2, 1876 Wilkes-Barre, Pa.	Dec. 15, 1905 Troop A
Phillip Roller	Aug. 22, 1870 Fort Wayne, Ind.	Dec. 15, 1905 Troop A
James J. Stinson	Dec. 26, 1880 Warrior Run, Pa.	Dec. 15, 1905 Troop A
Paul B. Stout	Apr. 29, 1876 Milton, Pa.	Dec. 15, 1905 Troop A
George W. Wilkinson	Aug. 21, 1880 Beverly. N. J.	Dec. 15, 1905 Troop A
Frederick E. Borman	Jan. 2, 1881 Hanover, Germany	Dec. 15, 1905 Troop B
William A. Clark	May 26, 1881 Philadelphia, Pa.	Dec. 15, 1905 Troop B
Joseph Cooley	Mar. 22, 1877 Philadelphia, Pa.	Dec. 15, 1905 Troop B
Francis L. Drake	Dec. 12, 1874 Philadelphia, Pa.	Dec. 15, 1905 Troop B
James D. Dunsmore	Apr. 7, 1876 Harrisburg, Pa.	Dec. 15, 1905 Troop B
James G. Ernst	Nov. 24, 1878 Stockertown, Pa.	Dec. 15, 1905 Troop B
George W. Freeman	Sept. 23, 1880 Latrobe, Pa.	Dec. 15, 1905 Troop B
Romanus Fellman	Mar. 5, 1879 Hatfield, Pa.	Dec. 15, 1905 Troop B
Mortimer C. Funston	Jan. 25, 1872 Catawissa, Pa.	Dec. 15, 1905 Troop B
John S. Garland	Dec. 2, 1884 Chester Centre, Pa.	Dec. 15, 1905 Troop B
Charles O. Hart	July 29, 1872 Baden, Germany	Dec. 15, 1905 Troop B
Joseph P. Halloran	Sept. 8, 1879 Philadelphia, Pa.	Dec. 15, 1905 Troop B
Walter S. Hennig	Nov. 13, 1882 Philadelphia, Pa.	Dec. 15, 1905 Troop B
William Haler	Feb. 17, 1880 Allegheny, Pa.	Dec. 15, 1905 Troop B

Name	Date of Birth and Birthplace	Enlistment Date and Assignment
Newton Kelly	Jan. 1, 1880 Philadelphia, Pa.	Dec. 15, 1905 Troop B
William Lane	Aug. 3, 1870 Philadelphia, Pa.	Dec. 15, 1905 Troop B
Francis P. McGinnis	Sept. 3, 1876 Philadelphia, Pa.	Dec. 15, 1905 Troop B
John B. Mountjoy	Nov. 28, 1884 Boyertown, Pa.	Dec. 15, 1905 Troop B
Frank J. Murray	Jan. 7, 1872 Philadelphia, Pa.	Dec. 15, 1905 Troot B
William R. MacSherry	Jan. 29, 1877 Philadelphia, Pa.	Dec. 15, 1905 Troop B
Alexander C. Reamer	June 2, 1871 Harrisburg, Pa.	Dec. 15, 1905 Troop B
Harry Smith	May 9, 1881 Philadelphia, Pa.	Dec. 15, 1905 Troop B
Robert G. Tait	Apr. 26, 1871 Sank County, Wisc.	Dec. 15, 1905 Troop B
Leonce J. Tierce	May 11, 1880 New York, N. Y.	Dec. 15, 1905 Troop B
Robert E. Tipton	Jan. 15, 1877 Gettysburg, Pa.	Dec. 15, 1905 Troop B
Charles S. Weaver	June 26, 1868 Neuchlan, Pa.	Dec. 15, 1905 Troop B
Anthony W. Shelmerdine	May 4, 1870 Philadelphia, Pa.	Dec. 15, 1905 Troop B
Walter W. Ambrose	Apr. 16, 1881 Shenandoah, Pa.	Dec. 15, 1905 Troop C
Loyd E. Booth	July 2, 1884 DuBois, Pa.	Dec. 15, 1905 Troop C
Marshall J. Booth	Feb. 12, 1882 Forty-Fort, Pa.	Dec. 15, 1905 Troop C
Marvin C. Beck	July 26, 1879 Pottsville, Pa.	Dec. 15, 1905 Troop C
William A. Boyd	July 13, 1876 Philadelphia, Pa.	Dec. 15, 1905 Troop C
Alonzo B. Cady	Aug. 9, 1868 Spring Hill, Pa.	Dec. 15, 1905 Troop C
John Dugan	Feb. 18, 1874 Locust Gap, Pa.	Dec. 15, 1905 Troop C
Ross C. Fetterolf	Sept. 8, 1872 Royersford, Pa.	Dec. 15, 1905 Troop C
Isaac Fleming	Sept 20, 1878 Belfast, Ireland	Dec. 15, 1905 Troop C

Name	Date of Birth and Birthplace	Enlistment Date and Assignment
William R. Johnston	Feb. 22, 1870 Salem, Pa.	Dec. 15, 1905 Troop C
Thomas J. Garrity	Feb. 4, 1880 Philadelphia, Pa.	Dec. 15, 1905 Troop C
Louis F. Koch	July 20, 1880 Allegheny, Pa.	Dec. 15, 1905 Troop C
William H. Keogh	Aug. 11, 1876 Allegheny, Pa.	Dec. 15, 1905 Troop C
Timothy Kelleher	Mar. 18, 1878 Cork, Ireland	Dec. 15, 1905 Troop C
Thomas C. Lott	Nov. 4, 1877 Philadelphia, Pa.	Dec. 15, 1905 Troop C
Meyer VanLewen	Jan. 30, 1878 Pittsburgh, Pa.	Dec. 15, 1905 Troop C
Howard G. Mercer	Aug. 17, 1882 Philadelphia, Pa.	Dec. 15, 1905 Troop C
George C. Miller	Dec. 18, 1880 Philadelphia, Pa.	Dec. 15, 1905 Troop C
Thomas B. Naughton	Feb. 11, 1873 Philadelphia, Pa.	Dec. 15, 1905 Troop C
James E. Nilon	June 13, 1876 Montgomery County, Pa.	Dec. 15, 1905 Troop C
Mark A. Prynn	Nov. 19, 1879 Tywardreath, England	Dec. 15, 1905 Troop C
Daniel G. Steiner	Dec. 22, 1874 Erie, Pa.	Dec. 15, 1905 Troop C
Thomas Stables	Jan. 2, 1881 Cheshire County, England	Dec. 15, 1905 Troop C
William R. Smith	Dec. 30, 1879 Philadelphia, Pa.	Dec. 15, 1905 Troop C
Walter C. Snyder	Dec. 27, 1879 Chester County, Pa.	Dec. 15, 1905 Troop C
James L. Sullivan	Oct. 23, 1879 York Furnace, Pa.	Dec. 15, 1905 Troop C
Herman Thomas	May 9, 1876 New York, N. Y.	Dec. 15, 1905 Troop C
Benjamin F. Tinney	Dec. 29, 1876 Clio, Mich.	Dec. 15, 1905 Troop C
Richard H. Tremaine	Apr. 29, 1869 London, England	Dec. 15, 1905 Troop C
William E. Wilson	Feb. 7, 1867 Punxsutawney, Pa.	Dec. 15, 1905 Troop C
Thomas F. Wiechard	June 24, 1878 Philadelphia, Pa.	Dec. 15, 1905 Troop C

Name	Date of Birth and Birthplace	Enlistment Date and Assignment
Adam Wreath, Jr.	Mar. 3, 1876 Philadelphia, Pa.	Dec. 15, 1905 Troop C
Edward J. Baker	Apr. 29, 1880 Reading, Pa.	Dec. 15, 1905 Troop D
Wilbert Brooks	Aug. 23, 1871 Philadelphia, Pa.	Dec. 15, 1905 Troop D
Eugene V. Calvert	Feb. 14, 1879 Loyalsock, Pa.	Dec. 15, 1905 Troop D
Harry E. Carroll	Aug. 25, 1882 Baltimore, Md.	Dec. 15, 1905 Troop D
Thomas L. Casey	Sept. 6, 1878 Scranton, Pa.	Dec. 15, 1905 Troop D
Homer A. Chambers	July 26, 1881 Allegheny, Pa.	Dec. 15, 1905 Troop D
Joseph M. Curts	Mar. 17, 1876 Antes Fort, Pa.	Dec. 15, 1905 Troop D
John Devlin	Oct. 12, 1876 Armagh, Ireland	Dec. 15, 1905 Troop D
Emery Edwards	July 7, 1877 Plymouth, Pa.	Dec. 15, 1905 Troop D
Charles S. Everitt	Jan. 4, 1875 Philadelphia, Pa.	Dec. 15, 1905 Troop D
George W. Haas	Oct. 1, 1881 Riverside, Pa.	Dec. 15, 1905 Troop D
William E. Hess	Nov. 18, 1878 Reading, Pa.	Dec. 15, 1905 Troop D
Tyson C. Heller	Sept. 6, 1872 Reading, Pa.	Dec. 15, 1905 Troop D
John F. Henry	Aug. 10, 1875 New York, N.Y.	Dec. 15, 1905 Troop D
John L. Keogh	Apr. 17, 1884 Allegheny, Pa.	Dec. 15, 1905 Troop D
Frank Kettle	Oct. 7, 1877 Plymouth, Pa.	Dec. 15, 1905 Troop D
Nathan Kohut	Sept. 29, 1876 Austria	Dec. 15, 1905 Troop D
George H. Koons	Sept. 1, 1875 Buck Mountain, Pa.	Dec. 15, 1905 Troop D
Robert Lindsay	July 25, 1877 Philadelphia, Pa.	Dec. 15, 1905 Troop D
William E. Lyter	Nov. 13, 1881 Harrisburg, Pa.	Dec. 15, 1905 Troop D
Claude R. Masters	Aug. 27, 1880 Scranton, Pa.	Dec. 15, 1905 Troop D

Name	Date of Birth and Birthplace	Enlistment Date and Assignment
Joseph R. McIlvain	Mar. 4, 1884 Philadelphia, Pa.	Dec. 15, 1905 Troop D
Warren J. Meade	Dec. 12, 1876 Sinnamahoning, Pa.	Dec. 15, 1905 Troop D
Roy Nevins	Nov. 18, 1874 Savage, Md.	Dec. 15, 1905 Troop D
Charles L. Ohliger	May 24, 1875 Canton, Ohio	Dec. 15, 1905 Troop D
Clarke Read	Jan. 9, 1875 Harnesburg, N. J.	Dec. 15, 1905 Troop D
George S. Schollenberger	Feb. 12, 1881 Philadelphia, Pa.	Dec. 15, 1905 Troop D
Charles F. Smith	Apr. 13, 1880 Philadelphia, Pa.	Dec. 15, 1905 Troop D
Francis S. Strawser	Aug. 3, 1880 Freeburg, Pa.	Dec. 15, 1905 Troop D
George Wagner	May 14, 1879 Conynham, Pa.	Dec. 15, 1905 Troop D
Francis A. Zehringer	Feb. 18, 1872 Conshohocken, Pa.	Dec. 15, 1905 Troop D
Reginald H. Gibson	Apr. 14, 1868 Cork, Ireland	Dec. 15, 1905 Troop C
Walter W. Duffield	June 14, 1880	Dec. 19, 1905 Troop D
Frederick D. Frasch	Mar. 14, 1875 Harrisburg, Pa.	Dec. 20, 1905 Troop A
Giles L. Tompkins	Oct. 16, 1878 Meshoppen, Pa.	Dec. 20, 1905 Troop A
James Sutton, Jr.	Mar. 25, 1872 Clearfield, Pa.	Dec. 15, 1905 Troop D
Joseph D. Carroll	July 15, 1875 Norristown, Pa.	Dec. 20, 1905 Troop B
Frank M. Class	Mar. 14, 1875 Philadelphia, Pa.	Dec. 20, 1905 Troop B
John W. Coover	Apr. 30, 1876 Ephrata, Pa.	Dec. 20, 1905 Troop B
Maurice J. Welsh	Mar. 1, 1878 Philadelphia, Pa.	Dec. 21, 1905 Troop C
Charles H. Hanover	Feb. 15, 1878 Allegheny, Pa.	Dec. 15, 1905 Troop D
Lewis E. Lardin	Sept. 29, 1879 Johnstown, Pa.	Dec. 15, 1905 Troop D
J. Cheston Morris, Jr.	April 1, 1861 Philadelphia, Pa.	Dec. 26, 1905 Headquarters

Name	Date of Birth and Birthplace	Enlistment Date and Assignment
Ernest V. B. Douredoure	July 27, 1883 Philadelphia, Pa.	Dec. 27, 1905 Troop B
George L. Boyle	May 9, 1875 Philadelphia, Pa.	Jan. 3, 1906 Troop A
Frederick C. Vail	July 31, 1875 Germantown, Pa.	Jan. 4, 1906 Troop B
Joseph H. Randolph	Oct. 25, 1880 West Point, Miss.	Jan. 6, 1906 Troop D
Benjamin F. Rothstein	May 8, 1875 Petrolia, Pa.	Jan. 9, 1906 Troop D
Robert Cummings	Aug. 26, 1882 Wilkes-Barre, Pa.	Jan. 10, 1906 Troop D
August Grosser	May 13, 1883 Germany	Jan. 10, 1906 Troop D
Chalkley N. Booth	Aug. 11, 1877 Brandywine, Del.	Jan. 25, 1906 Troop B
Arthur Bates	Apr. 4, 1870 Philadelphia, Pa.	Jan. 26, 1906 Troop C
Henry Hilton	Dec. 30, 1884 Pittsburgh, Pa.	Feb. 1, 1906 Troop D
Judson H. Rutledge	Dec. 23, 1873 Masonville, Pa.	Feb. 9, 1906 Headquarters
James W. Page	May 12, 1880 Scranton, Pa.	Feb. 10, 1906 Troop B
Edward Grubgeld	May 15, 1876 Philadelphia, Pa.	Feb. 15, 1906 Troop B
Frederick C. Fessman	Mar. 28, 1871 Philadelphia, Pa.	Feb. 15, 1906 Troop B
Leslie C. Gray	Nov. 7, 1880 Phillipsburg, Pa.	Feb. 15, 1906 Troop B
John P. Butler	Dec. 25, 1879 Glasgow, Scotland	Feb. 15, 1906 Troop B
Lewis L. Adleson	Feb. 15, 1878 Brookville, Pa.	Feb. 15, 1906 Troop B
William Boyd	May 29, 1876 Philadelphia, Pa.	Feb. 15, 1906 Troop B
William V. Casey	Apr. 20, 1882 Wilmington, Del.	Feb. 15, 1906 Troop B
William Weathers	Feb. 12, 1880 Wyoma, W. Va.	Feb. 15, 1906 Troop C
Arthur Crehan	Sept. 8, 1881 Allegheny, Pa.	Feb. 15, 1906 Troop C
Arthur G. Smith	Aug. 17, 1879 Altoona, Pa.	Feb. 15, 1906 Troop C

Name	Date of Birth and Birthplace	Enlistment Date and Assignment
George W. Magargel	Apr. 9, 1877 Lairdsville, Pa.	Feb. 15, 1906 Troop C
Hunter T. Nugent	Apr. 23, 1884 Bryn Mawr, Pa.	Feb. 15, 1906 Troop D
Edward D. Baker	Apr. 19, 1878 Hollenbach, Pa.	Feb. 15, 1906 Troop A
William H. Edwards	Jan. 11, 1876 Philadelphia, Pa.	Feb. 15, 1906 Troop A
Morris Isaacs	Jan. 15, 1878 New York, N.Y.	Feb. 15, 1906 Troop A
Charles F. Kohler	Jan. 12, 1878 Philadelphia, Pa.	Feb. 15, 1906 Troop A
Wilbert E. Myers	May 19, 1880 Bloomington, Kan.	Feb. 15, 1906 Troop A
Shockley D. Mullinix	May 22, 1876 Montgomery County, N.C	Feb. 21, 1906 Troop C
William E. Hamilton	Dec. 18, 1876 Reading, Pa.	Feb. 15, 1906 Troop A
George M. Fries	Mar. 12, 1876 Philadelphia, Pa.	Mar. 16, 1906 Troop B
Thomas M. Boettner	Dec. 10, 1876 Tamaqua, Pa.	Mar. 19, 1906 Troop B
Herbert Smith	Jan. 5, 1881 Riverside, N.J.	Mar. 19, 1906 Troop B
James Mottola	Feb. 8, 1879 Naples, Italy	Mar. 20, 1906 Troop B
Thomas Parkinson	Jan. 25, 1880 Philadelphia, Pa.	Mar. 20, 1906 Troop B
John G. Meyer	June 24, 1878 New York, N.Y.	Mar. 20, 1906 Troop B
Joshua M. Ludwig	Oct. 1, 1878 York, Pa.	Mar. 21, 1906 Troop A
Ira C. Stevenson	Dec. 9, 1880 Butler, Pa.	Mar. 22, 1906 Troop B
Frederick Wright	Apr. 8, 1876 Baltimore, Md.	Mar. 22, 1906 Troop B
Charles A. McHugh	Nov. 8, 1875 Eagle Pass, Texas	Mar. 25, 1906 Troop B
Jens K. Jensen	Nov. 5, 1880 Visborg, Denmark	Mar. 25, 1906 Troop C
Frederick Crossland	June 10, 1880 Ingleside, Md.	Mar. 26, 1906 Troop C
Peter Wanner	May 27, 1877 Reading, Pa.	Mar. 26, 1906 Troop C
Robert J. Hafer	Apr. 24, 1875 Bridgeport, Pa.	Mar. 27, 1906 Troop C

Name	Date of Birth and Birthplace	Enlistment Date and Assignment
Francis H. Grey	Apr. 26, 1879 Washington, D.C.	Mar. 27, 1906 Troop D
Olaf D. Carlton	May 15, 1883 Lorraine, Ohio	Mar. 27, 1906 Troop D
William B. Thomas	Nov. 8, 1881 Shenandoah, Pa.	Mar. 31, 1906 Troop C
Thomas Meikrantz	Aug. 23, 1880 Hazleton, Pa.	Mar. 31, 1906 Troop C
Jasper Oftedahl	Dec. 17, 1879 Stavanger, Norway	Apr. 1, 1906 Troop B
George C. Powell	July 26, 1877 Cape May, N.J.	Mar. 31, 1906 Troop C
Charles Savary	Apr. 26, 1881 Middlefield, Mass.	Apr. 3, 1906 Troop C
John C. Wilson	Jan. 5, 1878 Rockford, Tenn.	Apr. 3, 1906 Troop B
Frederick Montgomery	Dec. 9, 1882 Hot Springs, Ark	Mar. 31, 1906 Troop A
James M. Boland	Oct. 17, 1881 Philadelphia, Pa.	Apr. 2, 1906 Troop A
James Allen	May 29, 1880 Boston, Mass.	Apr. 3, 1906 Troop A
James W. Wykoff	Aug. 1, 1880 Sinnamahoning, Pa.	Apr. 4, 1906 Troop D
Walter J. Koch	June 29, 1870 Reading, Pa.	Apr. 5, 1906 Troop D
William C. Ramsey	Oct. 17, 1875 Centre Square, Pa.	Apr. 9, 1906 Troop A
Charles Heinze	July 2, 1875 Glashutten, Germany	Apr. 11, 1906 Troop A
George W. Shaw	Apr. 22, 1883 Hickman, Ky.	Apr. 19, 1906 Troop A
John E. Walsh	Nov. 27, 1879 San Francisco, Cal.	Apr. 19, 1906 Troop D
Matthew J. Moran	Mar. 21, 1879 Castle Bar, Ireland	Apr. 20, 1906 Troop B
Milton K. Sterner	Mar. 14, 1880 Easton, Pa.	Apr. 21, 1906 Troop D
Leonard M. Andress	June 19, 1879 Conshohocken, Pa.	Apr. 26, 1906 Troop A
Leslie B. Tally	July 2, 1881 Hardford, Ky.	Apr. 26, 1906 Troop C
Archie W. Smith	Dec. 20, 1879 Washington, D.C.	Apr. 25, 1906 Troop D
Charles M. Culver	Feb. 8, 1879 Lewistown, N.Y.	May 3, 1906 Troop C

Name	Date of Birth and Birthplace	Enlistment Date and Assignment
William C. Wilhelm	Apr. 9, 1874 Columbia, Pa.	May 7, 1906 Troop A
John C. Alvator	May 10, 1878 New York, N. Y.	May 9, 1909 Troop A
George Wisman	Aug. 31, 1880 Marietta, Pa.	May 8, 1906 Troop C
Edward J. Barr	Feb. 21, 1874 Philadelphia, Pa.	May 23, 1906 Troop A
Hugh L. Marshall	Feb. 8, 1880 Boston, Mass.	May 23, 1906 Troop A
Marshall Crawford	June 29, 1879 Miles, Iowa	June 16, 1906 Troop B
John W. Hall	Mar. 28, 1880 Philadelphia, Pa.	July 2, 1906 Troop C
William L. Dalton	Apr. 2, 1879 Iron Bluff, N.C.	Aug. 1, 1906 Troop A
Henry Herlichka	Feb. 22, 1880 Pilsen, Austria	Aug. 1, 1906 Troop B
William H. Ramsey	Jan. 31, 1872 Harrisburg, Pa.	Aug. 3, 1906 Troop A
George E. Wilson	Jan. 27, 1877 Boston, Mass.	Aug. 3, 1906 Troop C
Richard F. Gray	July 1, 1879 Catfish, Pa.	Aug. 4, 1906 Troop B
Frank Young	July 5, 1872 Towanda, Pa.	Aug. 8, 1906 Troop A
Thomas L. Davis	Aug. 17, 1881 Conrad, N.C.	Aug. 14, 1906 Troop A
John M. Doerr	Apr. 30, 1883 Camden, N.J.	Aug. 16, 1906 Troop A
Harry E. Loomes	Feb. 19, 1873 Elmira, N.Y.	Aug. 24, 1906 Troop B
William A. Morgan	Aug. 9, 1875 Philadelphia, Pa.	Aug. 21, 1906 Troop A
James F. Ely	Apr. 7, 1879 Stone Run, Pa.	Aug. 28, 1906 Troop C
Max Kibel	June 6, 1879 New York, N.Y.	Aug. 24, 1906 Troop A
Samuel B. Nissley	Oct. 4, 1884 Landisville, Pa.	June 6, 1906 Headqaurters
George G. Burnside	Jan. 23, 1875 Philadelphia, Pa.	Sept. 27, 1906 Troop C
William H. Evans	Feb. 17, 1877 Norristown, Pa.	Oct. 1, 1906 Troop B
Herman W. Parker	Mar. 16, 1878 Big Run, Pa.	Sept. 29, 1906 Troop D

Name	Date of Birth and Birthplace	Enlistment Date and Assignment
Oswald Heinrichs	Dec. 15, 1880 Philadelphia, Pa.	Oct. 17, 1906 Troop B
Howard L. Hickok	Aug. 27, 1880 Philadelphia, Pa.	Oct. 20, 1906 Troop D
Amos C. Books	July 12, 1882 Lexington, Pa.	Oct. 22, 1906 Troop A
John J. McShea	July 22, 1878 Schenectady, N.Y.	Oct. 23, 1906 Troop A
Clark J. Rainey	Apr. 22, 1875 LaJose, Pa.	Nov. 1, 1906 Troop B
George B. Chidsey	Sept. 13, 1880 Rocky Fork, Tenn.	Nov. 1, 1906 Troop B
Charles C. Boyd	Jan. 30, 1881 Baltimore, Md.	Nov. 13, 1906 Troop B
Edward B. Casner	Nov. 12, 1873 Maysville, Ohio	Nov. 24, 1906 Troop C
Edward Hallisey	June 9, 1883 Lynn, Mass.	Nov. 28, 1906 Troop C
Walter S. Smeaton	Aug. 16, 1876 Somerville, Mass.	Dec. 1, 1906 Troop C
Frederick S. White	Feb. 15, 1883 Media, Pa.	Dec. 3, 1906 Troop C
William Durkin	Oct. 27, 1876 Lawrence, Mass.	Dec. 4, 1906 Troop A
Andrew Duke	Nov. 4, 1876 Cheerch, Hungary	Dec. 4, 1906 Troop B
Joseph Lawrence	Oct. 7, 1872 New York, N.Y.	Dec. 6, 1906 Troop A
John Moughan	Oct. 14, 1877 Plains, Pa.	Dec. 10, 1906 Troop B
Charles W. Burkett	June 7, 1883 Troy, N.Y.	Dec. 11, 1906 Troop B
William Metcalf	Apr. 25, 1881 New York, N.Y.	Dec. 13, 1906 Troop B
George Witekosky	June 22, 1879 Edwardsville, Pa.	Dec. 15, 1906 Troop B
Robert Wager	Apr. 26, 1882 Hunters Land, N.Y.	Dec. 19, 1906 Troop A
Lee Harpole	Oct. 11, 1881 Junction City, Ore.	Dec. 24, 1906 Troop D
Richard D. Reed	May 18, 1884 Horresdale, Pa.	Dec. 25, 1906 Troop B
James Ziegler	Oct. 31, 1876 Philadelphia, Pa.	Dec. 26, 1906 Troop C

ENACTMENTS OF THE PENNSYLVANIA GENERAL ASSEMBLY AFFECTING PENNSYLVANIA STATE POLICE OPERATIONS

Act No.	Pamphlet Law No.	Date of Approval	Purpose
228	225	2-27-1865	Authorizing any corporation owning, or using, a railroad, in this state to apply to the governor to commission such persons as the corporations may designate to act as policemen with powers to arrest and incarcerate. (Railroad Police)
87	99	4-11-1866	Authorizing corporations owning and operating mines and steel mills in this state to apply to the governor to commission such persons as the corporations may designate to act as policemen with powers to arrest and incarcerate. (Coal and Iron Police)
			* * * * * * *
227	361	5-2-1905	Creating the Department of State Police; providing for four troops (228 officers and men).
198	259	5-25-1907	Requiring daily settlements with State Treasurer and Auditor General.
—	551	6-1-1911	Creating new positions and increasing salaries.
338	528	6-19-1913	Authorizing the carrying out of capital punishment by electrocution, and providing funds for the construction of necessary facilities at the Western Penitentiary at Rockview, Centre County.
338	736	6-2-1915	Enacting the Workmen's Compensation Act; defining the liability of an employer to pay damages for injuries received by an employe in the course of employment; establishing an elective schedule of compensation; and providing procedure for the determination of liability and compensation.
36	54	4-12-1917	Increasing salaries and creating a new complement of 330 officers and men.
201	600	6-7-1917	Authorizing payment of one-half salary, not to exceed $2,000, annually, to state employes serving in the Army and Navy during World War I.

Act No.	Pamphlet Law No.	Date of Approval	Purpose
314	814	7-11-1917	Requiring State Police assistance to state Highway Commissioner in the use of prison labor.
347	1062	7-18-1917	Authorizing a Volunteer Police Force to protect all Pennsylvania interests from subversive enemy activities during World War I. Applicants to be commissioned by the governor, serve without pay, and perform duty under the direction of organized police departments.
179	366	6-3-1919	Reorganizing State Police, duties and powers, to include a Bureau of Fire Protection and keeping of criminal records; adding a fifth troop; increasing salaries and complement to 415 officers and men.
283	678	6-30-1919	Authorizing State Police to arrest, upon view, for violations of the Motor Code.
286	710	7-1-1919	Establishing duties of State Police relative to fires and fire prevention.
234	500	5-11-1921	Permitting appeals from State Police orders and decisions relative to fire prevention.
279	657	5-16-1921	Reporting of stolen motor vehicles to State Highway Department.
297	847	5-17-1921	Authorizing arrests for shooting at targets or random.
386	1061	5-21-1921	Creating school troop; adjusting service pay; increasing complement to 421 officers and men.
168	259	5-18-1923	Authorizing the State Highway Commissioner to empower certain other employes of his department to perform such official acts as he may designate. (State Highway Patrol)
183	283	5-19-1923	Citing duties of State Police relative to anti-lynching law.
230	425	5-24-1923	Authorizing State Highway Commissioner to appoint employes to enforce provisions of Motor Vehicle Code. (State Highway Patrol)
274	498	6-7-1923	Enacting the Administrative Code; abolishing the Bureau of Fire Protection as a specific agency; abolishing Deputy Superintendent and Chief of Bureau of Fire Protection as specific officers under law; adjusting powers and duties of State Police; changing name from Department of State Police to Pennsylvania State Police.
296	718	6-14-1923	Authorizing "designated officers" of the State Highway Department to enforce Motor Vehicle Code. (State Highway Patrol)

Act No.	Pamphlet Law No.	Date of Approval	Purpose
140	214	4–8–1925	Expanding special police commissions and powers to employes of utilities (water and electric), mineral mining, quarries and express companies.
177	314	4–27–1925	Establishing term of superintendent for four years "from the third Tuesday of January next following the election of a governor and until his successor shall have been appointed and qualified"; increasing salaries and service pay for enlisted personnel.
270	414	4–27–1927	Establishing a formal system of maintaining criminal records.
291	450	4–27–1927	Citing powers and duties for fire prevention.
452	886	5–11–1927	Publishing new Vehicle Code; citing authority of State Highway Patrolmen (Sec. 1215); authorizing State Police and Highway Patrol to weigh motor vehicles and trucks (Sec. 905).
153	151	4–5–1929	Repealing P.L. 361 (1905) and P.L. 54 (1917) relative to salaries of officers and men.
175	177	4–9–1929	Enacting the Administrative Code of 1929; citing powers and duties of the superintendent and Pennsylvania State Police; transferring the State Highway Patrol to the Department of Revenue; requiring biennial reports to governor on even-numbered years.
243	546	4–18–1929	Creating a system for screening industrial security police prior to issuing commissions; modifying Coal and Iron Police authority; better known as Industrial Police Act of 1929.
403	905	5–1–1929	Enacting Vehicle Code of 1929; citing authority of State Highway Patrol.
463	1539	5–3–1929	Increasing salaries of enlisted personnel.
55-A	36	5–3–1929	Authorizing installation of electrically-operated telephone/typewriter system of communication and appropriating funds.
158	497	6–11–1931	Enacting the Uniform Firearms Act and placing enforcement with the Secretary of the Commonwealth.
255	694	6–22–1931	Requiring State Highway Patrol to assist Department of Revenue in the enforcement of Highway Use Excise Tax Law.
282	1139	6–1–1933	Abolishing certain fire prevention records and reports required by P.L. 450 (1927).
156	348	6–15–1935	Repealing enactments and abolishing Coal and Iron Police.

Act No.	Pamphlet Law No.	Date of Approval	Purpose
379	1169	7–18–1935	Adjusting complement and salaries; establishing a detective division.
411½	1314	7–18–1935	Authorizing training of municipal police at State Police Training School and appropriating funds.
355	1056	7–16–1935	Citing authority of police officers, including State Police; making it "unlawful for operators to refuse to comply with any lawful order, signal or direction of a peace officer who shall be in uniform and exhibit his badge or other sign of authority."
211	774	5–21–1937	Establishing the Pennsylvania Turnpike Commission and authorizing the commission to build and maintain a toll roadway from Middlesex, Cumberland County, to Irwin, Westmoreland County.
448	2403	6–29–1937	Citing duties relating to fires and fire protection; name changed to Pennsylvania Motor Police.
449	2410	6–29–1937	Updating statutes relative to training school to reflect merger of State Police and Highway Patrol.
450	2412	6–29–1937	Authorizing use of Motor License Fund for partial funding of Pennsylvania Motor Police.
451	2420	6–29–1937	Regulating hours of rest and vacation.
452	2421	6–29–1937	Enforcing act pertaining to dry cleaning.
453	2423	6–29–1937	Establishing and regulating retirement system; compulsory membership in system.
454	2433	6–29–1937	Updating statutes on maintaining criminal identification records to reflect change to Pennsylvania Motor Police.
455	2436	6–29–1937	Amending the Administrative Code of 1929 to reflect consolidation of Pennsylvania State Police and State Highway Patrol; providing Pennsylvania Motor Police with complement of 1,600 officers and men. Setting salary of commissioner at $8,000, annually, and limiting appointments to one deputy.
307	660	6–21–1939	Citing duty to return escaped convicts.
378	1080	6–26–1939	Authorizing return of parole violators at penitentiary expense.
400	1135	6–27–1939	Regulating the annual inspection of school buses by Motor Police.
91	207	6–25–1941	Regulating payment into retirement fund by members while in military and naval service.
117	249	7–3–1941	Specifying retirement system rights and obligations of members in active wartime service.

Act No.	Pamphlet Law No.	Date of Approval	Purpose
189	494	7-24-1941	Appointing a representative of Motor Police to Pennsylvania Highway Traffic Advisory Committee to assist U. S. War Department.
19	50	4-21-1942	Amending P.L. 600 (1917) relative to half-pay to dependents during military service; limited by combined service pay and allowances.
42	67	4-22-1943	Providing for pay increases and advancement in rank for members in active wartime service.
52	94	4-28-1943	Amending the Administrative Code to change name from Pennsylvania Motor Police to Pennsylvania State Police.
53	101	4-28-1943	Amending P.L. 2420 (1937) to reflect name change.
54	102	4-29-1943	Amending P.L. 494 (1941) to reflect name change.
55	104	4-28-1943	Amending P.L. 1314 (1935) to reflect name change.
56	106	4-28-1943	Amending P.L. 2423 (1937) to reflect name change.
57	110	4-28-1943	Amending P.L. 1046 (1929) to reflect name change.
58	111	4-28-1943	Amending P.L. 905 (1929) to reflect name change.
59	114	4-28-1943	Amending P.L. 249 (1941) to reflect name change.
60	118	4-28-1943	Amending P.L. 660 (1939) to reflect name change.
61	119	4-28-1943	Amending P.L. 414 (1927) to reflect name change.
62	122	4-28-1943	Amending P.L. 694 (1931) to reflect name change.
63	123	4-28-1943	Amending P.L. 450 (1927) to reflect name change.
216	485	5-21-1943	Amending the Penal Code sections relating to the Uniform Firearms Act and transferring enforcement to State Police.
211	538	5-15-1945	Amending P.L. 1019 (1933) relative to payment for removal of fire hazards.
239	583	5-16-1945	Providing for additional credit for war veterans taking examinations for State Police enlistment.
262	620	5-16-1945	Amending P.L. 450 (1927) relative to removal or change of building fire hazards by political subdivisions.
267	627	5-17-1945	Amending P.L. 787 (1937) relative to removal of fire hazards.

Act No.	Pamphlet Law No.	Date of Approval	Purpose
336	834	5–22–1945	Restoring retirement rights and specifying time for rejoining retirement system after military service.
375	945	5–24–1945	Amending P.L. 280 (1931) relative to payment of costs of eliminating fire hazards.
442	1388	6–4–1945	Providing right of appeal to Court of Common Pleas of Dauphin County, when aggrieved by action of the commissioner.
267	625	6–16–1947	Increasing state retirement annuities and further regulating allowances.
315	720	6–20–1947	Providing for payment of tax on premiums of foreign casualty insurance companies into state annuity accounts.
390	935	6–25–1947	Authorizing search without warrant to assist Department of Revenue in collecting cigarette tax.
497	1199	7–2–1947	Authorizing enforcement of Fuel Use Tax Act to assist Department of Revenue.
43	396	4–6–1949	Clarifying P.L. 450 (1927) relative to appeals to fire prevention orders.
192	776	4–28–1949	Increasing salary of commissioner to $15,000 and deputy to $8,500.
268	956	5–9–1949	Setting obligation of State Police to assist Department of Public Instruction in preparing text books relative to fire prevention.
402	1342	4–14–1949	Permitting State Police to inspect dry cleaning and dyeing plants.
425	1438	5–18–1949	Increasing complement to 1,800 officers and men. (Previously 1,600)
568	1903	5–27–1949	Enacting the Military Code of 1949 exempting members of State Police from militia duty except by voluntary enlistment.
4	28	3–19–1951	Creating the State Council of Civil Defense for the general purpose of assisting in the coordination of the state and local activities related to national and state civil defense.
9	53	3–22–1951	Subjecting control of special fire police to State Police.
14	57	3–22–1951	Imposing duties on State Police relative to fireworks.
561	2016	1–14–1952	Authorizing transfer of police and auxiliary police during disasters and emergencies under State Police direction.
609	2150	1–18–1952	Increasing salary of deputy commissioner to $10,000.

Act. No.	Pamphlet Law No.	Date of Approval	Purpose
254	1006	7–29–1953	Increasing complement to 1,900 officers and men. (Previously 1,800)
361	1273	8–21–1953	Regulating the business of private detectives, to be known as Private Detective Act of 1953.
83	259	7–7–1955	Authorizing payment for certain injuries, more commonly known as the Heart and Lung Act.
128	321	8–9–1955	Providing for additional credits to applicants serving in any armed conflict.
257	866	12–15–1955	Providing that State Policemen assigned to duty with the Pennsylvania Turnpike Commission shall not be counted in authorized complement of 1,900 officers and men.
446	1387	4–4–1956	Changing to biweekly pay periods effective 6–1–1956. (Previously paid twice a month)
657	1959	6–1–1956	Increasing salaries of commissioner to $20,000 and deputy to $13,500.
592	1761	5–28–1956	Providing funds for the construction of a new Pennsylvania State Police Training School at Hershey.
40	98	4–30–1957	Amending Private Detective Act of 1953 to include members of the State Police.
122	245	6–5–1957	Requiring insurance companies to report fire losses to State Police.
359	679	7–10–1957	Imposing duties on State Police relative to the sale and use of air rifles.
360	682	7–10–1957	Providing for mandatory retirement of enlisted men at age 60, and excluding commissioner and deputy, and any member with less than twenty years of service; effective 1–1–1958.
78	392	6–1–1959	Revising membership in Class C (Retirement System), effective 8–1–1959, to include only those having police powers.
112	487	6–29–1959	Changing name of Pennsylvania State Police Training School to Pennsylvania State Police Academy.
113	488	6–29–1959	Changing name of Pennsylvania State Police Training School to Pennsylvania State Police Academy.
327	838	9–8–1959	Making unlawful for State Police, or any state agency, to refuse employment to members of Pennsylvania National Guard not on extended active duty.
455	1334	10–21–1959	Entitling FOP representatives to leave of absence, with pay, to attend state and national lodge convention or conference.
533	1518	11–19–1959	Establishing procedure for furnishing abstract of accident investigations for a fee of $3.00.
696	1916	12–17–1959	Authorizing the carry-over of unused annual and sick leave entitlements and setting limits.

Act No.	Pamphlet Law No.	Date of Approval	Purpose
48	108	4–28–1961	Amending the Vehicle Code to authorize use of radar by State Police.
336	653	7–14–1961	Basing retirement on average compensation of highest five years.
356	820	7–20–1961	Providing for public liability insurance coverage while performing official duties.
430	965	8–7–1961	Authorizing Department of Property and Supplies to purchase radio communications system from Bell Telephone Company.
444	995	8–18–1961	Increasing complement to 2,100 officers and men. (Previously 1,900)
593	1341	9–15–1961	Clarifying provisions for disability retirement.
147	275	7–25–1963	Regulating dismissal, suspension, demotion and reenlistment.
148	278	7–25–1963	Specifying that no member shall be dismissed or reduced in rank except by court-martial.
85	123	6–8–1965	Providing for closed-secret vote by court-martial board and furnishing transcript to the accused.
112	193	7–9–1965	Increasing salary of commissioner from $20,000 to $25,000; applying this raise only to persons appointed to office after 7–9–1965.
323	657	11–9–1965	Authorizing enforcement of provisions of Hazardous Substance Transportation Act.
458	1164	12–22–1965	Providing for pensions to widows of enlisted members who died in the line of duty prior to January 1, 1938.
6	54	8–31–1966	Increasing complement to 2,350 officers and men. (Previously 2,100)
12	22	5–3–1967	Increasing salary of commissioner to $25,000, annually, and removing salary of deputy from legal restrictions.
48	172	7–12–1967	Increasing complement to 3,550 officers and men during 1967–1971 period (a 1200-man increase at a rate of 300 per year).
112	275	8–24–1967	Authorizing State Police to assist Department of Revenue with inspection of hold-down and tie-down devices.
140	321	10–5–1967	Eliminating two-year enlistments.
239	492	10–26–1967	Raising fee for copy of accident investigation record to $5.00.
312	671	12–5–1967	Amending Tenure Act to exclude cadets and troopers with less than eighteen months of service.

Act No.	Pamphlet Law No.	Date of Approval	Purpose
313	673	12–5–1967	Establishing an eighteen-month probationary period for cadets and troopers.
111	237	6–24–1968	Authorizing collective bargaining between policemen and public employers; providing for binding arbitration.
235	754	7–31–1968	Creating the Pennsylvania Crime Commission in the Department of Justice, consisting of the attorney general as chairman and four other commissioners appointed by the governor.
376	1202	12–12–1968	Forbidding the interception of police broadcast messages "for the purpose of aiding himself or others in the perpetration of any unlawful act."
188 (1969 Session)	460	1–13–1970	Providing for the mandatory reporting of crime data (UCR statistics) to the Department of Justice.
117	351	5–6–1970	Transferring 43.19 acres of land in Susquehanna Township, Dauphin County, from Department of Welfare to State Police for new Troop H headquarters building.
163	608	12–15–1971	Increasing complement to 3,790 officers and men. (Previously 3,550)
24	72	2–17–1972	Amending P.L. 450 (1927) relative to fire prevention laws and State Police duties.
349	1649	12–28–1972	Increasing complement to 3,940 officers and men. (Previously 3,790)
Reorganization Plan No. 7 of 1973	P.L. 464	10–10–1973	Amending act 188, P.L. 460 (1970) and transferring the administration of crime data collection (UCR program) from the Department of Justice to the State Police effective immediately.
31	125	3–1–1974	Enacting State Employees' Retirement Code; defining final average salary base on highest compensation received during any three non-overlapping periods of twelve consecutive months; allowing the return of accumulated contributions, and disallowing any amendment thereto by collective bargaining under Acts 111 and 195.
120	359	6–18–1974	Creating the Municipal Police Officers' Education and Training Commission, and citing duties of State Police commissioner to implement and administer the minimum courses of study and training for municipal police officers covered by this act.

Act No.	Pamphlet Law No.	Date of Approval	Purpose
235	705	10–10–1974	Enacting the Lethal Weapons Training Act; obliging State Police to educate, train and certify privately employed agents who, as an incidence of their employment, carry lethal weapons.
30 (HB-749)		4–7–1976	Amending the Crimes Code to permit police departments to record certain incoming telephone calls.
81 (HB-1817)		6–17–1976	Enacting a new Motor Vehicle Code with sweeping changes in the laws for the motoring public in Pennsylvania.
101 (HB-385)		6–24–1976	Providing for the payment of $25,000 to survivors of firemen and police officers killed in the performance of duty.
254 (HB-1945)		11–23–1976	Amending the Lethal Weapons Training Act of 1974.
227 (SB-21)		11–8–1976	Amending the Administrative Code of 1929; requiring a simple majority of twenty-six votes in the Senate to confirm the State Police commissioner instead of two-thirds vote.

BRIEF HISTORY OF PENNSYLVANIA STATE POLICE APPROPRIATIONS

From 1905 through 1960, the general assembly appropriated funds for two year periods. Except for convening in special sessions, the general assembly met only during odd-numbered years. The practice of annual appropriations was begun for the 1961–62 fiscal year which was thirteen months long (June 1, 1961, to June 30, 1962) in order to adjust to the federal fiscal year. Until 1923, appropriations were based on line-item budgets, wherein funds were designated for specific·purposes. When the Administrative Code of 1923 was enacted, appropriations were more generally applied to agency requirements.

In 1923, when the State Highway Patrol was organized, operational funds were drawn by warrant from the Motor License Fund by the Department of Highways. No appropriations enactments were required of the general assembly. When the Highway Patrol was transferred to the Department of Revenue in 1929, the same funding procedure was observed until the merger with the Pennsylvania State Police in 1937.

Beginning with 1937 through 1971, the State Police budget was largely a reflection of administrative costs and criminal activities on one hand and traffic operations on the other. The budget was proportioned according to the deployment of manpower during the previous year. Administrative costs and criminal activities, constituting approximately 20 percent of the total budget, were supported by General Fund appropriations; traffic operations, however, were supported by unappropriated transfers from the Motor License Fund. Later on the augmentation system was enlarged to include: (1) tranfers from the Motor License Fund, (2) refunds from the Turnpike Commission for salaries paid patrol personnel and an overhead percentage for benefits and equipment, (3) receipts from the sale of used patrol vehicles, (4) fees received from municipalities for training police officers at the academy (basically expenses for quarters and meals), and (5) federal funding as it became available in later years.

The augmentation program was discontinued with the 1971–72 fiscal period. Beginning with the State Police budget for that fiscal year, all funds, regardless of their intended usage, were appropriated by the general assembly. This procedure remains in effect.

PENNSYLVANIA STATE POLICE APPROPRIATIONS

Act No.	Pamphlet Law No.	Date	Amount	Remarks
227	361	5–2–1905	$425,000	Included $5,000 insurance coverage collected on Wyoming barracks fire of 1908.
673	752	6–14–1907	$512,600	
659	864	5–15–1909	$540,300	First salary increase and adjustment in ranks.
—	207A	6–14–1911	$647,340	
407	755	7–16–1913	$676,260	
429	33A	6–16–1915	$714,635	
37-A	34	6–22–1917	$7,262	Deficiency appropriations.
46-A	41	7–16–1917	$1,137,640	
42-A	34	7–16–1919	$1,766,775	Included appropriations for new Bureau of Fire Protection; Governor Sproul redlined $30,000.
1-A	3	3–2–1921	$6,000	Deficiency appropriations.
42-A	33	5–27–1921	$1,912,645	Governor Sproul redlined $125,000.
44-A	35	6–30–1923	$1,500,000	First budget not line-itemized.
328-A	190	5–14–1925	$1,662,000	
347-A	194	5–11–1927	$1,662,000	
55-A	36	5–3–1929	$260,000	Funding for new teletypewriter system; Governor Fisher redlined $115,000.
354-A	181	5–16–1929	$2,091,500	Included deficit from previous fiscal period.
133	289	5–29–1931	—	Authorized Dept. of Revenue to appropriate Motor License Fund money for the lease or purchase of land for the State Highway Patrol.
15-A	16	6–11–1931	$2,491,500	Included funds for teletypewriter system.
300-A	169	6–3–1933	$2,491,500	Deficiency appropriations—Special session.
67	288	1–19–1934	$93,000	For municipal police training.
411½	1314	7–18–1935	$20,000	
77-A	71	7–20–1935	$2,565,000	
53	131	8–7–1936	$9,000	Deficiency appropriations—Special session.
59-A	47	6–29–1937	$50,000	Motor License Fund to meet obligation of Motor Police Retirement System.
59½-A	47	6–29–1937	$50,000	General Fund to meet obligation of Motor Police Retirement System.

Act No.	Pamphlet Law No.	Date	Amount	Remarks
103-A	74	7-2-1937	$1,000,000	"And any additional sums, from time to time, transferred from Motor License Fund."
69-A	60	6-27-1939	$1,000,000	"And any additional sums, from time to time, transferred from Motor License Fund."
12-A	13	6-16-1941	$1,000,000	"And any additional sums, from time to time, transferred from Motor License Fund."
77-A	59	6-4-1943	$1,000,000	"And any additional sums, from time to time, transferred from Motor License Fund."
77-A	54	6-1-1945	$1,850,000	For purchase of land and construction of new buildings; Governor Martin withheld $200,000.
87-A	63	6-4-1945	$3,000,000	"And any additional sums, from time to time, transferred from Motor License Fund."
94-A	72	7-9-1947	$5,000,000	"And any additional sums, from time to time, transferred from Motor License Fund."
89-A	62	5-27-1949	$5,800,000	"And any additional sums, from time to time, transferred from Motor License Fund."
134-A (1951 Session)	87	1-21-1952	$6,330,000	"And any additional sums, from time to time, transferred from Motor License Fund."
78-A	54	8-22-1953	$6,906,000	"And any additional sums, from time to time, transferred from Motor License Fund."
592	1761	5-28-1956	$3,000,000	Authorized construction of new training school, troop headquarters buildings at Erie, Blakely, and other stations.
150-A	120	6-1-1956	$6,515,000	"And any additional sums, from time to time, transferred from Motor License Fund."
95-A	60	7-19-1957	$7,000,000	Motor License Fund, Turnpike Commission and training fees augmentations.
38-A	34	11-12-1959	$7,157,272	Motor License Fund, Turnpike Commission and training fees augmentations.
5-A	38	5-25-1961	$3,472,966	First annual budget, covering thirteen months 6-1-1961 to 6-30-1962 to establish new fiscal period.

Act No.	Pamphlet Law No.	Date	Amount	Remarks
1-A	5	3-7-1962	$3,421,553	Add augmentations.
45-A	33	8-13-1963	$2,939,124	Add augmentations.
50-A	36	6-18-1964	$3,157,858	Add augmentations.
19-A	19	7-9-1965	$3,157,858	Add augmentations.
69-A	59	8-24-1966	$4,068,696	Add augmentations.
31-A	29	8-30-1967	$5,856,175	Add augmentations.
72-A	55	6-27-1968	$7,495,084	Add augmentations.
12-A	14	7-31-1969	$7,995,000	Add augmentations.
78-A	86	3-24-1970	$8,695,000	Amended Act 12-A (1969) to increase General Fund appropriations for 1969–70 fiscal period. Add augmentations.
3-A	809	3-4-1971	$10,600,000	For 1970–71 fiscal period. Add augmentations. Final year for augmentations program.
24-A	870	8-3-1971	$45,842,000	Traffic control. (1971–72)
			$1,066,000	Traffic safety facilities. (1971–72)
27-A	878	8-31-1971	$14,836,000	General administration—criminal activities. (1971–72)
			$ 710,000	Narcotics control. (1971–72)
17-A	1849	6-7-1972	$20,423,000	General administration—criminal activities. (1972–73)
19-A	1891	7-7-1972	$55,093,000	Traffic control and safety facilities. (1972–73)
9-A	483	6-29-1973	$61,933,000	Traffic control and safety facilities. (1973–74)
11-A	489	7-12-1973	$22,026,000	General administration—criminal activities. (1973–74)
21-A	1371	6-26-1974	$25,240,000	General administration—criminal activities. (1974–75)
23-A	1412	6-27-1974	$70,276,000	Traffic control and safety facilities. (1974–75)
8-A	(HB-1336)	6-30-1975	$22,066,000	General administration—criminal activities. (1975–76)
9-A	(SB-823)	7-9-1975	$76,482,000	Traffic control and safety facilities. (1975–76)
			$1,600,000	Municipal Police Training. (1975–76)
7-A	(HB-568)	6-4-1976	$27,439,000	General administration—criminal activities. (1976–77)
15-A	(SB-1417)	6-30-1976	$83,484,000	Traffic control and safety facilities. (1976–77)
			$1,400,000	Municipal Police Training. (1976–77)

APPROPRIATIONS LISTED BY FISCAL PERIODS

Biennial Budgets			
1905–1907	$425,000	1951–1953	$31,650,000
1907–1909	$512,600	1953–1955	$34,530,000
1909–1911	$540,300	1955–1957	$32,575,000
1911–1913	$647,340	1957–1959	$35,000,000
1913–1915	$676,260	1959–1961	$35,786,360
1915–1917	$721,897	*Annual Budgets*	
1917–1919	$1,137,640	1961–1962	$17,364,483
1919–1921	$1,772,775	1962–1963	$17,107,765
1921–1923	$1,912,645	1963–1964	$14,695,620
1923–1925	$1,500,000	1964–1965	$15,789,290
1925–1927	$1,662,000	1965–1966	$15,789,290
1927–1929	$1,662,000	1966–1967	$20,343,480
1929–1931	$2,351,500	1967–1968	$29,280,875
1931–1933	$2,491,500	1968–1969	$37,475,420
1933–1935	$2,584,500	1969–1970	$43,475,000
1935–1937	$2,594,000	1970–1971	$53,000,000
1937–1939	$5,000,000	1971–1972	$62,454,000
1939–1941	$5,000,000	1972–1973	$75,516,000
1941–1943	$5,000,000	1973–1974	$83,959,000
1943–1945	$5,000,000	1974–1975	$95,516,000
1945–1947	$15,000,000	1975–1976	$100,148,000
1947–1949	$25,000,000	1976–1977	$112,323,000
1949–1951	$29,000,000		

ROSTER
Pennsylvania State Police
1936

Executive Office

Major Lynn G. Adams—Superintendent
Major Cecil M. Wilhelm—Deputy Superintendent
Silvus J. Overmiller—Comptroller
Guy E. Reichard—Chief Quartermaster
John R. Price—Accountant
Chester E. Shuler—Advanced stenographer-secretary
Carl A. Knorr—Principal statistical clerk
Gilbert W. Aungst—Head file clerk
Lloyd V. Becker—Radio announcer
Herman L. Breighner—Senior police clerk

Bureau of Criminal Indentification and Information

William F. Hoffman—Director
Charles Kunz—Supervising fingerprint operator
John A. Funck—Micro-ballistician
Vernon N. Clemmens—Fingerprint indentification clerk (Reading)
Earl T. Denton—Fingerprint identification clerk (Butler)
Benjamin K. Lee—Fingerprint identification clerk (Wyoming)
Harold Nifong—Fingerprint identification clerk (Harrisburg)
Paul J. Roche—Fingerprint identification clerk (Harrisburg)
Elmer H. Doll—Junior fingerprint identification clerk
Sam C. Garvin—Senior photographer
Stanford C. Smith—Senior fingerprint clerk
Harry J. Strine—Senior permit clerk
Ralph L. Fiscel—Junior photographer

Bureau of Fire Protection

William F. Treager—Fire marshall
Ralph D. Gardner—Senior investigator
Ethel M. Wright—Senior stenographer

Troop A, Greensburg

Captain Jacob C. Mauk
Lieutenant Charles C. Keller
First Sergeant John J. Tomek
Principal Police Clerk Blair D. O'Neal
Principal Clerk—Stenographer James K. Seacrist
Special Stenographer—Clerk Frank Hamm
Special Stenographer—Clerk Percy C. Kratzer

Sergeants—
  James V. Buckley
  Frank Gleason
  Vincent F. Bunch
  Jackson R. Dodson
  William R. Hanna
Corporals—
  James F. Maroney
  Hilding C. Johnson
  Joseph J. Conwell
  William Tevelin
  Francis J. Hanley
  Harry G. E. Wagner
  Eugene L. Fontaine
  Walter B. Kunkle
  Alfred W. Flinner
  Charles A. Haxton
Privates 1st Class—
  Adams, Glenn W.
  Ammerman, Emerick L.
  Beck, John C.
  Benson, George H.
  Bretz, Ralph S.
  Bricklemyer, John E.
  Brozenn, George J.
  Buck, Charles F.
  Chrin, John
  DeWitt, Charles H.
  Domin, Thomas B.
  Drenning, David A.
  Erickson, Carl A.
  Faber, Elmer W.
  Forney, Lester E.
  Gage, Leon H.

Gertzen, Rudolph F.
Gettier, John E.
Griffith, James H.
Grill, Alfred A.
Gunderman, Stacy B.
Hanmore, Clare M.
Hanna, Charles J.
Harrison, Edward P.
Helfenstein, John P.
Hoffer, Joseph A.
Kercher, George W.
Mannion, Joseph E.
Maurer, Carl A.
McAllister, Frederick P.
McKee, Robert C.
Miller, Leo R.
Miskill, Thomas G.
Moats, Troy A.
Moffatt, Charles R.
Morrison, Edward W.
Naughton, George D.
O'Mara, John F.
Regna, John R.
Rittelmann, Paul A.
Sanute, Anthony
Schmoyer, Elmer
Sherlock, Stephen
Stansfield, Harold W.
Thomas, Charles W.
Valentine, Aubert T.
Walsh, Raymond F.
Wasconis, George S.
Witzel, William J.
Wood, Arthur C.

Troop B, Wyoming

Captain William A. Clark
Lieutenant William D. Plummer
First Sereant Charles S. Cook
Principal Police Clerk Frank M. Barry
Principal Clerk—Stenographer George R. Naugle
Special Stenographer—Clerk Leo A. Garvey
Special Stenographer—Clerk Stanley A. Gabrysh

Sergeants—
  Norman E. Annick
  Joseph H. Miller
  Theodore W. Enoch
  Harold T. Newman
  Stanley S. Smith
Corporals—
  John A. Carr
  Joseph F. Santilli

Charles D. Santee
Jacob E. Hess
Robert C. Frick
Charles E. Stewart
Robert W. Knight
Leo R. Pope
Isador Brauch
Joseph A. Piorkowski

Privates 1st Class—

Bader, Worden A.
Baldieri, Albert F.
Banghart, Delroy
Barr, Edward E.
Bohr, Lynn H.
Bonfanti, Joseph F.
Boyer, George W.
Brand, Charles A.
Broski, John J.
Brown, Winfield M.
Coates, James W.
Connolly, Charles A.
Daubensqeck, Henry B.
Davis, Morgan B.
Deckard, Wilmer
Dixon, Edwin S.
Duffy, Francis M.
Dula, John K.
Emminger, Jonas G.
Eshlemann, Thomas E.
Fink, William G.
Garman, Earl L.
Green, Clifton D.
Green, David R.
Hartman, Charles
Jones, Arthur V.
Jones, Richard H.
Kisner, Howard W.
Klinger, Harry W.

Koval, John
Leh, Edward F.
Lesher, John R.
McCartney, Frank H.
McChesney, Lewis W.
McIlvaine, Joseph F.
McQuaid, Edward J.
Metz, Lester G.
Milligan, Jay C.
Minnich, Clarence R.
Murphy, William V.
Musser, Robert W.
Neilson, Russel R.
Neville, Charles H.
Reed, Warren A.
Reigel, Charles C.
Rowswell, William H.
Ryan, Michael C.
Ryan, Paul V.
Sapudar, Frank N.
Singer, Warren W.
Soule, Orin E.
Spence, Roger L.
Spotts, Sherman C.
Tissue, Kenneth N.
Unger, Donald K.
Weichel, Joseph C.
Werst, Kenneth H.
Wilson, Aloysius J.

Troop C, Reading

Captain Samuel W. Gearhart
Lieutenant Edwin C. Griffith
First Sergeant Edward C. Sickel
Principal Police Clerk Raymond S. Herb
Principal Clerk—Stenographer Paul E. Levan
Special Stenographer—Clerk Samuel A. Ely
Special Stenographer—Clerk Denver B. Barne

Sergeants

Reese L. Davis
Aaron P. Reichard
William W. Francis
Paul N. Wagner
Ray H. Simmons

Corporals—

William S. Bloom
Earl C. Pepple
Daniel C. Dean
William P. Snyder
John R. Stewart
John M. Wommer

William F. Herman
Michael J. Reilly
Carl Skup
Robert C. Mock

Privates 1st Class—

Amey, Douglas J.
Bast, Stanton L.
Bell, Harry E.
Boxler, Raymond G.
Brace, Thomas
Burkholder, James L.
Burtner, Bruce L.

Christ, Harry F.
Dando, Harold
Davey, Joseph R.
Dooner, Thomas W.
Edwards, Cyril G.
Eisenberger, Harry U.
Enck, Milton S.
Ericsson, Donald C.
Ertle, Walter
Farrell, John J.
Fisher, Charles H.
Fitzgerald, Harry E.
Frank, Norman W.
Gowan, Felix R.
Greblunas, Peter
Habig, Henry P.
Haman, Walter A.
Harbold, Charles E.
Hartman, Claude E.
Heston, Francis M.
Huzvar, John F.
Keuch, William J.
Lenker, John F.
Lichty, Benjamin O.
Lowson, Thomas
Lucas, Lester L.

Lyons, Joseph J.
Marshall, John A.
McBreen, Edward P.
McBride, Joseph W.
McDevitt, John F.
Moody, Charles G.
Paradiso, Anthony C.
Picton, Leonard
Ramer, Freeman R.
Ransom, Willis E.
Reed, John B.
Reilly, Peter J.
Roth, Rudolph
Sapudar, Lawrence
Sauer, George M.
Scheidel, John J.
Smith, George G.
Smith, Stiles H.
Soule, Howard D.
Strahan, Robert M.
Strickland, Edward J.
Taylor, Charles W.
Toye, Thomas F.
Wagner, Donald E.
Wert, William L.
Wilhelm, Marshall N.

Troop D, Butler

Captain Jasper Oftedahl
Lieutenant Thomas M. Boettner
First Sergeant Martin J. Crowley
Principal Police Clerk C. C. Bowman
Principal Clerk—Stenographer Carl A. Kennedy
Special Stenographer—Clerk Ambrose E. Bergan
Special Stenographer—Clerk Homer S. Hammond

Sergeants—
  Emmett J. Donovan
  Edward J. Price
  Edward C. Bergan
  John F. Mullany
  Harold W. Pierce
Corporals—
  Frank Milligan
  Charles E. Stacy
  Russell Barker
  Walter L. Gibbons
  Marcus White
  Joseph F. Schmidt
  James B. Brooks
  William R. Brush
  Joseph H. Wigton
  George W. Shiner

Privates 1st Class—
  Amos, Daniel O.
  Balsiger, James W.
  Banks, Steven C.
  Barone, Frank
  Bassler, Sherman G.
  Bradbury, Jack
  Croup, John C.
  Eben, John J.
  Edelman, John T.
  Engle, Paul T.
  Fitzgerald, Harold E.
  Foley, Claude H.
  Foley, Gordon H.
  Franko, William E.
  Gecelosky, Andrew M.
  Gibbons, Walter A.

Hartzell, George A.
Hayes, William J.
Hayman, Willis J.
Henicheck, Jacob J.
Hichenko, Andrew
Hughmanick, Andrew C.
James, Edward
Knudson, Albin L.
Limbers, Earl F.
Lloyd, Louis R.
Longo, Paul A.
Machin, Ray A.
Malloy, Raymond B.
Mathias, Cecil M.
May, Samuel
Mazza, George
McCullough, Robert O.
Mears, Ralph V.
Mehallick, John
Moran, Bernard J.

Mosier, James W.
Mullen, Charles E.
Munsee, Harold N.
Nevin, William L.
Redman, Edward G.
Rogosky, Anthony S.
Rothwell, John F.
Rousseau, Eugene
Schauer, Willard
Sedlock, Michael J.
Shulick, Michael T.
Sibley, Robert L.
Snipas, Clemence C.
Sorok, Charles
Steiner, Joseph E.
Stinnett, Harry A.
Stuck, James L.
Taylor, John E.
Weir, Albert R.
Zerbe, Michael J.

Troop E, Harrisburg

Captain Paul B. Stout
Lieutenant Montgomery B. Bennett
First Sergeant Donald H. Austin
Principal Police Clerk William N. Doll
Principal Clerk—Stenographer Fred J. Denn
Special Stenographer—Clerk W. Earl Gulden
Special Stenographer—Clerk Robert P. Maffett

Sergeants—
  Albert F. Dahlstrom
  Edwin J. Stroman
  Maurice O. Harnois
  Russell W. Frutchey
  Charles E. Weller
Corporals—
  Samuel S. Mollenkof
  William M. Lewis
  Arthur B. Snyder
  Albert Davis
  Joseph S. Holochwost
  Linton D. Gritman
  Henry W. Buckbee
  John P. Herman
  Alfred B. Verbecken
  DeWitt M. Nye
Privates 1st Class—
  Aitken, William E.
  Arms, Ervin M.
  Bouse, Edward F.
  Broderick, William J.
  Bushey, Joseph F.

Clemons, John F.
Davis, William B.
Eckenrode, Jesse W.
Engle, Chester A.
Fessler, John E.
Frank, John F.
Funk, George E.
Geiger, Leon R.
Gray, Richard D.
Gray, Wiley L.
Greenwood, Kelton H.
Gressang, William H.
Hahn, George A.
Hartman, Carl E.
Heckman, Guy R.
Heiser, Frank E.
Herman, Kenneth W.
Hilt, John B.
Hochreiter, John L.
Hoffman, Charles L.
Hooper, Thomas A.
Jones, Curven F.

Kane, James E.
Kasparavich, William
Kelly, Jeremiah F.
King, William M.
Knies, Russel K.
McCartney, Frank G.
Miller, William A.
Melick, Richard A.
Motter, Miles L.
Martin, Robert H.
Murray, James F.
Nerone, Angelo N.
Nicholson, Lloyd H.
North, Richard O.
Parsons, Reagle O.
Poorman, Arthur E.
Priar, Lawrence L.
Priest, Forest N.
Rheam, Robert

Riggs, Oran D.
Robenolt, Chester B.
Ruda, Paul T.
Salzinger, Joseph
Schuster, Paul F.
Scott, William H.
Schreckengast, George M.
Smith, Wallace H.
Stedman, George V.
Stone, Henry D.
Tacchi, Hugo J.
Tingley, Oscar N.
Walsh, Martin J.
Wassell, Michael J.
Wellen, Henry R.
Whitecotton, Lewis M.
Williams, John H.
Woodring, Melvin L.

School Troop, Hershey
Captain Thomas F. Martin
Lieutenant Andrew J. Hudock
Sergeant Edgar T. Strange
Corporal Frank R. Cooch
Corporal Clark E. Holland

Detective Division
Lieutenant Harry E. McElroy

ROSTER
State Highway Patrol
1925

Harrisburg
Captain Wilson C. Price, Superintendent
Captain Philip J. Dorr, Adjutant

Hershey

Lieutenant John R. Standiford, Inspection Officer
Lieutenant Lawrence Brosha, Supply Officer
Lieutenant John W. McCarthly, Examination Officer
Sergeant James H. Marshall, Training School Commandant
Sergeant William F. Mote, Mechanical Inspector
Sergeant George H. Keller
Sergeant John M. Bender
Corporal Charles F. Schroeder
Corporal Harry C. Gabel
Corporal Richard Pastorius
Corporal George N. Pickering
Corporal Henry M. Wakefield

Greensburg

Lieutenant David E. Miller, Inspection Officer
Sergeant John P. Peck
Corporal Lloyd Killinger

Butler

Sergeant Wilbur M. Parker
Corporal Jacob J. A. Fiscus

Wyoming

Sergeant Jesse C. McMurtry
Corporal Guy L. Stine

Wesleyville

Sergeant Walter B. Smoot
Corporal James S. Blair

Moscow

Sergeant Jesse C. McClung

Malvern

Sergeant Joseph R. Schubert
Corporal John H. Robinson
Corporal Leon L. Houpt

Hollidaysburg

Corporal Arthur J. Saline

Lancaster

Corporal Harry E. Edie

Uniontown

Corporal Arthur J. Oldham

Beaver Falls

Corporal Charles J. McRae

Gettyburg

Corporal John D. Kime

York

Corporal Nathaniel F. Martin

Wyomissing

Corporal Daniel R. Tobias

Franklin

Corporal Samuel P. Manross

Nicholson

Corporal Nicholas Sassong

Huntingdon

Corporal Charles V. Varner

Washington

Corporal Paul L. Stone

Bethlehem

Corporal William H. McClarin
Corporal Joseph J. Weinert

Mansfield

Corporal Ralph C. Day

Warren

Corporal James E. Springer

Pittsburgh

Corporal Lloyd H. Lease

Patrol Field Roster and Locations

Allison Park
  Melbourne A. Charles**
  Joe Frickanish
Beaver Falls
  Charles J. McRae**
  Frank L. Garnow

Bedford
  Fred G. McCartney**
  John J. Tallon
Bellefonte
  David Daniels**
  Millard Solt

Bethlehem
William H. McClarin**
John P. Yohe
James C. Campbell (Exam Detail)
John P. Hannon (Exam Detail)
Arthur C. Mantz (Exam Detail)
Joseph J. Weinert (Exam Detail)
Bloomsburg
William D. Brown**
John Cheloc
Brookville
Robert L. Christy**
Russell W. Cooper
Butler
Jacob J. A. Fiscus**
William J. Jurison
Wilbur M. Parker **
A. P. Reed
Andrew J. Gallick (Exam Detail)
Joseph L. O'Kane (Exam Detail) *
John D. Zimmerman (Exam Detail)
Chambersburg
Anson L. Bowman **
Mark L. Gemberling
Ellsworth E. Keckler
Clearfield
Arnold M. Flanigan **
Earl F. McGill
Joseph G. McCann (Exam Detail)
Walter F. O'Malloy (Exam Detail)
Clarence Zimmerman (Exam Detail) *
Collegeville
Roscoe H. Crouse **
Samuel J. Kennedy
Coudersport
Anthony J. Pulveno **
Edward J. Lutz
Doylestown
William Dwyer **
F. C. McLane
Harold M. Wynn
Franklin
Samuel P. Manross**
Willard Cyphers
Wilson A. Fackler (Exam Detail)
Earl C. Holder (Exam Detail)
Leo A. Miles (Exam Detail) *
Gettysburg
John D. Kime **
Thomas N. Boate
Roy M. Brinkman

Greensburg
David E. Miller ****
John P. Peck ***
Lloyd A. Killinger **
Ray Hoover
John William Reed
Clarence J. Hagen (Exam Detail) *
Joseph B. Haddad (Exam Detail)
William F. Halliman (Exam Detail)
Harrisburg
Henry Harner **
Willard Dauberman
Otis J. Deibler
Joseph F. Flounders
Robert Owesney
Earl C. Pepple
Joseph S. Rhine
Hazleton
Joseph E. Nelligan **
John W. Snyder
Hollidaysburg
Arthur W. Saline **
Geoge W. Gabrielson
George H. James
William A. Ent (Exam Detail) *
Melvin Hutzell (Exam Detail)
John H. Dodson (Exam Detail)
Paul F. Dawson (Exam Detail)
Huntingdon
Charles K. Varner **
Don L. Rupert
Indiana
Albert L. Reese **
Edward W. Allen
Jennerstown
Earl B. Ging **
F. N. McCartney
Kennett Square
Harvey Peiffer **
T. H. Dougherty
John W. Emrich
Lancaster
Harry A. Edie **
Ellwood S. Grimm
Melvin H. Snavely
Lewistown
R. E. Nash **
Herman Roush
Lock Haven
John M. Tolbert **
Joe B. Champion

Malvern
  Joseph R. Schubert ***
  J. H. Robinson **
  Edward Seerey
  Leon L. Houpt (Exam Detail) *
  Lee Diebler (Exam Detail)
  Graydon A. Meadows (Exam Detail)
  William J. Ruch (Exam Detail)
  M. E. Stone (Exam Detail)
Mansfield
  Ralph C. Day **
  James L. Utter
Meadville
  Raymond Nuhfer **
  Andrew W. Phillips
Moscow
  Jesse C. McClung ***
  Gifford B. Alexander **
  Harry V. Wilcom
Muncy
  C. A. Zarger **
  Albert L. Flick
  Daniel W. Cable (Exam Detail) *
  H. C. Fleming (Exam Detail)
  James A. Ryan (Exam Detail)
  Philip H. Sack (Exam Detail)
New Castle
  Chester M. Beatty **
  Arthur W. Schuler
Nicholson
  Nicholas Sassong **
  George C. Stocksdale
  Arthur Zimmerman
Philadelphia
  Richard T. Levis **
  George A. Drumbor
  Ellwood J. Markley
  Joseph A. Murphy
  Harold V. Piersol
  Joseph P. Sawaski
Pittsburgh
  Lloyd H. Lease**
  Frank Concilla
  Alvin Daughty
  George W. Kruse
Pottsville
  Earl J. Henry **
  Nathan Freed
  Lloyd A. Moyer

Selinsgrove
  Samuel H. Bard **
  Carl Musser
Stroudsburg
  Raymond C. Espenshade **
  Harvey A. Eby
Towanda
  Francis M. Mathers **
  Wilbur D. Grove
Uniontown
  Arthur J. Oldham **
  Russell O. Miller
Warren
  James E. Springer **
Washington
  Paul Stone **
  John J. Longhenry (Exam Detail) *
  J. F. Hossack (Exam Detail)
  Stanley L. Wheeler (Exam Detail)
Wesleyville
  Walter B. Smoot ***
  James S. Blair **
  Robert J. Valentine (Exam Detail) *
  Oscar E. Samson (Exam Detail)
  Thomas J. Bert
  T. Jenkins
Wyoming
  Jesse C. McMurtry ***
  Guy L. Stine **
  Clyde R. Jacoby
  Gilbert A. Newman
  Frederick J. Seitler
  Robert E. Cotter (Exam Detail) *
  Robert J. Hawley (Exam Detail)
  Joseph T. Laughlin (Exam Detail)
  Otto Brower (Exam Detail)
Wyomissing
  Daniel R. Tobias **
  Robert J. Burns
  John Grabert
York
  Nathaniel F. Martin **
  George Baughman

  ****Inspecting Officer
   ***Inspecting Sergeant
    **In Charge of Station
     *In Charge of Exam Detail

Highway Patrol Training School

Exam Detail	*Instructors, Mechanics, Cooks*
Simon C. Peffley	James L. Donnelly
Harold W. Neptune	Peter J. Byrne
John Grance	Leon J. Cole
	George E. Ehrhorn
	John James Jennings
	Percy A. Putt
	Oliver D. Thomas
	Henry M. Warfield

Recruit Class of March 3, 1925

John A. Boushell	Irvan C. Korman
Reuben C. Carlson	Frank J. Levendusky
John J. Connelly	Wilbur B. Mead
Fred W. Hafer	Lawrence A. Ross
Stephen F. Hartman	Michael P. Seibert
Thomas M. Jakeman	Alexander Tyhurst
Russel C. Judson	Gerald E. Watt
Clarence A. Keefer	Charles R. Williams
Harman S. Kessler	William R. Williams
Charles H. Killian	

ROSTER
State Highway Patrol
1937

Headquarters

Earl J. Henry	Captain (Acting Superintendent)
John R. Standiford	Captain (Adjutant)
James C. Taylor	Principal Enforcement Investigator
Harry B. Kerns	Sergeant
Frances LaPides	Stenographer
Eleanor J. McDermott	Principal Stenographer
Dorothy B. O'Brien	Senior Stenographer

Accounts Unit

William C. Burton	Bookkeeping Machine Operator
Robert J. Franklin	Expense Record Clerk
Janes M. Heefner	Bookkeeping Machine Operator
Mrs. L. P. Hicks	Junior Payroll Clerk
John H. Klinger	Typist Clerk
Gretchen L. Knox	File Clerk
E. Mae Twigg	Advanced File Clerk
Russell Wrightstone	Head Police Clerk

Mechanical Unit

Charles F. Schroeder	Lieutenant
Oliver D. Thomas	First Sergeant
Ralph C. Hoover	Corporal
Joseph J. Lennon	Troop Clerk C
Clell W. Ammerman	Mechanic 1st Class
Harry E. Bangs	Mechanic 1st Class
Russell R. Bechtel	Mechanic 3rd Class
Joseph M. Carey	Mechanic 3rd Class
Charles W. Crain	Mechanic 3rd Class
L. Jerome Cunningham	Troop Clerk C
Richard C. Davis	Mechanic 2nd Class
Edward S. Frey	Mechanic 1st Class
Harry B. Hawk	Mechanic 3rd Class
Morris S. Kendig	Mechanic 2nd Class
John Kinsky	Mechanic 2nd Class
Andrew S. Lieb	Mechanic 2nd Class
William J. McLaughlin	Mechanic 3rd Class
Roland Mallory	Mechanic 3rd Class
Delos M. Page	Mechanic 3rd Class
L. J. Robertson, Jr.	Mechanic 3rd Class
Russel B. Shank	Mechanic 2nd Class
Mervin G. Stump	Mechanic 2nd Class
Charles B. Sweigart	Mechanic 2nd Class

Supply Unit

Lawrence Brosha	Captain
Russell L. Ellis	Sergeant
William A. Ent	Corporal
David J. Falger	Troop Clerk B
William J. Garrick	Patrolman
Antonio Terrari	Patrolman

Training School

Arthur J. Oldham	Captain
Fred G. McCartney	Lieutenant
William J. Bynane	First Sergeant
Robert M. Bair	Sergeant
Joseph Goldstein	Sergeant
Harry E. Meyers	Sergeant
Benjamin P. Bretz	Corporal
Joseph G. Burkhart	Corporal

Joseph C. McCune   Corporal
Harold J. Berrean   Troop Clerk A
Harry R. McKenna   Troop Clerk C
Myron W. Thomas   Troop Clerk A
Willis W. Enck   Patrolman
Eston M. Enke   Patrolman
Charles E. Saul   Patrolman
Joseph E. Temple   Patrolman
Robert S. Zimmerman   Patrolman
James R. Carter   Advanced Cook
Andrew A. Henderson   Advanced Cook

Troop A–Harrisburg

Thomas N. Boate   Captain
Charles S. Graeff   Lieutenant
John D. Kime   Lieutenant
James J. Tooey   First Sergeant

Sergeants: Daniel Boas (Student)
  Charles E. Alexander   Francis J. Bonenberger
  John S. Garrett   W. Cleon Boston
  Charles W. Grein   Clarence D. Boyle
  Joseph S. Rhine   Adam J. Budjako
  Ethan R. Rubicam   Russel F. Cassel
  Singleton Sheaffer   Edward H. Crowthers (Student)
  Albert H. Shuller   Martin H. Cullen
  Frank L. Tuckey   Frank Damian
Corporals: Michael J. Dean
  Lloyd G. Adams   Robert E. Deitrich
  John A. Aumon   Sidney C. Deyo
  Arthur W. Ditchfield   George Durilla (Student)
  Lloyd B. Gibbs   Edward E. Egan (Student)
  Alphonse C. Glasser   Joseph P. English
  William R. Lammie   Walter J. Farra (Student)
  Clayton A. McHenry   Richard E. Fitzpatrick, Jr.
  Charles C. Naddeo   Francis A. Gavaghan
  Raymond E. Nash   Philip S. Gerhard
  Preston H. Ortmyer   George E. Goodhart
  John P. Peck   James J. Haggerty
  Lewis S. Small   George S. Harleman
  Ray E. Sprenkle   Donald Harris
  Clyde F. Stryker   Glenn F. Henry
  Gerald J. Sweeney   Carl J. Jeffries
  James G. Warren   Lodwick D. Jenkins
  Marion J. Wicker   John J. Julo (Student)
Troop Clerk A: Edward B. Keller
  Sylvester J. McKenrick   Joseph M. Kelly (Student)
Troop Clerk C: James F. Kennedy
  Donald D. Brink   Raphael M. King
Patrolmen: Anthony W. Krencewicz
  Cyrus W. Achenbach   Benedict Labenski
  Delroy M. Anderson   William N. Lesser

Charles W. Lutton
William B. McGuire, Jr.
Thomas H. McGurl
Edward R. McLister
Thomas C. Mahalik
Raymond E. Mathers
Harold C. Menegat
Ira W. Messersmith
John Micka
George E. Miller
John P. Monaghan
William C. Moran
Edward A. Moss
Edward F. Muldowney (Student)
Joseph J. Nork
George O'Day
William L. Peck
James W. Rankin
Milton Rauenzahn

Carl F. Renz
Herman A. Ries
Anthony J. Roskoski
Andrew J. Royko
Frank C. Russell
Harry E. Russell
Peter P. Salus (Student)
Paul R. Schappert (Student)
Harold C. Sheads
Vernon E. Simpson
Russell E. Stewart
Aleksander J. G. Swalinski
John S. Trease
Charles E. Waltermyer
Oliver H. Werner
Edward W. Wilanosky (Student)
Jerome J. Wychulis (Student)
Frank W. Yercavage

Troop B–Greensburg

Joseph G. McCann
John C. Bricker
Ray Hoover
Frank L. Garnow
Clyde Borror
John U. Colligan
Carrie Dowden
Mrs. Mary H. Sullen

Captain
Lieutenant
Lieutenant
First Sergeant
Troop Clerk B
Troop Clerk A
Kichen Helper A
Housekeeper C

Sergeants:
  Daniel Augustine
  James A. Blair
  Andrew D. Bowman
  Lewis R. Feloni
  Charles R. Kephart
  Earl F. McGill
  Carlton L. Stine
Corporals:
  Hilton D. Albert
  Micheal G. Barry
  Harold E. Beard
  Peter J. Byrne
  Francis R. Clark
  Edward J. Fox
  Harry A. Gidley
  Henry L. Isban
  Victor L. Jones
  Frank O. Lease
  Charles E. Loughner
  William G. McKee

Ernest C. Moore
Albert A. Myrter
John L. Peffer
George E. Rutledge
Patrolmen:
  Harold C. Armstrong
  Jasper Augustine (Student)
  Andrew Baigis
  Michael Benko
  Frank J. Bogatay
  Preston L. Burkett
  Francis J. Burns
  Arthur G. Cohen
  John C. Conway
  Albert McC. Cox (Student)
  Cornelius E. Coyle
  Joel E. Cree
  Samuel R. Davidson
  Karl H. Delbrook
  Harold L. Desch
  Thomas A. Dougherty

Lloyd G. Epler
Joseph M. Evans
John R. Fair
Edwin V. Gaffney
William J. Galvin
Frank S. Greggerson
Carl E. Gunnerson
Norman P. Holzapfel
William H. Hooke (Student)
James D. Hoye
Howard M. Jaynes
Batholomew V. Kilraine
William W. Kitch
Alfred H. Krull
Garwood K. Lodge
George E. McCloskey
Boyd W. McClusky
Thomas B. McDonough
Thomas W. McGuire
John A. Maggioncalda (Student)
Walter J. Marm
Joseph Y. Mermelstein
Paul W. Mihalko
Horace S. Miller
Emil A. Munson
William C. Munz, Jr.
Angelo J. Naddeo
Mattew J. O'Brien
Francis D. O'Donnell
Paul A. O'Mara (Student)

Emerson G. Palmer
Charles K. Pentz
Henry E. Poiser (Student)
Harlan E. Rarig
Ray L. Reck (Student)
Tyson E. Riggle
Walter C. Roth
John V. Roynan
Oscar E. Scott
Max D. Sherman
Merl R. Shetter (Student)
Charles T. Sieber (Student)
William J. Smith
Joseph C. Snyder
Carl E. Sproul
Howard A. Stephens
William A. Stile
Carl Stillwagon
Clarence F. Temke
Julius A. Trombetta (Student)
William J. Urick, Jr.
William C. Vilscek
Vincent E. Wadas
Leonard G. Washington
William C. Weaver
Harry J. Wertz
Benjamin J. Williams
Kenneth L. Williams
Albert Zavarello
Albert J. Ziola

Troop C–Bellefonte

Warren C. Baer
Charles J. McRae
George N. Pickering
John H. Hunchberger
Harry L. Price
George R. Gibboney
Sergeants:
  Walter K. Duhrkoff
  William J. Graham
  Elbert W. Lantz
  Martin V. Law
  Thomas G. Moriarity
Corporals:
  Herbert R. Anderson
  George A. Auten
  Alvin I. Barrett
  Lawrence M. Corson
  Uriah F. English
  George W. Gabrielson

Lieutenant
Lieutenant
Lieutenant
First Sergeant
Troop Clerk A
Troop Clerk B

  Neil J. Gallagher
  Joseph F. Hugar
  Carl W. Koperek
  Roger E. Pflugfelder
  John G. Rasavage
  Robert H. Raymond
  Leslie N. Shaw
  Clenmar W. Wagner
  Paul H. Winger
Patrolmen:
  Roy E. Bailey (Student)
  Victor E. Bell

Cornelius J. Conahan
William J. Carson
Robert J. Crozier
Robert J. Daley
John J. Daptula
Fordyce L. Deiter
William J. Earley
Goerge L. Finkbeiner
George W. Finnin
Oscar J. Finster
Leroy R. Foulkrod
Edward J. Gallagher
Joseph H. Garside
Henry F. Gorka (Student)
Charles S. Graci (Student)
Lewis F. Grebe (Student)
George J. Hirschmann
Arthur N. Isenberg
Bernard V. Johnston
John R. Juba
Edward E. Kissinger
Russell L. Knowles
Grant N. Kough, Jr.

James D. McGeehan
Frank M. Miller
Joseph E. Miller
James G. Olmes
Anthony J. Pulveno
Robert A. Rice
Charles C. Riggs
Paul M. Rittenhouse
John Rock
Alex A. Rudville
C. Fred Rugh
Peter A. Salamone
Clarence Schnabele
Grant E. Shannon
John H. Sheedy
John D. Simonson
James B. Snyder
Bruno P. Timpano
George J. Vanderslice (Student)
Nicholas A. Vicchiarelli (Student)
William J. Walters
Thomas G. Wells
John T. Ziegler

Troop D–Kingston

George H. Keller	Captain
John Grance	Lieutenant
Atreus H. Kratzke	Lieutenant
Frank T. Crum	First Sergeant
Joseph F. Hughes	Troop Clerk A
Carlton M. Mendenhall	Troop Clerk B

Sergeants:
A. W. Corbin
John C. Grey
Walter E. Price
Wilbur M. Smith
Ralph M. Stroh
Philip A. White
Corporals:
George J. Barkauskas
Thomas J. Betzko
Frank Evans
Benjamin Franklin
Charles S. Grow
Edward J. Holleran
Claire A. Johnson
John A. Kennedy
Robert J. Letteer
George F. O'Neill
Carson F. Overgard

Simon C. Peffley
John J. Pezzent
Melvin L. Reese
Edgar H. Stine
Patrolmen:
John W. Adams
Thomas G. Barclay
Joseph B. Barnauskas (Student)
John Barone
Ralph C. Bergstresser
John Billow
Daniel F. Brennan
Frank D. Burtner
Frank J. Cannon
Harold W. Casper (Student)
Melvin D. Clouser
William B. Cooper (Student)
Charles H. Craven

John A. Crissy
John R. Cummings (Student)
Donald S. Cutting
James J. Devine
Joseph A. DiPietro
John J. Donahue
Sherwood D. Dorman
James J. Durkin
Harold P. Farr (Student)
Bernard W. Fives
Harry S. Follmer
Edwin L. Gebhardt
Charles A. Givler, Jr.
James J. Grace
Malcolm E. Gramley
Samuel W. Greenawalt
Andrew F. Gregor
Walter J. Griffin
Calvin L. Hamberger
Clement W. Heist
Robert R. Ingram
David H. James
Floyd E. Kinley
Joseph R. Krushinski
William J. Kunigonis
William J. Kuprionas
John J. Laskos (Student)
Joseph F. Louches
Thomas J. McHugh

Joseph P. McNanaman
John Mancuso
Joseph T. Masnica
Nels G. Munson
Harry A. Nyman
Lawrence J. O'Rourke
Herbert A. Pecht
Stanley E. Petzak
Frank H. Phillips
John H. Rights
Harry B. Rinehart
Peter E. Sabinsky
Raymond G. Schwartz
Vincent R. Scolere
Robert M. Sewell
Edgar G. Shaffer
Sterling Sowden
James W. Supler
Frank J. Szostek
James J. Tama
Charles R. Taylor
Joseph F. Telban
Leroy Thomas
George W. Toth (Student)
Russell Walters
William F. Wendland
George J. Yashur (Student)
Herman R. Ziegler

Troop E–Philadelphia

William J. Ruch
Frank C. Miner
Melvin H. Snavely
Harold V. Piersol
Delbert A. Johnson
William J. Maher
Sergeants:
 Donald D. Davis
 Albert A. Discavage
 William R. Engle
 Herbert K. Gemmill
 Chester A. Lipp
 Lewis F. Owen
 Joseph J. Weinert
Corporals:
 Graham F. Boice
 Chester V. Cuddy
 David Daniels
 Arthur P. Diem
 Roslyn D. Evans
 Albert L. Henry

Captain
Lieutenant
Lieutenant
First Sergeant
Troop Clerk A
Troop Clerk C

 Frank X. Kelly
 John J. Kelly
 Millard B. McAfee
 John H. Morton
 E. Kriner Pote
 Chester W. Reitz
 Calvin M. Ross
 Irwin L. Rothermel
 Mike Stefanchick, Jr.
 Austin O. Steward
Patrolmen:
 Fred Arcamone
 James E. Badman
 Rudolph A. Balas

Adam Barron
Donald C. Beacraft (Student)
Harry C. Bensinger
John J. Boyle (Student)
James L. Brennan
Bernard F. Bride
Michael P. Burger
Stanley J. Butcavage
Thomas P. Cahalan
Thomas P. Carey
Gennaro F. Carfagno
Robert T. Chapman
Philip F. Chulick
Ignatz F. Clemens, Jr.
Reynolds V. Comstock
John J. Culp
Chester J. Czernik (Student)
Joseph Delaney
Thomas V. Devlin
Russell E. Dougherty
Woodrow W. Frank
Fred J. Gallagher
John B. George, Jr.
Joseph F. Graham
Francis P. Haffey
William S. Hall (Student)
James R. Harris
Donald E. Hatter
Alvin J. Herr
Amos O. Hess
Walter W. Hill
Dennis A. Hogan
Joseph F. Jacobe
Charles A. Jones
John A. Jones
John J. Kane

Regis P. Karadeema
Edward L. Konchar
Joseph F. Langan (Student)
Clyde A. Leftwich
Michael P. McGeary
Richard F. Mince
Charles L. Minnick
Wilbur D. Minor
John P. Mitchell (Student)
Edward W. Mooney (Student)
Stephen Morris
George D. Myers
Frank N. Nurthen, Jr.
James A. O'Brien (Student)
William J. Parkinson
Lawrence E. Perry
Anthony W. Poloncic
Leo Preitz
Daniel R. Purcell
George H. Rentz
Howard A. Rhodes
Francis O. Rodgers (Student)
John E. Sebesi
Samuel S. Semelsberger
James J. Shovelin (Student)
Jack F. Shubick
Bolick J. Tarlecky
William B. Templeton
Harry S. Trefsger
James F. Updyke
James P. White
Maurice F. Wilhere
Robert B. Wilt
Charles A. Winans
Joseph T. Winkler

Troop F–Franklin

Harry A. Edie
Albert L. Flick
Herman J. Roush
Alfred G. Wissinger
William F. Falger
Michael Donick, Jr.
Sergeants:
 Wilson A. Fackler
 Earl B. Ging
 Thomas E. Jones
 Raymond N. Nuhfer
 Clair B. Quiggle
 Oscar E. Samson

Lieutenant
Lieutenant
Lieutenant
First Sergeant
Troop Clerk A
Troop Clerk C
Corporals:
 Jack Bartlett
 Clyde H. Blocker
 John J. Burke
 Peter E. Carlson
 Leo R. Doolan
 Durward A. Gehr

John W. Heineman
Chester P. Hoover
Gerald F. Keck
Leon J. Lawton
John J. McGuire
James R. Vaughn
Alfred P. Vota
John E. Witherspoon
Patrolmen:
Donald M. Alexander
Robert E. Barry (Student)
Merrill A. Benner
David Berenson
Edward L. Betts
James W. Blythe
Raymond A. Blythe
William E. Boniger
Albert W. Boring
Paul T. Conner
Hugh F. Cunningham
Walter L. Cuthbert
Jack Dillman
James C. Elmer
Henry C. Fagley
William B. Flucker
Leslie G. Fobes
Louis Foradora
Leon J. Galavitz
Henry Gorski
Paul I. Gourley
Dennis L. Greenawalt
Ellis J. Hamaker
John Hardy, Jr.
Melvin Headley, Jr. (Student)
David C. Hoffman (Student)
Robert B. Hoke
Donald L. Holmes
Michael D. Hoyman
Theodore A. Hubley

Clarence W. Irwin (Student)
William James
Walter J. Jozefowicz
Anthony E. Kaleita (Student)
Bernard J. McCole
Chester R. McFarland
Frank S. McGregor
Joseph J. Mastrian
Joseph P. Milan, Jr. (Student)
Donald B. Miller
John H. Miller
Louis C. Miller
Marlin L. Miller
Joseph S. Moraski
Robert E. Parson
Herbert Perstein
Joseph F. Platt (Student)
Bruce A. Reeder
James W. Reese
Harold C. Ross
John T. Sarko
Albert E. Scheib
John P. Sharpe
William H. Shaw
George Sifter
William E. Stoops
William R. Sunday
Thomas C. Swarts
Stanley S. Szymanowicz (Student)
Joseph F. Vent
Francis Walters
Leroy C. Weiland
Delmar G. Williams (Student)
Roy O. Wyatt
Carl S. Wynn
Clifford G. Yahner
Lewis A. Yerskey
Joseph L. Young

RETIRED STATE POLICE ASSOCIATION OF PENNSYLVANIA

Incorporated June 24, 1950

The objects of this Association shall be to foster fellowship amongst its members, to keep alive the memories of service when members of the Pennsylvania State Police, to promote the welfare of its members and to inculate a spirit of friendly cooperation with members of the Pennsylvania State Police Civic Association.

Past Presidents

1950-51	Herbert Smith
1952-53	Joseph S. Rhine
1954-55	John P. Herman
1956-57	Edwin J. Stroman
1958	Harry E. Myers
1959	Frank C. Russell
1960	Fred G. McCartney
1961	Thomas E. Eshleman
1962	Walter B. Kunkle
1963	Alfred B. Verbecken
1964	Thomas E. Jones
1965	James J. Tooey
1966	Melvin L. Woodring
1967	Edgar K. Pote
1968	Charles H. DeWitt
1969	Ray Nighan
1970	Irwin L. Good
1971	Edward P. McBreen
1971-72	Willard Schauer
1973	Robert E. Deitrich
1974	Matthew J. O'Brien
1975	Benjamin P. Bretz
1976	Keith R. Dane
1977	Bernard J. Lebojesky

BIBLIOGRAPHY

American Academy of Political and Social Science, *Annals of the American Academy of Political and Social Science*, Vol. 146, No. 235, November, 1929.

Baldwin, Tom, "The Pennsylvania State Police," 7-part series, *Johnstown Tribune-Democrat,* November 20-26, 1974.

Baxter, Mike, "'Good, Gray Sheriff' Imagine Stands Fast After 5 Years," *The Miami Herald*, July 18, 1971.

Beitler, Lewis E. *Fiftieth Anniversary of the Battle of Gettysburg: Report of the Pennsylvania Commission, December 13, 1913*. Harrisburg, Pa.: William Stanley Ray, 1915.

Bell Telephone Company of Pennsylvania, *The Call*, Vol. 24, No. 3, 1966.

Bell Telephone Company of Pennsylvania, *The Telephone News*, September, 1924.

Bell Telephone Company of Pennsylvania, *The Telephone News*, Vol. 60, No. 4, 1964.

Burgoyne, Arthur C. *Homestead*, New York: Augustus M. Kelley Publishers, 1971.

Collier, Richard, *Plague of the Spanish Lady*, New York: Antheneum Publishers, 1974.

Colson, William W. *The State Capitol of Pennsylvania*, Harrisburg, Pa.: Telegraph Printing Company, 1907.

Commonwealth of Pennsylvania, *Official Opinions of the Attorney General of Pennsylvania 1935-1936*, Harrisburg, Pa., 1937.

Commonwealth of Pennsylvania, *Pennsylvania Manual*, Harrisburg, Pa., 1905-1975.

Cornell, Robert J. *The Anthracite Coal Strike of 1902*, New York: Russell and Russell, 1971.

Dacus, Joseph A. *Annals of the Great Strikes*, New York: Arno and The New York Times, 1969.

Department of State Police (Pennsylvania), *General Orders*, Harrisburg, Pa., 1905-1923.

Department of State Police (Pennsylvania), *History of the Department of State Police*, Harrisburg, Pa., 1917.

Department of State Police (Pennsylvania), *Payrolls*, Harrisburg, Pa., 1905-1923.

Donoghue, Frank Lee, *Guardians of the Mine Country*, Springfield, Mass.: McLoughlin Brothers, Inc., 1936.

Educational Review, *Educational Review of the Pennsylvania State Highway Patrol*, Harrisburg, Pa., 1925.

Fleming, Thomas J. "The Policeman's Lot," *American Heritage*, Volume 21, No. 2, February, 1970.

Gambino, Richard, *Blood Of My Blood*, Garden City, New York: Doubleday & Company, 1974.

Groome, John C. *Reply To The American Cossack*, Harrisburg, Pa.: Department of State Police, 1915.

Hepford, H. Joseph, *Report of Committee to Investigate the Administration of Justice*, Harrisburg, Pa., Pennsylvania House of Representatives, 1974.

Historical Society of Pennsylvania, *The Pennsylvania Magazine*, Vol. 41, 1917.

Hoehling, A. A. *The Great Epidemic*, Boston, Mass.: Little, Brown & Company, 1961.

Kohler, Saul, "Proud To Be A Trooper," *Today Magazine, The Philadelphia Inquirer*, June 25, 1961.

Kunitz, Stanley J., and Haycraft, Howard, *Twentieth Century Authors*, New York: The H. W. Wilson Company, 1942.

Lumb, George F. *Police Training and Survey*, Harrisburg, Pa.: The Police Training and Survey Company, 1919.

Maurer, Charles A. *The Constabulary of Pennsylvania*, Reading, Pa.: Allied Press, 1911.

Maurer, James H. *The American Cossack*, Reading, Pa.: Pennsylvania Federation of Labor, 1915.

Mayo, Katherine, *Justice To All*, New York: G. P. Putnam's Sons, 1917.

, *Mounted Justice*, New York: Houghton Mifflin Company, 1922.

, *The Standard-Bearers*, New York: Houghton Mifflin Company, 1918.

Milnor, Mark T. *The Harrisburg Military Association*, Harrisburg, Pa., 1967.

Pennsylvania Department of Highways, *Biennial Reports*, Harrisburg, Pa., 1918-1920, 1921-1922, 1926-1928, 1928-1930.

Pennsylvania Department of Highways, "Legislative History," *Publication L-514*, Harrisburg, Pa., 1954.

Pennsylvania Department of Highways, *Payrolls*, Harrisburg, Pa., 1923-1929.

Pennsylvania Department of Highways, *Publication No. 34*, Harrisburg, Pa., 1928.

Pennsylvania Department of Highways, "State Highway Patrol Rules and Regulations," *Bulletin No. 34*, Harrisburg, Pa., 1928.

Pennsylvania Department of Revenue, *Payrolls*, Harrisburg, Pa., 1929-1937.

Pennsylvania General Assembly, *Laws of Pennsylvania*, Harrisburg, Pa., 1865-1866, 1905-1974.

Pennsylvania General Assembly, *Legislative Journals*, Harrisburg, Pa., 1905-1972.

Pennsylvania Manufacturers' Association, *Monthly Bulletin*, August, 1914.

Pennsylvania Motor Police, *The Bulletin*, Harrisburg, Pa., 1938-1939.

Pennsylvania State Police, *Annual and Biennial Reports*, Harrisburg, Pa., 1906-1971.

Pennsylvania State Police, *The Communicator*, Harrisburg, Pa., 1963-1976.

Pennsylvania State Police, *General Orders*, Harrisburg, Pa., 1923-1937.

Pennsylvania State Police, *The Pennsylvania State Police*, Harrisburg, Pa., 1969.

Pennsylvania State Police, *Pennsylvania State Police: A Manual of Operations*, Harrisburg, Pa., 1963.

Pennsylvania State Police, *The Pennsylvania State Police Crime Laboratory, Technical Bulletin No. 1*, Harrisburg, Pa., 1962.

Pennsylvania State Police, *Personnel Ledgers*, Harrisburg, Pa., 1906-1937.

Pennsylvania State Police. *Public Information Bulletin No. 1*. Harrisburg, Pa., 1961.

Pennsylvania State Police. *Public Information Bulletin No. 1*. (revised), Harrisburg, Pa., 1962.

Pennypacker, Samuel Whitaker, *The Autobiography of a Pennsylvanian*, Philadelphia: John C. Winston Company, 1918.

Ralph, Chester Williams, M. D. *The United States Public Health Service 1798-1950*, Richmond, Virginia: Whittet & Shepperson, 1951.

Ruch, Walter M. "Memoirs of Col. Lynn G. Adams," a 6-part series, *The Sunday Patriot-News* (Harrisburg), February-April, 1952.

Smith, Bruce, *Police Systems in the United States*, New York: Harper and Brothers, 1940.

————, *The State Police*, Montclair, New Jersey: Patterson Smith Publishing Corporation, 1969.

State Police Civic Association (Pennsylvania), *Minutes*, Harrisburg, Pa., 1918-1976.

State Police Civic Association (Pennsylvania), *Rodeo Program Book*, Harrisburg, Pa., 1934.

The State Police Magazine, Spring Issue, 1928.

Teeters, Negley K. *Hang By The Neck*, Springfield, Illinois: Charles C. Thomas, 1967.

Wilson, Joseph Lapsley, *Book of the First Troop Philadelphia City Cavalry-1774-1914*, Philadelphia: Hallowell Company, 1915.